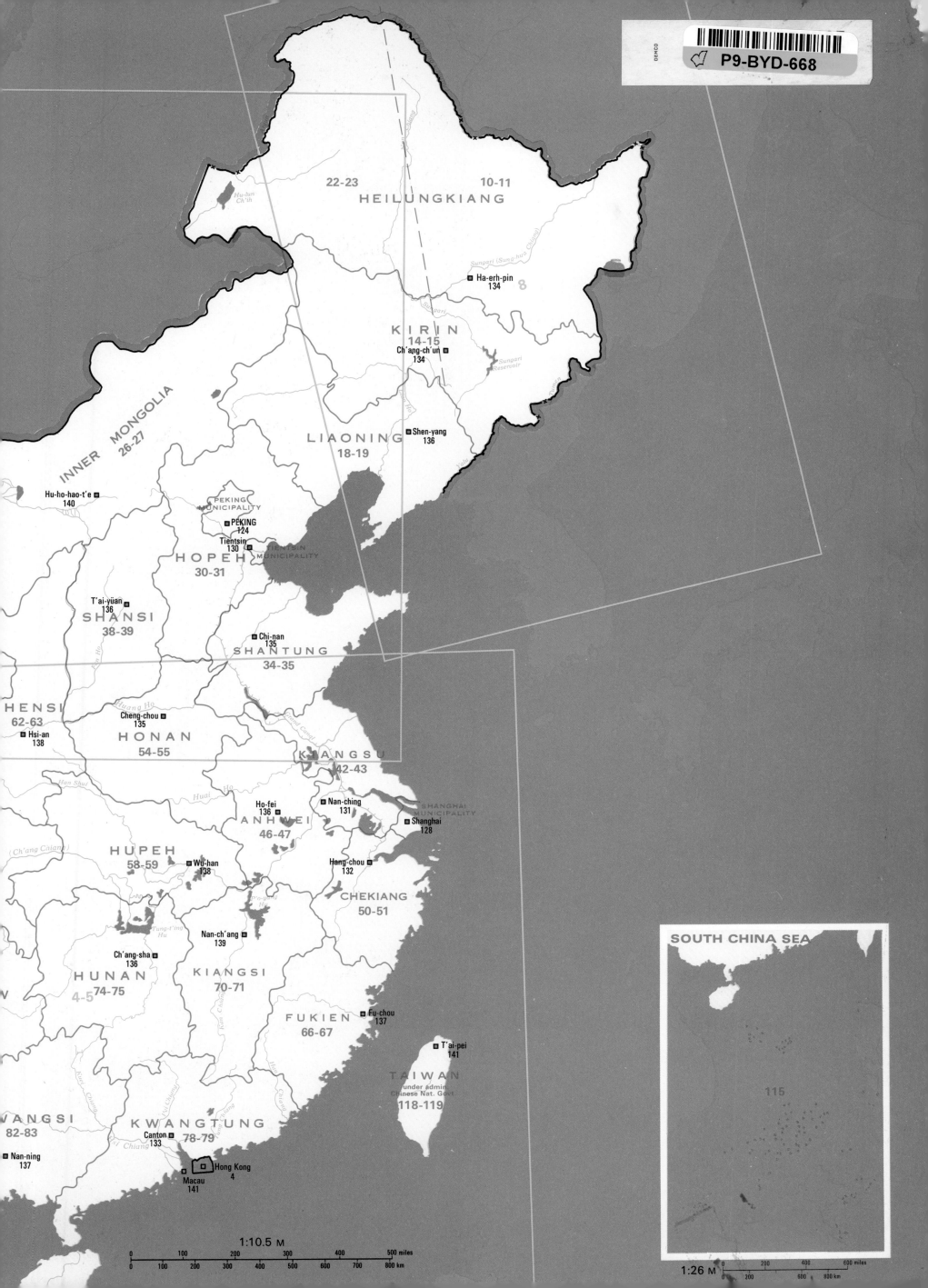

22-23   10-11
HEILUNGKIANG

Hu-lun Ch'ih

Sungari (Sung-hua Chiang)

□ Ha-erh-pin
134

8

KIRIN
14-15
Ch'ang-ch'un □
134

Sungari Reservoir

INNER MONGOLIA
26-27

LIAONING
18-19

□ Shen-yang
136

□ Hu-ho-hao-t'e
140

PEKING MUNICIPALITY

■ PEKING
124
Tientsin
130 □

TIENTSIN MUNICIPALITY

HOPEH
30-31

□ T'ai-yüan
136

SHANSI
38-39

□ Chi-nan
135

SHANTUNG
34-35

HENSI
62-63

□ Cheng-chou
135

■ Hsi-an
138

HONAN
54-55

Huang Ho

Grand Canal

KIANGSU
42-43

Huai Ho

Ho-fei
136 □

□ Nan-ching
131

SHANGHAI MUNICIPALITY
□ Shanghai
128

Han Shui

(*Ch'ang Chiang*)

HUPEH
58-59

□ Wu-han
138

P'o-yang Hu

Hang-chou
132 □

CHEKIANG
50-51

Tung-t'ing Hu

□ Nan-ch'ang
139

□ Ch'ang-sha
136

HUNAN
4-5 74-75

KIANGSI
70-71

FUKIEN
66-67

□ Fu-chou
137

□ T'ai-pei
141

TAIWAN
under admin.
Chinese Nat. Govt.
118-119

WANGSI
82-83

KWANGTUNG
78-79

□ Canton
133

HONG KONG
4

□ Nan-ning
137

□ Macau
141

1:10.5 M

0   100   200   300   400   500 miles
0   100   200   300   400   500   600   700   800 km

SOUTH CHINA SEA

115

1:26 M

0   200   400   600 miles
0   200   400   600   800 km

THE TIMES
ATLAS
OF
CHINA

THE TIMES
ATLAS
OF
CHINA

QUADRANGLE/THE NEW YORK TIMES BOOK CO.

912.5'
Tim

Editors and chief contributors   **P. J. M. Geelan**
D. C. Twitchett
Professor of Chinese, University of Cambridge

LB 11/12/75

Cartographic consultant   **John C. Bartholomew**

Contributors   **Maurice Corina**
Industrial Editor, The Times

W. W. Easey
School of Oriental and African Studies,
University of London

K. C. Jordan FRGS

Richard King
Faculty of Oriental Studies, University of Cambridge

H. A. G. Lewis OBE

The publishers would like to thank
James L. Payne, U.S. Government Printing Office,
Washington, D.C. for permission to use maps from the
Atlas of China, published by the
Central Intelligence Agency, 1971
Theodore Shabad of the New York Times
C. Kumei and M. Kikuchi of Kyobunkaku Limited
and M. Nitta of Tokyo for their kind co-operation and
assistance.

Publishing Manager: Barry Winkleman
Publishing assistant: Elizabeth Bland
Design and art direction: Ivan and Robin Dodd

Cartography by Kyobunkaku Limited, Tokyo
John Bartholomew & Son Limited, Edinburgh
and Hunting Surveys Limited, Boreham Wood

Text set by Yendall and Company, London

Chinese and English lists set by
Regal Company, Hong Kong

Printed by John Bartholomew & Son Limited

Data processing of the index by
Computer Data Processing Limited, London

Index computer set by Computaprint Limited, London

Index printed and books bound by
Hazell Watson and Viney, Aylesbury

First published (in part) by
Kyobunkaku Limited, Tokyo, 1973
First published in Great Britain in 1974 by
Times Books, the book publishing division of
Times Newspapers Limited
New Printing House Square, Gray's Inn Road,
London WC1X 8EZ

CONTENTS

Introduction *vii*

INTRODUCTION

It is with some diffidence that *The Times* presents this atlas to a world increasingly interested in China. Modern Chinese cartography has as yet provided nothing comparable to the maps and atlases available for most other countries. Despite the ancient origins of map-making in China, the People's Republic was initially poorly endowed with maps. Even if a great part of the archival material which did exist had not been removed to Taiwan, the quality and extent of coverage fell far short of what would be required by a modern, industrialised nation. By the tenth anniversary of the People's Republic, however, the more densely settled areas had been newly surveyed and mapped. Mapping the rest, including the outlying regions of Sinkiang, Tibet and Inner Mongolia, which were virtually unmapped, will occupy cartographic staffs for decades to come. These remarkable achievements have, unfortunately, not resulted in the publication of general maps to satisfy the external demand for information about the immense and rapidly-changing country. Detailed geographical and particularly statistical information at the time of writing is, by Western standards, hard to come by, but in spite of these difficulties this book will, it is hoped, fulfil an essential function: to submit to the discipline of an atlas the wide variety of information available from disparate sources about the land and people of China.

The first section of the atlas comprises maps and text concerned with a variety of historical, economic and physical topics. Maps illustrate the settlement and frontiers of China as they evolved through the great dynasties to the era of Communism; the ethnic minorities, climate, agriculture, communications, minerals and energy resources, industry and administration of modern China. The second section is a series of maps showing the physical structure of the country. The third and principal section of the atlas consists of maps of the provinces of China. These were originally compiled by a Japanese publisher, Kyōbunkaku, and have been transcribed, extensively updated and have been supplemented by hill shading to indicate the relief of the terrain. The maps are accompanied by text and a list of regions, districts, counties and municipalities for each province, in English and Chinese. The Chinese characters used in the administrative summaries for all provinces with the exception of Taiwan are the modern simplified characters which are used in the People's Republic.

During the preparation of this atlas three major problems emerged. The first concerned the choice of transcription system for the place-names in the atlas. Place-names present enormous difficulties. Transcription of Chinese, complex enough in itself, offers unlimited scope to sinologists and others to create widely varying spelling systems. 'Hsüan Te' and 'Seuen Tih', for example, although apparently unrelated, are different transcriptions of the reign-name of a Ming emperor. Of the two principal transcription systems, Wade-Giles and Pinyin, the former was selected on the grounds that, although Pinyin is now used for certain purposes in the People's Republic itself, Wade-Giles has been used in almost all technical literature about China, and by British and American cartographers, for many years. A more detailed discussion of the arguments which influenced this decision will be found on page 142.

The second problem was that posed by the existence of conventional names for many Chinese provinces and cities. In the case of the provinces, conventional forms of the names have been used throughout this atlas, except in the administrative summaries which follow each province plate, where the full names in Chinese and in Wade-Giles have been given. Cities whose conventional names have become widely used seemed to demand similar treatment, but this led to many inconsistencies and the decision was taken to use Wade-Giles spellings throughout the atlas, with only four exceptions: Peking, Tientsin, Canton and Shanghai. In the index conventional names, Post Offices spellings and the variant spellings of Tibetan and other minority-language names are all cross-referenced to the Chinese names given on the maps.

A third problem was raised by a characteristic of local administration in China, particularly in the western part of the country; this is the constant shifting of *hsien* (county) centres. These are as often known by the names of the *hsien* as by their own names. Furthermore, when a town increases its status to become a *shih* (municipality), it may acquire a new name as well as additional territory. Ambiguities of nomenclature may result. In the atlas an attempt has been made to indicate visually such names which may for these reasons be difficult to identify. All *hsien* and *shih* are symbolised according to the location of their centres in December 1972; but where the *hsien* or *shih* name differs from that of the place in which it was then situated, it is shown in square brackets. Thus Chung-shu [Jen-huai] indicates that the place called Chung-shu currently serves as the centre of Jen-huai Hsien and will on that account often be called Jen-huai. The square brackets serve also as a warning that this is not a permanent situation: a map based on 1966 information will have applied the name of Jen-huai to a place some 20 kilometres north-west whose actual name is Mao-t'ai but which *at that time* was the centre of Jen-huai Hsien.

Names of minority administrative areas are often descriptive in character and unwieldy when transcribed from their full Chinese forms. They have been given in whole or partial translation on the province maps. Thus, in Sinkiang, the K'o-tzu-le-su K'o-erh-k'o-tzu Tzu-chih-chou is referred to as the Kizil Su Kirghiz Autonomous District; the Su-pei Meng-ku-tsu Tzu-chih-hsien appears as North Kansu Mongol A.H. The full Chinese forms of all such names will be found in the administrative summaries following each province plate. These lists also include the names of those few *hsien* whose centres lie in *shih* which carry their own symbol. No distinction is made in the lists between sub-province level and lower level municipalities, since precise information is not available. Municipalities of the first category are probably those whose known boundaries are shown on the province plates and on the map on pages xxxvi and xxxvii which also contains a general account of the administrative divisions of the People's Republic.

In recent years much political significance has been read into the work of map and atlas publishers as far as boundary depiction and the spelling of place-names are concerned. The position of *The Times* as publisher of this and other atlases is quite clear. Its role is not one of international arbitration, nor does it seek in the depiction of boundaries to apportion lands to one state or another. An atlas publisher strays beyond his proper sphere if he tries to adjudicate between the rights and wrongs of a dispute, rather than to set out facts as he can best determine them. It follows that *The Times* in its atlases aims to show the territorial situation obtaining at the time of going to press, without regard to the *de jure* position in contentious areas or the rival claims of the contending parties. The portrayal of boundaries and the spelling of place-names in such areas must not be taken to indicate approval by *The Times* of the political status of the territories. Still less must it be inferred that *The Times* propagates the views of the government of the United Kingdom, the United States of America or any other nation.

CHINA'S HISTORY

Pre-history and the Shang period The main developments in prehistoric times were concentrated in Northern China, particularly in the area of loess soils in the provinces of Shensi, Shansi, and Honan, where conditions favoured primitive agriculture. The Shang was the first highly organised state from which we have records. It was also the first culture using metal (bronze). Scattered Shang sites are found over a much wider area than that shown, which includes all the major sites indicating a high level of culture.

The Warring States period The Shang was replaced in the 11th century BC by the Chou, who controlled most of northern and north-eastern China, which was administered through a system of fiefs. Its first capital was near modern Hsi-an. After 771 BC its centre was moved to the vicinity of modern Lo-yang, and the central authority of the Chou declined. Gradually the larger feudal states absorbed the smaller, until by the 3rd century BC only a handful of powerful states remained. The Chou kings had by this time lost all political power.

The Han Empire The larger states had already become powerful and highly centralised by the 3rd century BC. The Ch'in state, centred in the Wei river valley in the north-west, was the most powerful. In 221 BC Ch'in overcame the last of its rivals and unified all of China under a single centralised imperial regime, and expanded its frontiers southwards into Kwangtung. The authoritarian Ch'in empire collapsed in 207–6 BC, however, and was replaced from 202 BC by the Han, who controlled China, with a brief inter-regnum (AD 9–25) until AD 220. The map shows China at the time of the first recorded census (AD 2), when the population was 57,671,000, the great majority of whom lived in the north.

The Three Kingdoms At the final collapse of the Han in AD 220 China was divided into three regional regimes. Although briefly reunited under the Western Chin in 265 China passed through a period of political disunion which lasted until 589.

The Northern and Southern Dynasties During the period of disunion the south remained under a series of comparatively stable regimes, which gradually extended Chinese settlement and administration over the south and south-east. The north was invaded by a series of foreign peoples, and politically fragmented during the 4th century AD. The north was eventually reunified under the Toba Turkish Wei dynasty during the 5th century.

T'ang China The empire was again reunited under the Sui in 589. The new dynasty overtaxed its resources in a series of foreign wars, and fell in 617 to be replaced by the T'ang (618–907). During the T'ang, Chinese power extended far into Central Asia, while Chinese culture and institutions were widely adopted in Japan, Korea and Vietnam. The map shows T'ang China (though not its Central Asian territories) at the height of its power in 742. From the 8th century major changes began – the rapid growth of central and southern China as the main economic region; widespread development of cities and urban growth. The highly centralised state was challenged by powerful regional regimes.

The Five Dynasties In 881 the T'ang capital fell, and although the dynasty lasted in name until 907, China was split up into a number of independent states. From 907–960 a series of five short-lived dynasties in the north claimed to be the legitimate rulers of the empire, but in fact China remained fragmented and the last of the states surrendered to the new dynasty of Sung only in 979. These independent regimes are known as the Ten Kingdoms (Shih-kuo).

The Southern Sung and Chin The Sung had never been able to reconquer the area around Peking taken during the early 10th century by the Khitans, who established a powerful semi-Chinese state (Liao) in modern Manchuria. In the north-west another highly organised state, Hsi-hsia, was set up by the Tanguts. In the early 12th century the Jurchen, a Tungusic people from Manchuria, vassals of the Liao, replaced their overlords and set up a new state of Chin, which in 1127 forced the Sung to abandon their capital, and conquered most of northern China. Large parts of northern China were thus under successive foreign dynasties from 936 until 1368. During this period Sung China co-existed with several other Chinese-style bureaucratic states under alien rulers.

Sung China The Sung arose as a purely northern dynasty in 960, and gradually incorporated the independent states into a single empire by 979, although it could not recover some northern territories occupied by foreign powers. Under the Sung China enjoyed great internal prosperity. The population doubled between 742 and 1080, and by the end of the 11th century was about 100,000,000. This growth was concentrated in south and central China, while northern China declined.

The Mongol World Empire The rise of the Mongols in the early 13th century led to the conquest of Chin in 1234, and later to the conquest of the Southern Sung in 1278. China now became a part of the Mongol Empire, which stretched across Eurasia. This empire, however, was divided into a number of very different Khanates.

The Mongol Yüan period In China, Mongol rule was imposed very harshly after the conquest of the Chin in 1234, and the northern territories which then became Mongol suffered great destruction. However, the Mongols gradually adopted many Chinese institutions, and by the time the south was conquered in 1278, the Mongols applied policies which were far less harsh. Under the Mongols south-western China, hitherto under a series of independent kingdoms, was finally incorporated into the empire.

Ming China In 1368, with the establishment of the Ming, China was reunited under a Chinese dynasty for the first time for more than four centuries. The Ming was an inward looking period after the mid-15th century, but internally China underwent steady growth. Trade flourished, agriculture and industry grew steadily more productive, and the population rose rapidly to 150,000,000 by 1600.

The Ming Voyages Under the Sung and the Mongols China had become a major sea power, with Chinese ships trading with Indonesia, south-east Asia, India and the Persian Gulf. In the early 15th century the Emperor Yung-lo sent a series of massive maritime expeditions to south-east Asia and into the Indian Ocean, where they ranged as far as the Red Sea and the East African coast. The voyages soon came to an end, however, and the Chinese abandoned the use of sea power, just as the first western penetration of the Indian Ocean was about to begin.

The Ch'ing Empire In 1644 the Ming empire came to an end, conquered by the Manchus, descendents of the Jurchen who had formed the Chin state from 1127–1234. The Manchus not only established a powerful internal regime under which China prospered as never before, with a population reaching 315,000,000 in 1800 and 430,000,000 by 1850; they also extended China's external frontiers to incorporate Mongolia, Manchuria, Sinkiang and Tibet within China's frontiers for the first time. China exercised, too, some influence over a further series of tributary states, including Korea, Vietnam and Nepal. At the height of its power in about 1800, Ch'ing China faced serious internal economic problems, widespread social unrest and rebellions. From 1840 the western powers also began to force trading concessions from the Chinese and to exert pressure on the Chinese government.

Foreign influence in China The Opium War (1839–42) exposed China's weakness in the face of modern western military technology. As a result Hong Kong was ceded to Britain, and a number of ports opened to foreign trade. In the 1850s China faced a series of internal rebellions during which the western powers extracted further concessions, and Russia secured extensive territories east of the rivers Amur and Ussuri. In 1894–5 Japan's easy victory over China led to a period when the great powers attempted to define spheres of influence in China, and to compete for economic concessions, particularly for the right to build railways. With the collapse of the Ch'ing empire Mongolia became an independent state, Chinese influence in Tibet lapsed, Sinkiang came increasingly under Soviet influence, and Manchuria under the dominance of Japan which had already annexed Taiwan in 1895. In 1932 Manchuria became the Japanese puppet state of Manchukuo. In 1937 Japan invaded China itself, and occupied large areas until 1945.

The growth of the Communist regime The Chinese Communist Party had controlled large parts of Kiangsi and some neighbouring areas in the early 1930s. They were driven out by the Nationalists and established their base at Yen-an in Shensi from which they conducted their war of resistance against the Japanese. During the war many liberated areas within Japanese territory were communist dominated. With the coming of peace in 1945 the Russian occupation of Manchuria and Inner Mongolia ensured Communist dominance of these areas. After the outbreak of Civil War with the Nationalists in 1946 the Communist armies rapidly over-ran the north, and in 1949 the People's Republic was established in Peking, while the remaining members of the Nationalist government fled to Taiwan.

PRE-HISTORY AND THE SHANG PERIOD

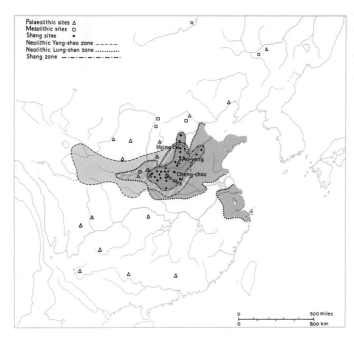

THE WARRING STATES PERIOD

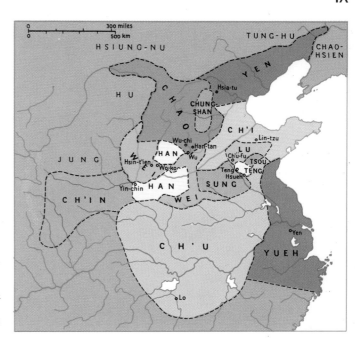

THE HAN EMPIRE 2 AD

THE THREE KINGDOMS 220–265 AD

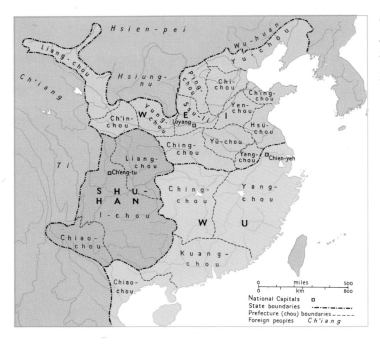

THE NORTHERN AND SOUTHERN DYNASTIES

T'ANG CHINA 742 AD

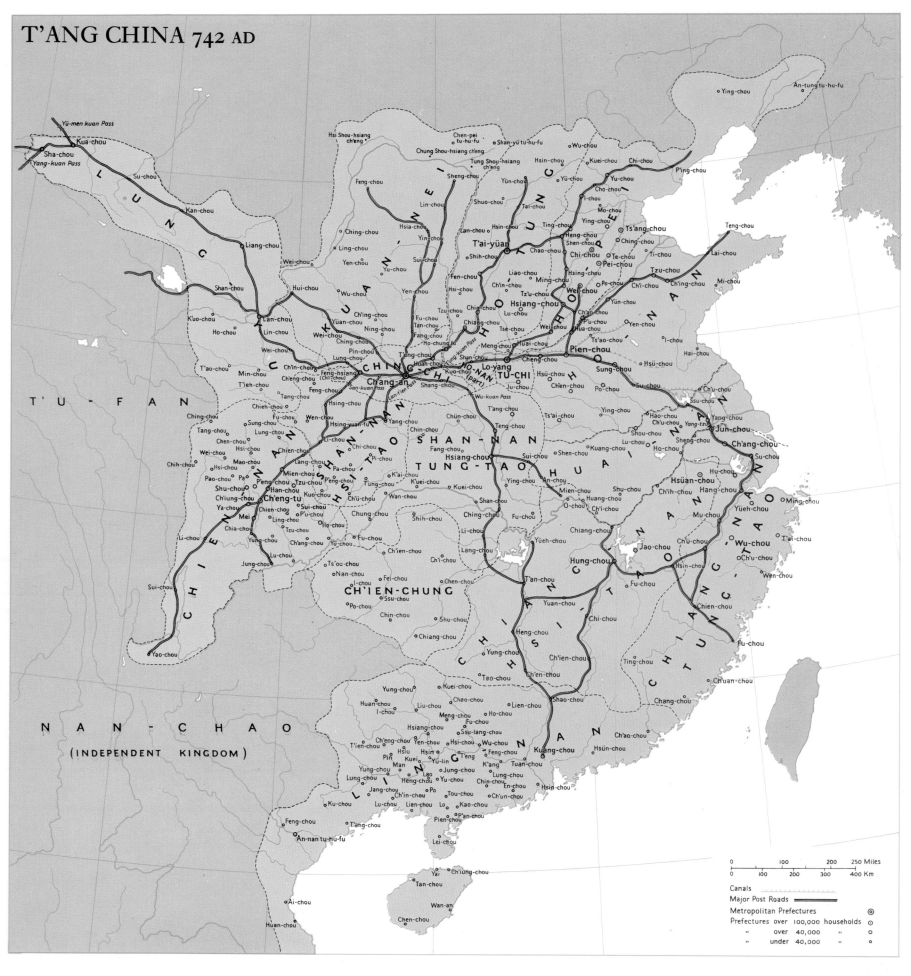

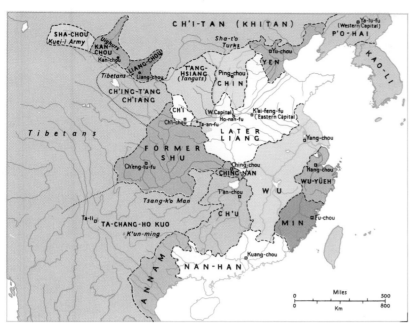

THE FIVE DYNASTIES

THE SOUTHERN SUNG AND CHIN

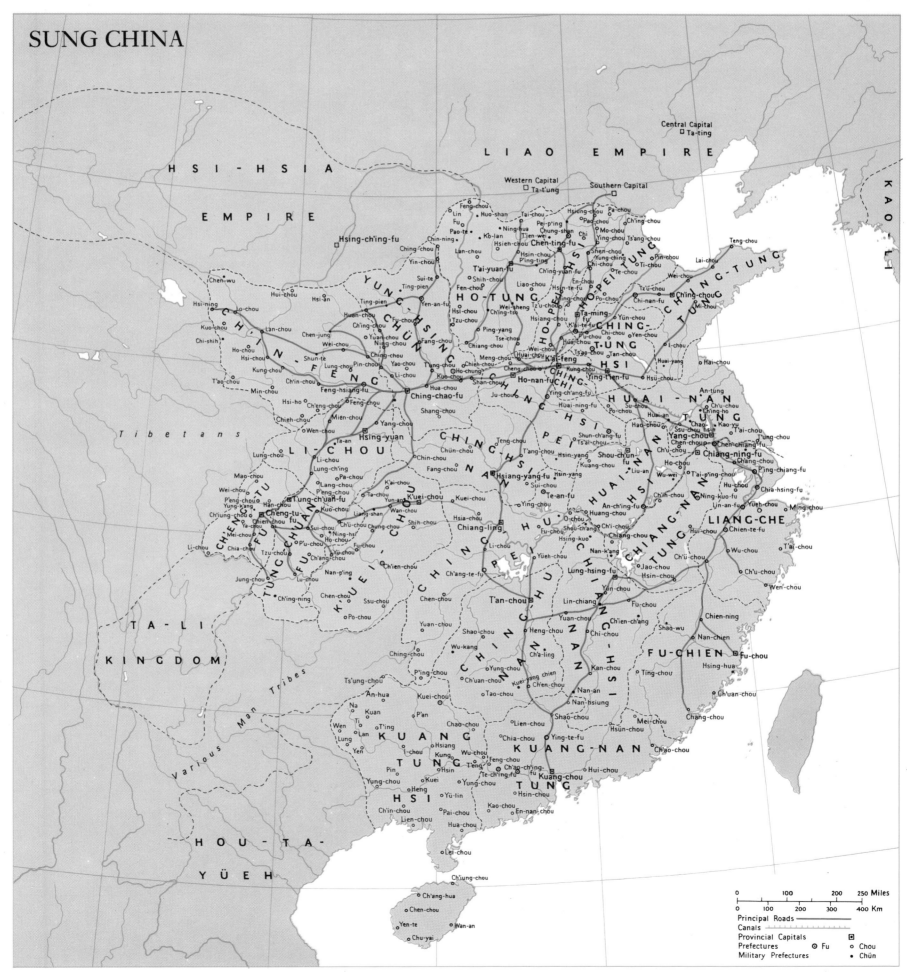

SUNG CHINA

THE MONGOL WORLD EMPIRE

Novgorod

Sibir

Moscow

Russian States

Kazan

Kiev

KIPCHAK EMPIRE

Sarai

GOLDEN HORDE

Ho-lin

Shang-tu

Liao-yang

Koryŏ

Ta-tu

E M P I R E

O F   T H E

G R E A T

Kan-chou

Pien-liang

Hang-chou

Wu-ch'ang

CHAGHATAI

Samarkand

Lop

K H A N

Feng-yuan

Tabriz

Mery

Kan-chou

Lung-hsing

Liu-ch'iu

EMPIRE

Ch'eng-tu

Ch'ang-te

ILKHAN

Baghdad

Isfahan

Herat

Leh

Mar-yul

Tibet

Shiraz

Kerman

Kabul

Lahore

Lhasa

Kuang-chou

EMPIRE

Multan

Delhi

Ta-li

Hainan

Sind

Empire of Delhi

Benares

Patna

MIEN

Annam

0 200 400 600 800 1000 miles

0 400 800 1200 1600 km

THE MONGOL (YÜAN) PERIOD 1300 AD

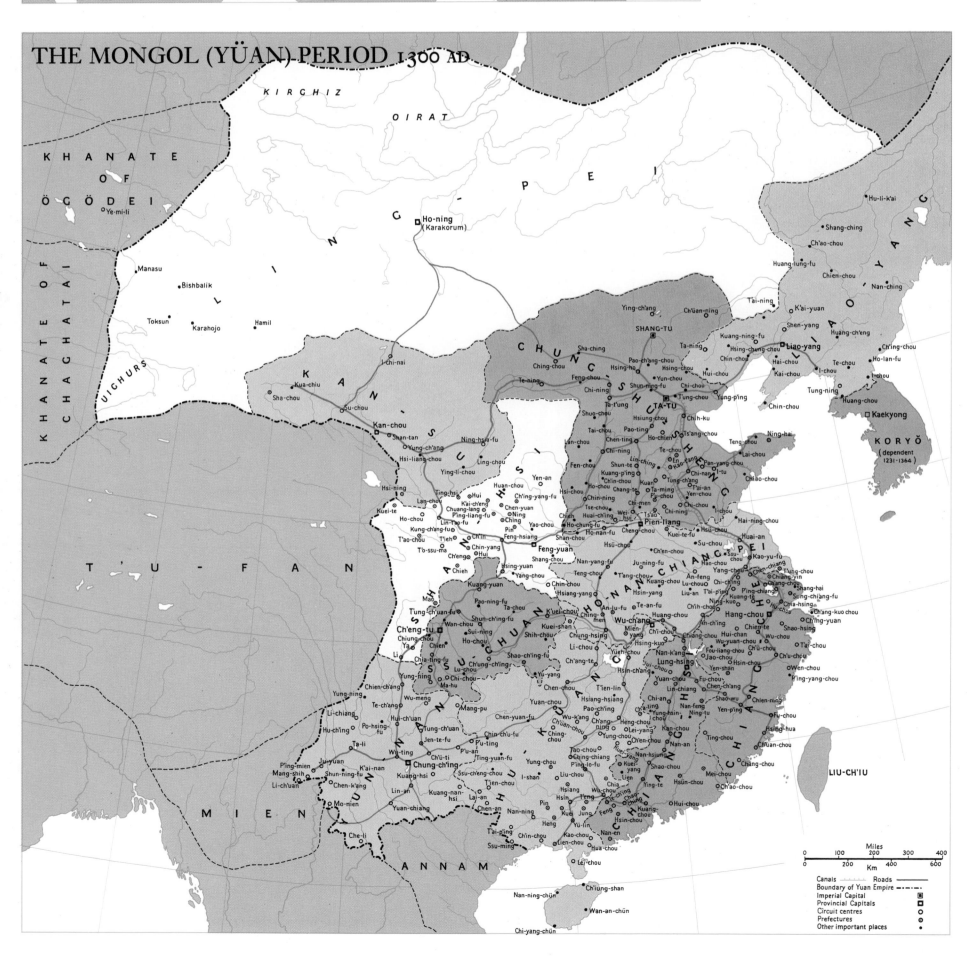

KIRGHIZ

OIRAT

KHANATE OF ÖGÖDEI

Ye-mi-li

L I N G   P E I

Ho-ning (Karakorum)

Hu-li-k'ai

Shang-ching

Ch'ao-chou

Nan-ching

KHANATE OF CHAGHATAI

Manasu

Bishbalik

Toksun

Karahojo

Hamil

UICHURS

I-chi-nai

KAN-SU

Kua-chiu

Sha-chou

Su-chou

Huang-lung-fu

Chien-chou

Ch'ing-chou

Ho-lan-fu

Ying-ch'ang

Ch'üan-ning

T'ai-ning

K'ai-yuan

Shen-yang

Huang-ch'eng

Shang-tu

Sha-ching

Ching-chou

CHUNG-SHU-SHENG

Liao-yang

KORYŎ (dependent 1231-1364)

Kaekyong

Te-ning

Feng-chou

Yun-nan

Chi-chou

Hsing-chung-chou

Chin-chou

Hai-chou

Te-chou

Ho-lan-fu

I-chou

Tung-ning

Huang-chou

Kan-chou

Shan-tan

Yung-ch'ang

Hsi-liang-chou

Ling-chou

Ning-hsia-fu

Ta-t'ung

Shuo-chou

Tai-chou

Lan-chou

Chen-ting

Te-chou

Ts'ang-chou

Teng-chou

Ning-hai

Lai-chou

T'U-FAN

Hsi-ning

Ting-hsi

Hui

Lan-chou

Kai-ch'eng

Chung-hsing

Ho-chou

Lin-t'ao-fu

Ping-liang-fu

Yao-chou

Ch'ing

Yen-an

Huan-chou

Chen-yuan

Chieh

Hsün-te

Chang-te

Ta-ming

T'ai-an

Yen-chou

I-chou

Hai-ning-chou

SHANSI

Shun-te

Ho-chung-fu

Tse-chou

Ts'ao

Chi-men

Yen-chou

Kuei-te-fu

Su-chou

Huai-an

Kao-yu-fu

CHIANG-PEI

T'ao-chou

T'ieh

Ch'in

Chin-yang

Feng-hsiang

Shan-chou

Hsü-chou

Nan-yang-fu

Kuei-te-fu

Su-chou

Kung-ch'ang-fu

T'o-ssu-ma

Ch'eng

Chieh

Hsing-yuan

Yang-chou

HONAN

Teng-chou

Hsin-yang

Liu-an

T'ai-p'ing

Ping-chiang

Shang-hai

Ch'ia-hsing

Ch'ang-kuo-chou

Ch'ing-yuan

Kuang-yuan

Pao-ning-fu

Ta-chou

K'uei-chou

Ju-ning-fu

An-feng

Yang-chou

Chien-yin

Pao-ting

Tz'ŭ

T'ung-ch'uan-fu

Shun-ch'ing-fu

Li-chou

Chung-ch'ing-fu

Ch'ang-te

Ch'ing-ho

Chien-te

Shao-hsing

SZU-CH'UAN

Ch'eng-tu

Wan-chou

HU-KUANG

Nan-k'ang

Wu-yuan-chou

Wu-chou

T'ai-chou

Chiung-chou

Ho-chou

Li-chou

Chung-ho-ch'ing-fu

Ch'ang-te

Yüeh-chou

Jao-chou

Ch'ü-chou

Wen-chou

Ya

Chien

Yü-yang

Hsiang-hsiang

Yuan-chou

Lung-hsing

CHIANG-CHE

Li-chiang

Chia-ting-fu

Lu-chou

Shih-chou

Chung-ch'ing-fu

Chi-an

Fu-chou

Hsing-hua

Yung-ning

Chien-ch'ang

Ma-hu

Yu-yang

T'ien-lin

Yen-shan

Shao-wu

Chien-ning

Te-ch'ang

Hui-ch'uan

Mang-pu

Chen-yuan-fu

Hsiang-hsiang

Pao-ch'ing

Heng

Yung-hsing

Shao

KIANGSI

Li-chiang

Po-hsing-fu

Tung-ch'uan

Jen-te-fu

Ch'ing-chou

Kan-chou

Ting-chou

Fu-chou

P'ing-mien

Shun-ning-fu

K'ai-nan

Chin-ch'u-fu

P'u-an

Yuan-yang-fu

Tao-chou

Nan-an

Lei-yang

Shao

Mei-chou

Ch'ao-chou

Mang-shih

Ch'ü-ti

Chung-ch'ing

Kuang-hsi

Ssu-ch'eng-fu

Tien-chou

I-shan

Liu-chou

Heng

Kuang

Ying-te

Hsün-chou

Lin-ch'uan

K'ai-nan

Laj-ni

Chen-an

Nan-ning

Kuei

Jung

Feng

Wu-chou

Hui-chou

Ch'ao-chou

MIEN

Mo-nien

Yuan-chiang

T'ai-ping

Ch'in-chou

Kao-chou

Nan-en

Che-li

Hsin

Hua-chou

ANNAM

Nan-ning-chün

Chiung-shan

Wan-an-chün

LIU-CH'IU

Chi-yang-chün

Miles 0 100 200 300 400

Km 0 200 400 600

Canals ...... Roads ———

Boundary of Yuan Empire —·—·—·—

Imperial Capital ■

Provincial Capitals ▣

Circuit centres ⊙

Prefectures ○

Other important places •

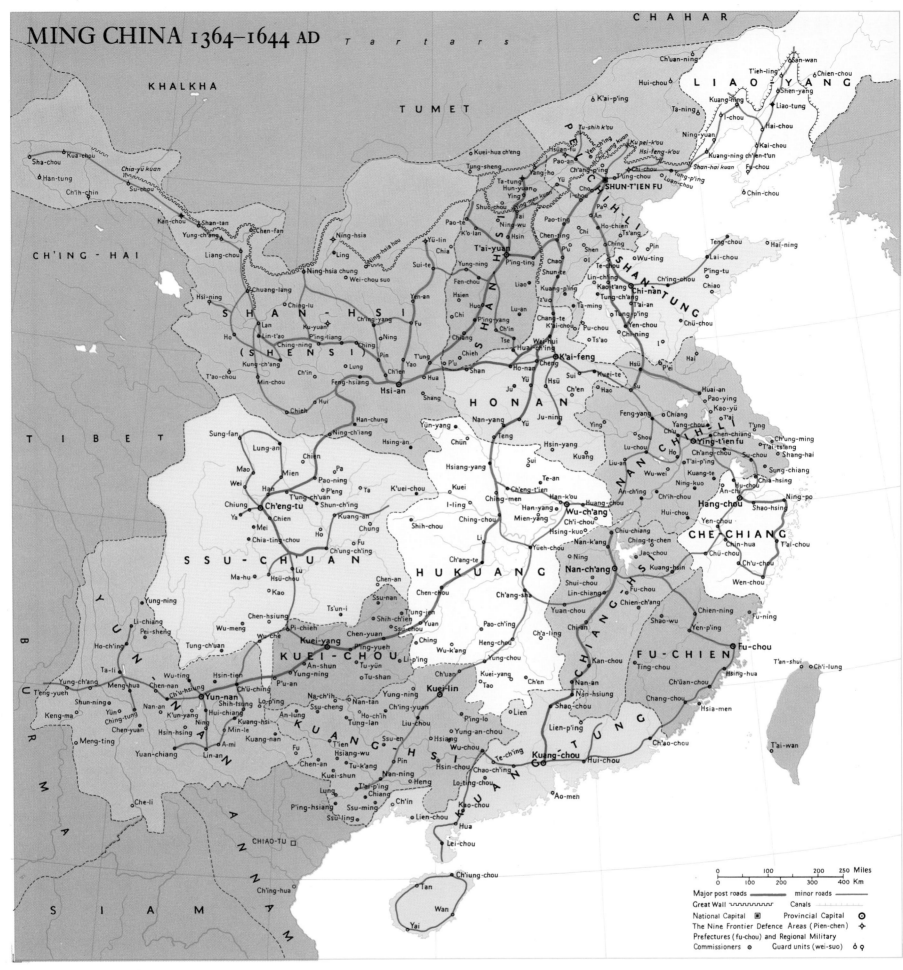

MING CHINA 1364–1644 AD

Tartars

CHAHAR

KHALKHA

TUMET

CH'ING-HAI

TIBET

BURMA

SIAM

SHAN-HSI (SHENSI)

SSU-CHUAN

YUNNAN

KUEI-CHOU

KWANG-HSI

HONAN

HUKUANG

KIANGSI

KWANGTUNG

FU-CHIEN

CHE-CHIANG

NAN-CHIH-LI

PEI-CHIH-LI

CHI-NAN-TUNG

LIAO-YANG

Major post roads — minor roads —
Great Wall ⌒⌒⌒⌒ Canals
National Capital ☐ Provincial Capital ◉
The Nine Frontier Defence Areas (Pien-chen) ✦
Prefectures (fu-chou) and Regional Military
Commissioners ◦ Guard units (wei-suo) ◦ ◦

0   100   200   250 Miles
0 100 200 300 400 Km

THE MING VOYAGES

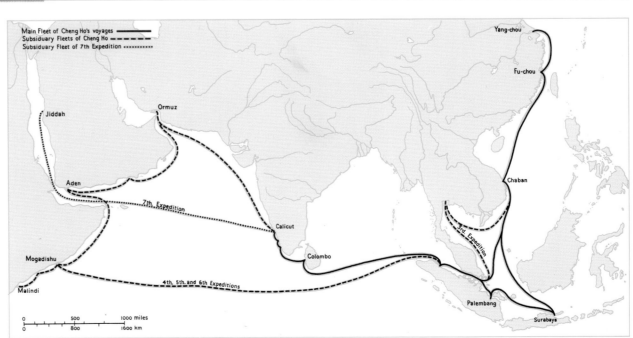

Main Fleet of Cheng Ho's voyages —
Subsidiary Fleets of Cheng Ho – – –
Subsidiary Fleet of 7th Expedition ·······

Jiddah

Ormuz

Aden

Mogadishu

Malindi

Calicut

Colombo

7th Expedition

4th, 5th, and 6th Expeditions

Palembang

Surabaya

Chaban

Fu-chou

Yang-chou

0   500   1000 miles
0   800   1600 km

THE CH'ING EMPIRE

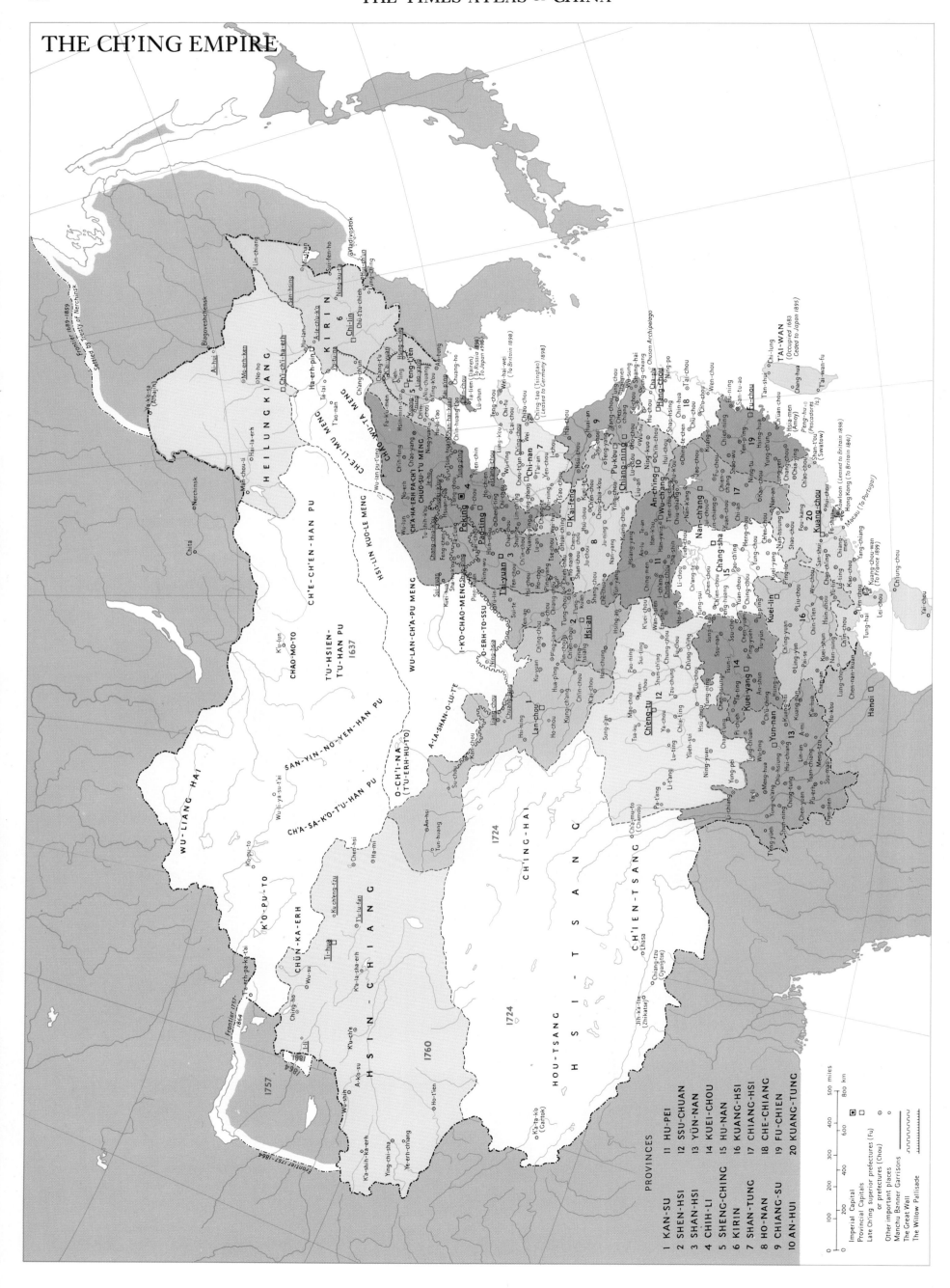

PROVINCES

1 KAN-SU	11 HU-PEI	
2 SHEN-HSI	12 SSU-CHUAN	
3 SHAN-HSI	13 YÜN-NAN	
4 CHIH-LI	14 KUEI-CHOU	
5 SHENG-CHING	15 HU-NAN	
6 KIRIN	16 KUANG-HSI	
7 SHAN-TUNG	17 CHIANG-HSI	
8 HO-NAN	18 CHE-CHIANG	
9 CHIANG-SU	19 FU-CHIEN	
10 AN-HUI	20 KUANG-TUNG	

Imperial Capital
Provincial Capitals
Late Ch'ing Superior prefectures (Fu)
  or prefectures (Chou)
Other important places
Manchu Banner Garrisons
The Great Wall
The Willow Pallisade

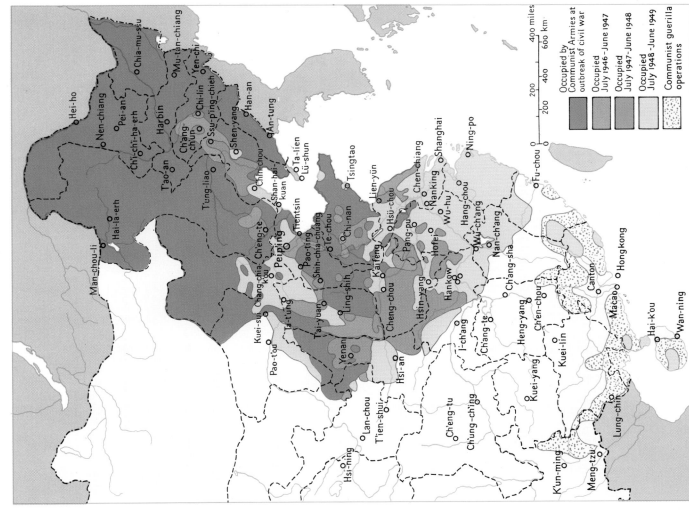

THE GROWTH OF THE COMMUNIST REGIME 1945–1949

Occupied by Communist Armies at outbreak of civil war

Occupied July 1946–June 1947

Occupied July 1947–June 1948

Occupied July 1948–June 1949

Communist guerilla operations

FOREIGN INFLUENCE IN CHINA

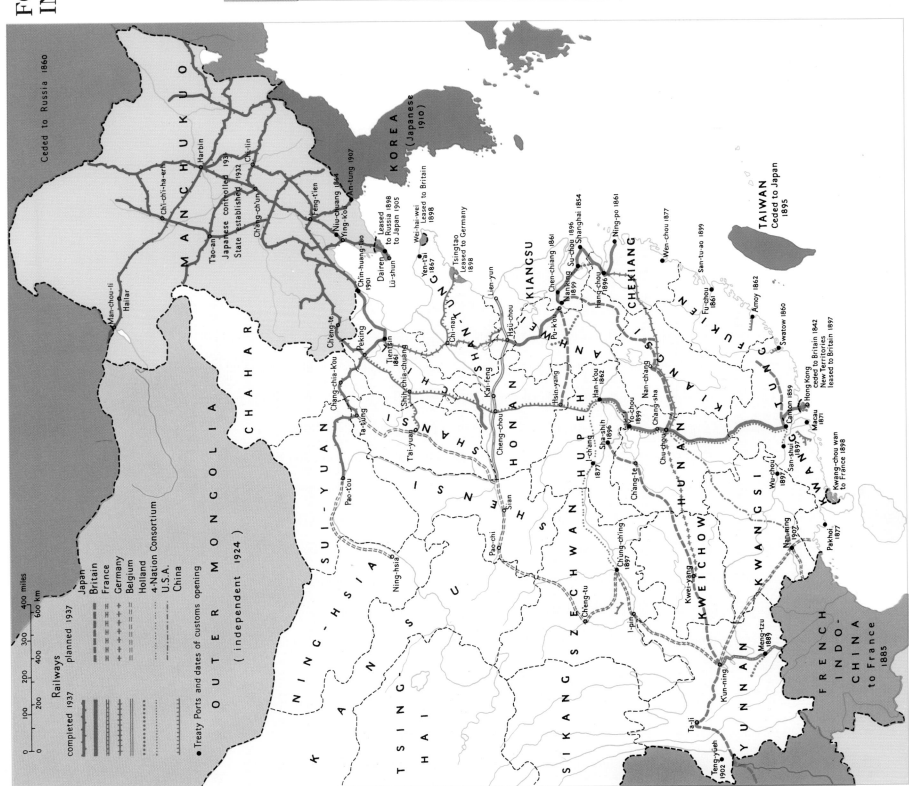

Railways

completed 1937
planned 1937

Japan
Britain
France
Germany
Belgium
Holland
4-Nation Consortium
U.S.A.
China

● Treaty Ports and dates of customs opening

ROUGHLY a quarter of the world's people live in China. The 1953 Census gave a total of 583,000,000. The exact figure at the present time is unknown, and estimates range from 750,000,000 to more than 900,000,000. The majority of observers place the total at more than 800,000,000.

The total Chinese population has always been very large by comparison with European countries, but has grown very rapidly in recent centuries. Until about AD 800 it remained stable at around 50,000,000. Between that date and AD 1200 it rose rapidly to more than 100,000,000 persons. Following the Mongol conquest it fell to about 65,000,000 in the late 14th century, and then rose steadily to about 150,000,000 in 1600. During the rebellions at the end of the Ming dynasty (1367–1644) and during the conquest of the Manchus, there was great loss of life, and the population only recovered to this level in the first decade of the 18th century. The peaceful and prosperous 18th century saw a tremendous population 'explosion'. From 150,000,000 in 1710 the total leapt to more than double (313,000,000) by 1800, and by 1850 had nearly trebled at 430,000,000.

The outbreak of the T'ai-p'ing rebellion and the series of risings and civil wars which followed, such as the Nien rebellion and the Moslem risings in Turkestan and Yunnan caused the loss of countless millions of lives, and in the 1870s and 1880s a series of terrible famines caused at least 20,000,000 deaths in northern China. These disasters led not only to a drop in the total population, but also prompted considerable internal migration and a marked fall in the rate of population increase. Under the Republic (1912–49) social and political instability, natural disasters and famines, and the massive loss of life during the war of resistance against the Japanese and the ensuing civil war, again kept population increase in check.

Nevertheless in 1953 the population had increased to nearly 600,000,000. Since 1949 internal peace and political stability, more adequate distribution of food supplies and rapidly improving standards of medical care and public hygiene have caused a further rapid population increase. A radical decrease in infant mortality has also led to a population whose average age is very young, when compared with the rapidly ageing populations of western countries. 86 per cent of the Chinese population is below 50, and 40 per cent under 18 years of age. At present the population is probably increasing at a rate of 15,000,000 per year.

Over-population was already becoming a problem at the end of the 18th century, when the necessity of feeding a rapidly increasing population began to strain the available food supply. In the mid-1950s this problem again became a subject of public debate, and a number of prominent economists began to advocate the limitation of runaway population growth by contraception, abortion and the encouragement of later marriages. This line was adopted by Chou En-lai in a speech in 1955, and became official policy. A widespread educational campaign began. However, at the time of the Great Leap Forward in 1958 there was a reversal of official policy, which promoted the theory that a large population and the largest possible labour force was an economic asset rather than a liability.

However, in the years of severe food shortages (1959–61) following the Great Leap Forward, official policy changed once again, and since 1962 the government has continued to encourage planned childbirth and late marriages. The 'normal' age of marriage is accepted as 25–29 for men, and 23–27 for women. These policy changes have had far greater impact upon the urban workers than among the rural population.

The Chinese population is almost entirely concentrated in the eastern half of the country. The western regions, Sinkiang, Tsinghai and Tibet, which only came under Chinese domination under the Manchu Ch'ing dynasty in the 18th century, and which are unsuited for permanent settlement, remain very sparsely peopled. Except for small oases they are largely inhabited by nomadic or semi-nomadic pastoral peoples. These three provinces, which comprise 37.5 per cent of the total land area of China, contain only 1.4 per cent of the population. Similarly the Inner Mongolian and Ningsia border areas, arid grasslands and semi-desert unsuited to permanent agriculture, which account for another 13 per cent of the total area, contain only 1.7 per cent of the population. Thus the arid western and north-western half of China contains barely 3 per cent of its people, and large areas are completely uninhabited.

In contrast to these areas, the eastern half of China is very densely peopled and the entire cultivable area has been settled for many centuries. Only the plains of the three provinces of the north-east, formerly the homeland of the Manchus, have been settled in the last century and a half. The only areas with low population densities are the mountainous regions, and marginal and uncultivated uplands. Something like 30 per cent of the total land area is under cultivation, and in these areas the population is extremely dense. Most of eastern China has population densities of more than 100 per square mile. In the fertile farmlands of the great eastern plain, the Yangtze valley, Szechwan and Kwangtung, densities are commonly over 500 per square mile, and in the great plain sometimes over 1,000 per square mile. Most densely peopled of all is the province of Szechwan. In the fertile plain around Ch'eng-tu the population density reaches 1,500 per square mile.

The great majority of the Chinese population remains rural and agricultural. At the time of the 1953 census only 13 per cent of the Chinese were urban dwellers. Even of this total, a third lived in small rural market towns and minor local administrative centres with less than 20,000 persons.

In the 1950s urban population was rapidly expanded as a result of the drive towards industrialisation, under the First Five Year Plan and the Great Leap Forward. Between 1957 and 1960 the total urban population shot up from 92,000,000 (14.3 per cent of the total) to 130,000,000 (18.5 per cent). Most of this increase resulted from the migration of workers from the countryside, but it was also affected by the abnormally high birth-rate in the cities, which was twice the national average. This enormous rate of increase among the urban population led to a shortage of urban housing, and consequent pressure on the construction industry which was unable to meet the demand for housing.

The collapse of the Great Leap Forward led to a considerable decrease in urban population. By 1962 some 20,000,000 urban workers had been returned to the countryside as the result of the closing down of many new and uneconomic industrial plants.

A third of the urban population live in the 17 great cities with populations of more than one million. These cities, which also accounted for more than 60 per cent of China's total industrial capacity in 1960, are concentrated in the coastal provinces and in Manchuria, with the exception of the great regional economic centres, T'ai-yüan, Hsi-an (Sian), Ch'eng-tu and Ch'ung-ch'ing, which were developed by deliberate policy in the 1950s. Besides these great metropolitan centres there are about a hundred regional urban centres with more than 100,000 people, and another hundred with more than 50,000. Well over 90 per cent of these urban centres are in eastern China, and a large proportion are in the north and north-east. The sparsely peopled western half of the country has very few urban centres of any size, and there are comparatively few large cities in southern China.

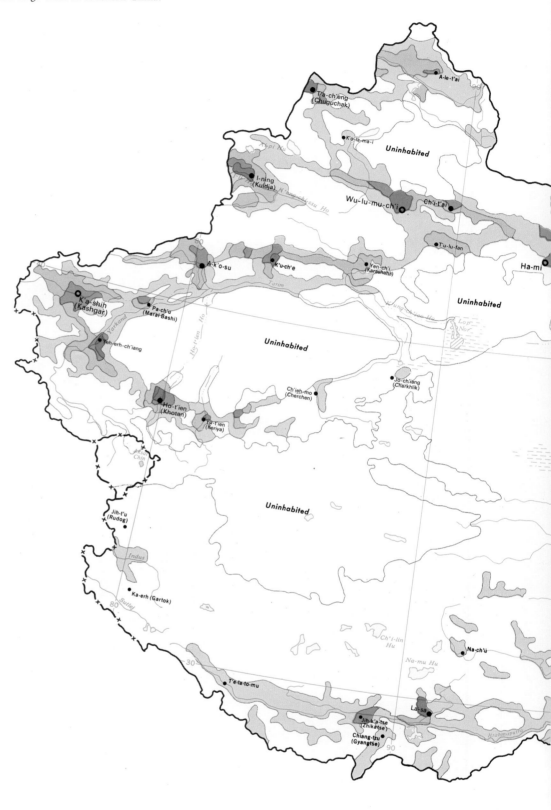

RURAL POPULATION
Persons per square mile

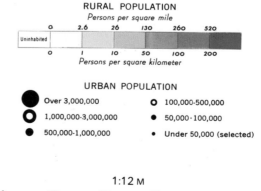

URBAN POPULATION

● Over 3,000,000 ○ 100,000-500,000

○ 1,000,000-3,000,000 ● 50,000-100,000

● 500,000-1,000,000 • Under 50,000 (selected)

1:12 M

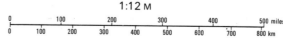

Population		Literacy	Structure of agricultural employment		
Population (1972) (1,000)	**Density per sq. km.**	**(% of Population over 15 years old)**	**(% of economically active population)**		
				1960	1970
PRC 750,000	79	N. America 99	Africa	80.5	75.5
Europe 469,000	95	Europe & USSR 96	**PRC**	**75.2**	**66.7**
Africa 364,000	12	Oceania 90	L. America	47.9	41.5
S. America 300,000	15	L. America 76	USSR/E. Europe	42.6	32.4
USSR 248,000	11	**PRC 60**	Japan	33.0	21.0
N. America 233,000	11	Asia (general) 53	W. Europe	23.5	17.2
Japan 106,000	287	Africa 26	Oceania	12.0	8.9
World 3,782,000	28		N. America	7.2	4.4
			World	57.8	51.4

ABOUT 95 per cent of the total Chinese population is composed of Han Chinese peoples, speaking one or other of the dialects of Chinese. The other 5 per cent is made up of the members of a great number of national minorities, ethnically and linguistically different from the Chinese. Despite their relatively small numbers, the minorities are politically significant for they occupy between them almost half of the area of China, including the vitally important strategic border areas with the Soviet Union, the Mongolian People's Republic, India, Burma, Vietnam and Korea.

The Tibetans There are about three million Tibetans, who occupy most of the Tibetan Autonomous Region, Tsinghai province, western Szechwan and north-western Yunnan. They were until recent times an independent people whose culture and social institutions have developed along quite different lines from the Chinese, and they remained to a large degree semi-autonomous, bound together by the complete political and social dominance of the Lamaistic church. Tibet was finally brought under firm Chinese central control after the rebellion of 1959, and in 1965 the Tibet Autonomous Region was set up to administer the area.

The Turkic peoples The various Turkic peoples, all of them Moslem, total about 4,300,000 and inhabit most of Sinkiang and the north-western parts of Tsinghai and Kansu. The most important of these peoples are the Uighurs, who inhabit the oases and towns of Sinkiang, and who were the dominant group in Central Asia until the Manchu conquest in the 18th century. The Uzbeks are also mostly settled in the oasis towns. The other main groups are the Kazakhs and the Kirghiz, pastoral nomads who live along the western border of Sinkiang and the Soviet Union, and whose peoples also live across the frontier. During their long and complex history, these Turkic peoples have enjoyed long periods of independence, but since 1949 many Chinese have been settled in the area, and although Sinkiang is an Autonomous Region, its Turkic peoples are no longer so dominant.

The Mongols The Mongols, totalling about one and a half million, inhabit the entire border region abutting on the Mongolian People's Republic, from Kansu in the west to Heilungkiang. The Mongols of this frontier zone comprise a great number of tribes speaking different dialects. They are organised into tribal Leagues and Banners each of which has its own territory. In the past the nomadic existence of the Mongols, in grasslands too dry for permanent agriculture, distinguished them from their Chinese neighbours, but since the late 19th century Chinese settlers have encroached on their pasturelands and attempted to open the frontier area for agriculture, and now many of the Mongols live in permanent settlements.

In addition to this main frontier zone of Mongol settlement there are scattered tribes and settlements of Mongols in the Dzungarian region of Sinkiang. In Tsinghai live the Monguor (Tu) people, who have been separated from the main Mongol peoples for many centuries and preserve an archaic form of the language and many ancient customs. Kansu is the home of the Pao-an and Tung-hsiang, Mongol peoples who live among the Chinese Moslems of the area and have been converted to Islam, although most of the Mongols were strongly influenced by Lamaistic Buddhism until recent times.

The Mongols, once rulers of all China and much of northern Asia, have always been very independent, even under the Manchu dynasty. In the early years of this century a powerful nationalist movement grew up, which led to the foundation of the independent Mongolian Republic. In 1947 an Inner Mongolian Autonomous District was established, which in 1954 was enlarged to form the Inner Mongolian Autonomous Region stretching from the borders of Heilungkiang to Sinkiang, with an area of 450,000 square miles. The Region was reduced, in 1969, to about a third of that area.

The Tungusic peoples The most important Tungusic people, the Manchus, who number perhaps two and a half millions, have been almost completely assimilated into the Han Chinese population, no longer speak their own language, and do not form separate ethnic communities. Most of them live in the provinces of Liaoning, Kirin and Heilungkiang.

The Koreans There is a considerable Korean minority numbering more than a million living in the north-east. The main community lives in the area around Yen-chi in eastern Kirin, where they settled as refugees in the 1870s.

The Chinese Moslems (Hui) The Chinese Moslems are not strictly an ethnic minority, since they are of Han Chinese descent and speak dialects of Mandarin. But they form a powerful religious minority which tends to live in separate communities concentrated in the north-west (Ningsia, for instance, forms a Hui Autonomous Region), in Peking and Tientsin, and among the city populations of Hopeh, Honan, Anhwei and Hunan.

The south-western minorities Most of the south-west, Kwangsi, Kweichow and Yunnan, has been colonised by Han Chinese only in comparatively recent times. Even today in these areas Chinese settlement is largely confined to the more fertile mountain basins and valleys, leaving the uplands and more remote districts in the hands of a great number of minority peoples. These peoples, whose insulation from Chinese influence until quite recently has made them China's most numerous, backward and fragmented minorities, divide into three main groups. The first includes half a million Thai tribesmen who live in the areas of Yunnan bordering on Burma, Laos and North Vietnam; the seven million Chuang who since 1958 have had their own province, Kwangsi Chuang Autonomous Region, and the Pu-yi. The second group comprises the three million Miao-Yao with settlements in southern Kweichow, in Yunnan, Kwangsi, Hunan and Kwangtung, and the She people who live in the mountains of Fukien and Chekiang. The third group includes the Sino-Tibetan peoples in western Yunnan and south-western Szechwan; the Min-chia living around Ta-li and the Tu-chia of western Hunan; the Hani on the Vietnamese border, and the Lisu and the Lahu in western Yunnan.

ALTAIC*		
TURKIC	1. Uighur	4. Salar
	2. Kazakh	5. Uzbek
	3. Kirghiz	
MONGOLIAN		
	6. Mongol	8. Tu(Mongor)
	7. Tung-hsiang	9. Daur
TUNGUSIC		
	10. Oronchon	12. Evenki
	11. Sibo	
KOREAN		
INDO-EUROPEAN		
TADZHIK		
AUSTROASIATIC		
MON-KHMER	13. Kawa	
	14. Puman (Pulang)	

SINO-TIBETAN		
HAN (CHINESE)		
△ **HUI (CHINESE MOSLEM)**		
TIBETO-BURMAN		
15. Tibetan	19. Hani (Woni)	
16. Yi (Lolo)	20. Lisu, Chingpo	
17. Pai	21. Lahu	
(Min-chia)	22. Nasi	
18. Tuchia		
TAI		
23. Puyi	25. T'ai	
(Chung-chia)	26. Chuang	
24. T'ung	27. Shui	
MIAO-YAO		
28. Miao	30. She	
29. Yao		

UIGHUR Language or dialect

*Language family

1:12 M

0	100	200	300	400	500 miles
0	100 200 300	400 500	600	700	800 km

CLIMATIC features, above all else, dictate the uses to which much of China's landscape can be put. The country is sharply divided into two parts, the north-western and western half, an arid or semi-arid region with less than 20 inches of annual precipitation, where temperature variations are extreme, and where permanent agriculture is possible only in sheltered or well-irrigated pockets; and, in contrast to this, the more humid regions of the south and south-east where the climate is much less variable.

The Chinese climatic pattern is dictated by the winter and summer monsoons. The monsoon pattern of climate is subject to wide local variation, and the continental high pressure and low pressure systems are far more extreme and more persistent in some years than in others. The annual variations have made the climate very unpredictable, and China has suffered seriously in the past from the effects of flood and, more particularly, of drought. In winter, the bitterly cold continental areas of Siberia and Central Asia become the centre of a massive and persistent high pressure system. Strong northerly or north-westerly winds (the winter monsoons) flow out from this system to the Pacific. Blowing into China from the Gobi desert, these winds generate frequent dust storms in northern China, but bring very little precipitation. Throughout China only a small proportion of the annual precipitation falls during the winter months and during the spring. From May onwards the air masses are reversed. Siberia and Central Asia heat up and become the centre of a low pressure system, and China's climate is dominated by southerly and south-easterly winds (the summer monsoons) flowing in from the Pacific. These are heavily moisture-laden and bring the summer rains (the 'plum rains'). Everywhere in China summer and autumn are the wettest seasons. This is especially the case in northern and north-eastern China where almost three-quarters of the annual rainfall comes between mid-June and mid-September.

In northern China spring droughts are frequent, and these are commonly followed by floods in early summer. Moreover, the summer rains fall during the period when losses through evaporation are highest, and their effects are thus significantly reduced. Although the concentration of rainfall in summer and autumn is almost universal, except in the western areas with minimum rainfall, it does not present such a serious problem in southern and south-eastern China. Here the annual rainfall rises to 50 or 80 inches, and even the drier winter months have adequate rainfall. Moreover, unlike northern China, the south is not subject to great variations in rainfall from one year to the next.

Average temperatures vary greatly throughout the country. The average January temperatures are below freezing throughout the west and north of the Chin-ling mountain range and the Huai river. In the north of Manchuria they fall well below −18°C (0°F) and there are areas where the subsoil is permanently frozen. In the north-east the winters are so severe that the rivers are icebound for upwards of 180 days each year. The average winter temperatures in central and southern China rise steadily towards the coastal zone of Fukien and Kwangtung, where they are about 15.5°C (60°F).

Whereas winter temperatures vary according to latitude, in summer the average temperatures are very much more uniform throughout the country. The average July temperatures are above 21°C (70°F) everywhere, and in general decrease from the coast westward. The average July temperatures in the south-east coastal zone, and in the Szechwan basin in the interior, are above 29.5°C (85°F).

The annual temperature range thus varies greatly. The most extreme variations of climate are to be found in northern Manchuria, where the average temperatures range from −25°C (−13°F) in January to 21°C (70°F) in July, and in the inland deserts of Sinkiang. The least variation is to be found in the southern coastal areas, where the seasons are far less sharply differentiated, and where the growing season lasts the whole year round.

These are broad generalisations. Local conditions and topography greatly influence climate, especially in the mountainous western half of the country. In the high plateaux of western China and Tibet sheer altitude also has a great effect. There are very great variations in the micro-climates of these areas, and for most of western China no adequate climatic data are available to permit of detailed description.

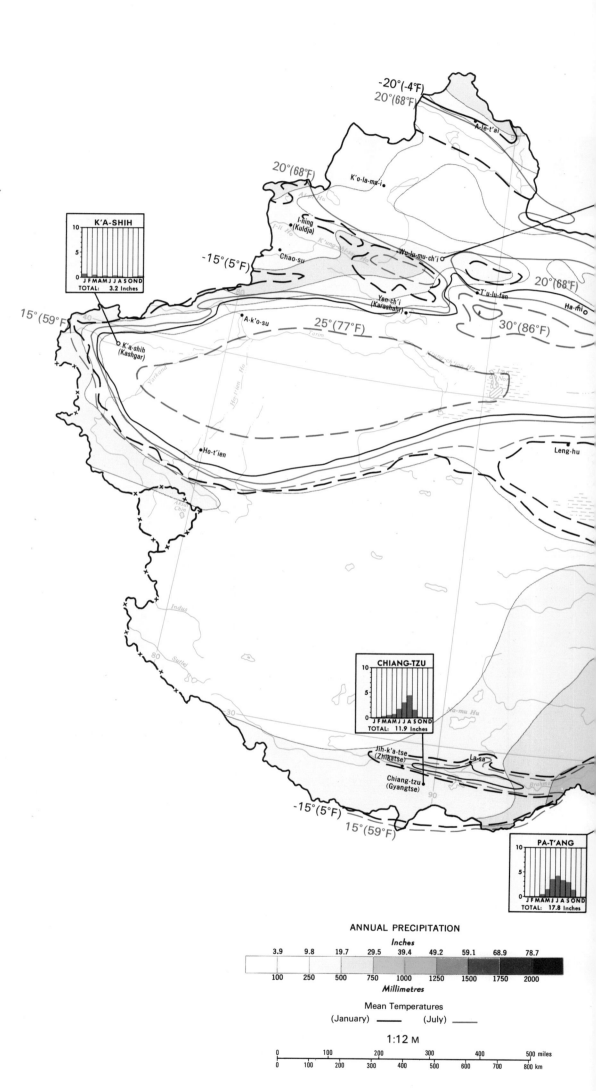

ANNUAL PRECIPITATION

Inches
3.9   9.8   19.7   29.5   39.4   49.2   59.1   68.9   78.7
100   250   500   750   1000   1250   1500   1750   2000
Millimetres

Mean Temperatures
(January) ——   (July) ——

1:12 M

20°(68°F)

20°(68°F)

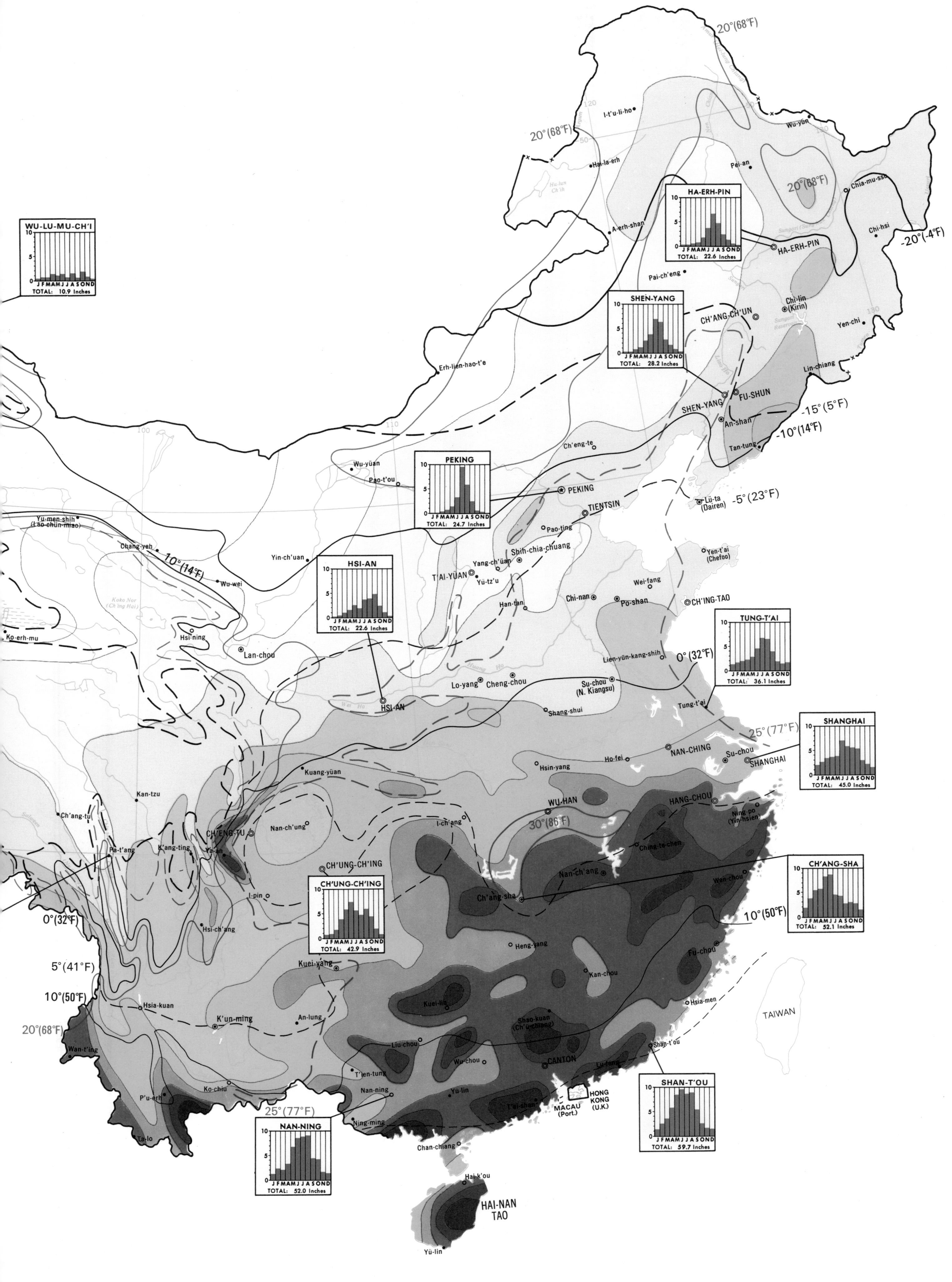

I-t'u-li-ho

Wu-yün

Hai-la-erh

Pei-an

Chia-mu-ssu

20°(68°F)

HA-ERH-PIN
10
5
0
J F M A M J J A S O N D
TOTAL: 22.6 Inches

Chi-hsi

A-erh-shan

HA-ERH-PIN

−20°(−4°F)

Pai-ch'eng

SHEN-YANG
10
5
0
J F M A M J J A S O N D
TOTAL: 28.2 Inches

CH'ANG-CH'UN

Chi-lin (Kirin)

Yen-chi

WU-LU-MU-CH'I
10
5
0
J F M A M J J A S O N D
TOTAL: 10.9 Inches

Erh-lien-hao-t'e

Lin-chiang

SHEN-YANG

FU-SHUN

An-shan

−15°(5°F)

−10°(14°F)

Ch'eng-te

Wu-yüan

Tan-tung

Pao-t'ou

PEKING
10
5
0
J F M A M J J A S O N D
TOTAL: 24.7 Inches

PEKING

TIENTSIN

Lü-ta (Dairen)

−5°(23°F)

Yü-men-shih (Lao-chün-miao)

Pao-ting

Chang-yeh

Yin-ch'uan

Yang-ch'üan

Shih-chia-chuang

Yen-t'ai (Chefoo)

10°(14°F)

Wu-wei

T'AI-YÜAN

Yü-tz'u

Wei-fang

HSI-AN
10
5
0
J F M A M J J A S O N D
TOTAL: 22.6 Inches

Han-tan

Chi-nan

Po-shan

CH'ING-TAO

Koko Nor (Ch'ing Hai)

Ko-erh-mu

Hsi-ning

Lan-chou

Lien-yün-kang-shih

0°(32°F)

TUNG-T'AI
10
5
0
J F M A M J J A S O N D
TOTAL: 36.1 Inches

Lo-yang

Cheng-chou

Su-chou (N. Kiangsu)

Tung-t'ai

HSI-AN

Shang-shui

25°(77°F)

SHANGHAI
10
5
0
J F M A M J J A S O N D
TOTAL: 45.0 Inches

Kuang-yüan

Hsin-yang

Ho-fei

NAN-CHING

Su-chou

SHANGHAI

Kan-tzu

WU-HAN

HANG-CHOU

Ch'ang-tu

i-ch'ang

30°(86°F)

Ning-po (Yin-hsien)

CH'ENG-TU

Nan-ch'ung

Ching-te-chen

Pa-t'ang

K'ang-ting

Ya-an

CH'UNG-CH'ING

Nan-ch'ang

Wen-chou

CH'ANG-SHA
10
5
0
J F M A M J J A S O N D
TOTAL: 52.1 Inches

I-pin

Ch'ang-sha

CH'UNG-CH'ING
10
5
0
J F M A M J J A S O N D
TOTAL: 42.9 Inches

10°(50°F)

0°(32°F)

Hsi-ch'ang

Heng-yang

Fu-chou

5°(41°F)

Kuei-yang

Kan-chou

10°(50°F)

Hsia-kuan

Kuei-lin

Hsia-men

20°(68°F)

K'un-ming

An-lung

Shao-kuan (Ch'ü-chiang)

TAIWAN

Wan-t'ing

Liu-chou

Shan-t'ou

P'u-erh

Ko-chiu

Wu-chou

Yü-lin

CANTON

Lu-feng

T'ien-tung

Nan-ning

T'ai-shan

MACAU (Port.)

HONG KONG (U.K.)

25°(77°F)

Ning-ming

SHAN-T'OU
10
5
0
J F M A M J J A S O N D
TOTAL: 59.7 Inches

Ta-lo

NAN-NING
10
5
0
J F M A M J J A S O N D
TOTAL: 52.0 Inches

Chan-chiang

Hai-k'ou

HAI-NAN TAO

Yü-lin

CHINA has always been an agrarian society, and agricultural techniques were already advanced by the 14th century when most of the crops, techniques and implements characteristic of Chinese agriculture were already in use. From that time onwards Chinese agriculture has had to support an ever-increasing population. By the end of the 16th century most of the good farmland in China itself was already under cultivation. Although new foreign crops, such as maize, sweet potatoes and ground nuts enabled farmers to utilise poor upland soils, much good land was devoted to the cultivation of another import – tobacco – and later of opium. Careless cultivation of hill lands also led to widespread soil erosion. In ordinary farming, few technical innovations were made. Farming became more and more labour-intensive and the average size of farms decreased. Although some frontier areas were brought under cultivation, climatic and physical conditions severely limited expansion of the cultivated area, and the same area which had fed 100,000,000 people in the 14th century had to feed more than 400,000,000 by the 19th century. By about 1800 China faced an economic crisis.

By the present century this crisis was acute. Although after 1850 Chinese settlers began to move into Manchuria and to open up some of the frontier zone in Inner Mongolia which had been traditional pasturelands of the Mongol tribes, there was little further room for expansion. Early in this century the population had reached 450,000,000 and famine was frequent, particularly in the poor northern provinces. Although about half of the farmers cultivated their own land, tenancy was widespread, particularly in the Yangtze provinces, in the south and in Szechwan. In the 1930s most people, of all political parties, believed that the inequalities of land-ownership were the source of China's agrarian problems, and landlordism, tenancy, indebtedness and the exploitation of the peasantry were blamed for agriculture's inefficiency. They believed that a more equitable redistribution of land would automatically increase the efficiency of agriculture. After 1949 planners continued to stress the primary need for such social and institutional changes. Although land reform was rapidly carried out throughout China, many inequalities persisted, and the average size of farms remained very small and uneconomic.

The next stage of planning was the organisation of individual farmers into larger productive units, first into mutual aid teams, whose members retained ownership of their lands, then into producer co-operatives and higher collectives in which all land was owned by the members. By 1956, 96 per cent were incorporated into producer co-operatives and 88 per cent were fully collectivised. These higher collectives averaged some 170 households – the equivalent of a large village – and were subdivided into production brigades of about 20 households. A further step towards full collectivisation came with the organisation of the People's Communes (Jen-min kung-she) in 1958. These combined the existing higher collectives into much larger units, which also took over the functions of the lowest level of local government, the *hsiang*. The communes, unlike the collectives, thus combined economic management with ordinary administrative functions. They were not only a step towards full communal control of all the means of production, but were also an essential part of the policy of administrative de-centralisation begun in 1957. By September 1958 the collectives had been merged into 26,400 communes, with an average size of 4,600 households or 25,000 persons. The largest were in the independent municipalities of Peking and Shanghai and in the most modernised areas with good communications – Hopeh, Honan, Kiangsu, Chekiang, the middle Yangtze plain around Wu-han and Kwangtung. The original communes proved to be too large, and after 1961 their number was greatly increased and their size reduced. By 1963 there were about 74,000 communes controlling the natural economic and social areas served by traditional local markets.

Internally the communes are divided into production brigades and smaller production teams which manage and perform agricultural work and production. The commune as a whole manages repair and construction work, handicrafts and small scale local industries, and has tended to become an organ of low-level local administration, with responsibility for law and order, rural education, health services, irrigation and water-control, and local transport. These changes in the nature of the communes occurred in the period of economic crisis and widespread shortages which followed the failure of the Great Leap Forward. The abandonment of very large productive units coincided with the end of attempts to impose a pattern of strictly communal living, and farmers regained control of their own private plots of land. At the same time the basic policy of the government towards agriculture changed. The social and institutional changes in favour of collective or communal use of land had now been pressed to completion, and the government now began to encourage technical improvement in agricultural production. Capital investment, which had been almost exclusively devoted to heavy industry in the 1950s was now diverted to the support of agriculture. Fertiliser production had been very backward but after 1962 many large plants and also a great number of small local factories were constructed. Although the use of chemical fertilisers still falls far below that of more highly developed countries, their wide-spread availability has led to great increases in crop yields. A further significant technical development was the mechanisation of agriculture. At the time of the Great Leap Forward local light engineering industries were established, mostly designed for the manufacture and repair of farm implements. The production of tractors began in the 1950s in large centralised plants built on Soviet models, producing machines designed for large scale farming. Since the early 1960s, however, many small local plants have been producing a wide range of tractors designed for Chinese conditions, while other local industries have developed seed-drills, earth-moving machinery and chemical sprays. Large scale rural electrification has also made possible the use of electrical pumping equipment for irrigation schemes and much of this equipment, too, is manufactured in local plants.

Great attention has also been given to the improvement of crop varieties. New strains of wheat have been cultivated in areas of the west and north with extremely harsh climates. New types of rice have pushed the limits both of rice cultivation and of double cropping of rice much farther north than in earlier times. The use of insecticides and pest control have also improved production. New techniques of cultivation have been tried and the terracing of fields, contour ploughing to check soil erosion, irrigation and afforestation schemes have considerably increased the area under cultivation.

In the early years, from 1949–61, agrarian production in China rose only very slowly, in spite of collectivisation, and the years 1959–61 were years of disastrous food shortages, crop failures and widespread hardship. Since 1962, however, grain production has risen steadily, and successfully provided for the increase in the population. Agriculture remains by far the most important sector of the Chinese economy, employing a very large proportion of the work-force, and providing both raw material for industry and roughly one-third of China's total exports.

Oases—Agricultural potential limited by availability of irrigation water. Wide variety of food grains, industrial crops (cotton), and fruit and vegetable specialties—grapes and melons.

Tibetan Highlands—High elevations limit cultivation mainly to fast-maturing barley. Some tubers and hardy vegetables grown; wheat and other grains planted at lower elevations.

Szechwan Rice—Single crop rice followed by wheat, rape, or peas is common cropping system. Corn and sweet potatoes extensively cultivated in non-irrigated fields.

PER CENT IN CULTIVATION

0   10   30   50

Non-cultivated

Oasis

Agricultural region boundary

Maximum length of growing season in days

1:12 M

0   100   200   300   400   500 miles

0   100   200   300   400   500   600   700   800 km

Corn-Kaoliang-Soybeans — Corn acreage recently increased; corn grown in rotation with kaoliang and leguminous crops, such as soybeans. Spring wheat, millet and other food grains grown; sugar beets locally important.

Spring Wheat—Spring wheat predominant grain. Yields fluctuate widely, except where irrigation water available. Millet, oats, buckwheat and oilseeds also significant crops.

Corn-Kaoliang-Winter Wheat — Corn planted in spring or summer following harvest of winter wheat, barley or peas. Rotations of corn and leguminous crops, such as soybeans, common. Kaoliang widely grown and cotton acreage significant.

Most significant agricultural division in China—along Huai Ho and upper Han Shui valleys—separates rice-growing southern provinces from the dry-grain-growing northern provinces where wheat, and coarse grains dominate. Sweet or white potatoes grown in all regions.

Rice-Winter Wheat — Agricultural transition zone between the North and South; to the north little rice grown; to the south some wheat is grown, but not as a major crop. One crop rice predominates, with wheat often sown in fall after rice harvest. Wheat also planted in dry fields. Cotton important industrial crop.

Rice-Tea—One crop rice traditional, but two crops harvested in some areas. Wheat, rape, or peas often follow single crop rice; green fertilizer crops usually follow in two crop rice areas.

Southwestern Rice — One crop of rice predominates. Wheat, beans, rapeseed, or green fertilizer crops commonly follow rice. Corn, particularly in the uplands, important secondary crop; subtropical crops commonly grown in the valleys.

Double-Crop Rice — Two crops of rice harvested annually throughout most of the region; three crops of rice grown in parts of Hainan. Some wheat, winter legumes, rapeseed or green fertilizer crops follow late rice crop. Sugarcane important secondary crop in Kwangtung; other subtropical crops widespread.

Production of selected crops (1971) 1,000 metric tons

	Europe	USSR	USA	PRC	Japan	World
Wheat	79,634	92,000	44,620	**32,000**	444	343.1
Rye	15,757	12,000	1,294	—	1	30.9
Barley	51,484	36,000	10,070	**18,500**	503	152.4
Oats	18,711	15,000	12,712	**1,690**	60	57.7
Maize	41,160	11,500	140,733	**28,500**	30	307.8
Millet & Sorghum	451	3,000	22,739	**22,000**	16	101.1
Rice paddy	1,841	1,420	3,820	**104,000**	14,139	307.4
includes mixed/misc. **All cereals**	231,212	172,640	236,146	**210,500**	15,207	1309.0
Sugar cane	462	—	21,769	**30,500**	815	585,482
Sugar beets	105,463	78,324	23,766	**5,200**	2,332	228,151
Centrifugal sugar	15,843	8,150	5,134	**3,300**	466	72,268
Non-centrifugal sugar	—	—	—	**726**	3	11,339
Potatoes	134,704	92,300	14,451	**27,000** 1965	3,156	306,445
Sweet potatoes & Yams	81	—	626	**81,000** 1965	2,564	147,713
Dry beans	913	68	744	**1,400**	167	11,686
Apples	12,533	—	2,791	**400**	1,050	19,954
Pears	4,509	—	665	**900**	470	7,399
Grapes	35,223	1,087	2,830	**135** 1970	234	54,838
Oranges/Tangerines	4,414	95	7,841	**700**	3,000	—
Soy beans	193	610	31,823	**11,500**	122	48,291
Groundnuts in shell	72	1	1,357	**2,700**	111	18,480
Cotton-seed	326	4,646	3,978	**3,036**	—	21,976
Rape-seed	2,076	3	1	**1,000**	25	7,880
Cotton (Lint)	183	2,394	2,299	**1,518**	—	11,799
Sesame-seed	78	1	4	**3,700**	30	20,981
Sunflower-seed	2,137	5,700	110	**70**	—	9,694
Castor beans	17	70	15	**90**	—	797
Jute	—	50	—	**500**	15	3,474
100 metric tons **Tung oil**	—	7	20	**900**	—	1,201
100 metric tons **Tea**	1	678	—	**1,730**	930	13,048
100 metric tons **Tobacco**	5,918	2,880	8,101	**7,850**	1,497	46,592

Meat, milk and egg production

	(1,000 metric tons)		(100 metric tons)	
	***meat**	****milk**	poultry	eggs
Europe	22,017	150,431	—	60,393
USSR	8,750	83,100	11,000	23,000
USA	16,939	53,796	63,321	42,185
PRC	***13,310**	**400,932**	**26,350**	**33,100**
Japan	941	5,004	3,810	18,500

—beyond estimate
*of which 3,460 pork
**cow, buffalo, goat, sheep
***beef-veal, mutton-lamb, pork

Raw silk

(not cocoons)
metric tons

Japan	20,515
PRC	10,200
USSR	3,020
Europe	801
USA	—
World	40,268

Wool Production

100 metric tons

	Greasy	Clean
USSR	4,240	2,544
Europe	2,620	1,421
USA	871	385
PRC	**600**	**360**
Japan	2	1
World	27,368	15,865

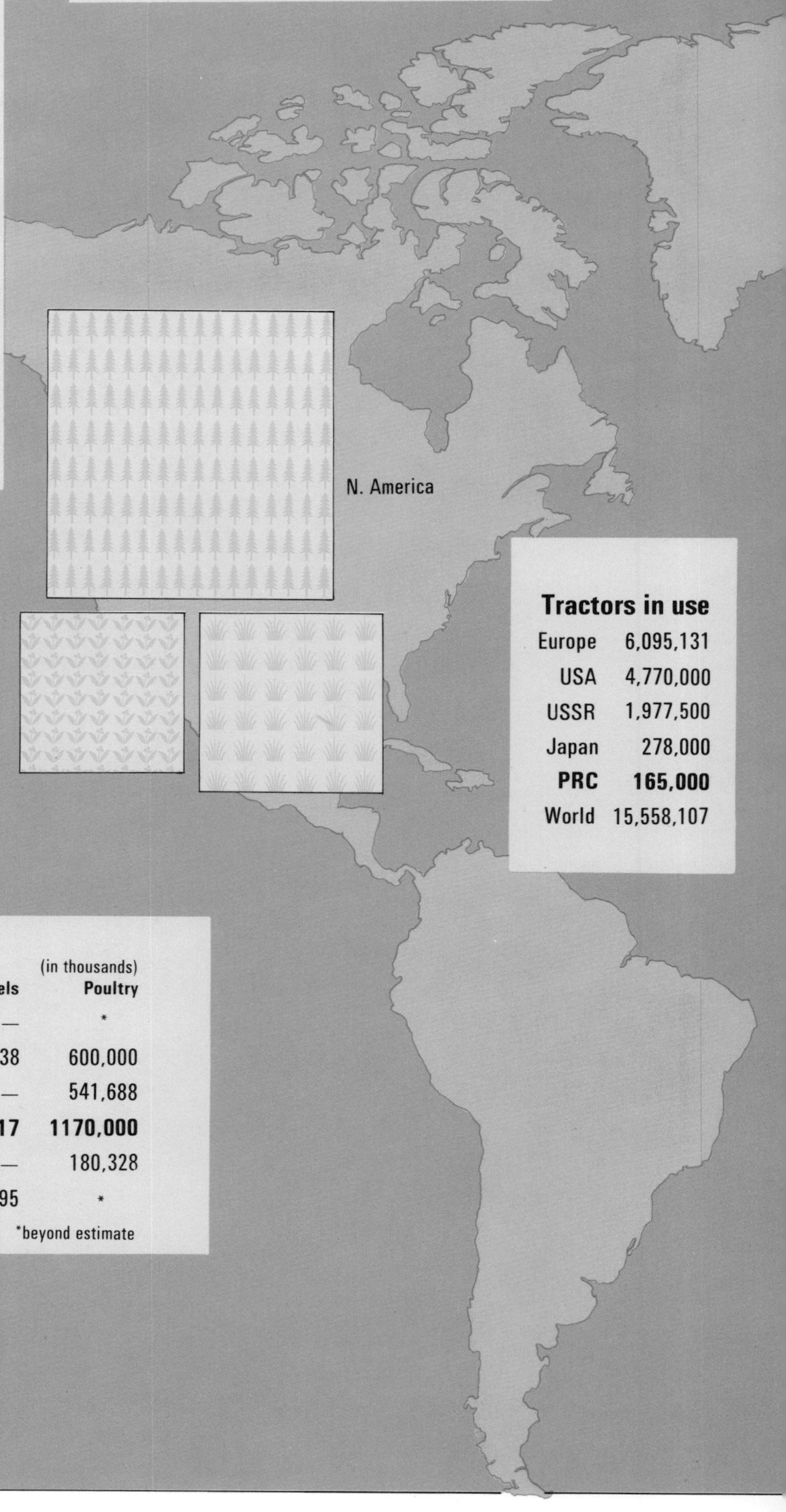

N. America

Tractors in use

Europe	6,095,131
USA	4,770,000
USSR	1,977,500
Japan	278,000
PRC	**165,000**
World	15,558,107

Livestock and poultry numbers

	(in millions)									(in thousands)
	Horses	Mules	Asses	Cattle	Pigs	Sheep	Goats	Buffaloes	Camels	Poultry
Europe	7.7	1.1	1.7	122.6	139.4	127.4	12.6	0.3	—	*
USSR	7.4	—	0.6	99.1	67.4	137.9	5.4	0.5	238	600,000
USA/Canada	8.1	—	—	126.8	75.2	20.3	2.1	—	—	541,688
PRC	**7.2**	**1.6**	**11.7**	**63.2**	**223.0**	**71.0**	**57.5**	**29.4**	**17**	**1170,000**
Japan	0.1	—	—	3.6	6.9	0.2	0.2	—	—	180,328
World	66.3	14.7	41.9	1141.2	667.7	1074.7	383.0	125.3	145.95	*

—Figures not available   *beyond estimate

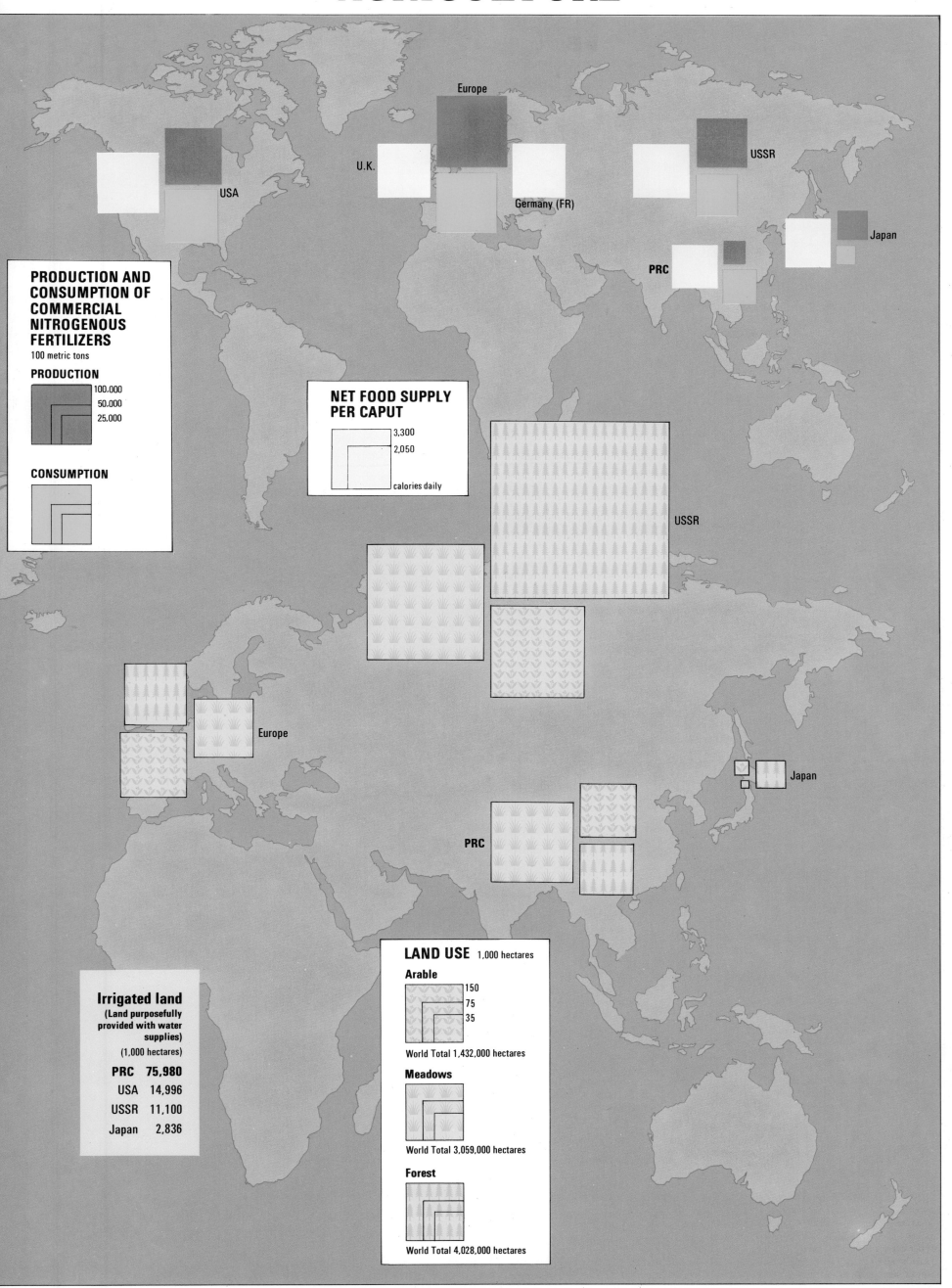

USA

Europe

U.K.

Germany (FR)

USSR

Japan

PRC

PRODUCTION AND CONSUMPTION OF COMMERCIAL NITROGENOUS FERTILIZERS
100 metric tons

PRODUCTION
- 100,000
- 50,000
- 25,000

CONSUMPTION

NET FOOD SUPPLY PER CAPUT
- 3,300
- 2,050

calories daily

USSR

Europe

Japan

PRC

Irrigated land
(Land purposefully provided with water supplies)
(1,000 hectares)

PRC	75,980
USA	14,996
USSR	11,100
Japan	2,836

LAND USE 1,000 hectares

Arable
- 150
- 75
- 35

World Total 1,432,000 hectares

Meadows

World Total 3,059,000 hectares

Forest

World Total 4,028,000 hectares

UNTIL the construction of railways, China depended upon its traditional transport network. The country was divided into roughly 60,000 primary market areas, which formed the basic social and economic divisions of the country, and which were the centres of perhaps three-quarters of all commerce. Within these areas the peasant producers carried their own goods to market, delivered their own rents to landlords, paid their taxes to the authorities and carried home their own purchases. Transfer of goods between these markets, and from the local markets to larger commercial centres was undertaken partly by professional carriers, partly by peasants working for hire as a subsidiary means of livelihood. Such local transport depended in northern China largely upon the roads, goods being carried by carts drawn by oxen, mules or horses, by pack animals, by wheelbarrows and human porters. In southern China, the natural river systems and a dense network of canals provided a means of transport. In general, the waterways, which also served the needs of drainage, flood control and irrigation, were much better maintained than the primitive roads of the north, and though water transport was still expensive, it was much cheaper than transport by road, which gave central and southern China a marked economic advantage over the north.

The long-distance transport system which was superimposed on the dense network of local communication was supported and maintained by the central government. Although the Ch'in and Han built a system of trunk highways in the 3rd and 2nd centuries BC, these were allowed to fall into disrepair and the road system remained poor and ill-maintained. However a nationwide network of post stations and courier services for official communications was maintained and these trunk routes became important routes for ordinary trade and travel. Besides maintaining communications throughout their empire, the government also had to collect vast revenues, and to transfer huge quantities of grain to provision their armies. Water transport was the only practicable means of handling such traffic. The main grain surplus areas were in central China, and the capitals and the bulk of the military establishment were in the north. Since the main river systems of the great eastern plain (the Yangtze, Huai Ho and Huang Ho) ran west to east, canals were built to join these river systems and carry the south to north traffic. The first canal between the Yangtze and Huai was built during the Warring States period. Under the Sui, in AD 607–9, a canal was built linking the Huang Ho to the Huai river and thence to the Yangtze and beyond to Hang-chou. Another canal joined the Huang Ho to a place near modern Tientsin. In the 14th century this canal system was replaced by the Grand Canal which linked Peking to the Yangtze by a different route. Until the 18th century this provided a very efficient transport system, with its own administrative and maintenance staff and large fleets of barges. In the middle of the 19th century, however, the system was seriously damaged. In 1851–5 the Huang Ho, which had flowed into the sea south of the Shantung peninsula, changed its course, blocking the northern section of the Grand Canal. Subsequently the southern sections of the canal were seriously damaged during the T'ai-p'ing and Nien rebellions. The Chinese government began to ship grain and other goods from Shanghai to Tientsin by sea, using both foreign steamers and ships of its own Chinese Merchants' Steam Navigation Company. Chinese owned steamboats became numerous and by 1913 over 1,000 steamers were in use on inland waterways. Although steamships were much faster, the costs of transport were about the same as for native junks, and these continued to carry the bulk of the goods.

As the steamship gradually changed the long-distance transport of bulk cargoes, the government communications system was also completely revolutionised in the late 19th century. A telegraph system was begun in 1881, a modern postal service was founded in 1896 and a telephone service in 1903, and the Chinese statesmen, who were convinced of the necessity of an effective system of transport as a means of strengthening the country, put all their efforts into railway construction. The beginnings of a modern highway system came much later than railways – in 1912 there were no roads fit for motor traffic at all – but rapid progress was made, and under the Nationalist government, from 1928–37, there was a serious attempt to build a planned highway network in the provinces of Chekiang, Kiangsu, Anhwei, Honan, Kiangsi, Hunan and Hopeh. By 1937 there were 114,000 kilometres of highway, more than two-thirds of which had been built since 1928, and almost all of which was in the coastal provinces. The outbreak of war, and the flight of the Chinese government to the south-west led to extensive highway construction in western China and the interior. A highway carried heavy truck traffic through the north-west and Sinkiang to the Soviet Union, and in the south-west a road was built through Yunnan to Burma. However, road transport remained severely hampered by the lack of automotive industry, a chronic shortage of fuels and a lack of technical skills and maintenance facilities. In 1949 the traditional forms of transport, slow, inefficient and extremely costly, continued to carry most goods.

Since 1949 the highway system has been extended and improved, and existing highways renovated. A network of strategic highways has been built to open up the sparsely peopled and remote areas of the south-west and west and have played a major role in the firm integration into the Chinese state of the ethnic minorities of these outlying areas. They have also made possible the exploitation of economic resources such as the oil fields of K'o-la-ma-i (Karamai) and the Tsaidam Basin. The road network of China is now estimated to total some 500,000 kilometres but well over half of this total is merely unsurfaced earth tracks, and there are still only a few thousand kilometres of modern concrete or bituminous-surfaced roads. Traffic is very light, however, as vehicles are few and petrol scarce. The Chinese automotive industry, concentrated in Ch'ang-ch'un, with smaller plants in Tientsin, Shanghai, Wu-han, Nan-ch'ang and Canton, is still very small. The first trucks were produced in 1957, but production virtually came to a halt in 1961, and only began to recover in about 1966. In 1971 output of trucks was about 75,000.

Waterways remain an important part of the transport system, although water transport in the north is badly limited by severe winters. In the 1950s, after a long period of neglect, considerable investment was made in the waterways. A major scheme, begun under the First Five Year Plan, to repair and re-open the Grand Canal as a trunk route has apparently been completed as far as the borders of Shantung, and the water-control and conservancy schemes on the Hai Ho, Huang Ho and Huai Ho systems, and improvements to the upper course of the Yangtze, have all added to the mileage of waterway navigable by small craft. As on the roads, however, traditional forms of transport prevail, and most water traffic is still carried by shallow-draught junks.

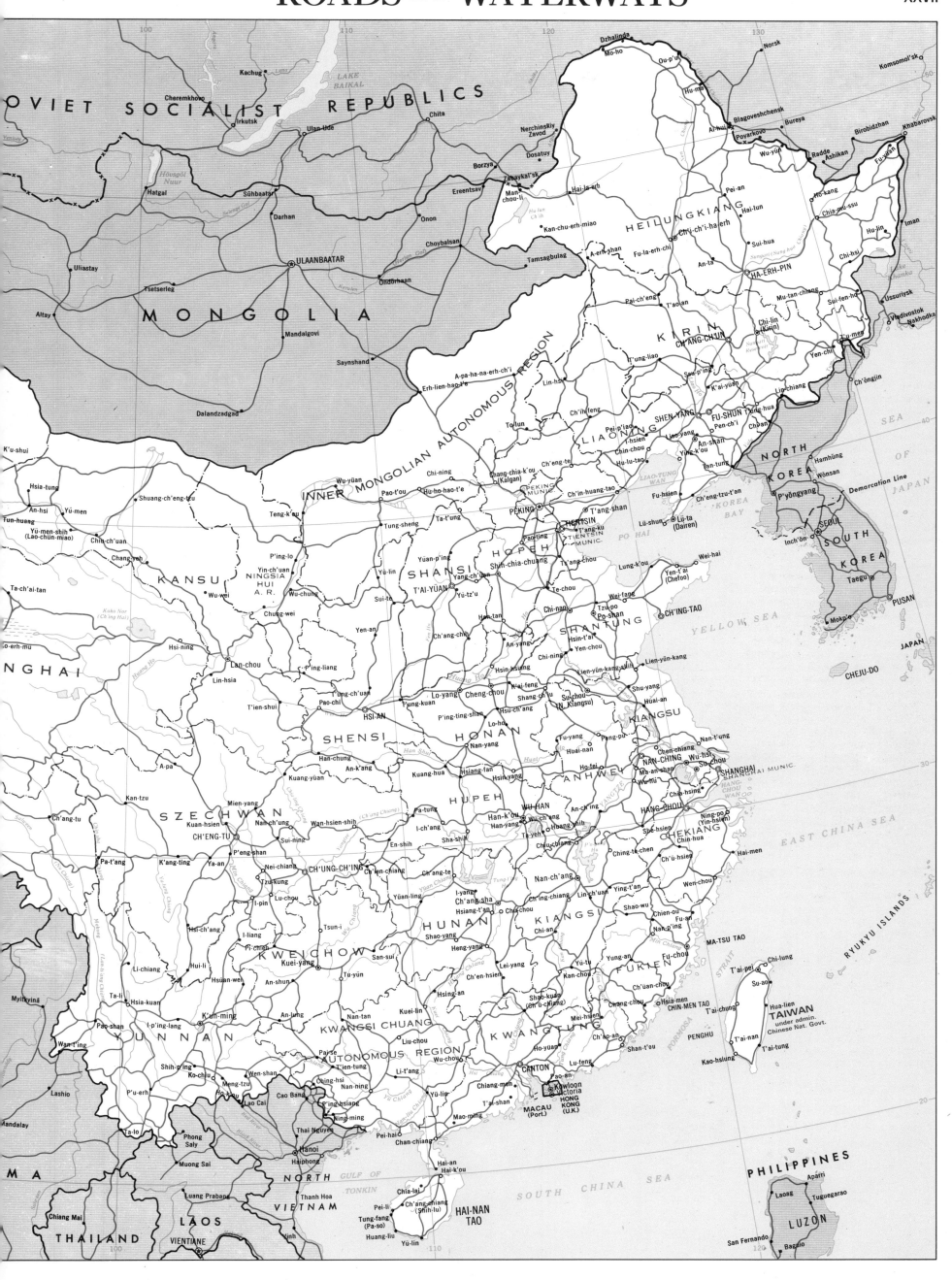

THE development of railways in China began only late in the 19th century. Although some modernising statesmen had advocated building a rail system in the 1860s, as a means of unifying the country, attempts to build railways met strong opposition, and the first experimental line built in 1876 from Shanghai to Wu-sung had to be dismantled. The government later built a short line from the T'ang-shan coal mines to Tientsin in 1881, but as late as 1895 there were only 288 kilometres of railway in the whole country.

After China's defeat by Japan in the war of 1894, the inevitability of modernisation was accepted, and opposition to railways ceased. From 1898 to 1911 there was a great wave of railway construction, almost all of it undertaken by foreign companies and financed by foreign loans. Resentment against the foreign influence represented by the railways and concessions led to powerful popular protest, and a campaign for the nationalisation of the rail network played a large part in the fall of the empire in 1911. But by this time 9,600 kilometres of track had been laid. These first lines were designed primarily for strategic rather than economic purposes, and for long-distance traffic. Peking and Tientsin were linked to Manchuria, a line was built by Chinese engineers to Chang-chia-k'ou (Kalgan) on the Mongolian border, and two great trunk lines were built from the north to the Yangtze, one from Peking to Han-k'ou (modern Wu-han), the other from Tientsin to P'u-k'ou on the Yangtze opposite Nanching. The Russians built the Chinese Eastern Railway, linking the Trans-Siberian line with Vladivostok across Manchuria, and a branch linking this line to the new port they developed at Lü-ta (Dairen), and in Shantung the Germans built a line from their new port Ch'ing-tao (Tsingtao).

After 1912 railway development came to a virtual halt. Internal instability and civil war prevented long-term planning and disrupted what services there were, and foreign investment ceased with the outbreak of the First World War. Between 1912 and 1927 only 3,400 kilometres of new lines were constructed, more than half of this in Manchuria where the Japanese had established a sphere of influence after the Russo-Japanese War. The railway, however, was extended further along the Mongolian border, and a beginning was made to two important trunk routes, from Han-k'ou to Canton, and the Lung-hai railway from the coast at Lien-yün-kang to the west. The restoration of some degree of political stability in 1927 improved the situation, and between 1928 and 1937 the Lung-hai and Canton-Han-k'ou lines were completed and a major line was built from Chekiang into Kiangsi and Hunan provinces. But the greatest progress continued to be in Manchuria, where some 4,500 kilometres were built by the Japanese after 1931 – 50 per cent more than in all the rest of China. After the outbreak of the Sino-Japanese War in 1937 there was some limited construction for strategic purposes, but immense damage was done to the existing railway system. Even greater damage was done during the civil war before 1949.

Throughout this early period only a narrow belt of territory along the railways found its economy much affected by the new form of transport. No network of feeder lines was built, and the traditional transport system – carriers and animal-drawn carts – operating on extremely primitive roads was both slow and expensive. All the railways were heavily in debt to foreign creditors, and their revenues were used in the repayment of loans and interest. Capital equipment was neglected, and maintenance kept to the barest minimum. By 1949 almost all of China's railways were obsolescent, with the exception of the Manchurian rail network which was better planned and dense enough to affect the economy of the whole region. After a programme of repair and reconstruction was completed, however, much of the old system was re-equipped and a major expansion of the rail system was undertaken between 1952 and 1960. A great new trunk line joined the new industrial centres of Pao-t'ou and Lan-chou in the north-west with the existing system, and a line was constructed into Szechwan. Another major trunk line was built into Sinkiang in the far west, designed to link up with the Soviet system and to serve the new oil fields at Yü-men and K'o-la-ma-i (Karamai). This line was completed only as far as Wu-lu-mu-ch'i (Urumchi) when the Sino-Soviet dispute broke out, though another line, connecting with the Soviet system via Mongolia, had been opened in 1956. In the south-west, Kwangsi and Kweichow provinces were given rail access to a new port developed at Chan-chiang, and in the south-western province of Fukien a railway was built to Hsia-men (Amoy) and Fu-chou.

In 1960 the collapse of the Great Leap Forward brought an end to new railway construction. Development started again only in 1964, and further growth was planned under the Third Five Year Plan for 1966–70, but this again suffered a setback with the disruption resulting from the Cultural Revolution during 1967–68. Since 1968, however, some new construction has been completed, particularly in the south-west, and much track has been doubled, modern marshalling yards constructed, major bridges built across the Yangtze at Nan-ching, Wu-han and Ch'ung-ch'ing, and new industrial plant built.

Even after half a century of carefully planned growth, the Chinese rail system is inadequate. It is still concentrated in the north-east and the coastal regions; it is still very sparse compared with the rail network of Europe or North America; it still remains a network of strategic trunk lines, dependent on the traditional forms of transport for the distribution and collection of goods. Most of the network remains single tracked and steam traction is almost universal. However, as internal air traffic is very meagre, the highway system remains poor and motor transport comparatively rare, the railway retains the sort of monopoly for long-distance passenger traffic and freight which it enjoyed in western countries at the turn of the century.

Rail traffic		Railway track	
(Passenger miles)		(km)	
Japan	179,037,000,000	USSR	135,200
USSR	164,915,000,000	USA	127,408
PRC	13,644,000,000	India	59,500
USA	10,770,000,000	PRC	35,000
		Japan	27,855

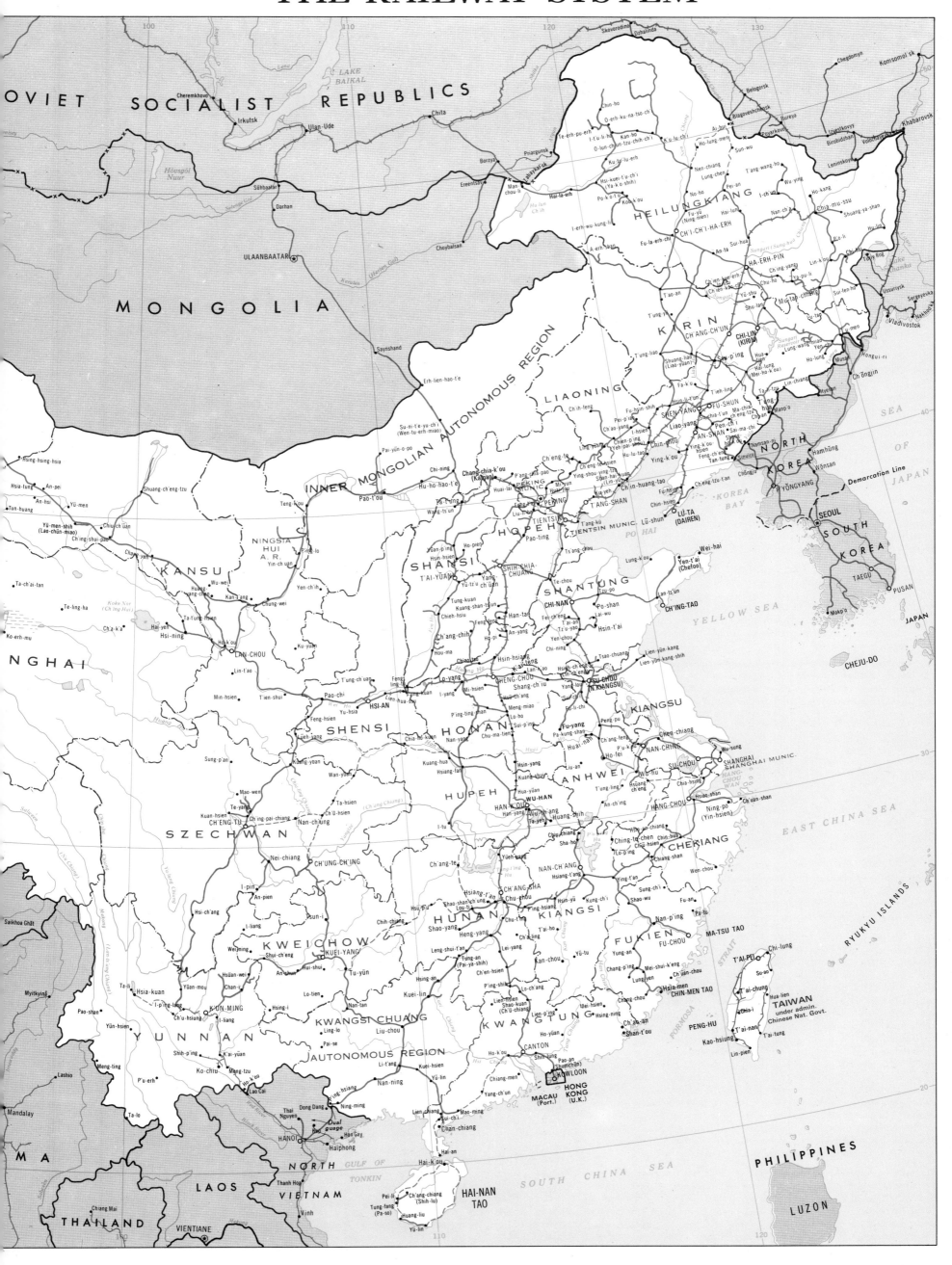

CHINA'S very considerable mineral resources are more than adequate to support her industry. Modern large-scale mining was situated originally in the coastal provinces and in Manchuria, and most mines were financed by foreign capital. The exploitation, though, of mineral resources was hampered by lack of detailed geological surveys until the 1920s and 1930s, lack of capital and poor transport facilities. Since 1949 extensive surveying has discovered many new mineral resources and the extension of the rail-network has made the exploitation of new mines possible. The government has invested heavily in mining, and in spite of a sharp decrease in mineral and metal production after 1960, by 1970 production was again increasing steadily while notable advances had been made in the techniques both of mining and ore processing.

Iron and steel China has very large iron reserves, although a large part of these consist of very low grade ores. The first modern ironworks in China was Han-yeh-ping, established at Wu-han at the end of the 19th century. In 1937 the iron and steel industry was almost entirely confined to southern Manchuria, at Pen-ch'i and at An-shan. Smaller ironworks were set up at Shih-ching-shan outside Peking, at T'ai-yüan and, during the war at Ch'ung-ch'ing. After 1945 the Soviet occupying forces dismantled most of the An-shan plant, and in 1949 iron and steel production had virtually ceased. Under the Communist regime iron and steel production was given the highest priority, both during the years of reconstruction (1949–52) and under the First Five Year Plan. During this period An-shan was developed into a large integrated iron and steel complex, which was supplemented by other new plants developed under the programme for the relocation of industry in the interior. During the Great Leap Forward a large number of iron and steel works were established, though many of these new developments proved uneconomical and inefficient and were shut down or abandoned in the years following the collapse of the Great Leap Forward in 1960. Overall production revived by 1966 and is now running well above the peak level of 1960. In recent years small scale local mining and smelting has been encouraged. There are eight major centres for the iron and steel industry. An-shan is still the largest integrated plant in China, and Pen-ch'i produces a wide range of special steels and steel products. Lung-yen, in northern Hopeh, is a major source of iron ore used by iron and steel complexes at Shih-ching-shan outside Peking, and at T'ai-yüan. Pao-t'ou has a new complex, started in the 1950s, using ore from the rich mines at Pai-yün-o-po to the north, and Wu-han has a large iron and steel plant supplied from Ta-yeh in Hupeh. Ma-an-shan on the Yangtze, is a major centre of iron mining, which was first exploited by the Japanese during the Second World War and has been a steel-making centre since 1964. Ch'ung-ch'ing has a large complex and Chiu-ch'üan, in the Kansu corridor, began production in the late 1960s. Hai-nan Island is also a major source of iron ore.

Ferrous alloys Although China is deficient in chrome, nickel and cobalt, there is however a large surplus over current needs of tungsten, of which China is a major world producer (15.4 per cent of the world supply). Tungsten is mined in many areas of the Nan-ling mountains in Kwangtung, Fukien and particularly in southern Kiangsi and Hunan. China also has more than adequate supplies of molybdenum, mostly from Chin-hsi in Liaoning, and manganese from Liaoning and Hunan.

Light metals Aluminium was first produced by the Japanese at Fu-shun and this plant was rehabilitated in 1957. Production is also reported from small plants in Shantung, Hopeh, Inner Mongolia, Kansu, Honan, Szechwan, Hunan and Chekiang. Magnesium metal is refined at Ying-k'ou in Liaoning.

Non-ferrous metals Copper deposits are widely scattered but small and production remains deficient. The most important producers are T'ung-ch'uan in Yunnan, Hwang-shih in Hupeh, Pai-yin and Wu-wei in Kansu and Hung-tao-shan in Liaoning. Two important centres have recently been brought into large scale production: T'ung-ling on the south bank of the Yangtze and Shou-wang-fen in Hopeh. Lead and zinc are produced in Hunan, Anhwei and Kiangsi, and a large amount of lead in southern Yunnan. Tin, of which China provides 4.6 per cent of the world's supply, is produced in Yunnan, Kwangsi and Kiangsi. China produces 18.3 per cent of the world's antimony, mainly from central Hunan, from Kwangsi and from Kwangtung. Most of the production of mercury, for export as well as for domestic use, is in Kweichow and Hunan.

By western standards China's consumption of fuels and energy is very low and in many fields human and animal power still provide a major resource. Coal is estimated to account for almost 90 per cent of China's energy resources, though the generation of hydro-electric power has increased steadily since 1960.

Coal China's coal reserves are perhaps between 70 and 80 billion tons, a total exceeded only by the USA and the USSR. Large scale coal mining was one of the first modern industries to be developed in the late 19th century. By the 1930s more than thirty million tons were produced annually, and nearly 66 million tons during the Japanese war effort in occupied China, though by 1949, as a result of the destruction and deliberate closure of mines in the intervening war years, production had fallen to about 32 million tons. By 1957 total production had reached 131 million tons, 123 million of which came from large modernised mines. Production was still further increased during the Great Leap Forward and a target of 425 million tons was set for 1960 (actual production in 1960 was perhaps 300 million tons), but the collapse of the Great Leap Forward led to a sharp cut-back to 160 million tons in 1961. Production slowly recovered to about 200 million tons in 1966 and has risen steadily to about 300 million tons in 1970. Some two-thirds of the total production comes from the established coal fields of the north-east and is used to feed the industrial base in Manchuria and northern China. Since the 1950s important new coal fields have been developed in Honan and Anhwei and on the borders of Ningsia and Inner Mongolia, but the south and west remain deficient in coal.

Petroleum Before 1949 oil production in China was minimal. After 1949 extensive prospecting was carried out and important new reserves were discovered. The small Yü-men field in western Kansu was greatly developed and linked by rail to a new refinery at Lan-chou and in the 1950s a much more important field was discovered at K'o-la-ma-i (Karamai) in Sinkiang, which was also linked by rail to Lan-chou and central China, and fields were brought

into production in the remote Tsaidam region of Tsinghai and at Nan-ch'ung in Szechwan. By 1960 total production had reached about 3 million tons. Up to this point, however, China continued to rely heavily on supplies from the Soviet Union, and the major refinery centre at Lan-chou was constructed with Soviet aid in 1958. The country was self-sufficient by 1966, though, when domestic output reached 8 million tons, following the discovery of major oil fields at Ta-ch'ing and Sheng-li which were developed entirely by Chinese technicians. By 1970 total output was about 20 million tons. Oil refining plant is concentrated in the coastal consuming areas at Shanghai, Lü-ta (Dairen) and Chin-hsi, and major modern refineries have been built at Nan-ching and Peking. There are smaller refineries at Nan-ch'ung, Yü-men, K'o-la-ma-i and Leng-hu. Shale-oil extraction, established by the Japanese in Manchuria, continues at the old plant at Fu-shun in Liaoning and at a new plant at Mao-ming in Kwangsi. Total production is over 2 million tons.

Natural gas Natural gas, has been used as a fuel for the evaporation of brine from salt wells in parts of Szechwan since the middle ages. This field, centred at Tzu-kung, is still exploited and a large gas field was brought into production in the 1960s near Ch'ung-ch'ing.

Electric power Coal-fired thermal plants, concentrated in the north and north-eastern regions, provide most of China's installed generating capacity, 90 per cent of which is used by industry. Rural electrification is largely supplied by small local generating plants. The development of hydro-electric schemes was comparatively late – the only major schemes brought into operation before 1949 were the large Feng-man and Sup'ung schemes built by the Japanese in Manchuria – but during the 1950s great stress was laid on electrification, and Soviet and East European engineers installed many new plants. Two huge projects on the Huang Ho, at Liu-chia and San-men were begun. There are three areas with a co-ordinated power system connected to a regional grid. The most advanced of these remains the Manchurian system which in 1957 produced almost half of China's electric power. It has now been linked with the Peking-Tientsin-T'ang-shan industrial area, which also has considerable generating capacity. A second power grid, fed by the very large hydro-electric station at Hsin-an-chiang in Chekiang, links Shanghai, Hang-chou and Nan-ching. The third power system was designed to take power from the San-men scheme on the Huang Ho (which was left unfinished by the withdrawal of Soviet aid) and joins the newly-developed industrial centres of Hsi-an (Sian), Lo-yang, Cheng-chou and T'ai-yüan. The electricity generating industry has expanded steadily and in 1970 installed capacity had reached 18 million kilowatts, compared with 11 million in 1960 and 1.8 million in 1949. However, in spite of China's immense potential hydro-electric resources and although the Chinese can now themselves manufacture most necessary equipment, hydro-electricity remains relatively undeveloped by western standards.

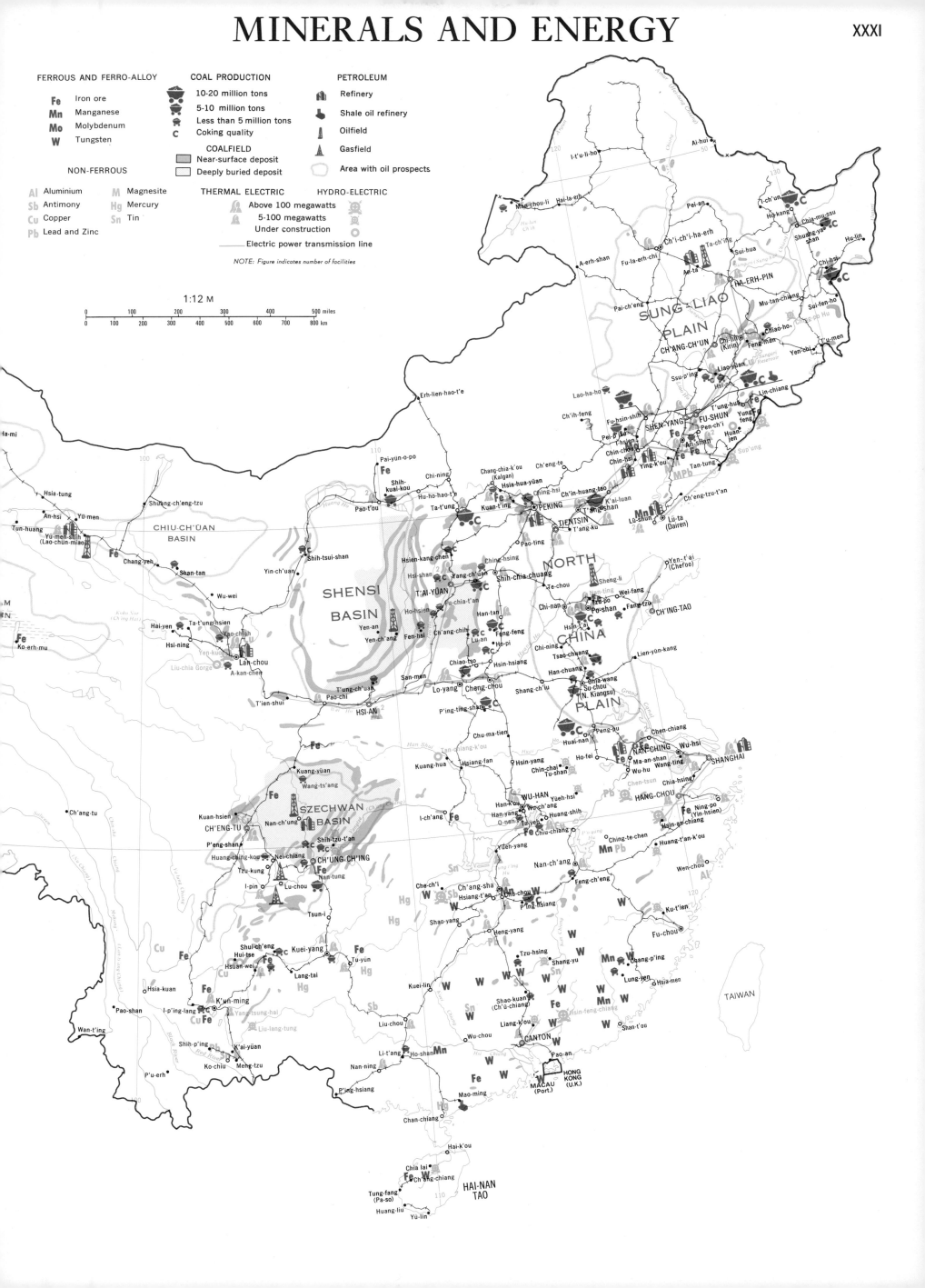

MINERALS AND ENERGY COMPARISONS

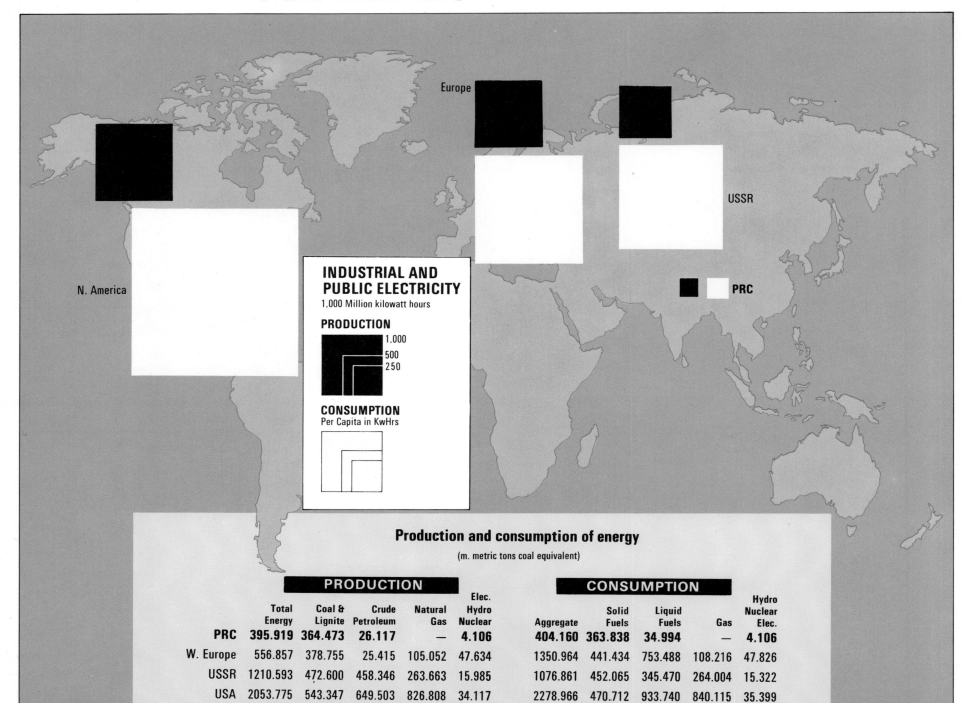

INDUSTRIAL AND PUBLIC ELECTRICITY
1,000 Million kilowatt hours

PRODUCTION

1,000
500
250

CONSUMPTION
Per Capita in KwHrs

Production and consumption of energy

(m. metric tons coal equivalent)

	PRODUCTION					CONSUMPTION				
	Total Energy	Coal & Lignite	Crude Petroleum	Natural Gas	Elec. Hydro Nuclear	Aggregate	Solid Fuels	Liquid Fuels	Gas	Hydro Nuclear Elec.
PRC	**395.919**	**364.473**	**26.117**	—	**4.106**	**404.160**	**363.838**	**34.994**	—	**4.106**
W. Europe	556.857	378.755	25.415	105.052	47.634	1350.964	441.434	753.488	108.216	47.826
USSR	1210.593	472.600	458.346	263.663	15.985	1076.861	452.065	345.470	264.004	15.322
USA	2053.775	543.347	649.503	826.808	34.117	2278.966	470.712	933.740	840.115	35.399
Japan	54.822	39.759	1.006	3.499	10.558	332.370	89.394	227.250	5.168	10.558

Aluminium
Production (1,000 metric tons)

USA	3,739.8
W. Europe	2,500.3
USSR	1,750.0
PRC	**155.0**
World	11,505.6

Tin
Mine Production (1,000 metric tons)

PRC	**23.0**
USSR	12.0
W. Europe	4.5
USA	—
World	235.6

Asbestos fibre
(1,000 short tons)

N. America	1,827
USSR	1,350
PRC	**190**
World	4,160

Antimony
Mine Production (metric tons)

Africa	15,543
PRC	**14,000**
Bolivia	13,105
Asia	7,580
USSR	7,500
W. Europe*	4,132
USA	411
World	69,029

*includes Yugoslavia: 2,100

Tungsten ores and Concentrates output
(metric tons)

PRC	**8,000**
USSR	6,500
USA	4,266
World	32,700

Copper
Mine Production (1,000 metric tons)

USA	1,490.3
USSR	1,050.0
W. Europe	272.1
PRC	**135.0**
World	7,022.0

Zinc
(million metric tons)

W. Europe	740.6
USSR	620·0
USA	476.8
PRC	**150.0**
World	5,661.5

Phosphate rock
(1,000 metric tons)

USA	38,500
USSR	21,000
PRC	**2,600**
World	91,616

Lead
Mine Production (1,000 metric tons)

USA	584.9
USSR	495.0
W. Europe	466.9
PRC	**125.0**
World	3,523.5

Iron ore
(million metric tons)

USSR	196.00
W. Europe	117.00
USA	89.00
PRC	**40.00**
World	750.00

Crude oil production
(million tons)

M. East	895
USA	532
USSR	394
PRC	**30**
W. Europe	22

Europe

USSR

PRC

N. America

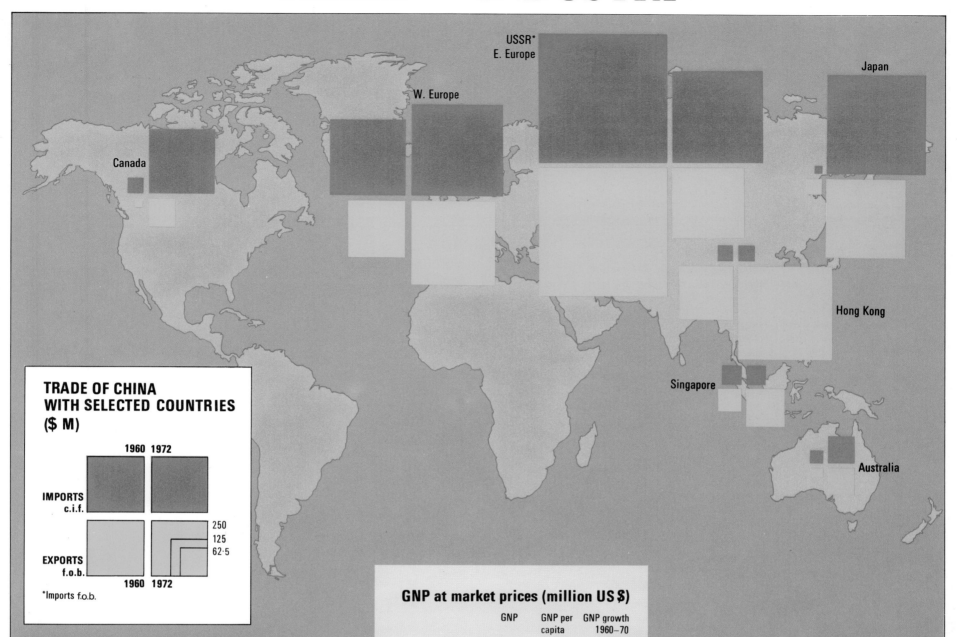

Canada

USSR*
E. Europe

Japan

W. Europe

Hong Kong

Singapore

Australia

TRADE OF CHINA WITH SELECTED COUNTRIES ($ M)

1960 1972

IMPORTS c.i.f.

EXPORTS f.o.b.

250
125
62·5

1960 1972

*Imports f.o.b.

GNP at market prices (million US $)

	GNP	GNP per capita	GNP growth 1960–70
USA	975,240	4,760	3.2%
USSR	434,870*	1,790	5.8%
Japan	198,840	1,920	9.6%
F. R. Germany	180,260	2,930	3.5%
PRC	**121,870***	**160**	**2.1%**
India	57,290	110	1.2%

*Net material product, converted

Cement / Cotton yarn

	Cement (1,000 short tons)	Cotton yarn (1,000 short tons)
USSR	104,992	1,582
USA	74,684	1,670
Japan	63,039	559
PRC	**11,016**	**1,602**

Steel (1,000 metric tons)

	Crude steel output	Finished steel products
EEC	139	101
USSR	126	**90
USA	121	*80
Japan	97	82
PRC	**23**	****14**

*deliveries **estimate

Cars in use / Motor vehicles

	Cars in use	Motor vehicles
USA	92,082,000	10,671,654
Europe	71,057,000	12,727,000
Japan	10,572,000	5,810,774
USSR	1,600,000	1,130,000
PRC (1970)	**133,000**	**160,000**
World	199,000,000	*32,944,068

Production (inc. cars)
*Main Producing countries only.

Radio sets / TV sets

	Radio sets (1,000)	TV sets (1,000)
USA	290,000	84,600
USSR	94,600	34,800
Japan	25,742	22,658
PRC	**11,500**	**300**

Merchant shipping fleet (1,000 gross tons)

Japan	30,509
USA	16,266
USSR	16,194
PRC	**1,022**

Non-cellulosic man made fibre

USA	3,893
Japan	1,520
USSR	330
PRC	**26**
World	9,975

Paper and Board (1,000 metric tons)

	Consumption	Production
USA	49.2	45.2
Japan	12.6	12.9
USSR	6.8	6.5
PRC	**3.4**	**1.7**

THE development of modern industry in China began in the period following the T'ai-p'ing rebellion in the 1860s, when although manufacturing by foreign firms was illegal, some small factories were established in the Treaty Ports, first at Shanghai and later also at Tientsin. After 1895 the Treaty of Shimonoseki legalised foreign industry in the Treaty Ports, and a large number of foreign companies began operations not only in Shanghai and Tientsin, but also in Wu-han, Shantung and in Manchuria. Chinese-controlled modern industry had meanwhile followed a different course. It had begun as an off-shoot of the 'self-strengthening' movement of the 1860s and 1870s and was predominantly military. The first enterprises were shipyards and arsenals, in Shanghai (1865), Nan-ching (1865), Fu-chou (1867) and Wu-han (1890). These arsenals not only manufactured modern weapons and built modern ships, but also conducted training programmes for engineers, technicians and translators, who were familiar with western technology and ideas and who were far more important in China's modernisation than the weapons produced by the arsenals. From 1872–95, however, a number of Chinese owned and managed modern industrial enterprises were founded with commercial objectives. Some of the larger ones were official or semi-official enterprises, but many were private concerns, engaged in mining, metal-working, textiles, paper-making and flour-milling. Most were poorly managed and under-capitalised and eventually many came under the control of foreign interests.

After 1895 Chinese industry expanded rapidly and a large number of companies, concerned mostly with mining, public utilities, food-processing and tobacco manufacture were founded in the early years of this century. By the end of the Ch'ing empire in 1911, however, industry was still of only very minor importance in the economy, and foreign investment was concentrated in mining, communications and finance. The outbreak of the First World War altered the Chinese economy in two ways. First, the Japanese came to control more and more of the foreign industry and eventually established economic control over Manchuria, where they had been predominant since their defeat of the Russians in the Russo-Japanese War. Until about 1931 they treated Manchuria simply as a market for their goods and as a source of raw material for Japanese industry. After this, when their control of Manchuria was complete, they formulated a long-term plan to transform Manchuria into a base of heavy industry, with large scale modern iron and steel, engineering and chemical industries, and highly productive mining, forestry and agriculture. The other major consequence of the War was that the involvement of the western powers in war production reduced the availability of imported goods in China, and Chinese industry expanded to meet the demand. It was not until the war ended, however, that this expansion was fully realised and 1918–22 was the period of most rapid growth in Chinese industry, with new investment in the traditional fields of textiles, food processing and mining. By 1922, political unrest had seriously disrupted the production of raw materials for industry and the distribution of manufactured goods, and the Chinese again began to invest their capital in the Treaty Ports under foreign protection. At the outbreak of war with Japan in 1937, industry was limited to Manchuria, then under Japanese control, to the coastal provinces, and to the Treaty Ports. The war prompted the Chinese to move many strategic plants from Shanghai and Wu-han into Szechwan and Yunnan, and at the same time the Japanese began to plan the relocation of industry in occupied China, expanding industry in Shansi and founding iron and steel works at Pao-t'ou in Inner Mongolia and at Ma-an-shan on the Yangtze.

In 1945 Chinese industry lay in ruins and before any real progress could be made to restore order, civil war, the inefficiency of the Kuomintang government and ever-spiralling inflation had effectively ruined the economy. The first years of the Communist regime were devoted to the restoration of basic industries and of the transport network. In 1952 this stage was completed and most industries were roughly back to where they had been in 1936. Between 1953 and 1957 the First Five Year Plan was put into operation. Rapid increase in industrial production was the first aim, using the existing base of heavy industry in Manchuria. This plan involved the relocation of industry and its development in the interior provinces, partly for strategic reasons, and some two-thirds of the new industrial installations and of the plants installed with Soviet aid were situated inland. Major concentrations of industry grew up in T'ai-yüan and Ta-t'ung; in Pao-t'ou; in Hsi-an (Sian) and Lan-chou; in Lo-yang and Cheng-chou; in Ch'eng-tu and Ch'ung-ch'ing. After 1957, however, growth once again tended to be concentrated in the established industrial complexes of Manchuria, Shanghai, Peking-Tientsin and the old Treaty Ports.

The Great Leap Forward, set in motion in 1958, attempted to accelerate industrial growth at an impossible pace. During 1958–60 every type of industrial enterprise was set enormously inflated targets, and great numbers of small plants were built in the provinces, many of them hopelessly inefficient and uneconomic. Over-extension of industrial effort was accompanied by a major agricultural crisis in 1959–61, and as a final blow, in 1960 the Soviet Union suddenly ceased all economic assistance to China and many crucial Soviet-planned projects were abandoned. Government investment in industry fell back to the level of 1953 and 20,000,000 urban workers were sent back to the countryside.

After 1963 a gradual recovery began. The earlier exclusive concentration on heavy industry was replaced by a diversified and more local spread of industry, and a great deal of production was now devoted to the support of agriculture. Investment was concentrated in chemical and fertiliser plants and in the production of tractors and agricultural implements. Another setback in industrial production followed the outbreak of the Cultural Revolution and only in mid-1969 did it recover to 1966 levels, but since then there has been a steady improvement. The lack of skilled technicians and managers has been made good, although China continues to rely heavily on foreign technology and design, and great attention is now paid to the development of local technical skills. The most marked feature of recent growth has been the development in parallel of modern, highly mechanised industry concentrated in large central plants and of small scale, often technically primitive, local industries designed to serve the needs of rural agriculture. Today, for example, there are more than one thousand small chemical fertiliser plants, which account for 60 per cent of the country's total output. The decentralisation of plants is partly due to the continuing shortcomings of the transport system, but is also designed as a deliberate policy to spread simple technology to the countryside, and as a means of absorbing local labour surpluses. Some of the local industries – electrical plants, cement and iron works, engineering shops – are run by the counties, others by the communes. Similar local organisations manage other industries processing agricultural goods, oil extraction, flour milling, cotton ginning, sugar refining, small scale canning and preservation of foods, and also textile manufacture and a wide variety of local handicrafts.

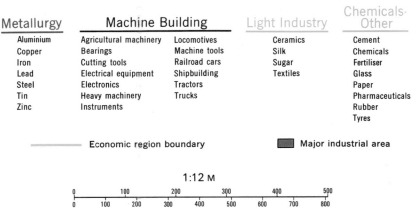

Metallurgy	Machine Building		Light Industry	Chemicals-Other
Aluminium	Agricultural machinery	Locomotives	Ceramics	Cement
Copper	Bearings	Machine tools	Silk	Chemicals
Iron	Cutting tools	Railroad cars	Sugar	Fertiliser
Lead	Electrical equipment	Shipbuilding	Textiles	Glass
Steel	Electronics	Tractors		Paper
Tin	Heavy machinery	Trucks		Pharmaceuticals
Zinc	Instruments			Rubber
				Tyres

————— Economic region boundary   ■ Major industrial area

1:12 M

0   100   200   300   400   500

0   100   200   300   400   500   600   700   800

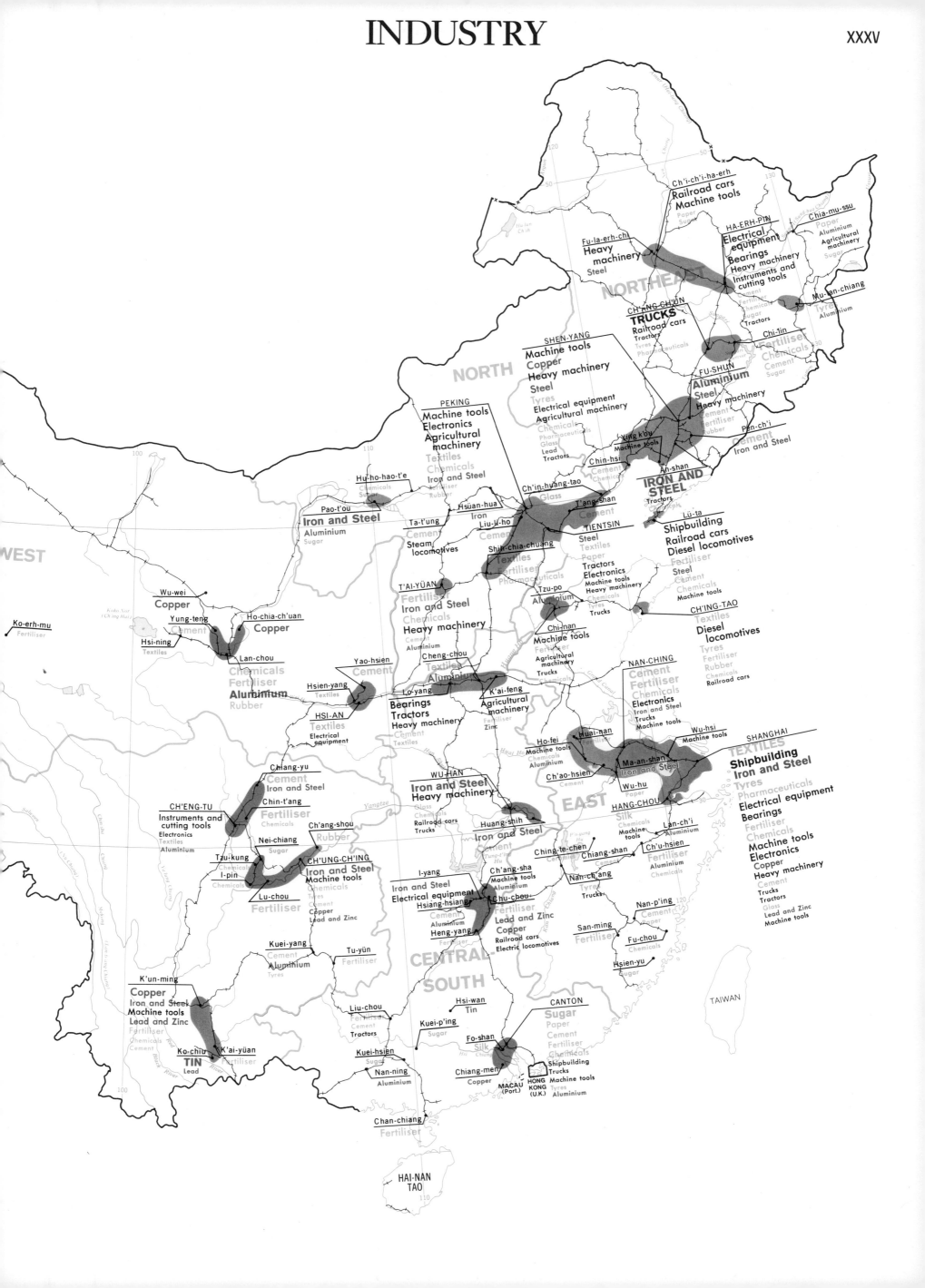

NORTHEAST

Ch'i-ch'i-ha-erh
Railroad cars
Machine tools

Chia-mu-ssu
Paper
Aluminium
Agricultural
machinery
Sugar

HA-ERH-PIN
Electrical
equipment
Bearings
Heavy machinery
Instruments and
cutting tools

Fu-la-erh-chi
Heavy
machinery
Steel

Mu-tan-chiang
Tyres
Aluminium

NORTH

CH'ANG-CH'UN
TRUCKS
Railroad cars
Tractors
Tyres
Pharmaceuticals

Chi-lin
Fertiliser
Chemicals
Cement
Sugar

SHEN-YANG
Machine tools
Copper
Heavy machinery
Steel
Electrical equipment
Agricultural machinery
Chemicals
Pharmaceuticals
Glass
Lead
Tractors

FU-SHUN
Aluminium
Steel
Heavy machinery
Cement
Fertiliser
Chemicals
Rubber

Pen-ch'i
Iron and Steel
Cement

PEKING
Machine tools
Electronics
Agricultural
machinery
Textiles
Chemicals
Iron and Steel
Fertiliser
Rubber

Hu-ho-hao-t'e
Chemicals
Sugar

Ying k'ou
Machine tools

Lü-ta
Shipbuilding
Railroad cars
Diesel locomotives
Fertiliser
Steel
Cement
Chemicals
Machine tools

Pao-t'ou
Iron and Steel
Aluminium
Sugar

Ta-t'ung
Cement
Steam
locomotives

Hsüan-hua
Iron
Cement

Ch'in-huang-tao
Glass

T'ang-shan
Cement

An-shan
IRON AND STEEL
Tractors

Chin-hsi
Cement
Chemicals

Liu-li-ho
Cement

TIENTSIN
Steel
Textiles
Paper
Tractors
Electronics
Machine tools
Heavy machinery
Chemicals
Tyres
Trucks

Shih-chia-chuang
Textiles
Fertiliser
Pharmaceuticals

T'AI-YÜAN
Fertiliser
Iron and Steel
Chemicals
Heavy machinery
Cement
Aluminium

Tzu-po
Aluminium

CH'ING-TAO
Textiles
Diesel
locomotives
Tyres
Fertiliser
Rubber
Chemicals
Railroad cars

Chi-nan
Machine tools
Fertiliser
Agricultural
machinery
Trucks
Chemicals

Cheng-chou
Textiles
Aluminium

Wu-wei
Copper

Ko-erh-mu
Fertiliser

Yung-teng
Cement

Ho-chia-ch'uan
Copper

Hsi-ning
Textiles

Lan-chou
Chemicals
Fertiliser
Aluminium
Rubber

Yao-hsien
Cement

Hsien-yang
Textiles

Lo-yang
Bearings
Tractors
Heavy machinery
Cement
Textiles

K'ai-feng
Agricultural
machinery
Fertiliser
Zinc

HSI-AN
Textiles
Electrical
equipment

NAN-CHING
Cement
Fertiliser
Chemicals
Electronics
Iron and Steel
Trucks
Machine tools

Ho-fei
Machine tools
Chemicals
Aluminium

Huai-nan

Wu-hsi
Machine tools

SHANGHAI
TEXTILES
Shipbuilding
Iron and Steel
Tyres
Pharmaceuticals
Electrical equipment
Bearings
Fertiliser
Chemicals
Machine tools
Electronics
Copper
Heavy machinery
Cement
Trucks
Tractors
Glass
Lead and Zinc
Machine tools

Ch'ao-hsien
Cement

Ma-an-shan
Iron and Steel

Wu-hu
Paper

EAST

Chiang-yu
Cement
Iron and Steel

Chin-t'ang
Fertiliser
Chemicals

CH'ENG-TU
Instruments and
cutting tools
Electronics
Textiles
Aluminium

Nei-chiang
Sugar

Ch'ang-shou
Rubber

WU-HAN
Iron and Steel
Heavy machinery
Glass
Chemicals
Railroad cars
Trucks

Huang-shih
Iron and Steel
Cement

HANG-CHOU
Silk
Chemicals
Machine
tools
Aluminium

Ching-te-chen
Cement

Chiang-shan

Ch'u-hsien
Fertiliser
Chemicals

Lan-ch'i
Aluminium

Tzu-kung
Chemicals
Tyres
Cement

I-pin
Chemicals

CH'UNG-CH'ING
Iron and Steel
Machine tools
Chemicals
Cement
Copper
Lead and Zinc

Lu-chou
Fertiliser

I-yang
Iron and Steel
Electrical equipment
Hsiang-hsiang
Cement
Aluminium

Ch'ang-sha
Machine tools
Aluminium

Chu-chou
Fertiliser
Lead and Zinc
Copper
Railroad cars
Electric locomotives

Nan-ch'ang
Tyres
Trucks

Nan-p'ing

San-ming
Fertiliser

Fu-chou
Chemicals

Kuei-yang
Cement
Aluminium
Tyres

Tu-yün
Fertiliser

Heng-yang

Hsien-yu
Sugar

K'un-ming
Copper
Iron and Steel
Machine tools
Lead and Zinc
Fertiliser
Chemicals
Cement

**CENTRAL
SOUTH**

Liu-chou
Fertiliser
Cement

Hsi-wan
Tin

CANTON
Sugar
Paper
Cement
Fertiliser
Chemicals

TAIWAN

Kuei-p'ing
Sugar

Fo-shan
Silk

Ko-chiu
TIN
Lead

K'ai-yüan
Fertiliser

Kuei-hsien
Sugar

Nan-ning
Aluminium

Chiang-men
Copper

MACAU
(Port.)

HONG
KONG
(U.K.)

Shipbuilding
Trucks
Machine tools
Tyres
Aluminium

Chan-chiang
Fertiliser

HAI-NAN
TAO

SINCE the foundation of the People's Republic of China in 1949, there have been many changes in its internal administration. By that year the country had passed through several decades of unrest, civil war, foreign invasion and a general decline of civil order. In many areas central control had been totally lacking for many years. The country was divided into 35 provinces, within which there was great variation of local government. From 1949 to 1958 there were constant changes and rationalisation of the local administrative structure, leading to amalgamation of some of the smaller provinces in Manchuria and the north-eastern border areas, and to many changes at lower levels. Since 1958 the administrative structure at the provincial level has remained comparatively unchanged, with the exception of the redistribution of a large part of the territory of the Inner Mongolian Autonomous Region to other provinces in 1969.

Provincial Level At the highest level of local administration the country is divided into units of three distinct types. In most of China the highest unit is the province (*sheng*). In the areas inhabited largely by national minorities, however, the province is replaced by the Autonomous Region (*tzu-chih-ch'ü*). These were established in Inner Mongolia (1947, but boundary changes were frequent until 1966 and further changes occurred in 1969); Sinkiang (1955); Ningsia (1958); Kwangsi (1958) and Tibet (1965). Finally Peking, Shanghai and Tientsin and their surrounding areas form provincial level municipalities (*chih-hsia-shih*) directly subordinate to central government.

Sub-provincial Level The level of administrative unit directly under the province subsumes several different types of administrative unit. The normal unit is the 'region' (*ti-ch'ü*) which was usually called 'special district' (*chuan-ch'u*) until 1971. Areas with substantial minority populations, however, are administered as 'autonomous districts' (*tzu-chih-chou*). In Inner Mongolia the equivalent administrative division is the 'league' (*meng*) or tribal federation. Important cities are given status as sub-provincial municipalities (*sheng-hsia-shih*), which have equivalent standing with the 'region' or local municipalities (*ti-hsia-shih*). 178 cities currently have such semi-autonomous status. The island of Hai-nan, under Kwangtung province, has a unique sub-provincial status as an 'administrative district' (*hsing-cheng-ch'ü*).

County Level The basic level of local administration is the 'county' (*hsien*). In minority areas some non-Chinese peoples are organised in 'autonomous hsien' (*tzu-chih-hsien*), and in Inner Mongolia the equivalent level of local administration is the 'banner' (*ch'i*) a tribal unit dating from Manchu times. The Mongol minority in Western Heilungkiang province is also organised in 'autonomous banners' (*tzu-chih-ch'i*). In Tibet, although the official term used is the *hsien*, the common local name for this level of administration is the *dzong*, rendered in Chinese as *tsung*.

Local Level Beneath the county level administrations, the traditional level of rural organisation until the mid-1950s was the 'locality' (*hsiang*). During the successive stages of collectivisation, however, the *hsiang* was gradually replaced in its administrative functions by the collectives and then by the people's communes (*jen-min kung-she*). These number some 75,000 at the present time, whereas there were formerly some 200,000 *hsiang*. Each commune is normally subdivided into production brigades (*sheng-chang ta-tui*) usually co-extensive with a village unit, and production teams (*sheng-chan tui*). Urban administrations beneath the county level are called 'towns' (*chen*). These are normally local market centres, the status of which is purely administrative.

Administrative changes at the lower levels have been frequent and continuous. The county seems to have been the level at which change was least frequent, but even here the administrative seat of counties has been frequently changed from one local town to another.

Parallel with the civil administration outlined above are two higher level regional organisations. For planning purposes China is organised in six economic co-ordination regions:
1 North-east: Heilungkiang, Kirin and Liaoning provinces.
2 East: Shantung, Kiangsu, Anhwei, Chekiang, Kiangsi and Fukien provinces, with Shanghai municipality.
3 North: Hopeh and Shansi provinces, Peking and Tientsin municipalities, with Inner Mongolia.
4 Central-south: Honan, Hupeh, Hunan, Kwangtung provinces and Kwangsi Autonomous Region.
5 South-west: Szechwan, Kweichow and Yunnan provinces and Tibet.
6 North-west: Kansu, Tsinghai, and Shensi provinces, Ningsia and Sinkiang Autonomous Regions.

These correspond roughly to the six 'greater administrative regions' (*ta hsing-cheng-ch'ü*) established in 1950 to oversee the work of reconstruction. These were reduced to a supervisory role in 1952 and abolished as administrative entities in 1954, although the Communist Party continued to maintain regional bureaux which had supra-provincial powers.

The second large-scale organisation is the military command system. China is divided into twelve major military commands:
1 Shen-yang: Heilungkiang, Kirin and Liaoning provinces.
2 Peking: Hopeh, Shansi, Peking, Tientsin and Inner Mongolia.
3 Chi-nan: Shantung.
4 Nan-ching: Kiangsu, Anhwei, Chekiang, Shanghai.
5 Fu-chou: Fukien and Kiangsi.
6 Wu-han: Hupeh and Honan.
7 Canton: Kwangtung, Kwangsi and Hunan.
8 Lan-chou: Kansu, Shensi, Ningsia and Tsinghai.
9 Sinkiang (Wu-lu-mu-ch'i): Sinkiang Autonomous Region.
10 Ch'eng-tu: Szechwan.
11 K'un-ming: Yunnan and Kweichow.
12 Tibet (La-sa): the Tibet Autonomous Region.

These military command areas played an important role in the period following the Cultural Revolution in 1966, when the Party regional bureaux ceased to function, and the military began to play a major role in civilian administration. Each province also functions as a military district.

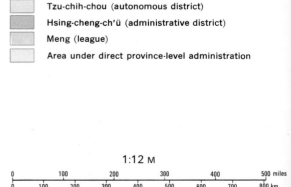

—— Province-level boundary
- - - Subprovince-level boundary
■ Shih (municipality)
□ Ti-ch'ü (region)
▨ Tzu-chih-chou (autonomous district)
▩ Hsing-cheng-ch'ü (administrative district)
▦ Meng (league)
▢ Area under direct province-level administration

1:12 M

0 — 100 — 200 — 300 — 400 — 500 miles
0 — 100 — 200 — 300 — 400 — 500 — 600 — 700 — 800 km

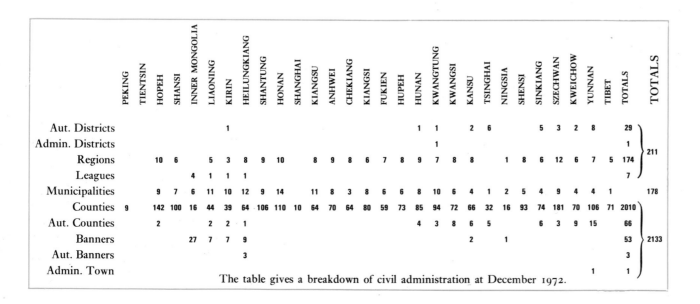

	PEKING	TIENTSIN	HOPEH	SHANSI	INNER MONGOLIA	LIAONING	KIRIN	HEILUNGKIANG	SHANTUNG	HONAN	SHANGHAI	KIANGSU	ANHWEI	CHEKIANG	KIANGSI	FUKIEN	HUPEH	HUNAN	KWANGTUNG	KWANGSI	KANSU	TSINGHAI	NINGSIA	SHENSI	SINKIANG	SZECHWAN	KWEICHOW	YUNNAN	TIBET	TOTALS
Aut. Districts					1													1	1		2	6			5	3	2	8		29
Admin. Districts																			1											1
Regions			10	6		5	3	8	9	10		8	9	8	6	7	8	9	7	8	8	1		8	6	12	6	7	5	174
Leagues					4	1	1	1																						7
Municipalities	9	7	6	11	10	12	9	14	11	8	3	8	6	6	8	10	6	4	1	2	5	4				9	4	4	1	178
Counties	9		142	100	16	44	39	64	106	110	1	64	70	64	80	59	73	85	94	72	66	32	16	93	74	181	70	106	71	2010
Aut. Counties			2			2	2	1										4	3	8	6	5			6	3	9	15		66
Banners					27	7	7	9													2		1							53
Aut. Banners					3																									3
Admin. Town																													1	1

Grouped totals: Aut. Districts + Admin. Districts + Regions + Leagues = 211; Counties + Aut. Counties + Banners + Aut. Banners + Admin. Town = 2133.

The table gives a breakdown of civil administration at December 1972.

ADMINISTRATIVE DIVISIONS

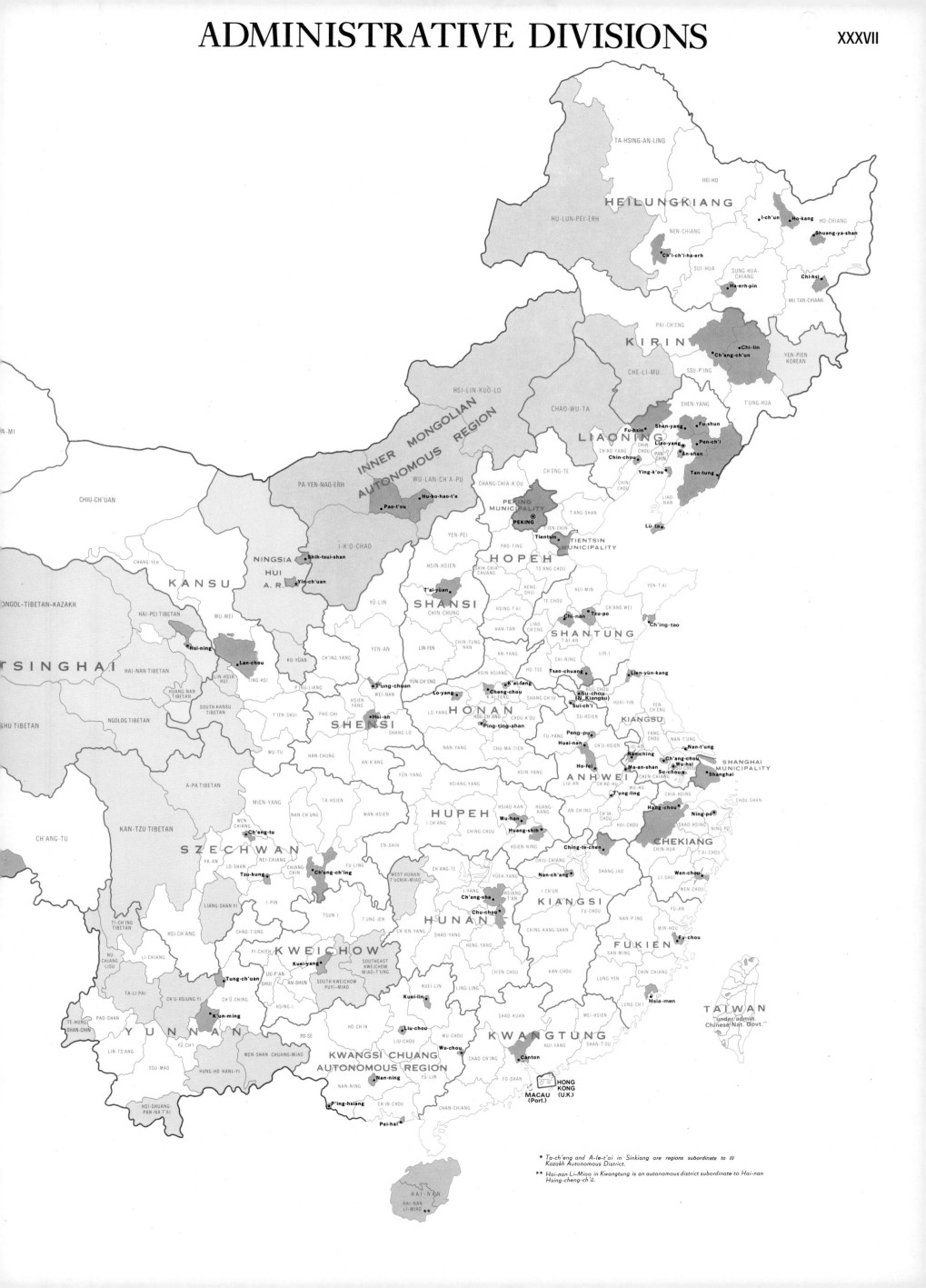

TA-HSING-AN-LING

HEILUNGKIANG

HU-LUN-PEI-ERH

NEN-CHIANG

HEI-HO

HO-CHIANG

•I-ch'un •Ho-kang

•Shuang-ya-shan

•Ch'i-ch'i-ha-erh

SUI-HUA

SUNG-HUA-CHIANG

Chi-hsi•

•Ha-erh-pin

MU-TAN-CHIANG

PAI-CH'ENG

KIRIN

CHE-LI-MU

•Ch'ang-ch'un •Chi-lin

SSU-P'ING

YEN-PIEN KOREAN

T'UNG-HUA

SHEN-YANG

HSI-LIN-KUO-LO

CHAO-WU-TA

CH'ENG-TE

Fu-hsin• Shen-yang• •Fu-shun

LIAONING

CHAO-YANG

Liao-yang• •Pen-ch'i

Chin-chou• •An-shan

PAN-CHIN

INNER MONGOLIAN AUTONOMOUS REGION

WU-LAN-CH'A-PU

CHANG-CHIA-K'OU

Ying-k'ou• •Tan-tung

CHIN CHOU

LIAO-NAN

Lü-ta•

PA-YEN-NAO-ERH

•Hu-ho-hao-t'e

PEKING MUNICIPALITY

•Pao-t'ou

⊛ PEKING

T'IEN-CHIN

T'ANG-SHAN

I-K'O-CHAO

YEN-PEI

Tientsin•

TIENTSIN MUNICIPALITY

CHIU-CH'UAN

NINGSIA HUI A.R.

•Shih-tsui-shan

CHANG-YEH

PAO-TING

HOPEH

TS'ANG-CHOU

KANSU

HUI-MIN

YEN-T'AI

HSIN-HSIEN

SHIH-CHIA-CHUANG

•Yin-ch'uan

HSIN-CHIANG

HENG-SHUI

MONGOL-TIBETAN-KAZAKH

HAI-PEI TIBETAN

WU-WEI

•T'ai-yüan

SHANSI

CHIN-CHUNG

TE-CHOU

CH'ANG-WEI

•Ch'ing-tao

•Hsi-ning

Chi-nan• Tzu-po•

SHANTUNG

TSINGHAI

HAI-NAN TIBETAN

LIN-HSIA HUI

•Lan-chou

LING-HSI

HUANG-NAN TIBETAN

SOUTH KANSU TIBETAN

T'AI-AN

LIAO-CH'ENG

CHI-NING

LIN-I

NGOLOG TIBETAN

SHU TIBETAN

TIEN-SHUI

KU-YÜAN

P'ING-LIANG

CH'ING-YANG

YEN-AN

LIN-FEN

CHIN-TUNG NAN

AN-YANG

HO-TSE

Tsao-chuang•

•Lien-yün-kang

T'ung-chuan•

WEI-NAN

HSIEN YANG

YÜN-CH'ENG

Lo-yang•

•K'ai-feng

•Cheng-chou

K'AI-FENG

SHANG-CH'IU

HSU-CHOU (N. Kiangsu)

•Su-chou

KIANGSU

•Sui-ch'i

•Hsi-an

LO-YANG

HONAN

HSU-CH'ANG

SHENSI

SHANG-LO

Ping-ting-shan•

SU-CHOU

FU-YANG

YANG CHOU

•Peng-pu

HUAI-YIN

YEN-CH'ENG

NAN-T'UNG

•Nan-t'ung

WU-TU

HAN-CHUNG

NAN-YANG

CHU-MA-TIEN

•Huai-nan

CH'U-HSIEN

LIU-HO

•Ho-fei

Nanching•

Ch'ang-chou•

•Wu-hsi

A-PA TIBETAN

MIEN-YANG

YÜN-YANG

HSIN-YANG

ANHWEI

•Ma-an-shan

•Su-chou

•Shanghai

SHANGHAI MUNICIPALITY

KAN-TZU TIBETAN

NAN-CH'UNG

TA-HSIEN

WAN-HSIEN

I-CH'ANG

HSIAO-KAN

HUANG-KANG

AN-CH'ING

CHEN-CHIANG

CHIA-HSING

CHOU-SHAN

CH'ANG-TU

TI-CH'ING TIBETAN

WEN CHIANG

•Ch'eng-tu

HUPEH

HSIEN-NING

CH'IH CHOU

HUI-CHOU

•T'ung-ling

WU-HU

SZECHWAN

NEI-CHIANG

LO-SHAN

EN-SHIH

CHING-CHOU

HANG-CHOU

•Hang-chou

•Ning-po

NING-PO

YA-AN

CHIANG CHIN

FU-LING

WEST HUNAN TUCHIA-MIAO

CH'ANG-TE

YÜEH-YANG

Tzu-kung•

•Ch'ung-ch'ing

•Ching-te-chen

CHEKIANG

SHAO-HSING

LIANG-SHAN YI

I-PIN

TSUN-I

T'UNG-JEN

I-YANG

HSIANG T'AN

I-CH'UN

SHANG JAO

CHIN-HUA

T'AI-CHOU

HSI-CH'ANG

CHAO-TUNG

CHAO-YANG

SHAO-YANG

•Ch'ang-sha

•Chu-chou

KIANGSI

•Wen-chou

LI-SHUI

WEN-CHOU

TE-HUNG SHAN-CHIN

PAO-SHAN

CH'U-HSIUNG YI

HUNAN

HENG-YANG

KAN-CHOU

CHING KANG-SHAN

NAN-P'ING

FUKIEN

JEN-CHOU

LI-CHIANG

PI-CHIEH

KWEICHOW

SOUTHEAST KWEICHOW MIAO-T'UNG

CH'EN-CHOU

SAN-MING

MIN-HOU

•Fu-chou

FU-AN

TA-LI PAI

CHÜ-CHING

•Kuei-yang

AN-SHUN

LIU-P'AN SHUI

KUEI-TING

LING-LING

FU-CHOU

LUNG-CH'I

NU-CHIANG LISU

HSING-I

•Tung-ch'uan

SOUTH KWEICHOW PUYI-MIAO

KUEI-LIN

KAN-CHOU

•Hsia-men

YUNNAN

•K'un-ming

KUEI-LIN

•Kuei-lin

SHAO-KUAN

LUNG-YEN

MEI-HSIEN

TAIWAN "under admin. Chinese Nat. Govt."

YÜ-CH'I

HO-CH'IH

•Liu-chou

WU-CHOU

KWANGTUNG

LIN-TS'ANG

WEN-SHAN CHUANG-MIAO

KWANGSI CHUANG AUTONOMOUS REGION

LIU-CHOU

•Wu-chou

CHAO-CH'ING

HUI-YANG

SHAN-T'OU

SSU-MAO

HUNG-HO HANI-YI

•Canton

FO-SHAN

HSI-SHUANG PAN-NA T'AI

•Nan-ning

NAN-NING

YÜ-LIN

HONG KONG (U.K.)

MACAU (Port.)

•P'ing-hsiang

CHAN-CHIANG

•Pei-hai

HAI-NAN

HAI-NAN LI-MIAO **

* Ta-ch'eng and A-le-t'ai in Sinkiang are regions subordinate to Ili Kazakh Autonomous District.

** Hai-nan Li-Miao in Kwangtung is an autonomous district subordinate to Hai-nan Hsing-cheng-ch'ü.

TOPOGRAPHIC surveys and maps, for use in the planning of the country's reconstruction, were pressing needs of the People's Republic of China in its first years. Although the bulk of the professionally qualified had departed for Taiwan, taking with them much archival material, Russian advisers assisted during the first decade and progress was swift. For public use only a few small scale maps and atlases were issued, but these did intimate China's standpoint on her national frontiers. Since that time, China has on several occasions declared her resolve to settle international boundary questions by discussion but has expressed equal determination to oppose unilateral action by others. In pursuance of this policy, agreement has been reached with Afghanistan (1963), Burma (1960), Mongolia (1962), Nepal (1961) and Pakistan (1963). Boundary agreements have also been made with Korea and Vietnam. Borders with the USSR and India and sovereignty of the islands in the South China Sea (see page 116) have yet to be finally resolved.

The Sino-Russian Frontier Towards the end of the 16th century Russian expansion into Siberia began in earnest. New towns were established from the Urals to the Pacific in a little over sixty years. The first expeditions were small, often numbered in tens, rarely in hundreds, but they were followed by the settlers who were to make their homes in Siberia. At this time China had no real frontiers in the sense of definable lines: the limits of Chinese territory were the most distant lands tributary to China.

From about 1573 the Ming Empire began its decline. In 1644 Manchu tribes overran China and founded the Ch'ing or Manchu Dynasty.

A party of 130 Russians reached the Amur river just when the Ming Dynasty was in its death throes. They travelled down it to the Sea of Okhotsk and founded the port of Okhotsk. When Khabarovsk arrived six years later he met stiff Manchu resistance which he successfully quelled but found himself and his country engaged in conflict with Manchu China. Forty years of hostilities ended in the Treaty of Nerchinsk, the first treaty ever signed by the Chinese Empire. The Russians gave up the Amur and agreed on a boundary which followed the Argun river to its confluence with the Amur and then along the Shilka river to the Stanovoy and Yablonovyy mountains. In 1850, however, a military detachment, seeking an alternative to the difficult overland route to Okhotsk, hoisted the Russian flag on the north bank of the river and in 1854 they were joined by a force which sailed in from the Pacific. China had no power to resist, after the crushing defeat of the Opium Wars (1838–42). The Treaties of Aigun (1858) and Peking (1860) made the Amur river the boundary and gave Russia the land between the Ussuri river and the Pacific. The USSR regards the boundary in this area as following Pritok (channel) Kazakevicheva thus making the island of Hei-hsia-tzu Soviet. China claims a 'thalweg' boundary – the line followed by the main navigational channels of the rivers. This would place the confluence at Khabarovsk and would make Hei-hsia-tzu Chinese (see section A).

Sixty-four villages on the north bank of the Amur lying between the rivers Zeya (Zela) and Bureya were to remain Manchu. The inhabitants were ejected during the Boxer Rebellion (1900). China has yet to agree the resulting river boundary (see section B).

A subsequent treaty (Tsitsihar, 1911) moved the Russian boundary a few miles further into China in two areas each about 50 miles in extent. China did not ratify this treaty although it was signed (see section C).

By 1850 Russian occupation of Siberia extended to Lake Balkhash, the Ili river and Lake Issyk-Kul'. Appeals for help from various Kirgiz tribes brought the Russians deeper into Kirgizia. In 1871 disorder reigned further up the Ili river in the region of Kul'dzha. The Russians moved in to restore order. Ten years later the Ili valley and Kul'dzha were returned to China. Treaties of 1864, 1870 and 1881 were signed with China to define the boundaries in this area (see section D).

Russian expansion towards India alarmed the British. A treaty was signed in 1895 in which the Wakhan corridor, a salient of Afghan territory, barred further Russian progress southwards. China was not a party to the Treaty but since the Russians had achieved a common frontier with Afghanistan in the Pamirs, the Khrebet Sarykol'skiy watershed became the Russo-Chinese boundary south of Kizil-Jik-Dawan (see section E).

The Sino-Indian Frontier Tibet was nominally under Chinese suzerainty at the fall of the Manchu Empire in 1911. At Simla in 1914 Britain and China discussed the division of Tibet into a western, autonomous region and an eastern, Chinese-administered region. At the same time a line, the McMahon Line–named after the British representative–was added to the final map to define the boundary between Tibet and India, including a part of what is now Burma. All three representatives signed the map and documents relating to the proposed boundaries. The Chinese Government, however, rejected their plenipotentiary's agreement, on the grounds of the portrayal of the boundary between Tibet and China (see section G). Chinese agreement with Burma (1960) includes acceptance of part of the McMahon Line, but China has yet to reach agreement with India and claims the correct boundary is in the foothills, thus excluding the North East Frontier Agency which India claims has long been under Indian administration.

Equally serious are the rival claims in Aksai Chin. China occupies this area, which India claims is her territory. A road built by China to link Sinkiang with Tibet now runs through it (see section F).

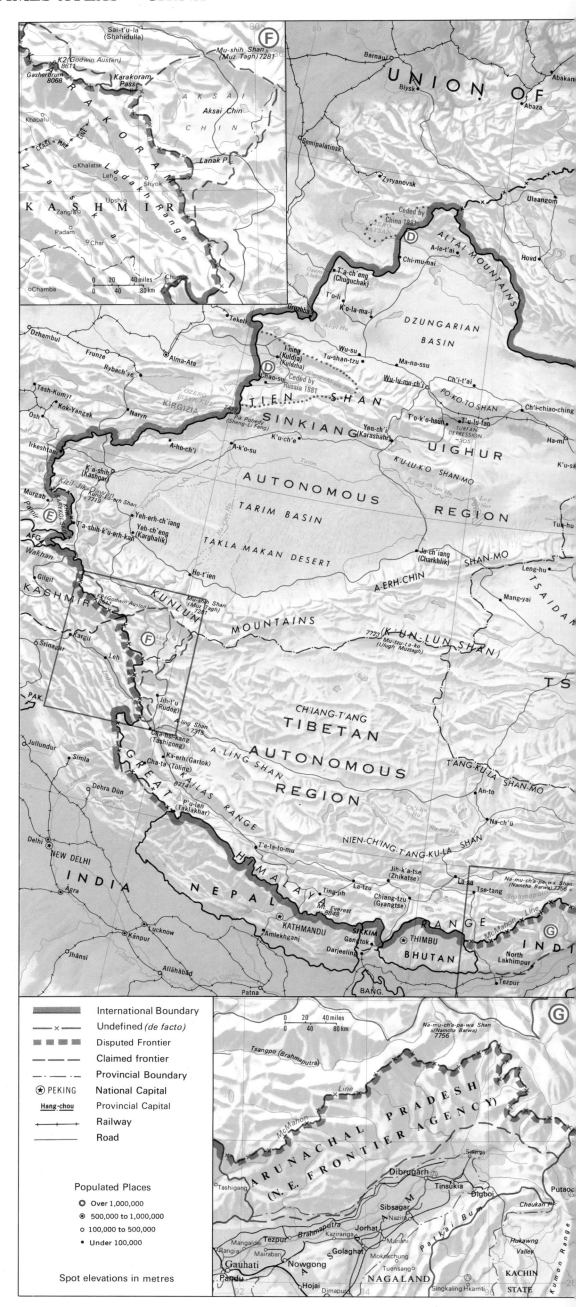

SYMBOLS

PHYSICAL MAPS (2-8)

Boundaries

International

Undelimited

Administrative

Communications

Railways

Roads

Tracks

Navigable Canals

Airports

Other Features

River, Stream

Seasonal Watercourses

Seasonal Flood-Plain

Pass ; Gorges

Dam, Barrage

Waterhole, Well

Summit, Peak

Ancient Walls

Lake Types

Fresh-water

Perennial Salt Lake

Seasonal Salt Lake

Saline Mud Flat

Salt Flat

Landscape Features

Ice-field and Glaciers

Sand Desert, Dunes

Saline Marsh, Salt Desert

Marsh, Swamp

Tidal Area

PROVINCIAL MAPS (10-119)

Administrative Centres

Provincial Capital

Shih (Municipality)

Hsien (County) or
Ch'i (Banner) centre

Other populated place

[Ta-pu] Name of Shih, Hsien or Ch'i
where different from
name of centre

Wu-hu Centre of Autonomous District,
League or Region

N.B. Regional name is shown only where
different from name of centre

Boundaries

International

Undelimited

Provincial

Autonomous District (A.D.);
Meng (League)
Hsien (Taiwan only)

Shih (Municipality)
Ti - ch'ü (Region)

Abbreviations

A.D. - Autonomous District
A.H. - Autonomous Hsien
Aut. Bann. - Autonomous Banner
E. Bann. - Eastern Banner
W. Bann. - Western Banner

Communications

Railway

Road, Track

Waterway

Shipping Route

Port ; Airport

Other Features

River, Stream

Seasonal Watercourse

Subterranean Stream

Undefined River Course

Canal, Ditches

Dam, Reservoir

Seasonal Lake

Marsh, Flood area

Salt Marsh

Desert

Reef, Shoal

Ancient Wall

Historic Site

Summit, Peak

Pass

Gorge

Hot Spring

CITY PLANS (124-141)

Built-up area

Railway

Trolley-bus/bus route; stop

Ferry

Airport

Bridge

Park, Recreation Area

City Wall

Named buildings

Tomb

Memorial

Stadium

UNION OF SOVIET SOCIALIST REPUBLICS

MONGOLIA

INNER MONGOLIA

MANCHURIA

SINKIANG

Chinese Turkestan

TIBET (Plateau of Tibet) — Ch'iang-tang

Kun-lun Shan

CHINA (PEOPLES REPUBLIC)

Nan Ling

PAKISTAN

INDIA

NEPAL

BHUTAN

BANGLA DESH

BURMA

THAILAND (SIAM)

LAOS

INDO-VIETNAM CHINA

KHMER REP.

NORTH / SOUTH

MALAYSIA

PENINSULAR MALAYSIA

SARAWAK

SABAH

BORNEO

KALIMANTAN

SUMATRA

INDONESIA

SULAWESI (CELEBES)

PHILIPPINES

TAIWAN (FORMOSA) [under admin. Chinese Nat. Govt.]

KOREA — NORTH KOREA / SOUTH KOREA

JAPAN

SAKHALIN

Hokkaido

SRI LANKA (Ceylon)

Seas and oceans

SEA OF OKHOTSK

SEA OF JAPAN

YELLOW SEA

EAST CHINA SEA

SOUTH CHINA SEA

BAY OF BENGAL

INDIAN OCEAN

Gulf of Tongking

Gulf of Siam

Gulf of Martaban

PO HAI

SULU SEA

CELEBES SEA

MOLUCCA SEA

BANDA SEA

JAVA SEA

Selected cities

Yakutsk, Omsk, Novosibirsk, Novokuznetsk, Krasnoyarsk, Irkutsk, Ulan Ude, Chita, Khabarovsk, Vladivostok, Karaganda, Semipalatinsk, Alma Ata, Frunze, Ulaanbaatar, Urumchi, Peking (Pei-p'ing), Tientsin, Tai-yuan, Lan-chou, Hsi-an (Sian), K'ai-feng, Shanghai, Nanking, Wu-han, Hang-chou, Ch'eng-tu, Ch'ung-ching (Chungking), Ch'ang-sha, Fu-chou, K'un-ming, Canton, Hong Kong (UK), T'ai-pei, T'ai-nan, Ha-erh-pin (Harbin), Ch'ang-ch'un, Shen-yang (Mukden), P'yongyang, Soul (Seoul), Inchon, Pusan, Nagasaki, Nagoya, Osaka, Tokyo, Sapporo, Delhi, Jaipur, Agra, Lucknow, Kanpur, Patna, Calcutta, Dacca, Mandalay, Rangoon, Moulmein, Chiang Mai, Vientiane, Bangkok (Krung Thep), Hanoi, Haiphong, Hue, Da Nang (Tourane), Phnom Penh, Saigon, Kuala Lumpur, Singapore, Kuching, Kota Kinabalu, Bandar Seri Begawan, Manila, Quezon City, Iloilo, Davao, Jakarta (Batavia), Surabaya, Yogyakarta, Palembang, Padang, Madras, Bangalore, Hyderabad, Colombo

Tropic of Cancer

Arctic Circle

Equator

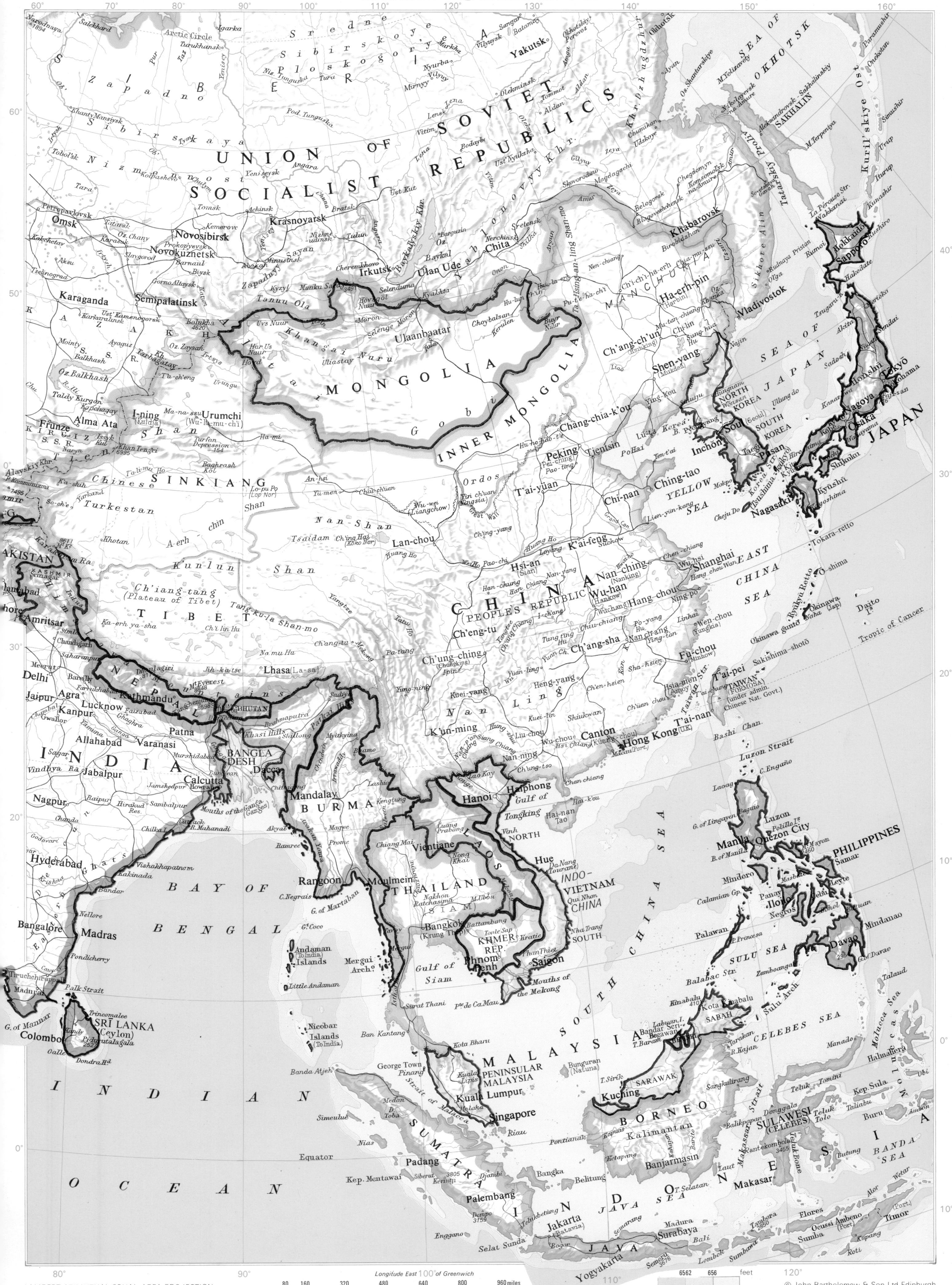

LAMBERT AZIMUTHAL EQUAL-AREA PROJECTION

1:24 M

80 160 320 480 640 800 960 miles
160 320 640 960 1280 1600 km

Longitude East of Greenwich

6562 656 feet
2000 200 m

© John Bartholomew & Son Ltd Edinburgh

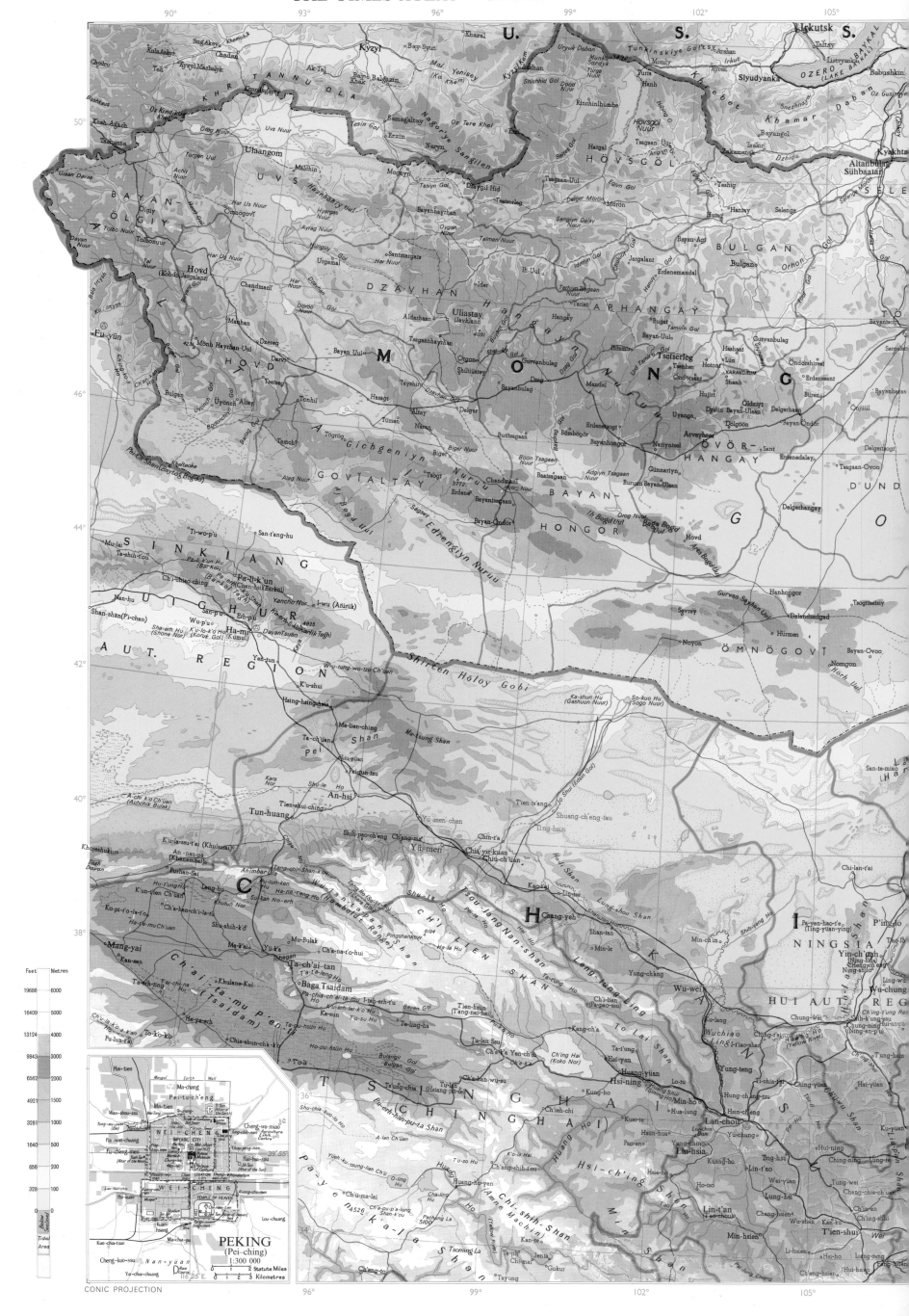

MONGOLIA

HENTIY

DORNOD

SÜHBAATAR

DORNOGOVĬ

INNER MONGOLIA REGION

LIAONING

HOPEH

SHANSI

SHANTUNG

SHENSI

HONAN

ANHWEI

KIANGSU

Ulan-Ude
ULAANBAATAR (ULAN BATOR)
Chita
Nerchinsk
Borzya
Man-chou-li
Choybalsan
Saynshand
Erh-lien-hao-t'e
Dzamïn Uüd
Hai-la-erh (Hu-lun)(Hailar)
Ch'i-ch'i-ha-erh (Tsitsihar)
Pai-ch'eng
T'ao-an
Shuang-liao
T'ung-liao
K'ai-lu
Fu-shun
Shen-yang
An-shan
Liao-tung Wan
Chin-chou
Hsin-min
Ch'in-huang-tao
LÜ-TA
Ta-lien (Dairen)
Lü-shun
PO HAI (GULF OF CHIHLI)
Po Hai Wan
PEI-CHING (Peking)
T'ien-chin (Tientsin)
T'ang-shan
Pao-ting
Chang-chia-kou
Hsüan-hua
Ta-t'ung
Pao-t'ou
Kweisui
Ning-wu
Shih-chia-chuang
T'ai-yüan
Fen-yang
Hsing-t'ai
Te-chou
Chi-nan
Wei-fang
Ch'ing-tao
SHANTUNG PAN-TAO
Yen-t'ai   Wei-hai
Lin-i
Lien-yün-kang
Han-tan
An-yang
Hsin-hsiang
Chi-ning
Lo-yang
Cheng-chou
K'ai-feng
Hsü-chou
Huai-pei
Hsi-an (Sian)
Pao-chi
Yü-lin
Yen-an

Heights in metres

Longitude East of Greenwich

1:6 M
km   miles

© John Bartholomew & Son Ltd.

HONG KONG
1:300 000

CONIC PROJECTION

SOUTH CHINA

YELLOW SEA
(HUANG HAI)

SHANTUNG

KIANGSU

HONAN

ANHWEI

HUPEH

C H I N A

CHEKIANG

HUNAN

KIANGSI

FUKIEN

FORMOSA STRAIT
(T'AI-WAN HAI-HSIA)

TAIWAN
(FORMOSA)
(under admin.
Chinese Nat. Govt.)

KWANGTUNG

Canton

HONG KONG (To U.K.)
Macau (To Port.)

SOUTH

CHINA SEA

(NAN HAI)

HAI-NAN
TAO

Shanghai

SHANGHAI
1:300 000

1:6 M
km miles

Longitude East of Greenwich   Heights in metres

© John Bartholomew & Son Ltd, Edinburgh

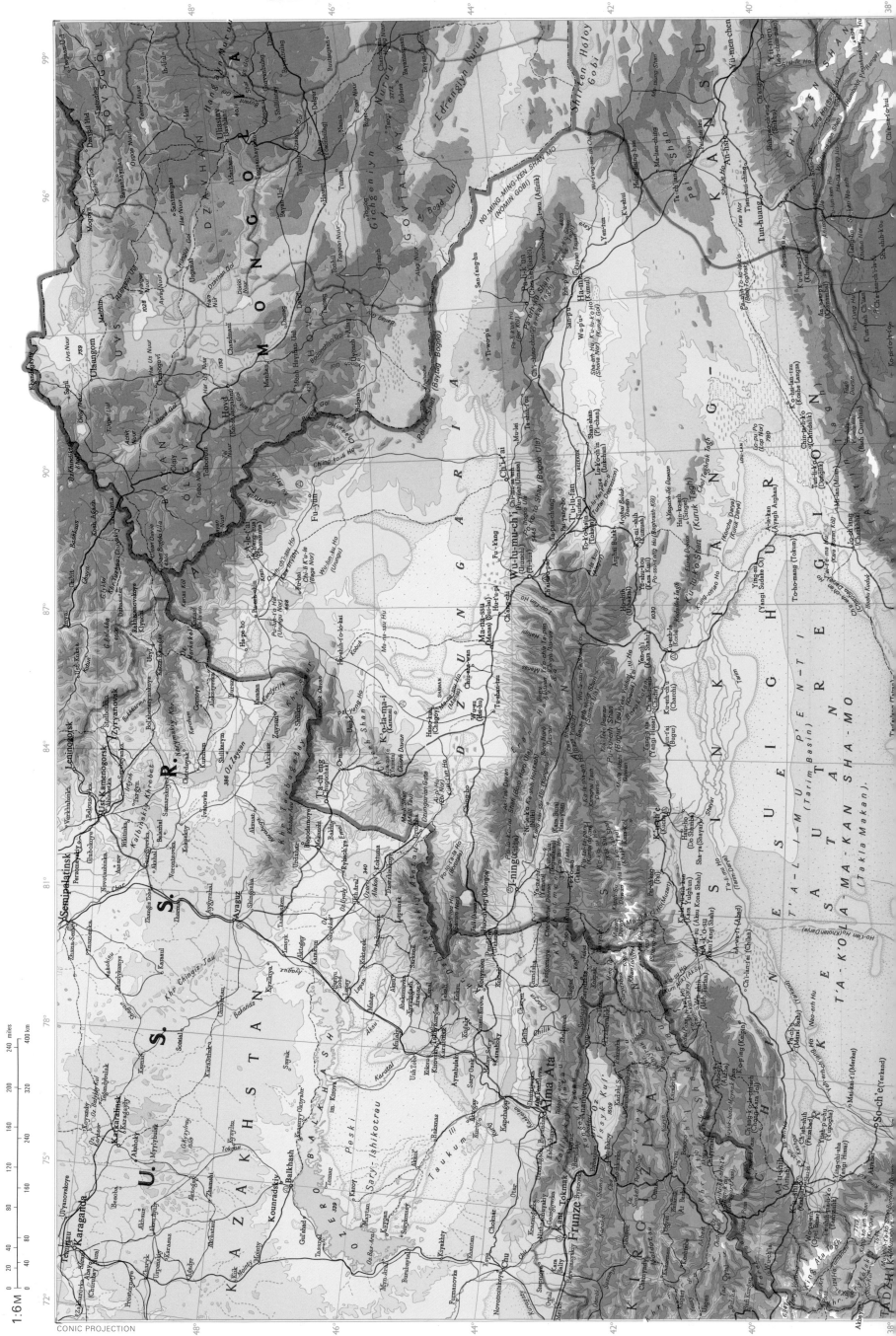

Heights in metres

© John Bartholomew & Son Ltd, Edinburgh

Longitude East 87° of Greenwich

Feet	Metres
19686	6000
16409	5000
13124	4000
9843	3000
6562	2000
4921	1500
3281	1000
1640	500
656	200
328	100
0	0

NORTH-EAST CHINA

U. S. S. R.

MANCHURIA CHINA

HEILUNGKIANG

KIRIN

LIAONING

NORTH KOREA

SOUTH KOREA

JAPAN

SEA OF JAPAN

KOREA BAY

YELLOW SEA (HWANG HAI)

Choson-Man

Shilka · Amur · Mo-ho · Zeya · Magdagachi · Shimanovsk · Svobodnyy · Belogorsk (Kuybyshevka-Vostochnaya) · Blagoveshchensk · Zavitinsk · Raychikhinsk · Birobidzhan · Khabarovsk · Fu-yüan · Komsomol'sk-na-Amure

Khrebet Dzhagdy · Khrebet Turana · Khr. Bureinskiy · Khr. Dusse Alin · Khr. Yam-Alin · Khr. Magu · Khrebet Chay · Ul'banskiy Zaliv · Chukchagirskoye Oz · Oz Zvoron · Oz Bolon · Anyuy

Khr. Dzhaki-Unakhta Yakbyyana

Hai-la-erh (Hu-lun) (Hailar) · Ya-k'o-shih · P'o-k'o-t'u · Man-kuei · Nen-chiang · Cha-lan-t'un · Ch'i-ch'i-ha-erh H (Tsitsihar) · Fu-yü · Hai-lun · I-ch'un · Ho-kang · Fu-chin · Bikin · Dal'nerechensk · Lesozavodsk

Nen Chiang (Nonni River) · Sui-hua · An-ta · Ha-erh-pin (Harbin) · A-ch'eng · Chiamu-ssu (Sungari River) · Shuang-ya-shan · Pao-ch'ing · Mi-shan (Tung-an) · Chi-hsi · Ozero Khanka · Spassk Dal'niy · Rudnaya Pristan'

Chang-hsing · Pai-ch'eng · T'ao-an · K'ai-lu · Ch'ang-ling · Nung-an · Ch'ang-ch'un · Chi-lin (Kirin) · Mu-tan-chiang · Tung-ning · Ussuriysk · Artem · Vladivostok · Partizansk · Nakhodka

Shuang-liao (Cheng-chia-t'un) · Ssu-p'ing · Liao-yüan (Pei-feng) · Kung-chu-ling · Hai-lung · Yen-chi · Tu-men · Hun-ch'un · Unggi · Najin · Zaliv Petra Velikogo

Fu-hsin · Hsin-min · Fu-shun · Shen-yang (Mukden) · Liao-yang · T'ieh-ling · Ch'ing-yüan · Hun-chiang · Tung-hua · Chang-pai · Ch'ŏngjin · Nanam · Kilchu

Chin-chou · An-shan · Pen-ch'i · Ying-k'ou · Liao-tung Wan (Gulf of Liaotung) · Tan-tung · Shuiju · Kanggye · Hyesanjin · Hamhŭng · Hŭngnam · Wŏnsan

LÜ-TA · Ta-lien (Daizen) (Lü-ta Shih) · Lü-shun · Chin-chou Wan · Pyongyang · Haeju · Kaesŏng · Inch'ŏn · SŎUL (SEOUL) (Yŏngsong) · Ch'unch'ŏn

Yen-t'ai (Chefoo) · Wei-hai · Taejŏn · Kunsan · Andong · Chŏngju

Take shima (Liancourt Rocks) · Ullŭng do (Dagelet) · Oki shotō · Sado · Takaoka · Toyama · Nagano · Kanazawa · Fukui

SKHOTE ALIN · SIKHOTE ALIN

CONIC PROJECTION
19686 13124 6562 656 328 164 0 328 656 1640 3281 4921 6562 9843 Feet
6000 4000 2000 200 100 50 0 100 200 500 1000 1500 2000 3000 Metres

Longitude East 129° of Greenwich

Heights in metres

1 : 6 M

0 20 40 80 120 160 200 240 miles
0 40 80 160 240 320 400 km

© John Bartholomew & Son Ltd, Edinburgh

HEILUNGKIANG
PROVINCE

HEILUNGKIANG is the most northerly of all the Chinese provinces, and one of the largest since the boundary changes of 1969. It is an area which was until recent times on the fringe of the Chinese empire. First incorporated in a Chinese-style state under the Liao (937–1125) Khitan dynasty and then under the larger and more sinified Chin (1125–1234) Jurchen dynasty, this area remained under a degree of central control during the period of the Mongol dynasty (1234–1368). In the late 14th century and the early 15th the Chinese Ming dynasty (1368–1644) attempted to exercise a form of indirect rule over the tribal population, but this gradually became ineffective. During the Manchu Ch'ing dynasty, which had its origins in the north-east, Russian expansion across Siberia reached the Amur river region in the mid-17th century. This was checked, and the Treaty of Nerchinsk (1689) recognised Chinese sovereignty over the whole Amur region to the north of the present boundary. This northern area was placed under a Manchu military governor. In 1858–60 Russia annexed the whole area north of the Amur river, and the coastal area south to Vladivostok.

Until this time the province remained very thinly peopled, with few Chinese farmers. Settlement in the plains of the Sungari (Sung-hua) and Nonni (Nen Chiang) rivers began only in the late 19th century. Heilungkiang, even more than Kirin and Liaoning, remained largely peopled by various Tungusic peoples. At the end of the 19th century, when the foreign powers began to divide China into spheres of influence, Heilungkiang came under Russian domination. The Russians constructed the Chinese Eastern Railway across the province to Vladivostok, and after the Boxer rebellion occupied the railway zone for some years. Russian influence remained here, even after the Russo–Japanese War of 1904–5, and a large number of White Russians settled in the cities after the Revolution of 1917. In 1931 the province, with the rest of Manchuria, came under Japanese control. By this time there had already been considerable Chinese immigration into Heilungkiang, and this continued. The Japanese also built a railway network, and began the exploitation of the province's resources. Under the Communist regime this growth has continued. The population rose from about 12,000,000 in 1953 to 21,000,000 by 1964. The increase is partly the result of extensive immigration from other parts of China.

In the post-war years the western section of the province, with a large Mongol population, became a part of the Inner Mongolian Autonomous Region, forming the Hu-lun-pei-erh (Hulunbuir) League. Late in 1969 this area was transferred to Heilungkiang.

Heilungkiang has a very harsh climate. Even the southern plain has average winter temperatures of −20.1°C (−4°F). In the Amur valley in the north temperatures drop to −27.6°C (−18°F). The winters are very long and there are many areas of permafrost. The summers are short and hot ranging from 20°C to 24°C (68°F to 75°F). The growing season is about 165 days in the Sung-hua plain, and less than 160 days in the north. Rainfall is adequate, about 500 mm to 600 mm in the plain, decreasing towards the west. Most of this falls in the summer months.

The natural vegetation of the central plains was steppe grassland, while the mountains are covered in dense mixed forest. There are still very large areas of natural forest, and Heilungkiang produces about 40 per cent of China's timber.

The Sung-hua river plain This is an area of natural grassland with extremely rich black soils, which was first brought into cultivation on a large scale in the early part of this century, when the coming of the railway gave it good communications with the outside. This is the most important agricultural area of Heilungkiang, where grain (corn, spring wheat, millet, kaoliang) soy beans, flax and sugarbeet are grown. There is also a dairy industry, and animal husbandry is important.

Ha-erh-pin (Harbin), the provincial capital, is the main city of this region. At the beginning of this century it was a small river port on the Sung-hua, but the railways transformed it into the natural communication centre for the province. Already a city of 380,000 in 1932, it doubled in the next decade under the Japanese, when it developed extensive food processing industries. Since 1949 Ha-erh-pin has developed more varied industry. It has become a major producer of heavy machinery (especially turbines and boilers) for power generating, for electrical equipment, for precision tools and bearings and for tractors. It also produces cement, fertilisers and chemicals, and refines sugar. Its population has continued to grow and is currently estimated at about 2,000,000.

Shao-tung and *Hu-lan* are important industrial satellite towns.

The Nen-chiang river plain lies to the west and north-west. It is slightly less fertile, and has a somewhat lower rainfall and a shorter growing season. It is mainly a grain-growing area, with winter wheat, corn, kaoliang and rice taking up most of the land. Soy beans and sugarbeet are also important economic crops. This area has well developed animal husbandry and a dairy industry concentrated around Ch'i-ch'i-ha-erh and An-ta.

Ch'i-ch'i-ha-erh is the main city of the area. An old post town under the Manchus, this was the first area settled by Chinese in the 18th century. It began to develop rapidly after 1903 when the Chinese Eastern Railway was completed, and by the 1930s already had a wide range of industries. Further industrial development followed under the Japanese and this has continued under the Communist regime. Ch'i-ch'i-ha-erh has a major engineering industry, producing railway locomotives and rolling stock, machine tools and mine machinery. It also has a large sugar-refining industry and paper mills, as well as extensive food-processing plants.

Fu-la-erh-chi is a satellite industrial city, with a steel plant, and heavy machinery factories.

Ta-ch'ing oilfield This oilfield, the precise location of which has never been specified, but which is south-west of An-ta, was discovered in 1959, and began production in 1962. By 1965 the field produced half of China's total oil production, 3,500,000 tons. Production has increased considerably since. Part of this oil is refined locally, the rest shipped by rail to refineries at Ta-lien and Chin-chou in Liaoning. The field remains China's largest source of oil, and has made a considerable contribution to China's self-sufficiency.

The Ho Chiang plain This is the plain where the Amur, Sungari and Ussuri rivers converge. It is a low-lying ill-drained area, with many swamps and a tendency to flood. There has been considerable work on water-conservancy schemes in the area since 1949, and there are many large state farms. The main crops are spring wheat, corn, kaoliang and rice, and sugarbeet, soy beans and flax are also grown.

Chia-mu-ssu is the principal route centre and market of this area. Its growth was comparatively late, dating from the completion of the railways in 1939 and the beginning of coal-mining in the nearby region. Growth has continued since 1949. It has a large power plant, and much diversified industry, including paper making, using wood from the forests of the Hsiao-hsing-an range to the north, sugar refining, the manufacture of farm equipment and aluminium smelting. It is also important for the lumber trade and for transport of coal.

Ho-kang is a major coal field, which first came into operation in 1936. It was producing 2,500,000 tons by 1943. Production has been greatly increased since 1949. It was nearly 5,000,000 tons in 1957, and is now probably about 10,000,000 tons.

Shuang-ya-shan, south-east of Chia-mu-ssu, is another important coal town, which was developed in the 1940s and has continued to grow. It produced 2,300,000 tons in 1957 and now probably produces about 5,000,000 tons.

The Hsiao-hsing-an mountains This heavily-forested mountain belt lies between the Amur and the Sungari plain. It is sparsely peopled, has little cultivated land, and is important mainly as a lumbering region.

I-ch'un is the main town of the area and the centre of the lumber industry.

The Hei-ho area This includes the lower and middle plain of the Amur and the northern slopes of the Hsiao-hsing-an range. It is extremely cold, and apart from the narrow alluvial plain along the Amur, has difficult and complex terrain, heavily covered with forest. It developed very late. Settlement began around Hei-ho early in this century, after a minor gold-rush in the 1880s. Extensive settlement took place in the 1950s, and there is now a small population producing spring wheat, corn and soy beans, with some hardy rice. Agriculture, however, is still confined to a very small area. The timber industry is very important, but communications are very poor.

South-eastern Heilungkiang uplands This area was virtually unpopulated virgin forest until the construction of the Chinese Eastern railway in the early years of this century, when lumbering became a major industry and Chinese settlers moved into the area. The main crops grown here are soy beans, corn, spring wheat and some rice.

Mu-tan-chiang is the region's major city. Formerly a small settlement, as the traditional regional centre had been Ning-an, it grew to importance as a lumbering centre, where the Mu-tan Chiang river crossed the new railway route. It retains its importance as a lumbering centre, but has also developed other industries in recent times, including aluminium smelting, a tyre manufacturing plant and, more recently, a small iron and steel plant.

Chi-hsi to the north-east is a very important coal mining centre. First developed by the Japanese in the 1930s, it has continued to grow steadily. It produced 5,800,000 tons in 1957, and now probably produces over 10,000,000 tons annually.

See also notes on page 21.

AREA
710,000 square kilometres

POPULATION
21,390,000 (other estimates up to 25,000,000)

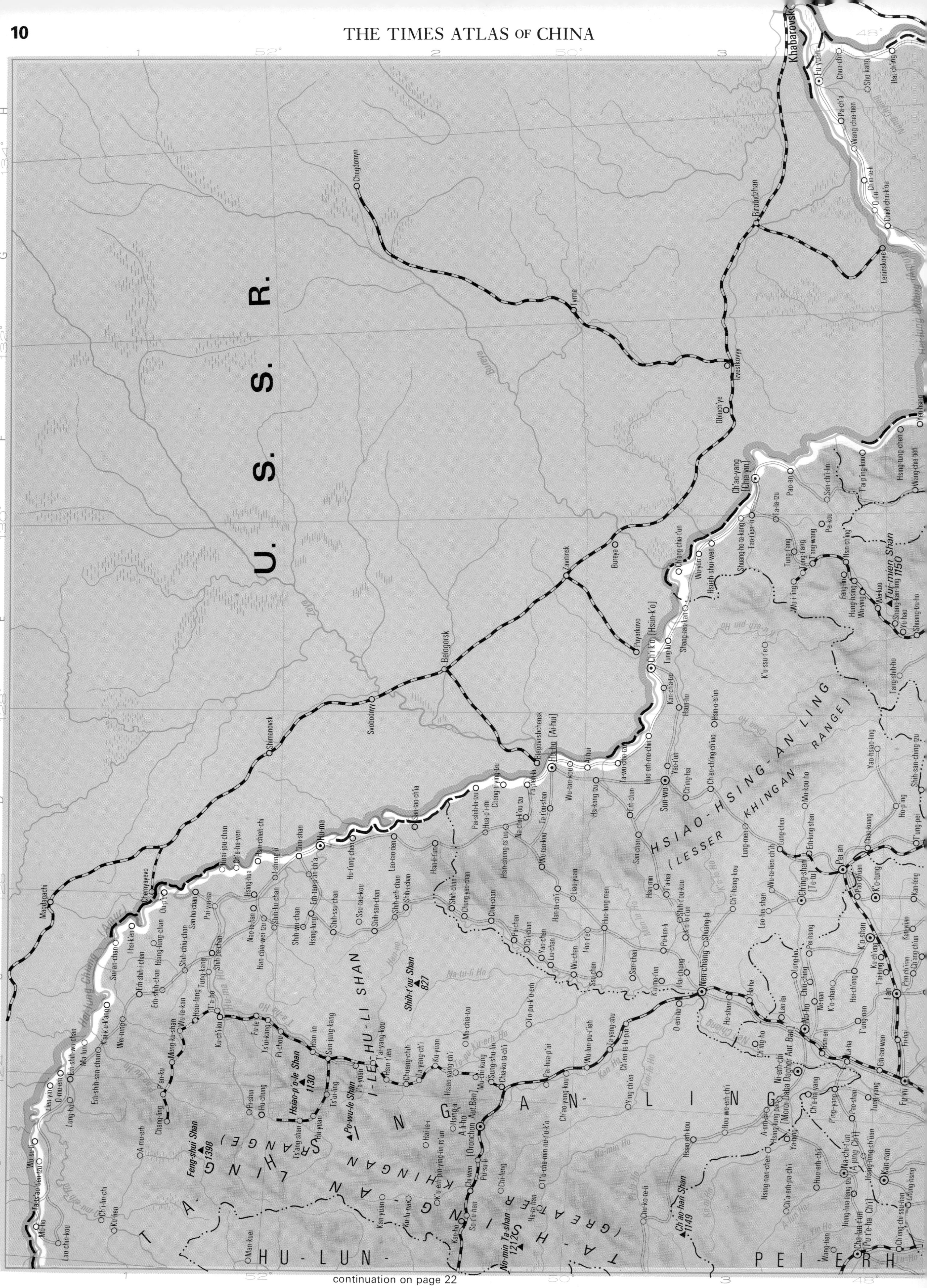

Khabarovsk

U. S. S. R.

Chegdomyn

Tyrma

Birobidzhan

Leninskoye

Izvestkovyy

Obluch'ye

Ch'ao-yang [Chia-yin]

Bureya

Poyarkovo

Belogorsk

Zeya

Blagoveshchensk

Svobodnyy

Ch'i-k'o [Hsün-k'o]

Hei-ho [Ai-hui]

Shimanovsk

Fa-pieh-la

HSIAO-HSING-AN-LING
(LESSER KHINGAN RANGE)

Sun-wu

Pei-an

K'o-tung

Ch'ernyayevo

Mandzhachi

Sui-an-chan

Harbin

Shih-t'ou Shan 827

Na-tu-li Ho

I-LE-HU-LI SHAN

Feng-shui Shan 1398

Hsiao-p'o-le Shan 1130

Po-wu-le Shan

TA-HSING-AN-LING (GREAT KHINGAN RANGE)

No-min Ta-shan 1212

Ch'ao-han Shan 1149

Tui-mien Shan 1150

Wen-ch'iang

Nu-ho

I-an

HU-LUN-

PEI-ERH

continuation on page 22

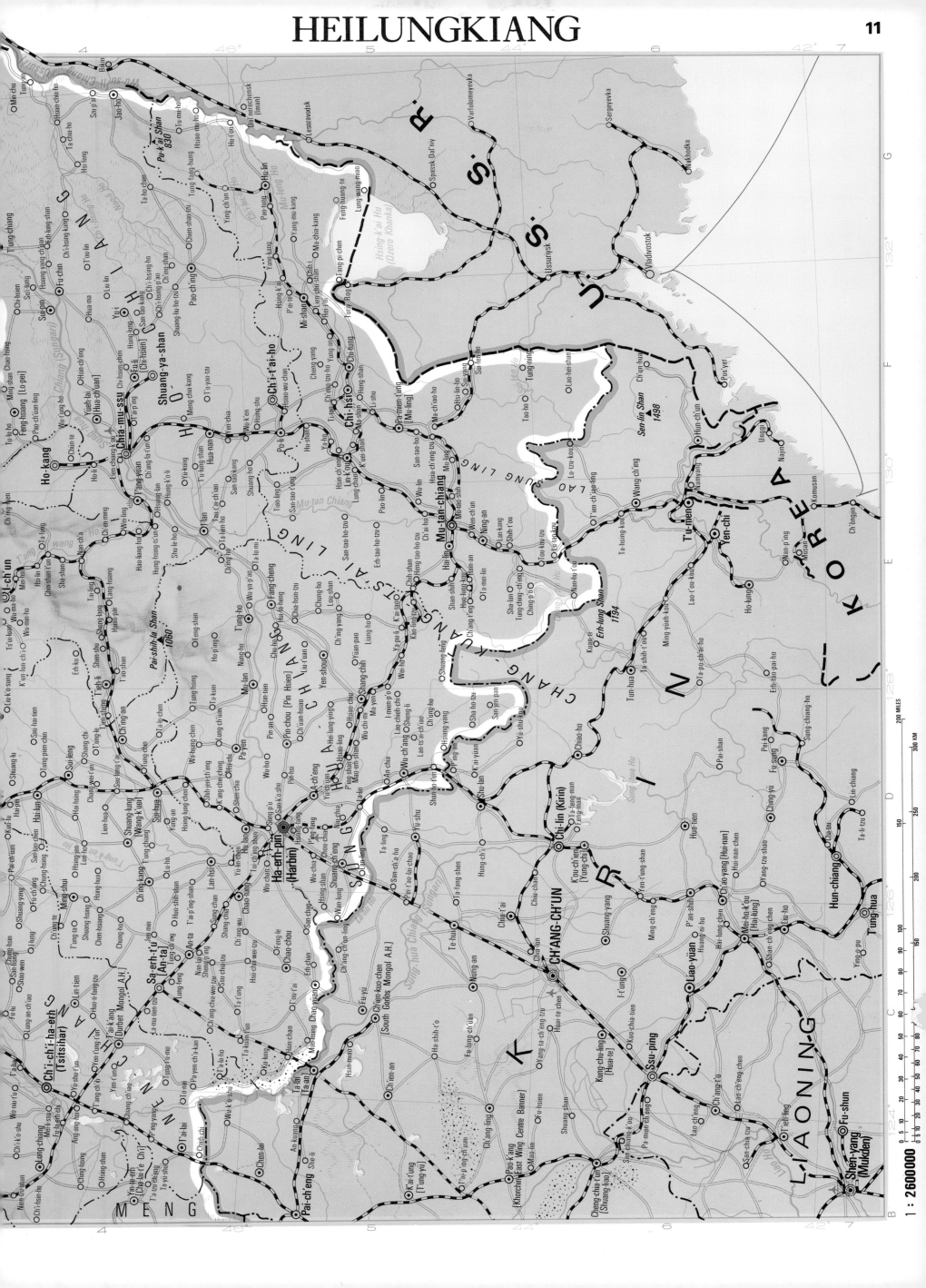

HEILUNGKIANG PROVINCE
HEI-LUNG-CHIANG SHENG
黑龙江省

12 shih	*municipalities*
1 meng	*league*
8 ti-ch'ü	*regions*
64 hsien	*counties*
1 tzu-chih-hsien	*autonomous county*
9 ch'i	*banners*
3 tzu-chih-ch'i	*autonomous banners*

capital **Ha-erh-pin Shih**	D5	哈尔滨市
An-ta Shih	C4	安达市
Chia-mu-ssu Shih	G4	佳木斯市
Ch'i-ch'i-ha-erh Shih	B4	齐齐哈尔市
Chi-hsi Shih	F5	鸡西市
Ch'i-t'ai-ho Shih	F5	七台河市
Hai-la-erh Shih	A3	海拉尔市
Ho-kang Shih	F4	鹤岗市
I-ch'un Shih	E4	伊春市
Man-chou-li Shih	B3	满州里市
Mu-tan-chiang Shih	E5	牡丹江市
Shuang-ya-shan Shih	F4	双鸭山市

Hei-ho Ti-ch'ü		黑河地区
Ai-hui Hsien		爱辉县
centre: Hei-ho	D2	黑河
Hsün-k'o Hsien		逊克县
centre: Ch'i-k'o	E3	奇克
Nen-chiang Hsien	C3	嫩江县
Pei-an Hsien	D3	北安县
Sun-wu Hsien	D3	孙吴县
Te-tu Hsien		德都县
centre: Ch'ing-shan	D3	青山

Ho-chiang Ti-ch'ü		合江地区
centre: Chia-mu-ssu	G4	佳木斯
Chi-hsien Hsien		集贤县
centre: Fu-li	F4	福利
Fu-chin Hsien	G4	富锦县
Fu-yüan Hsien	H3	抚远县
Hua-ch'uan Hsien		桦川县
centre: Yüeh-lai	F4	悦来
Hua-nan Hsien	F4	桦南县
I-lan Hsien	E4	依兰县
Jao-ho Hsien	G4	饶河县
Lo-pei Hsien		萝北县
centre: Feng-hsiang	F4	凤翔
Pao-ch'ing Hsien	G4	宝清县
Po-li Hsien	F5	勃利县
Sui-pin Hsien	F4	绥滨县
T'ang-yüan Hsien	E4	汤原县
T'ung-chiang Hsien	G4	同江县
Yu-i Hsien	F4	友谊县

Hu-lun-pei-erh Meng		呼伦贝尔盟
centre: Hai-la-erh	A3	海拉尔
A-jung Ch'i		阿荣旗
centre: Na-chi-t'un	B3	那吉屯
Cha-lai-t'e Ch'i		扎赉特旗
centre: Yin-te-erh	B4	晋德尔
Ch'en-pa-erh-hu Ch'i	C3	陈巴尔虎旗
Old Barga Banner		
centre: Pa-yen-k'u-jen		巴彦库仁
Hsi-kuei-t'u Ch'i	D3	喜桂图旗
centre: Ya-k'o-shih		牙克石
Hsin-pa-erh-hu Tso-ch'i	C3	新巴尔虎左旗
New Barga East Banner		
centre: A-mu-ku-lang		阿穆古郎
Hsin-pa-erh-hu Yu-ch'i	B3	新巴尔虎右旗
New Barga West Banner		
centre: A-erh-t'ai-mien-chen		阿尔太面镇
O-erh-ku-na Tso-ch'i	D2	额尔古纳左旗
Argun East Banner		
centre: Ken-ho		根河
O-erh-ku-na Yu-ch'i	D2	额尔古纳右旗
Argun West Banner		
centre: La-pu-ta-lin		拉布达林
O-wen-k'o Tzu-chih-ch'i	C3	鄂温克自治旗
Evenki Autonomous Banner		
centre: Nan-t'un		南屯
Pu-t'e-ha Ch'i		布特哈旗
centre: Cha-lan-t'un	B3	札兰屯

I-ch'un Ti-ch'ü		伊春地区
Chia-yin Hsien		嘉荫县
centre: Ch'ao-yang	F3	朝阳
T'ien-li Hsien	E4	铁力县

Mu-tan-chiang Ti-ch'ü		牡丹江地区
Chi-tung Hsien	F5	鸡东县
Hai-lin Hsien	E5	海林县
Hu-lin Hsien	G5	虎林县
Lin-k'ou Hsien	F5	林口县
Mi-shan Hsien	F5	密山县
Mu-ling Hsien		穆棱县
centre: Pa-mien-t'ung	F5	八面通
Ning-an Hsien	E5	宁安县
Tung-ning Hsien	F5	东宁县

Nen-chiang Ti-ch'ü		嫩江地区
centre: Ch'i-ch'i-ha-erh	B4	齐齐哈尔
Fu-yü Hsien	C4	富裕县
I-an Hsien	C4	依安县
Kan-nan Hsien	B4	甘南县
K'o-shan Hsien	C3	克山县
K'o-tung Hsien	D3	克东县
Lin-tien Hsien	C4	林甸县
Lung-chiang Hsien	B4	龙江县
No-ho Hsien	C3	讷河县
Pai-ch'üan Hsien	D4	拜泉县
T'ai-lai Hsien	B4	泰来县
Tu-erh-po-t'e Meng-ku-tsu		杜尔伯持蒙古族
Tzu-chih-hsien		自治县
Durbet Mongol Autonomous Hsien		
centre: T'ai-k'ang	F4	泰康

Sui-hua Ti-ch'ü		绥化地区
An-ta Hsien	C4	安达县
Chao-chou Hsien	C5	肇州县
Chao-tung Hsien	C4	肇东县
Chao-yüan Hsien	C5	肇源县
Ch'ing-an Hsien	D4	青安县
Ch'ing-kang Hsien	D4	青冈县
Hai-lun Hsien	D4	海伦县
Lan-hsi Hsien	D4	兰西县
Ming-shui Hsien	C4	明水县
Sui-hua Hsien	D4	绥化县
Sui-leng Hsien	D4	绥棱县
Wang-k'uei Hsien	D4	望奎县
centre: Shuang-lung	D4	双龙

Sung-hua-chiang Ti-ch'ü		松花江地区
centre: Ha-erh-pin	D5	哈尔滨
A-ch'eng Hsien	D5	阿城县
Fang-cheng Hsien	E5	方正县
Hu-lan Hsien	D4	呼兰县
Mu-lan Hsien	E5	木兰县
Pa-yen Hsien	D4	巴彦县
Pin Hsien		宾县
centre: Pin-chou	D5	宾州
Shang-chih Hsien	D5	尚志县
Shuang-ch'eng Hsien	D5	双城县
T'ung-ho Hsien	E4	通河县
Wu-ch'ang Hsien	D5	五常县
Yen-shou Hsien	E5	延寿县

Ta-hsing-an-ling Ti-ch'ü		大兴安岭地区
centre: Chia-ko-ta-ch'i	C2	加格达奇
Hu-ma Hsien	C1	呼玛县
Mo-li-ta-wa Ta-wo-erh-tsu		莫力达瓦达斡尔族
Tzu-chih-ch'i		自治旗
Moroi-Daba Daghor Autonomous Banner		
centre: Ni-erh-chi	C3	尼尔基
O-lun-ch'un-tsu Tzu-chih-ch'i		鄂伦春族自治旗
Oronchon Autonomous Banner		
centre: A-li-ho	B2	阿里河

KIRIN
PROVINCE

KIRIN (Chi-lin) was first created as a province in 1907, when the restrictions on Chinese settlement in Manchuria were finally lifted. Its present boundaries were established in 1954, with the exception of the sections of the Hu-lun pei-erh and Che-li-mu Leagues which were detached from Inner Mongolia in 1969. Its administrative capital was moved from Chi-lin (Kirin city) to Ch'ang-ch'un in 1954. This region was always on the border of the Chinese cultural sphere. From the 8th century it formed a part of the powerful Po-hai state, which was destroyed in 927 by the Khitan, who in turn established a powerful Chinese-style dynasty, the Liao, which controlled Manchuria and parts of north-eastern China. In the 12th century the Jurchen, one of the Liao's subject peoples of Tungusic stock, who inhabited central Kirin and Heilungkiang, established their own independent state, which in 1125 destroyed the Liao and went on to conquer all northern China. They were destroyed in 1234 by the Mongols, whose control extended over this region. After the restoration of Chinese rule under the Ming in 1368, Manchuria remained a tributary region. In the late 16th century the Jurchen again grew powerful, and in 1616 set up an independent state in Manchuria, which included parts of Liaoning as well as Kirin and Heilungkiang. In 1633 this state took the name of Manchu, and in 1644 conquered China, establishing the Ch'ing empire which was to last until 1911. The Manchus, in an attempt to preserve their racial and cultural identity, forbade Chinese settlement in Kirin. But some Chinese peasants had begun to settle in Kirin in the 18th century, and after 1860, with the Russian occupation of the region beyond the Amur, this ban was not strictly enforced. It lingered until 1907, however, and it was not until the very end of the 19th century and early in the present century that large-scale settlement began.

In 1931 Kirin was occupied by the Japanese, and in 1932 became part of the puppet state of Manchukuo. It was during this period that the province developed a rail and power network, and large-scale industrial development began. Since 1949 the population has continued to grow, as industry and agriculture have become more and more productive.

Kirin is a transitional area between the bleak northern climate of Heilungkiang and the comparatively mild Liaoning. Winters are extremely cold. Ch'ang-ch'un's average January temperature is −16.9°C (1°F). The rivers are frozen for at least five months per year, and the growing season is between 160-170 days. Summers are very hot, with July average of 23.6°C (75°F). The rainfall, most of which falls in the summer months, decreases westwards from 1,000 mm in the Ch'ang-pai Shan mountains to only 400 mm in the western plateau. The natural vegetation was dense mixed forest in the eastern mountain areas, and good natural grassland in the plains.

The Ch'ang-ch'un plain This is a flat fertile plain, with rich, black earth soils. It is densely cultivated, the most important crops being corn, kaoliang, soy beans, sugar beet and millet.

Ch'ang-ch'un is the dominant city in the area, and has been, since 1954, the provincial capital. Ch'ang-ch'un is a modern city, which grew up as a major railway junction after 1905 and became a major market for the agriculture of the region. In 1932 it was selected by the Japanese as the capital of the Manchukuo state, and grew into a fine modern city. Its population rose by 1945 to 862,000 people, many of whom were Japanese, and it became a major cultural centre as well as an administrative capital. After the war it declined somewhat, but by 1957 its population had reached 975,000. It is currently estimated at over one million. After 1949, however, Ch'ang-ch'un's character changed. Previously its dominant industry had been food-processing. In the 1950s it was developed into a major heavy industrial city. It has the largest automotive industry in China, which began producing lorries in 1956, diesel engine and tractor works, tyre manufacturing, and a major plant producing railway locomotives, rolling stock and equipment. It also has a pharmaceutical chemicals industry. It has many institutions of higher education, and is a major centre of the film industry.

The Ssu-p'ing plain This is the southern part of the central plain, separated from the Ch'ang-ch'un area by the low watershed between the Sung-hua (Sungari) river system and the drainage basin of the Liao river system. This, too, is a fertile plain, the main grain producing area of the province, growing corn, kaoliang, millet, soy beans and sugar beet.

Ssu-p'ing, like Ch'ang-ch'un, developed early in this century as a railway junction and as a market and collecting centre for local agricultural produce. The city was almost destroyed during the civil war. After 1949 it developed into a minor industrial city, with farm-machinery and chemical plants, and oil-extraction, flour milling and lumber working industries. Although the city was designated for further development in the late 1950s, this does not seem to have taken place.

Liao-yüan, to the south-east, is the centre of a major coalfield, producing some three million tons per annum of good quality steam coal. It has a large thermal generating plant, and some industry, including fertiliser and paper manufacturing.

The Chi-lin area This is a region of hills, quite high in the east, more rounded and rolling in the west, with only a small area of plain. The mountains are deeply dissected by the headwaters of the Sung-hua river. Above Chi-lin these were dammed at Feng-man to form a very large hydro-electric scheme. This was completed by the Japanese before 1942. Other schemes were planned in the same area in the 1950s.

The lowlands of this area grow soy beans and rice, with less concentration on corn and kaoliang than elsewhere in Kirin. Flax and tobacco are also cultivated. The hills are mostly forested, although much of the forest has been cut over.

Chi-lin, unlike Ch'ang-ch'un, is an old Chinese city, first established in the 17th century. Early in this century it was predominantly a centre of lumbering, and a regional market centre. As the Japanese began to develop Manchuria as a base for war industry in the 1930s, industries with a stress on chemicals concerned with the production of petroleum from coal, cement, and paper-making were established. In the 1950s the Fengman hydro-electric plant, which had been partly dismantled during the Russian occupation, was restored, and industrial growth resumed. A number of very large chemical and fertiliser plants, and a major ferro-alloy industry were set up. Chi-lin is also a centre for sugar refining.

The Yen-pien mountain region This is the most mountainous and rugged area of Kirin, with a series of ranges, the Ch'ang-pai Shan, Nan-kang Shan, Wei-hu Ling, and Lao-sung Ling, whose peaks rise from 1,000 m to 1,600 m. It is still heavily forested, and was settled later than the plain areas to the east. It is the centre of a large Korean minority, who emigrated into the Yen-chi-T'u-men area in the 1870s and 1880s. They now number about 600,000 in this area alone. This area is essentially a lumbering district, with timber exported by rail to Chi-lin or to the Mu-tan-chiang area of Heilungkiang. There is also some copper mining at T'ien-pao-shan. The agriculture of the area concentrates on rice, soy beans and millet.

Yen-chi is the administrative centre of this Korean Autonomous District and the main market for the agriculture of the surrounding area.

T'u-men, on the North Korean border, is a major rail junction, and also a centre of the paper-making industry.

The T'ung-hua area This comprises the south-eastern corner of Kirin. It is a mountainous area drained by the headwaters of the Sung-hua and of the Ya-lu rivers. More than two-thirds of the area remains under dense forest, and forestry is a major industry. It also has rich reserves of iron ore and coal. Agriculture is confined to limited areas, and corn, soy beans, millet and kaoliang are grown.

T'ung-hua is the main city of this area. A centre of the lumber industry from the late 19th century, it was reached by a railway in 1937, and later became important as a transportation centre for the local coalfield at Hun-chiang and the iron mines at Ta-litzu, to which branch lines were built. In the late 1950s the construction of a major iron and steel plant was planned here, but it was never built. Local coal and iron-ore is transported by rail to An-shan.

Hun-chiang, to the north-east of T'ung-hua, is a major coal mining city, producing some two to three million tons of good coking coal annually.

See also notes on page 21.

AREA
290,000 square kilometres

POPULATION
17,890,000 (other estimates up to 21,000,000)

continuation on page 230

HOPEH PROVINCE

PEKING AND TIENTSIN MUNICIPALITIES

THIS region comprises the province of Hopeh and the province-level municipalities of Peking and Tientsin. It includes not only the traditional province of Hopeh (known under the Manchus as Chih-li) but also the northern plateau and hill areas which once formed parts of the provinces of Chahar and Jehol. These areas have very different environments and histories. The Great Plain of southern Hopeh was already incorporated in the Chinese cultural area by the end of the second millenium BC. Although it was many centuries before the poorly drained marshy plain itself was brought under cultivation, the foothill zone along the T'ai-hang range in the west already had a number of notable cities. Under the unified empire of the Han (206 BC–AD 220) the plain itself was drained and brought under cultivation, and maintained a very dense population. It continued to be the most densely peopled and productive area in China until about the 8th century, when the economic centre of the empire shifted to the Yangtze valley. In the early 10th century the northern half of Hopeh came under the dominance of the Khitan state of Liao in 936, and remained under foreign rulers – first the Jurchen and then the Mongols until 1368. During this period Peking first became a national capital, and after the restoration of Chinese rule under the Ming in 1368, Peking again became the capital in 1421. Hopeh province suffered badly from floods and drought during the late 19th century. There was considerable emigration to Manchuria, to the borderlands of Inner Mongolia, and into the north-west.

The northern section of the province, beyond the Great Wall, has a very different environment, dry uplands unsuited to traditional Chinese farming. This has always remained a frontier zone comparatively sparsely peopled, and administratively distinct from Hopeh province. Apart from minor adjustments, the province took its present shape in 1956.

The Southern Hopeh plain This area forms a vast alluvial plain, almost entirely below 50 m, watered by a series of rivers. From south to north the Wei Ho, Chang Ho, Fu-yang Ho, Hu-t'o Ho, Ta-ch'ing Ho and Yung-ting Ho flow together in the vicinity of Tientsin to form the Hai Ho. The whole region is one of very poor drainage, with many large areas of marsh, such as the Wen-an marsh and the Pai-yang lake, and large tracts of saline land. Formerly an area perennially devastated by widespread flooding, since 1949 very extensive water control works have been carried out. Additional outlets to the sea have been constructed to reduce the build up of spring flood waters around Tientsin; dams constructed on the upper streams of the various rivers to control their flow and reduce their silt-load; extensive dykes and retention basins constructed, and some attempt made to reduce the salinity of the soil.

The area has a very hard climate. Average temperatures in January are about −4°C (25°F), and the rivers are icebound for about three months in winter. Summers are very hot, with average July temperatures of 25°C (77°F) in the north. Rainfall is low: below 750 mm everywhere, and below 500 mm in the central part of the plain. It is subject to great annual variations, spring droughts being very common, and almost three quarters of the rain falls in June, July and August. The growing season is about 260 days in the south, falling to 220 days in the Peking area.

Agriculture is extremely intensive. Apart from the saline soils of the coastal belt, and the marshlands west and south-west of Tientsin, a very large proportion of the total area is farmed. The commonest crops are winter wheat, barley or peas followed by corn. Kaoliang and soy beans are widely grown, and cotton is a very important crop, especially in the south and west.

The main cities lie at the foot of the T'ai-hang mountains, which rise from the plain to the west and form the border with Shansi province. This higher ground has been a major communications route since pre-historic times, and since the early years of this century has been followed by the main Peking to Han-k'ou railway. The area has also some important coal deposits.

Han-tan is an ancient city, which was a minor commercial and administrative centre until recent times. In the 1950s it became an important cotton textile town. Later, important coal mines were opened at Feng-feng, and iron mines at Tz'u-shan provided raw materials for an iron and steel plant, built in 1958–60. Another mining centre is nearby at K'uang-shan-ts'un. Large cement and thermal power plants have also been built.

Shih-chia-chuang, the provincial capital, is an entirely modern city. A small satellite village of the old administrative city of Cheng-ting until the beginning of the century, Shih-chia-chuang became a rail junction for the railway to T'ai-yüan, growing into an important commercial centre and a centre of light industry in the 1920s and 1930s. In 1939 another rail line linked it with Te-chou and Chi-nan in Shantung, increasing its commercial area. After 1949 it was built up into a major centre of the cotton textile industry, and has since developed a woollen industry and chemical and fertiliser plants. Its population rose from 373,000 in 1953 to 598,000 in 1958, when it became the provincial capital.

Pao-t'ing is another very ancient city and a former capital of Hopeh. It is the chief commercial and market centre for central Hopeh, and also an important cultural centre, with various museums and institutions of higher education. It has a variety of agriculture-based industries, flour milling, oil extraction, leather and woollen manufacture, and it produces rayon.

Ts'ang-chou, on the old Grand Canal near the coast, and on the Tientsin–P'u-k'ou railway, is the main administrative and commercial centre of the coastal plain. It has a variety of minor industries. Salt is produced in the nearby coastal area.

The Peking area Peking (Pei-ching), situated at the north of the great plain, and at the mouth of various routes into the Mongolian borderlands, has been an important city throughout historical times, and the national capital, with brief intervals, since the 13th century, when the Mongols set their capital here. It became the terminus of the Grand Canal, which brought in supplies from southern China, and the focus of the national system of post-roads. In this century the rail system has converged upon Peking. Until the end of the Manchu regime in 1911, Peking remained essentially an administrative and cultural capital, with a flourishing commercial life, but little industry. Later some industry grew up to the west, with the exploitation of coal mines at Men-t'ou-kou and the construction of an iron and steel plant at Shih-ching-shan. During the 1950s there was rapid industrial growth in the east towards T'ung-hsien. Peking's iron and steel industry was also greatly developed, and fully integrated in 1969. The Shih-ching-shan plant now produces more than 1,000,000 tons of iron annually. Heavy engineering plant producing bridge girders, locomotives, machine tools, motor vehicles, ball-bearings and agricultural equipment was developed, and electronic, chemical and textile industries. Peking has a large thermal generating plant, and is joined by a power grid to a hydro-electric plant at Kuan-t'ing, to Tientsin, T'ang-shan, and to the Manchurian power grid.

Peking is not only the nation's political capital, but also its cultural centre, with many museums, universities and institutions of higher education and research.

The municipality includes a large area of hills to the north of the city, and includes the mining and industrial centres in the vicinity. Its population was 2,768,000 in 1953, and had grown to 4,010,000 in 1958. It is currently estimated at about 7,000,000.

Tientsin (T'ien-ching), like Peking, has the status of a provincial-level municipality, which it was granted in 1967. Although it is China's third largest city, Tientsin is not an ancient city like Peking, but a product of modern economic development. A minor port until the 19th century, it was opened to foreign trade in 1860, and in the various foreign concessions which were set up thereafter, western trade and industry began on a large scale, and Tientsin became a centre of modern and western ideas second only to Shanghai. Tientsin also became China's second port, although the Hai Ho was impassable for large ships, and an outport at Ta-ku had to tranship most goods. During the War the Japanese began to construct a modern port, and this was completed in 1952 at T'ang-ku. Tientsin was always an important centre for canal and river traffic, and had rail communications from the early years of this century. Before 1949 most of Tientsin's industry was textiles (both cotton and woollens) and food-processing. Textiles remain very important, but the city has more recently developed a steelworks, a diversified engineering industry producing heavy machinery, tractors, lorries, diesel engines and industrial equipment of various kinds, an electronic industry, chemical and paper plants, and a plant manufacturing automobile tyres.

Tientsin is also a very important centre for education, with several universities and institutes of higher education, museums and libraries. Its growth since 1949 has not been as rapid as Peking's. It had 2,694,000 people in 1953, 3,200,000 in 1957 and is estimated to have over 4,000,000 today.

Eastern Hopeh This area includes the coastal plain east of Tientsin, which gradually narrows until the hills of the interior meet the coast at Shan-hai-kuan. This is an area with an agriculture similar to that of the plain, although cotton is not so commonly grown. It is mainly remarkable for its coalfield.

T'ang-shan is the main centre of the mining area. Its growth began in the 1880s with the exploitation by British capital of the K'ai-luan coal mines, which exported their output, by China's first railway, to Lu-t'ai and thence by boat to Tientsin and Shanghai. These mines have since been greatly expanded, and the complex of mines now produces between 10,000,000 and 15,000,000 tons annually. T'ang-shan developed a large scale cement industry in the early years of this century, and a large thermal generating plant which provides power for Tientsin and Peking as well as for T'ang-shan industrial complex. It has recently developed a large iron and steel industry, engineering works and a variety of other industries including textiles, paper making and food processing.

The Jehol uplands lie to the north of the Great Wall and east of Peking. It is an area of complex hills of 500 m to 1,000 m, with individual peaks up to 1,500 m, and ranges striking roughly south-west to north-east. These ranges, known collectively as the Yen Shan, are rugged and sparsely peopled, but they enclose some small basins which are carefully cultivated. The climate is very severe here, with January temperatures down to −14°C (7°F), and the climate is drier towards the north-west. The growing season is much shorter than elsewhere in the province – about 190–200 days.

Ch'eng-te, formerly the capital of Jehol, is the main city. It is the commercial and market centre for the densely peopled basin, and the main administrative centre for north-eastern Hopeh.

The North-western plateau This area stretches from north-west of Peking municipality to the border of Inner Mongolia. An area of high plateau, rising to between 1,000 m and 1,500 m, it is crossed by the Hsiung-erh Shan and Ta-ma-chün Shan ranges, striking from south-west to north-east, and rising to the north-west of the province. This area was formerly part of the province of Chahar, and still retains a small Mongol minority. It is marginal land for permanent agriculture. In the latter part of the 19th century and during the present century, Chinese farmers attempted to expand the area under cultivation into what were traditional pasturelands, often with disastrous results, as they destroyed the natural grassland.

Chang-chia-k'ou (Kalgan) was the traditional centre of this region, a border trading city and garrison town, where there was a major market for trade from the steppes, the collection of wool and hides, and the export of Chinese goods to the Mongols. Chang-chia-k'ou's importance was greatly increased in 1909 when a railway was built from Peking, which was subsequently extended further west. It was already a large city with extensive food processing and similar industries, but since the 1950s it has grown further and developed woollen and cotton textile mills, a rayon plant, and a large industry building mining machinery.

Hsüan-hua is a satellite city of Chang-chia-k'ou, with important iron mines at Lung-yen, and coal mines. It has a major power plant, and an iron and steel plant. But most of the iron ore from Lung-yen is sent to the steel works in T'ai-yüan, Shih-ching-shan or An-shan.

HOPEH AREA
190,000 square kilometres

POPULATION
41,410,000 (other estimates up to 46,000,000)

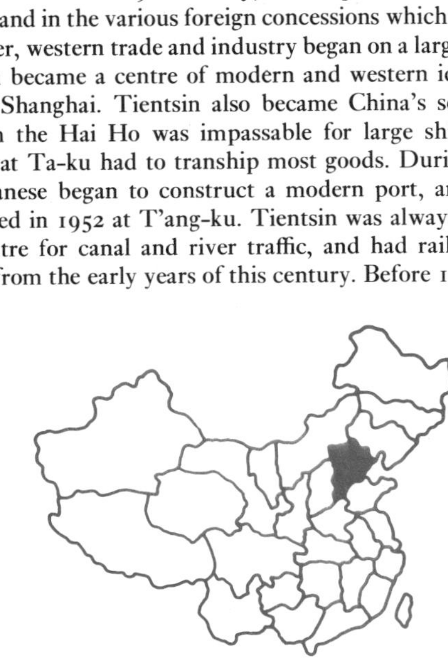

PEKING AREA
8,400 square kilometres

POPULATION
7,570,000

TIENTSIN AREA
3,900 square kilometres

POPULATION
4,280,000

LIAONING

NEI MONGGOL (MONGOLIA)

HOPEI

SHANSI

CH'I-LIAO-T'U SHAN

Chih-feng

Ch'eng-te

PEI-CHING (PEKING)

PEI-CHING SHIH

Chang-chia-k'ou (Kalgan)

T'ang-shan

Ch'in-huang-tao

TA-MA-CHÜN SHAN

HSIUNG-ERH SHAN

CHÜN-TU SHAN

Ming Tombs

Ta-sheng-t'ang Shan 1754

Yün-wu Shan 1964

Tu Shan 1677

Wu-chih Shan 1270

Wu-ling Shan

Chieh-shih Shan

Hsiao-wu-t'ai Shan 2870

Heng Shan 2052

T'ai-pai Shan 2298

330 km

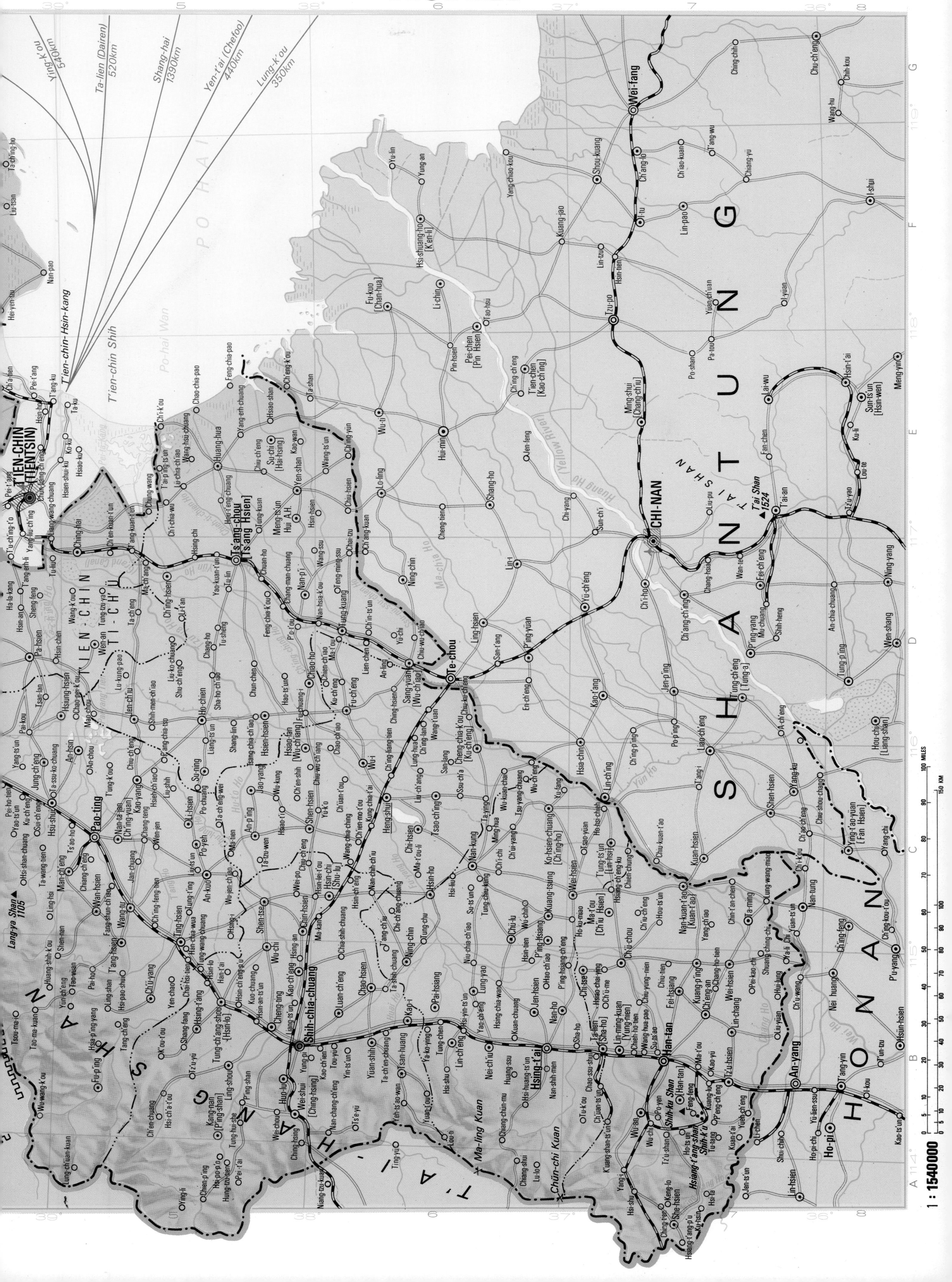

Ying-k'ou 540km
Ta-lien (Dairen) 520km
Shang-hai 1390km
Yen-t'ai (Chefoo) 440km
Lung-k'ou 350km

Tien-chin-Hsin-kang
Tien-chin Shih

P O - H A I

Po-hai Wan

TIEN-CHIN (TIENTSIN)

TIEN-CHIN TI-CH'U

PAO-TING

SHANSI

T'AI-HANG SHAN

Lang-ya Shan ▲ 1105

Shih-chia-chuang

Hsing-t'ai

An-yang

Han-tan

Shih-ku Shan ▲
Shih-ku

HONAN

Ho-pi

Te-chou

Tsang-chou [Tsang Hsien]

S H A N T U N G

CHI-NAN

TAI SHAN
Tai Shan ▲ 1524
T'ai-an

Wei-fang

Yellow River (Huang Ho)

Yün Ho (Grand Canal)

Hu-t'o Ho

Ma-ling Kuan

Chün-chi Kuan

100 MILES
150 KM

A 114° B 115° C D 116° E 117° F 118° G 119°

1 : 1 540 000

HOPEH PROVINCE 河北省
HO-PEI SHENG

9 shih	*municipalities*	
10 ti-ch'ü	*regions*	
142 hsien	*counties*	
2 tzu-chih-hsien	*autonomous counties*	

capital Shih-chia-chuang Shih	B5	石家庄市
Chang-chia-k'ou Shih	B3	张家口市
Ch'eng-te Shih	E3	承德市
Ch'in-huang-tao Shih	G4	秦皇岛市
Han-tan Shih	B7	邯郸市
Hsing-t'ai Shih	B6	邢台市
Pao-ting Shih	C5	保定市
T'ang-shan Shih	F4	唐山市
Ts'ang-chou Shih	D5	沧州市

Chang-chia-k'ou Ti-ch'ü — 张家口地区

Chang-pei Hsien	B2	张北县
Ch'ih-ch'eng Hsien	C3	赤城县
Cho-lu Hsien	C3	涿鹿县
Ch'ung-li Hsien		崇礼县
centre: Hsi-wan-tzu	C3	西湾子
Hsüan-hua Hsien	C3	宣化县
Huai-an Hsien		怀安县
centre: Ch'ai-kou-pao	B3	柴沟堡
Huai-lai Hsien		怀来县
centre: Sha-ch'eng	C3	沙城
K'ang-pao Hsien	B2	康保县
Ku-yüan Hsien		沽源县
centre: P'ing-ting-pao	C2	平定堡
Shang-i Hsien		尚义县
centre: Nan-haò-ch'ien	A2	南壕堑
Wan-ch'üan Hsien	B3	万全县
Yang-yüan Hsien		阳原县
centre: Hsi-ch'eng	B3	西城
Yü Hsien		蔚县
centre: Yü-hsien	B4	

Ch'eng-te Ti-ch'ü — 承德地区

Ch'eng-te Hsien		承德县
centre: Hsia-pan-ch'eng	F3	下扳城
Ch'ing-lung Hsien	F3	青龙县
Feng-ning Hsien		丰宁县
centre: Ta-ko-chen	D2	大阁镇
Hsing-lung Hsien	E3	兴隆县
K'uan-ch'eng Hsien	F3	宽城县
Luan-p'ing Hsien		滦平县
centre: An-chiang-ying	E3	鞍匠营
Lung-hua Hsien		隆化县
centre: Huang-ku-t'un	E2	皇姑屯
P'ing-ch'üan Hsien	F2	平泉县
Wei-ch'ang Hsien		围场县
centre: Chui-tzu-shan	E2	锥子山

Han-tan Ti-ch'ü — 邯郸地区

Ch'eng-an Hsien	B7	成安县
Chi-tse Hsien	B7	鸡泽县
Ch'iu Hsien		丘县
centre: Ma-t'ou	C7	马头
Ch'ü-chou Hsien	B7	曲周县
Fei-hsiang Hsien	B7	肥乡县
Han-tan Hsien		邯郸县
centre: not known	B7	
Kuang-p'ing Hsien	B7	广平县
Kuan-t'ao Hsien		馆陶县
centre: Nan-kuan-t'ao	C7	南馆陶
Lin-chang Hsien	B7	临漳县
She Hsien		涉县
centre: She-hsien	A7	
Ta-ming Hsien	C7	大名县
Tz'u Hsien		磁县
centre: Tz'u-hsien	B7	
Wei Hsien		魏县
centre: Wei-hsien	B7	
Wu-an Hsien	B7	武安县
Yung-nien Hsien		永年县
centre: Lin-ming-kuan	B7	临洺关

Heng-shui Ti-ch'ü — 衡水地区

An-p'ing Hsien	C5	安平县
Chi Hsien		冀县
centre: Chi-hsien	C6	
Ching Hsien		景县
centre: Ching-hsien	D5	
Fu-ch'eng Hsien	D6	阜城县
Heng-shui Hsien	C6	衡水县
Jao-yang Hsien	C5	饶阳县
Ku-ch'eng Hsien		故城县
centre: Cheng-chia-k'ou	C6	郑家口
Shen Hsien		深县
centre: Shen-hsien	C5	
Tsao-ch'iang Hsien	C6	枣强县
Wu-ch'iang Hsien		武强县

centre: Hsiao-fan	C5	小范
Wu-i Hsien	C6	武邑县

Hsing-t'ai Ti-ch'ü — 邢台地区

Ch'ing-ho Hsien		清河县
centre: Ko-hsien-chuang	C6	葛仙庄
Chu-lu Hsien	C6	巨鹿县
Hsing-t'ai Hsien	B6	邢台县
Hsin-ho Hsien	C6	新河县
Jen Hsien		任县
centre: Jen-hsien	B6	
Kuang-tsung Hsien	C6	广宗县
Lin-ch'eng Hsien	B6	临城县
Lin-hsi Hsien		临西县
centre: T'ung-ts'un	C7	童村
Lung-yao Hsien	B6	隆尧县
Nan-ho Hsien	B6	南河县
Nan-kung Hsien	C6	南宫县
Nei-ch'iu Hsien	B6	内丘县
Ning-chin Hsien	B6	宁晋县
Pai-hsiang Hsien	B6	柏乡县
P'ing-hsiang Hsien	C6	平乡县
Sha-ho Hsien		沙河县
centre: Ta-lien	B7	褡裢
Wei Hsien		威县
centre: Wei-hsien	C7	

Pao-ting Ti-ch'ü — 保定地区

An-hsin Hsien	C5	安新县
An-kuo Hsien	C5	安国县
Ch'ing-yüan Hsien		清苑县
centre: Nan-ta-jan	C5	南大冉
Cho Hsien		涿县
centre: Cho-hsien	C4	
Ch'ü-yang Hsien	B5	曲阳县
Fu-p'ing Hsien	B5	阜平县
Hsin-ch'eng Hsien		新城县
centre: Kao-pei-tien	C4	高碑店
Hsiung Hsien		雄县
centre: Hsiung-hsien	D4	
Hsü-shui Hsien	C4	徐水县
I Hsien		易县
centre: I-hsien	C4	
Jung-ch'eng Hsien	C4	容城县
Kao-yang Hsien	C5	高阳县
Lai-shui Hsien	C4	涞水县
Lai-yüan Hsien	B4	涞源县
Li Hsien		蠡县
centre: Li-hsien	C5	
Man-ch'eng Hsien	C5	满城县
Po-yeh Hsien	C5	博野县
T'ang Hsien		唐县
centre: T'ang-hsien	B5	
Ting Hsien		定县
centre: Ting-hsien	B5	
Ting-hsing Hsien	C4	定兴县
Wang-tu Hsien		望都县
Wan Hsien		完县
centre: Wan-hsien	C5	

Shih-chia-chuang Ti-ch'ü — 石家庄地区

Chao Hsien		赵县
centre: Chao-hsien	B6	
Cheng-ting Hsien	B5	正定县
Ching-hsing Hsien		井陉县
centre: Wei-shui	B5	微水
Chin Hsien		晋县
centre: Chin-hsien	C5	
Hsing-t'ang Hsien	B5	行唐县
Hsin-lo Hsien		新乐县
centre: Tung-ch'ang-shou	B5	东长寿
Huo-lu Hsien	B5	获鹿县
Kao-ch'eng Hsien	B5	藁城县
Kao-i Hsien	B6	高邑县
Ling-shou Hsien	B5	灵寿县
Luan-ch'eng Hsien	B6	栾城县
P'ing-shan Hsien		平山县
centre: Kang-nan	B5	岗南
Shen-tse Hsien	C5	深泽县
Shu-lu Hsien		束鹿县
centre: Hsin-chi	C6	辛集
Tsan-huang Hsien	B6	赞皇县
Wu-chi Hsien	B5	无极县
Yüan-shih Hsien	B6	元氏县

T'ang-shan Ti-ch'ü — 唐山地区

Ch'ang-li Hsien	G4	昌黎县
Ch'ien-an Hsien	F3	迁安县
Ch'ien-hsi Hsien		迁西县
centre: Hsing-ch'eng	F3	兴城
Feng-jun Hsien	F4	丰润县
Feng-nan Hsien		丰南县
centre: Hsü-ko-chuang	F4	胥各庄
Fu-ning Hsien	G4	抚宁县
Lo-t'ing Hsien	F4	乐亭县
Luan Hsien		滦县
centre: Luan-hsien	F4	
Luan-nan Hsien		滦南县
centre: Pen-ch'eng	F4	倴城
Lu-lung Hsien	F4	卢龙县
Tsun-hua Hsien	E3	遵化县
Yü-t'ien Hsien	E4	玉田县

T'ien-chin Ti-ch'ü — 天津地区

centre: Lang-fang	D4	
An-tz'u Hsien		安次县
centre: Lang-fang	D4	廊坊
Chi Hsien	E3	蓟县
centre: Chi-hsien		
Ching-hai Hsien	D5	静海县
Hsiang-ho Hsien	E4	香河县
Ku-an Hsien	D4	固安县
Ning-ho Hsien		宁河县
centre: Lu-t'ai	E4	芦台
Pa Hsien		霸县
centre: Pa-hsien	D4	
Pao-ti Hsien	E4	宝坻县
San-ho Hsien	E4	三河县
Ta-ch'ang Hui-tsu Tzu-chih-hsien — 大厂回族自治县		
Ta-ch'ang Hui Autonomous Hsien	D4	
Ta-ch'eng Hsien	D5	大城县
Wen-an Hsien	D5	文安县
Wu-ch'ing Hsien		武清县
centre: Yang-ts'un	E4	杨村
Yung-ch'ing Hsien	D4	永清县

Ts'ang-chou Ti-ch'ü — 沧州地区

Chiao-ho Hsien	D5	交河县
Ch'ing Hsien		青县
centre: Ch'ing-hsien	D5	
Hai-hsing Hsien		海兴县
centre: Su-chi	E5	苏基
Ho-chien Hsien	D5	河间县
Hsien Hsien		献县
centre: Hsien-hsien	D5	
Huang-hua Hsien	E5	黄骅县
Jen-ch'iu Hsien	D5	任丘县
Meng-ts'un Hui-tsu Tzu-chih-hsien — 孟村回族自治县		
Meng-ts'un Hui Autonomous Hsien	E5	
Nan-p'i Hsien	D5	南皮县
Su-ning Hsien	C5	肃宁县
Ts'ang Hsien		沧县
centre: Ts'ang-chou	D5	沧州
Tung-kuang Hsien	D6	东光县
Wu-ch'iao Hsien		吴桥县
centre: Sang-yüan	D6	桑园
Yen-shan Hsien	E5	盐山县

PEKING MUNICIPALITY 北京市
PEI-CHING SHIH — D4

9 hsien	*counties*	

Ch'ang-p'ing Hsien	D3	昌平县
Fang-shan Hsien	C4	房山县
Huai-jou Hsien	D3	怀柔县
Mi-yün Hsien	D3	密云县
P'ing-ku Hsien	E3	平谷县
Shun-i Hsien	D3	顺义县
Ta-hsing Hsien		大兴县
centre: Huang-ts'un	D4	黄村
T'ung Hsien		通县
centre: T'ung-chou	D4	通县
Yen-ch'ing Hsien	C3	延庆县

TIENTSIN MUNICIPALITY 天津市
T'IEN-CHIN SHIH — E5

SHANTUNG
PROVINCE

SHANTUNG is China's second most populous province (after Szechwan), with 8.3 per cent of the total population living on 1.6 per cent of the total area. Its density of population is exceeded only by Kiangsu.

It is a region which has been settled since Neolithic times, and in early Chinese history was one of the most important centres of Chinese culture. In the first millenium BC its principal state, Ch'i, was already famous for its teeming population, for its advanced economy, and for its political institutions. It continued to be important throughout the Chinese medieval period, when its ports became the chief outlets for the North China plain and for the trade with Korea and Japan. Under the Mongols its role as a communications link were strengthened by the construction of the new imperial canal route through western Shantung in 1293, and by a canal across the neck of the peninsula. These reduced the importance of its coastal trade. Although the first settlements in Shantung were in the uplands, the western and northern plains were already densely peopled by the 1st century BC. These areas, in spite of costly flood control works, were constantly threatened by floods as the Huang Ho changed its course. Particularly serious floods occurred at the end of the 12th century, when the Huang Ho left its northern course to discharge into the sea south of the Shantung peninsula, and in 1853–5 when it took its present course, which destroyed the northern section of the Grand Canal, flooded vast areas of rich farmland, and caused enormous loss of life. At the end of the 19th century, a series of droughts and famines, coupled with ever-increasing population pressure, led to large-scale emigration from Shantung to the newly-opened lands in Manchuria and along the Inner Mongolian border. This emigration, which began in the 1890s, reached a peak in the late 1920s, when more than four million people emigrated from the province between 1923 and 1930. Under the Communist regime, too, emigration has continued, both to Manchuria and to developing areas such as Sinkiang.

At the end of the 19th century Shantung came under strong foreign influence. In 1898 the Germans were granted a lease of the Chiao-chou bay, where they built a modern port, Ch'ing-tao (Tsingtao), while Britain leased Wei-hai-wei as a naval base. The Germans built a railway inland to Chi-nan (Tsinan) in 1905, and began to establish coal mines and other industries. During the First World War, in 1915, the Japanese took over German interests, and continued to occupy parts of Shantung until 1923.

Shantung divides into a number of very different regions.

The Shantung Peninsula The mountains of central Shantung and the Peninsula form part of the ancient mountain range which continues across the Gulf of Po-hai into the Liao-tung peninsula and the Chang-pai Shan range of eastern Manchuria. The average height of the hills of the peninsula is about 250 m. Individual peaks reach 900 m, but the landscape is one of rounded hills and small inter-montane basins. The coast is mostly sheer, and there are a series of good harbours. The climate is more temperate than the western areas of Shantung, and the growing season somewhat shorter. The agriculture of the area concentrates upon winter wheat and kaoliang, with foxtail millet and peanuts as important secondary crops. The hills were deforested in very early times, and the area has suffered badly from soil erosion. The area is also famous for wild silk, and for the production of fruit, particularly pears grown around Lai-yang, and grapes from Chi-mo.

Yen-t'ai (once known as Chefoo) was formerly a minor local port, which became the major centre of this area following the construction of a railway to Ch'ing-tao in 1955. It has recently seen the growth of some minor industry, including a small steel plant, and a major canning and processing industry. Yen-t'ai is a major fishing port. Its population was 116,000 in 1953.

The Chiao-lai plain This wide lowland plain separates the hills of the peninsula from the massif of central Shantung. A fertile and densely peopled agricultural area, it produces winter wheat, kaoliang, soy beans and sweet potatoes as staple crops, but is also an important producing area for cotton and tobacco, for which the Wei-fang area is famous. The area is traversed by the railway from Ch'ing-tao to Chi-nan.

Wei-fang is the major centre of this agricultural region, with processing plants for tobacco, peanut-oil extraction and flour milling. It is also close to a minor coalfield at Fang-tzu. Its population in 1953 was 149,000.

Ch'ing-tao, the largest city and industrial centre of Shantung, was the creation of western colonialisation. Although formerly a small fishing village, after the lease of the area to Germany in 1898, Ch'ing-tao was built up as a naval base and as the outlet for trade carried by the railway to Chi-nan. Ch'ing-tao remains a major port, exporting soy beans, peanuts and coal from the interior, and is also a fishing port even more important than Yen-t'ai. Ch'ing-tao's industrial growth began under the Germans, and was continued under the Japanese, who occupied the former German territory in 1915. Beside food manufacturing, oil extraction, and textiles, Ch'ing-tao is also a major centre of heavy industry, manufacturing diesel locomotives and railway rolling stock, rubber, especially automobile tyres, cement, chemicals and fertiliser. Its population was 1,121,000 in 1957.

The central Shantung massif This is a higher and more complex hill area than the peninsula. The northern section comprises three parallel ranges (from west to east, T'ai Shan, Lu Shan, I Shan) with a roughly south-west to north-east axis. They average 300–500 m, with peaks over 1,000 m, the highest being the most famous of China's traditional holy mountains, T'ai Shan (1,524 m). These ranges present a steep escarpment to the north. The southern and south-eastern sections of the massif are less rugged and lower, with broad cultivated river valleys draining south into the Huai. Once forested, these hills have long since been denuded of trees, with resultant soil erosion, although some attempt at reforestation has been made since 1949.

The agriculture of this area is mainly winter wheat, kaoliang, soy beans and millet, with areas specialising in production of wild silk and fruits, and peanuts as a widespread cash crop. Some sheep are also reared in the upland districts.

The area is important as a major coal producer, and centre of metal working. From very early times central Shantung was a major centre of the copper and iron industry. Modern development, however, began during the period of German influence before the First World War. The first major coal mines were those of Po-shan (in *Tzu-po* municipality) which produces some 10,000,000 tons annually. This mining centre has developed, since 1950, into an industrial district, with an important ceramic, refractory and glass industry, and an aluminium industry. To the north at Chin-ling-chen is a very rich source of high-grade iron ore. In recent years, following the discovery of the Sheng-li oilfield, Tzu-po has also become the centre of a petro-chemical industry. The municipality of Tzu-po, which includes the mining towns of Po-shan, Tzu-ch'uan, and Chin-ling-chen as well as the administrative centre Chang-tien, had a population in 1957 of 806,000.

Tsao-chuang in the south-west of the highlands was also developed as a coal mining centre before the First World War, when the Tientsin–Pu-k'ou railway first made it accessible. The mines were destroyed during the Second World War, but were rebuilt and modernised in the mid-1950s. The Tsao-chuang mines produce good coking coal, and output is estimated at over 6,000,000 tons. Another coalfield in this area is at Hsin-wen, which produces about 1,500,000 tons annually.

Chi-nan, the provincial capital and Shantung's second largest city, lies at the foot of the north-western corner of the massif. Chi-nan is an ancient city, a traditional administrative and transportation centre. Its modern growth began with the construction of the railway to Ch'ing-tao in 1905 and the Tientsin–Chi-nan–Pu-k'ou railway, which made it a major railway junction. It remains an important administrative and cultural centre. Industrial growth was at first concentrated in textiles, flour milling, oil extraction and similar processing industries, but in the late 1950s a small iron and steel complex was built, and Chi-nan has developed a large power plant, and a machine-building industry, specialising in machine tools, agricultural machinery, trucks, precision instruments and electrical equipment. It also manufactures fertilisers, industrial chemicals and paper.

The northern Shantung plain To the north of the central mountains is the flat, alluvial plain of the mouth of the Huang Ho. This is a rich area of farmland, whose only drawbacks are the highly saline soils of the delta area. In recent decades this plain has been extensively drained and irrigated. Its agriculture produces winter wheat, kaoliang, corn, soy beans and sweet potatoes. In the saline soils near the Huang Ho delta, cotton is a very important crop.

The area is also the site of a new oilfield, Sheng-li, the precise location of which is not clear. It is still a minor producer, with an output of 500,000 tons per year, but the field is thought to extend under the sea in the Po Hai gulf.

The coastal area is also a major source of salt, produced by evaporation.

Te-chou, at the point where the railway from Chi-nan to Tientsin crosses the Grand Canal and joins the railway to Shih-chia-chuang, is the main commercial and transportation centre of this area.

The western Shantung plain The plain lies to the west of the central massif. This is a part of the Great North China Plain of Hopeh and Honan, a rich alluvial area with a very dense agricultural population.

The area is traversed by the Grand Canal, which is supplied with water from a series of lakes in the south-west of the province. The agriculture of this region concentrates upon winter wheat, soy beans, kaoliang and cotton.

Chi-ning, the chief commercial and marketing centre of the region was formerly an important canal port, from which grain was shipped to Peking. The change of course of the Huang Ho in 1853–5, however, blocked the canal to the north, and ambitious plans to modernise and reopen the canal in the 1950s seem not to have been completed north of Chi-ning. Chi-ning is however linked to the Chi-nan–Pu-k'ou railway, and remains the chief city of this area. It had a population of 86,000 in 1953.

AREA
153,300 square kilometres

POPULATION
55,520,000 (estimate for 1970: 62,500,000)

SHANTUNG

P O   H A I

Huang Ho-k'ou

Tientsin 350km
Tientsin 440km
Ta-lien 240km
Ch'in-huang-tao 330km
Ta-lien 170km
Ta-lien—Wei-hai 170km
Ta-lien—Shih-tao 280km
Yen-t'ai—Shanghai 960km

Hsiao-ch'in Tao
Pei-huang-ch'eng Tao
Ta-ch'in Tao
Nan-huang-ch'eng Tao
MIAO-TAO CH'ÜN-TAO
T'o-chi Tao
Miao Tao
Pei-ch'ang-shan Tao
Ssu-hou [Ch'ang-tao]
Nan-ch'ang-shan Tao

Ch'i-mu Chiao
Lung-k'ou Wan

Yu-lin

Lai-chou Wan

Yang-chiao-kou
Ta-chia-wa
Nan-ho
Hou-chen
Shang-k'ou
Tao-t'ien
Shuang-yang-tien
Han-t'ing [Wei Hsien]
Wei-fang
Chu-liu-tien
h'ang-lo
Ta-yü-ho
Erh-shih-Li-p'u
Pei-yen
Ch'iao-kuan
Ma-sung
T'ang-wu
N G - W E I
Chao-k'ou-chuang
An-ch'iu
Ling-ho
Ching-chih
Kuan-chuang
Pao-ch'üan
Chang-chuang
Shi-pu-tzu
Ta-lao-ki
Chao-hsien
Meng-t'uan
Ku-yüeh
Wu-chi
Wang-hu
Kuan-chih
Chih-k'ou
Kao-tse
Lo-ho-ai
Hung-ning [Wu-lien]
Sung-pai-lin
Shih-ch'ang
Chü-hsien
Chi-chia-tien-tzu
San-chuang
Nan-ch'ao
Shih-ching
Huang-tun
Lao-p'o
Chü-feng
T'ao-lin
Shih-tzu-lu [Chü-nan]
P'ing-shang
Fang-ch'ien
San-chieh-shou
Che-wang
Hei-lin
Ch'ing-k'ou [Kan-yü]
Huan-tun-pu
Sha-ho
Tun-shang
Hsü-kou
Lien-yün-kang
Hai-chou
Pan-p'u
Yen-wei-kang

S U

SHAN-TUNG PAN-TAO

P'eng-lai
Pei-kou
Liu-chia-kou
Ch'ao-shui
Lung-k'ou
Huang-hsien
Huang-ch'eng-chi
Pei-ma
Ta-hsin-tien
Shih-Liang
Huang-shan-kuan
Hsin-chuang
Chang-hsing
Chao-ko-chuang
Ts'ang-ko-chuang
Chih-fu Tao
Chu-chi
Yen-t'ai (Chefoo)
Ku-hsien
Fu-shan
Ch'u-chia
K'ung-t'ung Tao
Wei-hai
Liu-kung Tao
Yang-ma Tao
Shang-chuang
Chiu-kuan
Lai-shan
Mou-p'ing
Pei-tien-tzu
Yang-t'ing
Wen-ch'üan-t'ang
Chiu-jung-ch'eng
Ch'eng-shan Chiao

Ai Shan ▲817
Sung-shan
Hsi-yu
Chu-ch'iao
Chao-yüan
Ssu-k'ou
Hsi-hsia
T'ieh-k'ou
Ch'en-chia-t'uan
Yüan-ko-chuang
Kao-ling
Shui-tao
923 ▲ K'un-yu Shan
Wen-teng
Ko-lü-chi
P'u-chi
Feng-chia
Sung-ts'un
Chang-chia-pu
Huang-shan
Ning-chin-so
Ch'iu-shan-ch'i
Mo-hsieh Tao
Ching-hai-wei
Jen-ho-chi

Ta-yüan
Yeh-hsien
Hu-t'ou-ya
P'ing-li-tien
Tao-t'ou
I-tao
Pi-kuo
Kuan-li
Yang-ch'u
T'ang-chia-p'o
T'ao-ts'un
Shan-ch'ien-tien
Ma-shih-tien
Yü-ko
Ch'e-an
Ya-tzu
Wu-chi
Nan-huang
Hai-yang-so

Kuo-chia-tien
Ma-lien-chuang
Ho-t'ou-tien
Feng-k'o-chuang
Lai-yang
Lai-yang-chan
Wan-ti
Chu-wu
Ju-shan-chai
Pai-shan-t'an
Ju-shan-k'ou
Su-shan Tao

Shui-chi [Lai-hsi]
Ma-ko-chuang
Lai-hsi-chan
Ta-k'uang
T'uan-wang
Hsiao-chi
Tung-ts'un [Hai-yang]
Liu-ko-chuang
Feng-ch'eng
Hsia-ying
Tung-chia
Hsin-ho
Ch'ang-i
Chang-she
P'ing-tu
Ma-ko-chuang
Shih-pu
Chin-t'ai
Ch'in-ma
Ts'ui-chia-chi
Lan-ts'un
Ma-lan
Ku-hsien
Kuo-chia-chuang
Hsia-ko-chuang
Hsüeh-fang
Hsüeh-k'ou
Chiang-shan-chen
Ta-shan
Hsing-ts'un

Ma-tien
Chiao-ting
Li-ko-chuang
Yao-ko-tun
Kao-mi
Ts'ai-chia-chuang
K'ang-chia-chuang
Chiang-chuang
Hsia-chuang
Chang-ling
Tsuo-shan
Nan-liu
Fang-tzu
Chin-t'ai
Liao-lan
Chang-ko-chuang
Liu-chia-chuang
Ling-shan
Niu-ch'i-p'u
Tien-chi
Wang-ts'un
Ao-shan-kung
T'ien-heng Tao

Chiao-hsien
Ch'ing Tao
Hsi-t'o
Ch'eng-yang
Hsien-chia-chai
Ts'ang-k'ou
Lao-shan
Lao Shan ▲
Ying-fang
Tung-wa-kou
Tu-ts'un
Ma-tien
Wang-t'ai
Li-ch'a
Hsin-an
Hsüeh-chia-chai
SHIH
Ch'ing-tao (Tsingtao)
Ssu-fang
Chiao-chou Wan
Ling-shan-wei
Wang-ko-chuang [Chiao-nan]
Chang-chia-lou
Shih-men
Ta-kung Tao
Chao-lien Tao
Ling-shan Wan
Ling-shan Tao
Hsia-ho-ch'eng
Po-li
▲ Lang-yeh Shan
Ta-lao-ki
Chi-chao
Shih-chiu-so

200km

P'ing Tao

Ch'e-niu Shan

Y E L L O W   S E A
(H U A N G   H A I)

Tsingtao—Shih-tao 240km
Tsingtao—Ta-lien 500km
Shanghai 740km
Shanghai 700km

1 : 1 350 000

0 5 10 20 30 40 50 60 70 80 90 100 MILES
0 5 10 20 30 40 50 60 70 80 90 100 150 KM

SHANTUNG PROVINCE 山东省
SHAN-TUNG SHENG

9 shih	*municipalities*	
9 ti-ch'ü	*regions*	
106 hsien	*counties*	

capital **Chi-nan Shih**	C3	济南市
Li-ch'eng Hsien		历城县
centre: Hung-chia-lou	C3	洪家楼
Ch'ing-tao Shih	F3	青岛市
Lao-shan Hsien		崂山县
centre: Li-ts'un	F3	李村
Chi-ning Shih	B4	济宁市
Te-chou Shih	B2	德州市
Tsao-chuang Shih	C5	枣庄市
Tzu-po Shih	D3	淄博市
centre: Chang-tien		张店
Wei-fang Shih	E3	潍坊市
Wei-hai Shih	H2	威海市
Yen-t'ai Shih	G2	烟台市

Ch'ang-wei Ti-ch'ü		昌潍地区
centre: Wei-fang	E3	潍坊
An-ch'iu Hsien	E3	安丘县
Ch'ang-i Hsien	E3	昌邑县
Ch'ang-lo Hsien	D3	昌乐县
Chiao Hsien		胶县
centre: Chiao-hsien	F3	
Chiao-nan Hsien		胶南县
centre: Wang-ko-chuang	E4	王哥庄
Chu-ch'eng Hsien	E4	诸城县
I-tu Hsien	D3	益都县
Kao-mi Hsien	E3	高密县
Lin-ch'ü Hsien	D3	临朐县
P'ing-tu Hsien	E3	平度县
Shou-kuang Hsien	D3	寿光县
Wei Hsien		潍县
centre: Han-t'ing	E3	寒亭
Wu-lien Hsien		五莲县
centre: Hung-ning	E4	洪凝

Chi-ning Ti-ch'ü		济宁地区
Chia-hsiang Hsien	B4	嘉祥县
Chin-hsiang Hsien	B4	金乡县
Chi-ning Hsien	B4	济宁县
Ch'ü-fu Hsien	B4	曲阜县
Ssu-shui Hsien	C4	泗水县
T'eng Hsien		滕县
centre: T'eng-hsien	C4	
Tsou Hsien		邹县
centre: Tsou-hsien	B4	
Wei-shan Hsien		微山县
centre: Hsia-chen	C5	夏镇
Wen-shang Hsien	B4	汶上县
Yen-chou Hsien	B4	兖州县
Yü-t'ai Hsien		鱼台县
centre: Ku-t'ing	B4	谷亭

Ho-tse Ti-ch'ü		菏泽地区
Ch'eng-wu Hsien	A5	成武县
Chüan-ch'eng Hsien	A4	鄄城县
Chü-yeh Hsien	B4	巨野县
Ho-tse Hsien	A4	菏泽县
Liang-shan Hsien		梁山县
centre: Hou-chi	B4	后集
Shan Hsien		单县
centre: Shan-hsien	B5	
Ting-t'ao Hsien	A4	定陶县
Ts'ao Hsien		曹县
centre: Ts'ao-hsien	A5	
Tung-ming Hsien	A4	东明县
Yün-ch'eng Hsien	A4	郓城县

Hui-min Ti-ch'ü		惠民地区
centre: Pei-chen	D2	北镇
Chan-hua Hsien		沾化县
centre: Fu-kuo	D2	富国
Huan-t'ai Hsien		桓台县
centre: So-chen	D3	索镇
Hui-min Hsien	C2	惠民县
Kao-ch'ing Hsien		高青县
centre: T'ien-chen	C2	田镇
K'en-li Hsien		垦利县
centre: Hsi-shuang-ho	D2	西双河
Kuang-jao Hsien	D2	广饶县
Li-chin Hsien	D2	利津县
Pin Hsien		滨县
centre: Pei-chen	D2	北镇
Po-hsing Hsien	D2	博兴县
Tsou-p'ing Hsien	C3	邹平县
Wu-ti Hsien	C2	无棣县
Yang-hsin Hsien	C2	阳信县

Liao-ch'eng Ti-ch'ü		聊城地区
Ch'ih-p'ing Hsien	B3	茌平县
Hsin Hsien		莘县
centre: Hsin-hsien	A3	
Kao-t'ang Hsien	B3	高唐县
Kuan Hsien		冠县
centre: Kuan-hsien	A3	
Liao-ch'eng Hsien	A3	聊城县
Lin-ch'ing Hsien	A3	临清县
Tung-a Hsien		东阿县
centre: T'ung-ch'eng	B3	铜城
Yang-ku Hsien	A3	阳谷县

Lin-i Ti-ch'ü		临沂地区
Chü Hsien		莒县
centre: Chü-hsien	D4	
Chü-nan Hsien		莒南县
centre: Shih-tzu-lu	D4	十字路
Fei Hsien		费县
centre: Fei-hsien	C4	
I-nan Hsien		沂南县
centre: Chieh-hu	D4	界湖
I-shui Hsien	D4	沂水县
I-yüan Hsien		沂源县
centre: Nan-ma	D3	南麻
Jih-chao Hsien	E4	日照县
Lin-i Hsien	D4	临沂县
Lin-shu Hsien		临沭县
centre: Hsia-chuang	D5	夏庄
Meng-yin Hsien	C4	蒙阴县
P'ing-i Hsien	C4	平邑县
T'an-ch'eng Hsien	D5	郯城县
Ts'ang-shan Hsien		苍山县
centre: Pien-chuang	D5	卞庄

T'ai-an Ti-ch'ü		泰安地区
Ch'ang-ch'ing Hsien	B3	长清县
Chang-ch'iu Hsien		章丘县
centre: Ming-shui	C3	明水
Fei-ch'eng Hsien	B3	肥城县
Hsin-t'ai Hsien	C4	新泰县
Hsin-wen Hsien		新文县
centre: Sun-ts'un	C4	孙村
Lai-wu Hsien	C3	莱芜县
Ning-yang Hsien	B4	宁阳县
P'ing-yin Hsien	B3	平阴县
T'ai-an Hsien	C3	泰安县
Tung-p'ing Hsien	B4	东平县

Te-chou Ti-ch'ü		德州地区
Ch'i-ho Hsien	B3	齐河县
Ch'ing-yün Hsien		庆云县
centre: Hsieh-chia-chi	C2	解家集
Chi-yang Hsien	C3	济阳县
Hsia-chin Hsien	A3	夏津县
Ling Hsien		陵县
centre: Ling-hsien	B2	
Lin-i Hsien	B2	临邑县
Lo-ling Hsien	C2	乐陵县
Ning-chin Hsien	B2	宁津县
P'ing-yüan Hsien	B2	平原县
Shang-ho Hsien	C2	商河县
Wu-ch'eng Hsien	A2	武城县
Yü-ch'eng Hsien	B3	禹城县

Yen-t'ai Ti-ch'ü		烟台地区
Ch'ang-tao Hsien		长岛县
centre: Ssu-hou	F2	寺后
Chao-yüan Hsien	F2	招远县
Chi-mo Hsien	F3	即墨县
Fu-shan Hsien	G2	福山县
Hai-yang Hsien		海阳县
centre: Tung-ts'un	G3	东村
Hsi-hsia Hsien	F2	栖霞县
Huang Hsien		黄县
centre: Huang-hsien	F2	
Jung-ch'eng Hsien		荣成县
centre: Ya-t'ou	H2	崖头
Ju-shan Hsien		乳山县
centre: Hsia-ts'un	G3	夏村
Lai-hsi Hsien		莱西县
centre: Shui-chi	F3	水集
Lai-yang Hsien	F3	莱阳县
Mou-p'ing Hsien	G2	牟平县
P'eng-lai Hsien	F2	蓬莱县
Wen-teng Hsien	H2	文登县
Yeh Hsien		掖县
centre: Yeh-hsien	E2	

SHANSI
PROVINCE

SHANSI province, especially the southern half, was one of the earliest areas of Chinese civilisation, the territory of the state of Chin. Later, after the unification of the empire in 221 BC the northern part of the province became one of the key defensive areas between China and her semi-nomadic northern neighbours. From the 3rd to the 6th century Shansi came under the control of a succession of alien dynasties. In AD 386–532 it was the base from which the Toba established the Northern Wei state (its first capital was at Ta-t'ung) which reunified northern China. In the early 7th century it was the power base for the establishment of the T'ang, and a crucial strategic area in their subsequent struggles with the Turks. In later times, when the political centre of China moved from the north-west, and the Shensi area went into an economic decline, Shansi remained relatively isolated and poor, bearing a heavy defensive establishment. During the late Ming and Ch'ing periods, the inhabitants of central Shansi became prominent in trade, and began to set up a widespread banking system, used for government transfers of funds, which had branches throughout China, but especially in the north and central provinces. These local banks ceased to be important after the end of the empire (1911). During the Republican period Shansi was controlled by Yen Hsi-shan, a powerful warlord whose autonomous regime attempted to institute some measure of industrial growth and modernisation. The first railway, joining T'ai-yüan to Shih-chia-chuang in Hopeh was built from 1904–7 by a Sino–French company, and Ta-t'ung was linked with Chang-chia-k'ou (Kalgan) and Peking shortly afterwards. Yen Hsi-shan built a further railway from Ta-t'ung to T'ai-yüan and later extended this to P'u-chou in the south-west of the province in 1937. Shansi was the scene of fierce resistance to the Japanese invasion and during the Second World War the Japanese carried out further development of industry and coal mining around T'ai-yüan, although the mountainous areas in both eastern and western Shansi were in the hands of Communist guerila forces.

Under the Communists, after 1949, the serious exploitation of Shansi's mineral wealth and the development of T'ai-yüan into a major industrial city have continued.

Shansi consists of a great upraised plateau, with an average height of from 500–1,000 m, broken by a series of fault trenches and basins down the middle of the province. It falls into a number of distinct regions.

Western Shansi The western edge of the plateau, north of the Fen river valley, is dominated by the folded range of the Lü-liang mountains, which average 1,500 m, with individual peaks of more than 2,500 m. To the west of this range, rivers drain into the Huang Ho, which runs through a series of gorges culminating at Lung-men, and is unnavigable. The climate is very dry, with 300–400 mm of rain, and the area, which is heavily loess covered, sustains rather poor agriculture, although spring wheat, millet and kaoliang are grown. The area has very poor communications, and is rather impoverished. In the 1950s various plans for improvements were made in connection with the reclamation plan for the Huang Ho basin, but few of these were implemented.

The An-i basin The extreme south-western corner of the province is occupied by the An-i basin, lying between the Chi-

wang Shan range to the north and the higher Chung-t'iao Shan range which forms the province's southern border. This is a heavily cultivated area, with a longer growing season (240 days or more) than other parts of Shansi. It grows winter wheat, corn, kaoliang and some cotton. This area, the main centre of which is Yün-ch'eng, is also a very important producer of salt, from the Chieh-i salt lake. This yields some 600,000 tons of household salt annually, and also sustains a small local chemical industry.

The Yang-ch'eng and Ch'ang-chih basins Drained by northern tributaries of the Huang Ho, the Ch'in Ho and Ta Ho respectively, these basins, which occupy the south-east of the province, are closely connected with Honan province. Intensively cultivated, this is the area of the province with the most rainfall (500 mm or more). Agriculture concentrates on winter wheat, corn, kaoliang, cotton and hemp. In addition to agriculture, the Ch'ang-chih area is an old-established centre of the iron industry. There is a coal field at Lu-an, north of Ch'ang-chih, which has been linked by rail to Honan since 1961. Ch'ang-chih itself has a small iron and steel works, cement manufacturing, and rubber works. Much of the coal from this area is shipped by rail to the industrial cities of Honan.

The Fen- Ho valley and T'ai-yüan basin The Fen Ho drains central Shansi, running from north-east to south-west through a series of fault basins. The valley has been irrigated from early times, but the irrigation system suffered neglect and was extensively repaired and broadened from the 1930s onwards. The agriculture is based on winter wheat, kaoliang and millet, while cotton and hemp are also widely grown. The largest and most productive area of cultivation is the basin around T'ai-yüan. These central basins have important coal mines, and the province as a whole has enormous reserves of coal. The Fen-hsi coal field on the west of the Fen Ho valley has mines at Ho-hsien, Fu-chia-t'un and Fen-hsi producing coking coal for the steel industry at T'ai-yüan. Further north is the newer I-t'ang field, developed in the 1960s. These fields are served by spur railways. A more important field is the Hsi-shan field west of T'ai-yüan itself which produces annually nearly 5 million tons of coking and steam coals.

T'ai-yüan is the provincial capital, the administrative centre and largest city of Shansi since very early historical times. Modern industry, together with western-style education, was established in the first years of this century, and further developed under the 'planned economy' instituted by warlord Yen Hsi-shan in the 1930s. It was not only an important food processing and textile centre, using locally grown cotton in modern mills, but it also had a wide range of engineering industries. After 1949 T'ai-yüan was one of the first inland centres to be developed into a major industrial complex under the industrial dispersion policy of the First Five Year Plan. The major industry first developed was iron and steel, using local coal and iron ore, and also ore from Lung-yen in Hopeh. In the late 1950s T'ai-yüan ranked after An-shan as China's second centre of steel production, although it has since been overtaken by Wu-han, Shanghai and possibly Pao-t'ou. Heavy machinery manufacture was also developed, and industrial chemical, ferti-

liser and plastics plants were set up after 1958. It has also become a major producer of aluminium. Yü-tz'u, a satellite city in the south-east, is a major producer of textile machinery. T'ai-yüan's population exceeded a million in 1957, and is estimated at about 1,100,000.

The Yang-ch'üan basin A small inter-montane basin situated west of the T'ai-hang mountains, east of T'ai-yüan. A minor agricultural district, Yang-ch'üan became an important producer of coal early in the century with the completion of the Shih-chia-chuang to Tai-yüan railway. Producing anthracite and low-sulphur coals, Yang-ch'üan yields between 5 and 10 million tons annually, much of which is exported to Hopeh as well as shipped to T'ai-yüan. There is also a local steel industry. The city has about 200,000 people.

The T'ai-hang mountains This is the general name given to the formidable mountain barrier which constitutes Shansi's eastern border with Hopeh. Presenting a steep 1,500–2,000 m escarpment to the east, broken only by a handful of passes cut by river valleys, these mountains have been a major cultural barrier throughout Chinese history. On the west the profile is much more gentle, and they slope down into the plateau. The northern end of the T'ai-hang proper is the valley of the Hu-t'o river. To the north are the complex series of north-east to south-west ranges making up the Wu-t'ai Shan and Heng Shan system, with peaks over 2,000 m. A largely barren area with only pockets of agriculture, this area was historically important as one of the great centres of Chinese Buddhism.

The Sang-kan basin The northernmost and largest of the basin plains in Shansi is that of the San-kan river, south of the great wall. This has always been a semi-frontier area for agriculture, because of its short growing season (less than 200 days) and low rainfall (below 500 mm). These, combined with bitterly cold winters, make it impossible to raise winter wheat, so agriculture largely depends on spring wheat, millet and kaoliang. Sesame and other oil seeds are important cash crops, and grazing of animals is important in the marginal lands.

Ta-t'ung is the chief city of the area. Traditionally an important political centre and a trading centre for the Inner Mongolian frontier, Ta-t'ung has been a major rail junction since the 1930s. Since the 1920s it has also been one of China's major coalfields, producing some ten million tons in the early 1960s. This field is of excellent bituminous coal. It is used for the generation of power, for the railways, and for the steel industries at Pao-t'ou and T'ai-yüan. Ta-t'ung also has a large cement industry, and engineering works specialising in railway plant and steam locomotives. It also remains a very important centre for local agricultural produce and for hides and wool from the Inner Mongolian frontier. It has a population of about 250,000.

Minority peoples Almost the entire population are Han Chinese, although on the northern border are a few Mongols and settlements of Chinese Moslems, who are also to be found in the T'ai-yüan and Ch'ang-chih areas.

AREA
157,000 square kilometres

POPULATION
Estimates range from 18,000,000 to 20,000,000

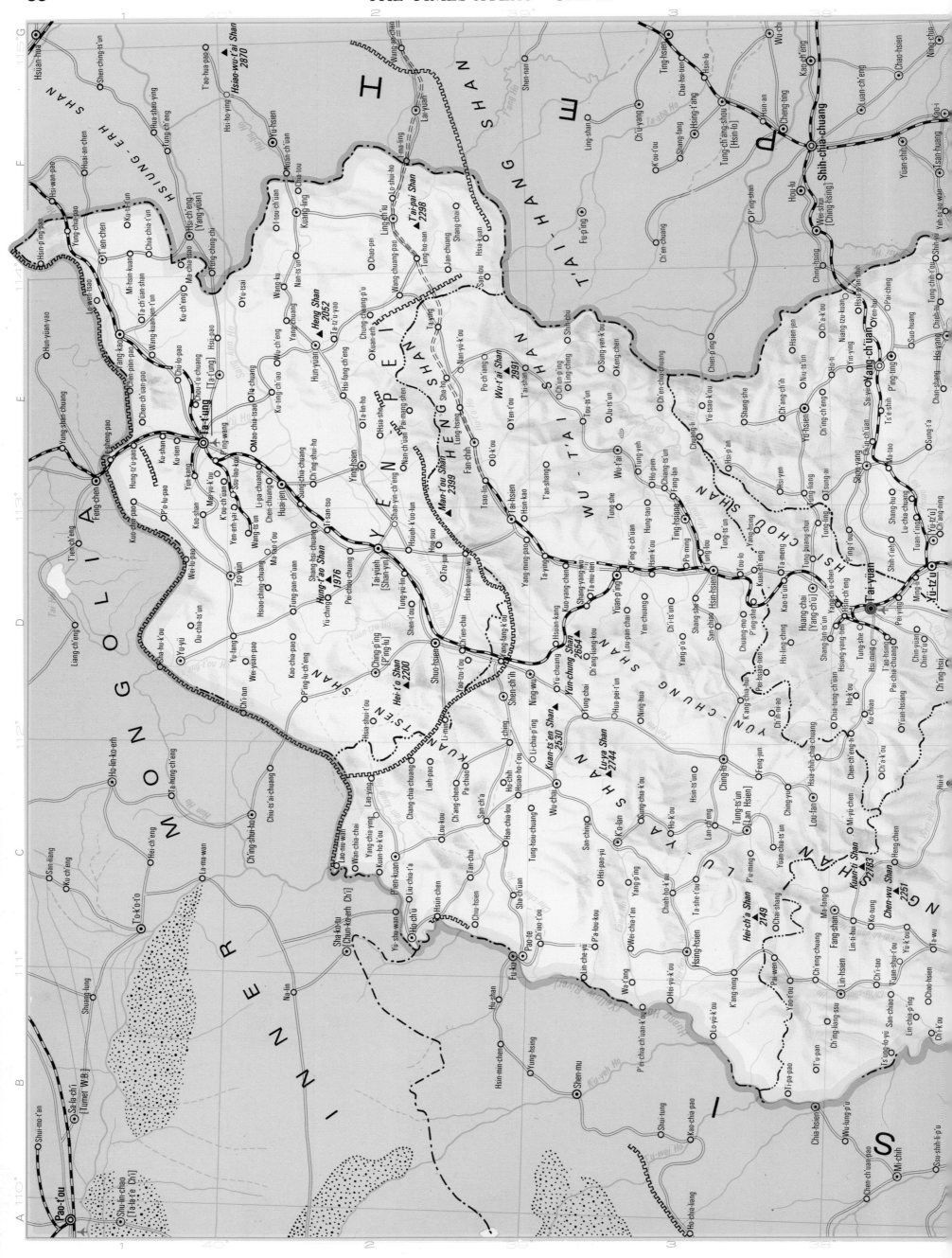

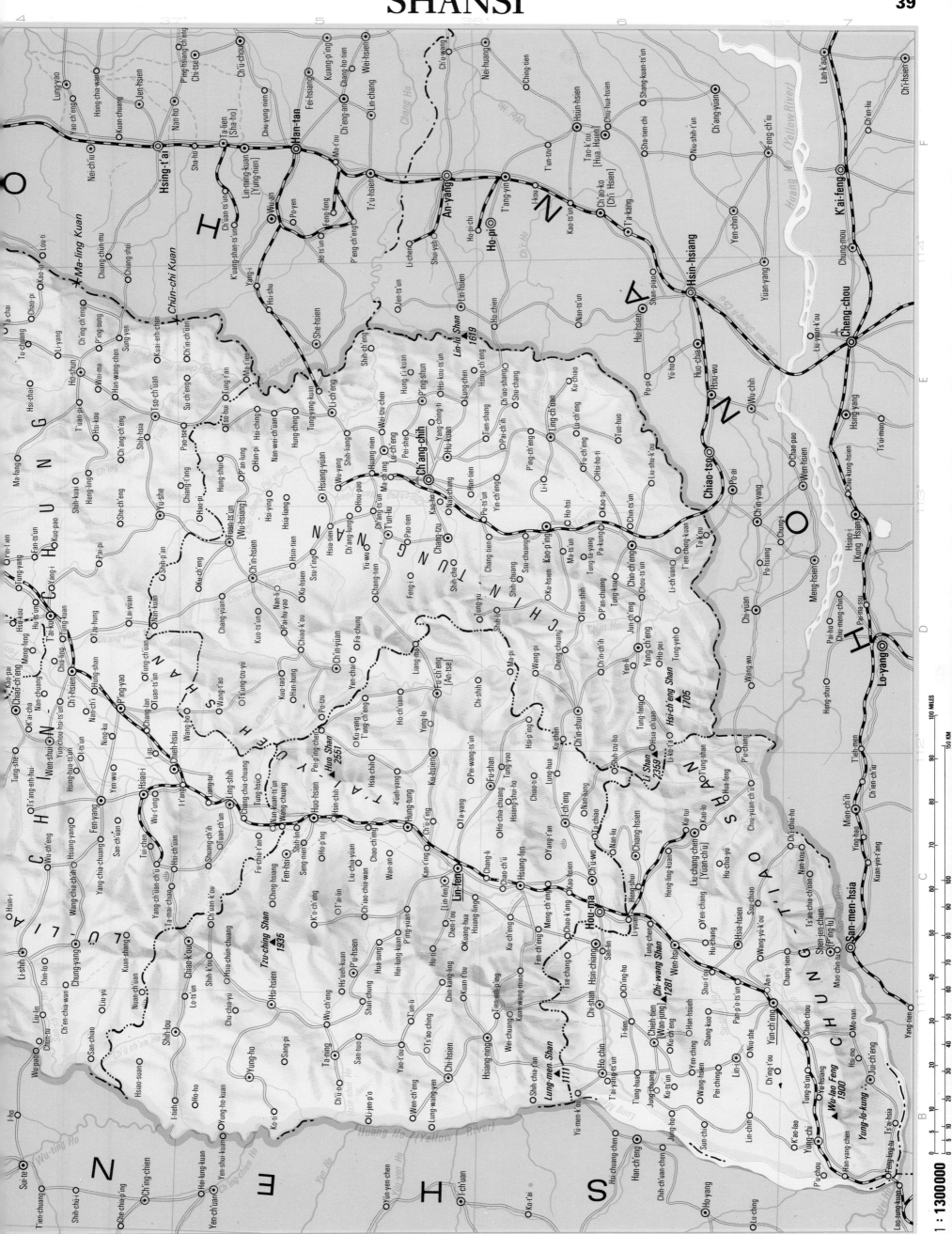

1 : 1300000

SHANSI PROVINCE
SHAN-HSI SHENG 山西省

7 shih	*municipalities*	
6 ti-ch'ü	*regions*	
100 hsien	*counties*	

capital T'ai-yüan Shih	D4	太原市
Ch'ing-hsü Hsien	D4	清徐县
Yang-ch'ü Hsien		阳曲县
centre: Huang-chai	D3	
Ch'ang-chih Shih	E5	长治市
Hou-ma Shih	C6	侯马市
Lin-fen Shih	C5	临汾市
Ta-t'ung Shih	E1	大同市
Yang-ch'üan Shih	E4	阳泉市
Yü-tz'u Shih	D4	榆次市

Chin-chung Ti-ch'ü 晋中地区
centre: Yü-tz'u	D4	榆次
Chiao-ch'eng Hsien	D4	交城县
Chieh-hsiu Hsien	C4	介休县
Ch'i Hsien		祁县
centre: Ch'i-hsien	D4	
Chung-yang Hsien	C4	中阳县
Fang-shan Hsien	C4	方山县
Fen-yang Hsien	C4	汾阳县
Ho-shun Hsien	E4	和顺县
Hsiao-i Hsien	C4	孝义县
Hsi-yang Hsien	E4	昔阳县
Ling-shih Hsien	C5	灵石县
Lin Hsien		临县
centre: Lin-hsien	B4	
Li-shih Hsien	C4	离石县
P'ing-ting Hsien	E4	平定县
P'ing-yao Hsien	D4	平遥县
Shou-yang Hsien	E4	寿阳县
T'ai-ku Hsien	D4	太谷县
Tso-ch'üan Hsien	E4	左权县
Wen-shui Hsien	D4	文水县
Yü Hsien		盂县
centre: Yü-hsien	E3	
Yü-she Hsien	D4	榆社县
Yü-tz'u Hsien		榆次县
centre: not known	D4	

Chin-tung-nan Ti-ch'ü 晋东南地区
centre: Ch'ang-chih	E5	长治
Ch'ang-chih Hsien	E5	长治县
Chang-tzu Hsien	D5	长子县
Chin-ch'eng Hsien	D6	晋城县
Ch'in Hsien		沁县
centre: Ch'in-hsien	D5	
Ch'in-shui Hsien	D6	沁水县
Ch'in-yüan Hsien	D5	沁源县
Hsiang-yüan Hsien	E5	襄垣县
Hu-kuan Hsien	E5	壶关县
Kao-p'ing Hsien	D6	高平县
Li-ch'eng Hsien	E5	黎城县
Ling-ch'uan Hsien	E6	陵川县
Lu-ch'eng Hsien	E5	潞城县
P'ing-shun Hsien	E5	平顺县
T'un-liu Hsien	D5	屯留县
Wu-hsiang Hsien		武乡县
centre: Tuan-ts'un	D5	段村
Yang-ch'eng Hsien	D6	阳城县

Hsin-hsien Ti-ch'ü 忻县地区
Ching-lo Hsien	C3	静乐县
Fan-chih Hsien	E2	繁峙县
Ho-ch'ü Hsien	C2	河曲县
Hsing Hsien		兴县
centre: Hsing-hsien	C3	
Hsin Hsien		忻县
centre: Hsin-hsien	D3	
K'o-lan Hsien	C3	岢岚县
Lan Hsien		岚县
centre: Tung-ts'un	C3	东村
Lou-fan Hsien	C3	娄烦县
Ning-wu Hsien	D2	宁武县
Pao-te Hsien	C2	保德县
P'ien-kuan Hsien	C2	偏关县
Shen-ch'ih Hsien	D2	神池县
Tai Hsien		代县
centre: Tai-hsien	D2	
Ting-hsiang Hsien	D3	定襄县
Wu-chai Hsien	C3	五寨县
Wu-t'ai Hsien	E3	五台县
Yüan-p'ing Hsien	D3	原平县

Lin-fen Ti-ch'ü 临汾地区
An-tse Hsien		安泽县
centre: Fu-ch'eng	D5	府城
Chiao-k'ou Hsien	C5	交口县
Chi Hsien		吉县
centre: Chi-hsien	B5	
Ch'ü-wo Hsien	C6	曲沃县
Fen-hsi Hsien	C5	汾西县
Fu-shan Hsien	C6	浮山县
Hsiang-fen Hsien	C6	襄汾县
Hsiang-ning Hsien	B6	乡宁县
Hsi Hsien		隰县
centre: Hsi-hsien	B5	
Hung-tung Hsien	C5	洪洞县
Huo Hsien		霍县
centre: Huo-hsien	C5	
I-ch'eng Hsien	C6	翼城县
Ku Hsien		古县
centre: Ku-hsien	C5	
Lin-fen Hsien		临汾县
centre: not known	C5	
P'u Hsien		蒲县
centre: P'u-hsien	C5	
Shih-lou Hsien	B4	石楼县
Ta-ning Hsien	B5	大宁县
Yung-ho Hsien	B5	永和县

Yen-pei Ti-ch'ü 雁北地区
centre: Ta-t'ung	E1	大同
Huai-jen Hsien	E2	怀仁县
Hun-yüan Hsien	E2	浑源县
Kuang-ling Hsien	F2	广灵县
Ling-ch'iu Hsien	F2	灵丘县
P'ing-lu Hsien		平鲁县
centre: Ching-p'ing	D2	井坪
Shan-yin Hsien		山阴县
centre: Tai-yüeh	D2	岱岳
Shuo Hsien		朔县
centre: Shuo-hsien	D2	
Ta-t'ung Hsien		大同县
centre: not known	E1	
T'ien-chen Hsien	F1	天镇县
Tso-yün Hsien	D2	左云县
Yang-kao Hsien	E1	阳高县
Ying Hsien		应县
centre: Ying-hsien	E2	
Yu-yü Hsien	D1	右玉县

Yün-ch'eng Ti-ch'ü 运城地区
Chiang Hsien		绛县
centre: Chiang-hsien	C6	
Chi-shan Hsien	B6	稷山县
Ho-chin Hsien	B6	河津县
Hsia Hsien		夏县
centre: Hsia-hsien	C6	
Hsin-chiang Hsien	C6	新绛县
Jui-ch'eng Hsien	B7	芮城县
Lin-i Hsien	B6	临猗县
P'ing-lu Hsien		平陆县
centre: Sheng-jen-chien	C7	圣人涧
Wan-jung Hsien		万荣县
centre: Chieh-tien	B6	解店
Wen-hsi Hsien	C6	闻喜县
Yüan-ch'ü Hsien		垣曲县
centre: Liu-chang-chen	C6	刘张镇
Yün-ch'eng Hsien	B6	运城县
Yung-chi Hsien	B7	永济县

KIANGSU PROVINCE
SHANGHAI MUNICIPALITY

THE Kiangsu–Shanghai region is the most populous and densely peopled area in China. Settled from very early times, this area, apart from its north-western extremity, formed part of the state of Wu from at least the 6th century BC. Wu was conquered by the Yüeh state in 473 BC, and then by the great Yangtze valley state of Ch'u in 334 BC. During this period the area developed a highly individual culture. Annexed by the Ch'in in 223 BC, the area became a part of the Chinese empire. But with the division of the empire in 220, the area became the main centre of a series of southern regimes, which were only reincorporated into the empire under the Sui in 589. After this the importance of Kiangsu grew rapidly. By the 8th century its population had grown and it had become a major grain-surplus area, exporting rice in huge quantities to the north via the canal system built by the Sui in the early 7th century. By the 12th century, this area had become the economic centre of the empire, with vastly productive agriculture, many great cities, and flourishing trade. With the conquest of northern China by the Chin in 1126, Hang-chou (Lin-an) became the capital of the Southern Sung empire, and grew into a huge and flourishing metropolis. The political capital of the empire remained in the south, at Nan-ching, when the Ming finally restored Chinese control over all of China in 1368. But even after 1421, when the seat of government moved, the region continued to prosper, and developed a highly productive economy, with a dense network of irrigation works and waterways, a complex textile industry, and a wealthy gentry which played a very important role in China's political and cultural life. Nan-ching once again became the political centre of China under the Nationalist government from 1928. But from the mid-19th century, with the growth of Shanghai as China's chief port and main centre of modern industry, the region became a centre for modernising influences. The present boundaries of the Shanghai Municipality and of Kiangsu date from 1958.

Virtually the entire region is a flat alluvial plain lying less than 50 m above sea-level. The hills are in the extreme north-west and the south-western corner of the province. A large proportion of the coastal areas have been reclaimed from the sea in historical times, and the coastline is constantly moving eastward. The plain is covered with a dense network of canals, irrigation ditches and canalised rivers, which form a very largely man-made landscape, intensively farmed.

Northern Kiangsu The area to the north of the Huai river was traditionally the poorest and most backward part of the province. It is drier than the rest of the province (less than 750 mm in the Hsü-chou area) and has a shorter growing season (250–260 days). As almost half of the annual rainfall comes in July and August, the area has a history of repeated droughts and disastrous floods. The main crops are winter wheat, followed by kaoliang or millet, with some corn. Sweet potatoes, peanuts and soy beans are also grown. Cotton cultivation has spread in this area since the mid-1950s, especially around Hsü-chou and the Huai valley. This area also has important coal deposits around Hsü-chou, an extension of the Tsao-chuang field in Shantung.

Hsü-chou, an important traditional route centre on the Grand Canal, became a major rail centre early in this century, at the point where the Tientsin–P'u-k'ou railway crossed the east–west Lung-hai route from the coast to the interior. Since the early 1950s, the Grand Canal south of Hsü-chou has been reconstructed, and has again become a major waterway. Hsü-chou's coalfield is at Chia-wang to the north-east, producing some 2,600,000 tons annually. Another coalfield to the south at Sui-ch'i produces some 5,000,000 tons. Hsü-chou is also a secondary industrial city, with textile and machine-making industries.

Lien-yün-kang is the port for the region. It is a modern city, built in the 1930s as the terminus of the Lung-hai railway, to replace the old port of Hai-chou which had silted up. It is the only port on the north Kiangsu coast, which is extremely shallow.

The Chiang-pei area The plain between the Huai and Yangtze rivers is divided into three zones. The coastal area, recently reclaimed from the sea, is an area of salt-pans which have been a major source of salt for many centuries. Further inland is an area of cultivated, but still very saline soils. This area is a major cotton-growing district. The western section is broken up by a series of lakes and marshes, and is largely a rice-producing area. The Chiang-pei area is served by a dense network of waterways, based on four main canals; the ancient Grand Canal between the Huai river at Huai-yin and the Yangtze near Yang-chou; the T'ung-yang canal running eastwards from Yang-chou to the coastal area of Huai-an; the Northern Kiangsu Canal, built to provide an adequate outlet from the Hung-tse lake to the sea; and the Ch'uan-ch'ang canal which runs parallel to the coast and was formerly much used by the salt industry. The most densely peopled and intensively farmed area lies in the south along the northern shore of the Yangtze mouth. In this area little rice is grown, the staple grains being wheat, barley and corn. Much of the land is planted to cotton, oilseeds, jute, soy beans, indigo and other specialised economic crops.

Yang-chou was, during the period from the 7th to the 11th centuries, one of China's richest trading cities, and the trans-shipment point for Yangtze trade on to the Grand Canal. Later it gradually declined, although it remained the home of the great salt merchants of Kiangsu. It is now mainly a commercial centre and market for northern Kiangsu salt and rice production.

Nan-t'ung began to rival Yang-chou as the chief city of the area at the end of the 19th century, when a local official, Chang Chien, provided it with modern schools, among the first in China, and various western-style industries. It now has cotton textiles, food processing, oil pressing and light engineering industries.

Ch'ing-chiang is the main town of the north, situated at the junction of the Grand Canal with the Huai. Once a major transport centre, much of its trade is now diverted to the railway further west in Anhwei. Like Yang-chou, it is now largely a commercial town and a major market for salt and rice.

Yen-ch'eng is the main centre of the coastal area, particularly for the salt industry.

The Nan-ching area comprises the part of Kiangsu south of the Yangtze and west of the T'ai Hu lake. This is the only hilly area in Kiangsu, but the hills, which have a south-west to north-east axis, do not exceed more than 200 m for the most part. The climate here is much more favourable than in the north of Kiangsu; rainfall is over 1,000 m and the growing season lasts for some 280 days. The lowland areas are intensively cultivated, largely double cropped with winter wheat followed by rice. Hill land occupies about a third of the region, and tea production is important, especially around I-hsing.

Nan-ching (Nanking) dominates this area. A major regional centre from at least the 2nd century BC, and from time to time the capital of various southern regimes, Nan-ching was the national capital from 1368–1421 and again from 1928–49. Until 1949 it was essentially a great administrative and commercial centre, with little industry. Since the early 1950s it has become a major industrial city. In addition to its traditional textile industry, it has become an important centre of the chemical industry; of fertiliser and cement manufacture; has a small iron and steel plant, engineering works producing lorries, machine tools and agricultural implements; electronics and plastics industries. Its communications were greatly improved in 1969 with the completion of a massive rail and road bridge across the Yangtze. Its population is estimated to be 1,700,000.

Chen-chiang is an old-established city at the northern end of the section of the Grand Canal south of the Yangtze. It became an important river port and centre of foreign trade in the late 19th century, but was gradually overshadowed by the growth of Shanghai. It remains a trading city, and its importance has been increased by the repairs to the Grand Canal, which leave it a major transfer point for goods from the area south of the Yangtze, like Yang-chou in the north. It has some minor industries – flour milling, oil-extraction and paper making. It is also an important centre of the lumber trade, where log rafts from the upper Yangtze are broken up for trans-shipment.

The T'ai Hu plain comprises the part of southern Kiangsu east of Chen-chiang. It is a huge, continuous expanse of alluvial plain, with only a few hills surrounding the T'ai Hu lake. The area has been heavily settled and intensively cultivated since at least the 6th century, and irrigation and reclamation work has been continuous for well over a thousand years. The soil is naturally fertile, the climate is warmer and wetter than other parts of Kiangsu, and the level of agricultural technique is extremely high. The basis of agriculture is doubled-cropped wheat and rice, but in some areas two crops of rice are grown. Grain is rotated with green fertiliser crops or rape-seed. Cotton is grown on the sandy lands in the north along the Yangtze. But the area is famous as one of China's chief districts for silk. The hills around T'ai Hu produce many fruits and also tea. Fresh-water fishing is also very important in this area.

Su-chou is a very ancient city, the capital of Wu in the 5th century BC, and a great administrative centre, famous for its cultured élite, its high level of education, its handicrafts and its wealth. It remains a tourist centre, with many beauty-spots and ancient monuments. Since 1949 it has become partially industrialised, although it has been rivalled by the growth of Shanghai and Wu-hsi. The old-established silk-industry has been greatly expanded; the city has developed a chemical industry, paper making, and has begun to produce cotton textiles.

Wu-hsi lies at the north-eastern corner of the T'ai Hu lake, also on the Grand Canal. It, too, is an ancient city, though of lesser importance than Su-chou until recent times. With the construction of the railway from Shanghai to Nan-ching in 1908, it grew into a very important market for the shipment of food to Shanghai, and grew rapidly into one of China's chief rice markets. Modern industry also began here rather early – the first modern textile mill was founded in 1894. Wu-hsi merchants played an important role in the industrial growth of Shanghai, and the city grew wealthy. After 1949 Wu-hsi's commercial role as a rice market diminished, and considerable industrial growth followed. Silk and cotton textiles are the main industry, but food processing, oil-extraction and machinery-making (diesel engines and machine tools) are of great importance.

Ch'ang-chou lies north-west of Wu-hsi, also on the canal and the railway. A local commercial city in former times, Ch'ang-chou developed a large-scale cotton textile industry after 1937. It is still the largest textile producer in the area, and also an important producer of textile machinery. It also has large engineering works, producing locomotives and railway rolling stock, diesel engines and electrical equipment.

The Shanghai Delta area Since 1958 this area, with Ch'ung-ming island in the mouth of the Yangtze, has formed the provincial-level municipality of Shanghai. The whole area is a flat plain broken by innumerable watercourses. Its agriculture is extremely intensive, and is largely concentrated on the production of foodstuffs for the Shanghai market, which dominates the whole area. Cotton and rice, wheat and rape-seed are the main crops, but vegetables and dairy produce are important commodities. Ch'ung-ming island is an important producer of cotton.

Shanghai is China's largest city, and one of its main industrial centres. Until 1842 Shanghai was a minor trading port, but once it had been opened up to foreign trade and foreign settlement, it grew at a phenomenal rate, outstripping the traditional ports of the Yangtze area, and the great cities like Su-chou in its hinterland. It became not only China's chief port, but also the major centre for modern western-owned industry, from which western ideas and modern technology were disseminated throughout the country.

Before 1937 Shanghai had a large share of Chinese industrial plant, industrial capital and modern industrial labour force, for the unsettled conditions in the inland provinces during the 1920s and 1930s encouraged industrial investment in Shanghai which was under western protection. Textiles and other light industries made up most of Shanghai's industry, and heavy industry was comparatively unimportant. After 1949, although the textile industry continued to grow – Shanghai is still by far the largest producer of textiles in China, manufacturing cotton, wool, silk and synthetic fibres – heavy industry was also developed. In the 1950s a major steel industry, using pig iron from Ma-an-shan and An-shan, was founded. This was converted in 1959–60 into a fully integrated iron and steel plant, producing 2 million tons of steel a year. Shanghai is also a major producer of copper, lead and zinc. There is a large and diversified engineering industry, and ship-building is a major industry. The chemical industry grew rapidly in the 1960s, producing industrial and pharmaceutical chemicals, plastics, synthetic fibres, and fertilisers. There is a large petro-chemical industry and refineries using crude oil from Ta-ch'ing in Manchuria.

Shanghai has three very large thermal power generating plants, and is the focus of a power grid, which connects it with Su-chou, Wu-hsi and Nan-ching, and with Hang-chou and the very large Hsin-an-chiang hydro-electric plant in Chekiang.

Shanghai's population is currently estimated at approximately twelve million.

KIANGSU AREA
102,200 square kilometres

POPULATION
45,230,000 (1957) (current estimates 47,000,000 to 51,000,000)

SHANGHAI AREA
5,600 square kilometres

POPULATION
12,000,000

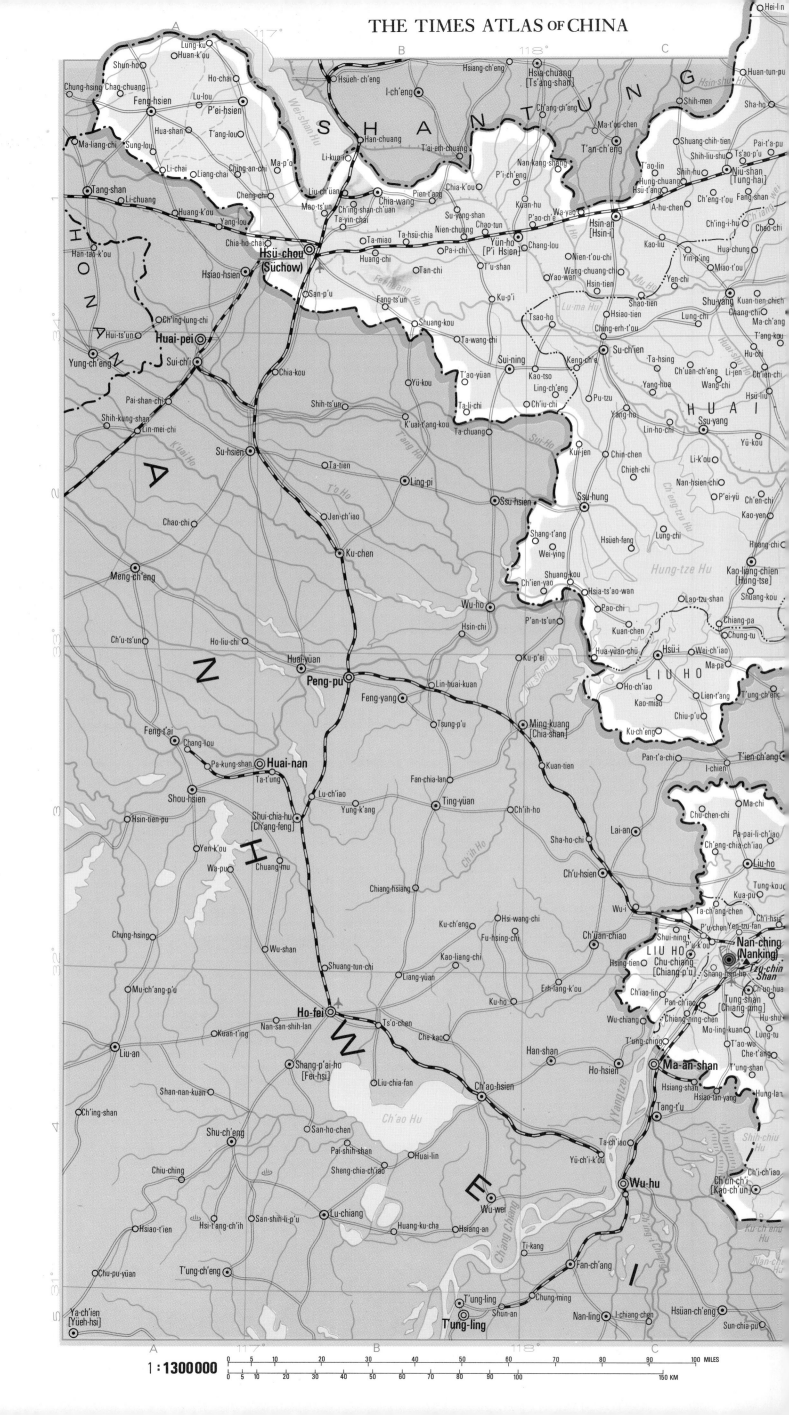

Hai-t'ou
Ch'in-shan Tao
Hai-chou Wan
Che wang
Ch'ing-k'ou [Kan-yü]
Tung-hsi-yün Tao
Hsü-kou
Lien-yün-kang
T'un-shang T'ai-pei
▲Yün-t'ai Shan
◉Lien-yün-kang
Hai-chou
Nan-ch'eng
Hsü-yü
Pan-p'u
Yen-wei-kang
Hsin-pa
Tung-chi
Lung-chü
T'ung-hsing-chieh
Ch'en-chia-kang
Ta-i-shan [Kuan-yün]
T'ien-lou
Hsin-shih-ts'un
Wu-chi
Pai-tsao
Ch'en-chi
Ta-yu
Ta-yu-chien
I-chi
Hsin-an-chen [Kuan-nan]
Kuo-chi
Pa-t'an
Liu-t'
Hsiang-shui
Liu-t'ao
Hsin-huai Ho
Kao-kou
Yung-ho-chi
Wu-fan
Pa-ta-chia
Hui-tun
Wu-kang
T'ang-chi
Ch'ien-ch'iu
Ssu-ming
T'ung-yang-kang
T'ung-hsing
Ch'eng-chi
Huang-ying
Ch'en-shih-an
Lien-shui
Yang-chai
Ch'en-chi
Fu-ning
Ho-te [She-yang]
YIN
Wang-ying
Ch'in-kung
Su-chia-tsui
Tung-kou
Kou-tun
Ch'en-yang
Chung-hsing-ch'iao
Ch'ing-chiang
Hsi-ch'iao
I-lin
Yung-hsing
Ts'ao-yen
Huang-chia-chien
San-lung
Pei Sha
Pan-cha
Huai-an
Ching-k'ou
Chien-yang
Hu-to [Chien-hu]
Hsin-hsing
Nan-yang
Ch'u-ch'iao
Tung-ch'iao
Kao-tso
Shang-kang
Yen-ch'eng
Wu-yu
Ssu-ch'a-ho
Yao Sha
P'ing-ch'iao
An-feng
She-yang
Lung-kang
Hsin-feng-chen
An Sha
Ching-ho
Ts'ao-tien
Lou-wang
Ch'in-nan
Yü-hua
Ch'a-ho
Pao-ying
Lu-to
Ta-kang
Ta-chung-chi [Ta-feng]
Liu-chuang
Nan-yang
Lü-liang-ch'iao
Liu-pao
Sha-kou
Ta-chou
An-feng
Pai-chü
Li-ch'eng [Chin-hu]
Fan-shui
Lin-tse
Hsiao-hai
Chieh-shou
Hsin-hsing [Hsing-hua]
Ta-to
Tai-chia-yao
Ts'ao-nien
Ch'en-tsao
Ta-ch'iao
Min-ch'iao
Ch'ing-shui-t'an
Ho-k'ou
Ti-to
Tung-t'ai
P'an-te-hsing
San-to
Chiang-miao
Ch'en-lun
Ssu-tsao
Ts'ao-p'ieh
Kao-yu
Tung-lo
Pa-ch'iao-chen
Tai-nan
Shih-yen
An-feng
San-ts'ang
Lu-chin
Fan-ch'uan
Liang-to
Fu-an
Ch'iang-kang
Hsiao-chi
Kang-k'ou
Ts'ou-t'ung
T'ang-yang
Li-li-she
P'ing-kou
Shao-po
Pai-mu
Hu-chi
Hai-an
Li-pao
Chiao-hsieh
Lang-chia Sha
T'ai-chou
Hsien-nü-miao [Chiang-tu]
Chiang-yen [T'ai Hsien]
Ssu-kang-k'ou
Ya-chou
Ting-chia-so
Pen-ch'a
Yang-chou
Chang-t'ien
Chiang-to
Ju-kao
Tung-ch'en
Ting-yen
Ch'a-ho
Ma-t'ang
Chüeh-kang [Ju-tung]
Wu-nan Sha
San-chiang-ying
Tao-p'u
K'ou-an
Hsüan-chia-p'u
Pan-ching
Mo-t'ou
Shih-kang
Ta-t'ung-chen
Chen-chiang
Tan-tou-chen
Yang-chung
Ma-tien
T'ai-hsing
Chi-chia-shih
Huang-ch'iao
Kuo-chia-yüan
P'ing-ch'iao
Hsi-t'ing
San-yü-chen
Lü-ssu
Lung-t'an
Hsia-shu
Kao-tzu
Chien-p'i
K'uai-ch'eng
Yü-fang
Hsin-feng
Ta-ch'eng-ch'iao
Kuang-ling
Hsieh-ch'iao
Erh-an
T'ien-sheng-kang
Chin-sha [Nan-t'ung]
Yü-hsi
Yü-tung
Hai-fu-chen
T'ang-shan
Meng-ho
Wei-ts'un
Shen-kang
Hsia-kang
Lu-yüan
Nan-t'ung
Erh-chia-chen
Ssu-chia-pa
San-yang-chen
T'u-ch'iao
Pai-mien
Lü-ch'eng
Hsü-shih-ch'iao
Chiao-ch'i
Chiang-yin
T'ang-cha
Hsiao-hai-chen
Ch'i-lin-chen
Hui-lung-chen [Ch'i-tung]
Chü-jung
Pao-nien
Yen-ling
An-chia-she
Ch'iang-ch'i
Ch'iao-ch'i
Yang-she [Sha-chou]
Fu-shan
Hsü-p'u
San-ch'ang
Ling-tien-chen
Chiu-lung-chen
Tung-an-chen
T'ai-an-kang
Yin-yang
Ch'ien-pai-shu
Hsieh-ch'iao
Chin-t'an
P'u-i-chen
Ch'i-shu-yen
Tse-yang-chen
Chu-t'ang
Mei-li
Hsü-shih
Miao-chen
Ch'ung-ming
Hsin-k'ai-ho
Ch'ang Chiang-k'ou
Kuo-chuang-miao
Ch'ih-ch'i-ch'iao
Ch'ang-chou
Hu-t'ang-ch'iao
Chang-ching-ch'iao
Ch'ien-mao
Huang-ching
Sha-ch'i
Fu-lu
Liu-ho
Hsin-k'ai-ho
Pao-chen
T'ien-wang-ssu
Hsüeh-pu
Chu-lin
Wu-huang
Li-chia-ch'iao
Lien-t'ang
Yü Shan
Ch'ang-shu
An-chen
Huang Sha
I-shih
P'i-ch'iao
Huang-li
Shang-huang
Lo-she
Hui Shan
Hu-tai
Wu-hsi
T'ang-k'ou
O'ang-shih
Shuang-feng
Pa-ch'eng
T'ai-ts'ang
Ch'ang-hsing Tao
Shang-hsing-chen
Chu-tse-ch'iao
Kuan-lin
Yang-hsiang
Ho-ch'iao
Hsin-hsien-ch'iao
Hsin-chuang
Wei-ching-t'ang
K'un-shan
Lo-tien
Wu-sung
K'ung-ch'ien
Li-yang
Hsin-an
Wang-t'ing
Nan-fang-ch'üan
Huang-tai-chen
Lu-mu
Cheng-i
Lu-chia
Nan-hsiang
Ta-ch'ang
SHANG-HAI SHIH
MAO SHAN
Ch'a-t'ing
Hsü-she
Hu-kuan-chen
Kuang-fu
Su-ch'ang
Su-ting
Lu-chih-chen
Chang-pu
An-t'ing
Kao-ch'iao
Ya-ch'i
She-chu
Tai-pu
Ting-shu-chen
Ling-yen Shan
Su-chou [Soochow]
Yü-fang
Ch'ing-pu
Ch'i-pao
◉SHANG-HAI
Tung-pa
Mei-chu
Chang-chu
Pen-tu
Heng-ching
T'ung-li
Ch'en-mu
Ching-k'ou
Ssu-ching
Ch'uan-sha
Lang-ch'i
Yang-tien
Hsi-tung-t'ing Shan
Tung-tung-t'ing Shan
Wu-chiang
Chou-chuang
Chou-chuang
Sung-chiang
Hsin-chuang [Shang-hai]
Nan-hui
Shan-pei
Tung-shan
Li-li
Lu-hsü
Hsin-ch'ang
Shih-tzu-p'u
Ssu-an
Li-chia-kang
P'ing-wang
Sheng-tse
Chen-tse
CHEKIANG
Kang-ch'ing
Chin-shan
Lü-kang
Che-lin
Kuang-te
Chieh-p'ai
Hu-chou [Wu-hsing]
Nan-hsün
Chia-shan
Chin-yen
Chin-shan-wei
T'ing-lin
Nan-ch'iao [Feng-hsien]
Feng-ch'eng
Ni-ch'eng

YELLOW SEA (HUANG HAI)
Ta Sha
Ch'ang Sha
P'u-tzu Sha
Huang-tzu Sha
Chin-chia Sha
Chuang-chia Sha

Tsingtao–Shanghai 740km
Tan-tung 1150km
Ch'in-huang-tao 1280km
Ta-lien 1040km
Yen-t'ai 960km
Nagasaki
Hawaii
Canton
Ning-po

(Mouth of the Yangtze)
Ch'ang Chiang (Yangtze)
(Whangpoo R.)
T'ai Hu
Kao-yu Hu
Shao-po Hu

LIU-HO

KIANGSU PROVINCE
CHIANG-SU SHENG   江苏省

11 shih	*municipalities*	
8 ti-ch'ü	*regions*	
64 hsien	*counties*	

capital Nan-ching Shih	C3	南京市
Ch'ang-chou Shih	D4	常州市
Chen-chiang Shih	D3	镇江市
Ch'ing-chiang Shih	D2	清江市
Hsü-chou Shih	B1	徐州市
Lien-yün-kang Shih	D1	连云港市
Nan-t'ung Shih	E3	南通市
Su-chou Shih	E4	苏州市
T'ai-chou Shih	D3	泰州市
Wu-hsi Shih	E4	无锡市
Yang-chou Shih	D3	扬州市

Chen-chiang Ti-ch'ü		镇江地区
Chiang-ning Hsien		江宁县
centre: Tung-shan	C4	东山
Chin-t'an Hsien	D4	金坛县
Chü-jung Hsien	D4	句容县
I-hsing Hsien	D4	宜兴县
Kao-ch'un Hsien		高淳县
centre: Ch'un-ch'i	C4	淳溪
Li-shui Hsien	D4	溧水县
Li-yang Hsien	D4	溧阳县
Tan-t'u Hsien		丹徒县
centre: Chen-chiang	D3	镇江
Tan-yang Hsien	D4	丹阳县
Wu-chin Hsien		武进县
centre: Ch'ang-chou	D4	常州
Yang-chung Hsien	D3	扬中县

Hsü-chou Ti-ch'ü		徐州地区
Feng Hsien		丰县
centre: Feng-hsien	A1	
Hsin-i Hsien		新沂县
centre: Hsin-an	C1	新安
Kan-yü Hsien		赣榆县
centre: Ch'ing-k'ou	D1	青口
P'ei Hsien		沛县
centre: P'ei-hsien	A1	
P'i Hsien		邳县
centre: Yün-ho	B1	运河
Sui-ning Hsien	B2	睢宁县
Tung-hai Hsien		东海县
centre: Niu-shan	C1	牛山
T'ung-shan Hsien		铜山县
centre: Hsü-chou	B1	徐州

Huai-yin Ti-ch'ü		淮阴地区
centre: Ch'ing-chiang	D2	清江
Huai-an Hsien	D2	淮安县
Huai-yin Hsien		淮阴县
centre: Ch'ing-chiang	D2	清江
Hung-tse Hsien		洪泽县
centre: Kao-liang-chien	C2	高良涧
Kuan-nan Hsien		灌南县
centre: Hsin-an-chen	D1	新安镇
Kuan-yün Hsien		灌云县
centre: Ta-i-shan	D1	大伊山
Lien-shui Hsien	D2	连水县
Shu-yang Hsien	C1	沭阳县
Ssu-hung Hsien	C2	泗洪县
Ssu-yang Hsien	C2	泗阳县
Su-ch'ien Hsien	C2	宿迁县

Liu-ho Ti-ch'ü		六合地区
Chiang-p'u Hsien		江浦县
centre: Chu-chiang	C3	珠江
Chin-hu Hsien		金湖县
centre: Li-ch'eng	D2	黎城
Hsü-i Hsien	C2	盱眙县
I-cheng Hsien	D3	仪征县
Liu-ho Hsien	C3	六合县

Nan-t'ung Ti-ch'ü		南通地区
Ch'i-tung Hsien		启东县
centre: Hui-lung-chen	F4	汇龙镇
Hai-an Hsien	E3	海安县
Hai-men Hsien		海门县
centre: Mao-chia-chen	F4	茅家镇
Ju-kao Hsien	E3	如皋县
Ju-tung Hsien		如东县
centre: Chüeh-kang	F3	掘港
Nan-t'ung Hsien		南通县
centre: Chin-sha	F3	金沙

Su-chou Ti-ch'ü		苏州地区
Ch'ang-shu Hsien	E4	常熟县
Chiang-yin Hsien	E4	江阴县
K'un-shan Hsien	E4	昆山县
Sha-chou Hsien		沙州县
centre: Yang-she	E4	杨舍
T'ai-ts'ang Hsien	F4	太仓县
Wu-chiang Hsien	E4	吴江县
Wu-hsi Hsien	E4	无锡县
Wu Hsien		吴县
centre: Su-chou	E4	苏州

Yang-chou Ti-ch'ü		扬州地区
Chiang-tu Hsien		江都县
centre: Hsien-nü-miao	D3	仙女庙
Ching-chiang Hsien	E3	靖江县
Han-chiang Hsien		邗江县
centre: Yang-chou	D3	扬州
Hsing-hua Hsien		兴化县
centre: Hsin-hsing	D3	新兴
Kao-yu Hsien	D3	高邮县
Pao-ying Hsien	D2	宝应县
T'ai Hsien		泰县
centre: Chiang-yen	E3	姜堰
T'ai-hsing Hsien	E3	泰兴县

Yen-ch'eng Ti-ch'ü		盐城地区
Chien-hu Hsien		建湖县
centre: Hu-tuo	D2	湖垛
Fu-ning Hsien	D2	阜宁县
Hsiang-shui Hsien	D1	响水县
Pin-hai Hsien		滨海县
centre: Tung-k'an	D1	东坎
She-yang Hsien		射阳县
centre: Ho-te	E2	合德
Ta-feng Hsien		大丰县
centre: Ta-chung-chi	E2	大中集
Tung-t'ai Hsien	E3	东台县
Yen-ch'eng Hsien	E2	盐城县

SHANGHAI MUNICIPALITY

SHANG-HAI SHIH	F4	上海市
Chia-ting Hsien	F4	嘉定县
Ch'ing-p'u Hsien	F4	青浦县
Chin-shan Hsien	F5	金山县
Ch'uan-sha Hsien	F4	川沙县
Ch'ung-ming Hsien	F4	崇明县
Feng-hsien Hsien		奉贤县
centre: Nan-ch'iao	F5	南桥
Nan-hui Hsien	F4	南汇县
Pao-shan Hsien	F4	宝山县
Shang-hai Hsien		上海县
centre: Hsin-chuang	F4	莘庄
Sung-chiang Hsien	F4	松江县

ANHWEI
PROVINCE

ANHWEI province took its present form for the first time under the Ch'ing dynasty (1644–1911), and has remained the same since then, apart from minor changes to the boundary with Kiangsu. It falls into two quite distinct areas. The north of the province forms a part of the great plain of eastern China; this was settled heavily in Han times. The southern area between the Yangtze and the Huai river was first heavily settled in the 7th and 8th centuries. The section of Anhwei south of the Yangtze was settled somewhat later, but developed a distinct character of its own, as it was the home of a remarkably successful group of merchants (the Hui-chou or Hsin-an merchants), who played a most important role in China's internal trade during the Ming and early Ch'ing period, and became immensely wealthy.

The North Anhwei plain This is a great area of level plain lying to the north of the Huai Ho river, and drained by a series of tributaries running into the Huai. The plain is broken only by some low hills in the area where Shantung, Kiangsu and Anhwei meet. There is no natural watershed between the Huai and the Huang Ho, and on many occasions there has been disastrous flooding in this area caused by the diversion of waters from the Huang Ho into the Huai river system. The last of these was deliberately caused in 1938 by the Nationalist army as a means of halting the Japanese armies. This caused immense destruction, and gravely damaged the drainage system of northern Anhwei, which suffered badly from flooding throughout the 1940s. Since 1951 a great deal of work has been done to control the Huai. It has been dyked, its headwaters dammed to provide irrigation waters and hydro-electricity, and more recently a canal (the New Pien canal) was constructed across the north of the area to relieve its tributary rivers. These works have increased the amount of irrigated land, reduced the danger of floods, and improved river transport. In the past northern Anhwei was largely an area of dry farming, with winter wheat or barley followed by a summer crop of corn. Soy beans and kaoliang were also commonly grown. Recently rice has begun to rival wheat as the staple grain crop in some southern areas. Cotton and various oilseeds such as rape are widely cultivated.

In the northern tip of the province there is an important coalfield known as the Huai-pei field. This is centred on Sui-ch'i, which was designated a municipality in 1961. The field is estimated to produce five million tons per annum.

Pang-pu is the chief city of northern Anhwei, at the point where the Tientsin–Pu-k'ou railway crosses the Huai river. A traditional river port and market centre, it grew rapidly in the early part of this century. Since the 1950s, while retaining its role as the centre of this rich agricultural area, and as a major market for wheat and other farm produce, it also developed considerable industry. Beside food processing and cotton textiles, and glass and paper manufacture, it has an engineering industry.

The Huai-nan hills Between the Huai river and the Yangtze valley lies a belt of hilly land, the eastward extension of the Ta-pieh Shan range on the border between Honan and Hupeh. In the west, on the Hupeh border, the hills are high and mountainous, with considerable areas over 1,500 m, and a peak, T'ien-chu Shan, of 1,751 m. The axis of these hills is mainly south-west to north-east. In the east the hills are low, rarely over 300 m, and rounded. In the middle is the basin of a large lake, the Chao Hu. The richest and most closely cultivated area is the central zone around the Chao Hu, which is carefully irrigated and is primarily a rice producing district. The southern basin of the upper Huai around Liu-an was formerly badly affected by flooding. It has greatly benefited from the works completed to control the Huai headwaters. Flooding is now less common, and irrigation has been greatly extended. Although wheat used to be the major crop, rice has become more widespread in the last decades. The high hills and mountains of the Ta-pieh Shan in the west still have much forest cover. The area produces wheat, corn, sweet potatoes and hemp. But it has suffered seriously from erosion in the past. Tea is also an important crop. The hilly area north and east of the Chao Hu lake is also a rice producing area, although it is not as intensively cultivated. The area suffers from drought in spring, and has a rather low rainfall (750 mm or below). Irrigation is common, but the schemes are very small and often inefficient. Rice, with winter wheat, is grown in low irrigated land. On the hilly uplands wheat, barley, sweet potatoes and corn are the main crops. Tobacco and peanuts are also grown.

Ho-fei (formerly Lu-chou) is the main city and the provincial capital. Situated on the Huai-nan railway, near the Chao Hu lake, it also has water communication with the Yangtze. Until 1950 Ho-fei was a small administrative city with only 40,000 people and no industry. Since then it has grown greatly. In the early years of the Communist period many light industries were relocated here from Shanghai. In the late 1950s a small steel plant was built, and an engineering industry grew up, manufacturing machine tools and mining equipment. There is also an aluminium plant. The population rose from 183,000 in 1953 to 360,000 in 1957, and is now estimated at about 500,000.

Huai-nan on the south bank of the Huai is the centre of a rich coalfield which began operations in 1929, and grew rapidly after the construction of a rail link to Yü-ch'i-k'ou on the Yangtze in 1936. Production was greatly increased after 1950, and the field is one of the biggest in China, with an annual output of more than 10,000,000 tons. Huai-nan also has a large thermal power plant, which is linked by a grid with various small hydro-electric schemes on the upper Huai tributaries, and with Pang-pu and Wu-hu south of the Yangtze.

The Yangtze valley This broad alluvial plain broken by low hills has a much warmer, wetter climate than the northern areas of Anhwei, with about 1,000 mm of rain, and a growing season of 230–250 days. Almost all of the cultivated land is irrigated paddy field. It is a great rice producing region, with very high yields. In the western part of the valley double-cropped rice is very common. In the east rice is usually grown following winter wheat. Cotton and rape-seed are widely grown, and some ramie and sugar cane. Tea is produced in the hills on the southern bank of the Yangtze.

Wu-hu was the traditional centre of the rice trade in southern Anhwei, and the building of the railway to Nan-ching increased its importance. Wu-hu remains an extremely important commercial and transport centre, but it has little industry except for paper and board manufacturing, cotton spinning, and food processing.

An-ch'ing, formerly the provincial capital, had a similar role on the northern bank of the Yangtze. It has no rail communications, however, and since losing its administrative status it has remained comparatively unimportant and little industry has been developed in the city.

Ma-an-shan on the southern bank of the Yangtze is a very important source of iron ore, first exploited by the Japanese during the Second World War, when blast furnaces were installed. In the early 1950s these were restored, and Ma-an-shan began to produce pig-iron in bulk for the Shanghai steel industry. It was greatly expanded in the late 1950s and early 1960s, and converted into an integrated iron and steel complex. Most of its pig-iron is still shipped to Shanghai, however.

T'ung-ling, also on the southern bank of the Yangtze, is an important mining centre for copper. There is also an iron mine at T'ao-chung to the east.

The Southern Anhwei hills The south of the province is an area of rugged hills and mountains, with rather narrow valleys and little cultivated land. Most of the uplands are between 600 m and 100 m, but individual peaks rise to 1,323 m (Chiu-hua Shan) and 1,841 m (Huang Shan). The climate is sub-tropical, with a growing season of 300 days or more, and abundant rainfall (1,750 mm to 2,000 mm). The area is thickly forested, and timber is an important product. Farming is concentrated in the valleys, where rice, wheat, barley, sweet potatoes, corn and rape-seed are the main crops. Tea production is a very important local industry – the area produces about a tenth of China's total tea crop.

T'un-ch'i is the chief route centre and communication node for this area. The city has replaced, in this respect, the older cities of She-hsien and Chi-men, although the latter remains an important centre of tea production.

Hsuan-ch'eng plays a similar role in the eastern mountains, with routes reaching into Chekiang, with which the area is closely linked.

AREA
130,000 square kilometres

POPULATION
31,240,000 (other estimates up to 39,000,000)

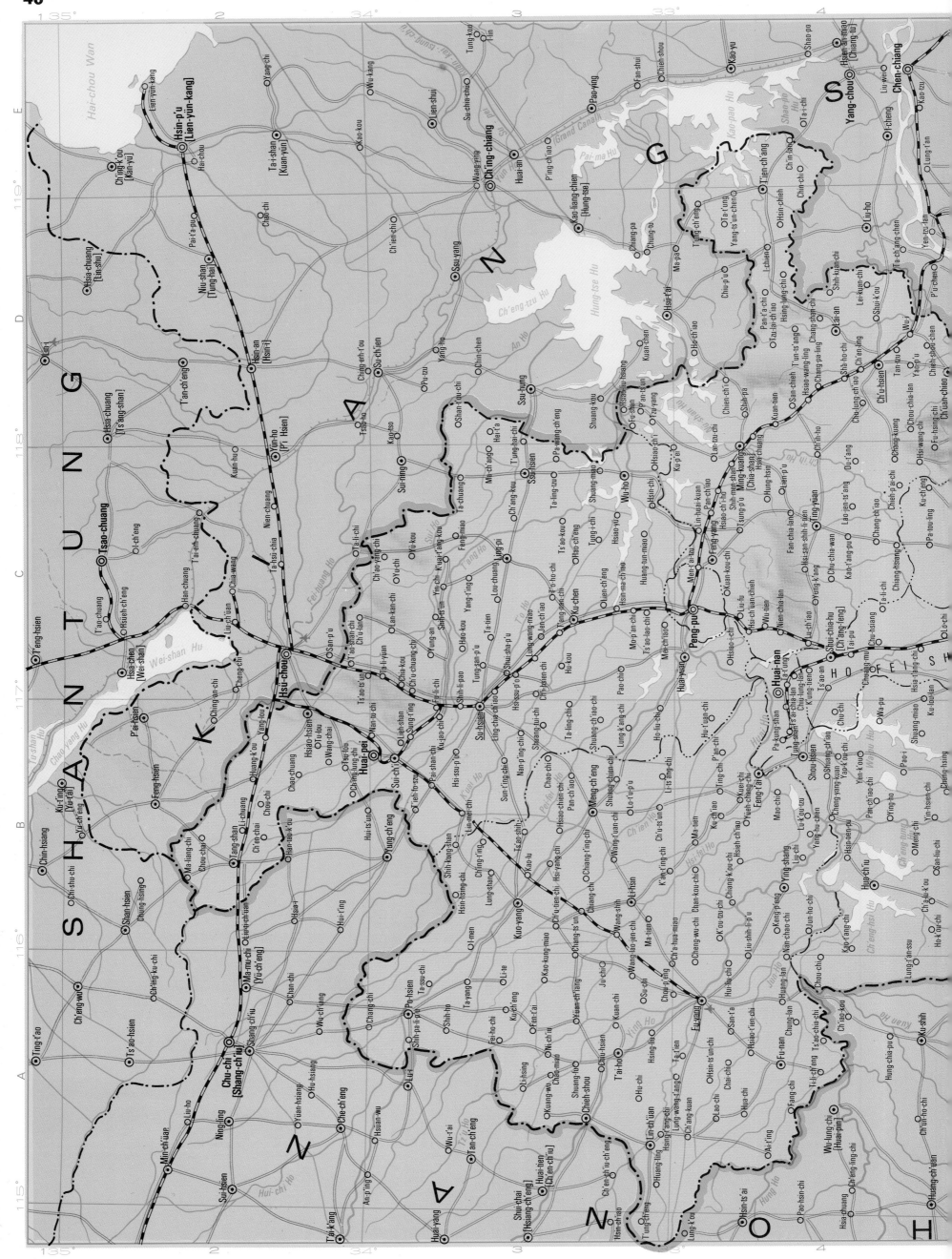

NAN-CHING (NANKING)

Ma-an-shan · Wu-hu · Ho-fei · An-ch'ing · Tung-ling · Chiu-chiang · Ching-te-chen · Huang-shih

TA-PIEH SHAN · CHAO-HU · HUI-CHOU · Ch'ao Hu · Ch'ang Chiang (Yangtze) · P'o-yang Hu

Ta-pieh Shan · Tien-chu Shan 1751 · Huang Shan 1841 · Chiu-hua Shan 1323 · Shih-erh Shan · Lu Shan 1426 · Hsieh Shan · Hung-mao Chien · Tung-t'ien-mu Shan 1479 · Hsi-t'ien-mu Shan 1507 · Ch'ien-ch'iu Kuan

KIANGSU · CHEKIANG · KIANGSI · HUPEH

Scale 1 : 1300000

ANHWEI PROVINCE
AN-HUI SHENG   安徽省

8 shih   *municipalities*
9 ti-ch'ü   *regions*
70 hsien   *counties*

capital Ho-fei Shih	D5	合肥市
Ch'ang-feng Hsien		长丰县
centre: Shui-chia-hu	D4	水家湖
An-ch'ing Shih	D6	安庆市
Huai-nan Shih	D4	淮南市
Huai-pei Shih	C3	淮北市
Ma-an-shan Shih	E5	马鞍山市
Peng-pu Shih	D4	蚌埠市
T'ung-ling Shih	D6	铜陵市
Wu-hu Shih	E5	芜湖市

An-ch'ing Ti-ch'ü		安庆地区
Ch'ien-shan Hsien	C6	潜山县
Huai-ning Hsien		怀宁县
centre: Shih-p'ai	C6	石牌
Su-sung Hsien	C6	宿松县
T'ai-hu Hsien	C6	太湖县
Tsung-yang Hsien	D6	枞阳县
T'ung-ch'eng Hsien	C5	桐城县
Wang-chiang Hsien	C6	望江县
Yüeh-hsi Hsien		岳西县
centre: Ya-ch'ien	C6	衙前

Ch'ao-hu Ti-ch'ü		巢湖地区
centre: Ch'ao-hsien	D5	巢县
Ch'ao Hsien		巢县
centre: Ch'ao-hsien	D5	
Fei-tung Hsien		肥东县
centre: Tien-pu	D5	店埠
Han-shan Hsien	E5	含山县
Ho Hsien		和县
centre: Ho-hsien	E5	
Lu-chiang Hsien	D5	庐江县
Wu-wei Hsien	D5	无为县

Ch'ih-chou Ti-ch'ü		池州地区
Ch'ing-yang Hsien	D6	青阳县
Kuei-ch'ih Hsien		贵池县
centre: Ch'ih-chou	C6	池州
Shih-t'ai Hsien		石台县
centre: Ch'i-li	D6	七里
Tung-chih Hsien		东至县
centre: Yao-tu	D6	尧度
T'ung-ling Hsien	D6	铜陵县

Ch'u-hsien Ti-ch'ü		滁县地区
Chia-shan Hsien		嘉山县
centre: Ming-kuang	D4	明光
Ch'üan-chiao Hsien	E4	全椒县
Ch'u Hsien		滁县
centre: Ch'u-hsien	E4	
Feng-yang Hsien	D4	凤阳县
Lai-an Hsien	E4	来安县
T'ien-ch'ang Hsien	E4	天长县
Ting-yüan Hsien	D4	定远县

Fu-yang Ti-ch'ü		阜阳地区
Chieh-shou Hsien	B3	界首县
Feng-t'ai Hsien	C4	凤台县
Fu-nan Hsien	B4	阜南县
Fu-yang Hsien	B4	阜阳县
Kuo-yang Hsien	C3	涡阳县
Li-hsin Hsien	C3	利辛县
Lin-ch'üan Hsien	B3	临泉县
Meng-ch'eng Hsien	C3	蒙城县
Po Hsien		亳县
centre: Po-hsien	B3	
T'ai-ho Hsien	B3	太和县
Ying-shang Hsien	C4	颖上县

Hui-chou Ti-ch'ü		徽州地区
centre: T'un-ch'i	E7	屯溪
Chi-ch'i Hsien	E6	绩溪县
Ch'i-men Hsien	D7	祁门县
Ching-te Hsien	E6	旌德县
Hsiu-ning Hsien	E7	休宁县
I Hsien		黟县
centre: I-hsien	D7	
Ning-kuo Hsien		宁国县
centre: Ho-li-ch'i	E6	河历溪
She Hsien		歙县
centre: Hui-ch'eng	E7	徽城
T'ai-p'ing Hsien		太平县
centre: Kan-t'ang	E6	甘棠

Liu-an Ti-ch'ü		六安地区
Chin-chai Hsien		金寨县
centre: Mei-shan	B5	梅山
Fei-hsi Hsien		肥西县
centre: Shang-p'ai-ho	D5	上派河
Huo-ch'iu Hsien	C4	霍丘县
Huo-shan Hsien	C5	霍山县
Liu-an Hsien	C5	六安县
Shou Hsien		寿县
centre: Shou-hsien	C4	
Shu-ch'eng Hsien	C5	舒城县

Su-hsien Ti-ch'ü		宿县地区
Hsiao Hsien		萧县
centre: Hsiao-hsien	C2	
Huai-yüan Hsien	D4	怀远县
Ku-chen Hsien	D3	固镇县
Ling-pi Hsien	D3	灵璧县
Ssu Hsien		泗县
centre: Ssu-hsien	D3	
Su Hsien		宿县
centre: Su-hsien	C3	
Sui-ch'i Hsien	C3	濉溪县
Tang-shan Hsien	C2	砀山县
Wu-ho Hsien	D3	五河县

Wu-hu Ti-ch'ü		芜湖地区
Ching Hsien		泾县
centre: Ching-hsien	E6	
Fan-ch'ang Hsien	E5	繁昌县
Hsüan-ch'eng Hsien	E6	宣城县
Kuang-te Hsien	F6	广德县
Lang-ch'i Hsien	F5	郎溪县
Nan-ling Hsien	E6	南陵县
Tang-t'u Hsien	E5	当涂县
Wu-hu Hsien		芜湖县
centre: Wan-chih	E5	湾址

CHEKIANG
PROVINCE

THE smallest of the mainland provinces of China, Chekiang has a dense population, and an importance out of proportion with its size. The province falls into two quite different parts, the area north of Hang-chou, which forms a part of the Yangtze delta region, very similar to southern Kiangsu, and the southern part of the province, which is mountainous, and is really a continuation of the mountains of northern Fukien. The first of these areas originally formed part of the Wu state, and was incorporated into the Ch'in and Han empires after 223 BC. The southern and eastern sections formed part of the territory occupied by the Yüeh peoples. Although the Han gradually claimed control of it, it was only slowly incorporated into the empire and settled. Its final period of growth began in the 6th and 7th centuries. After this it became increasingly important, particularly after the capital of the southern Sung was established at Hang-chou (1127–1280). The area became famous for its tradition of education and culture.

The whole province has a warm, damp, sub-tropical climate. In winter, January temperatures average about 4°C (39°F) in the north, 7.5°C (45.5°F) in the southern coastal area. In summer the whole province has average July temperatures of around 28–29°C (82–84°F). All of Chekiang has more than 1,000 mm of rainfall, with considerably more on the mountains of the south. The north, which has been intensively cultivated for well over a thousand years, long ago lost its natural vegetation cover. The mountains of the south are still richly covered with mixed forest.

The northern Chekiang plain This comprises the southern half of the Yangtze delta plain, to the south of the T'ai Hu lake. It is a continuation of the plain of Kiangsu and Shanghai, and the provincial boundary is purely arbitrary. It is a flat, featureless plain with a dense network of waterways, canals and irrigation channels, the most important of which is the Grand Canal, leading from Chia-hsing to Hang-chou. The chief crop is rice, grown after a spring crop of rape-seed, wheat or beans. Jute and cotton are widely grown, and fine tobacco around Tung-hsiang. The area raises many sheep, and in the Hu-chou and Wu-hsing areas silk culture is very important. In the hills to the south-west of the T'ai Hu lake, which occupy the west of this region, tea, bamboo and timber are important products.

Chia-hsing is a transport centre on the Grand Canal, and the main market and commercial centre for the north-east of the plain. It had 78,000 people in 1953. It is a silk manufacturing centre, with some modern engineering and chemicals.

Hu-chou plays a similar role in the area along the southern shore of the T'ai Hu lake. It has an old-established silk industry, and is a very important rice market.

Hang-chou is the provincial capital, and by far the largest city

in Chekiang. An ancient city, which rose to prominence in the 7th and 8th centuries, and which later became the immensely wealthy capital of the Southern Sung empire. Hang-chou became important as the southern terminus of the Grand Canal. Although it was once a seaport, its harbour has for many centuries been fit only for the smallest coastal shipping, and for river shipping on the Ch'ien-t'ang river leading into the interior of the province. Traditionally the centre of a wide variety of handicrafts, producing silks, cottons and paper, Hang-chou has been considerably industrialised since 1949. The silk industry has been greatly expanded, and some plants installed for the manufacture of cotton textiles and burlap from local jute. There is a small steel plant, some engineering works and a diversified chemical industry. It also remains a major transport centre, both for canal traffic, and for rail traffic from Kiangsi and Hunan. Hang-chou is a great beauty spot, with many famous historical sites, and remains a major cultural centre, with a number of institutions of higher education.

The Shao-hsing–Ning-po plain Along the southern shore of Hang-chou bay are a series of low alluvial plains, backed by the hilly uplands of the Kuiai-chi Shan, Ssu-ming Shan and T'ien-t'ai Shan ranges, which rise to 1,000 m or so. Here the valleys are cultivated in paddy fields, while much of the hill land remains wooded. The coastal plain has a dense irrigation system and canals linking Ning-po with the estuary of the Ch'ien-t'ang river. Flood control works have made life in this plain more secure in recent years. The main crop is rice. Double-cropped rice was first cultivated in this area, and is sometimes grown with a third spring-ripening crop. In the uplands, rice is usually grown with wheat or barley. Cotton, mostly exported to Shanghai is widely grown, and jute, ramie and rape-seed are important economic crops. The uplands are one of the great tea-producing areas of China. Timber is an important local resource, although most of the primary forest was cut long ago, and silk is produced widely. Along the coast fisheries are important, particularly in the Chou-shan archipelago off the coast. Salt is also produced in large quantities in the coastal districts.

Shao-hsing is situated in the middle of the waterway system of the plain and has been a major administrative town since early times. Famous in the past for its handicrafts, and above all for its rice wines, it remains largely an agricultural market centre, although some modern industry, including a small steel plant, was developed in the late 1950s.

Ning-po rose to importance later than Shao-hsing, during the 7th and 8th centuries, when it became a major port. It was a port for both the coastal trade, and also for the trade with the Ryukyu Islands and Japan. It later flourished as a trading city for exports from Chekiang, and its merchants were very impor-

tant as bankers in the 18th and early 19th centuries. As Shanghai rose, however, Ning-po's importance dwindled, although it remained an important second rank port. There was some industrial development before the Second World War, and the city's importance grew after 1955 when it first received a rail link. Traditionally its industries were textiles and food-processing. These were greatly expanded in the 1950s, and an engineering industry was founded, making diesel engines, agricultural implements, and building small ships for the fishing industry. It is a very important fishing port.

The south-western uplands These comprise the upper basin of the Ch'ien-t'ang river and its tributaries. It is the most sparsely peopled and backward port of Chekiang, a region of wooded hills, mostly under 1,000 m, separated by valleys and river basins. In these plains paddy fields make up most of the acreage, growing double-cropped rice often with corn, wheat or barley. Sugar-cane is grown in the Chin-hua and I-niao areas. Since 1949 the silk industry has been considerably developed and tea is produced around Ch'un-an and Chien-te. The Chin-hua basin is famous for its citrus fruits and there is a great deal of excellent timber. Although Chekiang has little coal, there is considerable development of hydro-electric power. There are two major schemes on the Ch'ien-t'ang river, one at Huang-t'an-k'ou near Chü-hsien, the other, a very large project on the Hsin-an Chiang near the Anhwei border. This plant is linked by a power grid to Hang-chou and Shanghai.

Chin-hua on the railway from Hang-chou to Kiangsi, is the main market centre of this region. It has developed some food-processing industry.

Lan-ch'i has developed an aluminium industry, using electric power from the Hsin-an Chiang scheme.

The south-eastern uplands This area of coastal highlands is drained by the Ou Chiang and Ling Chiang. It is the highest and most rugged land in Chekiang, with steep slopes and narrow valleys with little cultivable land. What land there is is intensively farmed using double-cropped rice, with green fertiliser crops of wheat, barley, rape-seed, sweet potatoes. Sugar cane is widely grown on the coast, and jute, ramie and cotton are important economic crops. Citrus fruits are a speciality of the area, and there is a good deal of tea production. Forestry is also important, and the area produces timber and wood oils, which are collected for shipment at Wen-chou.

Wen-chou is the region's main city and commercial centre. Although the city is hampered by poor communications with its hinterland, it is an important local port, exporting tea, timber and fruits. It has a paper industry, and various food-processing industries. Most of its exports go to Shanghai.

AREA
101,800 square kilometres

POPULATION
31,000,000

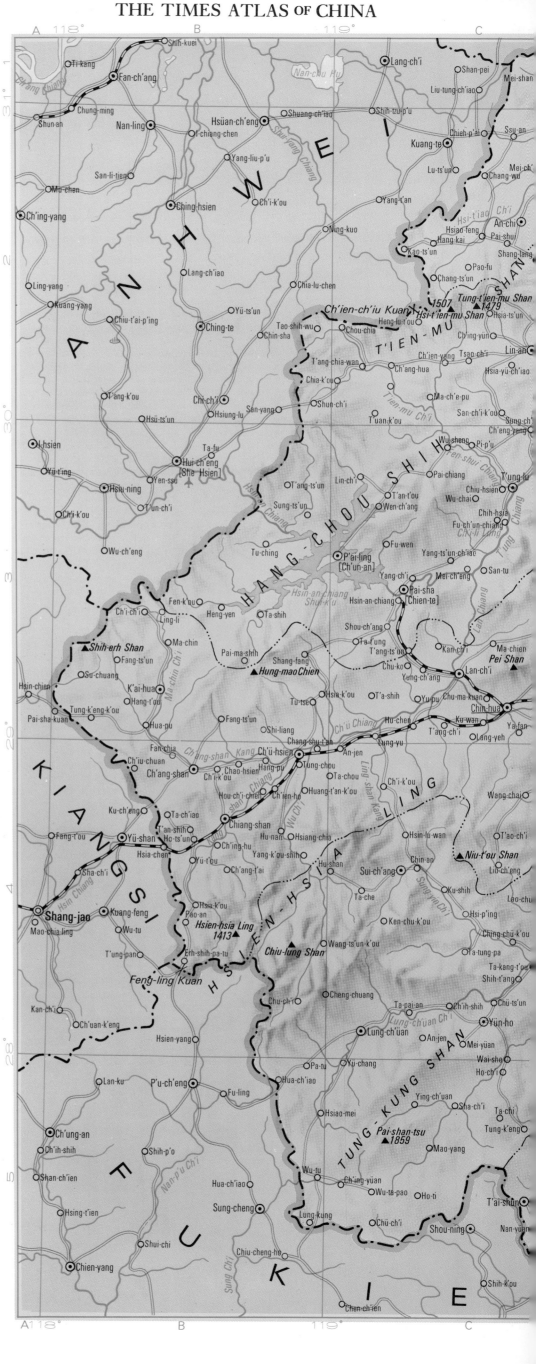

1:1 320 000

CHEKIANG PROVINCE
CHE-CHIANG SHENG
浙江省

3 shih	*municipalities*	
8 ti-ch'ü	*regions*	
64 hsien	*counties*	

capital **Hang-chou Shih**	D2	杭州市
Chien-te Hsien		建德县
centre: Pai-sha	C3	白沙
Ch'un-an Hsien		淳安县
centre: P'ai-ling	C3	排岭
Fu-yang Hsien	C2	富阳县
Hsiao-shan Hsien	D2	萧山县
Lin-an Hsien	C2	临安县
T'ung-lu Hsien	C3	桐庐县
Yü-hang Hsien		余杭县
centre: Lin-p'ing	D2	临平县
Ning-po Shih	E3	宁波市
Wen-chou Shih	D5	温州市

Chia-hsing Ti-ch'ü		嘉兴地区
centre: Hu-chou	D2	湖州
An-chi Hsien	C2	安吉县
Ch'ang-hsing Hsien	C1	长兴县
Chia-hsing Hsien	D2	嘉兴县
Chia-shan Hsien	D2	嘉善县
Hai-ning Hsien		海宁县
centre: Hsia-shih	D2	硖石
Hai-yen Hsien		海盐县
centre: Wu-yüan-chen	D2	武原镇
P'ing-hu Hsien	E2	平湖县
Te-ch'ing Hsien	D2	德清县
T'ung-hsiang Hsien	D2	桐乡县
Wu-hsing Hsien		吴兴县
centre: Hu-chou	D2	湖州

Chin-hua Ti-ch'ü		金华地区
Ch'ang-shan Hsien	B4	常山县
Chiang-shan Hsien	B4	江山县
Chin-hua Hsien	C3	金华县
Ch'ü Hsien		衢县
centre: Ch'ü-hsien	B4	
I-wu Hsien	D3	义乌县
K'ai-hua Hsien	B3	开化县
Lan-ch'i Hsien	C3	兰溪县
P'u-chiang Hsien	C3	浦江县
Tung-yang Hsien	D3	东阳县
Wu-i Hsien	C4	武义县
Yung-k'ang Hsien	D4	永康县

Chou-shan Ti-ch'ü		舟山地区
centre: Ting-hai	F2	定海
P'u-t'o Hsien	F3	普陀县
Sheng-ssu Hsien		嵊泗县
centre: Ts'ai-yüan-chen	F2	菜园镇
Tai-shan Hsien		岱山县
centre: Kao-t'ing-chen	F2	高亭镇
Ting-hai Hsien	F2	定海县

Li-shui Ti-ch'ü		丽水地区
Ch'ing-t'ien Hsien	D4	青田县
Chin-yün Hsien	D4	缙云县
Li-shui Hsien	C4	丽水县
Lung-ch'üan Hsien	C4	龙泉县
Sui-ch'ang Hsien	C4	遂昌县
Yün-ho Hsien	C4	云和县

Ning-po Ti-ch'ü		宁波地区
Chen-hai Hsien	E3	镇海县
Feng-hua Hsien	E3	奉化县
Hsiang-shan Hsien		象山县
centre: Tan-ch'eng	E3	丹城
Ning-hai Hsien	E3	宁海县
Tz'u-ch'i Hsien		慈溪县
centre: Hu-shan	E2	浒山
Yin Hsien		鄞县
centre: Ning-po	E3	宁波
Yü-yao Hsien	E2	余姚县

Shao-hsing Ti-ch'ü		绍兴地区
Sheng Hsien		
centre: Sheng-hsien	D3	嵊县
Chu-chi Hsien	D3	诸暨县
Hsin-ch'ang Hsien	D3	新昌县
Shang-yü Hsien		上虞县
centre: Pai-kuan	D2	百官
Shao-hsing Hsien	D2	绍兴县

T'ai-chou Ti-ch'ü		台州地区
Hsien-chü Hsien	D4	仙居县
Huang-yen Hsien	E4	黄岩县
Lin-hai Hsien		临海县
centre: T'ai-chou	E4	台州
San-men Hsien		三门县
centre: Hai-yu	E3	海游
T'ien-t'ai Hsien	E3	天台县
Wen-ling Hsien	E4	温岭县
Yü-huan Hsien		玉环县
centre: Huan-shan	E4	环山

Wen-chou Ti-ch'ü		温州地区
Jui-an Hsien	D5	瑞安县
Lo-ch'ing Hsien	D4	乐清县
P'ing-yang Hsien	D5	平阳县
T'ai-shun Hsien	C5	泰顺县
Tung-t'ou Hsien	E5	洞头县
Wen-ch'eng Hsien		文城县
centre: Ta-hsüeh	D5	大峃
Yung-chia Hsien	D4	永嘉县

HONAN
PROVINCE

HONAN is one of the smallest Chinese provinces, and one of the most densely peopled. Only Kiangsu and Shantung have denser populations. It is also one of the oldest settled areas of China. The north of the province was the site of various neolithic cultures, the homeland of the Shang state in the 2nd century BC, and the first Chinese bronze culture. The area of Lo-yang became the second capital of the Chou dynasty, and the capital of the Later Han and of many other dynasties during the first millenium. During this period the plain of eastern Honan was the most populous and heavily peopled area of China. In the 10th century K'ai-feng, already one of China's richest commercial cities, became the capital of the Sung dynasty (from 960–1127). Although the area never regained its former political eminence, it has remained an important economic region, in spite of the fact that it has suffered a succession of natural disasters: flooding of the Huang Ho, which has changed its course several times, causing great destruction, droughts, and plagues of locusts. Since 1949 water-control schemes have been constructed both on the Huang Ho and on the Huai river in the south of the province, which have reduced the danger of floods and made irrigation possible over far more of the plain. In addition, the region including Cheng-chou, Lo-yang and K'ai-feng was built up during the 1950s as a centre of modern industry.

Northern Honan This area, which lies to the north of the Huang Ho at the foot of the towering T'ai-hang range on the Shansi border, forms a part of the great plain of Hopeh and western Shantung. Apart from some saline areas in the north-east, it is a fertile alluvial plain. Its climate is harsher than that of the rest of the province, with a rainfall of 500 mm to 650 mm and a growing season of 240 frost-free days. January temperatures average only −2°C (28°F). The rainfall is very largely confined to the summer; spring droughts are common. The summers are hot, with average temperatures around 27°C (81°F). Much of the land has traditionally been farmed in dry fields, the main crops being winter wheat followed by kaoliang or corn. New varieties of wheat introduced in the 1950s greatly increased production. The main economic crop is cotton, which is widely cultivated between Hsin-hsiang and An-yang. On the poor lands along the Huang Ho peanuts are an important crop. Elsewhere rape-seed and sesame are grown. Tobacco is grown to some extent.

River control on the Huang Ho has strengthened the dykes, and also involved the construction of a canal from the Huang Ho to the Wei river. This has provided a water route from Hsin-hsiang to Tientsin, and also made possible a system of irrigation in the plain north of the Huang Ho between Cheng-chou and Hsin-hsiang. This was completed in 1953.

Along the foot of the T'ai-hang mountains are a number of important coal-mining centres. The oldest of these is at *Chiao-tso*, which produces over five million tons of anthracite per annum. Further north, near An-yang, are a series of mines at *Ho-pi*, which produce a further three million tons per year.

The main cities of the area all lie on the ancient road along the foot of the T'ai-hang range, followed since early in this century by the Peking–Han-k'ou railway.

An-yang, the last capital of the Shang, and an ancient administrative city is the northernmost. An-yang's modern industrial growth began in 1957 with the development of the nearby Ho-pi coalfield. A small iron and steel plant was built in 1958–60 using local iron ore.

Hsin-hsiang further south is a major transport centre, where the Peking–Han-k'ou railway crosses the Wei, which provides a water route to Tientsin. It also has a railway to the coal mines at Chiao-tso, which has been extended to Ch'ang-chih and the coalfield at Lu-an in south-eastern Shansi. It remains an important regional centre and an industrial town with textile and food-processing plants. It also has cement and rayon factories.

The Lo-yang – Cheng-chou – K'ai-feng region This belt of the middle Huang Ho valley has characteristics similar to those of the northern plain, but it is notable as the main industrial region of the province. It was an ancient east-west route, unified in this century by the Lung-hai railway. The main industrial centres are linked by a power grid which was to have been fed by the ambitious San-men hydro-electric scheme, left uncompleted in the early 1960s when Soviet aid ceased. The grid is fed by thermal generating plants at Lo-yang and Cheng-chou.

Lo-yang, one of China's most ancient cities and several times a dynastic capital, declined after the 10th century AD into a provincial administrative centre. Under the First Five Year Plan, it was chosen as a new industrial city under the scheme to relocate industry. It rapidly became a very important centre of the engineering industry, producing heavy machinery, mining plant, ball bearings and tractors. It also produces cotton textiles and cement on a large scale.

Cheng-chou became the provincial capital in 1954. It too had been an ancient city, the seat of one of the capitals of the Shang in the second millenium BC, but had later declined into a small provincial city. Its modern growth began with the construction of the Peking–Han-k'ou railway, and then the Lung-hai railway, which made it a vital rail junction. It rapidly rivalled and surpassed K'ai-feng as the chief market and communication centre for the rich Honan plain. In the 1950s it was selected for industrial development, particularly as a centre of the cotton textile industry. It also builds textile machinery on a large scale, and has large flour mills and oil-extraction plants. In recent times it has also become a major centre of aluminium production.

K'ai-feng was formerly the provincial capital. It first became important as a major commercial centre in the 7th and 8th centuries, as a port at the head of the Pien Canal, joining the Huang Ho to the Huai and the Yangtze. From 907 until 1127 it was the national capital. Later, the new Grand Canal built under the Mongols passed further east, and K'ai-feng gradually declined. With the coming of railways K'ai-feng was again left on one side, until the construction of the Lung-hai line, and its function as a regional market centre was assumed by Cheng-chou. In the 1950s, however, it too began a period of industrial growth, as a centre of production for agricultural machinery. In the 1960s it acquired a large fertiliser plant, and began smelting zinc. It has not, however, undergone rapid expansion on the scale of Lo-yang or Cheng-chou.

The western Honan mountains The western third of Honan is taken up by a complex of mountain ranges and basins, which represent the eastern extremity of the great Chin-ling range. The main ranges are the south-west to north-east Hsiung-erh Shan range in the north, mainly between 1,000 and 1,500 m, the hills south of the Lo valley culminating in the ancient holy mountain of Sung Shan (1,359 m), and the Fu-niu range with peaks up to 2,343 m, which strikes north-west to south-east. This region is comparatively sparsely peopled, and much of it still has forest cover. In the valleys and basins, the agriculture is mainly based on winter wheat grown in combination with millet, corn or kaoliang. Oats and buckwheat are grown in the upland areas. Goats and sheep are raised in considerable numbers. The area has poor communications and few towns of any size. In the north the Huang Ho flows in a narrow valley between the mountains of Honan and those of south-western Shansi. At one point it flows through a series of narrow gorges at San-men. This was the site of the hydro-electric scheme begun in the late 1950s.

The Nan-yang basin In the south-west of the province, between the Fu-niu Shan and T'ung-pai Shan ranges is the fertile basin around Nan-yang, part of the drainage basin of the Han Shui and its tributaries. This area, sheltered by the mountains, has a much warmer climate, with winter temperatures about 3°C (37°F), about 1,000 mm of rainfall and a growing season of more than 280 days. This area grows rice and winter wheat. Cotton, sesame, rape-seed are also important. It is also a major silk producing area.

Nan-yang is its commercial centre, and the centre of an extensive highway network. It was joined by rail to Lo-ho in 1969. However, its natural connections have always been with Hsiang-fan in northern Hupeh, rather than with Honan.

The east Honan plain This flat, featureless alluvial plain forms part of the drainage basin of the Huai river. In the 1950s much work was done on flood control in this area and a series of dams were built on various headwaters of the Huai Ho, in the foothills of the western mountains. In the mid-1960s the new Pien-ho canal was built to relieve the overloaded northern tributaries of the Huai, diverting some of their waters through northern Anhwei. The climate of this area becomes both warmer and wetter towards the south. In the north annual rainfall is about 750 mm, in the south 1,000 mm, with a growing season of more than 280 days. Most of this plain is devoted to the cultivation of winter wheat with corn, kaoliang and sweet potatoes. Cotton is also an important crop, and tobacco is grown widely in the region around Hsü-ch'ang. Along the foothills of the western mountains are a series of important coal mining centres. In the north are two new and comparatively small mines at Mi-hsien and Yi-yang near Lo-yang. The most important mining centre, producing somewhat less than 10,000,000 tons annually, and with vast reserves, is P'ing-ting-shan. These mines began production in the late 1950s, and produce coking coal, much of which is sent to the iron and steel complex at Wu-han.

The main regional market centres of the plain are *Hsü-ch'ang*, which is the chief outlet for the south-western district around Nan-yang, and the centre of the tobacco trade; *Shang-ch'iu*, which is the main market and collecting centre for the eastern plain and for the adjoining areas in Shantung and Anhwei; and *Hsin-yang* in the upper Huai Ho valley in the extreme south. Hsin-yang is the centre of an area where extensive irrigation works have been built since the 1950s, and where rice and winter wheat are the main crops. It is a market for rice and wheat, and for sesame, which is an important local crop.

AREA
167,000 square kilometres

POPULATION
50,320,000 (other estimates up to 55,000,000)

36°1

P'ing-shun

Ch'ang-chih

Fu-hsien   I-ch'uan   Chi-hsien   Chin-kang-ling   Ku-hsien   Fu-ch'eng [An-tse]   Ch'ang-tzu   Hu-kuan

Lo-ch'uan   Lin-fen   Tung-yü

Huai-pai   Liang-tzu-chia   Hsiang-ning   Fu-shan   Shu-chang

S H A N S I

Huang-ling   Shih-pao [Huang-lung]   Ku-ch'eng   Hsiang-fen   Hsi-p'ing   Kao-p'ing   Ling-ch'uan

Fen-ch'eng   Ch'in-shui   Yuan-shih   Fu-ch'eng

Feng-yüan   Yü-men-k'ou   I-ch'eng   Ch'ü-wo   Hou-ma   Yang-ch'eng   Chin-ch'eng

T'AI-HANG

35°   Ch'eng-ch'eng   Han-ch'eng   Ho-chin   Chi-shan   Hsin-chiang   Li-yüan   Wu-ts'un

Pai-shui   Chiang-hsien   Ta-k'ou   Chiao-tso

Ho-yang   Chieh-tien [Wan-jung]   Wen-hsi   Li Shan 2359   Hsia-ch'uan   Po-shan   Po-ai   Tai-wang   Hsiu-wu

Jung-ho   Li-ko-t'a

Lin-chin   Yen-ching   Liu-chang-chen [Yüan-ch'ü]   Hsi-ch'eng Shan 1705   Shao-yüan   K'o-ching   Shang-chuang   Hsi-hsiang

Lin-i   Hsia-hsien   Huang-pei-chiao   Wang-wu   Ssu-li   Chi-yüan   Ch'in-yang   Ta-hung-ch'iao

P'u-ch'eng   Yün-ch'eng   An-i   Chiu-yüan-ch'ü   Shih-ching   Chiao-ti   Ch'eng-liu   Pai-hsiang   Ch'ung-i   Chao-pao   Tao-hua-yü   Wen-hsien

Tang-mu   Ta-li   Ch'iao-i   Chieh-chou   C H U N G - T ' I A O   S H A N   Sheng-jen-chien [P'ing-fu]   Yang-shao   P'o-t'ou   Nan-chuang   Meng-hsien   Ssu-shui

Yung-chi   Yü-hsiang   Mao-chin-tu   Chiao-ti   Men-ch'ih   Heng-shui   Ch'ang-hua [Meng-chin]   Chiu-meng-chin   Chiu-kung-hsien   Sha-yü-kou

Wu-lao Feng 1900   San-men-hsia [Shan Hsien]   Ying-hao   Ch'ien-ch'iu   T'ieh-men   Ch'ang-hua   P'ing-lo   Hsiao-i [Kung Hsien]   Her-shih-kuan   Hsing-yang

Jui-ch'eng   Chang-mao   Kuan-yin-t'ang   I-ma   Hsin-an   Yen-shih   Ts'ui-miao

Feng-ling-tu   Wu-yüan-ts'un   Kung-ch'ien   Ho-ti-ts'un   Hsi-ts'un   Tzu-chien   Ku-shui   Lo-yang

Wei-nan   Ch'ih-shui   Hua-yin   T'ung-kuan   Yang-p'ing   Chiao-ts'un   Yang-tien   Ch'uan-k'ou   Han-ch'eng   Liu-ch'üan   Yen-ch'iu   Yüan-ya   Lung-men   Li-ts'un   Fu-tien   Kou-shih   Sung Shan 1359   M-hsien

3   Ling-k'ou   Hua-hsien   Hsüeh-chia-ying   Kuo-lüeh-chen [Ling-pao]   I-yang   P'eng-p'o-chen   Teng-feng   Lu-tien   Ch'ao-hua

Hsin-feng-chen   Lu-ling Kuan   San-hsiang   Lo Ho   Ch'ün-chao   Ta-chin-tien   Pai-sha Shui-k'u

Chin-tui-ch'eng   Hsün-chien-ssu   Chu-yang-chen   Kuan-tao-k'ou   Ch'ang-shui   Lo-ning   Tung-chao-pao   Pai-yang   Ying-yang   Pai-sha   Rai-sha

H S I A O   S H A N   Wang-fan   Pai-ho   Ming-kao   Nei-pu   Lin-ju-chen   Shun-tien

Hou-tzu-chen   Tu-kuan   Hsing-hua   T'ien-hu   Miao-hsia   Lin-ju   Yü-hsien

Ku-hsieu   Chin-pao Shan 2094   Ju-yang   Hsiao-tien   Chih-fang   Shen-kou

Lan-t'ien   Fan-li   Shang-tien   San-t'un   Chi-liao-chieh   Ching-chia-wa   Hung-ch'ang-ssu   Hsüeh-tien

Yung-feng   Lo-nan   P'an-ho   Lu-shih   Wen-yü   H S I U N G - E R H   S H A N   Ta-chang   Sung-hsien   Shang-chiu   Chung-t'ou

Hei-lung-k'ou   San-yao-ssu   T'an-t'ou   Chiu-hsien   Pei-tzu-chieh   Ta-ying   Pao-feng   Chia-hsien

34°   Shang-hsien   Mo-kou-k'ou   Heng-chien   San-ch'uan   Wa-wu-miao   Liang-wa   Hsiang-ch'eng

Kuan-p'o   W A I - W A N   S H A N   Ch'e-ts'un   Chao-ts'un   Hsia-t'ang   Lu-shan   Shen-lou   P'ing-ting-shan

Chao-chia-wan   Luan-ch'uan   Ho-yü   Erh-lang-miao   Jang-ho   Sha Ho   Chih-yang

Lung-chü-chai [Tan-feng]   Wu-li-ch'uan   Miao-tzu   F U - N I U   S H A N   Mo-t'ien-ling   Chang-liang-tien   Yeh-hsien   Ch'ang-ts'un

Wu-kuan   Mu-miao Ling 2343   Hei-yen-chen   Ch'iao-tuan   Ma-shih-p'ing   Ch'ang-ts'un   Chiu-hsien

Shan-yang   Shang-nan   T'ai-p'ing-chen   Nan-chao   Yün-yang   Sun-kou   Pao-an

Kao-pa-tien   T'u-men   Erh-lang-p'ing   Tung-chieh   Liu-shan   Tu-shu

4   She-wei   Pan-shan-p'ing   Pai-t'u-kang   Shih-men   Kuang-tien   Fang-ch'eng   Shang-tien

Hsi-p'ing   Chung-yang-tien   Hsia-kuan   Tu-li-p'ing   Nan-ho-tien   Huang-lu-tien   Chao-ho

Hsiang-ho   Ting-ho   Hsia-hsia   Ma-shan-k'ou   Shih-ch'ia   Po-wang   Hsiao-shih-tien   Hsiang-ho-kuan

Yün-hsi   Ching-tzu-kuan   Tan-shui   Ch'ih-mei   Chao-tien   An-kao   Mo-p'o   Ch'un-shu

Huang-yün-p'u   Ssu-wan   Shang-chi [Hsi-ch'uan]   Lu-i-miao   Shih-fo-ssu   Hsin-tien   Ch'iao-t'ou   She-ch'i   Yang-ts'e

33°   Nan-hua-t'ang   Nei-hsiang   Ch'ao-p'o   Chen-p'ing   Nan-yang   Kuo-chi

Chin-chia-ying   Chiu-hsi-ch'uan   Kuan-chang-p'u   Lao-ho   Ching-t'ai   Yüan-t'an   Chien-ling   Pi-yang

Pai-ho   Pai-sang   Sung-wan   Ma-teng   Shih-kang   Chia-sung   Hou-chi   Jang-tung   T'ung-ho   Jao-liang   Kuan-chuang   Ku-lou

Yün-hsien   Chang-ts'un   Pu-k'ou-chieh   Pai-niu   Wai-tzu   T'ung-chai-p'u   Wa-tien   Kao-i   Ma-ku-t'ier

Pao-hsia   Yün-yang   Chiu-chün-hsien   Hou-p'o   Wen-ch'ü   Chieh-chung-tien   Pai-ch'iu   Ta-ho-t'un   Pi-tien

Li-kuan-ch'iao   P'eng-ch'iao   Teng-hsien   Shang-t'un

Shih-yen   P'ing-li   T'ang-ho   Chien-ling   Pi-yang

5   Chu-ch'i   Tan-chiang [Chün Hsien]   San-kuan-tien   Lin-p'a   Sang-chuang   Kuo-t'an   Shang-t'un   P'ing-shih

Te-sheng-p'u   Liu-li-p'ing   Ts'ao-tien   Meng-chia-lou   Hsin-yeh   Hei-lung-chen   Ch'i-i   Ku-miao

Hsiao-tien-tzu   Kou-lin   Tung-kao-ying   Hu-yang-chen   T'ung-pai

Wei-chia-chi   Hsin-tien

Kuang-hua [Lao-ho-k'ou]   Heng-ch'ü-ho   San-ho-tien

Shih-hua-chieh

6   Ch'uan-ch'i   Shuang-ho   Chang-wan   Tsao-yang   Wu-shan

32°   T'ai-p'ing-tien   Fan-ch'eng   Hsing-lung

K'ai-feng   Hsiang-fan   Huang-lung   Wu-tien   T'ang-hsien-chen

Pao-k'ang   Hsiao-ho   Hsin-chi   T'a-erh-war

S Z E C H W A N   I-ch'eng   Huan-t'an

H U P E H   Shuang-ho   Mao-tz'u-fan   Sui-hsien

A   110°   B   111°   C   112°   D   113°

S H E N S I

H A N   S H U I

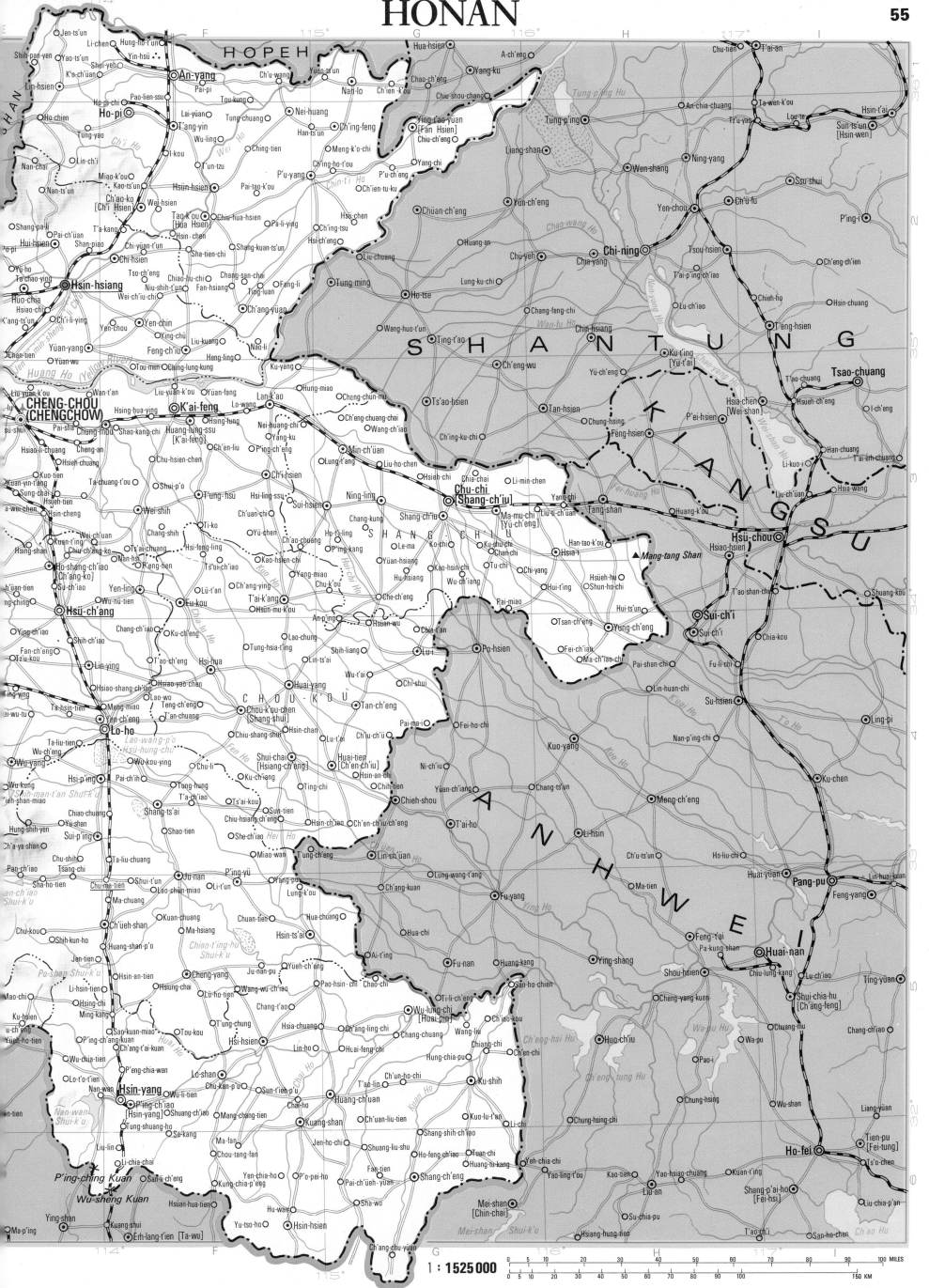

HONAN PROVINCE
HO-NAN SHENG
河南省

14 shih	*municipalities*	
10 ti-ch'ü	*regions*	
110 hsien	*counties*	

capital Cheng-chou Shih	E3	郑州市
An-yang Shih	F1	安阳市
Chiao-tso Shih	E2	焦作市
Ho-pi Shih	F2	鹤壁市
Hsin-hsiang Shih	E2	新乡市
Hsin-yang Shih	F5	信阳市
Hsü-ch'ang Shih	E3	许昌市
K'ai-feng Shih	F3	开封市
Lo-ho Shih	F4	漯河市
Lo-yang Shih	D3	洛阳市
Nan-yang Shih	D4	南阳市
P'ing-ting-shan Shih	E4	平顶山市
San-men-hsia Shih	C3	三门峡市
Shang-ch'iu Shih		喬丘市
centre: Chu-chi	G3	朱集

An-yang Ti-ch'ü — 安阳地区

An-yang Hsien	F1	安阳县
Ch'ang-yüan Hsien	F2	长垣县
Ch'i Hsien		淇县
centre: Ch'ao-ko	F2	朝歌
Ch'ing-feng Hsien	G2	清丰县
Fan Hsien		范县
centre: Ying-t'ao-yüan	G2	樱桃园
Hsün Hsien		浚县
centre: Hsün-hsien	F2	
Hua Hsien		滑县
centre: Tao-k'ou	F2	道口
Lin Hsien		林县
centre: Lin-hsien	E1	
Nan-lo Hsien	G1	南乐县
Nei-huang Hsien	F2	內黄县
P'u-yang Hsien	G2	濮阳县
T'ang-yin Hsien	F2	汤阴县

Chou-k'ou Ti-ch'ü — 周口地区

centre: Chou-k'ou-chen	F4	周口镇
Ch'en-ch'iu Hsien		沈丘县
centre: Huai-tien	G4	槐店
Fu-kou Hsien	F3	扶沟县
Hsiang-ch'eng Hsien		项城县
centre: Shui-chai	F4	水寨
Hsi-hua Hsien	F4	西华县
Huai-yang Hsien	F4	淮阳县
Lu-i Hsien	G4	鹿邑县
Shang-shui Hsien		商水县
centre: Chou-k'ou-chen	F4	周口镇
T'ai-k'ang Hsien		太康县
Tan-ch'eng Hsien	G4	郸城县

Chu-ma-tien Ti-ch'ü — 驻马店地区

Cheng-yang Hsien	F5	正阳县
Ch'üeh-shan Hsien	F5	确山县
Hsin-ts'ai Hsien	F5	新蔡县
Hsi-p'ing Hsien	E4	西平县
Ju-nan Hsien	F5	汝南县
P'ing-yü Hsien	F5	平舆县
Pi-yang Hsien	E5	泌阳县
Shang-ts'ai Hsien	F4	上蔡县
Sui-p'ing Hsien	E4	遂平县

Hsin-hsiang Ti-ch'ü — 新乡地区

Chi Hsien		汲县
centre: Chi-hsien	F2	
Ch'in-yang Hsien	D2	沁阳县
Chi-yüan Hsien	D2	济源县
Feng-ch'iu Hsien	F2	封丘县
Hsin-hsiang Hsien	E2	新乡县
Hsiu-wu Hsien	E2	修武县
Hui Hsien		辉县
centre: Hui-hsien	E2	
Huo-chia Hsien	E2	获嘉县
Meng Hsien		孟县
centre: Meng-hsien	D3	
Po-ai Hsien	E2	博爱县
Wen Hsien		溫县
centre: Wen-hsien	E3	
Wu-chih Hsien	E2	武陟县
Yen-chin Hsien	F2	延津县
Yüan-yang Hsien	E2	原阳县

Hsin-yang Ti-ch'ü — 信阳地区

Hsi Hsien		息县
centre: Hsi-hsien	F5	
Hsin Hsien		新县
centre: Hsin-hsien	F6	
Hsin-yang Hsien		信阳县
centre: P'ing-ch'iao	F5	平桥
Huai-pin Hsien		淮滨县
centre: Wu-lung-chi	G5	乌龙集
Huang-ch'uan Hsien	G5	潢川县
Kuang-shan Hsien	F5	光山县
Ku-shih Hsien	G5	固始县
Lo-shan Hsien	F5	罗山县
Shang-ch'eng Hsien	G6	商城县

Hsü-ch'ang Ti-ch'ü — 许昌地区

Ch'ang-ko Hsien		长葛县
centre: Ho-shang-ch'iao	E3	和尚桥
Chia Hsien		郏县
centre: Chia-hsien	E4	
Hsiang-ch'eng Hsien	E4	襄城县
Hsü-ch'ang Hsien	E3	许昌县
Lin-ying Hsien	E4	临颖县
Lu-shan Hsien	D4	鲁山县
Pao-feng Hsien	E4	宝丰县
Wu-yang Hsien	E4	舞阳县
Yeh Hsien		叶县
centre: Yeh-hsien	E4	
Yen-ch'eng Hsien	E4	郾城县
Yen-ling Hsien	F3	鄢陵县
Yü Hsien		禹县
centre: Yü-hsien	E3	

K'ai-feng Ti-ch'ü — 开封地区

Ch'i Hsien		杞县
centre: Ch'i-hsien	F3	
Chung-mou Hsien	F3	中牟县
Hsin-cheng Hsien	E3	新郑县
Hsing-yang Hsien	E3	荥阳县
K'ai-feng Hsien		开封县
centre: Huang-lung-ssu	F3	黄龙寺
Kung Hsien		巩县
centre: Hsiao-i	D3	孝义
Lan-k'ao Hsien	F3	兰考县
Mi Hsien		密县
centre: Mi-hsien	E3	
Teng-feng Hsien	E3	登封县
T'ung-hsü Hsien	F3	通许县
Wei-shih Hsien	F3	尉氏县

Lo-yang Ti-ch'ü — 洛阳地区

Hsin-an Hsien	D3	新安县
I-ch'uan Hsien	D3	伊川县
I-yang Hsien	D3	宜阳县
Ju-yang Hsien	D3	汝阳县
Ling-pao Hsien		灵宝县
centre: Kuo-lüeh-chen	B3	虢略镇
Lin-ju Hsien	D3	临汝县
Lo-ning Hsien	C3	洛宁县
Luan-ch'uan Hsien	C4	栾川县
Lu-shih Hsien	C3	卢氏县
Meng-chin Hsien		孟津县
centre: Ch'ang-hua	D3	长华
Mien-ch'ih Hsien	C3	渑池县
Shan Hsien		陕县
centre: San-men-hsia	C3	三门峡
Sung Hsien		嵩县
centre: Sung-hsien	D3	
Yen-shih Hsien	D3	偃师县

Nan-yang Ti-ch'ü — 南阳地区

Chen-p'ing Hsien	D4	镇平县
Fang-ch'eng Hsien	D4	方城县
Hsi-ch'uan Hsien		淅川县
centre: Shang-chi	C4	上集
Hsi-hsia Hsien	C4	西峡县
Hsin-yeh Hsien	D5	新野县
Nan-chao Hsien	D4	南召县
Nan-yang Hsien	D4	南阳县
Nei-hsiang Hsien	C4	內乡县
She-ch'i Hsien	D4	社旗县
T'ang-ho Hsien	D5	唐河县
Teng Hsien		邓县
centre: Teng-hsien	D5	
T'ung-pai Hsien	E5	桐柏县

Shang-ch'iu Ti-ch'ü — 喬丘地区

centre: Chu-chi	G3	朱集
Che-ch'eng Hsien	G3	柘城县
Hsia-i Hsien	H3	夏邑县
Min-ch'üan Hsien	G3	民权县
Ning-ling Hsien	G3	宁陵县
Shang-ch'iu Hsien	G3	商丘县
Sui Hsien		睢县
centre: Sui-hsien	G3	
Yü-ch'eng Hsien		虞城
centre: Ma-mu-chi	G3	马牧集
Yung-ch'eng Hsien	H4	永城县

HUPEH
PROVINCE

HUPEH province comprises two quite different regions. The eastern two-thirds of the province is an area of low-lying plain forming the northern half of the central Yangtze basin, bounded on the north by the Huai-yang ranges and on the southeast by the Mu-fu Shan range. This plain is drained by the Yangtze and its main northern tributary, the Han Shui. The western third of the province is a very different area, of rugged highlands with small cultivated basins and valleys, which divide Hupeh from Szechwan. The plain area has been settled by the Chinese since the first millenium BC. From the 7th century onwards it was intensively settled, and in the 11th century was already a rice-surplus producing area. In the late 19th century it was the first area in the Chinese interior to undergo considerable modern industrial growth. The mountainous west was very sparsely peopled until comparatively recent times.

The whole province is sheltered from northerly air masses by the northern mountains. It has winter temperatures of about 5°C (41°F), and very hot humid summers with average temperatures of 29°C (84°F) and more. The annual rainfall is over 1,000 mm except in the extreme north of the Han Shui valley, and very much more (1,500 mm and more) in the south-western mountains. The growing season is about 280 days in the north and 300 days in the south. Most of the rain falls in summer, but there is more winter rainfall than in northern China. The whole area was naturally forested, but the lowlands have long ago been cleared. The western mountains, however, are still heavily forested.

South-eastern Hupeh Apart from an area of forested hills and mountains on the south-east border with Kiangsi, along the Mu-fu Shan range, this region consists of a great alluvial plain drained by the Yangtze and the lower course of the Han Shui. The area was originally very swampy. There are still vast areas of lakes, and the Yangtze and other rivers meander through a landscape covered with a dense network of waterways. In the past this area was frequently flooded, and since 1954 two large retention basins have been built, one south of the Yangtze near Sha-shih, the other between the Han Shui and Yangtze west of Han-yang, to accommodate flood water in times of critical flooding. The plain is very intensively cultivated. The main crops are rice, winter wheat, barley and corn, with large areas devoted to the cultivation of cotton and of ramie. The hills of the south are an important tea-producing district.

The main importance of this area, however, is as the industrial region of Hupeh. The south-eastern hills have extremely important iron mines at Ta-yeh and some small anthracite mines. This area was the site of the first modern iron and steel plant in China. The Ta-yeh mines were first operated in the 1890s to feed an iron and steel works at Han-yang (Wu-han). Coal was brought from P'ing-hsiang in Kiangsi. Later the ironworks passed into the possession of the Japanese, who shut down local production of steel, but exported ore from Ta-yeh to Japan. During the Second World War, the plant of the Han-yang iron works was moved to Ch'ung-ch'ing.

Wu-han is by far the region's largest city, and one of the most important industrial complexes in China. It consists of three separate cities, at the confluence of the Han Shui and Yangtze; Han-k'ou, the largest, which developed into a major commercial centre for foreign trade in the Yangtze area during the late 19th century; Han-yang, site of the old iron and steel complex and a major industrial area; and Wu-ch'ang, the administrative centre

of the province, with universities and other public buildings. This is the oldest of the three cities, which replaced Chiang-ling as the main administrative and commercial centre of Hupeh during the Ming period. The three cities were joined by two rail and road bridges over the Han (1954) and the Yangtze (1957). Although the old iron and steel plant was dismantled during the war, Wu-han was designated a major centre for industrial growth in the 1950s, and a huge integrated iron and steel complex was constructed between 1956 and 1959, and later extended. Wu-han produces steel rails and constructional steel, and supplies a varied engineering industry, which manufactures heavy machinery, boilers, diesel engines, lorries, railway rolling stock, ball bearings etc. An aluminium plant was also installed in 1971, and there are various chemical industries and glass-making plants and cement works. Han-k'ou and Han-yang have also large cotton textile mills, and paper mills.

Wu-han's combined population rose from 1,400,000 in 1953 to 2,100,000 in 1957 and is currently estimated to be about 2,700,000.

Huang-shih, about 80 km downstream from Wu-han, is a new industrial centre established in 1950, to include the iron-mining centre of Ta-yeh, Shih-hui-yao the port from which the ore was shipped, and Huang-shih-kang, a major cement manufacturing centre. Huang-shih has an old-established iron and steel plant rebuilt in the late 1950s. But most of the local ore is sent by rail to Wu-han.

O-ch'eng, between Huang-shih and Wu-han on the railway, also has a small iron and steel complex, built between 1958–60.

Sha-shih is the principal city of the western section of the Hupeh plain. It is not only an important port on the Yangtze, but also has a more direct water-route to Wu-han through the maze of waterways north of the river. Sha-shih's growth began in the last century, when it was opened to foreign trade. It rapidly displaced nearby Chiang-ling, the traditional administrative centre of the area. After 1949 there was a good deal of industrial growth here, and Sha-shih has become an important manufacturing city for cotton textiles and cotton yarn, and has many other small food-processing and other industries. It also remains a very important local commercial and marketing centre.

The middle Han Shui basin is an area of flat alluvial plains and low hills, rising to little more than 150 m to 400 m. Intensively cultivated and heavily peopled, though not to the extent of the southern plain, it too is a productive area where agriculture concentrates upon rice, winter wheat, barley, corn, rape-seed and cotton. Wheat is far more important than in the south-eastern plain, since the climate is noticeably cooler, with a shorter growing season, and rice is mostly confined to the area around Hsiang-fan.

Hsiang-fan is the main city of the area, formed in 1950 by the amalgamation of the ancient administrative city of Hsiang-yang and the newer city of Fan-ch'eng. Traditionally a transport centre at the junction of the Han Shui with its northern tributaries the Pei Ho and T'ang Ho, which provide an easy route into Ho-nan, Hsiang-yang lost some of its importance when the Peking–Han-k'ou railway was constructed on a route further east, although it remained the commercial and market centre of the region and an important river port. In 1965 it was connected with Wu-han by rail, as the first stage of a line designed to follow the Han valley westwards. It supports a variety of minor textile and food-processing industries.

Kuang-hua (also known as Lao-ho-k'ou), further up the Han valley, is at the western extremity of the plain, and also plays an important role in trade from the mountainous district of the north-west, and from the Nan-yang basin in southern Honan. A very important trading city before the Second World War, its role has largely been assumed by Hsiang-fan.

North-western Hupeh is a rugged mountainous area drained by the Han Shui and its tributaries. The mountains are not very high – mostly below 1,000 m – but the small basins around Yün-hsien, Chün-hsien, Fang-hsien and Chu-shan are the only areas with any considerable agricultural population. The area is colder than other areas of Hupeh, and has a rainfall below 750 mm, with frequent winter droughts. Wheat, corn, sweet potatoes, some rice, cotton and sesame are the main crops. The productivity of the area, however, is low. Forest products are cultivated; pears, persimmons, walnuts and tung-oil are important. The area has no sizeable towns, and little industry of any sort. At the eastern edge of this region, the Han Shui flows through steep gorges. In 1958 a hydro-electric scheme was inaugurated at Tan-chiang, but has not, apparently, been completed.

North-eastern Hupeh This area consists of the hilly land rising to the ranges known collectively as the Huai-yang ranges – the T'ung-pai Shan and Ta-pieh Shan forming the border with Honan and Anhwei, and the Ta-hung Shan forming the area's western border. The hills are mostly very low (200 m to 300 m), and there are extensive plains. The mountain ranges themselves are formed of much weathered granite and gneiss, and the highest peaks are only about 1,000 m. With the exception of the mountain ranges, this is a densely peopled and highly cultivated area. Rice is the main crop, grown with wheat, cotton, soy beans, ramie, sesame and rape-seed. There is little industry.

The south-western Hupeh mountains This is the most mountainous region of the province, an area of rugged topography with many mountains above 1,000 m, comprising the Wu Shan ranges, which form the boundary between Hupeh and Szechwan, and through which the Yangtze runs in a series of spectacular gorges, and the mountainous basin of the Ch'ing Chiang on the Hunan border. It is an area with large areas of natural forest cover, and with a climate which varies widely. In general it has warmer winters than the Wu-han area, because of the protection given by the mountains against cold winter winds. It also has a very abundant rainfall. Only the area of the Yangtze valley around I-ch'ang, and the basins around En-shih and Hsüan-en, are heavily cultivated. The main crops are rice, corn, wheat, sweet potatoes, yams and soy beans. Corn is the main staple crop in the uplands. Rape-seed, ramie and cotton are also grown. Livestock are extensively raised, and tea production is widespread. Citrus fruits and forest products like tung-oil, varnish and tallow are important. The population is very sparse, however, and the area is the most backward in Hupeh.

I-ch'ang, a river port at the western end of the Yangtze gorges, is the area's only sizeable city. Always an important commercial centre, since the 1950s it has developed chemical and food-processing industries.

I-tu, further downstream, is the main commercial outlet for the Ch'ing Chiang valley, exporting timber, tea and other forest products.

AREA
180,000 square kilometres

POPULATION
33,710,000 (other estimates up to 35,000,000)

SHENSI

SZECHWAN

HUPEI

HUNAN

TA-PA-SHAN

WU-TANG SHAN

YÜN-YANG

HSIANG

Chen-an · Hu-chia-yüan · T'u-men · Shang-nan · Hsi-p'ing · She-wei · Erh-lang-p'ing

Man-ch'uan-kuan · Hsiang-ho · Chung-yang-tien · Hsi-hsia · Ma-shan-k'ou

Hu-pei K'ou · Shang-tien-tzu · Shang-chin · Huang-yün-p'u · Nan-hua-t'ang · Hsiao-tien-tzu · Nei-hsiang · Chen-p'ing

Shih-ch'üan · Kuan-fang-p'u · T'u-men · Ma-an · Yün-hsi · Pai-sang · Kuan-chang-p'u

Han-yin · Lan-ho-p'u · Chia-ho · Tien-ho · Ta-yen · Yün-hsien · An-yang · Shih-ku-kuan · P'eng-ch'iao · Teng-hsien

Yüan-k'ou · Pai-ho · Yang-wei · Chiang-chün-ho · Pao-hsia · Huang-lung-t'an · Chiu-chün-hsien · Lang-ho-tien · Ch'ing-shan-kang · Tan-chiang [Chün Hsien] · San-kuan-tien

An-k'ang · Chia-tzu-chieh · Te-sheng-p'u · Yün-yang · Shih-yen · Liu-li-p'ing · Ts'ao-tien · Hsiao-tien-tzu · Lao-ho-k'ou [Kuang-hua]

Lao-hsien · P'ing-li · Chu-ch'i · Hsien-ho-p'u · Pao-feng · Ta-mu-ch'ang · Wu-tang Shan 1613 · Shih-hua-chieh · Leng-chi · Hsien-jen-tu · Huang-chi

Tso-lung-kou · Kuan-ya-tzu · Chung-feng · Shui-p'ing · Chu-shan · Tung-lang · Shih-ku-ch'eng · Ku-ch'eng · Lung-wang-chi · Lü-yen-i

Lan-kao · Tso-lung-kou · Hsiao-ho-k'ou · Ch'üan-ch'i · Hsia-pa · Men-ku · Chün-tien · Fang-hsien · Ch'ing-feng · Su-ku · Tzu-chin · Sheng-tai · Miao-t'an · T'ai-p'ing-tien · Niu-shou · Chang-wan

Wen-ch'uan · Kuan-tu-k'ou · T'u-ch'eng · Hsi-hao-p'ing · Wang-chia-t'an · Chin-tou · Ssu-p'ing · K'ai-feng · Chao-chia-tien · Shih-men · Lung-chung · Hsiang-fan [Hsiang-yang]

K'ai-hsien · Chiang-k'ou-chen · Tao-shih-p'ing · Fan-chia-ya · Shang-k'an · Pao-k'ang · Hou-p'ing · Huang-hua · Ch'ang-p'ing · Huang-t'an-chou · Nan-chang

Lin-chiang · Hsüeh-chia-p'ing · Ta-shen-nung-chia 3052 · Shen-nung-chia · Cheng-chia-p'ing · Hsieh-ma-ho · Hsüeh-p'ing · Wu-chen · Hsiao-h · Lei-k'ou

Ta-shen-nung-chia · Chen-tsu-ling · Ma-lang-p'ing · Pan-chiao · Liu-chi · An-chi · K'ung-chia-wan

Feng-chieh · Chü-t'ang Hsia · Wu-shan · Wu Hsia · Kuan-tu-k'ou · Hsing-shan · Huang-liang-p'ing · Chang-shu-p'ing · Ma-t'ou-ya · Yang-p'ing · Hsia-k'ou · Hsün-chien-ssu · Chiu-hsien · Hsiao-yen · Hsien-chu · Tung-kung · Su-ch'i · Shih-ch'iao · Nan-ch'iao

Wan-hsien · Yen-tu-ho · Ta-hsia-k'ou · Wu-tu-ho · Hsi-pei-k'ou · Yüan-an · Kuan-yin-ssu

Lung-chü-pa · Chiang-k'ou-chen · Shen-chen-ch'i · Tzu-kuei · Hsiang-ch'i · Lo-t'ien-ch'i · Lien-t'o · Fen-hsiang-ch'ang · Yü-ch'i · Ching-men · o-tao

Chien-nan · Mou-tao · Nan-mu-yüan · Pa-tung · Hsia-pao-p'ing · Mao-p'ing · Huang-ling-miao · Nan-chin-kuan · P'ing-shan-pa · Ta-ch'iao-pien · Hsiao-ch'i-t'a [I-ch'ang] · I-ch'ang · Ya-ch'üeh-ling · T'u-men-ya · Wu-li-p'ing · Tang-yang · Tzu-hua · Ho-jung · T'uan-hu

Pai-yang-pa · Yu-p'i-tse · Mu-fu · Ch'a-tien-tzu · Lung-p'ing · Lü-ts'ung-p'o · Ma-sha · Lang-p'ing · Ho-chia-p'ing · Kao-chia-yen · Ku-lao-pei · Chin-yang-k'ou · Hung-hua-t'ao · Wen-an · Ch'üan-hsin-tien · Shih-hui-ch'iao

Chien-shih · Mao-tien · Chia-shu-p'ing · Wang-p'ing · Ch'ang-liang-tzu · San-li-pa · Kao-tien-tzu · Yeh-san-kuan · Ch'ing-t'ai-p'ing · Huo-shao-p'ing · Tzu-ch'iu · Tu-chen-wan · Ch'ang-yang · Tung-shih · Ma-chia-tien · Chiang-k'ou · Sha-shih

En-shih · Pai-yang-p'ing · Ts'ui-chia-pa · Hung-yen-ssu · Ya-ch'üeh-shui · Lung-feng-pa · Sha-tzu-ti · Hung-r'u-hsi · Yang-liu-ch'ih · Wu-feng · Nieh-chia-ho · P'an-chia-wan · Lao-ch'eng · Yang-hsi · Hsing-chiang-k'ou [Sung-tzu] · T'ai-p'ing-k'ou · Ch'ien-chiang · Pu-i

Lung-chü-pa · Pai-yang-pa · Mou-tao · T'un-pao · San-ch'a · Hsin-t'ang · Kuan-tien-k'ou · Chin-ch'i · Chin-ch'-k'ou · Wu-feng · Ts'ai-hua · Yü-yang-kuan · Ch'ang-lo-p'ing · Liu-chia-ch'ang · Ching-chou · Chiang-ling · Pu-i

Wang-chia-ying · Li-ch'uan · Liang-wu-shan · P'ien-ch'üan · Liang-ho-k'ou · Pa-chiao · Ch'un-mu-ying · Hsia-p'ing · Wan-t'an · Ch'ing-shui-wan · Hsi-chai · Chieh-ho-shih · Tou-shih [Kung-an]

Na-shui-ch'i · Wei-kan-pao · Chiao-yüan · Mao-pa · Hei-tung · Ta-chi-ch'ang · Hsüan-en · Hsiao-kuan · Pai-kou-pa · Ch'i-feng Kuan · T'ai-p'ing-chen · Tsou-ma-p'ing · Wu-li-p'ing · Ch'ing-kuan-tu · Mo-p'an-chou · Tung-yüeh-miao · Nan-p'ing · Huang-shan-t'o

Lo-shui-k'an · Chung-lu · Wen-tou · Ch'ing-p'ing · Kao-lu · Sha-tao-kou · Chiang-k'ou · Mo-shih · Hsieh Shui · Shih-men · Hsin-an · Li-hsien · Chin-shih

Chien-shan · Shih-hui · Hsieh-feng · Chung-pao · Li-chia-ho · Hsin-ch'e · Lung-chia-chai · Ta-yung · Ch'i-chia-ho · Shih-pan-an · Tsou-shih

Ch'ien-chiang · Shih-men-k'an · Ting-chai · Lai-feng · Chiu-ssu · Lung-shan · Sang-chih · Lung-tung-p'ing · Yen-p'o-tu · Tzu-li · Yü-shih-ch'iao · Lin-li

Yü-shan-chen · Chia-ma-ch'ih · Mao-pa · Ch'ang-te

Pao-chia-lou · Cho-shui · Man-shui · Pai-fu-ssu · Nung-ch'e · Lung-chia-chai · Ta-yung · Ch'ih-chia-ho · Shih-pan-an

Kung-t'an · Liang-ho-k'ou · Tang-yen Ho · Ling-ch'i [Yung-shun] · K'o-sha · Shih-t'i-ch'i · Yü-chia-ch'i · Tsou-shih

T'ao-yüan

Map labels

Provinces/regions: HONAN, ANHWEI, KIANGSI

Mountain ranges: TA-PIEH SHAN, MU-FU SHAN, HUANG-SHIH SHIH, TUNG-PAI SHAN

Rivers: Han Shui, Sha Ho, Huai Ho, Chu-kan Ho, Tang Ho, Chueh Ho, Kun Ho, Yun Shui, Han Shui, Tien-men Ho, Chang Chiang (Yangtze)

Major cities: Nan-yang, Hsin-yang, WU-HAN, Hankow [Han-kou], Han-yang, Wu-ch'ang, Huang-shih, Chiu-chiang

Selected place names (north to south, west to east):
Nan-chao, Liu-shan, Yün-yang, Chiu-hsien, Wu-yang, Wu-ch'eng, Shui-chai [Hsiang-ch'eng], Huai-tien [Ch'en-ch'iu], Kou-yang, Chang-ts'un, Pao-an, Wu-kung, Hsi-p'ing, Yüan-ch'iang, T'ai-ho, Fang-ch'eng, Chiao-chuang, Shang-ts'ai, Ch'en-ch'iu-ch'eng, Chieh-shou, Li-hsin, Shih-ch'iao, Sui-p'ing, She-ch'i, Yang-ts'e, Pan-ch'iao, Chu-ma-tien, Ju-nan, P'ing-yü, Lung-k'ou, Fu-yang, Nan-yang, Wa-tien, Pi-yang, Ch'üeh-shan, Cheng-yang, Hsin-ts'ai, Fu-nan, Ying-shang, T'ang-ho, Chu-kou, Huang-shan-p'o, Yüeh-ch'eng, Wu-lung-chi [Huai-pin], Ti-li-ch'eng, Huo-ch'iu, Hsin-yeh, P'ing-shih, Li-hsin-tien, Ming-kang, Hsi-hsien, Lo-shan, Huang-ch'uan, T'ao-lin, Ku-shih, Chung-hsing-chi, Hu-yang-chen, T'ung-pai, Hsiao-lin-tien, Ch'ang-t'ai-kuan, P'ing-ch'iao [Hsin-yang], Chai-ho, Kuang-shan, Tuan-chi, Huo-shan, Fo-tzu-ling

Peaks with elevations: 1078, T'ung-pai Shan, Ta-hung Shan, Ta-wu Shan 783, Chi-kung Shan, Ta-pieh Shan, T'ien-chu Shan 1751

Passes: P'ing-ching Kuan, Wu-sheng Kuan, Sung-tzu Kuan

KIANGSI
PROVINCE

KIANGSI province was first incorporated into the Chinese empire at an early stage but remained sparsely peopled until the 8th century AD. Before this the main expansion of the Chinese settlement south of the Yangtze had been in Hunan, through which ran the main route to Kwangtung. Later the route through Kiangsi became the more important, after the construction of the canal system in the early 7th century diverted traffic to southern China through Yang-chou and the lower Yangtze. The prosperity of Kiangsi developed with the growth of tea planting and silver mining in the province in the late 8th century, when Kiangsi merchants became famous for their wealth. In the late T'ang and Sung (8th to 13th centuries) the area was rapidly settled by Chinese farmers, and became renowned for its academies, and for its scholars and statesmen. In the 19th century Kiangsi's role as a major transport route from Canton to the north was much reduced by the opening of coastal ports to foreign shipping. In the early part of this century Kiangsi first suffered from war-lordism, and later, after 1927, became one of the main bases of the Communist movement. After years of fighting and destruction, the Nationalist government drove the Communists from Kiangsi, on the Long March to the north (1934–5). Almost immediately afterwards came the war with Japan, and Kiangsi was under Japanese occupation from 1938–45.

Kiangsi is more or less co-extensive with the drainage basin of the Kan Chiang, the great tributary of the Yangtze which flows into the Po-yang lake. It is surrounded by mountains, but these have many gaps and easy passes into the neighbouring provinces. Apart from the alluvial plains around the Po-yang lake and the major river in the north, most of the province is hilly country lying between 200 m and 1,000 m.

The climate is sub-tropical, with a growing season lasting about 320 days in the north, and all year round in the far south. The rainfall is abundant – most of the province has more than 1,500 mm per year, apart from the Kan-chou area in the south, which has about 1,250 mm. The north and north-east have considerably more, in some places more than 2,000 mm. There is a marked maximum in the summer months, but even in the winter there is adequate rain. Temperatures average 4° to 5°C (39° to 41°F) in January, slightly lower in the north. The summers are very hot (average 29°C; 84°F) and extremely humid. The province was originally an area of sub-tropical forest. Most of the central areas have long ago been cleared, but the mountainous areas still have very extensive areas of forest.

The central Kiangsi plain The area around the southern side of the Po-yang lake, the lower valleys of the Kan Chiang and Fu Ho rivers, form a broad, low-lying, featureless, alluvial plain with some higher hills to the south and west. The Po-yang lake, which varies greatly in size and shape from season to season, has been surrounded by a complex network of flood-prevention works, and the whole plain has a dense network of waterways, used for drainage, irrigation and local transport. This area is economically the longest settled, most intensively cultivated and most developed part of Kiangsi, forming not only an important route south from the Yangtze, but also a major east-west route

from Chekiang and Shanghai to Hunan. Agriculture concentrates mainly on very intensive cultivation of double-cropped rice with winter wheat. Cotton, sesame and soy beans are important crops.

Nan-ch'ang is the traditional provincial capital, the main trade and administrative centre of the province. The city was formerly a very important staging post on the main trunk route from Peking and Nan-ching to Canton, but suffered something of an eclipse after the 1860s. However, it remained the major regional centre for a rich and productive area, and its importance revived with the building of a rail link to the coast in 1936–7. Since 1949 it has been steadily industrialised and has grown considerably. Its industry largely concentrates on agriculture-based industries (food-processing, cotton textiles, oil extraction), on lumbering and paper-making. But there is also an important engineering industry producing tractors, diesel engines, lorries and aircraft. It also makes automobile tyres. It has a large thermal generating plant using coal from the Shang-t'ang coalfield, near Feng-ch'eng to the south-west. This field, developed since 1959, produces some 2,000,000 tons per year.

Fu-chou is the main regional market centre for the south-eastern plain. It has some rice-milling and fertiliser manufacture.

North-east Kiangsi comprises a hilly and mountainous area to the south of the Yangtze. The only extensive flat areas lie along the valley of the Hsin Chiang and on the eastern shores of the Po-yang lake. These lowlands are intensively farmed and densely populated. Rice predominates. Double cropped rice is common, or rice grown together with winter wheat, rape-seed or soy beans. Cotton, jute, and sesame are also grown. In the uplands single-crop rice is grown in the valleys; wheat, soy beans, corn and sesame on dry upland fields. The uplands are one of China's most important tea-planting areas, particularly in the north and east of the region.

Shang-jao is the traditional economic centre for north-eastern Kiangsi, situated on the railway between Nan-ch'ang and Chekiang. It has some minor industry engaged in tea-processing and waxed paper making.

Ying-t'an, the junction between the Nan-ch'ang–Chekiang railway and the newer railway to Hsia-men and Fu-chou in Fukien was a minor market town until the 1950s but has to some extent replaced Shang-jao as an outlet for goods from Fukien.

Ching-te-chen, in the uplands to the north, is the centre of China's largest and most famous ceramic industry. Although the production of porcelain fell off during the early years of this century, the industry has been revived and extensively modernised since 1949, and the population of Ching-te-chen, most of whom are engaged in the industry in some way, has grown from 50,000 in 1949 to 270,000 today.

North-western Kiangsi This, too, is an area of rugged uplands, the only lowlands being the Yangtze valley and the valley of the Hsiu Shui. The Yangtze lowland, an area of dyked reclaimed land, is largely cultivated with cotton, ramie and rape-seed. In the hilly districts, wheat is more important than rape-seed. In the hilly districts, wheat is more important than

rice as a grain crop. Cotton is also grown, tea is cultivated, and potatoes and sweet potatoes are common crops.

Chiu-chiang is the main city. Situated near the Po-yang lake where it drains into the Yangtze, it was the natural outlet for Kiangsi's trade, and a major river port. It was opened to foreign trade in 1858 and became the port not only for Kiangsi, but also for eastern Hupeh and Anhwei. It remained very important until the 1930s, when first the civil disturbances in Kiangsi, and then the construction of the railway to Shanghai, giving Nan-ch'ang a direct outlet to the sea, diverted a good deal of its trade. It remains the economic centre for northern Kiangsi, a major market for grain, tea, tobacco and ramie, and has an important cotton textile and food-processing industry.

Western Kiangsi This area comprises the hilly middle basin of the Kan Chiang, rising to the series of ranges which form the border with Hunan. Apart from the narrow river plains, much of this area remains forest covered. It is comparatively sparsely peopled, and agriculture is much less intensive and productive than in the northern plains. Rice, sweet potatoes, soy beans and rape-seed are the main crops. The area around Chi-an produces cotton, jute, sesame and sugar cane.

Chi-an is the main economic centre of the middle Kan Chiang valley. A river port, above which the Kan Chiang flows through a series of rapids, it has some industry, including rice mills and a camphor factory.

P'ing-hsiang in the extreme west, on the railway to Ch'ang-sha, is the centre of the most densely peopled area. It is also important as the centre of a very productive coalfield. This was first extensively developed in the 1890s as a fuel source for the Han-yeh-p'ing iron works at Han-yang (Wu-han). After the iron industry closed down in the late 1920s, coal production fell off drastically. However, since the 1950s it has again been developed, and is now the biggest coalfield in southern China, producing somewhat less than 10,000,000 tons per year, much of which is shipped to the industrial cities of Hunan and to the steel complex at Wu-han. It also has an important ceramic industry.

South-eastern Kiangsi This is a very hilly and mountainous area, above 500 m except a few valleys and basins. It has a very warm, wet climate with a very long growing period. The cultivated valleys produce rice, which is mainly double-cropped, soy beans, rape-seed and sweet potatoes. The uplands produce peanuts. In the valleys, jute and sugar cane are important crops. The mountains still have extensive forests, and lumbering is a major winter occupation. Rafts of pine and cedar are floated down to Kan-chou. The forests also produce pitch, resin and turpentine.

The region has considerable mineral reserves. Tungsten is mined in several districts and tin and copper near Ta-yü.

Kan-chou is the main regional centre, a market for grain, sugar, timber and tungsten ore. It has some miscellaneous manufacturing, producing paper, and farming and mining equipment. Its industry is supplied with power from a hydro-electric scheme at Shang-yu, completed between 1954–7.

AREA
160,000 square kilometres

POPULATION
21,070,000 (other estimates up to 25,000,000)

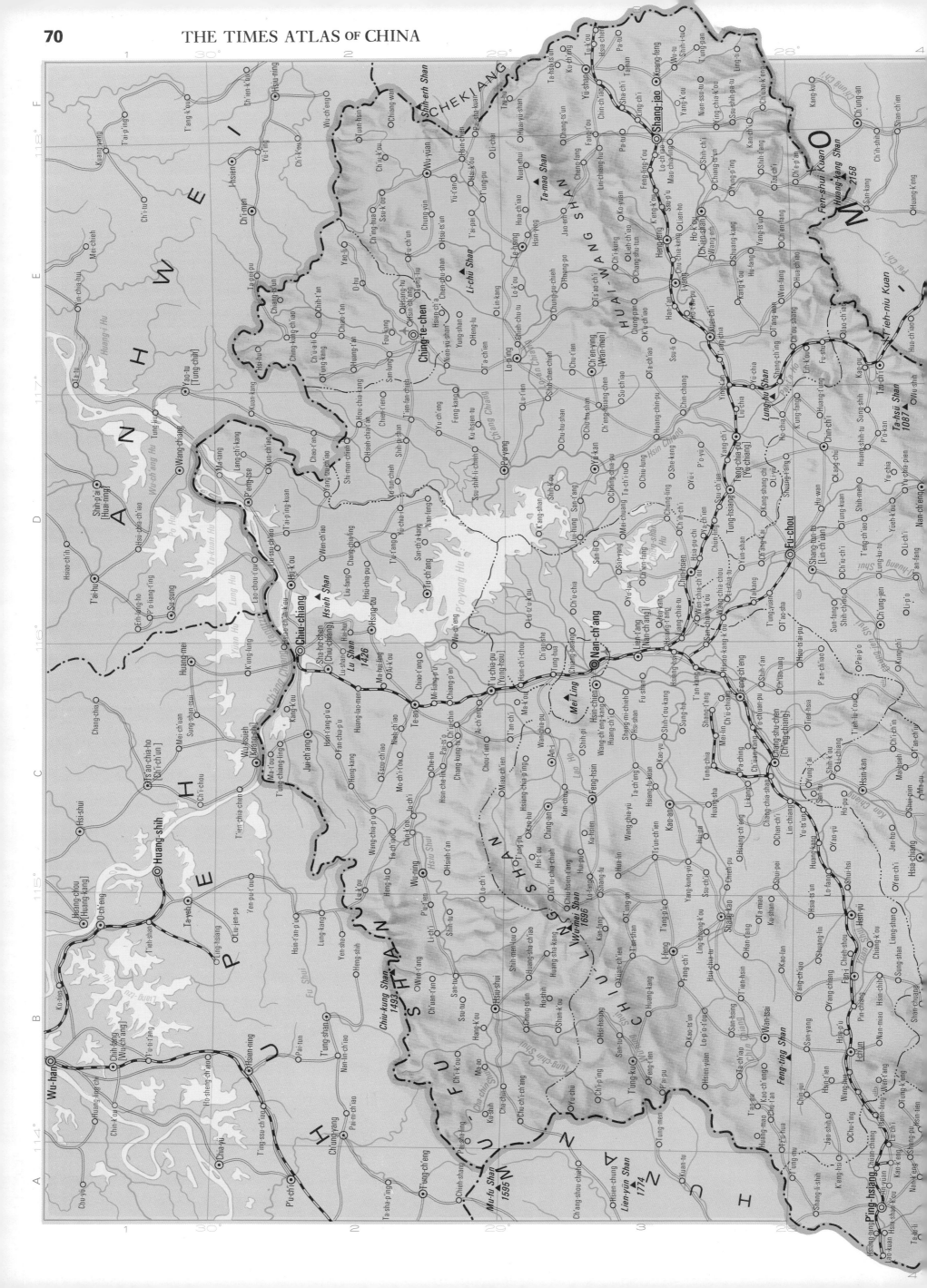

Hsin-ch'ing · Chien-yang · Feng-lo · Fang-tao · Nan-p'ing · Hsia-yang · Hsi-ch'in · Kao-sha · Kuan-p'ing · An-ch'i · T'ung-an · Hsia-men (Amoy)

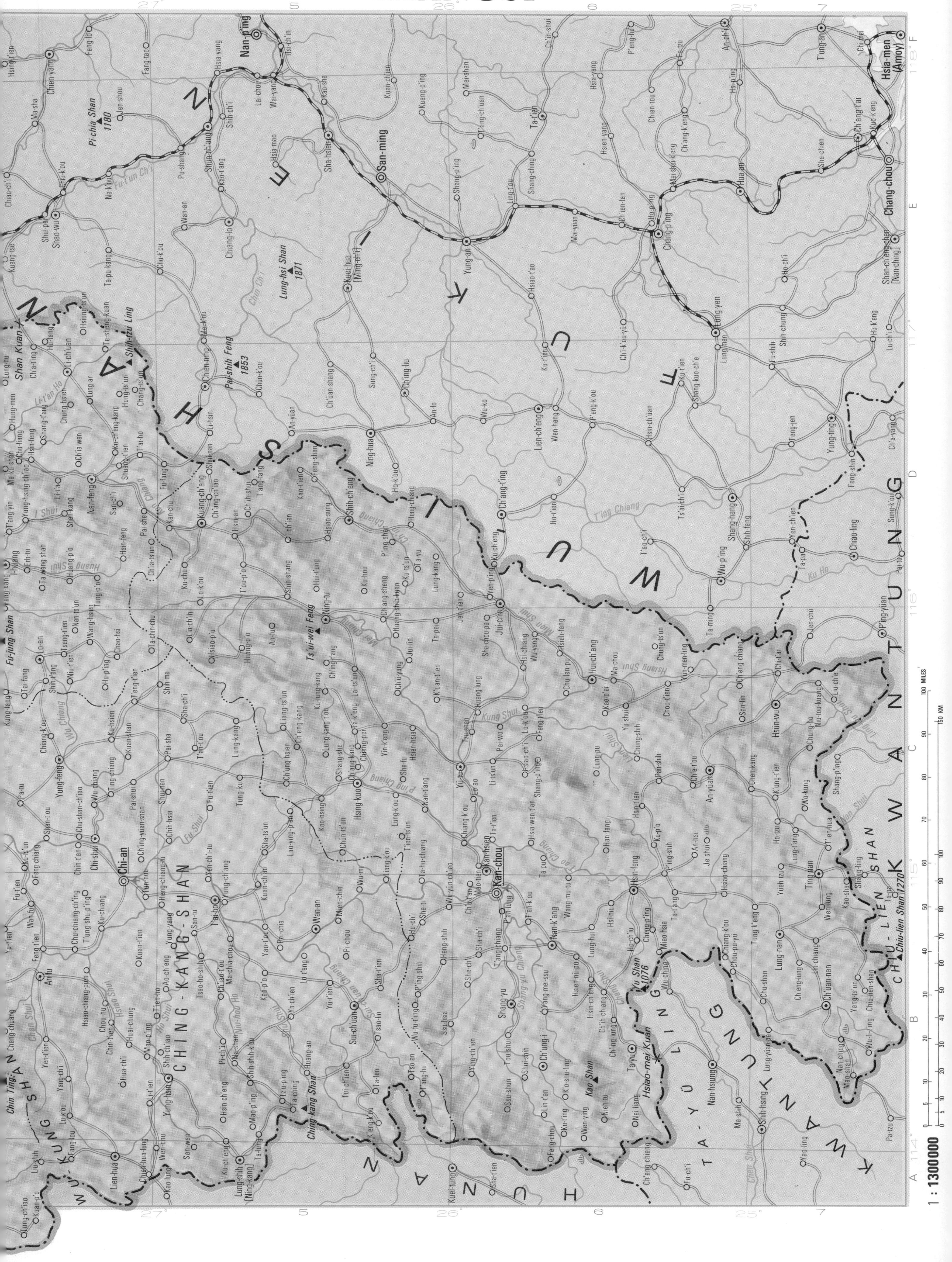

Hsing-tzu · Ma-sha · Shih-pei · Shao-wu · Na-k'ou · Pu-shang · Shuang-ch'ang · Shih-ch'i · Lai-yang · Wan-yang · Shang-p'ing · Mei-shan · Hsiang-yang · P'eng-hu · Ta-tien · Ch'ang-k'eng · Sha-chien · Kuo-k'eng · Chu-ch'ien

Chiao-ch'i · Shui-pei · Shao-wu · Wan-an · Chiang-lo · Hsia-mao · Sha-hsien · San-ming · Kuei-hua [Ming-ch'i] · Kuang-p'ing · Kuan-p'ing · Ta-lien · Chien-tou · Chiang-k'eng · Hsien-yang · Chang-p'ing · Shan-ch'eng [Nan-ching] · Chang-chou

Pi-chia Shan 1180

Lung-hsi Shan 1871

Pai-shih Feng 1853

Shih-tzu Ling

Shan Kuan

Fu-jung Shan

Ts'ui-wei Feng

CHING-KANG-SHAN · Ching-kang Shan

Kao Shan · **Yu Shan 1076** · **Chiu-lien Shan 1270** · CHIU-LIEN SHAN

Hsiao-mei Kuan

TA-YÜ LING

WU-KUNG SHAN

Chi-an · Kan-chou · Nan-k'ang · Jui-chin · Ning-hua · Ch'ang-t'ing · Lien-ch'eng · Yung-ting · Lung-yen · Yung-an · Shang-hang · Wu-p'ing · Hsin-feng · Hsin-fu · Lung-nan · Ting-nan

WANTUNG · KWANTUNG · HUNAN

1 : 1300000

0 10 20 30 40 50 60 70 80 90 100 MILES

0 20 40 60 80 100 120 140 150 KM

KIANGSI PROVINCE
CHIANG-HSI SHENG   江西省

8 shih	municipalities
6 ti-ch'ü	regions
80 hsien	counties

capital Nan-ch'ang Shih	C3	南昌市
Chi-an Shih	B4	吉安市
Ching-te-chen Shih	E2	景德镇市
Chiu-chiang Shih	C2	九江市
Fu-chou Shih	D3	抚州市
Kan-chou Shih	B6	赣州市
P'ing-hsiang Shih	A4	萍乡市
Shang-jao Shih	E3	上饶市

Ching-kang-shan Ti-ch'ü   井冈山地区

centre: Chi-an	B4	吉安
An-fu Hsien	B4	安福县
Chi-an Hsien	B4	吉安县
Chi-shui Hsien	C4	吉水县
Hsia-chiang Hsien	C4	峡江县
Hsin-kan Hsien	C4	新干县
Lien-hua	A4	莲花县
Ning-kang Hsien		宁冈县
centre: Lung-shih	A5	砻市
Sui-ch'uan Hsien	B5	遂川县
T'ai-ho Hsien	B5	泰和县
Wan-an Hsien	B5	万安县
Yung-feng Hsien	C4	永丰县
Yung-hsin Hsien	B5	永新县

Chiu-chiang Ti-ch'ü   九江地区

Chiu-chiang Hsien		九江县
centre: Sha-ho-chen	C2	沙河镇
Hsing-tsu Hsien	D2	星子县
Hsiu-shui Hsien	B2	修水县
Hu-k'ou Hsien	D2	湖口县
Jui-ch'ang Hsien	C2	瑞昌县
P'eng-tse Hsien	D2	彭泽县
Te-an Hsien		德安县
Tu-ch'ang Hsien	D2	都昌县
Wu-ning Hsien	C2	武宁县
Yung-hsiu Hsien		永修县
centre: T'u-chia-pu	C2	涂家埠

Fu-chou Ti-ch'ü   抚州地区

Chin-ch'i Hsien	D4	金溪县
Ch'ung-jen Hsien	D4	崇仁县
I-huang Hsien	D4	宜黄县
Li-ch'uan Hsien	D4	黎川县
Lin-ch'uan Hsien	D4	临川县
centre: Shang-tun-tu	D4	上顿渡
Lo-an Hsien	C4	乐安县
Nan-ch'eng Hsien	D4	南城县
Nan-feng Hsien	D4	南丰县
Tzu-ch'i Hsien	E3	资溪县

I-ch'un Ti-ch'ü   宜春地区

An-i Hsien	C3	安义县
Ching-an Hsien	C3	靖安县
Ch'ing-chiang Hsien		清江县
centre: Chang-shu-chen	C3	樟树镇
Chin Hsien		进县
centre: Chin-hsien	D3	
Feng-ch'eng Hsien	C3	丰城县
Feng-hsin Hsien	C3	奉新县
Fen-i Hsien	B4	分宜县
Hsin-chien Hsien	C3	新建县
Hsin-yü Hsien	B4	新余县
I-ch'un Hsien	B4	宜春县
I-feng Hsien	B3	宜丰县
Kao-an Hsien	C3	高安县
Nan-ch'ang Hsien		南昌县
centre: Lien-t'ang	C3	莲塘
Shang-kao Hsien	B3	上高县
T'ung-ku Hsien	B3	铜鼓县
Wan-tsai Hsien	B3	万载县

Kan-chou Ti-ch'ü   赣州地区

An-yüan Hsien	C6	安远县
Ch'üan-nan Hsien	B7	全南县
Ch'ung-i Hsien	B6	崇义县
Hsin-feng Hsien	B6	信丰县
Hsing-kuo Hsien	C5	兴国县
Hsün-wu Hsien	C7	灵乌县
Hui-ch'ang Hsien	C6	会昌县
Jui-chin Hsien	D6	瑞金县
Kan Hsien		赣县
centre: Kan-hsien	C6	
Kuang-ch'ang Hsien	D5	广昌县
Lung-nan Hsien	B7	龙南县
Nan-k'ang Hsien	B6	南康县
Ning-tu Hsien	C5	宁都县
Shang-yu Hsien	B6	上犹县
Shih-ch'eng Hsien	D5	石城县
Ta-yü Hsien	B6	大余县
Ting-nan Hsien	C7	定南县
Yü-tu Hsien	C6	于都县

Shang-jao Ti-ch'ü   上饶地区

Ch'ien-shan Hsien		铅山县
centre: Ho-k'ou	E3	河口
Heng-feng Hsien	E3	横峰县
I-yang Hsien	E3	弋阳县
Kuang-feng Hsien	F3	广丰县
Kuei-ch'i Hsien	E3	贵溪县
Lo-p'ing Hsien	E3	乐平县
Po-yang Hsien	D2	波阳县
Shang-jao Hsien	E3	上饶县
Te-hsing Hsien	E3	德兴县
Tung-hsiang Hsien	D3	东乡县
Wan-nien Hsien		万年县
centre: Ch'en-ying	E3	陈营
Wu-yüan Hsien	E2	婺源县
Yü-chiang Hsien		余江县
centre: Teng-chia-pu	D3	邓家埠
Yü-kan Hsien	D3	余干县
Yü-shan Hsien	F3	玉山县

HUNAN
PROVINCE

HUNAN, particularly the northern area around Ch'ang-sha, was the seat of one of the most important and powerful Chinese states, Ch'u, from the 7th to the 3rd centuries BC. Ch'u was a rich and influential state with an artistic and literary culture very different from that of northern China. Under the Ch'in and Han dynasties (221 BC to AD 220) its former territories became a part of the newly unified Chinese empire, and many settlers from the north occupied the Ch'ang-sha area and the Hsiang Chiang valley, which formed the main route to Canton and the south. The hill areas remained in the hands of various aboriginal peoples. The main period of growth came between the 8th and 11th centuries, when its population increased five-fold. Under the Ming (1368–1644) and Ch'ing (1644–1911) Hunan became a great grain producing area, shipping vast quantities of rice to the cities of the lower Yangtze region. It also developed a strong sense of regional identity. By the 19th century it began to suffer from population pressure, land shortage, and landlordism, and from the mid-19th century there was a great deal of peasant unrest, among both the Chinese farmers and the minority peoples of the border areas. In the 1920s and 1930s the border area with Kiangsi became a principal stronghold of the Chinese Communists, and Mao Tse-tung and many other prominent leaders came from the province.

Hunan comprises the drainage basin of the Tung-ting lake, into which four major tributaries of the Yangtze flow. These are the Hsiang Chiang, the Tzu Shui, the Yüan Chiang and Li Shui. Apart from the northern plain, most of the province is hilly, and large areas are still forest-covered. The climate is wet, with 1,500 mm of rain in the north and east, and 1,200 mm in the west. The mountainous areas have as much as 1,900 mm. Seventy per cent of the rain falls in summer. Winters are short, dry and cold, with January averages of 3°C to 5°C (37°F to 41°F), and occasional waves of severe cold. Summer temperatures average about 28°C (82°F), and 30°C (86°F) and more in the humid low-lying northern plain. The frost-free growing period is about 260 days in the north and 300 days in the south of the province.

The Tung-ting Lake plain The north of the province is occupied with the flat lacustrine basin around the southern shores of the Tung-ting Lake. This lake has been silting up, and its area has been much reduced since the beginning of this century. The shorelands are gradually being reclaimed, and flood control works extended to bring the polders under cultivation. Most of the land in this region is irrigated paddy field, and has traditionally been a very important rice surplus area. Much of the land is double cropped. The dry, unirrigated fields are largely used for the cultivation of cotton, which is grown in rotation either with wheat or soy beans, or with rape-seed. Ramie is another important fibre crop, grown in the Yüan Chiang valley and around Han-shou. Jute is grown widely on poor, dry fields unsuitable for cotton.

Ch'ang-te is a major port and trans-shipment point not only for agricultural produce of the Tung-ting plain, but also for the upper valley of the Yüan Chiang. It has a large trade in timber and tung oil as well as in rice and cotton.

Yueh-yang is another port and commercial centre at the outlet from the lake into the Yangtze. It too is an important centre of the timber trade, lumber being shipped downstream in rafts to Wu-han, or exported by rail.

The lower Hsiang Chiang basin This area of alluvial plain is surrounded by low, gently rolling hills, rising to the series of south-west to north-east ranges forming the Kiangsi border in the east. It is the oldest, most intensively cultivated, most densely peopled and most highly developed area in the province. As in the northern plain, most of the cultivated area is irrigated paddy field, devoted largely to the production of rice. Multiple cropping has been practised at least since the 18th century. Corn, sweet potatoes, wheat and buckwheat are also grown, but the tendency has been to concentrate more and more on intensive rice culture. Rape-seed, grown for oil, is the only major economic crop. This area, the main industrial district of Hunan, uses power generated in thermal power stations at Ch'ang-sha and Chu-chou, and also hydro-electricity from the Che-ch'i scheme on the Tzu Shui river further west. There are some coal deposits, but coal is brought by rail from the P'ing-hsiang mines in Kiangsi.

Ch'ang-sha is the traditional centre of Hunan, the provincial capital and its main cultural centre. It is a major port, long prosperous as a major rice market, and as a centre of trade in tea, lumber, cotton, ramie and livestock. Since the beginning of the century it has had a diversity of industry, cotton textiles, foodstuffs, rice milling, tea processing, oil extraction, tobacco making. Its growth was accelerated by the extension of a railway from Wu-han in 1918. More recently it has become a centre of precision engineering and machine tool manufacture, agricultural equipment and agricultural chemicals. In the early 1970s an aluminium industry was developed. The population of Ch'ang-sha was 703,000 in 1957.

Chu-chou, unlike Ch'ang-sha, is an entirely modern town. Formerly a small market town, it became the river port for the P'ing-hsiang coal mines at the beginning of the century, when it was connected with P'ing-hsiang by rail. It later became a very important railway junction with the Canton-Wu-han line, and grew into a centre for the manufacture of railway equipment, locomotives and rolling stock. It has also become an important centre of the copper and lead and zinc industries, processing ore from Shui-k'ou-shan, and has established a major chemical fertiliser industry. Its population is estimated at 500,000.

Hsiang-tan was a river port and market centre, which stagnated early in this century when the railway took away much of its trade. Its industrial growth began in 1937. In 1947 its major modern industry, the production of electrical equipment, electric cables and wire was founded. A steel industry was founded in 1959–60 and expanded in the late 1960s. Hsiang-tan also has a large cement works, and cotton textile mills. A recent development has been aluminium smelting. Its population is estimated at about 400,000.

The central Hunan hills This region comprises the middle and upper valleys of the Tzu Shui, Lien Shui and Wu Shui rivers. To the west of the Tzu Shui are quite rugged hills, 500 m and more high. The western part of the region has lower hills, and a larger proportion of the land under cultivation.

The valleys of this area are intensively farmed, but there is a much higher proportion of dry farming than in the north, and there is little grain surplus. Rice is important, but wheat, corn and sweet potatoes are also staples. Rape-seed, peanuts and tobacco are grown as cash crops. This area is the main tea-producing district of Hunan. Tea production began here in the 10th century, and reached a peak in the 19th century. By 1949 the industry had fallen into a decline, but it has since been

revived. Timber is also a very important resource of the area, and there is considerable mineral wealth as Hsi-k'uang-shan, near Hsin-hua, is a very important source of antimony. There are considerable coal and iron reserves, and tungsten is also mined.

Shao-yang is the chief communication and market centre of the area, joined by rail to Ch'ang-sha in 1960. It is an important centre of handicrafts, especially wood and bamboo working, and has a large paper industry. Its population had risen to 118,000 in 1953.

Southern Hunan The south of the province is an area of hills rising to the complex ranges of the Nan-ling, which reach 500–1,000 m. Much of the area is still thickly forested. The main settlements are in the broad upper valleys of the Hsiang Chiang and its tributaries. These valleys are intensively farmed and well irrigated. Paddy rice is the major crop, but double cropping is rare. Dry fields are cultivated with sweet potatoes and wheat. Some peanuts and rape-seed are grown. Timber and forest products, particularly tea-oil are very important. Leng-shui-t'an is the major centre of the lumber industry. The area also has great mineral wealth. There are major lead and zinc mines at Shui-k'ou-shan, south of Heng-yang, and at Ch'en-hsien; reserves of tungsten at I-chang, Ju-ch'eng and elsewhere; tin mines, sulphur, and copper deposits near Ch'en-hsien.

Heng-yang is the major city of southern Hunan, with a population estimated at 300,000. An old-fashioned strategic and route centre, it grew rapidly after the construction of the Canton-Wu-han railway in 1937, and became an important Nationalist base until 1944, when there was considerable industrial growth. Badly damaged in the latter stages of the Second World War, its industry was restored after 1949, but has been overshadowed by the growth of Chu-chou and Ch'ang-sha. It manufactures mining equipment and machinery, diesel and electric motors, tractors, agricultural chemicals and agricultural implements. It has a large thermal generating station. Heng-yang remains a very important rail junction and regional transportation and market centre for the area.

Western Hunan Uplands In the upper valleys of the Yüan Chiang and Li Shui, the country is rugged highlands rising to the Kweichow plateau. The mountains rise to 500–1,000 m and have steep slopes and narrow valleys, with little land suitable for cultivation. The rivers are of little use for navigation and transport is difficult. Much of the area is still settled by minority peoples who cultivate scattered areas in the hills. The uplands produce corn, sweet potatoes and wheat. The valleys are cultivated with rice, wheat and corn, and some cotton, ramie and rape-seed are grown. Timber, tea-oil, tung-oil and tea are important products. But communications are poor, the population sparse, and towns few and small.

Minority Peoples About 97 per cent of Hunan's population are Han Chinese. There are four important minorities. In the western uplands live the Miao (370,000) and T'u-chia (390,000). They have their own autonomous districts. In the extreme south-west are some 125,000 T'ung, a Tai people who have assimilated Chinese culture. They too have their own autonomous *hsien*. Lastly, along the southern border of the province are numerous scattered communities of Yao peoples (70,000) engaged in hill farming and forestry.

AREA
210,500 square kilometres

POPULATION
41,000,000

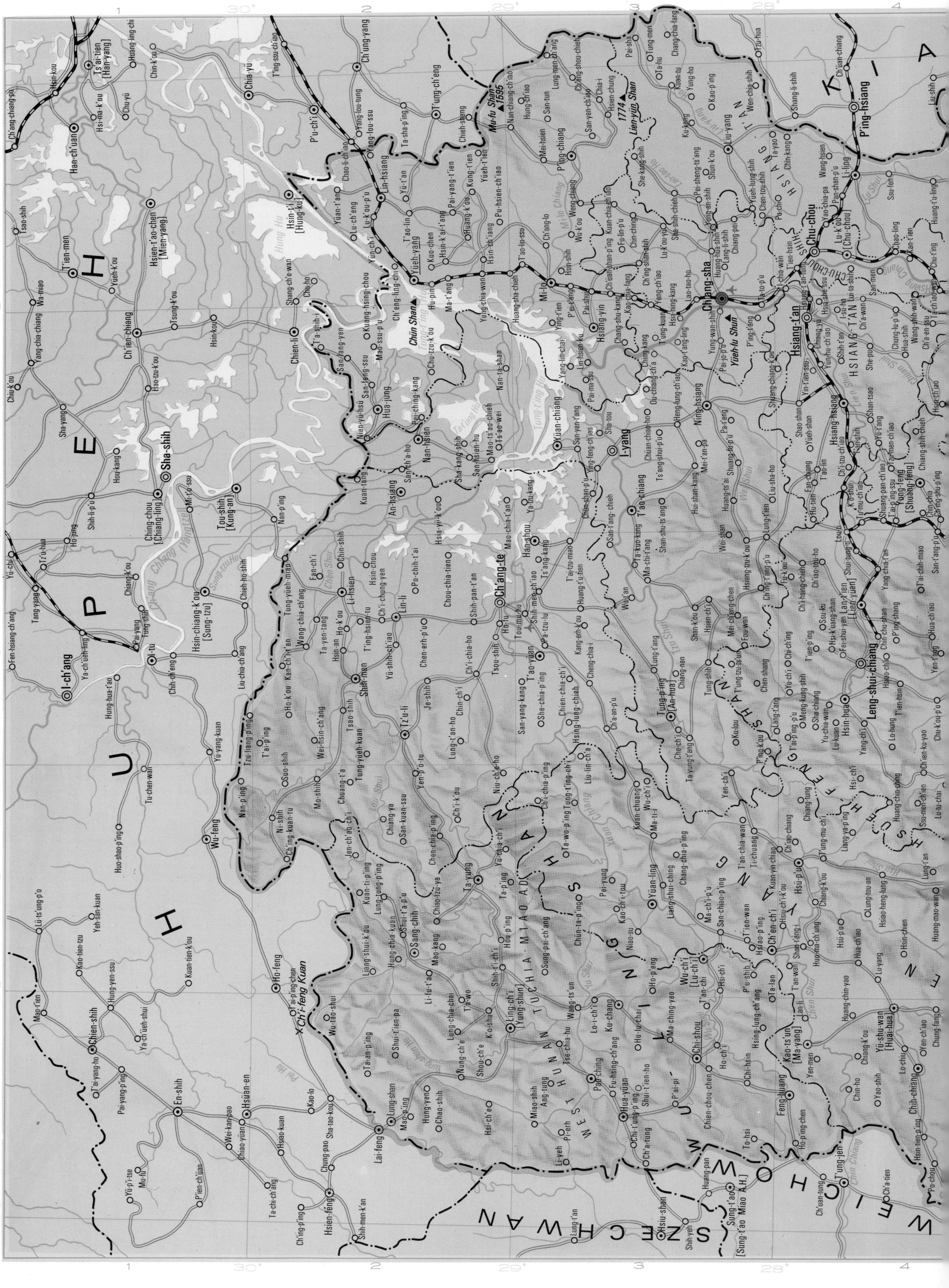

HUPEH
HUNAN
SZECHWAN
KIANGSI
KWEICHOW
Ch'ang-sha
Yüeh-yang
Ch'ang-te
I-yang
Hsiang-t'an
Chu-chou
Sha-shih
I-ch'ang
Shih-men
Tz'u-li
Ta-yung
Yüan-ling
Chi-shou
Wu-ch'i [Lu-ch'i]
Hua-yüan
Lung-shan
Lai-feng
Hsien-feng
En-shih
Hsüan-en
Chien-shih
Ho-feng
Wu-feng
Leng-shui-chiang
Hsin-hua
Lien-yüan
Shao-shan
P'ing-hsiang
Liu-yang
Ning-hsiang
Hsiang-yin
Mi-lo
Han-shou
Yüan-chiang
Nan-hsien
An-hsiang
Hua-jung
Chien-li
Hsin-t'i [Hung-hu]
Hsien-t'ao-chen [Mien-yang]
T'ien-men
Han-ch'uan
Ching-chou [Chiang-ling]
Tou-shih [Kung-an]
Hsin-chiang-k'ou [Sung-tzu]
Tung-t'ing Hu
Chün Shan
Hung Hu
Yüeh-lu Shan
Mu-fu Shan 1595
Lien-yün Shan 1774
Ch'i-feng Kuan
Ch'ang Chiang (Yangtze)
TUCHIA MIAO A.D.
WEST HUNAN
Sung-t'ao Miao A.H.
Feng-huang
Ch'en-ch'i
Hsü-p'u
Yü-shu-wan [Huai-hua]
Kao-ts'un [Ma-yang]
Chih-chiang
Ling-ch'i [Yung-shun]
Sang-chih
Lin-li
Li-hsien
T'ao-yüan
T'ao-chiang
Tung-p'ing [An-hua]

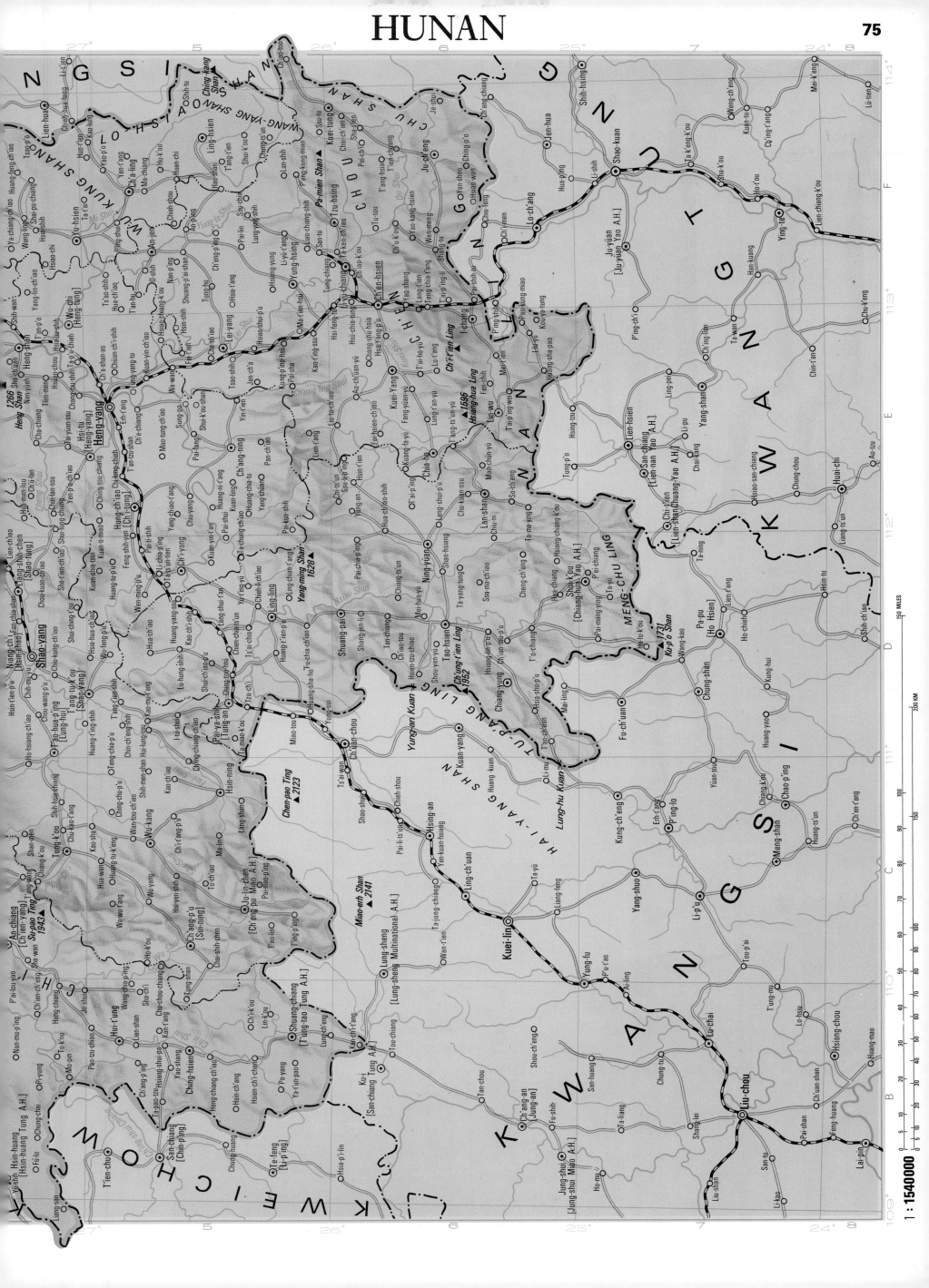

HUNAN PROVINCE
HU-NAN SHENG

8 shih	*municipalities*
1 tzu-chih-chou	*autonomous district*
9 ti-ch'ü	*regions*
85 hsien	*counties*
4 tzu-chih-hsien	*autonomous counties*

湖南省

capital **Ch'ang-sha Shih**	E3	长沙市
Ch'ang-sha Hsien	E3	长沙县
Ch'ang-te Shih	D2	常德市
Chu-chou Shih	F4	株州市
Chu-chou Hsien		株州县
centre: Lu-k'ou	F4,	渌口
Heng-yang Shih	E5	衡阳市
Hsiang-t'an Shih	E4	湘潭市
I-yang Shih	E3	益阳市
Leng-shui-chiang Shih	D4	冷水江市
Shao-yang Shih	D4	邵阳市
Ch'ang-te Ti-ch'ü		常德地区
An-hsiang Hsien	E2	安乡县
Ch'ang-te Hsien	D2	常德县
Han-shou Hsien	D3	汉寿县
Li Hsien		沣县
centre: Li-hsien	D2	
Lin-li Hsien	D2	临澧县
Shih-men Hsien	D2	石门县
T'ao-yüan Hsien	D3	桃源县
Tz'u-li Hsien	D2	慈利县
Ch'en-chou Ti-ch'ü		郴州地区
centre: Ch'en-hsien	F6	郴县
An-jen Hsien	F5	安仁县
Ch'en Hsien		郴县
centre: Ch'en-hsien	F6	
Chia-ho Hsien	E6	嘉禾县
I-chang Hsien	E6	宜章县
Ju-ch'eng Hsien	F6	汝城县
Kuei-tung Hsien	F6	桂东县
Kuei-yang Hsien	E6	桂阳县
Lei-yang Hsien	E5	耒阳县
Lin-wu Hsien	E6	临武县
Tzu-hsing Hsien	F6	资兴县
Yung-hsing Hsien	F5	永兴县
Ch'ien-yang Ti-ch'ü		黔阳地区
Ch'en-ch'i Hsien	C3	辰溪县
Ch'ien-yang Hsien		黔阳县
centre: An-chiang	C4	安江
Chih-chiang Hsien	B4	芷江县
Ching Hsien		靖县
centre: Ching-hsien	B5	
Hsin-huang T'ung-tsu Tzu-chih-hsien		新晃侗族 自治县
Hsin-huang Tung Autonomous Hsien		
centre: Hsin-huang	B4	
Hsü-p'u Hsien	C4	溆浦县
Huai-hua Hsien		怀化县
centre: Yü-shu-wan	B4	榆树湾
Hui-t'ung Hsien	B5	会同县
Ma-yang Hsien		麻阳县
centre: Kao-ts'un	B4	高村
T'ung-tao T'ung-tsu Tzu-chih-hsien		通道侗族自治县
T'ung-tao Tung Autonomous Hsien		
centre: Shuang-chiang	B5	双江
Yüan-ling Hsien	C3	沅陵县
Heng-yang Ti-ch'ü		衡阳地区
Ch'ang-ning Hsien	E5	常宁县
Ch'i-tung Hsien		祁东县
centre: Hung-ch'iao	E5	洪桥
Ch'i-yang Hsien	D5	祁阳县
Heng-nan Hsien		衡南县
centre: Heng-yang	E5	衡阳
Heng-shan Hsien	E4	衡山县
Heng-tung Hsien		衡东县
centre: Wu-chi	E4	吴集
Heng-yang Hsien		衡阳县
centre: Hsi-tu	E5	西渡

Hsiang-hsi T'u-chia-tsu Miao-tsu Tzu-chih-chou		湘西土家族苗族 自治州
West Hunan Tuchia-Miao Autonomous District		
centre: Chi-shou	B3	吉首
Chi-shou Hsien	B3	吉首县
Feng-huang Hsien	B4	凤凰县
Hua-yüan Hsien	B3	花垣县
Ku-chang Hsien	B3	古丈县
Lu-ch'i Hsien		沪溪县
centre: Wu-ch'i	C3	武溪
Lung-shan Hsien	B2	龙山县
Pao-ching Hsien	B3	保靖县
Sang-chih Hsien		桑植县
Ta-yung Hsien	C2	大庸县
Yung-shun Hsien		永顺县
centre: Ling-ch'i	B2	灵溪
Hsiang-t'an Ti-ch'ü		湘潭地区
Ch'a-ling Hsien	F5	茶陵县
Hsiang-hsiang Hsien	E4	湘乡县
Hsiang-t'an Hsien	E4	湘潭县
Li-ling Hsien	F4	醴陵县
Ling Hsien		酃县
centre: Ling-hsien	F5	
Liu-yang Hsien	F3	浏阳县
Yu Hsien		攸县
centre: Yu-hsien	F4	
I-yang Ti-ch'ü		益阳地区
An-hua Hsien		安化县
centre: Tung-p'ing	D3	东坪
I-yang Hsien	E3	益阳县
Nan-Hsien		南县
centre: Nan-hsien	E2	
Ning-hsiang Hsien	E3	宁乡县
T'ao-chiang Hsien	E3	桃江县
Yüan-chiang Hsien	E3	沅江县
Ling-ling Ti-ch'ü		零陵地区
Chiang-hua Yao-tsu Tzu-chih-hsien		江华瑶族自治县
Chiang-hua Yao Autonomous Hsien		
centre: Shui-k'ou	D7	水口
Chiang-yung Hsien	D6	江永县
Hsin-t'ien Hsien	E6	新田县
Lan-shan Hsien	E6	蓝山县
Ling-ling Hsien	D5	零陵县
Ning-yüan Hsien	D6	宁远县
Shuang-pai Hsien	D6	双牌县
Tao Hsien		道县
centre: Tao-hsien	D6	
Tung-an Hsien		东安县
centre: Pai-ya-shih	D5	白牙市
Shao-yang Ti-ch'ü		邵阳地区
Ch'eng-pu Miao-tsu Tzu-chih-hsien		城步苗族自治县
Ch'eng-pu Miao Autonomous Hsien		
centre: Ju-lin-chen	C5	儒林镇
Hsin-hua Hsien	D4	新化县
Hsin-ning Hsien	C5	新宁县
Hsin-shao Hsien		新邵县
centre: Niang-ch'i	D4	酿溪
Lien-yüan Hsien		涟源县
centre: Lan-t'ien	D4	蓝田
Lung-hui Hsien		隆回县
centre: T'ao-hua-p'ing	D4	桃花坪
Shao-tung Hsien		邵东县
centre: Liang-shih-chen	D4	两市镇
Shao-yang Hsien		邵阳县
centre: T'ang-tu-k'ou	D5	塘渡口
Shuang-feng Hsien		双峰县
centre: Yung-feng	E4	永丰
Sui-ning Hsien		绥宁县
centre: Ch'ang-p'u	C5	长铺
Tung-k'ou Hsien	C4	洞口县
Wu-kang Hsien	C5	武冈县
Yüeh-yang Ti-ch'ü		岳阳地区
Hsiang-yin Hsien	E3	湘阴县
Hua-jung Hsien	E2	华容县
Lin-hsiang Hsien	F2	临湘县
Mi-lo Hsien	F3	汨罗县
P'ing-chiang Hsien	F3	平江县
Yüeh-yang Hsien	F2	岳阳县

KWANGTUNG
PROVINCE

THE Kwangtung area was first included in China by the Ch'in in 214 BC, when the Chinese general, Chao T'o, subdued the area. After the fall of Ch'in he set up an independent state, which resisted the Chinese until the end of the 2nd century BC, when the Chinese finally conquered all Kwangtung, and incorporated it into the empire. Thereafter the Chinese maintained a strong control over Canton and the surrounding delta area, and a general control over other parts of the province. It was, however, many centuries before the province was settled by Chinese. As late as the T'ang period (AD 618–907), although Canton was a major seaport for trade with South-east Asia, India and the Persian Gulf, with a large foreign trading community the rest of the province had only small, scattered Chinese settlements among a predominantly aboriginal population. The region was considered a place of banishment. At the fall of the T'ang, Kwangtung was for a while an independent kingdom, Nan-Han, but after re-unification with the empire under the Sung, Chinese settlement began again in earnest, accelerating after the 12th century. Chinese settlers continued to pour into the region, some of whom formed the distinct K'o-chia (Hakka) group, who, as late-comers, were largely forced to occupy the less fertile and productive lands.

The growth of Kwangtung was particularly rapid under the Ming (1368–1644) and by the 17th century the pressure of population led to extensive emigration. Cantonese moved into the adjoining province of Kwangsi, into the ravaged and depopulated areas of Szechwan after the mid-17th century rebellions there, and into Taiwan and south-east Asia. In the mid-19th century emigration spread to America and even to South Africa.

From the 17th century onwards the area around Canton was a focus for foreign influence: Canton increasingly became China's major port for foreign trade, which was channelled through its immensely rich, licensed merchants (cohong); Macau had been a Portuguese enclave since the 16th century; Hong Kong became a British colony in 1842, following the Opium War. As a result, when relations between China and the western powers became strained, the tension was concentrated in the Canton area.

The entire province has a wet, tropical or sub-tropical climate. The average temperatures in January range from 13°C to 16°C (55°F to 61°F), and those in July from 28°C to 30°C (82°F to 86°F). There is virtually no winter and frost is extremely rare except on high land in the north. Rainfall is heavy – over 2,000 mm along the coast, but gradually decreasing towards the north-west. Only western Hainan, the Lei-chou peninsula and the Mei-hsien area in the north-east have less than 1,500 mm. The rainfall comes very largely in summer, from mid-April until October. The growing season lasts throughout the year.

The Pearl River Delta The centre of the province is the alluvial delta plain of the Chu Chiang (Pearl River), into which flow the Hsi Chiang from Kwangsi, the Pei Chiang from the northern mountains of the Nan-ling, and the Tung Chiang draining north-eastern Kwangtung. The plain, some 11,000 square kilometres in extent, is crossed by a dense network of distributary streams and canalised rivers, broken by some outlying hills. Much of the land is reclaimed, and reclamation continues. The area supports an extraordinary density of population. The main crop is rice, which produces two crops a year, but sweet potatoes, wheat and rape-seed are also important. The area is a major producer of silk, and there are a large number

of other subsidiary crops – tobacco in the western delta, jute in the east, tropical fruits of many types, sugar cane. The area also produces large quantities of livestock, particularly hogs for the urban markets of Canton and Hong Kong. Fish rearing, in ponds, is also a very important local industry.

To the west, in the valley of the Hsi Chiang, the plain merges into an area of hills with some remnants of forest cover. On these uplands the main crops are wheat, sweet potatoes, taro, kaoliang, rape-seed and peanuts.

Canton (Kuang-chou) is the largest city in Kwangtung. The provincial capital since Han times, Canton has always been a port and a centre of foreign trade, although it can only take ships of medium tonnage. It has become a major industrial city in recent times and a very important centre of sugar refining, the waste from which is used in a large newsprint mill, one of the largest in China. There is a large cement industry, and chemical and fertiliser plants. There is a small iron and steel works and a varied engineering industry, producing machine tools, trucks, and small ships. Other plants produce aluminium and automobile tyres. There is also much light industry, food-processing and textile manufacture. Canton is also a very important cultural and educational centre. Its population was 1,800,000 in 1957, and is currently estimated at 3,000,000, including the suburbs within its municipal area.

Fo-shan (Fatshan, Namhoi) lies south-west of Canton. It is the centre of the silk industry of the delta, it produces ceramics, and has recently acquired a large chemical plant.

Chiang-men (Kongmoon), with 85,000 people in 1953, is the major centre of the western delta. Primarily a major trading and market centre it has a copper industry, and is a producer of paper and board.

Eastern Kwangtung This area, forming the drainage basins of the Tung Chiang and the Han Chiang is a region of low hills, long ago denuded of natural cover, which have suffered seriously from erosion. The northern part of the region rises to the high watershed of the Nan-ling ranges, which still have more extensive areas of forest cover. In general the north-eastern area around Mei-hsien is comparatively unproductive. The chief areas of intensive agriculture are in the lower valley of the Tung Chiang, where rice and sugar cane are important crops, and above all the alluvial plain around Shan-t'ou, the delta of the Han Chiang. This area is intensively farmed for rice, sugar and sweet potatoes, with some jute production. It is a very important producer of citrus fruits.

Shan-t'ou (Swatow) is the major city of this area. An old-established port, with 280,000 people in 1953, Shan-t'ou is the natural outlet and market centre not only for the surrounding plain, but also for the Han Chiang valley and the Mei-hsien region. It has little industry.

Northern Kwangtung This area is largely the drainage basin of the Pei Chiang, to the north of the Canton delta. Rising to the Nan-ling ranges of the Hunan–Kiangsi borders, the northern areas still have rich forest reserves, and important mineral resources, especially tungsten, antimony and iron. Agriculture in the area is mainly confined to the valleys. Rice is the main crop, double-cropped in the southern districts. Tobacco, sugar cane and ramie are grown extensively, and the area is an important tea producing centre.

Shao-kuan is the focus of this region, historically important

as a route centre controlling the access to Kwangtung from both Hunan and Kiangsi. There is a small coalfield nearby (the only major source of coal in Kwangtung), which provides fuel for a thermal generating plant and a small iron and steel works. There are important smelters for non-ferrous metals produced in the area, and some machine building.

South-western Kwangtung This is an area of low hills, with few rivers and much poor barren land. It has a very hot tropical climate, with more than 1,500 mm of rain, mostly falling in summer. The only comparatively dry area is the Lei-chou peninsula. It is an area where three crops per year are possible. Paddy rice is the main crop, where conditions are suitable, but tubers – sweet potato, cassava, taro – are important. It is an area which produces various tropical crops – jute, sisal, sea island cotton, sugar cane. Tropical fruits (bananas, pineapples, mangoes) are widely grown. Rubber has also been extensively planted in the north and south of the Lei-chou peninsula since the 1950s.

Chan-chiang (Tsamkong) on the eastern side of the Lei-chou peninsula, is the area's most important city. Formerly the centre of the French leased territory of Kwangchowwan, it was returned to China in 1945. In 1955 it was linked by rail to Kwangsi, since when it has grown into a major port. It has two large fertiliser plants, and an important coastal salt industry.

Mao-ming, which is linked to Chan-chiang by rail, is important as a producer of oil from oil-shale. This industry has been developed since 1958, and the town has its own refineries producing a variety of fuel oils and gasoline.

Hainan Island Hainan has a tropical climate with an annual average temperature of 25°C (77°F), with a year-round growing season. The mountainous centre of the island is still densely forested, and the south still has a large non-Chinese minority of Li peoples (360,000 in all). The coastal areas produce rice (three crops a year in some places), and large quantities of sugar cane. There have been attempts to plant rubber, coconuts, coffee, sisal and other tropical crops.

Iron ore of very high quality is produced in the west near Ch'ang-chiang, which is linked by rail to the port of Tung-fang, from where it is exported to Chan-chiang on the mainland. There is a small local iron smelting industry.

Hai-k'ou on the north coast is the chief city of Hainan, and the port for the fertile agricultural plain of the north of the island. It has some minor food processing industry.

Kwangtung province also administers the various islands in the South China Sea, belonging to China.

Minority Peoples The vast majority of the population of mainland Kwangtung are Han Chinese, speaking the Cantonese dialects. Among these live the Hakka, speaking a different language, with different customs. They immigrated into Kwangtung some time after the Cantonese population, perhaps from Sung times onwards, from northern and central China, by way of Fukien and Kiangsi. There was much friction between these two groups, which lead to extensive warfare in the mid-19th century. The only minority people on the mainland are the small settlements of Yao living along the Hunan border, in the far north. The Chinese population of Hainan is largely composed of speakers of Min (i.e. Fukien) dialects. The Li peoples, who inhabit the mountains and most of southern Hainan, are of Thai race. There are also a small number of Miao people in Hainan.

AREA
220,000 square kilometres

POPULATION
42,800,000 (other estimates up to 48,000,000)

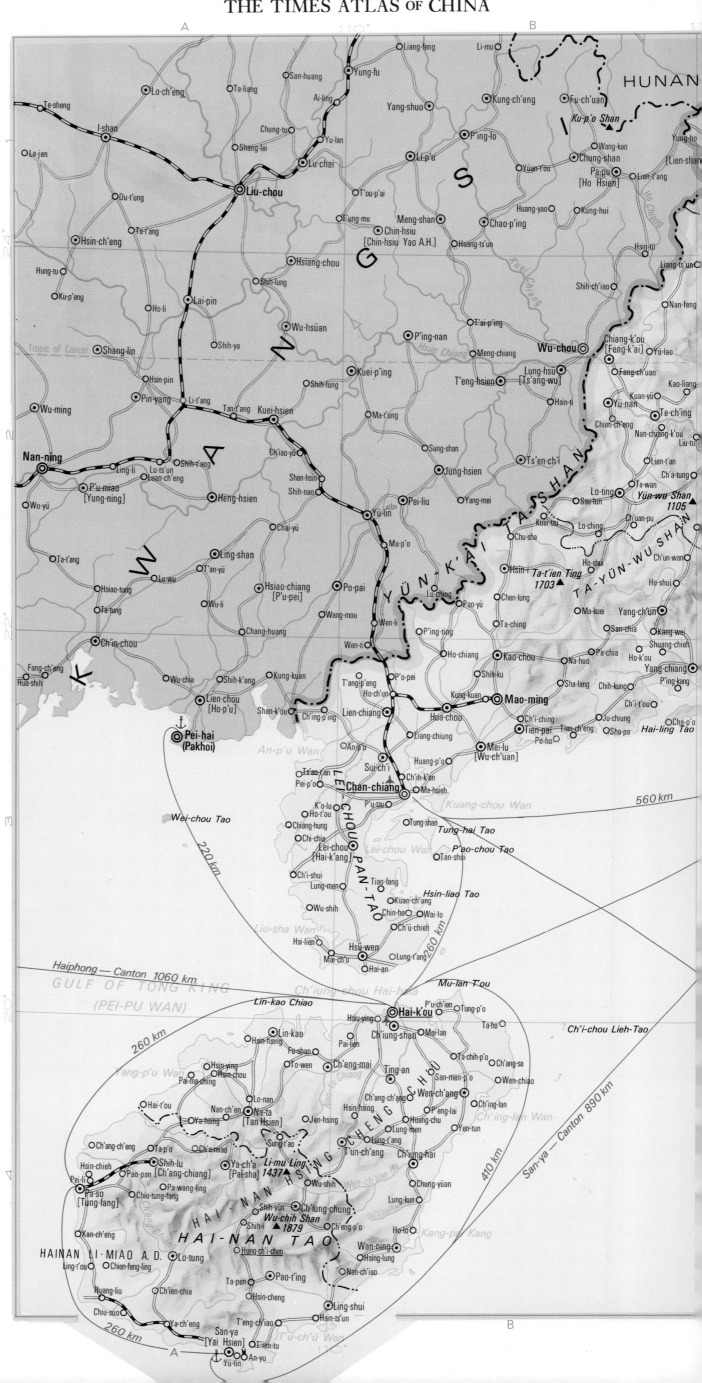

KIANGSI

FUKIEN

YAO SHAN

CHIU-LIEN SHAN

CANTON (KUANG-CHOU)

HONG KONG (To U.K.)

Macau (To Port.)

Kowloon

Shan-t'ou (Swatow)

SOUTH CHINA SEA

(NAN HAI)

Canton — Swatow 540 km
Canton — Shanghai 1690 km
Hong Kong — Yokohama 2930 km
Hong Kong — Kao-hsiung 630 km
Singapore — Hong Kong 2670 km
Hong Kong — Manila 1170 km
Conakry — Canton 19220 km
Jakarta — Canton 3340 km
Chan-chiang — Singapore 2480 km

1 : 2180000

0 5 10 20 30 40 50 60 70 80 90 100 150 200 MILES

0 10 20 30 40 50 60 70 80 90 100 150 200 250 300 KM

KWANGTUNG PROVINCE
KUANG-TUNG SHENG 广东省

10 shih	municipalities	
1 hsing-cheng-ch'ü	administrative district	
1 tzu-chih-chou	autonomous district	
7 ti-ch'ü	regions	
94 hsien	counties	
3 tzu-chih-hsien	autonomous counties	

capital Kuang-chou Shih	C2	广州市
Hua Hsien		花县
centre: Hua-hsien	C2	
Ts'ung-hua Hsien	C2	从化县
Chan-chiang Shih	B3	湛江市
Chao-ch'ing Shih	C2	肇庆市
Chiang-men Shih	C2	江门市
Fo-shan Shih	C2	佛山市
Hai-k'ou Shih	B3	海口市
Hui-chou Shih	D2	惠州市
Mao-ming Shih	B3	茂名市
Shan-t'ou Shih	E2	汕头市
Shao-kuan Shih	C1	韶关市

Chan-chiang Ti-ch'ü		湛江地区
Hai-k'ang Hsien		海康县
centre: Lei-chou	B3	雷州
Hsin-i Hsien	B2	信宜县
Hsü-wen Hsien	B3	徐闻县
Hua-chou Hsien	B3	化州县
Kao-chou Hsien	B3	高州县
Lien-chiang Hsien	B3	廉江县
Sui-ch'i Hsien	B3	遂溪县
Tien-pai Hsien	B3	电白县
Wu-ch'uan Hsien	B3	吴川县
centre: Mei-lu	B3	梅绿
Yang-chiang Hsien	B3	阳江县
Yang-ch'un Hsien	B2	阳春县

Chao-ch'ing Ti-ch'ü		肇庆地区
Feng-k'ai Hsien		封开县
centre: Chiang-k'ou	B2	江口
Hsin-hsing Hsien	C2	新兴县
Huai-chi Hsien	C2	怀集县
Kao-yao Hsien	C2	高要县
centre: Chao-ch'ing	C2	肇庆
Kuang-ning Hsien		广宁县
centre: Nan-chieh		南街
Lo-ting Hsien	B2	罗定县
Ssu-hui Hsien	C2	四会县
Te-ch'ing Hsien	B2	德庆县
Yü-nan Hsien	B2	郁南县
Yün-fu Hsien	C2	云浮县

Fo-shan Ti-ch'ü		佛山地区
Chu-hai Hsien		珠海县
centre: Hsiang-chou	C2	香州
Chung-shan Hsien		中山县
centre: Shih-ch'i	C2	石岐
En-p'ing Hsien	C2	恩平县
Hsin-hui Hsien	C2	新会县
K'ai-p'ing Hsien		开平县
centre: San-pu	C2	三埠
Kao-ho Hsien		高鹤县
centre: Sha-p'ing	C2	沙坪
Nan-hai Hsien		南海县
centre: Fo-shan		佛山
P'an-yü Hsien		番禺县
centre: Shih-ch'iao	C2	市桥
San-shui Hsien		三水县
centre: Hsi-nan	C2	西南
Shun-te Hsien		顺德县
centre: Ta-liang	C2	大良
T'ai-shan Hsien	C2	台山县
Tou-men Hsien		斗门县
centre: Ching-an	C2	井岸

Hai-nan Hsing-cheng-ch'ü		海南行政区
centre: Hai-k'ou	B3	海口
Ch'eng-mai Hsien	A4	澄迈县
Ch'iung-hai Hsien	B4	琼海县
Ch'iung-shan Hsien	B4	琼山县
Lin-kao Hsien	A4	临高县
Tan Hsien		儋县
centre: Na-ta	A4	那大
Ting-an Hsien	B4	定安县
T'un-ch'ang Hsien	B4	屯昌县
Wan-ning Hsien	B4	万宁县
Wen-ch'ang Hsien	B4	文昌县

Hai-nan Li-tsu Miao-tsu Tzu-chih-chou		海南黎族苗族自治州
Hainan Li-Miao Autonomous District		
centre: Hung-ch'i-chen	A4	红旗镇
Ch'ang-chiang Hsien		昌江县
centre: Shih-lu	A4	石碌
Ch'iung-chung Hsien	A4	琼中县
Ling-shui Hsien	B4	陵水县
Lo-tung Hsien	A4	乐东县
Pao-t'ing Hsien	A4	保亭县
Pai-sha Hsien		白沙县
centre: Ya-ch'a	A4	牙叉
Tung-fang Hsien		东方县
centre: Pa-so	A4	八所
Yai Hsien		崖县
centre: San-ya	A4	三亚

Hui-yang Ti-ch'ü		惠阳地区
centre: Hui-chou	D2	惠州
Ho-p'ing Hsien		和平县
centre: Yang-ming	D1	阳明
Ho-yüan Hsien	D2	河源县
Hui-tung Hsien		惠东县
centre: P'ing-shan	D2	平山
Hui-yang Hsien		惠阳县
centre: Hui-chou	D2	惠州
Lien-p'ing Hsien	D1	连平县
Lung-ch'uan Hsien		龙川县
centre: Lao-lung	D1	老隆
Lung-men Hsien	D2	龙门县
Pao-an Hsien		宝安县
centre: Shen-chen	D2	深圳
Po-lo Hsien	D2	博罗县
Tseng-ch'eng Hsien	C2	增城县
Tung-kuan Hsien	C2	东莞县
Tzu-chin Hsien	D2	紫金县

Mei-hsien Ti-ch'ü		梅县地区
Chiao-ling Hsien	E1	蕉岭县
Feng-shun Hsien	E2	丰顺县
Hsing-ning Hsien	D1	兴宁县
Mei Hsien		梅县
centre: Mei-hsien	E1	
P'ing-yüan Hsien	D1	平远县
Ta-pu Hsien		大埔县
centre: Hu-liao	E1	湖寮
Wu-hua Hsien	D2	五华县

Shan-t'ou Ti-ch'ü		汕头地区
Ch'ao-an Hsien	E2	潮安县
Ch'ao-yang Hsien	E2	潮阳县
Ch'eng-hai Hsien	E2	澄海县
Chieh-hsi Hsien		揭西县
centre: Ho-p'o	D2	河婆
Chieh-yang Hsien	E2	揭阳县
Hai-feng Hsien	D2	海丰县
Hui-lai Hsien	E2	惠来县
Jao-p'ing Hsien		饶平县
centre: Huang-kang	E2	黄岗
Lu-feng Hsien	D2	陆丰县
Nan-ao Hsien	E2	南澳县
P'u-ning Hsien	E2	普宁县

Shao-kuan Ti-ch'ü		韶关地区
Ch'ing-yüan Hsien	C2	清远县
Ch'ü-chiang Hsien		曲江县
centre: Ma-pa	C1	马坝
Fo-kang Hsien		佛冈县
centre: Shih-chiao	C2	石角
Hsin-feng Hsien	D1	新丰县
Jen-hua Hsien	C1	仁化县
Ju-yüan Yao-tsu Tzu-chih-hsien		乳源瑶族自治县
Ju-yüan Yao Autonomous Hsien		
centre: Ju-yüan	C1	
Lien Hsien		连县
centre: Lien-hsien	C1	
Lien-nan Yao-tsu Tzu-chih-hsien		连南瑶族自治县
Lien-nan Yao Autonomous Hsien		
centre: San-chiang	C1	三江
Lien-shan Chuang-tsu Yao-tsu Tzu-chih-hsien		连山壮族瑶族自治县
Lien-shan Chuang-Yao Autonomous Hsien		
centre: Chi-t'ien	C1	吉田
Lo-ch'ang Hsien	C1	乐昌县
Nan-hsiung Hsien	D1	南雄县
Shih-hsing Hsien	D1	始兴县
Weng-yüan Hsien		翁源县
centre: Lung-hsien	D1	龙仙
Yang-shan Hsien	C1	阳山县
Ying-te Hsien	C1	英德县

KWANGSI CHUANG
AUTONOMOUS REGION

KWANGSI first came into the political orbit of the Chinese under the Ch'in, when in 214 BC a large army was sent to conquer Kwangtung, and also the eastern sections of Kwangsi. At this time Chinese authority was not securely established, and for the next centuries the area lay on the periphery of the Chinese empire, with Chinese occupation of the eastern and south-eastern parts of the province, and a system of indirect rule through chieftains of the aboriginal Chuang peoples in the more westerly districts. This situation was complicated by the settlement in the northern parts of the province of Yao and Miao tribesmen, driven from their homes in southern Hunan and Kiangsi by the advance of Chinese settlement. Unlike the Chuang, who easily assimilated Chinese customs, the Miao and Yao remained in the hills districts, often harshly oppressed by Chinese settlers. There was continuous trouble, with major risings in the 1830s, and the initial outbreak of the T'ai-p'ing rebellion occurred in Kwangsi, involving many Hakka, as well as some Chuang. The province remained a comparatively poor area until the present century. In the Republican period its military leaders formed the Kwangsi Clique, the principal opposition to Chiang Kai-shek within the Kuomintang, and controlled much of Kwangtung, Hunan and Hupeh for long periods between 1926–37. During this time some effort was made to modernise Kwangsi itself. After the outbreak of the war with Japan, the province was the scene of much fighting and destruction. Since 1949, the province has been enlarged by the addition of the coastal area, giving Kwangsi an outlet to the port of Pei-hai (Pakhoi).

The province is almost coextensive with the basin of the Hsi Chiang river system, which provides good water communications throughout the region. The topography is mostly hilly, with rather poor, infertile soils. The land gradually rises to the north, where it merges into the Kweichow plateau in the west, and the steep ranges of the Nan Shan on the Hunan and Kwangtung borders. The climate is tropical in the south and sub-tropical in the northern half of the province, where the mountains are comparatively cool. Temperatures have a rather small seasonal range. At Kuei-lin January averages 9–10°C (48–50°F); July about 26°C (79°F). The rainfall is heavy – above 1,000 mm everywhere except in the west and north-west, and up to 2,000 mm on the coast and in mountainous districts in the east. Most rain falls from May to October, and the summers are extremely hot and humid. The growing seasons lasts throughout the year.

South-west Kwangsi This is a very hilly area, drained by the Yu Chiang and Tso Chiang rivers, with comparatively narrow river plains, and rather a low proportion of cultivated land. Rice is the main crop. Double-cropping is normal in the east around Nan-ning. In the west single-cropped rice grown together with corn is more common. Sugar cane is an important crop in the east and south. It is mostly refined at Nan-ning. Peanuts are widely grown, and tobacco is grown in the eastern valleys, to be processed in Liu-chou.

Nan-ning, the provincial capital, is the centre of this region. It is an old-established route centre, and became the provincial capital in 1912. It is the main cultural and educational city in Kwangsi. Traditionally a river port, its importance has grown greatly since the construction of the railway in the early 1950s. It has a thermal generating station using coal from the Ho-shan mines at Lai-pin to the north-east. Its industry concentrates on processing local agricultural produce such as sugar. But some modern industry has also grown up – engineering and machine building, a wide range of chemicals and fertilisers, and aluminium are local industries. Its population is now estimated at about 400,000.

The Coastal Area Acquired finally by Kwangsi in 1965, the coastal area mostly consists of rather barren hills. Agriculture concentrates on rice, with much cultivation of tubers such as taro, sweet potatoes and cassava. Jute, sugar and ramie are important economic crops.

Pei-hai (Pakhoi) is an old-established port, but too shallow for modern shipping and it has lost much of its trade to Chanchiang in Kwangtung, the terminus of the railway to Kwangsi. Pei-hai, however, remains a very important fishing port.

South-eastern Kwangsi This area, which is the part of the province that has been settled the longest, has a well developed agriculture. Double-cropped rice is normal, often with a third winter crop such as wheat, tobacco, vegetables or sweet potatoes. Ground nuts are widely grown on sandy soils. Sugar cane and jute are important industrial crops, and there are sugar refineries at Wu-chou and Kuei-hsien. The area to the west of Wu-chou has some manganese mines.

Wu-chou is the chief centre of this district. Before the railways were constructed, most of Kwangsi's trade went via Wu-chou to Canton, and it remains a very important river port and market centre, although the railway has taken away some of its trade. It has recently become a centre of sugar refining, and the largest manufacturer of pitch in China.

North-eastern Kwangsi The basin of the Kuei Chiang river is a very hilly area, much of it composed of limestone with spectacular karst landscapes. Although it was one of the first settled areas of Kwangsi, it has a very low proportion of cultivated land. Rice is the main crop, but double cropping is only slowly spreading from the south. Ramie fibre is an important crop, grown on hill slopes and terraced fields. Peanuts are also important. Some tea of good quality is grown.

Kuei-lin is the regional centre. It is an ancient city, and was the provincial capital until 1912. It supports a very wide range of local handicraft industries, and various food-processing industries based on local agriculture.

North-western Kwangsi This area, too, is very hilly with a very low proportion of cultivated land. Much of the area is composed of limestone, and lack of water is a major problem. Agriculture is mainly rice growing, with double cropping in the south, and corn grown extensively on upland fields. Cotton, ramie, hemp, peanuts and some sugar cane are also grown in the south.

The area still has a good deal of natural forest, and lumbering is an important industry in the valleys of the Hung Shui and Liu Chiang. The main trees are pine, fir, oak, maple and camphor. Lumber is floated down the rivers to lumber-mills at Liu-chou.

This region also has some minerals. Coal is mined at Ho-shan, south of Liu-chou, and antimony is produced near Nan-tan.

Liu-chou is the main route centre of this area, and its importance has grown greatly since the railways were constructed. It is the junction of main lines to Kuei-yang, and to Kuei-lin and Hunan. It has become the major industrial city of the province. It has a large thermal generating plant, using coal from Ho-shan, and a small steel works at Lu-sai, a few miles to the north-east. Liu-chou has developed an engineering industry, making tractors, farm-machinery and railway equipment. It has large fertiliser and cement works, an electronic industry, and a major lumber-milling industry.

National Minorities The main minority people in Kwangsi are the Chuang, a Thai people, of whom there are 6,500,000 living in the province. They are China's largest national minority. Kwangsi was constituted a Chuang Autonomous Region in 1958. The Chuang have assimilated Chinese culture and generally speak Chinese. They form the bulk of the population in the more sparsely peopled western half of the province. Other minorities are the Tung living on the Hunan border; the Yao and the Miao, who live in scattered communities in the north, in the coastal zone, and along the Vietnamese border. There are estimated to be about 470,000 Yao, 200,000 Miao and 150,000 Tung in the province.

AREA
230,000 square kilometres

POPULATION
20,840,000 (other estimates up to 25,000,000)

HUNAN

KWEICHOW

KWANGTUNG

Te-feng [Li-p'ing]
Mao-kung
P'ing-yung
Tsai-ma
Ku-chou [Jung-chiang]
Ping-mei [Ts'ung-chiang]
Shuang-chiang [T'ung-tao Tung A.H.]
T'ing-p'ing
P'ing-teng
Ch'e-t'ien
Tzu-yüan
Chen-pao Ting 2123
Mei-ch'iu
Huang-t'u-ching
Ta-hsi-chiang
Miao-tou
Ling-ling
Yang-ming Shan 1628
Hsin-t'ien
Ao-ch'üan-yü

Miao-erh Shan 2141
Lung-sheng [Lung-sheng Multi national A.H.]
YÜEH-CH'ENG LING
HAI-YANG SHAN
Kuei-lin
Ling-ch'uan
Hsing-an
TA-YAO SHAN
Liu-chou
Lai-pin
I-shan
Kuei-hsien
Kuei-p'ing
Wu-chou (Feng-k'ai)
Yü-lin
TA-JUNG SHAN
YÜN-KAI TA SHAN
TA-YÜN-WU SHAN
Chao-ch'ing
Ta-ming Shan
K'un-lun Kuan
Yung-ning
Ch'in-chou (Yamchow)
Pei-hai (Pakhoi)
Wei-chou Tao
Chan-chiang
Mao-ming
Hua-chou
Lien-chiang
Sui-ch'i
Lei-chou [Hai-k'ang]

GULF OF TONGKING (PU WAN)
SOUTH CHINA SEA (NAN HAI)
Tropic of Cancer
Canton
Singapore

Liu-wan Shan 1103
Yüan-pao Shan 2081
Ku-p'o 1731 Shan
Ying-yang Kuan
Lung-hu Kuan
Yung-an Kuan
Ch'ung-t'ien Ling 1952
MENG-CHU LING
TA-PANG LING

1 : 1750000

0 5 10 20 30 40 50 60 70 80 90 100 150 MILES
0 5 10 20 30 40 50 60 70 80 90 100 150 200 KM

KWANGSI CHUANG AUTONOMOUS REGION
KUANG-HSI CHUANG-TSU TZU-CHIH-CH'Ü

广西壮族自治州

6 shih	*municipalities*	
8 ti-ch'ü	*regions*	
72 hsien	*counties*	
8 tzu-chih-hsien	*autonomous counties*	

capital **Nan-ning Shih**	E5	南宁市
Kuei-lin Shih	G2	桂林市
Liu-chou Shih	F3	柳州市
Pei-hai Shih	F6	北海市
P'ing-hsiang Shih	C5	凭祥市
Wu-chou Shih	H4	梧州市

Ch'in-chou Ti-ch'ü		钦州地区
Ch'in-chou Hsien	E6	钦州县
Ho-p'u Hsien		合浦县
centre: Lien-chou	F6	廉州
Ling-shan Hsien	F5	灵山县
P'u-pei Hsien		浦北县
centre: Hsiao-chiang	F5	小江
Shang-ssu Hsien	D5	上思县
Tung-hsing Ko-tsu Tzu-chih-hsien		东兴各族自治县
Tung-hsing Multi-national Autonomous Hsien		
centre: Tung-hsing	E6	

Ho-ch'ih Ti-ch'ü		河池地区
Feng-shan Hsien	D3	凤山县
Ho-ch'ih Hsien		河池县
centre: Chin-ch'eng-chiang	E3	金城江
Huan-chiang Hsien	E3	环江县
I-shan Hsien	E3	宜山县
Lo-ch'eng Hsien	E3	罗城县
Nan-tan Hsien	D3	南丹县
Pa-ma Yao-tsu Tzu-chih-hsien		巴马瑶族自治县
Pa-ma Yao Autonomous Hsien		
centre: Pa-ma	D3	
T'ien-o Hsien		天峨县
centre: Liu-p'ai	D2	六排
Tu-an Yao-tsu Tzu-chih-hsien		都安瑶族自治县
Tu-an Yao Autonomous Hsien		
centre: Tu-an	E4	
Tung-lan Hsien	D3	东兰县

Kuei-lin Ti-ch'ü		桂林地区
Ch'üan-chou Hsien	H2	全州县
Hsing-an Hsien	G2	兴安县
Kuan-yang Hsien	H2	灌阳县
Kung-ch'eng Hsien	G3	恭城县
Ling-ch'uan Hsien	G2	灵川县
Lin-kuei Hsien		临桂县
centre: Kuei-lin	G2	桂林
Li-p'u Hsien	G3	荔浦县
Lung-sheng Ko-tsu Tzu-chih-hsien		龙胜各族自治县
Lung-sheng Multi-national Autonomous Hsien		
centre: Lung-sheng	G2	
P'ing-lo Hsien	G3	平乐县
Tzu-yüan Hsien	G1	资源县
Yang-shuo Hsien	G3	阳朔县
Yung-fu Hsien	G2	永福县

Liu-chou Ti-ch'ü		柳州地区
Chin-hsiu Yao-tsu Tzu-chih-hsien		金秀瑶族自治县
Chin-hsiu Yao Autonomous Hsien		
centre: Chin-hsiu	G3	
Hsiang-chou Hsien	F4	象州县
Hsin-ch'eng Hsien	E3	忻城县
Jung-an Hsien		融安县
centre: Ch'ang-an	F2	长安
Jung-shui Miao-tsu Tzu-chih-hsien		融水苗族自治县
Jung-shui Miao Autonomous Hsien		
centre: Jung-shui	F2	
Lai-pin Hsien	F4	来宾县
Liu-ch'eng Hsien		柳城县
centre: Ta-p'u	F3	大埔
Liu-chiang Hsien	F3	柳江县
Lu-chai Hsien	F3	鹿寨县
San-chiang T'ung-tsu Tzu-chih-hsien		三江洞族自治县
San-chiang Tung Autonomous Hsien		
centre: Ku-i	F2	古宜
Wu-hsüan Hsien	F4	武宣县

Nan-ning Ti-ch'ü		南宁地区
Ch'ung-tso Hsien	D5	崇左县
Fu-sui Hsien	D5	扶绥县
Heng Hsien		横县
centre: Heng-hsien	F5	
Lung-an Hsien	D4	隆安县
Lung-chou Hsien	C5	龙州县
Ma-shan Hsien	E4	马山县
Ning-ming Hsien	D5	宁明县
Pin-yang Hsien	E4	宾阳县
Shang-lin Hsien	E4	上林县
Ta-hsin Hsien	D5	大新县
T'ien-teng Hsien	D4	天等县
Wu-ming Hsien	E4	武鸣县
Yung-ning Hsien		邕宁县
centre: P'u-miao	E5	蒲庙

Po-se Ti-ch'ü		百色地区
Ching-hsi Hsien	C4	靖西县
Hsi-lin Hsien		西林县
centre: Pa-ta	B3	八达
Ling-yün Hsien	C3	凌云县
Lo-yeh Hsien	C3	乐业县
Lung-lin Ko-tsu Tzu-chih-hsien		隆林各族自治县
Lung-lin Multi-national Autonomous Hsien		
centre: Lung-lin	B3	
Na-p'o Hsien	B4	那坡县
Po-se Hsien	C4	百色县
P'ing-kuo Hsien	D4	平果县
Te-pao Hsien	C4	德保县
T'ien-lin Hsien		田林县
centre: Lo-li	C3	乐里
T'ien-tung Hsien		田东县
centre: P'ing-ma	D4	平马
T'ien-yang Hsien	C4	田阳县

Wu-chou Ti-ch'ü		梧州地区
Chao-p'ing Hsien	G3	昭平县
Chung-shan Hsien	H3	钟山县
Fu-ch'uan Hsien	H3	富川县
Ho Hsien		贺县
centre: Pa-pu	H3	八步
Meng-shan Hsien	G3	蒙山县
T'eng Hsien		藤县
centre: T'eng-hsien	G4	
Ts'ang-wu Hsien		苍梧县
centre: Lung-hsü	H4	龙圩
Ts'en-ch'i Hsien	H5	岑溪县

Yü-lin Ti-ch'ü		玉林地区
Jung Hsien		容县
centre: Jung-hsien	G5	
Kuei Hsien		贵县
centre: Kuei-hsien	F4	
Kuei-p'ing Hsien	G4	桂平县
Lu-ch'uan Hsien	G5	陆川县
Pei-liu Hsien	G5	北流县
P'ing-nan Hsien	G4	平南县
Po-pai Hsien	F5	博白县
Yü-lin Hsien	G5	玉林县

SZECHWAN
PROVINCE

SZECHWAN, one of the largest provinces in China, and the most populous, contains over 11 per cent of the total population. The present province was formed in 1955 by the fusion of the old province of Szechwan with Sikang in the western highlands. Although the new territory is almost half of the area, it is sparsely peopled, with probably about 4,000,000 people.

The two areas have had a very different history. Szechwan, although it had been peopled from much earlier times, first became a part of the Chinese political system in the late 4th century BC, when it was invaded by the state of Ch'in. In the 3rd century BC, the Ch'in government first built the irrigation system in the plain around Ch'eng-tu, which was to remain the economic centre of the province. Szechwan grew steadily until the 13th century, when it had already a dense population engaged in intensive farming. It was much damaged by the Mongol invasion, and again seriously depopulated and ravaged in the wars at the end of the Ming period (1368–44). After this, the province was largely resettled by people from Central and Southern China. In the early Republican period it was very unstable, the scene of constant fighting between rival war-lords. Its modern development dates from the Second World War, when the Nationalist government, in the face of the Japanese advance, withdrew to the south-west, bringing with it many industries dismantled in the coastal cities, and many institutions of higher learning.

Since the beginning of the Communist regime Szechwan has been more firmly integrated into the Chinese state by the construction of railways. The first line reached Ch'eng-tu from Pao-chi in 1956, and the province now also has rail links with Yunnan and Kweichow. The Yangtze, formerly the chief artery for Szechwan's trade, has also had its channels through the gorges in the east of the province cleared and improved for shipping. The western and north-western sections of the province have also been given a much improved highway system.

The Szechwan Basin The eastern half of the province is a basin, drained by the Yangtze and its tributaries, and surrounded by high mountains. It lies at an altitude of about 1,000 m. The south-eastern part of this basin is quite hilly, with a series of steep ranges with a south-west to north-east axis. To the south of the Yangtze valley these rise to the Kweichow plateau. In the extreme east of the province the ranges join the Ta-pa Shan, a very high and rugged range which forms the border with Shansi. This eastern knot of mountains is traversed by the Yangtze in a series of spectacular gorges. The western part of the basin is also hilly. The only area of flat land is the Ch'eng-tu plain in the north-west. The whole basin has a moist humid and temperate climate, protected from north and north-westerly winds by the great mountain ranges. Rainfall is between 750 and 1,250 mm, with even heavier falls in the south-western mountains. Most rain falls in summer. Winter temperatures average 10°C (50°F); summers average 29°C (84°F) and are very humid. The growing season lasts eleven months throughout the basin, and virtually the whole year in the southern section.

The Ch'eng-tu plain The major agricultural region of Szechwan, this is a large alluvial fan formed by the Min Chiang river which has been irrigated since the 3rd century BC and now supports one of the densest rural populations in the world. Most of the land is rice-paddy, the rice crop being followed by wheat, rape-seed or peas as a winter crop. On the higher ground corn, sweet potatoes, cotton and hemp are grown, and on the hilllands citrus fruits, especially tangerines, are widely cultivated.

Ch'eng-tu is the traditional centre of this area, and the provincial capital. Founded in the 4th century BC it was always an important regional metropolis and trading city, the centre of a very important silk industry. During the Second World War modern industry begun to grow, and this was accelerated after the completion of a railway to Ch'ung-ch'ing in 1952, and a rail-

way linking Ch'eng-tu with Pao-chi in Shensi in 1956, connecting with the main Chinese rail network. Industry has continued to grow, but not on the scale of Ch'ung-ch'ing. Ch'eng-tu has a large textile industry, and precision engineering, instrument making, and radio plants. A large thermal power plant is fed by coal from nearby Kuan-hsien.

Chin-t'ang to the north-east is a centre of the chemical and fertiliser industries, with a large plant built by the Czechs and completed in 1959–60.

Chiang-yu, even further to the north-east, is a major producer of cement, and has a small iron and steel industry.

The South-western basin This area is bounded by the lower courses of the Min Chiang and To Chiang and the valley of the Yangtze. An area of alluvial plain separated by areas of low hills, it is hotter and wetter than the Ch'eng-tu area. The northern part is very intensively farmed. Rice is the main crop, and in the river valleys is widely grown, usually in rotation with corn, sweet potatoes or peanuts. On higher land corn and cotton are widely grown. The upland western area around Lo-shan is a major silk producing area.

Nei-chiang is a major market and route centre, and an important rail junction. It is the main centre of the sugar refining industry, also has light engineering and textile (cottons) plants, and produces paper.

Tzu-kung is the main city of the region. The centre of an ancient salt industry, using brine from deep wells, Tzu-kung has developed into a centre of the chemical industry, and also manufactures machine tools and electrical equipment.

I-pin, the traditional market on the Yangtze, has also developed a chemical industry.

The Ch'ung-ch'ing area occupies the south-east of the Szechwan basin. This, too, is a very warm and wet area, with intensive irrigation and a 320-day growing period. It is a major rice-producing region, where double cropping of rice is common. Wheat, corn, sweet potatoes and kaoliang are important subsidiary crops. Oranges, tangerines, lichees and longan fruits are widely grown, and the area is an important producer of silk.

Ch'ung-ch'ing (Chungking) is the chief centre of the area. A traditional regional centre and river port, with routes across Szechwan and into Kweichow by river and rail, Ch'ung-ch'ing's modern growth began during the Second World War, when it became the capital of the Nationalist government. This period was also the beginning of its transformation into a major centre of heavy industry. A steel industry was founded here in 1940, using plant dismantled in Han-yang. Building on this base, the Communist regime developed Ch'ung-ch'ing into a major heavy industrial base for south-western China. In 1960 it became a fully integrated iron and steel complex, producing over 1 million tons of steel annually. It has also developed other industry, producing machine tools, electrical equipment, small ships, railway rolling stock, cement, copper, lead and zinc, plastics and chemicals. Its population (1,770,000 in 1953), is now estimated at over 4,400,000.

Ch'ang-shou, a small industrial town downstream on the Yangtze, is a major centre of the synthetic rubber industry.

Lu-chou, the main market centre for the western part of the area, has also developed a large fertiliser and chemical industry.

The Eastern Basin This area, the lower basins of the Chia-ling and Ch'ü rivers, is comparatively hilly, with little flat land. The valleys grow rice, wheat and sweet potatoes, and cotton and silk are also produced. The higher north-eastern sections have still much forested land, and grow tea, tree oils and citrus fruits, and draft animals are bred in large numbers.

Nan-chung is a major route and market centre for this area, and the traditional centre of the silk industry. In recent times its

importance has grown, owing to the discovery in 1956 of a major oil-field, which began production in 1958, and produces between 500,000 and 1,000,000 tons annually. Some of this is refined locally, but most is sent down the Yangtze by tanker.

The Northern Basin lies east of the Ch'eng-tu plain and south of the Lung-men Shan range and occupies the upper basins of the Fu Chiang and Chia-ling rivers. It is mostly a hilly district, with little level land except in the valleys in the south-west. Much of the area is under dry farming, producing corn, soy beans, cotton and tea. It also has a very old-established silk industry.

Mien-yang is the traditional market for this region, and also an important centre of the silk industry.

Kuang-yuan, on the railway to Pao-chi, is the centre of the north-eastern part of this area. It produces iron ore on a small scale and has coal mines at Wang-tsang and Pai-shui.

The Yangtze Gorge region This eastern extremity of Szechwan is mountainous with a complex, difficult terrain, and poor communications. There is little cultivation, except in the valleys, where rice, wheat and rape-seed are the main crops. The forested mountains produce tung- and tea-oil.

Wan-hsien, a minor port city on the Yangtze, is the main outlet for the area north of the river and the adjoining parts of Hupeh.

Fu-ling plays the same role for the areas of the Chien Chiang valley, which provides a route into northern Kweichow.

The Apa region This region occupies the mountains and plateaux of north-western Szechwan, beyond the basin itself, and is a high area of rugged ranges and high plateaux, with very varied climatic regimes. The area is only sparsely peopled. Chinese (Han) settlement is confined to the southern and north-eastern valleys, where rice, corn, buckwheat and potatoes with some rape-seed and tobacco are grown. Most of the area is inhabited by Tibetans, who make up 70 per cent of the population. Pastoral industry is very important. Much of the land remains forested, and there is some lumbering.

The Kan-tzu-Ya-an region Formerly a part of Sikang province, this area comprises the towering Ta-hsüeh Shan range, the eastern border of the Szechwan basin, and the high plateau broken by another high north-south range, the Sha-lu-li Shan, to the west. Much of this region lies above 3,000 m. It has a short growing season of between 100 and 200 days. Agriculture is confined to the lower valleys in the south-east around Ya-an, where wheat, barley and peas are the main crops. Tea is also grown extensively in the Ya-an and Jung-ching areas. The northern and western parts of this area are sparsely peopled, largely by Tibetans, and are mainly pastoral areas, where sheep, horses and yaks are bred. Grain is imported into this area from Ya-an. Along the valleys of the Ta-tu and Ya-lung rivers are extensive forests.

Ya-an is the traditional market town of the southern area, and an important trading town on the highway to Tibet. It was capital of Sikang from 1950–55.

K'ang-ting, the main centre of the Tibetan population of the western plateau, and a traditional trading centre between Chinese and Tibetans, with a woollen manufacturing industry, was capital of Sikang until 1950. It is an important route centre with highways leading into both Tibet and Tsinghai.

The South-western plateau The plateau of the south-west is slightly lower (2,000–2,500 m), warmer and wetter than the Kan-tzu area. Most parts have a 200–300-day growing period, and agriculture is important. Where possible, corn, paddy rice, wheat or buckwheat are grown, according to the altitude. Rape-seed and peanuts are important crops, and livestock, especially cattle, are raised by farmers.

AREA
560,000 square kilometres

POPULATION
67,960,000 (other estimates up to 75,000,000)

TSINGHAI

PA-YEN-K'A-LA SHAN

Huang Ho (Yellow River)

KANSU

MIN SHAN

T I B E T

ERH SHAN

SHA-LU-LI SHAN

A-PA TIBETAN A.D.

KAN-TZU TIBETAN A.D.

Chin-sha Chiang (Yangtze)

Ya-lung Chiang

CHIUNG-LAI SHAN

TA-HSÜEH SHAN

CHE-TO SHAN

TA-HSIANG LING

NING-CHING SHAN

Lan-ts'ang Chiang (Mekong)

TA-NIEN-T'A-WENG SHAN

PO-SHU-LA LING

Nu Chiang (Salween)

HENG-TUAN SHAN

YÜN-NAN

LIANG-SHAN YI A.D.

BURMA

INDIA

Cha-ka
Ch'ing-shui-ho
Shang-kung-ma
Chi-mei [Ta-jih]
Lang-mu-ssu
Jan-tao [Tieh-pu]
Tien-ka-ssu

Chiang-nan
Hsia-man-ssu
Kao-lung-kung-pa

Hsieh-wu-ssu
Chih-ch'ing-sung-to [Chiu-chih]
So-ko-ts'ang-ssu
Jo-erh-kai

Chieh-ku [Yü-shu]
Chih-men-ta
Se-hsü-ssu
Pai-yü-ssu
T'ang-k'o
Wa-ch'ieh
Mo-wa

Ma-ta-ssu
Shih-ch'ü
Sai-lai-t'ang [Pan-ma]
Cheng-ta-sang
Shang-a-pa
A-pa
Mai-erh-ma
Ch'a-li-ssu
Ha-la-ma [Hung-yüan]
Ma-t'i-ssu

Hsiang-ta [Nang-ch'ien]
O-niu-ssu
Wen-po-ssu
Meng-lung-ssu
P'u-wu-ssu
Lo-hsüeh
Nan-mu-ta
T'a-wa
An-ch'iang
An-ch'ü
Mao-erh-kai

Teng-k'o
Chiao-wu-ssu
O-chih
Ch'a-cha-ssu
K'o-kuo
Kang-mu-ta [Jang-t'ang]
Shang-lang-t'ang
Lung-jih-pa
Chung-lang-k'ou

Chieh-cha
Hsia-cha-ssu
Pi-lung
Ta-t'ang-pa
Jan-ch'ung
Chia-ch'ung-ma
Kan-la
I-li
Erh-ka-li
Ch'o-ssu-chia
Ta-ts'ang-ssu
Hsia-lang-k'ou
Hei-shui

Se-ta
Lo-jo-ssu
San-ku
Weng-ta
Shua-ching-ssu
Sung-kang
Ma-erh-k'ang
Cho-k'o-chi

Ch'üeh-erh Shan-k'ou
K'o-lo-tung
Ma-ni-kan-ko
Yü-lung
Hsi-ch'ing-ssu
O-jih
Hsia-chai
Chin-ch'uan
Mi-ya-lo
T'ung-hua

Te-ko
Hsin-lu-hai
Pa-hsi-to-ch'ia
Kan-tzu
Chu-wo
Hsüeh-ch'eng
Wen-ch'üan
Wei-chou

Kung-ya
Jung-pa-ch'a
Pai-li
Hsiung-chi-ling
Wa-wu-k'ou
Chin-ta
Yü-k'o
Liang-ho-k'ou
Tsa-ku-nao [Li Hsien]

Kang-to
Chiang-ta
Ho-po
Ta-she-tung
Lu-huo
Tan-tung
An-ning
Mien-hu-chen

Lei-wu-ch'i
Ch'ing-ni-tung
Pai-yü
Ma-jung
Ch'ieh-i
Jen-ta
Peng-lung-ssu
Pien-erh
Pa-wang
Hsiang-chin
Ta-wei
Teng-sheng

Ch'ang-tu
Jung-kai
Te-lai
Hsin-lung
Ku-lo
Ma-hsi
Tao-fu
Ko-ch'ia
Yüeh-cha
Huai-yüan
Shuang-sheng
Ta-i

Ên-ta
Ma-ni-kan-ko
Ch'ü-teng
Lo-ku-ssu
Chi-ssu-chung
Mao-niu
Ch'iao-ch'i
Pao-hsing
Ch'iung-lai

Chi-t'ang
I-tun
Jan-mo-ch'ü-teng
Ko-mo-t'ung
Ch'ien-ning
Chin-t'ang
Lu-shan
Pai-chang
P'u-chiang

Pai-ma [Pa-su]
Ya-wa
Po-k'o-hsi
T'a-tzu-pa
T'a-kung-ssu
So-ô-to
Wo-lung-shih
Chiang-chü
Lu-ting
Tien-ch'üan
Ming-shan
Tan-leng

Pa-t'ang
Li-t'ang
O-lo
Ya-chiang
Hsin-tu-ch'iao
K'ang-ting
Tzu-shih
Ya-an
Ts'ao-pa

Pang-ta
Niu-ku-tu
Chia-wai
Cho-sang
Mu-la
T'ang-o
Jen-chu-t'o
Kung-ka Shan 7590
Che-to Shan-k'ou
Leng-ch'i
Ying-ching
Hung-ya

Jan-wu
Chu-pa-lung
Po-mi
Tzu-ho
Sha-te
Hua-t'an
O-mei Shan 3092
O-mei
Sha-wan-chen

Ka-te
Fu-lin [Han-yüan]
Hsin-min
Lung-ch'i-k'ou
O-pien

Se-pa
La-po
Chi-chü
Chüeh-i
Chiu-lung
Li-tzu-p'ing
An-shun-ch'ang
Shih-mien
Ta-pa

Chung-tsa
Tao-hsüeh
Sang-tui
Tao-ch'eng
Jo-tsa
Pa-wo-lung
T'o-wu
Ta-ch'iao
Miao-ning
Hsi-ho
Hsin-shih-pa [Kan-lo]
Le-wu

Yen-ching
Ch'a-ch'ia
Chung-hsin-jung
Hsiang-ch'eng
Mai-ti-lung
Lu-ning
Ma-fang-kou
Lu-ku
Mien-shan
Kan-hsiang-ying [Hsi-te]
P'u-hsiung
Hung-ch'i
Hsi-ning

Hei-ta
Kung-chia-ling
Wa-erh-chai
Chin-k'uang
Li-chou
Shan-leng-kang
Mei-ku

Te-jung
Pai-ting
Weng-shui
Ch'ia-hsin
Wa-ch'ang
K'ang-wu
Wa-li
Chao-chiao
Lan-pa
Wu-p'o

Te-ch'in
Ku-hsüeh
Pen-tzu-lan
Tung-i
Po-wa [Mu-li Tibetan A.H.]
Hsi-ch'ang
Ho-hsi
P'u-t'o
Chin-yang

Renam
Chung-tien
P'ing-ch'uan
Ma-li
T'o-mu-kou

Putao
Yan-wa
Mei-yü
Wei-ch'eng
Yen-yüan [Yen-yüan Yi A.H.]
Te-ch'ang
P'u-ko
Wen-p'ing-chen [Lu-tien]

Chü-tien
T'u-kuan-ts'un
Ning-lang [Ning-lang Yi A.H.]
Tan-kuei
Yung-ting-ying
Ning-nan

Yi-lung Shan 5950
Chan-ho
P'u-wei

Pai-han-ch'ang
Li-chiang [Li-chiang Nasi A.H.]
Yen-pien
Sa-lien
Mi-i
I-men
Hsin-chieh
Ch'iao-chia
Hui-t'o

Lan-p'ing
Chien-ch'uan
Yung-sheng
Hua-p'ing
Tu-k'ou
Cha-shih
Ta-ch'ang
Hui-li
Ta-ch'iao
Hui-tung
Chiang-chou

Chin-chiang
Li-ch'i
T'ung-an
Ta-ch'iao

Yung-jen
Tung-ch'uan

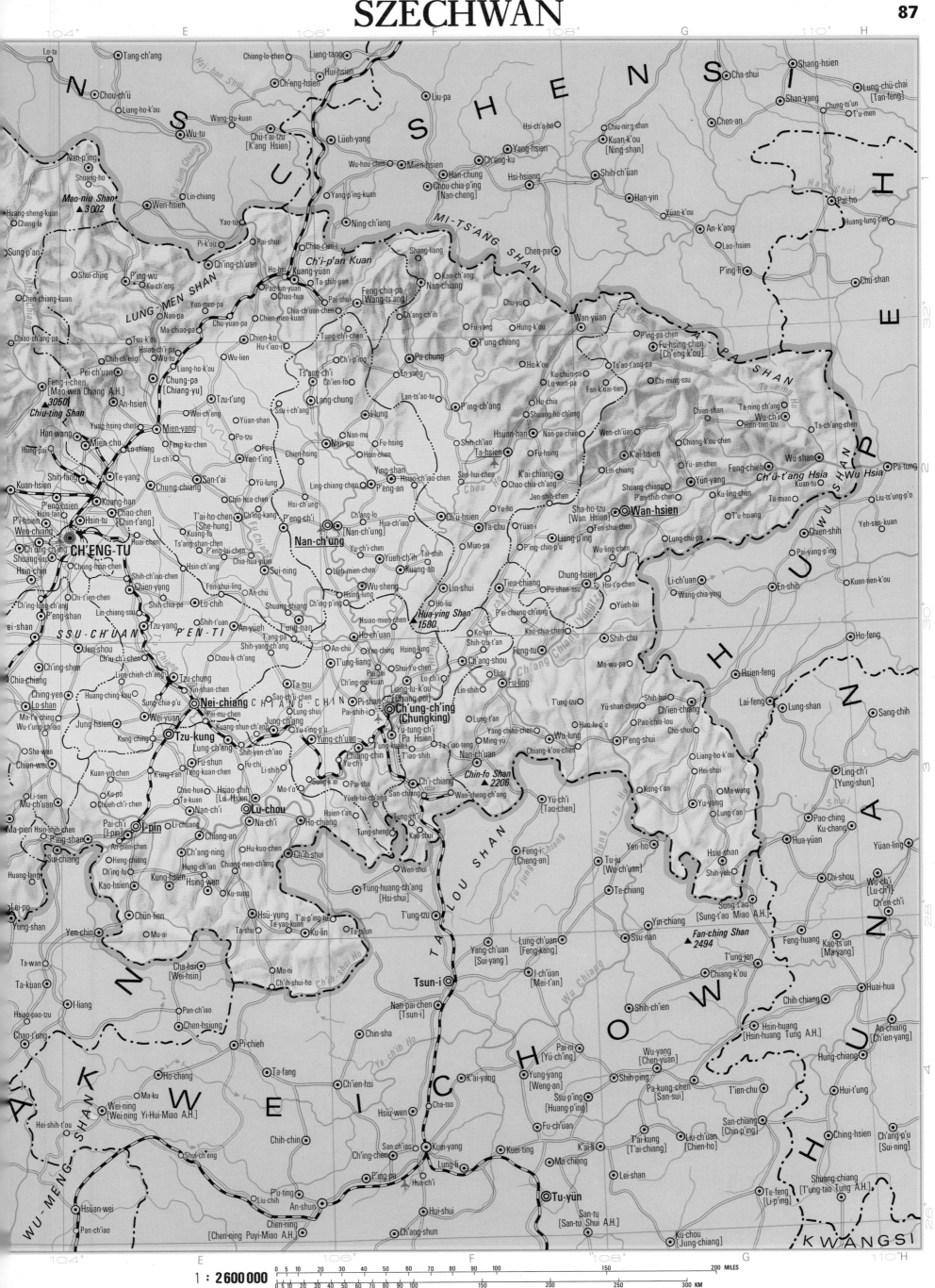

SZECHWAN PROVINCE 四川省
SSU-CH'UAN SHENG

9 shih	municipalities	
3 tzu-chih-chou	autonomous districts	
12 ti-ch'ü	regions	
181 hsien	counties	
3 tzu-chih-hsien	autonomous counties	

Name	Code	Chinese
capital Ch'eng-tu Shih	E2	成都市
Ch'ung-ch'ing Shih	F3	重庆市
Ch'ang-shou Hsien	F3	长寿县
Ch'i-chiang Hsien	F3	綦江县
Pa Hsien		巴县
centre: Yü-tung-ch'i	F3	鱼洞溪
I-pin Shih	E3	宜宾市
Lu-chou Shih	E3	泸州市
Nan-ch'ung Shih	F2	南充市
Nei-chiang Shih	E3	內江市
Tu-k'ou Shih	C4	渡口市
Tzu-kung Shih	E3	自贡市
Wan-hsien Shih	G2	万县市

A-pa Tsang-tsu Tzu-chih-chou 阿坝藏族自治州
A-pa Tibetan Autonomous District

Name	Code	Chinese
centre: Ma-erh-k'ang	D2	马尔康
A-pa Hsien	C1	阿坝县
Chin-ch'uan Hsien	D2	金川县
Hei-shui Hsien	D1	黑水县
Hsiao-chin Hsien	D2	小金县
Hung-yüan Hsien	D2	红原县
centre: Ha-la-ma	D1	哈拉玛
Jang-t'ang Hsien		壤塘县
centre: Kang-mu-ta	C1	刚木达
Jo-erh-kai Hsien	D1	若尔盖县
Li Hsien		理县
centre: Tsa-ku-nao	D2	杂谷脑
Ma-erh-k'ang Hsien	D2	马尔康县
Mao-wen Ch'iang-tsu Tzu-chih-hsien		茂汶羌族自治县
Mao-wen Chiang Autonomous Hsien		
centre: Feng-i-chen	D2	凤仪镇
Nan-p'ing Hsien	E1	南坪县
Sung-p'an Hsien	D1	松潘县
Wen-ch'uan Hsien	D2	汶川县
centre: Wei-chou	D2	威州

Chiang-chin Ti-ch'ü 江津地区

Name	Code	Chinese
centre: Yung-ch'uan	E3	永川
Chiang-chin Hsien	F3	江津县
Chiang-pei Hsien		江北县
centre: Liang-lu-k'ou	F3	两路口
Ho-ch'uan Hsien	F2	合川县
Jung-ch'ang Hsien	E3	荣昌县
Pi-shan Hsien	F3	璧山县
Ta-tsu Hsien	F3	大足县
T'ung-liang Hsien	F3	铜梁县
Yung-ch'uan Hsien	E3	永川县

Fu-ling Ti-ch'ü 涪陵地区

Name	Code	Chinese
Ch'ien-chiang Hsien	G3	黔江县
Feng-tu Hsien	F3	丰都县
Fu-ling Hsien	F3	涪陵县
Hsiu-shan Hsien	G3	秀山县
Nan-ch'uan Hsien	G3	南川县
P'eng-shui Hsien	G3	彭水县
Shih-chu Hsien	G3	石柱县
Tien-chiang Hsien	F2	垫江县
Wu-lung Hsien	G3	武隆县
Yu-yang Hsien	G3	酉阳县

Hsi-ch'ang Ti-ch'ü 西昌地区

Name	Code	Chinese
Hsi-ch'ang Hsien	D4	西昌县
Hui-li Hsien	D4	会理县
Hui-tung Hsien	D4	会东县
Mien-ning Hsien	D3	昆宁县
Mi-i Hsien	D4	米易县
Mu-li Tsang-tsu Tzu-chih-hsien		木里藏族自治县
Mu-li Tibetan Autonomous Hsien		
centre: Po-wa	C4	博瓦
Ning-nan Hsien	D4	宁南县
Te-ch'ang Hsien	D4	德昌县
Yen-pien Hsien	C4	盐边县
Yen-yüan I-tsu Tzu-chih-hsien		盐源彝族自治县
Yen-yüan Yi Autonomous Hsien		
centre: Yen-yüan	C4	

I-pin Ti-ch'ü 宜宾地区

Name	Code	Chinese
Ch'ang-ning Hsien	E3	长宁县
Chiang-an Hsien	E3	江安县
Chün-lien Hsien	E3	筠连县
Fu-shun Hsien	E3	富顺县
Ho-chiang Hsien	E3	合江县
Hsing-wen Hsien	E3	兴文县
Hsü-yung Hsien	E3	叙永县
I-pin Hsien		宜宾县
centre: Pai-ch'i	E3	柏溪
Kao Hsien		高县
centre: Kao-hsien	E3	
Ku-lin Hsien		古蔺县
Kung Hsien		珙县
centre: Kung-hsien	E3	
Lu-Hsien		泸县
centre: Hsiao-shih	E3	小市
Lung-ch'ang Hsien	E3	隆昌县
Na-ch'i Hsien	E3	纳溪县
Nan-ch'i Hsien	E3	南溪县
P'ing-shan Hsien	E3	屏山县

Kan-tzu Tsang-tsu Tzu-chih-chou 甘孜藏族自治州
Kan-tzu Tibetan Autonomous District

Name	Code	Chinese
centre: K'ang-ting	C2	康定
Ch'ien-ning Hsien	C2	乾宁县
Chiu-lung Hsien	C3	九龙县
Hsiang-ch'eng Hsien	B3	乡城县
Hsin-lung Hsien	C2	新龙县
I-tun Hsien	B2	义敦县
K'ang-ting Hsien	C2	康定县
Kan-tzu Hsien	B2	甘孜县
Li-t'ang Hsien	C2	理塘县
Lu-huo Hsien	C2	炉霍县
Lu-ting Hsien	D3	泸定县
Pai-yü Hsien	B2	白玉县
Pa-t'ang Hsien	B2	巴塘县
Se-ta Hsien	C1	色达县
Shih-ch'ü Hsien	B1	石渠县
Tan-pa Hsien	C2	丹巴县
Tao-ch'eng Hsien	C3	稻城县
Tao-fu Hsien	C2	道孚县
Te-jung Hsien	B3	得荣县
Te-ko Hsien	B2	德格县
Teng-k'o Hsien	A1	邓柯县
Ya-chiang Hsien	C2	雅江县

Liang-shan I-tsu Tzu-chih-chou 凉山彝族自治州
Liang-shan Yi Autonomous District

Name	Code	Chinese
centre: Chao-chiao	D3	昭觉
Chao-chiao Hsien	D3	昭觉县
Chin-yang Hsien	D4	金阳县
Hsi-te Hsien	D3	喜德县
centre: Kan-hsiang-ying	D3	甘相营
Kan-lo Hsien	D3	甘洛县
centre: Hsin-shih-pa	D3	新市坝
Lei-po Hsien	D3	雷波县
Ma-pien Hsien	D3	马边县
Mei-ku Hsien	D3	美姑县
O-pien Hsien	D3	峨边县
P'u-ko Hsien	D4	普格县
Pu-t'o Hsien	D4	布拖县
Yüeh-hsi Hsien	D3	越西县

Lo-shan Ti-ch'ü 乐山地区

Name	Code	Chinese
Chia-chiang Hsien	D3	夹江县
Chien-wei Hsien	D3	犍为县
Ch'ing-shen Hsien	D3	青神县
Ching-yen Hsien	E3	井研县
Hung-ya Hsien	D3	洪雅县
Jen-shou Hsien	E3	仁寿县
Lo-shan Hsien	D3	乐山县
Mei-shan Hsien	D2	眉山县
Mu-ch'uan Hsien	D3	沐川县
O-mei Hsien	D3	峨眉县
P'eng-shan Hsien	D2	彭山县
Tan-leng Hsien	D2	丹棱县

Mien-yang Ti-ch'ü 绵阳地区

Name	Code	Chinese
An Hsien		安县
centre: An-hsien	E2	
Chiang-yu Hsien		江油县
centre: Chung-pa	E2	中坝
Chien-ko Hsien	E1	剑阁县
Ch'ing-ch'uan Hsien	E1	青川县
Chung-chiang Hsien	E2	中江县
Kuang-yüan Hsien	E1	广元县
Mien-chu Hsien	E2	绵竹县
Mien-yang Hsien	E2	绵阳县
Pei-ch'uan Hsien	E2	北川县
P'eng-ch'i Hsien	E2	蓬溪县
P'ing-wu Hsien	E1	平武县
San-t'ai Hsien	E2	三台县
She-hung Hsien		射洪县
centre: T'ai-ho-chen	E2	太和镇
Sui-ning Hsien	E2	遂宁县
Te-yang Hsien	E2	德阳县
T'ung-nan Hsien	E2	潼南县
Tzu-t'ung Hsien	E2	梓潼县
Wang-ts'ang Hsien		旺苍县
centre: Feng-chia-pa	F1	冯家坝
Yen-t'ing Hsien	E2	盐亭县

Nan-ch'ung Ti-ch'ü 南充地区

Name	Code	Chinese
Hsi-ch'ung Hsien	E2	西充县
I-lung Hsien	F2	仪陇县
Kuang-an Hsien	F2	广安县
Lang-chung Hsien	E2	阆中县
Nan-ch'ung Hsien		南充县
centre: not known	F2	
Nan-pu Hsien	F2	南部县
P'eng-an Hsien	F2	蓬安县
Ts'ang-ch'i Hsien	E2	苍溪县
Wu-sheng Hsien	F2	武胜县
Ying-shan Hsien	F2	营山县
Yüeh-ch'ih Hsien	F2	岳池县

Nei-chiang Ti-ch'ü 內江地区

Name	Code	Chinese
An-yüeh Hsien	E2	安岳县
Chien-yang Hsien	E2	简阳县
Jung Hsien		荣县
centre: Jung-hsien	E3	
Lo-chih Hsien	E3	乐至县
Nei-chiang Hsien	E3	內江县
Tzu-chung Hsien	E3	资中县
Tzu-yang Hsien	E2	资阳县
Wei-yüan Hsien	E3	威远县

Ta-hsien Ti-ch'ü 达县地区

Name	Code	Chinese
Ch'ü Hsien		渠县
centre: Ch'ü-hsien	F2	
Hsüan-han Hsien	F2	宣汉县
K'ai-chiang Hsien	F2	开江县
Lin-shui Hsien	F2	邻水县
Nan-chiang Hsien	F1	南江县
Pa-chung Hsien	F2	巴中县
P'ing-ch'ang Hsien	F2	平昌县
Ta-chu Hsien	F2	大竹县
Ta Hsien		达县
centre: Ta-hsien	F2	
T'ung-chiang Hsien	F2	通江县
Wan-yüan Hsien	G1	万源县

Wan-hsien Ti-ch'ü 万县地区

Name	Code	Chinese
Ch'eng-k'ou Hsien		城口县
centre: Fu-hsing-chen	G2	复兴镇
Chung Hsien		忠县
centre: Chung-hsien	G2	
Feng-chieh Hsien	G2	奉节县
K'ai Hsien		开县
centre: K'ai-hsien	G2	
Liang-p'ing Hsien	F2	梁平县
Wan Hsien		万县
centre: Sha-ho-tzu	G2	沙河子
Wu-ch'i Hsien	G2	巫溪县
Wu-shan Hsien	G2	巫山县
Yün-yang Hsien	G2	云阳县

Wen-chiang Ti-ch'ü 温江地区

Name	Code	Chinese
Chin-t'ang Hsien		金堂县
centre: Chao-chen	E2	赵镇
Ch'iung-lai Hsien	D2	邛崃县
Ch'ung-ch'ing Hsien	D2	崇庆县
Hsin-chin Hsien	D2	新津县
Hsin-tu Hsien	E2	新都县
Kuang-han Hsien	E2	广汉县
Kuan Hsien		灌县
centre: Kuan-hsien	D2	
P'eng Hsien		彭县
centre: P'eng-hsien	D2	
P'i Hsien		卑县
centre: P'i-hsien	D1	
P'u-chiang Hsien	D2	蒲江县
Shih-fang Hsien	E2	什邡县
Shuang-liu Hsien	D2	双流县
Ta-i Hsien	D2	大邑县
Wen-chiang Hsien	D2	溫江县

Ya-an Ti-ch'ü 雅安地区

Name	Code	Chinese
Han-yüan Hsien	D3	汉源县
centre: Fu-lin	D3	富林
Lu-shan Hsien	D2	芦山县
Ming-shan Hsien	D2	名山县
Pao-hsing Hsien	D3	宝兴县
Shih-mien Hsien	D3	石棉县
T'ien-ch'üan Hsien	D2	天全县
Ya-an Hsien	D3	雅安县
Ying-ching Hsien	D3	荥经县

KWEICHOW
PROVINCE

KWEICHOW province was until recent times one of the most backward and sparsely peopled areas in China. Although a Chinese administration was set up in the area under the Han (206 BC–AD 220), the Chinese officials merely attempted to maintain some measure of control over the non-Chinese tribes which occupied the area, and Chinese penetration was confined to the north and east of the modern province. The area was provided with a provincial government and took the name Kuei-chou under the Ming (1368–1644). From the 16th century onward Chinese began to settle and farm the valleys of the eastern part of Kweichow, many of them impoverished Hakka, gradually forcing the native minority peoples out of the most fertile areas. Another wave of migration in the late 19th century brought many settlers from Hunan and Szechwan into the province in search of land. But Kweichow remained poor and backward, the communications of the province very poor, and transport costs prohibitive. When the Japanese invasion forced the Nationalist government to retreat to the south-west, the modernisation of the province was begun. Highways to the neighbouring provinces were constructed, a rail link built to Kwangsi, and some industries set up in Kuei-yang and Tsun-i. Much of this activity ceased with the end of the Second World War, and modern growth was revived only with the construction of railways in the late 1950s. Kuei-yang was connected with the Kwangsi province in 1958, with Szechwan in 1966, and with Yunnan in about 1969. Modern transport has made possible some industrial development, and the exploitation of mineral resources. Highways have also made accessible the southern and western districts.

The Kuei-yang Basin This area is centred on the valleys of the Wu Chiang and its tributaries, which have provided the main east-west route through the province. Its role as the communication centre of Kweichow has been further strengthened since the construction of railways. It has grown into the main industrial area of Kweichow, producing over two thirds of its total industrial output. The area is also well developed agriculturally. The main crops are rice and wheat in the valleys, with corn and rape-seed on upland fields. Tobacco is grown on fertile, sandy soils where irrigation is possible. The tobacco curing industry is centred at Kuei-ting.

The area has scattered coal deposits, considerable reserves of iron and, in the area north of Kuei-yang, reserves of bauxite.

Kuei-yang is the main city. The provincial capital since Ming times, it is an old-established administrative and communications centre, the nodal point of the highway system, and since the 1960s a major rail junction. Apart from temporary industrial growth through the Second World War, it had little industry apart from food processing and handicrafts before 1949. Under the first Five Year Plan it was industrialised to some degree, and its population grew from 271,000 to 504,000 between 1953–7. A large thermal generating station using local coal was built, and since then there has been much diversified industrial growth. A small iron and steel complex was established during the Great Leap Forward. A machine building industry was set up to produce electrical equipment, diesel engines, railway rolling stock

and mine machinery. There is a large cement works, and a chemical industry making fertilisers. More recently a rubber tyre industry has gained importance, and Kuei-yang has become a producer of aluminium. In addition, there are still important textile, food processing, leather and paper-making industries. Kuei-yang produces 75 per cent of the province's industrial output. Its population has been recently estimated at approximately 800,000.

An-shun is the chief commercial centre of the western part of this central basin, and its importance has grown since the construction of the Kweichow–Yunnan rail link in 1969. It has some small scale oil-extraction, flour-milling and iron-working industries.

Northern Kweichow This area comprises the lower valley of the Wu Chiang, and the valleys of the Ch'ih Shui and other rivers flowing north into the Yangtze in Szechwan. It is a high plateau area, climbing northwards to the series of ranges such as the Ta-lou Shan, rising to 1,500 m and more, which form the border with Szechwan. This is the main agricultural region of Kweichow, with better developed irrigation systems than elsewhere. In the east (the Wu Chiang area) rice and wheat are the main crops, with cotton which was formerly exported to Shanghai and Canton, an important cash crop. In the northern area (the Fu-yung Chiang and Ch'ih Shui valleys) rice and sweet potatoes are the main crops, and ramie is widely grown.

Tsun-i is the main centre of this area. The area is an important producer of manganese, which is exported to the steel complex at Ch'ung-ch'ing. There is a small local iron industry, machinery making, and a large phosphate fertiliser plant. It also has a textile industry, using local cotton and ramie, and rice and flour mills.

Eastern Kweichow This is the area drained by the headwaters of the Yuan Chiang on the border of Hunan. Comparatively sparsely peopled, much of this area is occupied by Miao and Tung minority peoples. In the valleys paddy rice, wheat, rape-seed and cotton are the main crops. In the more westerly areas tobacco is widely grown and sent to be processed in Kuei-ting. There has been considerable reafforestation in this region as forestry is very important among the Miao and Tung peoples and fir, tung-oil and camellia oil are produced. Mining is also significant – the area has one of China's main sources of mercury at Wan-shan.

K'ai-li is the main town, the chief commercial centre, and has some industry: engineering, soft wood working, and news-print production.

T'ung-jen is the chief market centre for the north of this region, with oil extraction, small fertiliser plants and agricultural implement manufacture.

Southern Kweichow This area is the drainage basin of the Hung-shui Ho which forms the border with Kwangsi. It is lower than most of Kweichow, has extensive areas of karst landscape similar to Kwangsi, and has a much warmer sub-tropical climate than the centre and north of the province.

Over half of the population are Pu-i and Miao minority peoples, who lived formerly by shifting 'slash and burn' farming, but are now mostly settled. In the valleys paddy rice is grown intensively, particularly around Tu-yün, Tu-shan and An-lung. A very important product in the extreme south-west of the province is sugar cane, which is refined at a plant in Hsing-i. The area around Tu-yün is an important producer of ramie fibre. Much of the area is densely forested, and lumbering is an important industry. Lumber is floated down the Hung-shui Ho to Kwangsi. The area is also an important producer of mercury, which is mined at Hsing-i.

Tu-yün was a minor town of about 10,000 people in the 1930s. Temporarily important as the railhead into the province after 1940, it revived after the railway was rebuilt in 1958. It has some local coalmines and a thermal power station. There is some minor industry – engineering, textiles (ramie linen), iron working and paper making.

Tu-shan is an important local market and commercial centre in the east of the region.

Western Kweichow The west of the province is a high, cold, mountainous plateau area rising to above 2,000 m, with peaks of almost 3,000 m. A remote, sparsely peopled area, it has recently been linked by rail both to Kuei-yang and to Yunnan province. It was traditionally an area where pastoral industry was important, as it has a cool climate and a short growing season, and the production of sheep, goats and horses represents about one third of all agricultural production. Agriculture in this area is comparatively recent. The main crops in the lower valleys are corn and rice, with some wheat, barley, rape-seed and beans. In the uplands the principal crops are potatoes, buckwheat and oats.

Hua-chieh is the main market and communication centre for the north-eastern part of this region, with communications with south-east Szechwan.

Shui-ch'eng is the main centre of the more southerly area bordering on Yunan. It has been connected with Kuei-yang by rail since 1969. There are important coal mines and iron mines in the vicinity. Since the coming of the railway it has largely displaced Wei-ning, further west, as the main commercial centre of this region.

National Minority Peoples Kweichow has a very complex ethnic population, which is reflected in the various autonomous administrative units. The Pu-i (Chung-chia) who inhabit much of southern Kweichow are a Thai people related to the Chuang of Kwangsi. They live interspersed with communities of Miao. They total 1,200,000 people. In the far west live the Yi (about 275,000). East of the Pu-i live the Tung and Shui, also of Thai stock. They number 700,000 and 134,000 respectively. The north-eastern border region is largely peopled by Miao, whose settlements are also found scattered all over the south of the province. They total 1,400,000. In general, the minority peoples are concentrated in the southern, eastern and western border areas of the province. Han Chinese settlement has been mainly in the centre and north, in the lowlands, leaving much of the higher land to the minority peoples.

AREA
174,000 square kilometres

POPULATION
17,000,000 (some estimates as high as 20,000,000)

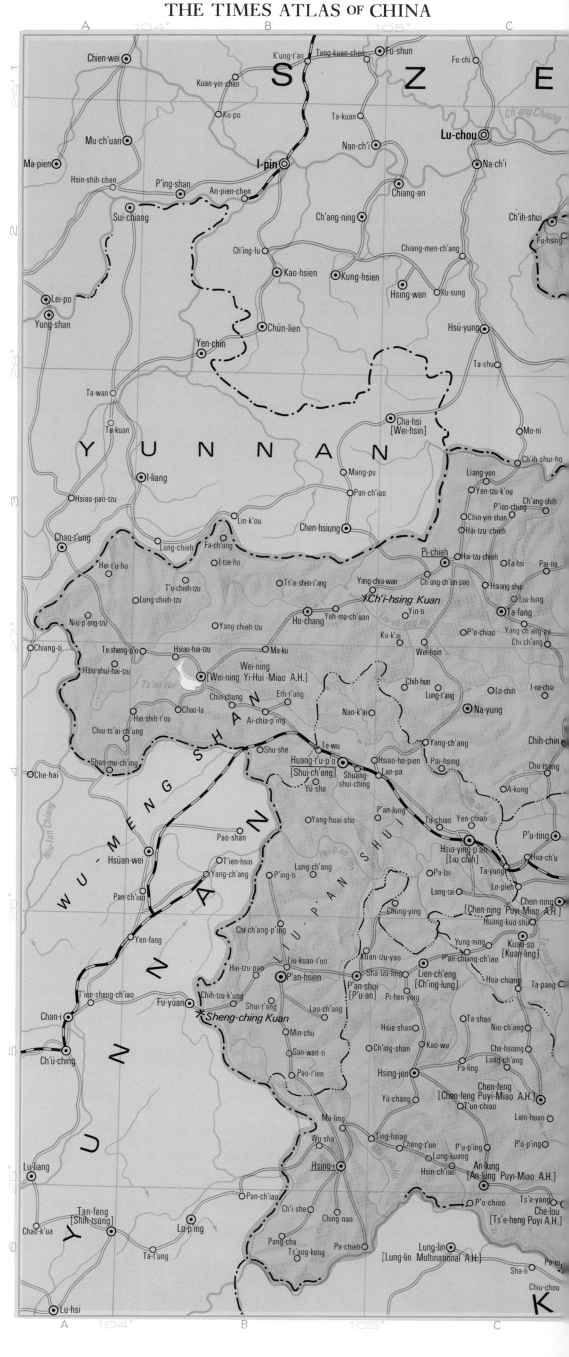

KWEICHOW

C H W A N
H U N A N
K W A N G S I
TA LOU SHAN
SOUTH EAST KWEICHOW MIAO-TUNG A.D.
SOUTH KWEICHOW PUYI-MIAO A.D.
Nan-ch'uan
2206 Chin-fo Shan
Yu-ch'i
Lo-lung
Hei-shui
Ch'i-chiang
Wan-sheng-ch'ang
San-chiang
Yüeh-lai-ch'ang
Ho-chiang
Ta-lien
Chung-hsin
Yü-ch'ing [Tao-chen]
Cho-shui
Hou-p'ing
T'an-chia-ch'ang
Yu-yang
Hsin-chou
Shang-ba
Shui-pa-t'ang
Kan-shui
Han-chia-kou
Chiu-ch'eng
Chen-nan
Lung-t'an
Pao-ching
Tung-sheng
Yang-teng
Hai-lung-pa
Lung-hsing
An-ch'ang-chen
Szu-ch'ü
Kuan-chou
Yen-ho
Hua-yuan
Ch'a-tung
Wang-lung
Kuan-tu
Ch'ai-pa
Sung-k'an
Feng-i [Cheng-an]
Miao-t'ang
Ko-lin
Fu-yang
Hsiao-ma-ts'un
Ta-chin-sha
Shih-pao-ssu
Chieh-ch'en-hsi
Hsien-yuan
T'ai-pai
Tu-ju [Wu-ch'uan]
T'u-ti-ao
Hsiu-shan
P'ai-pi
Chi-shou
Shih-yeh
Yüan-hou
Wen-shui
Liang-ts'un
Hsin-chan
Lin-ch'i
T'u-p'ing
Liu-tu
Kan-hsi
Ch'iao-chia-p'u
Wen-p'ing
T'u-ch'eng
Tung-huang-ch'ang [Hsi-shui]
Kuan-tien
Hsin-ch'ang
K'uan-k'uo-pa
Wen-ch'üan
T'u-hsi
Feng-lo
Te-chiang
Huang-pan
Hsing-chueh-hsi
Sang-mu
Li-tzu-pa
Yuan-t'ien
Sha-tzu-p'o
Sung-t'ao [Sung-t'ao Miao A.H.]
T'ung-tzu
Yung-an
Sui-yang-ch'ang
Chien-ch'a-hsi
T'ien-t'ang-shao
T'ai-p'ing-tu
Hua-ch'iu
Hung-hua-yüan
Wang-ts'ao-pa
P'ing-yuan
Pan-ch'i
Wu-lo
Ta-p'ing-ying
San-ho
Kao-ch'iao
Lou-shan-kuan
Ma-t'ou-shan
Ying-wu-hsi
Ch'ao-ti
Yin-chiang
Ho-shui
Mu-huang
P'an-hsin
Ku-lin
Ta-pa
Hua-p'ing
P'u-chüeh
Feng-huang
Pan-ch'iao
Yang-ch'uan [Sui-yang]
Lung-ch'üan [Feng-kang]
Ssu-nan
Fan-ching Shan 2494
Jen-huai
Shan-p'en
Sha-wan
Hsin-chou
Hsü-chia-pa
Ch'an-hsi
Niu-lang
Ta-hsing
P'u-lao-ch'ang
Yu-ch'uan-pa
Sui-chia-pa
T'ao-ying
Chung-shu [Jen-huai]
Kao-p'ing
Yung-hsing
Te-wang
Ch'uan-tung
I-ch'üan [Mei-t'an]
Feng-yen
Pa-huang-ch'ang
T'ung-jen
Mao-ts'ao-p'u
T'ang-t'ou
Ta-pa-ch'ang
Chiang-k'ou
Tsun-i
Lao-p'u-ch'ang
Huang-chia-pa
Hsing-lung
Ya-ch'uan
Chin Chiang
Ch'en Shui
Lu-pan
Shui-k'ou-szu
Hsia-tzu-ch'ang
Wen-chia-tien
Min-hsiao
Yen-wu-p'ing
Ch'ang-kang
Nan-pai-chen [Tsun-i]
Kao-t'ai
Sung-yen
Lung-t'ang
Ch'a-tien
Ch'ing-ch'ih
Mao-pa
Feng-hsiang-pa
Ya-hsi
Lung-p'ing
Shih-ch'ang
Ta-p'ing
Wan-shan
Chih-chiang
Pai-la-k'an
Ao-ch'i
Pai-sha
P'an-shui
Hou-pa-ch'ang
Shih-ch'ien
Hua-ch'iao
Hsin-tien-p'ing
T'ien-p'ing
Shih-ch'ang
T'uan-hsi
Mao-p'ing
Chü-feng
K'ai-pen
Chin-sha
An-ti
Sha-t'u
San-ho
Ta-wu-chiang
Chia-ao
T'ien-ma
Tao-pa-shui
Chu-tsang
Chiang-chieh-ho
Lung-hsi
Ma-hsi
Lung-t'ien
Hsin-huang [Hsin-huang Tung A.H.]
San-chung-yen
Wu-chiang-tu
Ma-ch'ang
Yang-lung-chan
Wu Chiang
Pai-ni [Yü-ch'ing]
Yang-ch'ang
Ssu-yang [Ts'en-kung]
Yü-p'ing
Sha-ch'ang
Wen-ch'üan
Niu-ch'ang-p'o
Hei-shen-miao
Chiu-chuang
Hua-li
Chung-p'ing
Ts'ao-t'ang
Tzu-ching-kuan
Kan-hsi
Wu-yang [Chen-yüan]
Ch'ing-hsi
Yang-p'ing
Weng-tung
Hsi-feng
Hsieh-ho
Lin-ch'üan
Ch'ien-hsi
Shih-tung
K'ai-yang
Yung-yang [Weng-an]
Shih-p'ing
Chiao-hsi
Chu-p'ing
Lan-t'ien
Shuang-liu
Liu-kuang
Ku-li
Chiu-chou
Pa-kung-chen [San-sui]
T'ung-lin
Pang-tung
Sha-wo
Chiu-ch'ang
Ma-ch'ang
Lung-kang
Tao-p'ing
Niu-ch'ang
T'ien-chu
Hui-t'ung
Ta-kuan
Cha-tso
Ssu-p'ing [Huang-p'ing]
Shuang-ching
Hsüan-tung
T'ai-lieh
Kao-niang
Yüan-k'ou
Pa-pu
Hsiu-wen
Yang-ch'ang
Hsin-tien
Chung-an-chiang
San-chiang [Chin-p'ing]
Wei-ch'eng
Lu-p'ing
Pa-ch'ang
Hua-ch'i
Lin-tai
Tu-la-ying
Hsi-ma-ho
Fu-ch'üan
Ch'ing-p'ing
T'ai-kung [T'ai-chiang]
Ko-tung
Liu-ch'üan [Chien-ho]
Kao-hsien
Hsiang-shui-pa
Liu-ch'ang
Wu-tang
Hsin-liu
Hua-ch'iao
Hsiao-mao-ch'ang
San-ch'iao
Kuei-yang (Kweiyang)
Ma-ch'ang-p'ing
Kan-pa-shao
Lung Ho
P'ai-yang
Ching-hsien
Kuei-ting
Hsia-ssu
K'ai-li
Lei-kung Shan 2168
Nan-chia
Ch'ing-chen
Ch'i-meng
Mao-ch'ang
Ku-chiao
Ta-yung
Chung-huang
Ch'ü Shui
Hsiao-pi
Lung-li
Ku-tung
Ma-chiang
Lung-ch'ang
P'ing-pa
Hu-ch'ao
Pu-lang
Hua-ch'i
Yen-shan
Ao-shih
Yang-liu-chieh
Hsuan-wei
Lei-shan
Shang-chung
Ma-ch'ang
T'ien-lung
Mao-mao-tung
Erh-p'u
Ch'ang-ming
Ch'ing-yen
Sha-pao-pao
Lang-tung
Hsing-jen
Ta-t'ang
An-shun
Yang-ch'ang
P'ing-fa
Tu-yün
Yün-wu Shan
Lung-ch'üan [Tan-chai]
Wu-lo
Lo-li
Te-feng [Li-p'ing]
Shuang-chiang [T'ung-tao Tung A.H.]
An-shun-chou
Lin-shao
Pai-mang
Chai-hao
Chung-ch'ao
Yao-chia-shao
Chiang-chou
Wang-ssu
Mao-kung
Kung-chou
Ma-p'u
Ta-shan-shao
Hui-shui
Kuang-shun
Pai-chin
P'ing-lang
P'u-an
P'ing-yung
Tsai-ma
Yung-ts'ung
Chi-ch'ang
Ch'ang-shun
K'ai-k'ou
Mo-ch'ung
San-tu [San-tu Shui A.H.]
Chung-ch'eng-pao
San-tu
Hsia-p'i-lin
Shui-k'ou
Chiang-lung
Mao-ying
Pai-so
Chia-jung
Keng-ting Shan 1663
Tu-chiang
P'ing-chiang
Ku-chou [Jung-chiang]
Shuang-chiang
Ku-i [San-chiang Tung A.H.]
Kou-ch'ang
Ya-chou
Shui-lung
Sha-tzu-kou
Tzu-yun [Tzu-yün Miao-Puyi A.H.]
Tuan-shan
Hsien-t'ang
P'ing-hu [P'ing-t'ang]
Tu-shan
Ting-tan
Pa-k'ai
T'ing-tung
Hsia-chiang
Kuan-tung
Pa-lo
Ping-mei [Ts'ung-chiang]
Tou-chiang
Ch'ia-p'u
Tai-hua
Yang-ch'ang
Lo-lu
T'ung-chou
Che-mi
Ch'iao-t'ou
Chi-ch'ang
San-tung
Huo-hung
Pien-yang
K'o-tu
Liu-ma
Hou-ch'ang
Shang-ssu
Chou-t'an
Chiu-ch'ien
P'ing-cheng
Tsai-pien
Chia-ya
Feng-tung
Chia-liang
Hsia-ssu
Pan-keng
Hsing-lang
Chia-ch'iao
Yüan-pao Shan 2081
Tan-chou
P'eng-t'ing
Ling-yang
Lung-p'ing [Lo-tien]
Po-huan
Li-po
Ch'ao-yang
Ma-wei
Pai-ts'eng
Ta-i
Pa-ta
Liu-chai
Ch'ang-an [Jung-an]
Lo-wang
Sang-lang
Lo-k'un
Ssu-t'ing
Lo-yüan
Fu-hsing [Wang-mo Puyi-Miao A.H.]
Mang-ch'ang
Fu-shih
Jung-shui [Jung-shui Miao A.H.]
Liu-p'ai [T'ien-o]
Tu-i
Che-hsiang
Nan-tan
Hsia-nan
Shui-yuan
San-huang
Hung-shui Ho
Ho-mu
Yang-pa
Ta-pin
Ch'e-ho
Ta-ch'ang
Tse-ling
Huan-chiang
Ta-liang
Kao-lou Ling 1424
Lo-yeh
Liu-chia
Tung-chiang
Lo-ch'eng
Ch'ang-lao
Chin-ch'eng-chiang [Ho-ch'ih]
Te-sheng
Ta-p'u [Liu-ch'eng]
Chung-tu
Ch'iao-yin
Kan-t'ien
Feng-shan
Ai-tung
Huai-yüan
Shang-lei
106°
107°
108°
109°
D
E
F
G

1 : 1540 000

0 5 10 20 30 40 50 60 70 80 90 100 MILES

0 5 10 20 30 40 50 60 70 80 90 100 150 KM

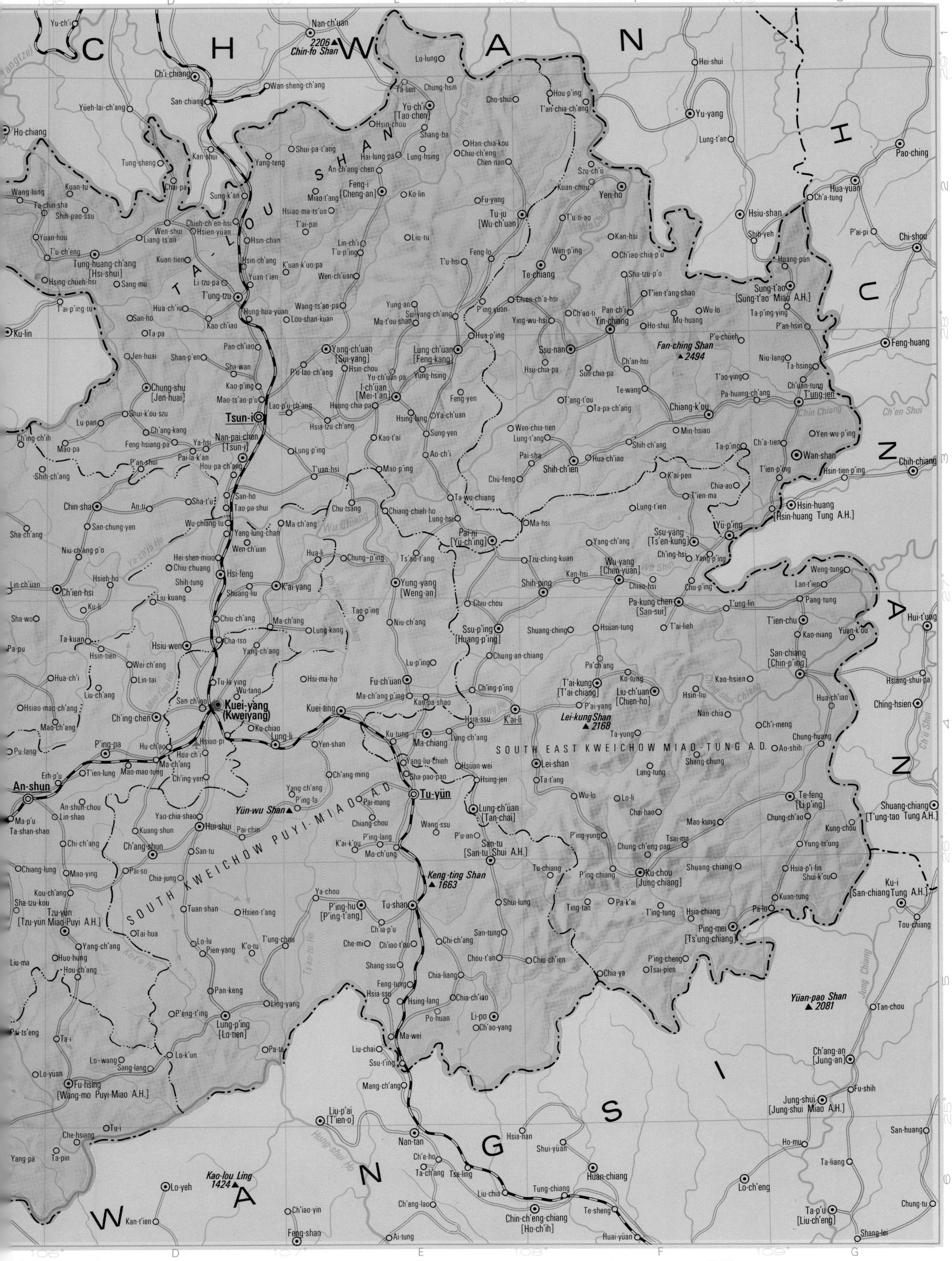

KWEICHOW PROVINCE
KUEI-CHOU SHENG   贵州省

4 shih	*municipalities*	
2 tzu-chih-chou	*autonomous districts*	
6 ti-ch'ü	*regions*	
70 hsien	*counties*	
9 tzu-chih-hsien	*autonomous counties*	

capital Kuei-yang Shih	D4	贵阳市
An-shun Shih	C4	安顺市
Tsun-i Shih	D3	遵义市
Tu-yün Shih	E4	都匀市

An-shun Ti-ch'ü   安顺地区

An-shun Hsien	C4	安顺县
Chen-ning Pu-i-tsu Miao-tsu		镇宁布依族苗族
Tzu-chih-hsien		自治县
Chen-ning Puyi-Miao Autonomous Hsien		
centre: Chen-ning	C4	
Ch'ing-chen Hsien	D4	清镇县
Hsi-feng Hsien	D3	息烽县
Hsiu-wen Hsien	D4	修文县
K'ai-yang Hsien	D3	开阳县
Kuan-ling Hsien		关岭县
centre: Kuan-so	C5	关索
P'ing-pa Hsien	D4	平坝县
P'u-ting Hsien	C4	普定县
Tzu-yün Miao-tsu Pu-i-tsu		紫云苗族布依族
Tzu-chih-hsien		自治县
Tzu-yün Miao-Puyi Autonorhous Hsien		
centre: Tzu-yün	D5	

Ch'ien-nan Pu-i-tsu Miao-tsu   黔南布依族苗族
Tzu-chih-chou   自治州
South Kweichow Puyi-Miao Autonomous District

centre: Tu-yün	E4	都匀
Ch'ang-shun Hsien	D4	长顺县
Fu-ch'üan Hsien	E4	福泉县
Hui-shui Hsien	D4	惠水县
Kuei-ting Hsien	E4	贵定县
Li-po Hsien	E5	荔波县
Lo-tien Hsien		罗甸县
centre: Lung-p'ing	D5	龙坪
Lung-li Hsien	D4	龙里县
P'ing-t'ang Hsien		平塘县
centre: P'ing-hu	E5	平湖
San-tu Shui-tsu Tzu-chih-hsien		三都水族自治县
San-tu Shui Autonomous Hsien		
centre: San-tu	E4	
Tu-shan Hsien	E5	独山县
Tu-yün Hsien	E4	都匀县
Weng-an Hsien		瓮安县
centre: Yung-yang	E3	雍阳

Ch'ien-tung-nan Miao-tsu T'ung-tsu   黔东南苗族侗族
Tzu-chih-chou   自治州
Southeast Kweichow Miao-Tung Autonomous District

centre: K'ai-li	E4	凯里
Chen-yüan Hsien		镇远县
centre: Wu-yang	F3	潕阳
Chien-ho Hsien		剑河县
centre: Liu-ch'uan	F4	柳川
Chin-p'ing Hsien		锦屏县
centre: San-chiang	G4	三江
Huang-p'ing Hsien		黄平县
centre: Ssu-p'ing	E4	四屏
Jung-chiang Hsien		榕江县
centre: Ku-chou	F5	古州
K'ai-li Hsien	E4	凯里县
Lei-shan Hsien	F4	雷山县
Li-p'ing Hsien		黎平县
centre: Te-feng	G4	德凤
Ma-chiang Hsien	E4	麻江县
San-sui Hsien		三穗县
centre: Pa-kung-chen	F4	八弓镇
Shih-ping Hsien	F3	施秉县
T'ai-chiang Hsien		台江县
centre: T'ai-kung	E4	台拱
Tan-chai Hsien		丹寨县
centre: Lung-ch'üan	E4	龙泉
T'ien-chu Hsien	G4	天柱县
Ts'en-kung Hsien		岑巩县
centre: Ssu-yang	F3	思旸
Ts'ung-chiang Hsien		从江县
centre: Ping-mei	F5	丙妹

Hsing-i Ti-ch'ü   兴义地区

An-lung Pu-i-tsu Miao-tsu		安龙布依族苗族
Tzu-chih-hsien		自治县
An-lung Puyi-Miao Autonomous Hsien		
centre: An-lung	C5	
Cheng-feng Pu-i-tsu Miao-tsu		贞丰布依族苗族
Tzu-chih-hsien		自治县
Chen-feng Puyi-Miao Autonomous Hsien		
centre: Chen-feng	C5	
Ch'ing-lung Hsien		晴隆县
centre: Lien-ch'eng	C5	莲城
Hsing-i Hsien	B5	兴义县
Hsing-jen Hsien	C5	兴仁县
P'u-an Hsien		普安县
P'an-shui	B5	盘水
Ts'e-heng Pu-i-tsu Tzu-chih-hsien		册享布依族自治县
Ts'e-heng Puyi Autonomous Hsien		
centre: Che-lou	C6	者楼
Wang-mo Pu-i-tsu Miao-tsu		望谟布依族苗族
Tzu-chih-hsien		自治县
Wang-mo Puyi-Miao Autonomous Hsien		
centre: Fu-hsing	D5	复兴

Liu-p'an-shui Ti-ch'ü   六盘水地区

centre: Huang-t'u-p'o	B4	黄土坡
Liu-chih Hsien		六枝县
centre: Hsia-ying-p'an	C4	下营盘
P'an Hsien		盘县
centre: P'an-hsien	B5	
Shui-ch'eng Hsien		水城县
centre: Huang-t'u-p'o	B4	黄土坡

Pi-chieh Ti-ch'ü   毕节地区

Ch'ien-hsi Hsien	D3	黔西县
Chih-chin Hsien	C4	织金县
Chin-sha Hsien	D3	金沙县
Ho-chang Hsien	B3	赫章县
Na-yung Hsien	C4	纳雍县
Pi-chieh Hsien	C3	毕节县
Ta-fang Hsien	C3	大方县
Wei-ning I-tsu Hui-tsu Miao-tsu		威宁彝族回族苗族
Tzu-chih-hsien		自治县
Wei-ning Yi-Hui-Miao Autonomous Hsien		
centre: Wei-ning	B4	

Tsun-i Ti-ch'ü   遵义地区

Cheng-an Hsien		正安县
centre: Feng-i	E2	凤仪
Ch'ih-shui Hsien	C2	赤水县
Feng-kang Hsien		凤冈县
centre: Lung-ch'üan	E3	龙泉
Hsi-shui Hsien		习水县
centre: Tung-huang-ch'ang	D2	东皇场
Jen-huai Hsien		仁怀县
centre: Chung-shu	D3	中枢
Mei-t'an Hsien		湄潭县
centre: I-ch'üan	E3	义泉
Sui-yang Hsien		绥阳县
centre: Yang-ch'uan	E3	洋川
Tao-chen Hsien		道镇县
centre: Yü-ch'i	E2	玉溪
Tsun-i Hsien		遵义县
centre: Nan-pai-chen	D3	南白镇
T'ung-tzu Hsien	D2	桐梓县
Wu-ch'uan Hsien		务川县
centre: Tu-ju	F2	都濡
Yü-ch'ing Hsien		余庆县
centre: Pai-ni	E3	白泥

T'ung-jen Ti-ch'ü   铜仁地区

Chiang-k'ou Hsien	F3	江口县
Shih-ch'ien Hsien	F3	石阡县
Ssu-nan Hsien	F3	思南县
Sung-t'ao Miao-tsu Tzu-chih-hsien		松桃苗族自治县
Sung-t'ao Miao Autonomous Hsien		
centre: Sung-t'ao	G2	
Te-chiang Hsien	F2	德江县
T'ung-jen Hsien	G3	铜仁县
Wan-shan Hsien	G3	万山县
Yen-ho Hsien	F2	沿河县
Yin-chiang Hsien	F2	印江县
Yü-p'ing Hsien	F3	玉屏县

YUNNAN
PROVINCE

YUNNAN, the large province occupying the south-west of China proper, became an integrated part of China at a comparatively late stage. Under the Han (206BC–AD220) the kingdom of Tien, in the area of modern K'un-ming, came under Chinese suzerainty, but Chinese control, never very strong, soon lapsed. The area was populated by a large number of non-Chinese aboriginal peoples, without any strong political organisation. In the 8th century the area was dominated by the powerful Nan-chao state, centred on Ta-li. This kingdom became very powerful, and for a while exerted great influence in parts of northern Burma and Thailand and north-western Vietnam. After it fell at the beginning of the 10th century, its place was taken by another independent state, the Ta-li kingdom. The area was finally incorporated into China under the Mongol Yüan dynasty in the 13th century. It remained a frontier area, however, with scattered Chinese garrisons and settlements in the valleys and intermontane basins living beside a very mixed aboriginal population which occupied the uplands. In the 17th and 18th centuries Yunnan became an important source of copper, but this trade died out in the mid-19th century. At this time the province was much disrupted by rebellions of the Chinese Moslem (Hui) population (1855–73), and by tribal risings. The province provided a great deal of opium in the 19th century, a trade which was encouraged as a source of revenue by the war-lords who controlled the province in the early republican period. Its modern development eventually began with the retreat of the government into the south-west during the war with Japan (1937–45). A highway system was built giving the province access to Kweichow and Szechwan, and to northern Burma, and many Chinese refugees moved into the province. After 1949 the Communist government further developed the highway system, and began to develop the railways. The French, who claimed Yunnan as part of their 'sphere of influence', built a first railway from Haiphong to K'un-ming early in the century. This was rebuilt after being destroyed during the war, and in 1969 K'un-ming was connected by rail with Kuei-yang, and with the main Chinese railway network. A direct rail link with Szechwan is also planned.

The whole province is situated on the high south-western plateau, at altitudes of 1,300 m and above, rising towards the west and the north. The plateau is deeply divided by river valleys, and by occasional low-lying basins, the most notable of which are those of the T'ien-ch'ih lake south of K'un-ming, and the Ta-li basin in the west. The western part of Yunnan is occupied by extremely high north-south mountain ranges separated by the deep and inaccessible valleys of the upper Salween, Mekong and Yangtze. Here peaks reach over 5,000 m. The climate is wet, with 750 mm of rain almost everywhere in the province, and as much as 1,750 mm in the extreme south-west. The winters are dry, almost all the rain falling between May and October. Temperatures are much modified by the great altitudes. Winter averages in the K'un-ming area are about 11°C (52°F), and the summers are cool at about 23°C (73°F).

The plateau is mostly covered with rich forest, zoned by altitude. Conifers predominate. Only about 5 per cent of the area is actually under cultivation.

North-eastern Yunnan This is the longest settled, most populous part of Yunnan, with a large proportion of the province's cultivated land, concentrated in the north-eastern plains along the Chin-sha (upper Yangtze) river, and in the lake basins around K'un-ming, where there are considerable areas of flat, cultivable land. The main crops are rice, wheat, corn (especially in the north-east) and rape-seed. Some cotton is grown around K'un-ming, tobacco is a very important cash crop everywhere, and some sugar cane is planted. Since 1949 great efforts have been made to increase productivity by irrigation works, by introducing new types of rice and by terracing hill-slopes. Pigs and sheep are reared in the mountainous areas.

Tung-ch'uan is the centre of Yunnan's copper industry. Very important in the 17th and 18th centuries, the mines in northern Yunnan were revived during the Second World War, and extended after 1954. Ore is smelted in K'un-ming.

The area also has important reserves of iron ore, which are mined at Wu-ting north-west of K'un-ming; and of coal, which is mined at I-p'ing-lang, west of K'un-ming.

K'un-ming is the provincial capital, and by far its largest city and cultural and industrial centre. Traditionally a provincial administrative centre, with about 85,000 people in 1910, its modern growth began with the construction by the French of a narrow-gauge railway to Haiphong in 1910. It then became a prosperous commercial city. Industrial growth came between 1939–45, when the government was removed to western China, and many industrial plants, banks, and businesses moved to K'un-ming from the coastal provinces. After 1940 it flourished as the terminus of the Burma Road, and of the air route to India. It rapidly grew into a large city. Its population, 147,000 in 1936, doubled by 1945 to 300,000. A temporary setback followed the end of the war, and the return of many enterprises to the east. But under the Communist regime a deliberate effort was made to build it up as an industrial base for the south-west. It has become a major producer of copper, lead and zinc. An iron and steel works has been built in nearby An-ning. K'un-ming produces machine-tools, electrical equipment, and since 1969, trucks. There are large chemical, fertiliser and cement plants. It has both hydro-electric and thermal power plants. The population of K'un-ming was estimated to be 900,000 in 1958.

The Ko-chiu region This occupies the south-east of the province. It is comparatively low-lying, at about 1,000–1,500 m, an area of limestone mountains and karst landscape similar to neighbouring parts of Kweichow and Kwangsi. The climate is temperate all year round and there is heavy rainfall, ranging from 1,200 mm in the north to 1,800 mm in the south-west. The valleys have a frost-free sub-tropical climate. Agriculture is rather ill-developed and there is little irrigated land. The main crops are rice and corn, with sugar cane grown on wet lowlands, and peanuts on dry upland fields. There is considerable timber, tea-oil and tung-oil production.

Ko-chiu is China's most important tin-mining centre producing over 90 per cent of the country's tin. Tin has been mined here since the late 18th century, but modern production began with the building of the railway to Haiphong. Before the Second World war the tin was exported to refineries in Hong Kong. During the 1950s the mines were expanded and refineries built on the spot. Lead is also produced locally, and some chemicals.

K'ai-yüan is the main transportation and commercial centre of the area. It also has important coal mines nearby at Hsiao-lung-tan, which feed a thermal generating station producing power for Ko-chiu.

North-west Yunnan This is the highest and most rugged part of the province, much of it above 3,000 m, an area of high mountain ranges divided by deep inaccessible valleys. There is much natural grassland on the higher slopes above the tree-line. The population is sparse. Cultivation is concentrated on the flat lands around lake Erh Hai and in the river valleys of the north and south-east. Rice and winter wheat are widely grown. Cotton is an important cash crop, and great efforts have been made to improve the crop strains. Sugar cane is grown in low, irrigated land. The area is also an important producer of tea, which was first introduced to the Ta-li area in the late 19th century. In the north-western uplands ranching is important and large flocks of cattle, sheep and yaks are reared by the Tibetan, Pai, Li-su, and I minority peoples. The area around Erh Hai is a famous dairy-farming district, producing large quantities of dried milk products. Forestry is also important.

Hsia-kuan is the area's major city, which has replaced nearby Ta-li, the traditional centre of the region, since the construction of the Burma Road. It is a major market for tea, cotton and sugar, and has various industries processing agricultural products.

South-west Yunnan This region is much lower-lying. Apart from mountain ranges such as the Ai-lao and Wu-liang, much of it is below 1,500 m. It is also much hotter. Areas below 1,000 m are virtually frost-free all the year. Rainfall is heavy, from 1,250–1,750 mm, 90 per cent of it falling between May and October. Agriculture is confined to the river valleys, and is rather primitive. The most important crops are rice, glutinous rice, corn, sweet potatoes, with some barley and soy beans. Tea is quite an important product, and its cultivation has a very long history. Most of it is grown by minority peoples.

Yün-ching-hung (Ching-hung) is the chief town of the south-west and the main political centre for the Tai peoples. The town has been linked to K'un-ming by a highway since 1953, and has some minor industry, but is mainly a market and commercial centre for the area.

Ssu-mao was opened up to foreign trade in the last years of the 19th century, and was a base for French enterprise in Yunnan. It fell into decay however, and was a ghost-town by 1949, although it has now recovered, and is again a regional town of some importance.

P'u-erh was the traditional centre of the tea trade.

Minority Peoples Yunnan has the most varied ethnic population in China. In the north-east the chief group are the I (Lolo, No-su). In the north-west there are a variety of Tibeto-Burman peoples, the Pai, I, Li-su, Na-si etc. In the north-east are communities of I, and of Chinese Moslems. The south-west is particularly complex, with Tibeto-Burman Hani, Lahu, and Tuchia; Tai peoples such as the T'ung and Pu-yi, and Mon-khmer peoples like the Puman and Kawa. The Ko-chiu area has many Hani, I, Chinese Moslems, Tai, and Miao and Yao tribes. There are altogether 28 different nationalities in Yunnan, totalling some 7 million persons.

AREA
380,000 square kilometres

POPULATION
20,510,000 (other estimates up to 24,000,000)

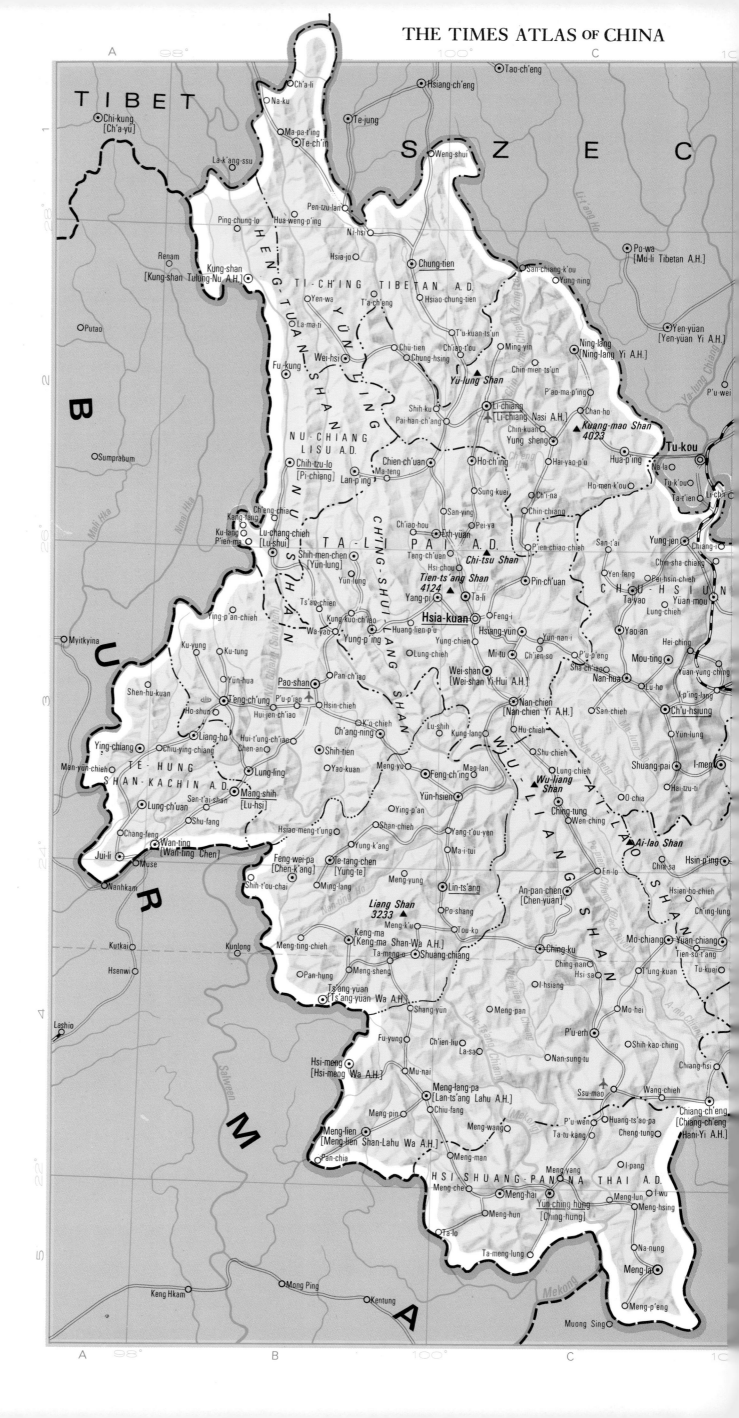

Yüeh-hsi • Hsin-shih-pa [Kan-lo] • Mu-ch'uan • Ma-pien • Ta-kuan • Nan-ch'i • Lu-chou • I-pin • Na-ch'i • Ho-chiang • San-chiang • Chen-nan • Yen-ho
Kan-hsiang-ying [Hsi-te] • Mei-ku • Shan-leng-kang • Hsin-shih-chen • P'ing-shan • An-pien-chen • Chiang-an • Ch'ih-shui • Wen-shui • Kan-shui • Feng-i [Cheng-an] • T'u-chi • Te-chiang • Sha-tzu-p'o
Chao-chiao • Wu-p'o • Lei-po • Yung-shan • P'u-erh-tu • Ch'ang-ning • Chiang-men-ch'ang • Wen-ch'üan • T'ien-t'ang-shao
Hsi-ch'ang • Kuei-hsi • Yen-chin • Kao-hsien • Hsing-wen • Ku-sung • Hsü-yung • T'ai-p'ing-tu • Tung-huang-ch'ang [Hsi-shui] • Lung-ch'üan [Feng-kang] • Ssu-nan • Chiang-k'ou
Te-ch'ang • P'u-ko • Mao-tsu • Shou-shan • Hsiao-ts'ao-pa • Lo-k'an • Ta-wan • Mo-ni • Ch'ih-shui-ho • T'a-p'ing-tu • Ku-lin • T'ung-tzu • TSUN-I • I-ch'üan [Mei-t'an] • Shih-ch'ien
Mi-i • I-men • Hui-li • Lien-feng • Ta-wan • I-liang • Mang-pu • Pan-ch'iao • Liang-yen • Nan-pai-chen [Tsun-i] • Pai-ni [Yü-ch'ing] • Wu-yang [Chen-yüan]
Ch'iao-chia • Ma-k'ou • Hsiao-pao-tzu • Lung-chieh • K'uei-hsiang • Chen-hsiung • Pi-chieh • Chin-sha • Tao-pa • Wu-yang • Weng-an • Pa-kung-chen [San-sui]
Chao-t'ung • Ho-chang • Ma-ku • Ta-fang • Chien-hsi • Hsi-feng • K'ai-yang • Ssu-p'ing [Huang-p'ing] • T'ai-kung [T'ai-chiang] • Liu-ch'üan [Chien-ho]
Che-fan • Hei-shih-t'ou • Wei-ning [Wei-ning Yi-Hui-Miao A.H.] • Na-yung • Chih-chin • Ch'ing-chen • San-ch'iao • KUEI-YANG • Kuei-ting • Fu-ch'uan • K'ai-li • Ku-chou [Jung-chiang]
Hui-tse • Shang-cha-k'o • Shuang-ho • Shui-ch'eng • Lung-li • Ma-chiang • Lei-shan
Yin-min • Lo-hsüeh • Che-chi-chieh • T'ang-t'ang • Pao-shan • Liu-chih • P'u-ting • AN-SHUN • Hua-ch'i • Hui-shui • Lung-ch'üan [Tan-chai]
TUNG-CH'UAN • Pan-ch'iao • Hsüan-wei • T'ien-hsin • Ch'ang-shun • San-tu [San-tu Shui A.H.] • Ku-chou
Sa-ying-p'an • Yang-ch'ang • Lien-ch'eng [Ch'ing-lung] • Kuan-so [Kuan-ling] • P'ing-hu [P'ing-t'ang] • Tu-shan
Tung-p'o • Lung-hai-t'ang • Tien-wei • Yen-fang • P'an-hsien • P'ing-pa • Tzu-yün [Tzu-yün Miao-Puyi A.H.] • Li-po
Kao-ch'iao • Ma-chieh • Kung-shan • Sung-shao-kuan • P'an-shui [P'u-an] • Lung-p'ing [Lo-tien] • Ma-wei
Lu-ch'üan • A-wang • Hsün-tien • Chan-i • Fu-yüan • Fu-ts'un • Chen-feng [Chen-feng Puyi-Miao A.H.] • An-lung [An-lung Puyi-Miao A.H.] • Liu-p'ai [T'ien-o] • Nan-tan
Wu-ting • Wang-chia-chuang • T'ung-ch'üan-chen [Ma-lung] • Fu-lo • Huang-ni-ho • Che-lou [Ts'e-heng Puyi A.H.] • Che-ho • Tse-ling
Lu-tz'u • Fu-min • Sung-ming • Ma-ming • Lao-hu • Lao-ch'ang • Hsing-i • Ting-hsiao • Kao-lou Ling • Lo-yeh • Chin-ch'eng-chiang [Ho-ch'ih] • I-shan
K'UN-MING • Yang-lin • Ta-pan-ch'iao • Pan-ch'iao • Hsing-jen • Lung-lin [Lung-lin Multinational A.H.] • Chiu-chou • Feng-shan • Tung-lan
Lu-feng • An-ning • Ch'eng-kung • Lu-liang • Ma-chieh • Lo-p'ing • Pa-ta [Hsi-lin] • Ling-yün
Lu-liang • Chin-ning • I-liang • Chao-k'ua • Tan-feng [Shih-tsung] • Ta-t'ung • Lo-li [T'ien-lin] • Pa-ma [Pa-ma Yao A.H.] • Hsia-yao
Tu-kuan-ts'un • Lu-nan [Lu-nan Yi A.H.] • Pan-ch'iao • Che-t'ai • Ti-hsü • Chu-chou • Pai-se • Tu-an [Tu-an Yao A.H.]
San-chia-ch'ang • Ch'eng-chiang • Hsia-chia-tu • Kuei-hsi • Lu-hsi • Yü-hsia • Pa-i • Lo-li [T'ien-lin] • Ma-shan
Pei-ch'eng • Chiang-ch'uan • Mi-le • Jih-che • Kuang-nan • Po-ai • T'ien-yang • P'ing-ma [T'ien-tung]
Fu-liang-p'eng • Yü-ch'i • Hsi-erh • Hsin-tien • Ni-chiao • Ch'iu-pei • Chu-lin • Hsi-yang-chieh • Pa-pao • Che-sang • Fu-ning • P'ing-ma • Ma-shan
Hua-hsien • O-shan [O-shan Yi A.H.] • Ho-hsi • Hua-ning • T'ung-hai • Chu-yüan • Kuang-nan • Na-p'o • Te-pao • P'ing-kuo • Lo-yü
Yang-wu • Lung-wu • Chung-ho-ying • A-meng • Na-sa • Ma-chieh • Hsi-ch'ou • Tung-kan • Ching-hsi • Lung-an • Wu-ming
Pao-hsiu • Hsin-chieh • Hsiao-lung-t'an • WEN-SHAN CHUANG-MIAO A.D. • P'ing-yüan-chieh • Ch'ang-shan • Yen-shan • Fu-ning • Hsin-yü • T'ien-teng • Ch'iao-chien • Nan-ning
Shih-p'ing • K'ai-yüan • Mien-tien • Ta-t'a • Te-hou-chieh • Ma-t'ang • Mu-kan-chieh • Na-p'o • Te-pao • T'ien-teng • Lung-ming • Ta-hsin
Pa-hsin • Chien-shui • Ts'ao-pa • Pi-se-chai • Fan-chih-hua • Wen-shan • Ma-li-p'o • Ping-kuo • T'ai-p'ing • Pou-miao [Yung-ning]
Hung-ho • Kou-chieh • Kuan-t'ing • KO-CHIU • Ta-t'un-chieh • Meng-tzu • Hsin-ts'un • Ko-ku • Ma-kuan • Na-p'o • NAN-NING • Fu-sui • Wu-yü
Yüan-yang • Tou-mu-ko • Man-hao • Wan-t'ang • Ku-mu • Tu-lung-hsin-chieh • Ha-giang • Lai-t'uan • Ch'ung-tso
Lü-ch'un • Chin-p'ing • A-te-po • P'ing-pien [P'ing-pien Miao A.H.] • La-ha-ti • Lang-son • Ch'ing-hsi • Ning-ming • Pan-ti • Shang-ssu
HUNG-HO HANIYI A.D. • Cao Bang • Lung-chou • T'ai-p'ing • Shang-ssu
Ho-k'ou [Ho-k'ou Yao A.H.] • Lang Xang • P'ing-hsiang • T'ien-hsi • Pan-ti • Mong Cai
Lao Cai • Bao Ha • Lang Son • Hon Gay
Phong Saly • Lai Chau • Song Hong (Red River) • Song Lo • NORTH • Song Da (Black River) • Lang Son
Tuyen Quang • Yen Bai • Phu Tho • Phuc Yen • Phulang Thuong • Dong Trieu
LAOS • Luan Giao • Thai Nguyen • Bac Ninh • Hon Gay
Dien Bien Phu • Son La • Phu Tho • VIETNAM • Ban Na Ngha • Son Tay • Hanoi • Bac Ninh

HWAN • KWEICHOW • KWANG SI

1 : 2600000

0 10 20 30 40 50 60 70 80 90 100 150 200 MILES
0 5 10 20 30 40 50 60 70 80 90 100 150 200 250 300 KM

Tropic of Cancer

YUNNAN PROVINCE 云南省
YÜN-NAN SHENG

4 shih	municipalities
8 tzu-chih-chou	autonomous districts
7 ti-ch'ü	regions
106 hsien	counties
15 tzu-chih-hsien	autonomous counties
1 chen	administrative town

Name	Ref	中文
capital K'un-ming Shih	D3	昆明市
An-ning Hsien	D3	安宁县
Ch'eng-kung Hsien	D3	呈贡县
Chin-ning Hsien	D3	晋宁县
Fu-min Hsien	D3	富民县
Hsia-kuan Shih	C3	下关市
Ko-chiu Shih	D4	个旧市
Tung-ch'uan Shih	D2	东川市
Chao-t'ung Ti-ch'ü		昭通地区
Chao-t'ung Hsien	D2	昭通县
Chen-hsiung Hsien	E2	镇雄县
Ch'iao-chia Hsien	D2	巧家县
I-liang Hsien	E2	彝良县
Lu-tien Hsien	E2	鲁甸县
centre: Wen-p'ing-chen	D2	文屏镇
Sui-chiang Hsien	D1	绥江县
Ta-kuan Hsien	D2	大关县
Wei-hsin Hsien	D1	威信县
centre: Cha-hsi	E2	扎西
Yen-chin Hsien	E1	盐津县
Yung-shan Hsien	D1	永善县
Ch'ü-ching Ti-ch'ü		曲靖地区
Chan-i Hsien	D3	沾益县
Ch'ü-ching Hsien	D3	曲靖县
Fu-yüan Hsien	E3	富源县
Hsüan-wei Hsien	E2	宣威县
Hsün-tien Hsien	D3	寻甸县
Hui-tse Hsien	D2	会泽县
I-liang Hsien	D3	宜良县
Lo-p'ing Hsien	E3	罗平县
Lu-liang Hsien	D3	陆良县
Lu-nan I-tsu Tzu-chih-hsien		路南彝族自治县
Lu-nan Yi Autonomous Hsien		
centre: Lu-nan	D3	
Ma-lung Hsien		马龙县
centre: T'ung-ch'üan-chen	D3	通泉镇
Shih-tsung Hsien		师宗县
centre: Tan-feng	D3	丹凤
Sung-ming Hsien	D3	嵩明县
Ch'u-hsiung I-tsu Tzu-chih-chou		楚雄彝族自治州
Ch'u-hsiung Yi Autonomous District		
Ch'u-hsiung Hsien	C3	楚雄县
Lu-ch'üan Hsien	D3	禄劝县
Lu-feng Hsien	C3	禄丰县
Mou-ting Hsien	C3	牟定县
Nan-hua Hsien	C3	南华县
Shuang-pai Hsien	C3	双柏县
Ta-yao Hsien	C3	大姚县
Wu-ting Hsien	D3	武定县
Yao-an Hsien	C3	姚安县
Yüan-mou Hsien	C3	元谋县
Yung-jen Hsien	C2	永仁县
Hsi-shuang-pan-na T'ai-tsu Tzu-chih-chou		西双版纳傣族自治州
Hsi-shuang-pan-na Thai Autonomous District		
centre: Yün-ching-hung	C5	允景洪
Ching-hung Hsien		景洪县
centre: Yün-ching-hung	C5	允景洪
Meng-hai Hsien	C5	勐海县
Meng-la Hsien	C5	勐腊县
Hung-ho Ha-ni-tsu I-tsu Tzu-chih-chou		红河哈尼族彝族自治州
Hung-ho Hani-Yi Autonomous District		
centre: Ko-chiu	D4	个旧
Chien-shui Hsien	D4	建水县
Chin-p'ing Hsien	D4	金平县
Ho-k'ou Yao-tsu Tzu-chih-hsien		河口瑶族自治县
Ho-k'ou Yao Autonomous Hsien		
centre: Ho-k'ou	D4	
Hung-ho Hsien	D4	红河县
K'ai-yüan Hsien	D4	开远县
Lü-ch'un Hsien	D4	绿春县
Lu-hsi Hsien	D3	泸西县
Meng-tzu Hsien	D4	蒙自县
Mi-le Hsien	D3	弥勒县
P'ing-pien Miao-tsu Tzu-chih-hsien		屏边苗族自治县
P'ing-pien Miao Autonomous Hsien		
centre: P'ing-pien	D4	
Shih-p'ing Hsien	D4	石屏县
Yüan-yang Hsien	D4	元阳县
Li-chiang Ti-ch'ü		丽江地区
Hua-p'ing Hsien	C2	华坪县
Li-chiang Na-hsi-tsu Tzu-chih-hsien		丽江纳西族自治县
Li-chiang Nasi Autonomous Hsien		
centre: Li-chiang	C2	
Ning-lang I-tsu Tzu-chih-hsien		宁浪彝族自治县
Ning-lang Yi Autonomous Hsien		
centre: Ning-lang	C2	
Yung-sheng Hsien	C2	永胜县
Lin-ts'ang Ti-ch'ü		临沧地区
Chen-k'ang Hsien		镇康县
centre: Feng-wei-pa	B4	凤尾坝
Feng-ch'ing Hsien	B3	凤庆县
Keng-ma T'ai-tsu Wa-tsu Tzu-chih-hsien		耿马傣族佤族自治县
Keng-ma Shan-Wa Autonomous Hsien		
centre: Keng-ma	B4	
Lin-ts'ang Hsien	C4	临沧县
Shuang-chiang Hsien	B4	双江县
Ts'ang-yüan Wa-tsu Tzu-chih-hsien		沧源佤族自治县
Ts'ang-yüan Wa Autonomous Hsien		
centre: Ts'ang-yüan	B4	
Yung-te Hsien		永德县
centre: Te-tang-chen	B3	德党镇
Yün Hsien		云县
centre: Yün-hsien	C3	
Nu-chiang Li-su-tsu Tzu-chih-chou		怒江傈僳族自治州
Nu-chiang Lisu Autonomous District		
centre: Chih-tzu-lo	B2	知子罗
Fu-kung Hsien	B2	福贡县
Kung-shan Tu-lung-tsu Nu-tsu Tzu-chih-hsien		贡山独龙族怒族自治县
Kung-shan Tulung-Nu Autonomous Hsien		
centre: Kung-shan	B2	
Lan-p'ing Hsien	B2	兰坪县
Lu-shui Hsien		沪水县
centre: Lu-chang-chieh	B3	鲁掌街
Pi-chiang Hsien		碧江县
centre: Chih-tzu-lo	B2	知子罗
Pao-shan Ti-ch'ü		保山地区
Ch'ang-ning Hsien	B3	昌宁县
Lung-ling Hsien	B3	龙陵县
Pao-shan Hsien	B3	保山县
Shih-tien Hsien	B3	施甸县
T'eng-ch'ung Hsien	B3	腾冲县
Ssu-mao Ti-ch'ü		思茅地区
Chen-yüan Hsien		镇源县
centre: An-pan-chen	C4	按板镇
Chiang-ch'eng Ha-ni-tsu I-tsu Tzu-chih-hsien		江城哈尼族彝族自治县
Chiang-ch'eng Hani-Yi Autonomous Hsien		
centre: Chiang-ch'eng	C4	
Ching-ku Hsien	C4	景谷县
Ching-tung Hsien	C3	景东县
Hsi-meng Wa-tsu Tzu-chih-hsien		西盟佤族自治县
Hsi-meng Wa Autonomous Hsien		
centre: Hsi-meng	B4	
Lan-ts'ang La-hu-tsu Tzu-chih-hsien		澜沧拉祜族自治县
Lan-ts'ang Lahu Autonomous Hsien		
centre: Meng-lang-pa	B4	孟朗坝
Meng-lien T'ai-tsu La-hu-tsu Wa-tsu Tzu-chih-hsien		孟连傣族拉祜族佤族自治县
Meng-lien Shan-Lahu-Wa Autonomous Hsien		
centre: Meng-lien	B4	
Mo-chiang Hsien	C4	墨江县
P'u-erh Hsien	C4	普洱县
Ta-li Pai-tsu Tzu-chih-chou		大理白族自治州
Ta-li Pai Autonomous District		
centre: Hsia-kuan	B2	下关
Chien-ch'uan Hsien	B2	剑川县
Erh-yüan Hsien	B2	洱源县
Ho-ch'ing Hsien	C2	鹤庆县
Hsiang-yün Hsien	C3	祥云县
Mi-tu Hsien	C3	弥渡县
Nan-chien I-tsu Tzu-chih-hsien		南涧彝族自治县
Nan-chien Yi Autonomous Hsien		
centre: Nan-chien	C3	
Pin-ch'uan Hsien	C3	宾川县
Ta-li Hsien	C3	大理县
Wei-shan I-tsu Hui-tsu Tzu-chih-hsien		巍山彝族回族自治县
Wei-shan Yi-Hui Autonomous Hsien		
centre: Wei-shan	C3	
Yang-p'i Hsien	B3	漾濞县
Yung-p'ing Hsien	B3	永平县
Yün-lung Hsien	B3	云龙县
centre: Shih-men-chen	B3	石门镇
Te-hung T'ai-tsu Ching-p'o-tsu Tzu-chih-chou		德宏傣族景颇族自治州
Te-hung Shan-Kachin Autonomous District		
centre: Mang-shih	B3	芒市
Jui-li Hsien	A3	瑞丽县
Liang-ho Hsien	B3	梁河县
Lu-hsi Hsien		潞西县
centre: Mang-shih	B3	芒市
Lung-ch'uan Hsien	A3	陇川县
Wan-ting Chen		畹町镇
centre: Wan-ting	B3	
Ying-chiang Hsien	A3	盈江县
Ti-ch'ing Tsang-tsu Tzu-chih-chou		迪庆藏族自治州
Ti-ch'ing Tibetan Autonomous District		
centre: Chung-tien	B2	中甸
Chung-tien Hsien	B2	中甸县
Te-ch'in Hsien	B1	德钦县
Wei-hsi Hsien	B2	维西县
Wen-shan Chuang-tsu Miao-tsu Tzu-chih-chou		文山壮族苗族自治州
Wen-shan Chuang-Miao Autonomous District	E4	
Ch'iu-pei Hsien	E3	丘北县
Fu-ning Hsien	E4	富宁县
Hsi-ch'ou Hsien	E4	西畴县
Kuang-nan Hsien	E3	广南县
Ma-kuan Hsien	E4	马关县
Ma-li-p'o Hsien	E4	麻栗坡县
Wen-shan Hsien	E4	文山县
Yen-shan Hsien	E4	砚山县
Yü-ch'i Ti-ch'ü		玉溪地区
Ch'eng-chiang Hsien	D3	澄江县
Chiang-ch'uan Hsien	D3	江川县
Hsin-p'ing Hsien	C3	新平县
Hua-ning Hsien	D3	华宁县
I-men Hsien	C3	易门县
O-shan I-tsu Tzu-chih-hsien		峨山彝族自治县
O-shan Yi Autonomous Hsien		
centre: O-shan	D3	
T'ung-hai Hsien	D3	通海县
Yüan-chiang Hsien	C4	元江县
Yü-ch'i Hsien	D3	玉溪县

KANSU
PROVINCE

KANSU is a large and diverse province, which has formed a part of the Chinese state since very early times, playing an extremely important role as the major route for Chinese commercial, political and cultural contacts with Central Asia and the West. It was, however, always on the edge of the empire, a semi-frontier area with a semi-arid climate, liable to frequent droughts and famines. It was an impoverished province, whose natives played little part in national politics. In the late 19th century it suffered terrible destruction and massive bloodshed in the Moslem rebellion which lasted from 1862–78, and in the brutal suppression which brought it to an end. Millions of lives were lost, and untold destruction of cities and property brought ruin to the province. In the late 19th century famine on a massive scale also brought death to millions of Kansu's people.

Kansu's boundaries have undergone many changes in recent times. From 1954 to 1958 the province included the Ningsia Hui Autonomous Region. From 1956 to 1969 the Alashan desert area was incorporated in the Inner Mongolian Autonomous Region, being returned to Kansu's jurisdiction after the dismemberment of Inner Mongolia in 1969.

Eastern Kansu This region, east of the Liu-pan range, forms an integral part of the Shensi plateau and peneplain some 800–1,000 m above sea level, covered in a thick but deeply dissected mantle of wind-blown loess soil. This area is drained by the Ching Ho and other tributaries of the Wei Ho. It is the only part of Kansu where winter temperatures (here only slightly below freezing) are warm enough to permit the growth of winter wheat. Its rainfall–around 500 mm annually, mostly in summer–is also higher than in the west, and the area grows grain crops such as kaoliang, millets and oats, with soy beans, cotton, hemp and tobacco as cash crops. The chief marketing and distribution centres are Ping-liang and Ching-yang.

The Liu-pan mountains These are formed by the upturned western edge of the Shensi plateau. The forest which once covered parts of the mountains was long ago destroyed and the area is badly eroded.

The Lung-hsi basin West of the Liu-pan range is the fertile basin around T'ien-shui and Lan-chou, traditionally known as the Lung-hsi basin. It is drained by the Huang Ho, which flows in through a series of gorges above Lan-chou, and by its southern tributary the T'ao Ho. On the south-west it is bounded by the extensions of the ranges of eastern Tsinghai, and in the north by the Wu-chiao range, an outlier of the Ch'i-lien Shan range. The basin is heavily covered with loess, and is the most fertile section of the province. The climate however is harsh. Winter temperatures between 6°C (43°F) and 10°C (50°F) and a low rainfall (below 500 mm, almost entirely in the summer when evaporation losses are high) make the climate precarious. The agriculture of the basin is founded on spring wheat, millet and kaoliang. Around Lan-chou, tobacco and melons are important crops. Fruit culture is also important, peaches being a speciality of T'ien-shui, and citrus fruits of Hsi-ku. In the uplands of the south-west, cattle and sheep rearing is important.

Lan-chou, the chief city of the area and provincial capital has been an important garrison town and transport centre since ancient times. Situated on major routes north-west along the Kansu corridor into Central Asia, westward into Tsinghai and Tibet, southward into Szechwan and north-west along the Huang Ho to Ningsia, Pao-t'ou and northern Shansi, Lan-chou was a major centre for caravan traffic into the border regions until the Second World War. During the war it became the terminus of a motor road across Sinkiang to the Soviet Union, which became a crucial source of wartime supplies. The first railway reached Kansu only in 1945, when the Lung-hai railway was extended from Pao-chi to T'ien-shui. This line reached Lan-chou in 1952, and in the 1950s was extended west to Wu-lu-mu-ch'i (Urumchi), with the intention of joining up with the Soviet system. In 1958 another line linked Lan-chou to Pao-t'ou, and in 1959 a line was begun westward into Tsinghai.

Following these developments, Lan-chou, which had previously had only minor processing industries based on local agriculture, was developed into a major industrial city destined to become the principal industrial base for the North-western Economic Region (Kansu, Shensi, and Sinkiang). A large thermal power plant, built with Soviet aid in 1957, employs coal from two large coalfields near Lan-chou, A-kan-chen and Yao-chieh, each producing between one and two million tons annually. In 1958–60 two very large hydro-electric schemes were also begun on the Huang Ho gorges west of Lan-chou, at Yen-kuo and Liu-chia. Neither, however, appears to have been completed. North of Lan-chou is one of China's largest sources of copper, Pai-yin Chang, which began production in 1958. This area has been incoporated into Lan-chou municipality. Lan-chou also produces aluminium on a large scale. It is the seat of various machine-making industries – producing oil-field equipment, railway equipment, machine tools and ball bearings. But the major industry is chemicals. The city has a large oil refinery, linked by a pipe line to Yü-men, which also processes crude oil from K'o-la-ma-i (Karamai) and the Ch'ai-ta-mu P'en-ti (Tsaidam Basin). There are plants for fertiliser, and for synthetic rubber. Since the early 1960s Lan-chou has been the centre of the Chinese atomic industry, with a uranium enrichment plant which began operations in 1963.

With this massive and rapid industrial growth, Lan-chou grew from a city of 200,000 in 1949 to 900,000 a decade later. It is also an important cultural centre, with several university and technical institutes.

T'ien-shui, until the early 1950s a major transport centre and railhead, has since been replaced in this function by Lan-chou, and is now merely the distribution and market centre of the eastern Lung-hsi basin.

The Kansu Corridor To the north-west of Lan-chou extends the Kansu corridor, a narrow belt of land extending along the northern piedmont of the towering Ch'i-lien ranges which form the border with Tsinghai. This is an area of inland drainage. A series of streams, fed by the snows on the Ch'i-lien ranges, flows out into the desert plateau to the north. Only two flows any considerable distance: the Jo Shui (Edsin Gol), which flows into two

saline lakes near the Mongolian border, and the Shu-le, which flows into the far north-west near An-hsi. The whole area has very little rainfall – less than 300 mm annually – and agriculture is confined to the ten or so oases ranging in size from 200 to 1,500 square kilometres watered by these mountain streams, where irrigation can be practised. In the most easterly oases, Wu-wei and Chang-ye, special hardy varieties of rice have long been cultivated. Elsewhere, millet, kaoliang and spring wheat are the important crops. In the foothills of the mountains there is a well developed pastoral economy, raising horses, cattle, sheep and camels.

The towns of the Kansu corridor were traditionally a series of oases on a major caravan route. However, the coming of modern transport has led to some industrial developments.

Yü-men was the first major oil-field developed in China. Production began on a small scale in 1939, and throughout the war about 100,000 tons were produced annually and shipped out by lorry. In 1956 a rail link was built to Lan-chou, and a pipe-line constructed in the next year. The refinery at Yü-men itself was enlarged and modernised. In the late 1960s annual production was about two million tons.

Chiu-ch'uan was designated as the site of a major iron and steel complex to serve the north-west in the late 1950s. Very large iron reserves were discovered in the Ch'i-lien range south of the town, while an important coal field was opened up at Shan-tan to the east, producing a million tons annually. The plans for an integrated iron and steel plant seem to have been abandoned when the Great Leap Forward collapsed, but it seems possible that work has gone ahead with this plan since 1965.

Shuang-ch'eng-tzu about 140 miles north-east of Chiu-ch'uan in the valley of the Jo Shui, is China's space and missile launching centre.

The Alashan Desert To the north of the Kansu corridor lies the forbidding Alashan Desert, a virtually uninhabited plateau broken by low ranges of hills, which stretches to the Mongolian border. With an annual rainfall of 100 mm or less, much of this area is true desert, the rest very sparse grassland. It is inhabited entirely by nomadic Mongol herdsmen.

Minority Peoples Kansu has considerable variety of minority peoples. Most numerous are the Chinese Moslems (Hui), who were even more numerous until the great Moslem rebellions of the 19th century, during which millions perished. Their most important settlement is around Lin-hsia in the plain south-east of Lan-chou. Another large community lives on the Shensi border north of Tien-shui. Associated with the Hui settlement around Lin-hsia is a community of Tung-hsiang, a Moslem Mongol minority.

Tibetan minorities occupy much of the mountainous border district in the south-west, and live scattered along the Ch'i-lien range, and in the Wu-chiao range north of Lan-chou.

All of northern Kansu is peopled by Mongols, and a separate Mongol community is to be found in the Ch'i-lien mountains on the Tsinghai border. In the extreme north-western tip of Kansu is a Kazakh minority.

AREA
530,000 square kilometres

POPULATION
12,650,000
Other estimates 13,000,000

Na-jan-pa-pu-ssu-t'ai-yin
Pu-la-ko

Ch'ing-ho-k'ou

Ka-shun No-erh
(Chü-yen Hai)

So-kuo No-erh

Chiu-yen   Ts'e-k'o

K'u-shui

Wei-ya

Ming-shui   Kung-p'o-ch'üan   I-k'en-kao-le

Hsing-hsing-hsia

Lo Ching   Shih-pan Ching

Ta-lan-k'u-pu
[O-ch'i-na Ch'i]

Hung-liu-ho   Ma-lien-ching   T'ung-ch'ang-k'ou   Ma-tsung Shan 2583   Lo-t'o-ching   Wu-lan-ch'üan-chi

SINKIANG   PEI   SHAN   P'ing-shan-t'ou   Chiang-chün-t'ai   Hung-lu-lu-yang-ta   Lao-hsi-miao   Hsi-miao (Shuang-ch'eng-tzu)

Ta-ch'üan   Hua-niu-shan   Hu-hsi-hsin-ts'ün

Pai Shan 2013   Hsiao-ch'üan-tung   Liu-yüan   Shuang-ch'eng-tzu

Hung-liu-yüan   Hsia-tung   Pei-shan   PA-TAN-CHI-LIN

K'u-shui-ching   Pai-tun-tzu   An-pei   T'ien-t'sang   Ta-wan

Chang-chia-ch'üan   P'ei-ta-ch'iao   Ch'iao-wan   Ch'ou-shui-tung   Ting-hsin   Shuang-ch'eng-tzu

Yü-men-kuan   T'ou-kung   An-hsi   Shuang-t'a-pao   Yin-ma-ch'ang   Tung-pa

Ku-yü-men-kuan   T'ien-shui-ching   Shih-kung   Shu-le-ho   Yü-men-chen   Hua-hai   HO-LI SHAN

Tun-huang   Chi-li-chen   T'a-shih   Ch'ang-ma-ta-pa   Ch'ih-chin-pao   Yao-ch'üan-tzu   Chin-t'a   T'ien-ch'eng   Hsin-ching

San-wei Shan   Tung-pa-r'u   Han-hsia   Hsin-min-pao   Chia-yü-kuan   Lo-ch'eng

Sha-tsao-yüan   Ch'ien-fo-tung   Shih-pao-ch'eng   Ch'ang-ma   Yü-men   Chin-chai   Ch'ing-shui

Nan-hu   Ta-kung-ch'a   Yü-men   Tung-chan   Chiu-ch'üan   Hei-ch'üan   Ta-ch'e-ch'ang

Tu-shan-tzu   Ma-tzu-hsüan-ch'üan   Hsi-kou   Ch'ing-shui   Kao-t'ai   Liao-ch'üan   O-k'en-hu-tu-ko [Alashan West Banner]

Po-lo-chuan-ching [Aksai Kazakh A.H.]   Ch'ang-ts'ao-kou   YEH-MA NAN-SHAN   Ta-ch'üan   Pai-t'u-wan-tzu   Hsü-san-wan   Hsin-hua   Pan-ch'iao

An-nan-pa   Yen-ch'ih-wan   Kan-kou   Ch'i-lien Shan 5564   Yuan-shan-tzu   Sha-ho-pao [Lin-tse]   Wu-chiang-pao

Tang-chin Shan-k'ou   WU-LAN TA-PAN   Hai-t'un   TSOU-LANG NAN-SHAN   Hung-wan-ssu   Chang-yeh   Ta-p'ing-pao   UNG-SHOU SHAN

Ting-tzu-k'ou   Hua-hai-tzu   T'o-le   [South Kansu Yuku A.H.]   Lung-tao-pao   Tung-le   Shan-tan

Leng-hu   Su-kan No-erh   CHI-LIEN SHAN   Hua-chai-tzu   Ma-lien-ching

Ha-na-t'eng Ho   Tang Ho   SHU-LE NAN-SHAN   T'O-LAI NAN-SHAN   Liu-pa   San-pao   Chi-ling

Ch'a-leng-k'ou   Yü-k'a   Ha-la Hu   Ko-tzu-tung   Pa-pao [Ch'i-lien]   Feng-ch'eng   Min-le   Shui-ch'üan-tzu

Sha-liang-tzu   CHAI-TA-MU P'EN-TI   Ta-ch'ai-tan   Mu-li   Yen-chih Shan   Yung-ch'ang

Hsi-t'ai-chi-nai-erh Hu   O-po   Hsin-ch'eng   Huang-ch'eng   LENG LU

Tung-t'ai-chi-nai-erh Hu   Huai-t'ou-t'a-lai   Te-ling-ha   Yeh-ma-t'an   [Kang-ch'a]   Ch'ing-shih-tsui

Nu-t'u-le   Ch'a-erh Yen-ch'ih   Te-ling-ha   Nung-ch'ang   Hsin-yüan [T'ien-chün]   Sha-lin-ho   Hao-men [Men-yüan Hui A.H.]

Ch'a-erh-han   Mao-niu-shan   Mo-ho   Ch'a-k'a   Ch'ing-hai Hu (Koko Nor)   Ha-erh-kai   San-chiao-ch'eng [Hai-yen]   Ta-t'ung

T'o-le   Ko-erh-mu (Golmo)   Hei-ma-ho   Huang-yüan   Hsi-ning (Sining)   Kan-li-p'u

No-mu-hung   TSINGHAI   Ch'a-han-wu-su [Tu-lan]   Ch'ia-pu-ch'ia [Kung-ho]   Tao-t'ang-ho   Ka-jang

Na-ch'ih-t'ou   Hsiang-jih-te   Ho-yin [Kuei-te]   Ma-k'o-t'ang (Chien-cha)

K'UN-LUN SHAN   Ta-ho-pa   Mang-la [Kuei-nan]   Hsin-chieh

Chi-ma-erh Ho   Tzu-k'o-t'an [Hsing-hai]   T'ang-nai-hai   Pa-t'an

Mien-ts'ao-wan   So-nai-hai [Tse-k'u]

Cha-ling   Hua-shih-hsia   La-chia-ssu   Yu-kan-t'an [Honan Mongol A.H.]

Se-wu-kou [Chü-ma-lai]   Ts'o-pa-jih-ka-tse   Huang-ho-yen [Ma-to]   Ma-la-i-wan   I-ch'i-kai

Yeh-ma-t'an   Ta-wu [Ma-ch'in]

Yeh-niu-kou   Ch'a-la-kou   Kan-te   Ou-la

Chia-chi-po-lo-ko [Chih-to]   Hsia-jih-ssu   Ch'ing-shui-ho   Hsiu-ma-t'an   Shang-kung-ma   Chih-ch'ing-sung-to [Chiu-chih]

Chia-lung-yün   Chi-mai [Ta-jih]   Pai-yü-ssu

Yü-yü-jih-pen [Tsa-to]   Ko-ma   Chiang-nan   Sang-jih-ma

Chieh-cha   Tzu-ch'i-u-tu-k'ou   Chieh-ku [Yü-shu]   Chih-men-ta   SZECH

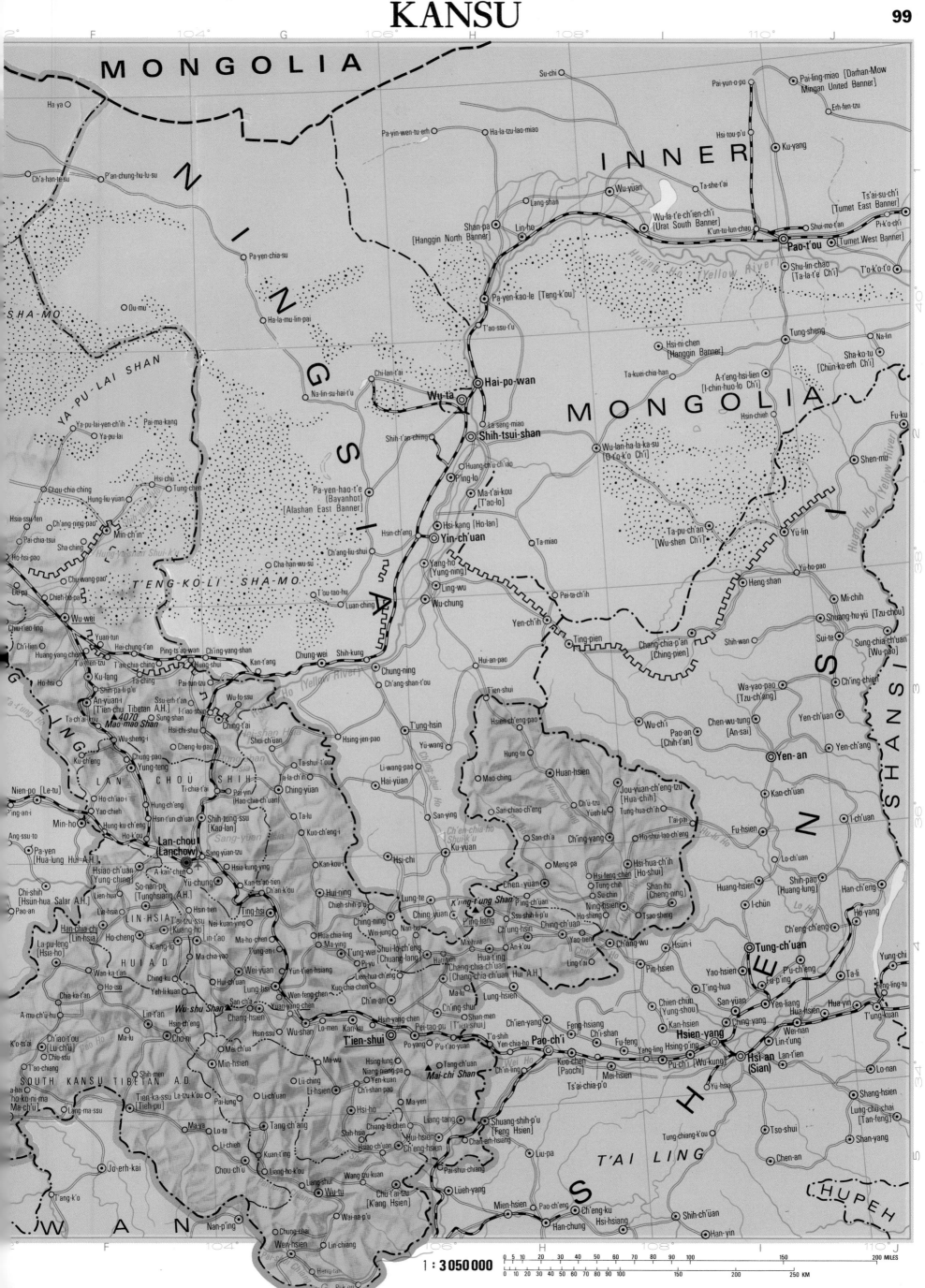

1 : 3 050 000

KANSU PROVINCE
KAN-SU SHENG 甘肃省

4 shih	*municipalities*	
2 tzu-chih-chou	*autonomous districts*	
8 ti-ch'ü	*regions*	
66 hsien	*counties*	
6 tzu-chih-hsien	*autonomous counties*	
2 ch'i	*banners*	

capital Lan-chou Shih	F4	兰州市
Kao-lan Hsien		皋兰县
centre: Shih-tung-ssu	F3	石洞寺
Yü-chung Hsien	G4	榆中县
Yung-teng Hsien	F3	永登县
Chia-yü-kuan Shih	D2	嘉峪关市
T'ien-shui Shih	H3	天水市
Yü-men Shih	C2	玉门市

Kan-nan Tsang-tsu Tzu-chih-chou 甘南藏族自治州
South Kansu Tibetan Autonomous District

centre: Ho-tso	F4	合作
Cho-ni Hsien	F4	卓尼县
Chou-ch'ü Hsien	G5	舟曲县
Hsia-ho Hsien		夏河县
centre: La-pu-leng	F4	拉卜楞
Lin-t'an Hsien	F4	临潭县
Lu-ch'ü Hsien		碌曲县
centre: Ch'iao-t'ou	F4	桥头
Ma-ch'ü Hsien		玛曲县
centre: Cho-ko-ni-ma	F4	卓格尼玛
Tieh-pu Hsien		迭部县
centre: Tien-ka-ssu	F4	电尕寺

Lin-hsia Hui-tsu Tzu-chih-chou 临夏回族自治州
Lin-hsia Hui Autonomous District

centre: Han-chia-chi	F4	韩家集
Ho-cheng Hsien	F4	和政县
K'ang-lo Hsien	F4	康乐县
Kuang-ho Hsien		广河县
centre: T'ai-tzu-ssu	F4	太子寺
Lin-hsia Hsien		临夏县
centre: Han-chia-chi	F4	韩家集
Tung-hsiang-tsu Tzu-chih-hsien		东乡族自治县
Tunghsiang Autonomous Hsien		
centre: So-nan-pa	F4	锁南坝
Yung-ching Hsien		永靖县
centre: Hsiao-ch'uan	F4	小川

Chang-yeh Ti-ch'ü 张掖地区

Chang-yeh Hsien	E2	张掖县
Kao-t'ai Hsien	D2	高台县
Lin-tse Hsien		临泽县
centre: Sha-ho-pao	E2	沙河堡
Min-le Hsien	E2	民乐县
Shan-tan Hsien	E2	山丹县
Su-nan Yü-ku-tsu Tzu-chih-hsien		肃南裕固族自治县
South Kansu Yüku Autonomous Hsien		
centre: Hung-wan-ssu	D2	红湾寺

Ch'ing-yang Ti-ch'ü 庆阳地区

centre: Hsi-feng-chen	H4	
Cheng-ning Hsien		正宁县
centre: Shan-ho	I4	山河
Chen-yüan Hsien	H4	镇原县
Ch'ing-yang Hsien	H4	庆阳县
Ho-shui Hsien		合水县
centre: Hsi-hua-ch'ih	I4	西华池
Hua-ch'ih Hsien		华池县
centre: Jou-yüan-ch'eng-tzu	H3	柔远城子
Huan Hsien		环县
centre: Huan-hsien	H3	
Ning Hsien		宁县
centre: Ning-hsien	H4	

Chiu-ch'üan Ti-ch'ü 酒泉地区

A-k'o-sai Ha-sa-k'o-tsu Tzu-chih-hsien		阿克塞哈萨克族自治县
Aksai Kazakh Autonomous Hsien		
centre: Po-lo-chuan-ching	B2	博罗转井
An-hsi Hsien	B1	安西县
Chin-t'a Hsien	D2	金塔县
Chiu-ch'üan Hsien	D2	酒泉县
O-chi-na Ch'i		额济纳旗县
Edsin Banner		
centre: Ta-lan-k'u-pu	E1	达兰库布
Su-pei Meng-ku-tsu Tzu-chih-hsien		肃北蒙古族自治县
North Kansu Mongol Autonomous Hsien		
centre: Tang-ch'eng-wan	B2	党城湾
Tun-huang Hsien	B1	敦煌县

P'ing-liang Ti-ch'ü 平凉地区

Ching-ch'uan Hsien	H4	泾川县
Ching-ning Hsien	G4	静宁县
Chuang-lang Hsien		庄浪县
centre: Shui-lo-ch'eng	H4	水洛城
Ch'ung-hsin Hsien	H4	崇信县
Hua-t'ing Hsien	H4	华亭县
Ling-t'ai Hsien	H4	灵台县
P'ing-liang Hsien	H4	平凉县

T'ien-shui Ti-ch'ü 天水地区

Chang-chia-ch'uan Hui-tsu Tzu-chih-hsien		张家川回族自治县
Chang-chia-ch'uan Hui Autonomous Hsien	H4	
Chang Hsien		漳县
centre: Chang-hsien	G4	
Ch'in-an Hsien	G4	秦安县
Ch'ing-shui Hsien	H4	清水县
Hsi-ho Hsien	G4	西河县
Hui Hsien		徽县
centre: Hui-hsien	H5	
Kan-ku Hsien	G4	甘谷县
Liang-tang Hsien	H5	两当县
Li Hsien		礼县
centre: Li-hsien	G4	
T'ien-shui Hsien		天水县
centre: Pei-tao-pu	G4	北道埠
Wu-shan Hsien	G4	武山县

Ting-hsi Ti-ch'ü 定西地区

Ching-yüan Hsien	G3	靖远县
Hui-ning Hsien	G4	会宁县
Lin-t'ao Hsien	F4	临洮县
Lung-hsi Hsien	G4	陇西县
Ting-hsi Hsien	G4	定西县
T'ung-wei Hsien	G4	通渭县
Wei-yüan Hsien	G4	渭源县

Wu-tu Ti-ch'ü 武都地区

Ch'eng Hsien		成县
centre: Ch'eng-hsien	G5	
K'ang Hsien	G5	康县
centre: Chü-t'ai-tzu	G5	咀台子
Min Hsien		岷县
centre: Min-hsien	F4	
Tang-ch'ang Hsien	G5	宕昌县
Wen Hsien		文县
centre: Wen-hsien	G5	
Wu-tu Hsien	G5	武都县

Wu-wei Ti-ch'ü 武威地区

A-la-shan Yu-ch'i		阿拉善右旗
Alashan West Banner		
centre: O-k'en-hu-tu-ko	E2	额肯呼都格
Ching-t'ai Hsien	G3	景泰县
Ku-lang Hsien	F3	古浪县
Min-ch'in Hsien	F2	民勤县
T'ien-chu Tsang-tsu Tzu-chih-hsien		天祝藏族自治县
T'ien-chu Tibetan Autonomous Hsien		
centre: An-yüan-i	F3	安远驿
Wu-wei Hsien	F3	武威县
Yung-ch'ang Hsien	E2	永昌县

CHENG-CHOU

(CHENGCHOW)

Population 595,000 (1953); 1,100,000 (1970 estimate)

The city has been provincial capital of Honan since 1954, situated to the south of the Huang Ho river and at the eastern extremity of the Hsiung-erh Shan mountain range. It is generally identified with the Shang capital city of Ao. It achieved its greatest importance under the Sui, T'ang and early Sung when, as the terminus of the Pien-ho canal, it was near a vast granary complex from which provisions were shipped westwards to the capitals at Lo-yang and Ch'ang-an, or northwards to the armies on the frontier around Peking. In 1903 the Peking–Han-k'ou railway arrived at Cheng-chou, and thereafter it became a major rail junction for handling agricultural produce. After 1949, because Cheng-chou was in the centre of a densely peopled cotton-growing district with excellent communications, it was deliberately developed into a modern industrial city. Its industries remain largely based on local agriculture and textiles. This rapid industrial growth has involved a phenomenal increase in the city's population, and there has been an enormous building programme, involving the reconstruction of much of the old city.

CHI-NAN

(TSINAN, JINAN)

Population 680,000 (1953); 862,000 (1958 estimate)

When Shantung province was created under the Ming (1368–1644), Chi-nan, a city which had enjoyed considerable importance as an administrative and religious centre for many centuries, was a natural choice as capital. The modern phase of Chi-nan's growth began in 1852, when the Huang Ho shifted its course to flow in the old bed of the Chi river just north of the city and provided a link for small craft with the Grand Canal and the waterways of Shantung and Hopeh. The construction of excellent rail communications in the early years of this century meant that Chi-nan rapidly became a commercial centre for the agricultural region to the north and developed much light industry.

Since 1949 it has been swiftly and deliberately developed both as an administrative centre and also as a major centre of modern industry. The pre-war textile and flour-milling industries have been expanded and iron and steel, automotive and machine-building industries established. Chi-nan has also become the chief cultural centre of Shantung, with agricultural, medical and engineering colleges and a large university.

T'AI-YÜAN

(TAIYUAN)

Population 721,000 (1953); 1,020,000 (1958 estimate)

Situated on both banks of the Fen Ho river, commanding the north–south route through Shansi and natural lines of communication through the mountains to Hopeh and northern Shansi, T'ai-yüan has been an important city throughout Chinese history. The modern city dates from the Sung period, when it was built to replace the old, heavily-fortified city a few miles further east, which had been destroyed to prevent rebellion. Under the Ming and the Ch'ing, Tai-yüan became the capital of Shansi province and grew in size and importance.

Shansi was fortunate that in the decades of political chaos after 1911 the province remained under a powerful war-lord, Yen Hsi-shan, who maintained political stability. Real growth began with Yen's adoption, in 1933, of a 10-year Industrial Development Plan, based on the Soviet model. Under this plan T'ai-yüan was to become the heavy industrial base for his regime and development was partly completed when the Japanese invaded in 1937. They developed the city's industry still further. Since 1949, in accord with the government's strategy of moving industry away from the coastal zone, T'ai-yüan has become a very large industrial centre, notable for the sheer size of its capacity and for its diversity. Local coal production is considerable; there is a large thermal generating plant; the iron and steel, engineering and chemical industries are extremely important. Industry is supported by many centres of education and research, particularly for technology and applied science.

CH'ANG-SHA

(CHANGSHA)

Population 651,000 (1953); 800,000 (1970 estimate)

The city has been the provincial capital of Hunan since 1664. Its position on the Hsiang Chiang river, some 50 km south of the Tung-t'ing Lake, with excellent water communications to southern and south-western Hunan, has made it a natural commercial centre for centuries. Under the Ming (1368–1644) and the Ch'ing (1644–1911) it became very wealthy as one of China's chief rice markets. Ch'ang-sha was opened to foreign trade in 1904, following the Treaty of Shanghai between China and Japan. Further development followed the opening of the railway to Han-k'ou in 1918.

Ch'ang-sha was in the front line of the Sino–Japanese War from 1938 onwards. It was the site of three major battles in 1939 and 1941 and was virtually destroyed by fire in 1938–9. Since 1949 the city has been rebuilt and has regained its former importance. It is now both a major port, handling enormous tonnages of rice, cotton, timber and livestock, and the most important collection and distribution point on the railway from Han-k'ou to Canton. It is also a major centre of industry and has plants for the manufacture of machine and precision tools, cement, ceramics and paper-making; plants for rice milling, and processing of agricultural products, such as oil-extraction, tea and tobacco curing and textiles; a large chemical and fertiliser industry, and a thermal generating station. Ch'ang-sha has a long tradition of learning and now has a variety of colleges and institutes of higher education.

SHEN-YANG

(MUKDEN)

Population 2,299,000 (1953); 3,000,000 (1970 estimate)

Shen-yang, which was known as Mukden under the Manchus, who made this city their capital before their conquest of China, is now the capital city of Liaoning province. Its position to the south of the Manchurian plain, at the junction of important north–south and east–west rail routes, has made the city the natural economic and political centre of Manchuria. Shen-yang developed particularly during the period of Japanese rule, when a new city was constructed in the former Japanese railway concession zone, to the west of the old Chinese city. The proximity of the city to the iron and steel plants of An-shan and Pen-ch'i has led to further development of heavy industry since the early 1950s, and Shen-yang is now one of the principal metal and machinery producers of China. It also produces electrical equipment, aircraft and vehicles, including tractors.

YIN-CH'UAN

(YINCHWAN)

Population 84,000 (1953)

Yin-ch'uan has been the capital of Ningsia Autonomous Region since its foundation in 1958. It is located on the upper Huang Ho river in the middle of the Ningsia plain. It has a river port at Heng-ch'eng, about 15 km to the east, and is a rail and road centre. The immediate plain area is intensely irrigated and extremely productive. Yin-ch'uan, traditionally an administrative and commercial centre, has grown considerably since 1949, although it is still largely non-industrial. It is primarily a grain market, with flour mills and rice hulling plants, and it serves as a market for the hides, wool and other animal products of the nomadic herdsmen from the surrounding grasslands. The wool produced in the steppe has been the foundation for a modern woollen textile mill which came into operation in 1954.

Yin-ch'uan is an important centre for the Moslem (Hui) minority peoples who constitute one third of the population, and who have established their own schools, cultural centres and hospitals.

HO-FEI

(HOFEI)

Population 184,000 (1953); 500,000 (1970 estimate)

Ho-fei, the provincial capital of Anhwei province, is an important natural communication centre, situated to the north of Ch'ao Hu lake, on a low saddle in the north-eastern extension of the Ta-pieh mountain range. Major east–west and north–south routes run through the city. In the pre-war period Ho-fei remained essentially a traditional city, an administrative centre and the regional market for the fertile plain to the south. The construction in 1912 of the Tientsin–P'u-k'ou railway for a while made Ho-fei a provincial backwater, but between 1932–6 a railway built primarily to exploit the rich coal field in northern Anhwei did much to revive the economy of the Ho-fei area.

Under the Communist regime, it has developed rapidly into a major industrial city. A very large thermal generating plant was established in the early 1950s and a cotton mill and iron and steel complex opened later in the decade. There is a chemical and an aluminium industry, engineering works and a variety of light industries.

FU-CHOU

(FOOCHOW)

Population 553,000 (1953); 700,000 (1970 estimate)

Fu-chou, the provincial capital of Fukien, is situated on the north bank of the estuary of Fukien's largest river, the Min Chiang. During Sung times (960–1278) the province became extremely prosperous, largely through overseas trade, and established itself as a centre of culture and education. Between the 16th and the 19th centuries the port of Fu-chou flourished, its prosperity reaching its highest point after it was opened as a Treaty Port in 1842 and became the chief port for the tea trade. The decline of the tea trade in the late 19th century reduced its importance, although Fu-chou remained a commercial centre and a port until the Second World War.

Since the start of the Communist regime, Fu-chou has developed considerably. Its communications with the interior have been greatly improved by the clearing of the Min Chiang for navigation by medium-sized craft and by the construction of the railway in 1956, which links the city with the main Chinese railway system. Fu-chou is no longer accessible to sea-going ships, but Ma-wei and an outer harbour at Kuan-t'ou handle the export of timber, fruits, paper and foodstuffs. Important chemical, engineering and textile industries have been established in the city.

KUEI-YANG

(KWEIYANG)

Population 271,000 (1953); 504,000 (1958 estimate)

Kuei-yang, provincial capital of Kweichow province, is a natural route centre, with comparatively easy access northwards to Szechwan and north-east to Hunan. Originally the area was peopled with non-Chinese tribes, and it was not until the Yüan invasion of the south-west in 1253 that it was made the seat of an army and a 'pacification office'. Chinese settlement in the area also began at this time. Although Kuei-yang was an important administrative and commercial centre, however, it remained merely the capital of one of China's backward provinces until progress was stimulated by the Second World War, and road and rail communications were greatly improved.

Since 1949 the development of the city has been accelerated and Kuei-yang has become a major industrial base. Coal is mined in the locality of Kuei-yang and An-shun and large deposits of bauxite have been discovered in the north. Aluminium is also produced. In the late 1950s an iron and steel plant was built and the city has become an important manufacturer of industrial, railway and mining plant. There are also large chemical, rubber and textile industries.

NAN-NING

(NANNING, YUNG-NING)

Population 195,000 (1953); 400,000 (1970 estimate)

Nan-ning became the provincial capital of Kwangsi province in 1949, and in 1958, the capital of the Kwangsi Chuang Autonomous Region which replaced it. Until this time Nan-ning, like the other major cities in Kwangsi, Liu-chou and Wu-chou, had been essentially a commercial centre dependent on Canton and on the Hsi Chiang river system. It had been laid out as a spacious modern city under the warlord Li Tsung-jen in the 1930s, but had been much affected by the war and had been occupied twice by the Japanese, in 1940 and 1944. Since 1949 the city's industry has grown considerably and its rail communications have been improved. It is in the middle of a fertile agricultural region and leather manufacture, flour milling, sugar refining, meat packing and the production of fertiliser are important industries. It is a centre of printing and paper manufacture and is also a major producer of aluminium and iron and steel.

After the establishment of the Chuang Autonomous Region in 1958, Nan-ning became the chief cultural centre for the training of cadres from the minority groups, as well as supporting Kwangsi University, a large medical school and a school of Agriculture.

WU-HAN

(WUHAN)

Population 1,427,000 (1953); 2,700,000 (1973 estimate)

Wu-han, situated at the confluence of the Han Shui and the Yangtze is the most extensive conurbation of central China, comprising three cities: Wu-ch'ang, Han-k'ou and Han-yang. The cities were formed into a single municipality in 1950. Wu-ch'ang has been the administrative capital of Hupeh since the 13th century. It is on the right bank of the Yangtze, opposite Han-k'ou and Han-yang, to which it was linked by a great bridge in 1957. It contains the administrative centre of the province, its universities and other public buildings. Outside the old city walls a very large industrial complex has grown up, based on an integrated iron and steel mill constructed in 1956–9 and later expanded. This mill produces steel rails and heavy constructional steel, and supplies a machine-building industry. There are also aluminium, glass and cement works.

Han-k'ou, the largest of the three cities, developed from the late 19th century into the chief centre of foreign trade in the central Yangtze area. It is linked by a second bridge, built in 1954, to Han-yang, which was the site of China's earliest iron and steel works, constructed at the beginning of this century. This was dismantled in 1937 and removed to Ch'ung-ch'ing. Han-yang and Han-k'ou are both centres of very large cotton textile mills and of paper making.

HSI-AN

(SIAN)

Population 787,000 (1953); 1,310,000 (1958 estimate)

The valley of the Wei Ho river, where Hsi-an, the capital of Shensi province, is situated has been one of the cradles of Chinese civilisation since Neolithic times. It was chosen as the seat of the Chou and Ch'in states. Their successors, the Han, built their capital at Ch'ang-an in 200 BC which became the hub of their vast empire's new administration and an important commercial centre. The city fell into decline at the end of the Former Han period and only revived at the re-unification of the empire by the Sui, who built a new city, Ta-hsing-ch'eng, just to the south-east of the Han city. It remained the capital of the T'ang empire under the old name of Ch'ang-an, and became the richest, most populous city in the world of its time. The decline of T'ang power after about AD 880, however, marked the end of the city's prosperity. In the suceeding periods the much reduced city, sacked in 882 and dismantled in 904, became the provincial capital of Shensi, a province which sank steadily in importance until in the

19th century it was one of the most backward in China. The name Hsi-an was given to the city under the Ming (1368–1644).

Its modern growth is very recent and has been remarkably rapid. After the Communist victory in 1949, it became a major centre in the north-west, not only of administration and politics, but also of industry. It has a very large electric generating station and is a centre for the production of electrical equipment and electronic instruments. The city also has one of China's largest modern cotton mills, and engineering and chemical industries.

Although little remains of the old capital, Hsi-an has many ancient monuments, a museum and a famous collection of stone inscriptions. It is a cultural centre with two universities and a number of technical institutes.

NAN-CH'ANG
(NANCHANG)
Population 398,000 (1953); 508,000 (1958 estimate)

Since the foundation and walling of the city in 201 BC, Nan-ch'ang, the provincial capital of Kiangsi on the Kan Chiang river, has been an important administrative and commercial centre. In the 1850s, however, it suffered considerably as a result of the T'ai-p'ing rebellion, and although it was afterwards ruled by a series of progressive governors, its pre-eminence as a commercial centre declined as overland trade routes were replaced by coastal steamship services, and Kiu-kiang, with direct access for the large ships of the Yangtze, became a rival.

Under the Communist regime, Nan-ch'ang has been extensively industrialised. It is a large-scale producer of cotton yarn and textiles and has large paper-making, food-processing and rice-milling industries. Heavy industry was developed in the mid-1950s, with the installation of a large thermal power plant, an iron-smelting plant, and a machinery industry concentrating on agricultural equipment and diesel engines. Later Nan-ch'ang became a centre of the automotive industry, producing trucks and tractors, and has developed a large chemical industry.

CH'UNG-CH'ING
(CHUNGKING)
Population 1,773,000 (1953); 4,400,000 (1970 estimate)

Situated to the south-east of the Szechwan basin, at the confluence of the Yangtze and the Chia-ling rivers, Ch'ung-ch'ing, the war-time capital of Nationalist China, is a centre of communications. Railways lead west to Ch'eng-tu and from there to north-west China, and south to Kuei-yang in Kweichow province, Kwangsi and Yunnan. Freight is trans-shipped between the railways and the Yangtze, which provides a route westward into central China.

Ch'ung-ch'ing is the largest and most rapidly growing industrial city in south-west China. This industrial growth is very recent. The iron and steel industry of Ch'ung-ch'ing was established after 1938 when plants were moved here from Han-yang and Huang-shih, out of the path of the Japanese advance, and the city now produces about one million tons of steel a year. Its other industries include engineering, shipyards, chemicals, fertilisers, plastics, textiles and a wide range of light industry.

Ch'ung-ch'ing has an important university, a number of specialised institutes, museums and libraries.

CH'ENG-TU
(CHENGTU)
Population 857,000 (1953); 1,700,000 (1970 estimate)

The provincial capital of Szechwan province, Ch'eng-tu, has always been a great city and administrative centre, with river communications throughout the Szechwan Basin and beyond, and overland communications north to Lan-chou, north-east to Hsi-an and the traditional centres of political authority, and south-west and west into Yunnan and Tibet. Ch'eng-tu grew rapidly during the Second World War, when many refugees from the east settled there, and its trade and commerce expanded. Since 1949 the growth of Ch'eng-tu has continued. Its road and rail communications have been modernised and improved and it now has air services to all parts of the south-west. It has become a major industrial centre. A very large thermal generating station and two important radio and electronic plants (installed by Soviet engineers) were built in the 1950s, and engineering, chemical and aluminium industries have been established. The city's oldest industry, textiles, is still flourishing and now produces not only the traditional silks but also some cotton and woollen textiles.

Ch'eng-tu is a city with strong local character, whose inhabitants are proud of their sophistication. Its three universities, many institutes and technical schools and historical monuments make it an important cultural centre.

K'UN-MING
(KUNMING)
Population 699,000 (1953); 880,000 (1958 estimate)

K'un-ming, the provincial capital of Yunnan province, has always played a very important part in the communications of the Chinese south-west as it was the junction of two major trading routes, one westwards into Upper Burma, the other southwards to northern Indo-China. Trade trails over the mountains ran east to Hunan and north-east to I-pin in Szechwan.

The opening of the K'un-ming area began with the completion in 1906–10 of the railway to Haiphong, and when K'un-ming became a Treaty Port in 1908 it rapidly became a major commercial centre. But K'un-ming's transformation into a great modern city resulted from the outbreak of the Japanese War in 1937 when great numbers of Chinese flooded into the south-west, bringing with them many dismantled industrial plants which were erected beyond the range of the Japanese bombers. In addition, many universities and institutes of higher education were evacuated here. After the beginning of the Communist period, the expansion of industry which had started during the Second World War continued. The chief industries remain the production of copper, lead and zinc; iron and steel; engineering and chemical works and textiles. K'un-ming is a major cultural centre—there are universities, technical colleges and a number of research institutes.

HSI-NING
(SINING)
Population 94,000 (1953); 300,000 (1970 estimate)

Hsi-ning, the provincial capital of Tsinghai province since 1928, has always been an important strategic point on the Chinese western frontier. It is situated in a fertile mountain basin in the valley of the Huang Shui river, on what were traditionally the main trade routes from northern China into Tibet and the Tsaidam basin, now replaced by modern highways. With the rise of Lamaistic Buddhism, it became an important religious centre, with Tsinghai's biggest Lamasery at Kun-bum to the south-east.

Since the late 1950s, when the Liu-chia Gorge dam and hydro-electric scheme came into operation, Hsi-ning has been linked by high-tension grid to Liu-chia and Lan-chou. It has also developed local coal supplies from mines at Ta-t'ung and has a medium-sized iron and steel works. The city has developed a woollen industry, using wool produced by the nomads of the surrounding pastoral areas, and has a thriving leather industry. It is also an important market for salt from the Tsaidam region.

WU-LU-MU-CH'I
(URUMCHI)
Population 141,000 (1953); 400,000 (1970 estimate)

The city, formerly known as Ti-hua, has been the provincial capital of Sinkiang since it became a province in 1882. It grew rapidly into the greatest city and centre of trade in Central Asia, with a population estimated at about 40,000 at the beginning of the Republic in 1912. Its commercial importance was coupled, in the last days of the empire, with its growing strategic significance as the British and Russians attempted to establish influence in Sinkiang.

Under the Communists, Wu-lu-mu-ch'i has been developed not only as the regional capital and cultural centre of Sinkiang, but also, with the aid of improved road and rail communications, as a major industrial base. Wu-lu-mu-ch'i's new prosperity derives from the oilfield discovered at Karamai in 1955, which has become one of China's major sources of oil, and from extensive coal deposits around the city. In the late 1950s large iron and steel and engineering industries were developed and cement works, chemical and fertiliser plants and cotton textile mills have also been founded.

Wu-lu-mu-ch'i remains an Uighur city with a predominantly Moslem population. There are many schools and institutes of higher education which include colleges for minorities, and for the study of the Russian language, medicine and agriculture.

HU-HO-HAO-T'E
(HUHEHOT)
Population 148,000 (1953); 320,000 (1958 estimate)

Since 1952 Hu-ho-hao-t'e has been the provincial capital of the Inner Mongolian Autonomous Region and Command Headquarters of the Inner Mongolian Military Region. The area was traditionally at the very edge of Chinese settlement and the city grew up as a frontier trading centre, but in the late 18th century Chinese settlers began to farm the fertile plain and a new Chinese city was founded to the north of the Mongol city. The cities later combined under the name of Kuei-sui and became a considerable market with a large Moslem community. Its importance grew rapidly after the completion in 1922 of the railway linking the city to Peking and Tientsin in the east, and Pao-t'ou to the west. Since 1949 Hu-ho-hao-t'e has developed into a fairly important centre of industry, with grain mills, tanneries, plants for oil extraction and a large woollen textile industry. The city also has iron and steel and chemical plants. Cultivation has recently expanded north of Hu-ho-hao-t'e and to support this a major tractor plant and diesel engine factory have been developed. In 1957 the city became the seat of the first university in Inner Mongolia, with an important Medical and Veterinary College. Schools, hospitals, a palace of culture and theatres have made it an important regional cultural centre.

LA-SA
(LHASA)
Population 85,000 (1973 estimate)

La-sa, capital city of the Tibetan Autonomous Region, was founded, according to tradition, in 600 AD by Srong-btsan sgam-po, architect of the first Tibetan state. Either La-sa itself or nearby Samye continued as the Tibetan capital until the dissolution of the kingdom in 842. After this La-sa remained an important religious centre. In 1642 the fifth Dalai Lama established La-sa as the capital of Tibet. Following the Manchu conquest in the 18th century, La-sa became the residence of the Manchu governor (Amban) and it has been the administrative centre of Tibet ever since. The Manchus were expelled in 1912.

Until the 1950s the country remained, in spite of Chinese government representatives, firmly in the hands of the Tibetan religious hierarchy. A third of its population were monks, and La-sa has many great religious buildings and monasteries, the most famous of which is the Potala, once the residence of the Dalai Lama. After the re-occupation of Tibet by the Chinese in 1951 there were some years of tension between the Communist administration and the Tibetan hierarchy, which led to the rebellion of 1959. Subsequently the Buddhist church was suppressed, many of the monks returned to lay life and the political control of the church destroyed completely.

La-sa has been greatly increased in size and the municipal area now covers some 30,000 square miles of central Tibet. Once almost exclusively Tibetan in population, the city now has large numbers of Chinese inhabitants and a military garrison. There has been some development of minor industry and pharmaceuticals, fertilisers and agricultural machinery are manufactured.

T'AI-PEI
(TAIPEI)
Population 1,117,000 (1964 estimate)

T'ai-pei is the chief city and provincial capital of Taiwan province and, since 1949, the seat of the Chinese Nationalist government in exile. A minor city, founded in 1708, it remained comparatively unimportant until 1887, when Taiwan became an independent province, and T'ai-pei replaced T'ai-nan as provincial capital in 1892. It remained the capital during the Japanese occupation of the island from 1895 to 1945. The city has a very large population of Chinese from the mainland.

Originally the centre of a fertile agricultural area and the hub of Taiwan's excellent rail and road systems, T'ai-pei has developed a considerable range of industries, particularly cotton and synthetic textiles, fertilisers, chemicals, cement and paper manufacture and a variety of consumer goods.

T'ai-pei has also become the cultural centre for the Nationalist regime. It has two major universities and several other institutes of higher education, theatres and museums.

MACAU
(MACAO)
Population 300,000

The oldest European foothold in the Orient, Macau is a Portuguese colony. It was ceded to the Portuguese as a trading outpost in 1557 as a reward for clearing the South China Sea of pirates. Rent was paid to Kwangtung province for the territory until Macau declared itself independent in 1849. China recognised this claim in 1887 when the Portuguese undertook not to alienate Macau without the agreement of China, but it was not officially declared an overseas province by Portugal until 1951.

Macau, a peninsula and two small islands, covers an area of six and a half square miles and lies 40 miles south-west of Hong Kong across the Pearl River estuary. An important bishopric and centre for missionary activity, it grew rich in the 17th century but declined when Japan closed its doors to foreign trade and later under competition from the English and Dutch traders. It is now principally a commercial and tourist dependency of Hong Kong but it has an important gold trade and some light industry based for the most part on textiles.

HONG KONG
Population 4,500,000

Hong Kong, one of the finest natural harbours of the Chinese coast, was founded as an entrepôt for the opium trade. The Chinese empire insisted that all foreign trade should be conducted at Canton and foreign traders settled in nearby Macau. The sale of tea and silk brought into China a great deal of silver. This adverse balance of bullion strained the resources of the Western traders and they began to sell Indian opium illegally to the Chinese in exchange for silver. Eventually the Chinese insisted that the trade should cease and this confrontation led to the Opium War of 1839–42. After their defeat the Chinese ceded Hong Kong Island to the British, and Kowloon peninsula was added in 1870. In 1898 Britain secured a 99-year lease on a further 366 square miles, which included the New Territories on the mainland and some islands.

Hong Kong thrived on trade between China and the West. When this was reduced by American policy in the 1950s and 1960s Hong Kong developed a successful light industrial sector. Today Hong Kong earnings are provided principally by textiles, electronics, banking and financial services, plastics and tourism. The population was 600,000 in 1945 but has swollen to its present level after several waves of immigration from the Chinese mainland. There is a railway from Kowloon to Canton through the New Territories. Frequent ferry services link Hong Kong Island to Kowloon and a road tunnel has been recently completed.

CITY PLANS

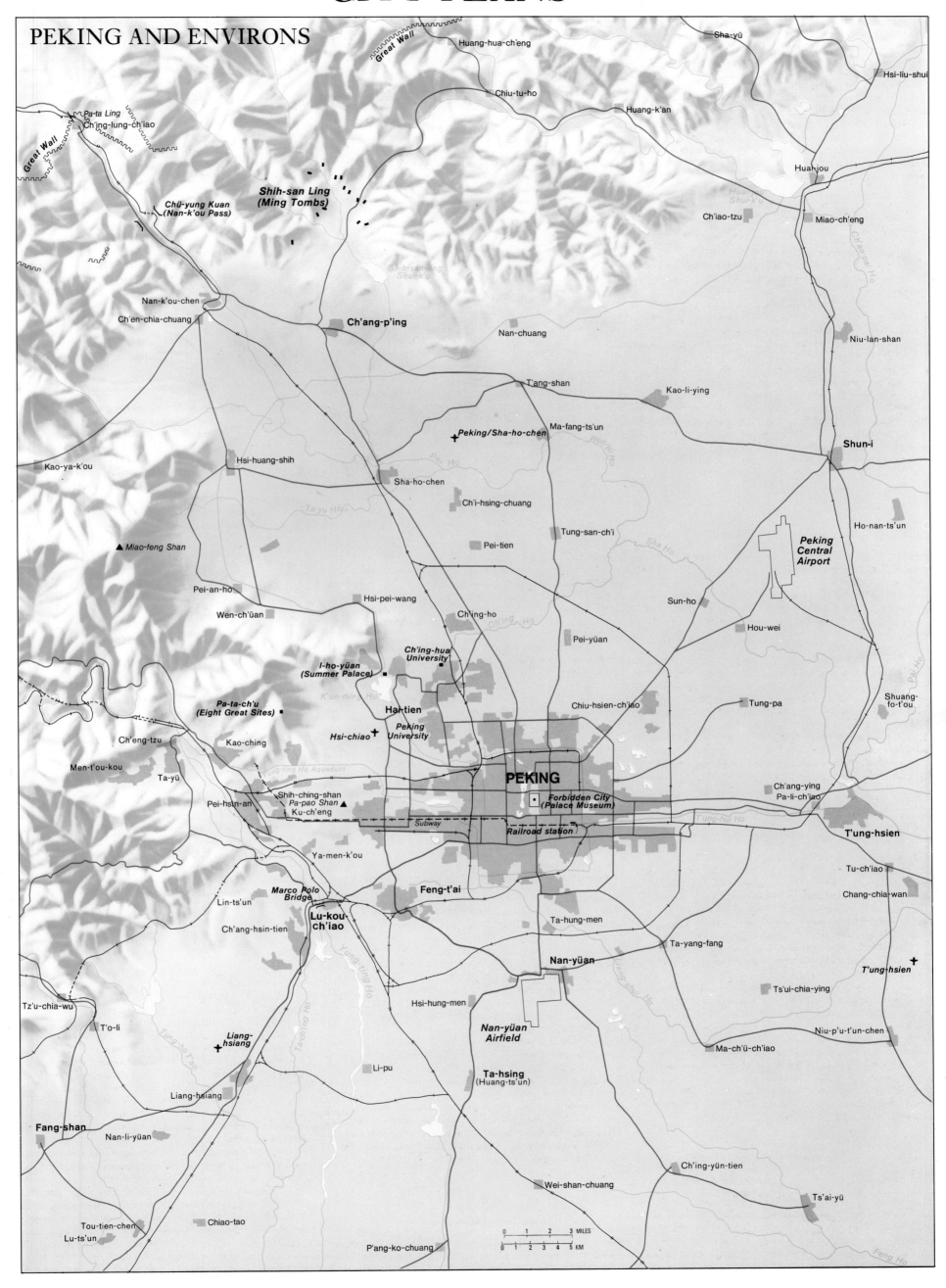

PEKING AND ENVIRONS

Great Wall
Huang-hua-ch'eng
Sha-yü
Hsi-liu-shui
Chiu-tu-ho
Huang-k'an
Pa-ta Ling
Ch'ing-lung-ch'iao
Great Wall
Hual-jou
Chü-yung Kuan
(Nan-k'ou Pass)
Shih-san Ling
(Ming Tombs)
Ch'iao-tzu
Miao-ch'eng
Nan-k'ou-chen
Ch'en-chia-chuang
Ch'ang-p'ing
Nan-chuang
Niu-lan-shan
Kao-ya-k'ou
T'ang-shan
Kao-li-ying
Peking/Sha-ho-chen
Ma-fang-ts'un
Shun-i
Hsi-huang-shih
Sha-ho-chen
Ch'i-hsing-chuang
Ho-nan-ts'un
Miao-feng Shan
Pei-tien
Tung-san-ch'i
Peking Central Airport
Pei-an-ho
Hsi-pei-wang
Ch'ing-ho
Sun-ho
Wen-ch'üan
Pei-yüan
Hou-wei
I-ho-yüan
(Summer Palace)
Ch'ing-hua University
Shuang-fo-t'ou
Pa-ta-ch'u
(Eight Great Sites)
Hai-tien
Chiu-hsien-ch'iao
Tung-pa
Ch'eng-tzu
Kao-ching
Peking University
Hsi-chiao
Men-t'ou-kou
Ta-yü
Ch'ang-ying
Pa-li-ch'iao
Shih-ching-shan
Pa-pao Shan
Ku-ch'eng
PEKING
Forbidden City
(Palace Museum)
Pei-hsin-an
Subway
Ya-men-k'ou
Railroad station
T'ung-hsien
Marco Polo Bridge
Lu-kou ch'iao
Feng-t'ai
Tu-ch'iao
Lin-ts'un
Chang-chia-wan
Ch'ang-hsin-tien
Ta-hung-men
Ta-yang-fang
Tz'u-chia-wu
Nan-yüan
T'ung-hsien
T'o-li
Hsi-hung-men
Ts'ui-chia-ying
Liang-hsiang
Nan-yüan Airfield
Niu-p'u-t'un-chen
Li-pu
Ma-ch'ü-ch'iao
Fang-shan
Nan-li-yüan
Ta-hsing
(Huang-ts'un)
Liang-hsiang
Ch'ing-yün-tien
Ts'ai-yü
Tou-tien-chen
Chiao-tao
Wei-shan-chuang
Lu-ts'un
P'ang-ko-chuang

I-ho Yüan
(Summer Palace)

I-ho-yüan Lu

Ch'ing-hua Nan-lu

CHUNG-KUAN-TS'UN

Ch'eng-fu Lu

K'un-ming Hu

Chin Ho

Hai-tien Lu

Hsüeh-yüan Lu

Wu-ts'un Lu

Su-chou Chieh

Pei-huan Hsi-lu

PEI-T'AI-P'ING-CHUANG

Pei-huan Hsi-lu

PEI-CHIAO-SHIH-CH'ANG

HAI-TIEN CH'Ü

Hsüeh-yüan Lu

Hsüeh-yüan Nan-lu

Wei-kung-ts'un Lu

Hsüeh-yüan Nan-lu

Hsin-chieh K'ou-wai

K'un-ming-hu Nan-lu

Su-chou Chieh

Pai-shih-ch'iao Lu

MA-T'I-HU-T'UNG

Hsing-shih-k'ou Lu

Kao-liang-ch'iao Lu

Hsi-chih-men
Ch'e-chan

Tzu-chu-yüan Lu

Wu-ko-sung Lu

Tzu-chu-yüan Kung-yüan
(Purple Bamboo Park)

Nan-han Ho

Ching-mi Ying shui-k'u (irrigation canal)

Municipal
Gymnasium

Peking Zoo

Hsi-chih Men-wai Ta-chieh

Hsi-chih Men-nei Ta-chieh

Chi-shui T'an

T'ien-ts'un Lu

Wu-lu-chü
Ch'e-chan

Pei-wa-ts'un Lu

PAI-SHIH-CH'IAO

TUNG-WU-YÜAN
Peking
Planetarium

ERH-LI-KOU-TUNG-K'OU

MA-HSIANG-HU-T'UNG

PING-AN-LI

Pa-li-chuang Lu

Ch'e-kung-chuang

Ta-chieh

Nan-hsiao Lu

Chung-hua Lu

Pei-ta-chieh

HUA-YÜAN-TS'UN

Tzu-chou-hung Lu

Pei-shih Lu

HSI-CH'ENG CH'Ü

Li-hsin Pei-lu

Yü-ch'üan Lu

Yung-ting Lu

Fu-ch'eng Lu

Fu-wai Ta-chieh

Fu-nei Ta-chieh

Yü-yüan-t'an Kung-yüan
(Jade Abyss Pool Park)

Yüeh-t'an Pei-lu

Hsi-tan Pei-ta-chieh

Hsi-ssu Pei-ta-chieh

Li-hsin Pei-lu

Wan-shou Lu

Wu-ko-sung

Ts'ui-wei Lu

San-ho Lu

Yü-yüan T'an

Yüeh-t'an
Kung-yüan

T'a-p'ing-ch'iao Ta-chieh

Nan-shih

Military Museum

SAN-LI-HO

Nationalities
Cultural
Palace

Hsi-tan
Shang-ch'ang
(market)

Hsi-ch

Pei-hsing-an Lu

Fu-hsing Lu

FU-HSING-LU

Fu-hsing Men-wai Ta-chieh

Fu-hsing Men-nei Ta-chieh

HSI-TAN

T'ai-p'ing Lu

Pei-li-ho Lu

Kuang-an-men Pei-pin-ho Lu

Hsin-wen-hua Chieh

Feng't'ai Lu

Lien-hua Ho

T'ieh-lu I-yüan
(hospital)

Lien-hua
Ch'ih

Huai-pai-shu Chieh

Hsüan-wu
Kung-yüan

Ch'u-ch'un Chieh

Hsüan-wu Men-wai Ta-chieh

Kuang-an Men-wai Ta-chieh

Kuang-an Men-nei Ta-chieh

Ma-lien-tao Lu

Kuang-an Men

HSÜAN-WU CH'Ü

Hung-wei Lu

Kuang-an Lu

Kuang-an-men Ch'e-chan

Ch'ing-nien Hu

Kuang-an-men Nan-pin-ho Lu

Nan-hsien-ko Chieh

Pai-kuang Lu

PAI-CHIH-FANG

HU-FANG-LU

Nan-heng Chieh

Wan-shou
Kung-yüan

Lu-kou-ch'iao Lu

Pai-chih-fang Hsi-chieh

Pai-chih-fang Tung-chieh

T'ao-jan-t'ing Kung-yüan
(Joyous Pavilion Park)

Yu-an Men

T'AO-JAN-T'ING Ho

Moat

Yung-ting-men
Ch'e-chan

Feng-t'sao-p'ai Shui-k'ou

Yü-an Men-wai Ta-chieh

HSI-CHUANG

FENG-T'AI CH'Ü

to Tientsin, Canton Shanghai

railways and stations
bus routes and stops
trolleybus routes and stops
underground railway line
terminal bus and trolleybus stops
theatres and cinemas
boundaries of the ch'ü
(metropolitian districts)

INDEX

INDEX

Sa-yen – Shih-t'i-ch'i 19

111 F3 Sa-yen *Sayan* Tibet
95 D2 Sa-ying-p'an *Sayingpan* Yun.
115 D3 Scarborough Reef China Sea
115 C5 Seahorse Breakers China Sea
115 D4 Seahorse Shoal China Sea
111 E3 Se-cha *Sezha* Tibet
115 C4 Second Thomas Shoal China Sea
63 E7 Se-ho-p'u *Sehepu* Shensi
86 A1 Se-hsü-ssu *Sexusi* Szech.
111 E3 Se-ju-sung-to *Serusongduo* Tibet
55 F6 Se-kang *Segang* Honan
111 E2 Se-kung *Segong* Tibet
Seling Tsho *see* Ch'i-lin Ts'o
102 B3 Se-li-pu-ya *Selibuya* Sink.
22 E2 Sen-ching *Senjing* Heilung.
30 D2 Sen-chi-t'u *Senjitu* Hopeh
39 C5 Seng-nien *Sengnian* Shansi
106 D2 Se-nieh Hu *Senie Hu* (lake) Tsing.
110 B2 Sen-ko Tsang-pu *Senge Zangbu* (river) Tibet
15 K4 Sen-lin Shan *Senlin Shan* (mt) Kirin
103 E1 Sen-t'a-ssu *Sentasi* Sink.
86 B3 Se-pa *Seba* Szech.
30 C4 Se-shu-fen *Seshufen* Hopeh
86 C1 Se-ta *Seda* Szech.
106 D3 Se-wu Ch'ü *Sewu Qu* (river) Tsing.
106 D3 Se-wu-kou *Sewugou* Tsing.
91 C3 Sha-ch'ang *Shachang* Kwei.
34 A3 Sha-chen *Shazhen* Shant.
58 C4 Sha-chen-ch'i *Shazhenqi* Hupeh
66 F3 Sha-ch'eng *Shacheng* Fukien
30 C3 Sha-ch'eng *Shacheng* Hopeh
50 C5 Sha-ch'i *Shaqi* Chek.
51 E3 Sha-ch'i *Shaqi* Chek.
75 B5 Sha-ch'i *Shaqi* Hunan
70 F3 Sha-ch'i *Shaqi* Kiangsi
71 B6 Sha-ch'i *Shaqi* Kiangsi
71 C5 Sha-ch'i *Shaqi* Kiangsi
43 F4 Sha-ch'i *Shaqi* Kiangsu
66 C4 Sha Ch'i *Sha Qi* (river) Fukien
67 C4 Sha Ch'i *Sha Qi* (river) Fukien
62 D4 Sha-chi *Shaji* Shensi
66 E4 Sha-chiang *Shajiang* Fukien
74 D4 Sha-chiang *Shajiang* Hunan
94 C3 Sha-ch'iao *Shaqiao* Yun.
67 C6 Sha-chien *Shajian* Fukien
19 I3 Sha-chien-tzu *Shajianzi* Liao.
110 B2 Sha-chih-ya *Shazhiya* Tibet
99 F2 Sha-ching *Shajing* Kansu
102 B2 Sha-ching-tzu *Shajingzi* Sink.
15 I5 Sha-chin-kou *Shajingou* Kirin
102 I1 Sha-ch'iu-ho *Shaqiuhe* Sink.
62 F3 Sha-chiu-tien *Shajiudian* Shensi
43 E4 Sha-chou Hsien *Shazhou Xian* Kiangsu
71 C6 Sha-chou-pa *Shazhouba* Kiangsi
75 E4 Sha-ch'üan *Shaquan* Hunan
38 C2 Sha-ch'üan *Shaquan* Shansi
26 D3 Sha-erh-mo-jen-so-mu *Shaermorensuomu* In. Mong.
114 B1 Sha-erh-pu-jih-tu *Shaerburidu* Ningsia
103 D1 Sha-erh-t'a-le *Shaertale* Sink.
Shag Paserab *see* Chia-pa-se-la
18 C3 Sha-hai *Shahai* Liao.
30 D3 Sha-ho *Shahe* Hopeh
31 B7 Sha-ho *Shahe* Hopeh
42 C1 Sha-ho *Shahe* Kiangsu
83 F5 Sha-ho *Shuhe* Kwangsi
54 D4 Sha Ho *Sha He* (river) Honan
59 E2 Sha Ho *Sha He* (river) Hupeh
34 C2 Sha Ho *Sha He* (river) Shant.
38 E2 Sha-ho *Shahe* Shansi
35 E2 Sha-ho *Shahe* Shant.
34 B4 Sha-ho-chan *Shahezhan* Shant.
70 C2 Sha-ho-chen *Shahezhen* Kiangsi
14 F5 Sha-ho-chen *Shahezhen* Kirin
46 E4 Sha-ho-chi *Shaheji* Anhwei
31 D5 Sha-ho-ch'iao *Shaheqiao* Hopeh
31 B7 Sha-ho Hsien *Shahe Xian* Hopeh
31 B7 Sha-ho Hsien *Shahe Xian* Hopeh
30 F4 Sha-ho-i *Shaheyi* Hopeh
63 C8 Sha-ho-k'an *Shahekan* Shensi
98 E2 Sha-ho-pao *Shahebao* Kansu
55 E5 Sha-ho-tien *Shahedian* Honan
11 D5 Sha-ho-tzu *Shahezi* Heilung.
87 G2 Sha-ho-tzu *Shahezi* Szech.
18 D4 Sha-hou-so *Shahousuo* Liao.
15 I4 Sha-ho-yen *Shaheyan* Kirin
66 C4 Sha-hsien *Shaxian* Fukien
59 F4 Sha-hu *Shahu* Hupeh
38 D1 Sha-hu-k'ou *Shahukou* Shansi
75 F4 Shai-pu-chiang *Shaibujiang* Hunan
59 E4 Sha-kang *Shagang* Hupeh
19 F4 Sha-kang *Shagang* Liao.
74 E2 Sha-kang-shih *Shagangshi* Hunan
110 B2 Sha-k'o-ti *Shakedi* Tibet
26 D5 Sha-ko-tu *Shagedu* In. Mong.
43 D2 Sha-kou *Shagou* Kiangsu
79 C1 Sha-k'ou *Shakou* Kwangt.
34 C5 Sha-kou *Shagou* Shant.
63 D7 Sha-kou-chieh *Shagoujie* Shensi
18 D3 Sha-kuo-t'un *Shaguotun* Liao.
19 E2 Sha-la *Shala* Liao.
Sha-la-mu-lun-miao *see* Sha-erh-mo-jen-so-mu
11 E5 Sha-lan *Shalan* Heilung.
78 B3 Sha-lang *Shalang* Kwangt.
82 B3 Sha-li *Shali* Kwangsi
110 C2 Sha-li *Shali* Tibet
104 C2 Sha-liang-tzu *Shaliangzi* Tsing.
14 A5 Sha-li-hao-lai *Shalihaolai* Kirin
23 D6 Sha-li-hao-lai *Shalihaolai* Kirin
19 F3 Sha-ling *Shaling* Liao.
19 G3 Sha-ling *Shaling* Liao.
30 B3 Sha-ling-tzu *Shalingzi* Hopeh
51 E3 Sha-liu *Shaliu* Chek.
30 E4 Sha-liu-ho *Shaliuhe* Hopeh
107 G2 Sha-liu-ho *Shaliuhe* Tsing.
118 B2 Sha-lu *Shalu* Taiwan
86 B2 Sha-lu-li Shan *Shaluli Shan* (mts) Szech.
118 C1 Sha-lun *Shalun* Taiwan
Shamal *see* Hsia-ma-le
62 F2 Sha-mao-t'ou *Shamaotou* Shensi
102 H1 Sha-men-tzu *Shamenzi* Sink.
102 H2 Sha-men-tzu *Shamenzi* Sink.
106 E5 Sha-mu-ta *Shamuda* Tsing.
67 C6 Shan-ch'eng-chen *Shanchengzhen* Fukien
14 F5 Shan-ch'eng-chen *Shanchengzhen* Kirin
51 D5 Shan-ch'i *Shanqi* Chek.
82 D3 Shan-chiao *Sanjiao* Kwangsi
94 B3 Shan-chieh *Shanjie* Yun.
66 C3 Shan-ch'ien *Shanqian* Fukien
35 F2 Shan-ch'ien-tien *Shanqiandian* Shant.
70 B4 Shan-chuang *Shanzhuang* Kiangsi
39 B5 Shan-chung *Shanzhong* Shansi
18 C4 Shan-chü-tzu *Shanjuzi* Liao.
86 C1 Shang-a-pa *Shangaba* Szech.
91 E2 Shang-ba *Shangba* Kwei.
38 F2 Shang-chai *Shangzhai* Shansi
86 C1 Shang-chai *Shangzhai* Szech.
95 D2 Shang-cha-ko *Shangzhage* Yun.
82 E2 Shang-ch'ao *Shangchao* Kwangsi
107 G3 Shang-cha-ssu *Shangzhasi* Tsing.
55 G6 Shang-ch'eng *Shangcheng* Honan
62 D5 Shang-chen-tzu *Shangzhenzi* Shensi
59 F5 Shang-ch'e-wan *Shangchewan* Hupeh
51 C3 Shang-ch'i *Shangqi* Chek.
11 D4 Shang-chi *Shangji* Heilung.
54 C4 Shang-chi *Shangji* Honan
11 C4 Shang-chia *Shangjia* Heilung.
19 H3 Shang-chia-ho *Shangjiahe* Liao.
51 C4 Shang-chiao-tao *Shangjiaodao* Chek.
11 D5 Shang-chih *Shangzhi* Heilung.
34 C4 Shang-chih *Shangzhi* Shant.
58 C1 Shang-chin *Shangjin* Hupeh
82 D5 Shang-chin *Shangjin* Kwangsi
67 C5 Shang-ching *Shangjing* Fukien
70 E3 Shang-ch'ing *Shangqing* Kiangsi
55 G3 Shang-ch'iu *Shangqiu* Honan
55 G3 Shang-ch'iu *Shangqiu* Honan
55 G3 Shang-ch'iu Ti-ch'ü *Shangqiu Diqu* Honan
54 D4 Shang-chiu-wu *Shangjiuwu* Honan
54 D2 Shang-chuang *Shangzhuang* Honan
30 B4 Shang-chuang *Shangzhuang* Hopeh
35 E4 Shang-chuang *Shangzhuang* Shant.
35 G2 Shang-chuang *Shangzhuang* Shant.
79 C3 Shang-ch'uan Tao *Shangchuan Dao* (island) Kwangt.
91 F4 Shang-chung *Shangzhong* Kwei.
50 B3 Shang-fang *Shangfang* Chek.
31 B5 Shang-fang *Shangfang* Hopeh
70 B3 Shang-fu *Shangfu* Kiangsi
43 F4 Shang-hai *Shanghai* Kiangsu
Shang-hai - city plan *see* Pages 128-129
43 F4 Shang-hai Hsien *Shanghai Xian* Kiangsu
43 F4 Shang-hai Shih *Shanghai Shi* Kiangsu
67 B5 Shang-hang *Shanghang* Fukien
34 C2 Shang-ho *Shanghe* Shant.
14 G3 Shang-ho-wan *Shanghewan* Kirin
38 D2 Shang-hsi-chuang *Shangxizhuang* Shansi
63 E7 Shang-hsien *Shangxian* Shensi
43 D4 Shang-hsing-chen *Shangxingzhen* Kiangsu
42 C3 Shang-hsin-ho *Shangxinhe* Kiangsu
51 D3 Shang-hu *Shanghu* Chek.
51 E3 Shang-hu *Shanghu* Chek.
38 E4 Shang-hu *Shanghu* Shansi
43 D4 Shang-huang *Shanghuang* Kiangsu
30 D2 Shang-huang-ch'i *Shanghuangqi* Hopeh
107 F2 Shang-huan-ts'ang *Shanghuancang* Tsing.
22 D2 Shang-hu-lin *Shanghulin* Heilung.
30 A2 Shang-i Hsien *Shangyi Xian* Hopeh
30 A2 Shang-i Hsien *Shangyi Xian* Hopeh
70 E3 Shang-jao *Shangrao* Kiangsi
75 D6 Shang-jen-li *Shangrenli* Hunan
67 E5 Shang-kan *Shanggan* Fukien
58 C3 Shang-k'an *Shangkan* Hupeh
43 E2 Shang-kang *Shanggang* Kiangsu
10 E4 Shang-kan-ling *Shangganling* Heilung.
70 B3 Shang-kao *Shanggao* Kiangsi
Shangkin *see* Shang-chin
Shangkiu *see* Shang-ch'iu
35 D3 Shang-k'ou *Shangkou* Shant.
30 F3 Shang-ku *Shanggu* Hopeh
55 F2 Shang-kuan-ts'un *Shangguancun* Honan
22 D2 Shang-k'u-li *Shangkuli* Heilung.
114 C3 Shang-kun-ch'üan *Shanggunquan* Ningsia
107 G4 Shang-kung-ma *Shanggongma* Tsing.
23 C6 Shang-kung-ti *Shanggongdi* Liao.
39 B6 Shang-kuo *Shangguo* Shansi
67 B5 Shang-kuo-ch'e *Shangguoche* Fukien
50 C2 Shang-lang *Shanglang* Chek.
86 C1 Shang-lang-t'ang *Shanglangtang* Szech.
38 D3 Shang-lan-ts'un *Shanglancun* Shansi
83 F3 Shang-lei *Shanglei* Kwangsi
87 F1 Shang-liang *Shangliang* Szech.
31 D5 Shang-lin *Shanglin* Hopeh
83 E4 Shang-lin *Shanglin* Kwangsi
79 C2 Shang-lin *Shanglin* Kwangt.
79 D1 Shang-ling *Shangling* Kwangt.
70 A4 Shang-li-shih *Shanglishi* Kiangsi
63 F7 Shang-lo *Shangluo* Shensi
63 F7 Shang-lo-chen *Shangluozhen* Shensi
63 F7 Shang-lo Ti-ch'ü *Shangluo Diqu* Shensi
66 D3 Shang-mei *Shangmei* Fukien
63 F7 Shang-nan *Shangnan* Shensi
59 H4 Shang-pa-ho *Shangbahe* Hupeh
47 D5 Shang-p'ai-ho *Shangpaihe* Anhwei
66 E3 Shang-pai-shih *Shangbaishi* Fukien
55 E2 Shang-pa-li *Shangbali* Honan
51 E4 Shang-p'an *Shangpan* Chek.
30 F3 Shang-pan-ch'eng *Shangbancheng* Hopeh
67 C5 Shang-p'ing *Shangping* Fukien
71 C6 Shang-p'ing *Shangping* Kiangsi
79 D1 Shang-p'ing *Shangping* Kwangt.
51 D3 Shang-p'u *Shangpu* Chek.
70 B4 Shang-pu *Shangbu* Kiangsi
71 C5 Shang-she *Shangshe* Kiangsi
38 D3 Shang-she *Shangshe* Shansi
38 E3 Shang-she *Shangshe* Shansi
55 G5 Shang-shih-ch'iao *Shangshiqiao* Honan
59 F3 Shang-shih-tien *Shangshidian* Hupeh
55 F4 Shang-shui Hsien *Shangshui Xian* Honan
82 D5 Shang-ssu *Shangsi* Kwangsi
91 E5 Shang-ssu *Shangsi* Kwei.
114 B1 Shang-tan *Shangdan* Ningsia
70 C3 Shang-t'ang *Shangtang* Kiangsi
71 D4 Shang-t'ang *Shangtang* Kiangsi
42 C2 Shang-t'ang *Shangtang* Kiangsu
18 D2 Shang-t'ang-kou *Shangtanggou* Liao.
10 E3 Shang-tao-kan *Shangdaogan* Heilung.
54 D3 Shang-tien *Shangdian* Honan
54 E4 Shang-tien *Shangdian* Honan
34 C2 Shang-tien *Shangdian* Shant.
58 B1 Shang-tien-tzu *Shangdianzi* Hupeh
55 F4 Shang-ts'ai *Shangcai* Honan
30 E4 Shang-ts'ang *Shangcang* Hopeh
75 F6 Shang-tu *Shangdu* Hunan
27 E4 Shang-tu *Shangdu* In. Mong.
54 D5 Shang-t'un *Shangtun* Honan
70 D4 Shang-tun-tu *Shangdundu* Kiangsi
119 B4 Shang-wu *Shangwu* Taiwan
22 D2 Shang-wu-erh-ken *Shangwuergen* Heilung.
38 D3 Shang-yang-wu *Shangyangwu* Shansi
51 D3 Shang-yen-t'an *Shangyantan* Chek.
15 H3 Shang-ying *Shangying* Kirin
82 C4 Shang-ying *Shangying* Kwangsi
71 B6 Shang-yu *Shangyou* Kiangsi
18 D3 Shang-yüan *Shangyuan* Liao.
71 B6 Shang-yu Chiang *Shangyou Jiang* (river) Kiangsi
51 D2 Shang-yü Hsien *Shangyu Xian* Chek.
102 C2 Shang-yu-i-ch'ang *Shangyouyichang* Sink.
22 D2 Shang-yu-ling *Shangyouling* Heilung.
94 B4 Shang-yün *Shangyun* Yun.
67 D5 Shang-yung *Shangyong* Fukien
102 C2 Shang-yu Shui-k'u *Shangyou Shuiku* (res.) Sink.
119 B5 Shan-hai *Shanhai* Taiwan
30 G3 Shan-hai-kuan *Shanhaiguan* Hopeh
99 I4 Shan-ho *Shanhe* Kansu
110 A2 Shan-ho *Shanhe* Tibet
11 D5 Shan-ho-t'un *Shanhetun* Heilung.
75 D6 Shan-hsiang *Shanxiang* Hunan
54 C3 Shan Hsien *Shan Xian* Honan
34 B5 Shan-hsien *Shanxian* Shant.
83 F5 Shan-hsin *Shanxin* Kwangsi
119 B3 Shan-hua *Shanhua* Taiwan
Shanjakur *see* Shang-chia-ssu
107 G2 Shan-ken *Shangen* Tsing.
114 C2 Shan-ken-ta-lai *Shangendalai* Ningsia
67 C6 Shan-ko *Shange* Fukien
51 D4 Shan-k'ou *Shankou* Chek.
74 D3 Shan-k'ou *Shankou* Hunan
70 B3 Shan-k'ou *Shankou* Kiangsi
83 F6 Shan-k'ou *Shankou* Kwangsi
63 E7 Shan-k'ou *Shankou* Shensi
103 F2 Shan-k'ou *Shankou* Sink.
66 C3 Shan Kuan *Shan Guan* (pass) Fukien
71 E4 Shan Kuan *Shan Guan* (pass) Kiangsi
86 D3 Shan-leng-kang *Shanlenggang* Szech.
47 D7 Shan-li *Shanli* Anhwei
118 C2 Shan-li *Shanli* Taiwan
51 D2 Shan-lien *Shanlian* Chek.
119 B4 Shan-lin *Shanlin* Taiwan
119 B3 Shan-mei *Shanmei* Taiwan
75 C4 Shan-men *Shanmen* Hunan
99 H4 Shan-men *Shanmen* Kansu
90 A4 Shan-mu-ch'ing *Shanmuqing* Kwei.
118 C2 Sha.ı-nan *Shannan* Taiwan
47 C5 Shan-nan-kuan *Shannanguan* Anhwei
111 D3 Shan-nan Ti-ch'ü *Shannan Diqu* Tibet
26 B4 Shan-pa *Shanba* In. Mong.
47 F5 Shan-pei *Shanbei* Anhwei
91 D3 Shan-p'en *Shanpen* Kwei.
55 E2 Shan-piao *Shanbiao* Honan
59 G4 Shan-p'o *Shanpo* Hupeh
102 I2 Shan-shan *Shanshan* Sink.
103 E2 Shan-shan *Shanshan* Sink.
11 E5 Shan-shih *Shanshi* Heilung.
118 A3 Shan-shui *Shanshui* Taiwan
114 C3 Shan-shui Ho *Shanshui He* (river) Ningsia
74 E3 Shan-shu-ts'ang *Shanshucang* Hunan
Shansi Province *see* Pages 37-40
14 G5 Shan-sung-kang *Shansonggang* Kirin
98 E2 Shan-tan *Shandan* Kansu
74 C4 Shan-t'ang-i *Shantangyi* Hunan
27 F3 Shan-tan-so *Shandansuo* In. Mong.
27 G3 Shan-tien Ho *Shandian He* (river) In. Mong.
34 C4 Shan-t'ing *Shanting* Shant.
26 D3 Shan-ting-hu-la-erh *Shandinghulaer* In. Mong.
71 C4 Shan-t'ou *Shantou* Kiangsi
79 E2 Shan-t'ou *Shantou* Kwangt.
46 E3 Shan-t'ou-chi *Shantouji* Anhwei
74 E4 Shan-tsao *Shanzao* Hunan
35 G2 Shan-tung Pan-tao *Shandong Bandao* (pen) Shant.
Shantung Province *see* Pages 33-36
47 C5 Shan-wang-ho *Shanwanghe* Anhwei
30 E1 Shan-wan-tzu *Shanwanzi* Hopeh
79 D2 Shan-wei *Shanwei* Kwangt.
66 E4 Shan-yang *Shanyang* Fukien
63 E7 Shan-yang *Shanyang* Shensi
67 D5 Shan-yao *Shanyao* Fukien
38 D2 Shan-yin-ch'eng *Shanyincheng* Shansi
38 D2 Shan-yin Hsien *Shanyin Xian* Shansi
82 D5 Shan-yü *Shanyu* Kwangsi
119 C4 Shan-yüan *Shanyuan* Taiwan
119 B4 Shao-chia *Shaojia* Taiwan
Shaohing *see* Shao-hsing
19 G4 Shao Ho *Shao He* (river) Liao.
51 D2 Shao-hsing *Shaoxing* Chek.
55 F3 Shao-kang-chi *Shaogangji* Honan
23 D6 Shao-ken *Shaogen* Liao.
79 C1 Shao-kuan *Shaoguan* Kwangt.
14 F4 Shao-kuo *Shaoguo* Kirin
14 D2 Shao-kuo-chen *Shaoguozhen* Kirin
43 D3 Shao-po *Shaobo* Kiangsu
74 E4 Shao-shan *Shaoshan* Hunan
83 G2 Shao-shui *Shaoshui* Kwangsi
55 F4 Shao-tien *Shaodian* Honan
42 C1 Shao-tien *Shaodian* Kiangsu
75 D4 Shao-tung Hsien *Shaodong Xian* Hunan
19 G4 Shao-tzu-ho *Shaozihe* Liao.
11 C4 Shao-wen *Shaowen* Heilung.
66 C3 Shao-wu *Shaowu* Fukien
75 D4 Shao-yang *Shaoyang* Hunan
75 D5 Shao-yang Hsien *Shaoyang Xian* Hunan
54 D2 Shao-yüan *Shaoyuan* Honan
78 B3 Sha-pa *Shaba* Kwangt.
91 E4 Sha-pao-pao *Shabaobao* Kwei.
19 F5 Sha-pao-tzu *Shabaozi* Liao.
79 C2 Sha-p'ing *Shaping* Kwangt.
114 B3 Sha-p'o-t'ou *Shapotou* Ningsia
59 G5 Sha-p'u *Shapu* Hupeh
83 F3 Sha-pu *Shabu* Kwangsi
Shara Bürdü *see* Sha-erh-pu-jih-tu
Shara M Süme *see* Sha-erh-mo-jen-so-mu
Shara Muren (river) *see* Hsi-la-mu-lun Ho
Sharasume *see* A-le-t'ai
Sharha *see* Hsia-jih-ha
Sharu Lake *see* Hsia-ju Ts'o
11 E4 Sha-shan *Shashan* Heilung.
102 C1 Sha-shan-tzu *Shashanzi* Sink.
58 E4 Sha-shih *Shashi* Hupeh
74 F3 Sha-shih-chieh *Shashijie* Hunan
Shasi *see* Sha-shih
114 C4 Sha-t'ang-pu *Shatangpu* Ningsia
58 B5 Sha-tao-kou *Shadaogou* Hupeh
58 D4 Sha-tao-kuan *Shadaoguan* Hupeh
86 C3 Sha-te *Shade* Szech.
71 B5 Sha-ti *Shadi* Kiangsi
79 C3 Sha-ti *Shadi* Kwangt.
75 F6 Sha-t'ien *Shatian* Hunan
59 G3 Sha-tien *Shadian* Hupeh
71 B5 Sha-t'ien *Shatian* Kiangsi
83 G5 Sha-t'ien *Shatian* Kwangsi
83 H3 Sha-t'ien *Shatian* Kwangsi
55 F2 Sha-tien-chi *Shadianji* Honan
111 E3 Sha-ting *Shading* Tibet
74 E3 Sha-tou *Shadou* Hunan
83 H4 Sha-t'ou *Shatou* Kwangsi
98 B2 Sha-tsao-yüan *Shazaoyuan* Kansu
71 C5 Sha-ts'un *Shacun* Kiangsi
91 D3 Sha-t'u *Shatu* Kwei.
34 A4 Sha-t'u-chi *Shatuji* Shant.
59 F5 Sha-tui *Shadui* Hupeh
106 D3 Sha-tung-t'a *Shadongta* Tsing.
83 G3 Sha-tzu *Shazi* Kwangsi
91 C5 Sha-tzu-kou *Shazigou* Kwei.
90 C5 Sha-tzu-ling *Shaziling* Kwei.
91 F2 Sha-tzu-p'o *Shazipo* Kwei.
58 B4 Sha-tzu-ti *Shazidi* Hupeh
Sha-wan *see* San-tao-ho-tzu
75 C4 Sha-wan *Shawan* Hunan
91 D3 Sha-wan *Shawan* Kwei.
87 D3 Sha-wan *Shawan* Szech.
86 D3 Sha-wan-chen *Shawanzhen* Szech.
102 D1 Sha-wan Hsien *Shawan Xian* Sink.
55 G6 Sha-wo *Shawo* Honan
91 C4 Sha-wo *Shawo* Kwei.
67 B4 Sha-wu-t'ang *Shawutang* Fukien
102 C2 Sha-ya *Shaya* Sink.
59 E4 Sha-yang *Shayang* Hupeh
Shayizamka *see* Chia-yü-ch'iao
54 D3 Sha-yü-kou *Shayugou* Honan
Shazga *see* Hsia-tzu-chieh
39 D4 She-ch'eng *Shecheng* Shansi
54 D4 She-ch'i *Sheqi* Honan
71 B6 She-ch'i *Sheqi* Kiangsi
55 F4 She-ch'iao *Sheqiao* Honan
74 D3 She-chia-p'ing *Shejiaping* Hunan
She Chu *see* Hsien-shui Ho
43 D4 She-chu *Shezhu* Kiangsu
63 E7 She-ch'uan Ho *Shechuan He* (river) Shensi
71 C5 She-fu *Shefu* Kiangsi
47 E7 She Hsien *She Xian* Anhwei
31 A7 She-hsien *Shexian* Hopeh
87 E2 She-hung Hsien *Shehong Xian* Szech.
74 F3 She-kang-shih *Shegangshi* Hunan
Shekar *see* Hsieh-ko-erh
70 D3 She-keng *Shigeng* Kiangsi
Shekki *see* Shih-ch'i
59 G4 She-k'ou *Shekou* Hupeh
14 D2 She-li *Sheli* Kirin
14 F2 She-li *Sheli* Kirin
23 E5 She-li *Sheli* Kirin
26 C5 She-li-miao *Shelimiao* In. Mong.
14 F4 She-ling *Sheling* Kirin
Shemen Lake *see* Ch'a-lo-erh Ts'o
110 D3 Shen-cha *Shenzha* Tibet
79 D2 Shen-chen *Shenzhen* Kwangt.
34 A4 Shen-chi *Shenji* Shant.
11 D4 Shen-chia *Shenjia* Heilung.
102 I2 Shen-chia *Shenjia* Sink.
59 E4 Shen-chia-chi *Shenjiaji* Hupeh
38 D2 Shen-ch'ih *Shenchi* Shansi
79 C3 Shen-ching *Shenjing* Kwangt.
114 B3 Shen-ching *Shenjing* Ningsia
30 B3 Shen-ching-ts'un *Shenjingcun* Hopeh
14 E3 Shen-ching-tzu *Shenjingzi* Kirin
19 G3 Shen-ching-tzu *Shenjingzi* Liao.
Shen-ch'iu *see* Ch'en-ch'iu
118 C2 Shen-ch'ou *Shenchou* Taiwan
51 E3 Shen-ch'üan *Shenquan* Chek.
79 E2 Shen-ch'üan *Shenquan* Kwangt.
79 E2 Shen-ch'üan Kang *Shenquan Gang* Kwangt.
47 D5 Sheng-chia-ch'iao *Shengjiaqiao* Anhwei
47 E6 Sheng-chia-ch'iao *Shengjiaqiao* Anhwei
90 B5 Sheng-ching Kuan *Shengjing Guan* (pass) Kwei.
102 I2 Sheng-chin-t'ai *Shengjintai* Sink.
103 E2 Sheng-chin-t'ai *Shengjintai* Sink.
51 D3 Sheng-hsien *Shengxian* Chek.
59 G4 Sheng-hung-ch'ing *Shenghongqing* Hupeh
11 E4 Sheng-lang *Shenglang* Heilung.
11 D5 Sheng-li *Shengli* Heilung.
59 H3 Sheng-li *Shengli* Hupeh
23 E5 Sheng-li *Shengli* Kirin
106 D2 Sheng-li-k'ou *Shenglikou* Tsing.
102 C2 Sheng-li-shih-chiu-ch'ang *Shenglishijiuchang* Sink.
102 H2 Sheng-li Ta-pan *Shendi Daban* (pass) Sink.
103 D2 Sheng-li Ta-pan *Shengli Daban* (pass) Sink.
70 C3 Sheng-mi-chieh *Shengmijie* Kiangsi
11 C4 Sheng-p'ing *Shengping* Heilung.
14 F5 Sheng-shui-ho-tzu *Shengshuihezi* Kirin
51 F2 Sheng-ssu Hsien *Shengsi Xian* Chek.
51 F2 Sheng-ssu Lieh-tao *Shengsi Liedao* (islands) Chek.
58 D2 Sheng-tai *Shengdai* Hupeh
79 C2 Sheng-t'ang *Shengtang* Kwangt.
43 E5 Sheng-tse *Shengze* Kiangsu
43 E3 Sheng-tz'u-chen *Shengcizhen* Kiangsu
63 E8 Shen-ho-k'ou *Shenhekou* Shensi
31 C5 Shen-hsien *Shenxian* Hopeh
67 D6 Shen-hu *Shenhu* Fukien
94 A3 Shen-hu-kuan *Shenhuguan* Yun.
39 C7 Shen-jen-chien *Shenrenjian* Shansi
71 D4 Shen-kang *Shengang* Kiangsi
43 E4 Shen-kang *Shengang* Kiangsu
54 E3 Shen-kou *Shengou* Honan
34 B4 Shen-li-p'u *Shenlipu* Shant.
54 E4 Shen-lou *Shenlou* Honan
62 F2 Shen-mu *Shenmu* Shensi
31 B5 Shen-nan *Shennan* Hopeh
58 C3 Shen-nung-chia *Shennongjia* Hupeh
31 D4 Shenq-fang *Shengfang* Hopeh
51 E2 Shen-shih-ch'iao *Shenshiqiao* Chek.
11 E4 Shen-shu *Shenshu* Heilung.
Shensi Province *see* Pages 61-64
51 D2 Shen-tang *Shendang* Chek.
38 D2 Shen-t'ou *Shentou* Shansi
34 B2 Shen-t'ou *Shentou* Shant.
31 C5 Shen-tse *Shenze* Hopeh
47 E7 Shen-tu *Shendu* Anhwei
67 C6 Shen-t'u *Shentu* Fukien
14 E4 Shen-yang *Shenyang* Kirin
19 G3 Shen-yang *Shenyang* Liao.
Shen-yang - city plan *see* Page 136
19 G2 Shen-yang Ti-ch'ü *Shenyang Diqu* Liao.
She-p'an Yang *see* San-men Wan
14 B3 She-po-t'u *Shebotu* Kirin
23 E5 She-po-t'u *Shebotu* Kirin
74 E4 She-pu *Shebu* Hunan
83 G4 She-pu *Shebu* Kwangsi
Shershik Gompa *see* Sa-hsi-k'o-kung-pa
75 C5 She Shui *She Shui* (river) Hunan
59 G3 She Shui *She Shui* (river) Hupeh
75 D4 She-t'ien-ch'iao *Shetianqiao* Hunan
Shetsuishan *see* Shih-tsui-shan
54 C4 She-wei *Shewei* Honan
43 D2 She-yang *Sheyang* Kiangsu
43 D2 She-yang Ho *Sheyang He* (river) Kiangsu
43 E2 She-yang Hsien *Sheyang Xian* Kiangsu
Shigatse *see* Jih-k'a-tse
Shigatse Region *see* Jih-k'a-tse Ti-ch'ü
Shigatze *see* Jih-k'a-tse
63 E9 Shih-chai-ho *Shizhaihe* Shensi
10 C2 Shih-chan *Shizhan* Heilung.
91 C3 Shih-ch'ang *Shichang* Kwei.
91 F3 Shih-ch'ang *Shichang* Kwei.
35 E4 Shih-ch'ang *Shichang* Shant.
18 C4 Shih-chang-tzu *Shizhangzi* Liao.
39 D5 Shih-che *Shizhe* Shansi
70 D3 Shih-chen-chieh *Shizhenjie* Kiangsi
67 E5 Shih-ch'eng *Shicheng* Fukien
71 D5 Shih-ch'eng *Shicheng* Kiangsi
79 D1 Shih-cheng *Shizheng* Kwangt.
19 H4 Shih-ch'eng *Shicheng* Liao.
39 E5 Shih-ch'eng *Shicheng* Shansi
118 C2 Shih-ch'eng *Shicheng* Taiwan
19 F5 Shih-ch'eng Tao *Shicheng Dao* (island) Liao.
66 C4 Shih-ch'i *Shiqi* Fukien
70 E3 Shih-ch'i *Shiqi* Kiangsi
14 F4 Shih-ch'i *Shiqi* Kirin
79 C2 Shih-ch'i *Shiqi* Kwangt.
83 F5 Shih-ch'ia *Shiqia* Kwangsi
47 C5 Shih-chia-ch'iao *Shijiaqiao* Anhwei
51 D2 Shih-chia-ch'iao *Shijiaqiao* Chek.
43 D3 Shih-chia-ch'iao *Shijiaqiao* Kiangsu
31 B5 Shih-chia-chuang *Shijiazhuang* Hopeh
47 F6 Shih-ch'iao *Shiqiao* Anhwei
54 D4 Shih-ch'iao *Shiqiao* Honan
55 E4 Shih-ch'iao *Shiqiao* Honan
58 E3 Shih-ch'iao *Shiqiao* Hupeh
70 D4 Shih-ch'iao *Shiqiao* Kiangsi
71 B5 Shih-ch'iao *Shiqiao* Kiangsi
83 H4 Shih-ch'iao *Shiqiao* Kwangsi
79 C2 Shih-chiao *Shijiao* Kwangt.
79 C2 Shih-ch'iao *Shiqiao* Kwangt.
79 C2 Shih-ch'iao *Shiqiao* Kwangt.
34 D3 Shih-ch'iao *Shiqiao* Shant.
34 D4 Shih-ch'iao *Shiqiao* Shant.
87 F2 Shih-ch'iao *Shiqiao* Szech.
87 E2 Shih-ch'iao-chen *Shiqiaozhen* Szech.
19 G3 Shih-ch'iao-tzu *Shiqiaozi* Liao.
87 E2 Shih-chia-pa *Shijiaba* Szech.
14 E4 Shih-chia-pao *Shijiabao* Kirin
18 E3 Shih-chia-pao *Shijiabao* Liao.
110 D2 Shih-chia-sha-lung *Shijiashalong* Tibet
39 B6 Shih-chia-t'an *Shijiatan* Shansi
30 C4 Shih-chia-ying *Shijiaying* Hopeh
15 I5 Shih-ch'i-chieh *Shiqijie* Kirin
47 F6 Shih-chieh-tu *Shijiedu* Anhwei
79 C2 Shih-chien *Shijian* Kwangt.
91 F3 Shih-ch'ien *Shiqian* Kwei.
47 D5 Shih-chien-pu *Shijianbu* Anhwei
67 D6 Shih-ching *Shijing* Fukien
54 D3 Shih-ching *Shijing* Honan
35 D4 Shih-ching *Shijing* Shant.
30 D4 Shih-ching-shan *Shijingshan* Hopeh
10 C1 Shih-chiu-chan *Shijiuzhan* Heilung.
47 E5 Shih-chiu Hu *Shijiu Hu* (lake) Anhwei
42 C4 Shih-chiu Hu *Shijiu Hu* (lake) Kiangsu
35 E4 Shih-chiu-so *Sijiusuo* Shant.
51 D4 Shih-chu *Shizhu* Chek.
14 G4 Shih-chü *Shiju* Kirin
83 G4 Shih-chü *Shiju* Kwangsi
38 E3 Shih-chü *Shiju* Shansi
86 B1 Shih-ch'ü *Shiqu* Szech.
87 G3 Shih-chu *Shizhu* Szech.
63 D7 Shih-ch'üan *Shiquan* Shensi
43 E3 Shih-chuang *Shizhuang* Kiangsu
39 D6 Shih-chuang *Shizhuang* Shansi
63 D6 Shih-ch'uan Ho *Shichuan He* (river) Shensi
110 A2 Shih-ch'üan-ho *Shiquanhe* Tibet
103 F2 Shih-ch'üan-tzu *Shiquanzi* Sink.
62 F3 Shih-chü-i *Shijuyi* Shensi
67 C6 Shih-chung *Shizhong* Fukien
10 C2 Shih-erh-chan *Shierzhan* Heilung.
50 B3 Shih-erh Shan *Shier Shan* (mt) Chek.
70 F2 Shih-erh Shan *Shier Shan* (mt) Kiangsi
15 H6 Shih-erh-tao-kou *Shierdaogou* Kirin
67 B5 Shih-fang *Shifang* Fukien
87 E2 Shih-fang *Shifang* Szech.
51 D3 Shih-feng Ch'i *Shifeng Qi* (river) Chek.
54 D4 Shih-fo-ssu *Shifosi* Honan
118 B3 Shih-fo-tung *Shifodong* Taiwan
34 B3 Shih-heng *Shiheng* Shant.
Shihhing *see* Shih-hsing
46 B3 Shih-ho *Shihe* Anhwei
18 E5 Shih-ho *Shihe* Liao.
102 D1 Shih-ho-tzu *Shihezi* Sink.
102 H1 Shih-ho-tzu *Shihezi* Sink.
99 G5 Shih-hsia *Shixia* Kansu
39 E4 Shih-hsia *Shixia* Shansi
75 C4 Shih-hsia-chiang *Shixiajiang* Hunan
79 D1 Shih-hsing *Shixing* Kwangt.
42 C1 Shih-hu *Shihu* Kiangsu
58 D2 Shih-hua-chieh *Shihuajie* Hupeh
87 G3 Shih-hui *Shihui* Szech.
59 E4 Shih-hui-ch'iao *Shihuiqiao* Hupeh
30 F3 Shih-hui-yao *Shihuiyao* Hopeh
19 G4 Shih-hui-yao *Shihuiyao* Liao.
102 H1 Shih-hui-yao-tzu *Shihuiyaozi* Sink.
78 A4 Shih-i *Shiyi* Kwangt.
10 C2 Shih-i-chan *Shiyizhan* Heilung.
70 F3 Shih-i-tu *Shiyidu* Kiangsi
43 E4 Shih-i-yü *Shiyiyu* Kiangsu
79 D1 Shih-jen-chang *Shirenzhang* Kwangt.
11 D4 Shih-jen-ch'eng *Shirencheng* Heilung.
30 E2 Shih-jen-kou *Shirengou* Hopeh
54 C5 Shih-kang *Shigang* Honan
43 E3 Shih-kang *Shigang* Kiangsu
83 F6 Shih-k'ang *Shikang* Kwangsi
94 C4 Shih-kao-ching *Shigaojing* Yun.
79 C1 Shih-k'eng k'ung *Shikeng Kong* (mt) Kwangt.
Shihkiachwang *see* Shih-chia-chuang
66 E3 Shih-k'ou *Shikou* Fukien
70 C4 Shih-k'ou *Shikou* Kiangsi
70 D3 Shih-k'ou *Shikou* Kiangsi
79 C2 Shih-kou *Shigou* Kwangt.
39 C5 Shih-k'ou *Shikou* Shansi
34 D2 Shih-k'ou *Shikou* Shant.
114 C3 Shih-kou-i *Shigouyi* Ningsia
78 B3 Shih-ku *Shigu* Kwangt.
94 B2 Shih-ku *Shigu* Yun.
39 E4 Shih-kuai *Shiguai* Shansi
26 D4 Shih-kuai-kou *Shiguaigou* In. Mong.
15 J4 Shih-kuan *Shiguan* Kirin
46 E4 Shih-kuan-chi *Shiguanji* Anhwei
47 E5 Shih-kuei *Shigui* Anhwei
58 D2 Shih-ku-kuan *Shiguguan* Hupeh
98 B1 Shih-kung *Shigong* Kansu
114 C3 Shih-k'ung *Shikong* Ningsia
46 C3 Shih-kung-shan *Shigongshan* Anhwei
55 E5 Shih-kun-ho *Shigunhe* Honan
31 B7 Shih-ku Shan *Shigu Shan* (mt) Hopeh
34 C4 Shih-lai *Shilai* Shant.
39 D6 Shih-li *Shili* Shansi
50 B3 Shih-liang *Shiliang* Chek.
55 G4 Shih-liang *Shiliang* Honan
39 E5 Shih-liang *Shiliang* Shansi
35 F2 Shih-liang *Shiliang* Shant.
19 G3 Shih-li-ho *Shilihe* Liao.
39 C5 Shih-lin *Shilin* Shansi
118 C1 Shih-lin *Shilin* Taiwan
14 E4 Shih-ling *Shiling* Kirin
106 C3 Shih-li-no-erh *Shilinuoer* Tsing.
46 C3 Shih-li-pao *Shilibao* Anhwei
15 K4 Shih-li-p'ing *Shiliping* Kirin
58 E4 Shih-li-p'u *Shilipu* Hupeh
10 C1 Shih-liu-chan *Shiliuzhan* Heilung.
67 C6 Shih-liu-fan *Shiliufan* Fukien
42 C1 Shih-liu-shu *Shiliushu* Kiangsu
39 B4 Shih-lou *Shilou* Shansi
78 A4 Shih-lu *Shilu* Kwangt.
82 C5 Shih-lung *Shilong* Kwangsi
83 F4 Shih-lung *Shilong* Kwangsi
79 C2 Shih-lung *Shilong* Kwangt.
67 C6 Shih-ma *Shima* Fukien
71 C5 Shih-ma *Shima* Kiangsi
79 D1 Shih-ma *Shima* Kwangt.
55 E4 Shih-man-t'an Shui-k'u *Shimantan Shuiku* (res) Honan
51 D2 Shih-men *Shimen* Chek.
54 D4 Shih-men *Shimen* Honan
30 C3 Shih-men *Shimen* Hopeh
30 E3 Shih-men *Shimen* Hopeh
30 F4 Shih-men *Shimen* Hopeh
74 D2 Shih-men *Shimen* Hunan
58 D3 Shih-men *Shimen* Hupeh
99 F4 Shih-men *Shimen* Kansu
70 D4 Shih-men *Shimen* Kiangsi
34 D5 Shih-men *Shimen* Shant.
35 E4 Shih-men *Shimen* Shant.
118 C1 Shih-men *Shimen* Taiwan
30 G3 Shih-men-chai *Shimenzhai* Hopeh
94 B3 Shih-men-chen *Shimenzhen* Yun.
31 D5 Shih-men-ch'iao *Shimenqiao* Hopeh
74 D3 Shih-men-ch'iao *Shimenqiao* Hunan
70 D2 Shih-men-chieh *Shimenjie* Kiangsi
58 A5 Shih-men-k'an *Shimenkan* Hupeh
70 B3 Shih-men-lou *Shimenlou* Kiangsi
46 D4 Shih-men-shan *Shimenshan* Anhwei
75 C5 Shih-men-shan *Shimenshan* Hunan
22 D3 Shih-men-tzu *Shimenzi* Heilung.
34 C2 Shih-miao *Shimiao* Shant.
86 D3 Shih-mien *Shimian* Szech.
83 F5 Shih-nan *Shinan* Kwangsi
67 D5 Shih-n'iu Shan *Shiniu Shan* (mt) Fukien
46 E4 Shih-pa *Shiba* Anhwei
10 C1 Shih-pa-chan *Shibazhan* Heilung.
22 F1 Shih-pa-chan *Shibazhan* Heilung.
27 E4 Shih-pa-ch'ing *Shibaqing* In. Mong.
47 C6 Shih-p'ai *Shipai* Anhwei
59 E4 Shih-p'ai *Shipai* Hupeh
46 B3 Shih-pa-li-p'u *Shibalipu* Anhwei
99 F3 Shih-pa-li-p'u *Shibalipu* Kansu
63 C7 Shih-pa-li-p'u *Shibalipu* Shensi
39 D4 Shih-p'an *Shipan* Shansi
98 D1 Shih-pan Ching *Shiban Jing* (well) Kansu
59 F3 Shih-pan-ho *Shibanhe* Hupeh
74 D2 Shih-pan-t'an *Shibantan* Hunan
55 E1 Shih-pan-yen *Shibanyan* Honan
63 E5 Shih-pao *Shibao* Shensi
98 C2 Shih-pao-ch'eng *Shibaocheng* Kansu
91 D2 Shih-pao-szu *Shibaosi* Kwei.
67 C5 Shih-pei *Shibei* Fukien
70 C3 Shih-pi *Shibi* Kiangsi
83 E3 Shih-pieh *Shibie* Kwangsi
27 G3 Shih-pieh-su-mu *Shibiesumu* In. Mong.
Shih-p'ing *see* Ch'ih-p'ing
91 F3 Shih-ping *Shibing* Kwei.
95 D4 Shih-p'ing *Shiping* Yun.
70 D2 Shih-pi-shan *Shibishan* Kiangsi
66 D3 Shih-p'o *Shipo* Fukien
63 F6 Shih-p'o *Shipo* Shensi
47 C5 Shih-p'o-tien *Shipodian* Anhwei
51 E3 Shih-p'u *Shipu* Chek.
35 E3 Shih-pu *Shibu* Shant.
10 C2 Shih-san-chan *Shisanzhan* Heilung.
22 F2 Shih-san-chan *Shisanzhan* Heilung.
103 E2 Shih-san-chien-fang *Shisanjianfang* Sink.
10 D4 Shih-san-ching-tzu *Shisanjingzi* Heilung.
67 D5 Shih-shan *Shishan* Fukien
18 E3 Shih-shan *Shishan* Liao.
71 D5 Shih-shang *Shishang* Kiangsi
67 D6 Shih-shih *Shishi* Fukien
71 B5 Shih-shih-k'ou *Shishikou* Kiangsi
59 E5 Shih-shou *Shishou* Hupeh
63 B6 Shih-shu-lin *Shishulin* Shensi
10 C2 Shih-ssu-chan *Shisizhan* Heilung.
15 H6 Shih-ssu-tao-kou *Shisidaogou* Kirin
47 D6 Shih-t'ai Hsien *Shitai Xian* Anhwei
74 E4 Shih-t'an *Shitan* Hunan
70 C3 Shih-t'an *Shitan* Kiangsi
79 C1 Shih-t'an *Shitan* Kwangt.
79 C2 Shih-t'an *Shitan* Kwangt.
118 B2 Shih-t'an *Shitan* Taiwan
114 C2 Shih-t'an-ching *Shitanjing* Ningsia
50 C4 Shih-t'ang *Shitang* Chek.
51 E4 Shih-t'ang *Shitang* Chek.
70 E3 Shih-t'ang *Shitang* Kiangsi
71 C4 Shih-t'ang *Shitang* Kiangsi
83 F5 Shih-t'ang *Shitang* Kwangsi
83 H2 Shih-t'ang *Shitang* Kwangsi
34 C3 Shih-t'an-wu *Shitanwu* Shant.
35 H3 Shih-tao *Shidao* Shant.
35 H3 Shih-tao Wan *Shidao Wan* (bay) Shant.
118 C1 Shih-ti *Shidi* Taiwan
74 C2 Shih-t'i-ch'i *Shitiqi* Hunan

20

Shih-t'ieh – Sutlej

38 D4 **Shih-t'ieh** *Shitie* Shansi
94 B3 **Shih-tien** *Shidian* Yun.
102 H2 **Shih-t'i-tzu** *Shitizi* Sink.
11 E5 **Shih-t'ou** *Shitou* Heilung.
94 B4 **Shih-t'ou-chai** *Shitouzhai* Yun.
70 C3 **Shih-t'ou-kang** *Shitougang* Kiangsi
10 C3 **Shih-t'ou-kou** *Shitougou* Heilung.
10 C2 **Shih-t'ou Shan** *Shitou Shan* (mt) Heilung.
59 H4 **Shih-t'ou-tsui** *Shitouzui* Hupeh
Shih-tsien-fu *see* **Shih-ch'ien**
114 C2 **Shih-tsui-shan** *Shizuishan* Ningsia
Shih-tsui-tzu *see* **Shih-tsui-shan**
46 D3 **Shih-ts'un** *Shicun* Anhwei
95 D3 **Shih-tsung Hsien** *Shizong Xian* Yun.
75 F5 **Shih-tu** *Shidu* Hunan
70 B2 **Shih-tu** *Shidu* Kiangsi
87 E2 **Shih-t'uan** *Shituan* Szech.
14 G3 **Shih-t'un** *Shitun* Kirin
79 C2 **Shih-tung** *Shidong* Kwangt.
91 D3 **Shih-tung** *Shidong* Kwei.
99 F3 **Shih-tung-ssu** *Shidongsi* Kansu
119 B4 **Shih-tzu** *Shizi* Taiwan
39 C6 **Shih-tzu-ho** *Shizihe* Shansi
30 C2 **Shih-tzu-kou** *Shizigou* Hopeh
63 D7 **Shih-tzu-kou-k'ou** *Shizigoukou* Shensi
71 D4 **Shih-tzu Ling** *Shizi Ling* (mt) Kiangsi
35 D4 **Shih-tzu-lu** *Shizilu* Shant.
47 F6 **Shih-tzu-p'u** *Shizipu* Anhwei
59 G4 **Shih-tzu-p'u** *Shizipu* Hupeh
87 F3 **Shih-tzu-t'an** *Shizitan* Szech.
119 B4 **Shih-tzu-t'ou** *Shizitou* Taiwan
75 E4 **Shih-wan** *Shiwan* Hunan
62 E3 **Shih-wan** *Shiwan* Shensi
82 E5 **Shih-wan Ta-shan** *Shiwan Dashan* (mts) Kwangsi
Shih-wei *see* **Chi-la-lin**
14 E4 **Shih-wu** *Shiwu* Kirin
23 F6 **Shih-wu** *Shiwu* Kirin
10 C2 **Shih-wu-chan** *Shiwuzhan* Heilung.
83 F4 **Shih-ya** *Shiya* Kwangsi
87 E3 **Shih-yang-ch'ang** *Shiyangchang* Szech.
99 F2 **Shih-yang Ho** *Shiyang He* (river) Kansu
102 I2 **Shih-yao-tzu** *Shiyaozi* Sink.
87 G3 **Shih-yeh** *Shiye* Szech.
58 C2 **Shih-yen** *Shiyan* Hupeh
43 E3 **Shih-yen** *Shiyan* Kiangsu
87 E3 **Shih-yen-ch'iao** *Shiyanqiao* Szech.
114 C3 **Shih-yen-ch'ih** *Shiyanchi* Ningsia
38 F4 **Shih-yü** *Shiyu* Shansi
78 A4 **Shih-yün** *Shiyun* Kwangt.
83 F6 **Shih-yung** *Shiyong* Kwangsi
Shilingol League *see* **Hsi-lin-kuo-le Meng**
Shinchiku *see* **Hsin-chu**
Shine Us *see* **Hsi-ni-wu-su**
35 E3 **Shi-pu-tzu** *Shibuzi* Shant.
Shi-tsui-tze *see* **Shih-tsui-shan**
Shiuchow *see* **Shao-kuan**
Shiuhing *see* **Chao-ch'ing**
Shiukwan *see* **Shao-kuan**
Shoka *see* **Chang-hua**
50 C3 **Shou-ch'ang** *Shouchang* Chek.
74 B2 **Shou-ch'e** *Shouche* Hunan
83 F2 **Shou-ch'eng** *Shoucheng* Kwangsi
34 B3 **Shou-chieh** *Shoujie* Shant.
118 C3 **Shou-feng** *Shoufeng* Taiwan
46 C4 **Shou-hsien** *Shouxian* Anhwei
34 D3 **Shou-kuang** *Shouguang* Shant.
66 E3 **Shou-ning** *Shouning* Fukien
19 G3 **Shou-shan** *Shoushan* Liao.
95 D2 **Shou-shan** *Shoushan* Yun.
30 E3 **Shou-wang-fen** *Shouwangfen* Hopeh
38 E4 **Shou-yang** *Shouyang* Shansi
63 D7 **Shou-yang Shan** *Shouyang Shan* (mt) Shensi
75 D6 **Shou-yen-yü** *Shouyanyu* Hunan
Showchow *see* **Shou-hsien**
86 D2 **Shua-ching-ssu** *Shuajingsi* Szech.
14 F6 **Shuang-ch'a** *Shuangcha* Kirin
102 I1 **Shuang-ch'a-ho-tzu** *Shuangchahezi* Sink.
11 D5 **Shuang-ch'eng** *Shuangcheng* Heilung.
14 E3 **Shuang-ch'eng-pao** *Shuangchengbao* Kirin
23 F5 **Shuang-ch'eng-p'u** *Shuangchengpu* Kirin
Shuang-ch'eng-tzu *see* **Hsi-miao**
51 C4 **Shuang-ch'i** *Shuangqi* Chek.
66 E3 **Shuang-ch'i** *Shuangqi* Fukien
66 E4 **Shuang-ch'i** *Shuangqi* Fukien
118 C1 **Shuang-ch'i** *Shuangqi* Taiwan
75 B5 **Shuang-chiang** *Shuangjiang* Hunan
91 F5 **Shuang-chiang** *Shuangjiang* Kwei.
87 E2 **Shuang-chiang** *Shuangjiang* Szech.
87 G2 **Shuang-chiang** *Shuangjiang* Szech.
94 B4 **Shuang-chiang** *Shuangjiang* Yun.
74 E4 **Shuang-chiang-k'ou** *Shuangjiangkou* Hunan
46 C4 **Shuang-ch'iao** *Shuangqiao* Anhwei
47 E6 **Shuang-ch'iao** *Shuangqiao* Anhwei
55 F5 **Shuang-ch'iao** *Shuangqiao* Honan
82 E4 **Shuang-ch'iao** *Shuangqiao* Kwangsi
46 C3 **Shuang-ch'iao-chi** *Shuangqiaoji* Anhwei
78 B3 **Shuang-chieh** *Shuangjie* Kwangt.
46 C3 **Shuang-chien-chi** *Shuangjianji* Anhwei
39 C5 **Shuang-ch'ih** *Shuangchi* Shansi
42 C1 **Shuang-chih-tien** *Shuangzhidian* Kiangsu
91 F4 **Shuang-ching** *Shuangjing* Kwei.
31 B7 **Shuang-ching-chi** *Shuangjingji* Hopeh
102 I1 **Shuang-ching-tzu** *Shuangjingzi* Sink.
10 C3 **Shuang-fa** *Shuangfa* Heilung.
11 E5 **Shuang-feng** *Shuangfeng* Heilung.
43 F4 **Shuang-feng** *Shuangfeng* Kiangsu
83 F5 **Shuang-feng** *Shuangfeng* Kwangsi
74 E4 **Shuang-feng Hsien** *Shuangfeng Xian* Hunan
30 E2 **Shuang-feng-ssu** *Shuangfengsi* Hopeh
46 B3 **Shuang-fu** *Shuangfu* Anhwei
74 E3 **Shuang-fu-p'u** *Shuangfupu* Hunan
67 D5 **Shuang-han** *Shuanghan* Fukien
47 B5 **Shuang-ho** *Shuanghe* Anhwei
47 C5 **Shuang-ho** *Shuanghe* Anhwei
11 F5 **Shuang-ho** *Shuanghe* Heilung.
54 D5 **Shuang-ho** *Shuanghe* Honan
58 E3 **Shuang-ho** *Shuanghe* Hupeh
59 E3 **Shuang-ho** *Shuanghe* Hupeh
63 D8 **Shuang-ho** *Shuanghe* Shensi
102 H1 **Shuang-ho** *Shuanghe* Sink.
86 D2 **Shuang-ho** *Shuanghe* Szech.
87 E1 **Shuang-ho** *Shuanghe* Szech.
95 E2 **Shuang-ho** *Shuanghe* Yun.
87 F2 **Shuang-ho-ch'ang** *Shuanghechang* Szech.
14 G4 **Shuang-ho-chen** *Shuanghezhen* Kirin
10 E3 **Shuang-ho-ta-kang** *Shuanghedagang* Heilung.
34 D4 **Shuang-hou** *Shuanghou* Shant.
11 C4 **Shuang-hsing** *Shuangxing* Heilung.
110 C2 **Shuang Hu** *Shuang Hu* (lake) Tibet
62 F3 **Shuang-hu-yü** *Shuanghuyu* Shensi
26 D4 **Shuang-i-ch'eng** *Shuangyicheng* In. Mong.
70 E3 **Shuang-kang** *Shuanggang* Kiangsi
14 C2 **Shuang-kang** *Shuanggang* Kirin
23 E5 **Shuang-kang** *Shuanggang* Kirin
30 E4 **Shuang-k'ou** *Shuangkou* Hopeh
59 E2 **Shuang-kou** *Shuanggou* Hupeh
42 B1 **Shuang-kou** *Shuanggou* Kiangsu
42 C2 **Shuang-kou** *Shuanggou* Kiangsu
42 C2 **Shuang-kou** *Shuanggou* Kiangsu
23 E6 **Shuang-liao** *Shuangliao* Kirin
14 D4 **Shuang-liao Hsien** *Shuangliao Xian* Kirin
51 D2 **Shuang-lin** *Shuanglin* Chek.
70 B4 **Shuang-lin** *Shuanglin* Kiangsi
91 D3 **Shuang-liu** *Shuangliu* Kwei.
87 D2 **Shuang-liu** *Shuangliu* Szech.
11 G4 **Shuang-liu-ho-tzu** *Shuangliuhezi* Heilung.
55 G6 **Shuang-liu-shu** *Shuangliushu* Honan
11 D4 **Shuang-lu** *Shuanglu* Heilung.
11 D4 **Shuang-lung** *Shuanglong* Heilung.
118 B3 **Shuang-lung** *Shuanglong* Taiwan
62 D5 **Shuang-lung-chen** *Shuanglongzhen* Shensi
46 C4 **Shuang-miao** *Shuangmiao* Anhwei
46 D3 **Shuang-miao** *Shuangmiao* Anhwei
14 F5 **Shuang-miao-tzu** *Shuangmiaozi* Kirin
19 H2 **Shuang-miao-tzu** *Shuangmiaozi* Liao.
75 D6 **Shuang-pai** *Shuangbai* Hunan
94 C3 **Shuang-pai** *Shuangbai* Yun.
75 F5 **Shuang-p'ai-shan** *Shuangpaishan* Hunan
74 E4 **Shuang-pan-ch'iao** *Shuangbanqiao* Hunan
14 D4 **Shuang-shan** *Shuangshan* Kirin
30 G3 **Shuang-shan-tzu** *Shuangshanzi* Hopeh
14 D4 **Shuang-sheng-t'un** *Shuanhshengtun* Kirin
63 B7 **Shuang-shih-p'u** *Shuangshipu* Shensi
90 B4 **Shuang-shui-ching** *Shuangshuijing* Kwei.
14 A4 **Shuang-t'ai-hsing** *Shuangtaixing* Kirin
23 D6 **Shuang-t'ai-hsing** *Shuangtaixing* Kirin
19 G2 **Shuang-t'ai-tzu** *Shuangtaizi* Liao.
70 D3 **Shuang-t'ang** *Shuangtang* Kiangsi
98 C1 **Shuang-t'a-pao** *Shuangtabao* Kansu
71 D4 **Shuang-t'ien** *Shuangtian* Kiangsi
43 E3 **Shuang-tien** *Shuangdian* Kiangsu
46 C3 **Shuang-tui-chi** *Shuangduiji* Anhwei
47 D4 **Shuang-tun-chi** *Shuangdunji* Anhwei
10 E4 **Shuang-tzu-ho** *Shuangzihe* Heilung.
67 C5 **Shuang-yang** *Shuangyang* Fukien
11 C4 **Shuang-yang** *Shuangyang* Heilung.
14 F4 **Shuang-yang** *Shuangyang* Kirin
18 E3 **Shuang-yang-tien** *Shuangyangdian* Liao.
35 E3 **Shuang-yang-tien** *Shuangyangdian* Shant.
11 F4 **Shuang-ya-shan** *Shuangyashan* Heilung.
39 E6 **Shu-chang** *Shuzhang* Shansi
47 C5 **Shu-ch'eng** *Shucheng* Anhwei
31 D5 **Shu-ch'eng** *Shucheng* Hopeh
47 E6 **Shu Ch'i** *Shu Qi* (river) Anhwei
94 C3 **Shu-chieh** *Shujie* Yun.
Shu-erh-kan Ho *see* **Hsiu-kou-kuo-le Ho**
94 B3 **Shu-fang** *Shufang* Yun.
102 A3 **Shu-fu** *Shufu* Sink.
34 D5 **Shu Ho** *Shu He* (river) Shant.
63 E8 **Shu-ho-k'ou** *Shuhekou* Shensi
47 D5 **Shu-ho-tun** *Shuhedun* Anhwei
51 D4 **Shu-hung** *Shuhong* Chek.
55 F4 **Shui-chai** *Shuizhai* Honan
34 C3 **Shui-chai** *Shuizhai* Shant.
106 B1 **Shui-chan** *Shuizhan* Tsing.
79 E1 **Shui-ch'e** *Shuiche* Kwangt.
90 B4 **Shui-ch'eng Hsien** *Shuicheng Xian* Kwei.
66 D3 **Shui-chi** *Shuiji* Fukien
35 F3 **Shui-chi** *Shuiji* Shant.
46 D4 **Shui-chia-hu** *Shuijiahu* Anhwei
75 D5 **Shui-ch'iao-p'u** *Shuiqiaopu* Hunan
66 B4 **Shui-ch'ien** *Shuiqian* Fukien
83 F3 **Shui-ching** *Shuijing* Kwangsi
87 E1 **Shui-ching** *Shuijing* Szech.
75 D4 **Shui-ching-t'ou** *Shuijingtou* Hunan
30 D2 **Shui-ch'üan** *Shuiquan* Hopeh
99 G3 **Shui-ch'üan** *Shinquan* Kansu
18 C3 **Shui-ch'üan** *Shuiquan* Liao.
98 E2 **Shui-ch'üan-tzu** *Shuiquanzi* Kansu
15 H3 **Shui-ch'ü-liu** *Shuiquliu* Kirin
47 C6 **Shui-hou-ling** *Shuihouling* Anhwei
70 C4 **Shui-hsi** *Shuixi* Kiangsi
Shuikiahu *see* **Shui-chia-hu**
46 E4 **Shui-k'ou** *Shuikou* Anhwei
66 D4 **Shui-k'ou** *Shuikou* Fukien
67 D5 **Shui-k'ou** *Shuikou* Fukien
75 D7 **Shui-k'ou** *Shuikou* Hunan
75 F5 **Shui-k'ou** *Shuikou* Hunan
79 D2 **Shui-k'ou** *Shuikou* Kwangt.
91 G5 **Shui-k'ou** *Shuikou* Kwei.
82 C5 **Shui-k'ou-kuan** *Shuikouguan* Kwangsi
75 E5 **Shui-k'ou-shan** *Shuikoushan* Hunan
91 D3 **Shui-k'ou-szu** *Shuikousi* Kwei.
34 C5 **Shui-kuo** *Shuiguo* Shant.
118 B3 **Shui-li** *Shuili* Taiwan
118 C3 **Shui-lien** *Shuilian* Taiwan
19 I2 **Shui-lien-tung** *Shuiliandong* Liao.
99 H4 **Shui-lo-ch'eng** *Shuiluocheng* Kansu
91 E5 **Shui-lung** *Shuilong* Kwei.
19 F5 **Shui-men-tzu** *Shuimenzi* Liao.
83 F5 **Shui-ming** *Shuiming* Kwangsi
114 C2 **Shui-mo-kou** *Shuimogou* Ningsia
Shui-mo-kou *Shuimogou* Sink.
102 I2 **Shui-mo-kou** *Shuimogou* Sink.
26 D4 **Shui-mo-t'an** *Shuimotan* In. Mong.
66 D3 **Shui-nan** *Shuinan* Fukien
71 C5 **Shui-nan** *Shuinan* Kiangsi
71 D5 **Shui-nan** *Shuinan* Kiangsi
42 C3 **Shui-ning** *Shuining* Kiangsu
91 E2 **Shui-pa-t'ang** *Shuibatang* Kwei.
66 C3 **Shui-pei** *Shuibei* Fukien
66 D3 **Shui-pei** *Shuibei* Fukien
70 C3 **Shui-pei** *Shuibei* Kiangsi
43 D4 **Shui-pei** *Shuibei* Kiangsu
70 C4 **Shui-pien** *Shuibian* Kiangsi
58 B2 **Shui-p'ing** *Shuiping* Hupeh
55 F3 **Shui-p'o** *Shuipo* Honan
119 B3 **Shui-shang** *Shuishang* Taiwan
46 D3 **Shui-sha-p'u** *Shuishapu* Anhwei
71 B6 **Shui-shih** *Shuishi* Kiangsi
18 E6 **Shui-shih-ying** *Shuishiying* Liao.
90 B5 **Shui-t'ang** *Shuitang* Kwei.
35 G2 **Shui-tao** *Shuidao* Shant.
74 C2 **Shui-t'a-p'u** *Shuitapu* Hunan
74 B3 **Shui-t'ien-ho** *Shuitianhe* Hunan
74 B2 **Shui-t'ien-pa** *Shuitianba* Hunan
102 C1 **Shui-ting** *Shuiding* Sink.
51 D5 **Shui-t'ou** *Shuitou* Chek.
67 D6 **Shui-t'ou** *Shuitou* Fukien
39 C6 **Shui-t'ou** *Shuitou* Shansi
118 B3 **Shui-t'ou** *Shuitou* Taiwan
87 F3 **Shui-t'u-chen** *Shuituzhen* Szech.
55 F5 **Shui-t'un** *Shuitun* Honan
47 E6 **Shui-tung** *Shuidong* Anhwei
62 F2 **Shui-tung** *Shuidong* Shensi
75 E4 **Shui-tung-chiang** *Shuidongjiang* Hunan
74 D4 **Shui-tung-ti** *Shuidongdi* Hunan
34 C2 **Shui-wan** *Shuiwan* Shant.
83 H5 **Shui-wen** *Shuiwen* Kwangsi
47 E5 **Shui-yang** *Shuiyang* Anhwei
47 E5 **Shui-yang Chiang** *Shuiyang Jiang* (river) Anhwei
55 F1 **Shui-yeh** *Shuiye* Honan
83 H3 **Shui-yen-pa** *Shuiyanba* Kwangsi
82 E3 **Shui-yüan** *Shuiyuan* Kwangsi
118 C2 **Shui-yüan** *Shuiyuan* Taiwan
10 H3 **Shu-kang** *Shugang* Heilung.
102 I2 **Shu-ko** *Shuge* Sink.
15 K5 **Shu-kuang** *Shuguang* Kirin
114 B1 **Shu-kuei** *Shugui* Ningsia
15 G3 **Shu-lan** *Shulan* Kirin
102 B3 **Shu-le** *Shule* Sink.
11 E4 **Shu-le-ho** *Shulehe* Heilung.
98 C1 **Shu-le-ho** *Shulehe* Kansu
103 F2 **Shu-le Ho** *Shule He* (river) Sink.
107 E1 **Shu-le Nan-shan** *Shule Nanshan* (mts) Tsing.
118 C2 **Shu-lin** *Shulin* Taiwan
119 B5 **Shu-lin** *Shulin* Taiwan
26 D4 **Shu-lin-chao** *Shulinzhao* In. Mong.
31 C6 **Shu-lu Hsien** *Shulu Xian* Hopeh
31 C6 **Shu-lu Hsien** *Shulu Xian* Hopeh
Shumkai *see* **Ts'en-ch'i**
14 A1 **Shu-mu-kou** *Shumugou* Kirin
23 D4 **Shu-mu-kou** *Shumugou* Kirin
47 D6 **Shun-an** *Shunan* Anhwei
66 C4 **Shun-ch'ang** *Shunchang* Fukien
50 B2 **Shun-ch'i** *Shunqi* Chek.
66 E3 **Shun-ch'ih** *Shunchi* Fukien
42 A1 **Shun-ho** *Shunhe* Kiangsu
55 H3 **Shun-ho-chi** *Shunheji* Honan
Shun-hua *see* **Ch'un-hua**
Shunhwa *see* **Chi-shih**
30 D3 **Shun-i** *Shunyi* Hopeh
74 F3 **Shun-k'ou** *Shunkou* Hunan
106 C4 **Shun-ta** *Shunda* Tsing.
Shuntak *see* **Shun-te**
79 C2 **Shun-te Hsien** *Shunde Xian* Kwangt.
54 E3 **Shun-tien** *Shundian* Honan
38 D2 **Shuo-hsien** *Shuoxian* Shansi
82 D4 **Shuo-liang** *Shuoliang* Kwangsi
111 E3 **Shuo-pan-to** *Shuobanduo* Tibet
90 B4 **Shu-she** *Shushe* Kwei.
Shushik *see* **Su-hsi-k'o**
71 B5 **Shu Shui** *Shu Shui* (river) Kiangsi
42 C1 **Shu-yang** *Shuyang* Kiangsu
Shwakingsze *see* **Shua-ching-ssu**
Shwangliao *see* **Shuang-liao**
Shwangyashan *see* **Shuang-ya-shan**
Siaho *see* **La-pu-leng**
Siahwayüan *see* **Hsia-hua-yüan**
Siakiang *see* **Hsia-chiang**
Siakwan *see* **Hsia-kuan**
Sian *see* **Liao-yüan**
Sian *see* **Hsi-an**
Siangcheng *see* **Hsiang-ch'eng**
Siangfan *see* **Hsiang-fan**
Siang Kiang *see* **Hsiang Chiang**
Siangshan Bay *see* **Hsiang-shan Kang**
Siangtan *see* **Hsiang-t'an**
Siangtu *see* **Hsiang-tu**
Siaoerhkow *see* **Hsiao-erh-kou**
Siaohsien *see* **Hsiao-hsien**
Siaokin *see* **Hsiao-chin**
Siaoshan *see* **Hsiao-shan**
Siaoshih *see* **Hsiao-shih**
Siaotsing River *see* **Hsiao-ch'ing Ho**
Siatsing *see* **Hsia-chin**
Siayi Zamka *see* **Chia-yü-ch'iao**
Sichang *see* **Hsi-ch'ang**
Sichow *see* **Chi-hsien**
Sienyang *see* **Hsien-yang**
Sienyu *see* **Hsien-yu**
Sifeng *see* **Hsi-feng**
Sihsien *see* **Hui-ch'eng**
Sihsien *see* **She Hsien**
Siking *see* **Hsi-an**
Sikwangshan *see* **Hsi-k'uang-shan**
Silingol League *see* **Hsi-lin-kuo-le Meng**
Simeng *see* **Hsi-meng**
Sinan River *see* **Hsin-an Chiang**
Sinchang *see* **Hsin-ch'ang**
Sincheng *see* **Hsin-ch'eng**
115 C4 **Sin Cowe Island** China Sea
Sine Usu *see* **Hsi-ni-wu-su**
Singtai *see* **Hsing-t'ai**
Singtze *see* **Hsing-tzu**
Sinhailien *see* **Lien-yün-kang**
Sinhsien *see* **Hsin-hsien**
Sinhwa *see* **Hsin-hua**
Sinhwang *see* **Hsin-huang**
Sining *see* **Hsi-ning**
Sinkan *see* **Hsin-kan**
Sin Kiang *see* **Hsin Chiang**
Sinkiang Uighur Autonomous Region *see* **Pages 101-104**
Sinlitun *see* **Hsin-li-t'un**
Sinmin *see* **Hsin-min**
Sinpu *see* **Hsin-p'u**
Sinsiang *see* **Hsin-hsiang**
Sintai *see* **Hsin-t'ai**
Sinwen *see* **Hsin-wen**
Sinyang *see* **Hsin-yang**
Sinyü *see* **Hsin-yü**
Sip Song Banna *see* **Hsi-shuang-pan-na Thai Autonomous District**
Sisia *see* **Hsi-hsia**
Si-siang *see* **Hsi-hsiang**
Sita *see* **Hsi-t'ai**
Siti *see* **Hsi-ti**
Sitsin *see* **Hsi-chin**
Siushan *see* **Hsiu-shan**
Siu Shui *see* **Hsiu Shui**
Siu-wen *see* **Hsiu-wen**
Siying *see* **Chan-chiang**
102 B3 **So-ch'e** *Suoche* Sink.
34 D3 **So-chen** *Suozhen* Shant.
75 E6 **So-ch'eng** *Suocheng* Hunan
118 A3 **So-chiang** *Suojiang* Taiwan
106 D4 **So-ch'ing-kung-pa** *Suoqinggongba* Tsing.
111 E2 **So Ch'ü** *Suo Qu* (river) Tibet
103 E3 **So-erh-k'u-li** *Suoerkuli* Sink.
Sogo Nur *see* **So-kuo No-erh**
106 C4 **So-hsiang-ch'a-shou** *Suoxiangchashou* Tsing.
So-hsien *see* **Ya-la**
111 E3 **So Hsien** *Suo Xian* Tibet
86 D1 **So-ko-ts'ang-ssu** *Suogecangsi* Szech.
98 E1 **So-kuo No-erh** *Suoguo Nuoer* (lake) Kansu
Soli *see* **Chi-shou**
23 D4 **So-lun** *Suolun* Kirin
107 G3 **So-nai-hai** *Suonaihai* Tsing.
99 F4 **So-nan-pa** *Suonanba* Kansu
Soochow *see* **Su-chou**
Soochow Creek *see* **Wu-sung Chiang**
86 C2 **So-o-lo** *Suoeluo* Szech.
10 B2 **So-t'u-han** *Suotuhan* Heilung.
67 D7 **South China Sea** Fukien
South China Sea Islands *see* **Pages 115-116**
91 E4 **South-east Kweichow Miao-Tung Autonomous District** Kwei.
14 E2 **South Gorlos Mongol Autonomous Hsien** Kirin
99 F4 **South Kansu Tibetan Autonomous District** Kansu
98 D2 **South Kansu Yüku Autonomous Hsien** Kansu
South Koko Nor Range *see* **Ch'ing-hai Nan-shan**
91 E4 **South Kweichow Puyi-Miao Autonomous District** Kwei.
115 C5 **South Luconia Shoals** China Sea
115 D1 **South Vereker Bank** China Sea
51 C2 **Sou-ts'un** *Soucun* Chek.
115 B4 **Spratly Island** China Sea
115 C4 **Spratly Islands** China Sea
50 C2 **Ssu-an** *Sian* Chek.
31 C6 **Ssu-ch'a** *Sicha* Hopeh
43 E2 **Ssu-ch'a-ho** *Sichahe* Kiangsu
30 D2 **Ssu-ch'a-k'ou** *Sichakou* Hopeh
10 C3 **Ssu-chan** *Sizhan* Heilung.
102 I1 **Ssu-ch'ang-hu** *Sichanghu* Sink.
103 E1 **Ssu-ch'ang-hu** *Sichanghu* Sink.
70 C3 **Ssu-ch'i** *Siqi* Kiangsi
118 C2 **Ssu-chi** *Siji* Taiwan
75 F5 **Ssu-chia** *Sijia* Hunan
39 C6 **Ssu-chiao** *Sijiao* Shansi
51 F2 **Ssu-chiao Shan** *Sijiao Shan* (island) Chek.
43 F3 **Ssu-chia-pa** *Sijiaba* Kiangsu
11 C4 **Ssu-chia-tzu** *Sijiazi* Heilung.
19 G2 **Ssu-chia-tzu** *Sijiazi* Liao.
66 C3 **Ssu-ch'ien** *Siqian* Fukien
70 D3 **Ssu-ch'ien** *Siqian* Kiangsi
79 D1 **Ssu-ch'ien** *Siqian* Kwangt.
43 F4 **Ssu-ching** *Sijing* Kiangsu
14 C3 **Ssu-ching-tzu** *Sijingzi* Kirin
23 E5 **Ssu-ching-tzu** *Sijingzi* Kirin
83 H3 **Ssu-ch'iu Shui** *Siqiu Shui* (river) Kwangsi
51 E3 **Ssu-chou-t'ou** *Sizhoutou* Chek.
39 D6 **Ssu-chuang** *Sizhuang* Shansi
87 E2 **Ssu-ch'uan P'en-ti** *Sichuan Pendi* Szech.
18 D4 **Ssu-erh-pao** *Sierbao* Liao.
99 F3 **Ssu-erh-t'an** *Siertan* Kansu
35 F3 **Ssu-fang** *Sifang* Shant.
11 D4 **Ssu-fang-t'ai** *Sifangtai* Heilung.
14 D1 **Ssu-fang-t'o-tzu** *Sifangtuozi* Kirin
74 F4 **Ssu-fen** *Sifen* Hunan
18 B2 **Ssu-fen-ti** *Sifendi* Liao.
30 D3 **Ssu-hai** *Sihai* Hopeh
11 D4 **Ssu-hai-tien** *Sihaidian* Heilung.
15 G3 **Ssu-ho** *Sihe* Kirin
34 B4 **Ssu Ho** *Si He* (river) Shant.
35 F2 **Ssu-hou** *Sihou* Shant.
71 B5 **Ssu-hsia** *Sixia* Kiangsi
46 D3 **Ssu-hsien** *Sixian* Anhwei
107 F2 **Ssu-hsin** *Sixin* Tsing.
79 C2 **Ssu-hui** *Sihui* Kwangt.
42 C2 **Ssu-hung** *Sihong* Kiangsu
30 E2 **Ssu-hu-yung** *Sihuyong* Hopeh
87 E2 **Ssu-i-ch'ang** *Siyichang* Szech.
26 C4 **Ssu-i-t'ang** *Siyitang* In. Mong.
43 D3 **Ssu-kang-k'ou** *Sigangkou* Kiangsu
14 D2 **Ssu-k'o-shu** *Sikeshu* Kirin
102 D1 **Ssu-k'o-shu** *Sikeshu* Sink.
102 H1 **Ssu-k'o-shu** *Sikeshu* Sink.
102 H1 **Ssu-k'o-shu Ho** *Sikeshu He* (river) Sink.
70 E2 **Ssu-k'ou** *Sikou* Kiangsi
35 F2 **Ssu-k'ou** *Sikou* Shant.
74 D4 **Ssu-ku** *Sigu* Hunan
19 F5 **Ssu-k'uai-shih** *Sikuaishi* Liao.
18 C3 **Ssu-kuan-ying-tzu** *Siguanyingzi* Liao.
38 E2 **Ssu-lao-kou** *Silaogou* Shansi
54 D2 **Ssu-li** *Sili* Honan
70 E3 **Ssu-li** *Sili* Kiangsi
83 E3 **Ssu-lien** *Silian* Kwangsi
82 D4 **Ssu-lin** *Silin* Kwangsi
75 E6 **Ssu-li-p'ing** *Siliping* Hunan
51 D3 **Ssu-lu-k'ou** *Silukou* Chek.
78 B2 **Ssu-lun** *Silun* Kwangt.
83 E4 **Ssu-lung** *Silong* Kwangsi
14 F2 **Ssu-ma-chia** *Simajia* Kirin
75 D6 **Ssu-ma-ch'iao** *Simaqiao* Hunan
94 C4 **Ssu-mao** *Simao* Yun.
79 E2 **Ssu-ma-p'u** *Simapu* Kwangt.
51 E2 **Ssu-men** *Simen* Chek.
74 C4 **Ssu-men-ch'ien** *Simenqian* Hunan
43 E2 **Ssu-ming** *Siming* Kiangsu
51 D3 **Ssu-ming Shan** *Siming Shan* (mt) Chek.
51 E3 **Ssu-ming Shan** *Siming Shan* (mts) Chek.
63 D7 **Ssu-mu-ti** *Simudi* Shensi
91 F3 **Ssu-nan** *Sinan* Kwei.
34 B2 **Ssu-nü-ssu** *Sinüsi* Shant.
83 E3 **Ssu-pa** *Siba* Kwangsi
83 F3 **Ssu-p'ai** *Sipai* Kwangsi
58 D3 **Ssu-p'ing** *Siping* Hupeh
14 E4 **Ssu-p'ing** *Siping* Kirin
23 F5 **Ssu-p'ing** *Siping* Kirin
91 E4 **Ssu-p'ing** *Siping* Kwei.
70 E3 **Ssu-p'u** *Sipu* Kiangsi
70 D2 **Ssu-shih-li-chieh** *Sishilijie* Kiangsi
99 H4 **Ssu-shih-li-p'u** *Sishilipu* Kansu
34 D4 **Ssu-shih-li-p'u** *Sishilipu* Shant.
62 D3 **Ssu-shih-li-p'u** *Sishilipu* Shensi
62 F3 **Ssu-shih-li-p'u** *Sishilipu* Shensi
70 F3 **Ssu-shih-pa-tu** *Sishibadu* Kiangsi
66 F4 **Ssu-shuang Leih-tao** *Sishuang Liedao* (island group) Fukien
54 E3 **Ssu-shui** *Sishui* Honan
34 C4 **Ssu-shui** *Sishui* Shant.
71 B6 **Ssu-shun** *Sishun* Kiangsi
82 C4 **Ssu-t'ang** *Sitang* Kwangsi
83 E5 **Ssu-t'ang** *Sitang* Kwangsi
83 G2 **Ssu-t'ang** *Sitang* Kwangsi
19 I3 **Ssu-tao-ho-tzu** *Sidaohezi* Liao.
10 C2 **Ssu-tao-kou** *Sidaogou* Heilung.
15 H6 **Ssu-tao-kou** *Sidaogou* Kirin
83 F2 **Ssu-ting** *Siding* Kwangsi
91 E5 **Ssu-t'ing** *Siting* Kwei.
39 D5 **Ssu-t'ing** *Siting* Shansi
114 B2 **Ssu-t'o-ching** *Situojing* Ningsia
43 E3 **Ssu-tsao** *Sizao* Kiangsu
67 C7 **Ssu-tu** *Sidu* Fukien
75 F5 **Ssu-tu** *Sidu* Hunan
70 B2 **Ssu-tu** *Sidu* Kiangsi
51 F2 **Ssu-tzu-mei Tao** *Sizimei Dao* (islands) Chek.
26 D4 **Ssu-tzu-wang Ch'i** *Suziwang Qi* In. Mong.
54 C4 **Ssu-wan** *Siwan* Honan
83 G4 **Ssu-wang** *Siwang* Kwangsi
42 C2 **Ssu-yang** *Siyang* Kiangsu
91 F3 **Ssu-yang** *Siyang* Kwei.
Süancheng *see* **Hsüan-ch'eng**
Süanhwa *see* **Hsüan-hua**
Süanwei *see* **Hsüan-wei**
118 C2 **Su-ao** *Suao* Taiwan
Subansiri *see* **Su-pan-hsi-li Ho**
Sucheng *see* **Su-hsien**
39 E5 **Su-ch'eng** *Sucheng* Shansi
46 B3 **Su-chi** *Suji* Anhwei
51 D3 **Su-ch'i** *Suqi* Chek.
31 E5 **Su-chi** *Suji* Hopeh
58 D3 **Su-ch'i** *Suqi* Hupeh
26 B3 **Su-chi** *Suji* In. Mong.
43 D2 **Su-chia-chü** *Sujiaju* Kiangsu
55 E3 **Su-ch'iao** *Suqiao* Honan
70 D3 **Su-ch'iao** *Suqiao* Kiangsi
83 G2 **Su-ch'iao** *Suqiao* Kwangsi
47 C5 **Su-chia-pu** *Sujiabu* Anhwei
19 G2 **Su-chia-t'un** *Sujiatun* Liao.
42 C2 **Su-ch'ien** *Suqian* Kiangsu
22 C2 **Su-ch'in** *Suqin* Heilung.
99 H4 **Su-chin** *Sujin* Kansu
Su-chou *see* **Chiu-ch'üan**
43 E4 **Su-chou** *Suzhou* Kiangsu
Su-chou Ho *see* **Wu-sung Chiang**
Süchow *see* **Hsü-chou**
50 B3 **Su-chuang** *Suzhuang* Chek.
Süehfeng Mts *see* **Hsüeh-feng Shan**
14 B5 **Su-erh-t'u** *Suertu* Kirin
23 D6 **Su-erh-t'u** *Suertu* Kirin
Suess Range *see* **Shu-le Nan-shan**
Su-fu *see* **Shu-fu**
Su-fu Hsien *see* **Shu-fu Hsien**
114 C1 **Su-hai-ao-pao** *Suhaiaobao* Ningsia
103 F1 **Su-hai-t'u Ch'üan** *Suhaitu Quan* (spring) Sink.
23 D4 **Su-ho** *Suhe* Kirin
46 C3 **Su-hsien** *Suxian* Anhwei
106 D1 **Su-hsi-k'o** *Suxike* Tsing.
114 B1 **Su-hung-t'u** *Suhongtu* Ningsia
107 F4 **Su-hu-t'ien-ma** *Suhutianma* Tsing.
10 C1 **Sui-an-chan** *Suianzhan* Heilung.
50 C4 **Sui-ch'ang** *Suichang* Chek.
31 C4 **Sui-ch'eng** *Suicheng* Hopeh
46 C3 **Sui-ch'i** *Suiqi* Anhwei
78 B3 **Sui-ch'i** *Suiqi* Kwangt.
79 C2 **Sui Chiang** *Sui Jiang* (river) Kwangt.
95 D1 **Sui-chiang** *Suijiang* Yun.
Sui-ch'i Shih *see* **Huai-pei**
71 B5 **Sui-ch'uan** *Suichuan* Kiangsi
71 B5 **Sui-ch'uan Chiang** *Suichuan Jiang* (river) Kiangsi
18 D4 **Sui-chung** *Suizhong* Liao.
11 F5 **Sui-fen-ho** *Suifenhe* Heilung.
11 F5 **Sui-fen Ho** *Suifen He* (river) Heilung.
46 D3 **Sui Ho** *Sui He* (river) Anhwei
55 G3 **Sui-hsien** *Suixian* Honan
59 F3 **Sui-hsien** *Suixian* Hupeh
11 D4 **Sui-hua** *Suihua* Heilung.
Suihwa *see* **Sui-hua**
Suikai *see* **Sui-ch'i**
Suiki *see* **Sui-ch'i Huai-pei**
11 D4 **Sui-leng** *Suileng* Heilung.
42 B2 **Sui-ning** *Suining* Kiangsu
87 E2 **Sui-ning** *Suining* Szech.
75 C5 **Sui-ning Hsien** *Suining Xian* Hunan
11 F4 **Sui-pin** *Suibin* Heilung.
55 E4 **Sui-p'ing** *Suiping* Honan
62 F3 **Sui-te** *Suide* Shensi
Sui-ting *see* **Shui-ting**
43 E4 **Sui-t'ing** *Suiting* Kiangsu
11 G4 **Sui-tung** *Suidong* Heilung.
11 F5 **Sui-yang** *Suiyang* Heilung.
59 E2 **Sui-yang** *Suiyang* Hupeh
91 E2 **Sui-yang-ch'ang** *Suiyangchang* Kwei.
91 E3 **Sui-yang Hsien** *Suiyang Xian* Kwei.
Suiyüan *see* **Hu-ho-hao-t'e**
101 D2 **Su-kai-t'i** *Sugaiti* Sink.
102 B3 **Su-kai-t'i** *Sugaiti* Sink.
106 D1 **Su-kan No-erh** *Sugan Nuoer* (lake) Tsing.
22 D3 **Su-ko-ho** *Sugehe* Heilung.
110 B2 **Su-ko-t'e** *Sugete* Tibet
58 D2 **Su-ku** *Sugu* Hupeh
14 D3 **Su-kung-t'o** *Sugongtuo* Kirin
Sula Gol *see* **Su-lin-kuo-le Ho**
102 B3 **Su-la-k'o** *Sulake* Sink.
107 E2 **Su-lin-kuo-le Ho** *Sulinguole He* (river) Tsing.
34 B2 **Su-liu-chuang** *Suliuzhuang* Shant.
Su-lo *see* **Shu-le**
Su-lo Hsien *see* **Shu-le Hsien**
102 D2 **Su-man-li** *Sumanli* Sink.
Sum Dzong *see* **Sung-tsung**
83 G3 **Su-mu** *Simu* Kwangsi
Su-mu Hai-tzu *see* **Huang-ch'i Hai**
Su-nan *see* **Hung-wan-ssu**
Su-nan Yü-ku-tsu Tzu-chih-hsien *see* **South Kansu Yüku Autonomous Hsien**
34 C2 **Sun-chen** *Sunzhen* Shant.
34 C2 **Sun-chen** *Sunzhen* Shant.
39 B6 **Sun-chi** *Sunji* Shansi
62 F1 **Sun-chia-ch'a** *Sunjiacha* Shensi
59 F3 **Sun-chia-ch'iao** *Sunjiaqiao* Hupeh
91 F3 **Sun-chia-pa** *Sunjiaba* Kwei.
15 G5 **Sun-chia-pao-tzu** *Sunjiabaozi* Kirin
47 E6 **Sun-chia-pu** *Sunjiabu* Anhwei
Sunchow *see* **Kuei-p'ing**
70 D4 **Sun-fang** *Sunfang* Kiangsi
51 E3 **Sung-ao** *Songao* Chek.
Sungari *see* **Sung-hua Chiang**
Sungari Reservoir *see* **Sung-hua Hu**
55 E3 **Sung-chai** *Songzhai* Honan
11 C4 **Sung-chan** *Songzhan* Heilung.
18 C3 **Sung-chang-tzu** *Songzhangzi* Liao.
66 D3 **Sung-cheng** *Songzheng* Fukien
50 C2 **Sung-ch'i** *Songqi* Chek.
66 B4 **Sung-ch'i** *Songqi* Fukien
66 D3 **Sung Ch'i** *Song Qi* (river) Fukien
43 D3 **Sung-chia-ch'iao** *Songjiaqiao* Kiangsu
62 F3 **Sung-chia-ch'uan** *Songjiachuan* Shensi
38 E2 **Sung-chia-chuang** *Songjiazhuang* Shansi
38 C3 **Sung-chia-kou** *Songjiagou* Shansi
43 F4 **Sung-chiang** *Songjiang* Kiangsu
15 H4 **Sung-chiang** *Songjiang* Kirin
15 H5 **Sung-chiang** *Songjiang* Kirin
15 I5 **Sung-chiang** *Songjiang* Kirin
15 H5 **Sung-chiang-ho** *Songjianghe* Kirin
87 E3 **Sung-chia-p'u** *Songjiapu* Szech.
34 A3 **Sung-chuang** *Songzhuang* Shant.
59 F3 **Sung-ho** *Songhe* Hupeh
51 D2 **Sung-hsia** *Songxia* Chek.
67 E5 **Sung-hsia** *Songxia* Fukien
54 D3 **Sung-hsien** *Songxian* Honan
38 F4 **Sung-hsi Ho** *Songxi He* (river) Shansi
70 C3 **Sung-hu** *Songhu* Kiangsi
14 F3 **Sung-hua-chiang** *Songhuajiang* Kirin
11 F4 **Sung-hua Chiang** *Songhua Jiang* (river) Heilung.
14 G3 **Sung-hua Chiang** *Songhua Jiang* (river) Kirin
23 F5 **Sung-hua Chiang** *Songhua Jiang* (river) Kirin
11 D5 **Sung-hua-chiang Ti-ch'ü** *Songhuajiang Diqu* Heilung.
11 D5 **Sung-hua-chiang Ti-ch'ü** *Songhuajiang Diqu* Heilung.
15 G4 **Sung-hua Hu** *Songhua Hu* (res) Kirin
87 E3 **Sung-k'ai** *Songkai* Szech.
91 D2 **Sung-k'an** *Songkan* Kwei.
79 C2 **Sung-kang** *Songgang* Kwangt.
86 D2 **Sung-kang** *Songgang* Szech.
Sungkiangho *see* **Sung-chiang-ho**
Sungkiapu *see* **Sung-chia-p'u**
67 B4 **Sung-k'ou** *Songkou* Fukien
67 D5 **Sung-k'ou** *Songkou* Fukien
79 E1 **Sung-k'ou** *Songkou* Kwangt.
94 C2 **Sung-kuei** *Songgui* Yun.
34 A3 **Sung-lin** *Songlin* Shant.
18 D3 **Sung Ling** *Song Ling* (mts) Liao.
30 C4 **Sung-lin-tien** *Songlindian* Hopeh
42 A1 **Sung-lou** *Songlou* Kiangsu
51 E4 **Sung-men** *Songmen* Chek.
95 D3 **Sung-ming** *Songming* Yun.
107 G2 **Sung-pa Hsia** *Songba Xia* (gorge) Tsing.
74 C3 **Sung-pai-ch'ang** *Songbaichang* Hunan
35 E4 **Sung-pai-lin** *Songbailin* Shant.
87 D1 **Sung-p'an** *Songpan* Szech.
111 D3 **Sung-p'an** *Songpan* Tibet
75 E5 **Sung-po** *Songbo* Hunan
11 D5 **Sung-p'u** *Songpu* Heilung.
59 G3 **Sung-pu** *Songbu* Hupeh
99 F3 **Sung-shan** *Songshan* Kansu
70 B4 **Sung-shan** *Songshan* Kiangsi
83 F6 **Sung-shan** *Songshan* Kwangsi
83 G5 **Sung-shan** *Songshan* Kwangsi
18 E3 **Sung-shan** *Songshan* Liao.
54 E3 **Sung Shan** *Song Shan* (mt) Honan
35 F2 **Sung-shan** *Songshan* Shant.
19 H2 **Sung-shan-pao** *Songshanbao* Liao.
59 H4 **Sung-shan-tsui** *Songshanzui* Hupeh
95 D3 **Sung-shao-kuan** *Songshaoguan* Yun.
102 H1 **Sung-sheng-kung** *Songshenggong* Sink.
70 D4 **Sung-shih** *Songshi* Kiangsi
19 F5 **Sung-shu** *Songshu* Liao.
15 H5 **Sung-shu-chen** *Songshuzhen* Kirin
10 C2 **Sung-shu-lin** *Songshulin* Heilung.
38 E4 **Sung-t'a** *Songta* Shansi
79 D1 **Sung-t'ang** *Songtang* Kwangt.
78 A4 **Sung-t'ao** *Songtao* Kwangt.
91 G2 **Sung-t'ao** *Songtao* Kwei.
91 G2 **Sung-t'ao Miao Autonomous Hsien** Kwei.
Sung-t'ao Miao-tsu Tzu-chih-hsien *see* **Sung-t'ao Miao Autonomous Hsien**
46 C3 **Sung-t'ing** *Songting* Anhwei
50 B3 **Sung-ts'un** *Songcun* Chek.
35 H2 **Sung-ts'un** *Songcun* Shant.
111 F3 **Sung-tsung** *Songzong* Tibet
58 D4 **Sung-tzu Ho** *Songzi He* (river) Hupeh
58 D4 **Sung-tzu Hsien** *Songzi Xian* Hupeh
59 H3 **Sung-tzu Kuan** *Songzi Guan* (pass) Hupeh
54 C5 **Sung-wan** *Songwan* Honan
91 E3 **Sung-yen** *Songyan* Kwei.
39 E4 **Sung-yen** *Songyan* Shansi
38 D3 **Sung-yen-k'ou** *Songyankou* Shansi
50 C4 **Sung-yin Ch'i** *Songyin Qi* (river) Chek.
67 D6 **Sung-yü** *Songyu* Fukien
79 E1 **Sung-yüan** *Songyuan* Kwangt.
Sunhing *see* **Hsin-hsing**
31 C5 **Su-ning** *Suning* Hopeh
27 E3 **Sunit East Banner** In. Mong.
Su-ni-t'e Tso-ch'i *see* **Sunit East Banner**
Su-ni-t'e Yu-ch'i *see* **Sunit West Banner**
27 E3 **Sunit West Banner** In. Mong.
34 C3 **Sun-keng** *Sungeng* Shant.
54 D4 **Sun-kou** *Sungou* Honan
114 B1 **Sun-pu-erh-mu-ch'ang** *Sunbuermuchang* Ningsia
111 D3 **Sunq-to** *Songduo* Tibet
34 B4 **Sun-shih-tien** *Sunshidian* Shant.
55 F5 **Sun-t'ieh-p'u** *Suntiepu* Honan
55 F4 **Sun-tien** *Sundian* Honan
46 C3 **Sun-t'ing-chi** *Suntingji* Anhwei
34 C4 **Sun-ts'un** *Suncun* Shant.
Sünwu *see* **Hsün-wu**
10 D3 **Sun-wu** *Sunwu* Heilung.
Sunyi *see* **Hsin-i**
38 E4 **Suo-huang** *Suohuang* Shansi
74 C2 **Suo-shih** *Suoshi* Hunan
67 C5 **Su-pang** *Subang* Fukien
111 E3 **Su-pan-hsi-li Ho** *Subanxili He* (river) Tibet
75 C4 **Su-pao Ting** *Subao Ding* (mt) Hunan
102 I2 **Su-pa-shih** *Subashi* Sink.
102 I2 **Su-pa-shih** *Subashi* Sink.
Su-pei *see* **Tang-ch'eng-wan**
43 D2 **Su-pei Kuan-kai-tsung-ch'ü** *Subei Guangaizongqu* (canal) Kiangsu
Su-pei Meng-ku-tsu Tzu-chih-hsien *see* **North Kansu Mongol Autonomous Hsien**
23 C5 **Su-pu-li-ka** *Sibuliga* Liao.
102 C2 **Su-pu-t'ai** *Subutai* Sink.
35 H3 **Su-shan Tao** *Sushan Dao* (island) Shant.
39 B6 **Su-shui Ho** *Sushui He* (river) Shansi
47 C6 **Su-sung** *Susong* Anhwei
Sutlej *see* **Hsiang-ch'üan Ho**

Su-ts'ai-k'o-su-a-chia-tzu – T'ang-yüan 21

106 C2 Su-ts'ai-k'o-su-a-chia-tzu *Sucaikesuajiazi* Tsing.
31 B7 Su-ts'ao *Sucao* Hopeh
31 C6 Su-ts'un *Sucun* Hopeh
34 D4 Su-ts'un *Sucun* Shant.
19 H3 Su-tzu Ho *Suzi He* (river) Liao.
19 G4 Su-tzu-kou *Suzigou* Liao.
42 B1 Su-yang-shan *Suyangshan* Kiangsu
82 E5 Su-yü *Suyu* Kwangsi
Swabue *see* Shan-wei
115 C5 Swallow Reef China Sea
Swatow *see* Shan-t'ou
Szechwan Basin *see* Ssu-ch'ua P'en-ti
Szechwan Province *see* Pages 85-88
Szefang *see* Ssu-fang
Szemao *see* Ssu-mao
Sze-nan-fu *see* Ssu-nan
Szeping *see* Ssu-p'ing
Szepingkai *see* Ssu-p'ing
Szeshui *see* Ssu-shui
Szewui *see* Ssu-hui
Szu- *see* Ssu-
91 F2 Szu-ch'ü *Siqu* Kwei.
11 G4 Szu-p'ai *Sipai* Heilung.

51 C5 Ta-an *Daan* Chek.
66 C3 Ta-an *Daan* Fukien
83 E3 Ta-an *Daan* Kwangsi
83 G4 Ta-an *Daan* Kwangsi
79 D2 Ta-an *Daan* Kwangt.
63 B7 Ta-an *Daan* Shensi
118 B2 Ta-an *Daan* Taiwan
14 E2 Ta-an Hsien *Daan Xian* Kirin
74 B2 Ta-an-p'ing *Daanping* Hunan
39 E4 Ta-chai *Dazhai* Shansi
99 F3 Ta-ch'ai-kou *Dachaigou* Kansu
106 C1 Ta-ch'ai-kou *Dachaigou* Tsing.
106 D2 Ta-ch'ai-ta-mu Hu *Dachaidamu* (lake) Tsing.
106 D2 Ta-ch'ai-tan *Dachaidan* Tsing.
102 D1 Ta-ch'a-k'ou *Tachakou* Sink.
102 H1 Ta-ch'a-k'ou *Tachakou* Sink.
51 F2 Ta-chan *Dazhan* Chek.
54 C3 Ta-chang *Dazhang* Honan
30 D4 Ta-ch'ang *Dachang* Hopeh
43 F4 Ta-ch'ang *Dachang* Kiangsu
82 D3 Ta-ch'ang *Dachang* Kwangsi
83 F4 Ta-chang *Dazhang* Kwangsi
106 E3 Ta-ch'ang *Dachang* Tsing.
42 C3 Ta-ch'ang-chen *Dachangzhen* Kiangsu
87 G2 Ta-ch'ang-chen *Dachangzhen* Szech.
67 E5 Ta-chang Ch'i *Dazhang Qi* (river) Fukien
30 D4 Ta-ch'ang Hui Autonomous Hsien Hopeh
30 D4 Ta-ch'ang Hui Autonomous Hsien *Dachang Hui* Hopeh
Ta-ch'ang Hui-tsu Tzu-chih-hsien *see* Ta-ch'ang Hui Autonomous Hsien
19 F5 Ta-ch'ang-shan Tao *Dachangshan Dao* (island) Liao.
51 F2 Ta-ch'ang-t'u Shan *Dachangtu Shan* (island) Chek.
30 F3 Ta-chang-tzu *Dazhangzi* Hopeh
55 E2 Ta-chao-ying *Dazhaoying* Honan
50 C4 Ta-che *Dazhe* Chek.
98 E2 Ta-ch'e-ch'ang *Dachechang* Kansu
51 D3 Ta-ch'en *Dachen* Chek.
62 E4 Ta-chen *Daozhen* Shensi
31 B6 Ta-ch'en-chuang *Dachenzhuang* Hopeh
31 D5 Ta-ch'eng *Dacheng* Hopeh
70 C3 Ta-ch'eng *Dacheng* Kiangsi
118 B3 Ta-ch'eng *Dacheng* Taiwan
102 C1 T'a-ch'eng *Tacheng* Sink.
94 B2 T'a-ch'eng *Tacheng* Yun.
43 D3 Ta-ch'eng-ch'iao *Dachengqiao* Kiangsu
19 F5 Ta-cheng-chia-t'un *Dazhengjiatun* Liao.
102 C1 T'a-ch'eng Ti-ch'ü *Tacheng Diqu* Sink.
18 C3 Ta-ch'eng-tzu *Dachengzi* Liao.
31 C5 Ta-ch'eng-wei *Dachengwei* Hopeh
50 C5 Ta-chi *Daji* Chek.
51 E4 Ta-ch'i *Daqi* Chek.
118 C2 Ta-ch'i *Daqi* Taiwan
118 B2 Ta-chia *Dajia* Taiwan
118 B2 Ta-chia Ch'i *Dajia Qi* (river) Taiwan
11 G4 Ta-chia-ho *Dajiahe* Heilung.
95 D4 Ta-chia-i *Dajiayi* Yun.
14 F3 Ta-chia-kou *Dajiagou* Kirin
83 F2 Ta-chiang *Dajiang* Kwangsi
83 G3 Ta-chiang *Dajiang* Kwangsi
47 E5 Ta-ch'iao *Daqiao* Anhwei
51 E4 Ta-ch'iao *Daqiao* Chek.
66 D4 Ta-ch'iao *Daqiao* Fukien
58 B4 Ta-ch'iao *Daqiao* Hupeh
70 B3 Ta-ch'iao *Daqiao* Kiangsi
70 C2 Ta-ch'iao *Daqiao* Kiangsi
70 E3 Ta-ch'iao *Daqiao* Kiangsi
43 D3 Ta-ch'iao *Daqiao* Kiangsu
43 E3 Ta-ch'iao *Daqiao* Kiangsu
15 I4 Ta-ch'iao *Daqiao* Kirin
83 G5 Ta-ch'iao *Daqiao* Kwangsi
79 C1 Ta-ch'iao *Daqiao* Kwangt.
39 C6 Ta-chiao *Dajiao* Shansi
86 D3 Ta-ch'iao *Daqiao* Szech.
86 D4 Ta-ch'iao *Daqiao* Szech.
95 D2 Ta-ch'iao *Daqiao* Yun.
55 F4 T'a-ch'iao *Taqiao* Honan
58 D4 Ta-ch'iao-pien *Daqiaobian* Hupeh
54 D4 Ta-ch'iao-wan *Daqiaowan* Hunan
19 F2 Ta-chia-tzu *Dajiazi* Liao.
35 D2 Ta-chia-wa *Dajiawa* Shant.
58 B5 Ta-chi-ch'ang *Dajichang* Hupeh
35 G2 Ta-chieh-shih *Dajieshi* Shant.
70 E2 T'a-ch'ien *Taqian* Kiangsi
83 E6 Ta-chih *Dazhi* Kwangsi
78 B4 Ta-chih-p'o *Dazhipo* Kwangt.
67 B5 Ta-ch'ih-yu *Dachiyu* Fukien
22 E3 Ta-chi-lu-ch'i-na Shan *Dajiluqina Shan* (mt) Heilung.
71 C4 Ta-chin-chu *Dajinzhu* Kiangsi
51 E4 Ta-ching *Dajing* Chek.
99 F3 Ta-ching *Dajing* Kansu
71 B5 Ta-ching *Dajing* Kiangsi
78 B2 Ta-ching *Dajing* Kwangt.
114 B3 Ta-ching *Dajing* Ningsia
34 B4 Ta-ching *Dajing* Shant.
63 E6 Ta-ching *Dajing* Shensi
102 I1 Ta-ching *Dajing* Sink.
95 D2 Ta-ching *Dajing* Yun.
14 F3 Ta-ch'ing-chü *Daqingju* Kirin
31 F4 Ta-ch'ing-ho *Daqinghe* Hopeh
31 D4 Ta-ch'ing Ho *Daqing He* (river) Hopeh
30 B2 Ta-ch'ing-kou *Daqinggou* Hopeh
26 D4 Ta-ch'ing Shan *Daqing Shan* (mts) In. Mong.
19 G2 Ta-ch'ing-tui-tzu *Daqingduizi* Liao.
59 H4 Ta-chin-p'u *Dajinpu* Hupeh
91 C2 Ta-chin-sha *Dajinsha* Kwei.
14 A5 Ta-ch'in-t'a-la *Daqintala* Kirin
23 D6 Ta-ch'in-t'a-la *Daqintala* Kirin
35 F1 Ta-ch'in Tao *Daqin Dao* (island) Shant.
54 D3 Ta-chin-tien *Dajindian* Honan
70 D3 Ta-ch'i-tu *Daqidu* Kiangsi
67 E5 Ta-ch'iu *Daqiu* Fukien
103 E3 Ta-chiu-pa *Dajiuba* Sink.
118 C2 Ta-cho-shui *Dazhuoshui* Taiwan
50 C4 Ta-chou *Dazhou* Chek.
43 D2 Ta-chou *Dazhou* Kiangsu
86 B1 Ta Ch'ü *Da Qu* (river) Szech.
87 F2 Ta-chu *Dazhu* Szech.
119 B4 Ta-chu *Dazhu* Taiwan
98 B1 Ta-ch'üan *Daquan* Kansu
98 C2 Ta-ch'üan *Daquan* Kansu
15 H4 Ta-ch'uan *Dachuan* Kirin
102 I1 Ta-ch'üan *Daquan* Sink.
46 D3 Ta-chuang *Dazhuang* Anhwei
67 D4 T'a-chuang *Tazhuang* Fukien
55 F3 Ta-chuang-t'ou *Dazhuangtou* Honan
38 E1 Ta-ch'üan-shan *Daquanshan* Shansi
103 F2 Ta-ch'üan-wan *Daquanwan* Sink.
14 F6 Ta-ch'üan-yüan *Daquanyuan* Kirin
110 D3 Ta-chu-ch'ia *Dazhuqia* Tibet
43 E2 Ta-chung-chi *Dazhongji* Kiangsu
75 D5 Ta-chung-ch'iao *Dazhongqiao* Hunan
51 F2 Ta-ch'ü Shan *Dagu Shan* (island) Chek.
110 D2 Ta-erh-cho *Daerzhuo* Tibet
Ta-erh-han-mao Ming-an Lien-ho-ch'i *see* Darhan-Mow Mingan United Banner
30 D2 Ta-erh-hao *Daerhao* Hopeh
26 B4 T'a-erh-hu *Taerhu* In. Mong.
102 I2 T'a-erh-lan *Taerlan* Sink.
106 C2 T'a-erh-ting *Taerding* Tsing.
59 F3 T'a-erh-wan *Taerwan* Hupeh
59 G5 Ta-fan *Dafan* Hupeh
90 C3 Ta-fang *Dafang* Kwei.
14 F3 Ta-fang-shen *Dafangshen* Kirin
18 E5 Ta-fang-shen *Dafangshen* Liao.
19 G2 Ta-fan-ho *Dafanhe* Liao.
71 B5 Ta-fen *Dafen* Kiangsi
11 E4 Ta-feng *Dafeng* Heilung.
43 E2 Ta-feng Hsien *Dafeng Xian* Kiangsu
15 G4 Ta-feng-man *Dafengman* Kirin
106 C1 Ta-feng-shan *Dafengshan* Tsing.
51 E3 Ta-fo Shan *Dafo Shan* (island) Chek.
47 E7 Ta-fu *Dafu* Anhwei
59 F3 Ta-fu Shui *Dafu Shui* (river) Hupeh
11 C4 T'a-ha *Taha* Heilung.
23 F4 T'a-ha *Taha* Heilung.
10 C2 T'a-ha Ho *Taha He* (river) Heilung.
22 F2 T'a-ha Ho *Taha He* (river) Heilung.
30 E4 Ta-hai-pei *Dahaibei* Hopeh
14 C4 Ta-han *Dahan* Kirin
23 E6 Ta-han *Dahan* Kirin
Tahcheng *see* T'a-ch'eng
26 D4 Ta-hei Ho *Dahei He* (river) In. Mong.
107 F3 Ta-hei Ho *Dahei He* (river) Tsing.
14 E4 Ta-hei Shan *Dahei Shan* (mts) Kirin
67 C5 Ta-heng *Daheng* Fukien
118 B2 Ta-heng-p'ing Shan *Dahengping Shan* (mt) Taiwan
67 B5 Ta-ho *Dahe* Fukien
78 B4 Ta-ho *Dahe* Kwangt.
79 C2 Ta-ho *Dahe* Kwangt.
10 C1 T'a-ho *Tahe* Heilung.
22 F1 T'a-ho *Tahe* Heilung.
11 G4 Ta-ho-chen *Dahezhen* Heilung.
27 G3 Ta-ho-k'ou *Dahekou* In. Mong.
27 G3 Ta-ho-k'ou *Dahekou* In. Mong.
63 D8 Ta-ho-k'ou *Dahekou* Shensi
30 C4 Ta-ho-nan *Dahenan* Hopeh
58 B5 Ta-ho-pa *Daheba* Hupeh
54 E5 Ta-ho-t'un *Dahetun* Honan
102 I2 Ta-ho-yen *Daheyan* Sink.
14 E3 Ta-hsi *Daxi* Kirin
90 C3 Ta-hsi *Daxi* Kwei.
102 D2 Ta-hsi *Daxi* Sink.
102 D3 T'a-hsi *Taxi* Heilung.
107 H2 Ta-hsia *Daxia* Tsing.
58 C3 Ta-hsia-k'ou *Daxiakou* Hupeh
26 D3 Ta-hsiang Ling *Daxiang Ling* (mts) Szech.
51 E3 Ta-hsieh-t'ou *Daxietou* Chek.
87 F2 Ta-hsien *Daxian* Szech.
103 D2 Ta-hsi-hai-tzu Shui-k'u *Daxihaizi Shuiku* (res.) Sink.
82 D5 Ta-hsin *Daxin* Kwangsi
83 G4 Ta-hsin *Daxin* Kwangsi
42 C2 Ta-hsing *Daxing* Kiangsu
14 D3 Ta-hsing *Daxing* Kirin
82 D3 Ta-hsing *Daxing* Kwangsi
91 G3 Ta-hsing *Daxing* Kwei.
95 D2 Ta-hsing *Daxing* Yun.
10 B2 Ta-hsing-an Ling *Daxingan Ling* (mts) Heilung.
10 C2 Ta-hsing-an-ling Ti-ch'ü *Daxinganling Diqu* Heilung.
14 F5 Ta-hsing-chen *Daxingzhen* Kirin
34 D5 Ta-hsing-chen *Daxingzhen* Shant.
30 D4 Ta-hsing Hsien *Daxing Xian* Hopeh
30 D4 Ta-hsing Hsien *Daxing Xian* Hopeh
15 J4 Ta-hsing-kou *Daxinggou* Kirin
30 D3 Ta-hsin-tien *Daxindian* Honan
34 D2 Ta-hsin-tien *Daxindian* Shant.
35 F2 Ta-hsin-tien *Daxindian* Shant.
51 E3 Ta-hsü *Daxu* Chek.
83 G4 Ta-hsüan *Daxuan* Kwangsi
42 B1 Ta-hsü-chia *Daxujia* Kiangsu
51 D5 Ta-hsüeh *Daxue* Chek.
118 C2 Ta-hsüeh Shan *Daxue Shan* (mt) Taiwan
86 C2 Ta-hsüeh Shan *Daxue Shan* (mts) Szech.
70 D4 Ta-hsü Shan *Daxu Shan* (mt) Kiangsi
70 F3 Ta-hsü-ts'un *Daxucun* Kiangsi
67 C4 Ta-hu *Dahu* Fukien
74 F3 Ta-hu *Dahu* Hunan
118 B2 Ta-hu *Dahu* Taiwan
82 D4 Ta-hua *Dahua* Kwangsi
79 C2 Ta-huai *Dahuai* Kwangt.
82 E2 Ta-huan Chiang *Dahuan Jiang* (river) Kwangsi
14 G5 Ta-huang-kou *Dahuanggou* Kirin
15 K4 Ta-huang-kou *Dahuanggou* Kirin
51 F2 Ta-huang-lung Shan *Dahuanglong Shan* (island) Chek.
71 B5 Ta-hu-chiang *Dahujiang* Kiangsi
70 C3 Ta-hu-lun *Dahulun* Hopeh
26 D4 Ta-hung-ch'eng *Dahongcheng* In. Mong.
19 F3 Ta-hung-ch'i *Dahongqi* Liao.
54 E2 Ta-hung-ch'iao *Dahongqiao* Honan
102 B4 Ta-hung-liu-t'an *Dahongliutan* Sink.
59 E3 Ta-hung Shan *Dahong Shan* (mt) Hupeh
106 D2 Ta-hung-shan *Dahongshan* Tsing.
14 C3 Ta-huo-fang *Dahuofang* Kirin
23 E5 Ta-huo-fang *Dahuofang* Kirin
19 F3 Ta-hu-shan *Dahushan* Liao.
91 D5 Ta-i *Dayi* Kwei.
34 B4 Ta-i *Dayi* Shant.
86 D2 Ta-i *Dayi* Szech.
19 F3 T'ai-an *Taian* Liao.
34 C3 T'ai-an *Taian* Shant.
118 B2 T'ai-an *Taian* Taiwan
43 F4 T'ai-an-kang *Taiangang* Kiangsu
111 E3 T'ai-chao *Taizhao* Tibet
51 D2 Tai-ch'i *Daiqi* Chek.
66 E4 Tai-ch'i *Daiqi* Fukien
43 D3 Ta-i-chi *Dayiji* Kiangsu
34 A5 Ta-i-chi *Dayiji* Shant.
34 B4 Ta-i-chi *Dayiji* Shant.
67 D4 T'ai-ch'i *Taiqi* Fukien
66 E4 Tai Chiang *Dai Jiang* (river) Fukien
91 E4 T'ai-chiang Hsien *Taijiang Xian* Kwei.
43 E3 Ta-i-chia-yao *Dajiayao* Kiangsu
14 A2 T'ai-chia-ying-tzu *Taijiayingzi* Kirin
23 D5 T'ai-chia-ying-tzu *Taijiayingzi* Kirin
54 D4 T'ai-chih-miao *Taizhimiao* Hunan
14 B2 Tai-ch'in-t'a-la *Daiqintala* Kirin
23 D5 Tai-ch'in-t'a-la *Daiqintala* Kirin
51 E4 T'ai-chou *Taizhou* Chek.
43 D3 T'ai-chou *Taizhou* Kiangsu
51 E4 T'ai-chou Lieh-tao *Taizhou Liedao* (islands) Chek.
51 E4 T'ai-chou Wan *Taizhou Wan* (bay) Chek.
Taichow *see* Tai-hsien
Taichow *see* T'ai-chou
118 B2 T'ai-chung *Taizhong* Taiwan
118 B2 T'ai-chung Hsien *Taizhong Xian* Taiwan
34 C5 T'ai-erh-chuang *Taierzhuang* Shant.
51 E3 Tai-fang *Daifang* Kiangsi
26 E4 Tai Hai *Dai Hai* (lake) In. Mong.
31 B4 T'ai-hang Shan *Taihang Shan* (mts) Hopeh
Taihing *see* T'ai-hsing
46 B3 T'ai-ho *Taihe* Anhwei
71 B5 T'ai-ho *Taihe* Kiangsi
71 D4 T'ai-ho *Taihe* Kiangsi
34 B3 T'ai-ho *Taihe* Shant.
119 B4 T'ai-ho *Taihe* Taiwan
87 E2 T'ai-ho-chen *Taihezhen* Szech.
Taihoku *see* T'ai-pei
75 E6 T'ai-ho-yü *Taiheyu* Hunan
118 B3 T'ai-hsi *Taixi* Taiwan
38 D2 Tai-hsien *Daixian* Shansi
43 E3 T'ai Hsien *Tai Xian* Kiangsu
43 D3 T'ai-hsing *Taixing* Kiangsu
47 C6 T'ai-hu *Taihu* Anhwei
43 E4 T'ai Hu *Taihu* (lake) Kiangsu
91 D5 Tai-hua *Daihua* Kwei.
11 C4 T'ai-k'ang *Taikang* Heilung.
23 F4 T'ai-k'ang *Taikang* Heilung.
55 F3 T'ai-k'ang *Taikang* Honan
Taikiang *see* T'ai-kung
39 D4 T'ai-ku *Taigu* Shansi
91 F4 T'ai-kung *Taigong* Kwei.
11 B4 T'ai-lai *Tailai* Heilung.
22 E4 T'ai-lai *Tailai* Heilung.
27 F2 Tai-la-min-su-mo *Dailaminsumo* In. Mong.
26 C4 T'ai-liang *Tailiang* In. Mong.
91 F4 T'ai-lieh *Tailie* Kwei.
39 C5 T'ai-lin *Tailin* Shansi
11 E4 Tai-ling *Dailing* Heilung.
118 C2 T'ai-lu-ko *Tailuge* Taiwan
118 C2 T'ai-lu-ko Hsia *Tailuge Xia* (gorge) Taiwan
118 C2 T'ai-lu-ko-ta Shan *Tailugeda Shan* (mt) Taiwan
79 D2 T'ai-mei *Taimei* Kwangt.
106 E4 T'ai-nai Ch'ü *Tainai Qu* (river) Tsing.
43 E3 Tai-nan *Dainan* Kiangsu
118 B3 T'ai-nan *Tainan* Taiwan
119 B3 T'ai-nan Hsien *Tainan Xian* Taiwan
66 C4 T'ai-ning *Taining* Fukien
67 B6 T'ai-pa *Taiba* Fukien
99 I3 T'ai-pai *Taibai* Kansu
70 E2 T'ai-pai *Taibai* Kiangsi
91 E2 T'ai-pai *Taibai* Kwei.
63 C6 T'ai-pai Hsien *Taibai Xian* Shensi
38 F2 T'ai-pai Shan *Taibai Shan* (mt) Shansi
63 C7 T'ai-pai Shan *Taibai Shan* (mt) Shensi
43 D1 T'ai-pei *Taibei* Kiangsu
118 C1 T'ai-pei *Taibei* Taiwan
T'ai-pei - city plan *see* Page 141
118 C2 T'ai-pei Hsien *Taibei Xian* Taiwan
27 H2 T'ai-pen-miao *Taibenmiao* In. Mong.
T'ai-p'ing *see* Wen-ling
66 D4 T'ai-p'ing *Taiping* Fukien
11 F4 T'ai-p'ing *Taiping* Heilung.
74 D2 T'ai-p'ing *Taiping* Hunan
75 E6 T'ai-p'ing *Taiping* Hunan
59 E2 T'ai-p'ing *Taiping* Hupeh
82 D4 T'ai-p'ing *Taiping* Kwangsi
82 D5 T'ai-p'ing *Taiping* Kwangsi
83 E3 T'ai-p'ing *Taiping* Kwangsi
83 E5 T'ai-p'ing *Taiping* Kwangsi
83 F5 T'ai-p'ing *Taiping* Kwangsi
79 C1 T'ai-p'ing *Taiping* Kwangt.
79 C2 T'ai-p'ing *Taiping* Kwangt.
118 B2 T'ai-p'ing *Taiping* Taiwan
83 E4 T'ai-p'ing-chai *Taipingzhai* Hopeh
79 C2 T'ai-p'ing-ch'ang *Taipingchang* Kwangt.
54 C4 T'ai-p'ing-chen *Taipingzhen* Honan
58 B5 T'ai-p'ing-chen *Taipingzhen* Hupeh
34 D2 T'ai-ping-chen *Taibingzhen* Shant.
34 B4 T'ai-p'ing-ch'iao *Taipingqiao* Shant.
22 D2 T'ai-p'ing-ch'uan *Taipingchuan* Heilung.
14 D3 T'ai-p'ing-ch'uan *Taipingchuan* Kirin
15 H5 T'ai-p'ing-ch'uan *Taipingchuan* Kirin
23 E5 T'ai-p'ing-ch'uan *Taipingchuan* Kirin
22 E2 T'ai-ping-chuang *Taibingzhuang* Hopeh
30 E6 T'ai-p'ing Hsien *Taiping Xian* Anhwei
10 F3 T'ai-p'ing-kou *Taipinggou* Heilung.
58 E4 T'ai-p'ing-k'ou *Taibingkou* Hupeh
15 K4 T'ai-p'ing-kou *Taipinggou* Kirin
18 C3 T'ai-p'ing-kou *Taipinggou* Liao.
18 D2 T'ai-p'ing-kuan *Taipingguan* Kiangsi
75 F6 T'ai-p'ing-li *Taipingli* Hunan
74 D4 T'ai-p'ing-p'u *Taipingpu* Hunan
11 D4 T'ai-p'ing-shan *Taipingshan* Heilung.
14 E3 T'ai-p'ing-shan *Taipingshan* Kirin
23 F5 T'ai-p'ing-shan *Taipingshan* Kirin
19 F4 T'ai-p'ing-shan *Taipingshan* Liao.
19 I4 T'ai-p'ing-shao *Taipingshao* Liao.
74 E4 T'ai-p'ing-ssu *Taipingsi* Hunan
58 D2 T'ai-p'ing-tien *Taipingdian* Hupeh
31 E5 T'ai-p'ing-ts'un *Taipingcun* Hopeh
87 F3 T'ai-p'ing-tu *Taipingdu* Szech.
75 E6 T'ai-p'ing-yü *Taipingyu* Hunan
46 D4 Tai-pu *Daibu* Anhwei
43 D4 Tai-pu *Daibu* Kiangsu
51 F2 Tai Shan *Dai Shan* (island) Chek.
43 D2 Tai-shan *Dayishan* Kiangsu
79 C2 T'ai-shan *Taishan* Kwangt.
34 C3 T'ai Shan *Tai Shan* (mt) Shant.
34 C3 T'ai Shan *Tai Shan* (mts) Shant.
38 E2 T'ai-shan *Taishan* Shansi
14 F6 T'ai-shang *Taishang* Kirin
51 F2 Tai-shan Hsien *Daishan Xian* Chek.
66 F4 T'ai-shan Lieh-tao *Taishan Liedao* (island group) Fukien
87 F2 Tai-shih *Daishi* Szech.
50 C5 T'ai-shun *Taishun* Chek.
103 E3 T'ai-t'e-ma Hu *Taitema Hu* (lake) Sink.
67 E5 Tai-t'ou *Daitou* Fukien
30 G3 T'ai-t'ou-ying *Taitouying* Hopeh
47 F4 T'ai-ts'ang *Taicang* Kiangsu
83 G2 T'ai-ts'un *Taicun* Kwangsi
10 C4 T'ai-tung *Taidong* Heilung.
119 C4 T'ai-tung *Taidong* Taiwan
119 B3 T'ai-tung Hsien *Taidong Xian* Taiwan
118 B3 T'ai-tzu *Taizi* Taiwan
19 G3 T'ai-tzu Ho *Taizi He* (river) Liao.
74 D3 T'ai-tzu-miao *Taizimiao* Hunan
99 F4 T'ai-tzu-ssu *Taizisi* Kansu
Taiwan *see* Pages 117-119
54 E2 Tai-wang *Daiwang* Honan
30 B4 Tai-wang-ch'eng *Daiwangcheng* Hopeh
82 C3 T'ai-wang Lao-shan *Taiwang Laoshan* (mt) Kwangsi
T'ai-wan Hai-hsia *see* Formosa Strait
T'ai-wan Hai-hsia *see* Formosa Strait
T'ai-wan Shan *see* Chung-yang Shan-mo
119 B4 T'ai-wu *Taiwu* Taiwan
58 B4 T'ai-yang-ho *Taiyanghe* Hupeh
10 C2 T'ai-yang-kou *Taiyanggou* Heilung.
63 B7 T'ai-yang Shan *Taiyang Shan* (mt) Shensi
39 B6 T'ai-yang-ts'un *Taiyangcun* Shansi
63 D6 T'ai-yü *Taiyu* Shensi
39 D4 T'ai-yüan *Taiyuan* Shansi
T'ai-yüan - city plan *see* Page 136
75 E4 Tai-yüan-ssu *Daiyuansi* Hunan
38 D2 Tai-yüeh *Daiyue* Shansi
39 D5 T'ai-yüeh Shan *Taiyue Shan* (mts) Shansi
Taiyuenfu *see* T'ai-yüan
67 D5 Tai-yün Shan *Daiyun Shan* (mt) Fukien
119 B4 Ta-jen *Daren* Taiwan
T'a-je Ts'o *see* T'e-li-na-mu Ts'o
Ta-jih *see* Chi-mai
107 F4 Ta-jih *Dari* Tsing.
107 F4 Ta-jih-chin-tu *Darijindu* Tsing.
111 D3 T'a-jung *Tavong* Tibet
83 G2 Ta-jung-chiang *Tarongjiang* Kwangsi
83 G4 Ta-jung Shan *Darong Shan* (mts) Kwangsi
66 C4 Ta-kan *Dagan* Fukien
70 D3 Ta-kang *Dagang* Kiangsi
43 D3 Ta-kang *Dagang* Kiangsu
43 E2 Ta-kang *Dagang* Kiangsu
55 F2 T'a-kang *Tagang* Honan
50 C4 Ta-kang-t'ou *Dagangtou* Chek.
75 F6 Ta-ken-ch'iao *Dagenqiao* Hunan
71 C5 Ta-k'eng *Dakeng* Kiangsi
79 C2 Ta-k'eng-k'ou *Dakengkou* Kwangt.
106 D1 Ta-k'en-ta-pan Shan *Dakendaban Shan* (mts) Tsing.
Takhing *see* Te-ch'ing
Taklakhar *see* P'u-lan
Taklakot *see* P'u-lan
Takla Makan *see* T'a-k'o-la-ma-kan Sha-mo
30 D2 Ta-ko-chen *Dagezhen* Hopeh
102 C3 T'a-k'o-la-ma-kan Sha-mo *Takelamagan Shamo* (desert) Sink.
102 B4 T'a-ko-ma-po *Tagemabo* Sink.
107 F1 Ta-ko-ta *Dageda* Tsing.
14 B2 T'a-k'o-t'u *Taketu* Kirin
23 D5 T'a-k'o-t'u *Taketu* Kirin
54 D2 Ta-k'ou *Dakou* Honan
39 D6 Ta-k'ou *Dakou* Shansi
30 E4 Ta-k'ou-t'un *Dakoutun* Hopeh
31 E5 Ta-ku *Dagu* Hopeh
119 B4 Ta-ku *Dagu* Taiwan
102 H1 Ta-kuai *Daguai* Sink.
91 D4 Ta-kuan *Daguan* Kwei.
87 E3 Ta-kuan *Daguan* Szech.
118 C3 Ta-kuan *Daguan* Taiwan
95 D2 Ta-kuan *Daguan* Yun.
35 F3 Ta-k'uang *Dakuang* Shant.
47 C6 Ta-kuan Hu *Daguan Hu* Anhwei
11 C4 Ta-kuan-t'un *Daguantun* Heilung.
19 H2 Ta-ku-chia *Dagujia* Liao.
19 G2 Ta-ku-chia-tzu *Dagujiazi* Liao.
11 D4 Ta-kuei *Dagui* Heilung.
35 F3 Ta-ku Ho *Dagu He* (river) Shant.
35 G2 Ta-ku Ho *Dagu He* (river) Shant.
110 C2 T'a-ku-k'o *Taguke* Tibet
51 E3 Ta-kung *Dagong* Chek.
98 C2 Ta-kung-ch'a *Dagongcha* Kansu
86 C2 T'a-kung-ssu *Tagongsi* Szech.
35 F4 Ta-kung Tao *Dagong Dao* (island) Shant.
34 C3 Ta-k'un-lun *Dakunlun* Shant.
74 D3 Ta-kuo-kang *Daguogang* Hunan
14 F4 Ta-ku-shan *Dagushan* Kirin
19 G3 Ta-ku-shan *Dagushan* Liao.
47 C5 Ta-ku-tien *Dagudian* Anhwei
15 I4 T'a-la-chan *Talazhan* Kirin
99 G3 Ta-la-ch'ih *Dalachi* Kansu
23 F4 T'a-la-ha *Talaha* Heilung.
11 C4 T'a-la-ho *Talahe* Heilung.
22 B3 Ta-lai *Dalai* Heilung.
14 E2 Ta-lai *Dalai* Kirin
23 F5 Ta-lai *Dalai* Kirin
22 D2 Ta-lai-kou *Dalaigou* Heilung.
102 D2 Ta-la-k'o *Dalake* Sink.
26 C4 T'a-la-kou *Talagou* In. Mong.
26 E4 Ta-la-ma-miao *Dalamamiao* In. Mong.
79 D2 Ta-lan *Dalan* Kwangt.
102 I2 Ta-lang-k'an *Dalangkan* Sink.
79 C3 Ta-lang-wan *Dalangwan* Kwangt.
98 E1 Ta-lan-k'u-pu *Dalankubu* Kansu
102 C2 Ta-lao-pa *Dalaoba* Sink.
62 E4 Ta-lao-shan *Dalaoshan* Shensi
35 D3 Ta-lao-tzu *Dalaozi* Shant.
14 E3 Ta-lao-yeh-fu *Dalaoyefu* Kirin
106 D4 Ta-la-ssu *Dalasi* Tsing.
26 D4 Ta-la-t'e Ch'i *Dalate Qi* In. Mong.
114 B2 T'a-la-t'u *Talatu* Ningsia
10 E3 Ta-la-tzu *Dalazi* Heilung.
15 J5 Ta-la-tzu *Dalazi* Kirin
82 C4 Ta-leng *Daleng* Kwangsi
82 D4 Ta-li *Dali* Kwangsi
63 E6 Ta-li *Dali* Shensi
118 C2 Ta-li *Dali* Taiwan
119 C3 Ta-li *Dali* Taiwan
94 C3 Ta-li *Dali* Yun.
30 E4 Ta-liang *Daliang* Hopeh
83 F3 Ta-liang *Daliang* Kwangsi
79 C2 Ta-liang *Daliang* Kwangt.
107 G2 Ta-liang *Daliang* Tsing.
119 B4 Ta-liao *Daliao* Taiwan
46 D4 Ta-li-chi *Daliji* Anhwei
42 B2 Ta-li-chi *Daliji* Kiangsu
34 B2 Ta-li-chia *Dalijia* Shant.
31 B7 Ta-lien *Dalian* Hopeh
91 E2 Ta-lien *Dalian* Kwei.
18 E6 Ta-lien *Dalian* Liao.
11 E4 Ta-lien-ho *Dalianhe* Heilung.
67 E5 Ta-lien Tao *Dalian Dao* (island) Fukien
19 F5 Ta-lien Tao *Dalian Dao* (island) Liao.
62 E3 Ta-li Ho *Dali He* (river) Shensi
66 C4 Ta-li-k'ou *Dalikou* Fukien
102 C2 Ta-li-mu *Dalimu* Sink.
102 D2 T'a-li-mu Ho *Talimu He* (river) Sink.
102 C3 T'a-li-mu P'en-ti *Talimu Pendi* Sink.
14 C4 Ta-lin *Dalin* Kirin
23 E6 Ta-lin *Dalin* Kirin
118 B3 Ta-lin *Dalin* Taiwan
34 C3 Ta-lin-ch'ih *Dalinchi* Shant.
14 E4 Ta-ling *Daling* Kirin
15 G2 Ta-ling *Daling* Kirin
82 D5 Ta-ling *Daling* Kwangsi
46 C3 Ta-ling-chi *Dalingji* Anhwei
18 D3 Ta-ling Chiang *Dalang Jiang* (river) Liao.
18 E3 Ta-ling-ho *Dalinghe* Liao.
46 D3 Ta-ling-tzu *Dalingzi* Anhwei
38 E2 Ta-lin-ho *Dalinhe* Shansi
23 B6 Ta-li No-erh *Dali Nuoer* (lake) Liao.
18 E3 Ta-lin-t'un *Dalintun* Kirin
23 D5 Ta-lin-t'un *Dalintun* Kirin
14 F2 Ta-lin-tzu *Dalinzi* Kirin
14 E2 Ta-li-pa *Daliba* Kirin
94 B2 Ta-li Pai Autonomous District Yun.
Ta-li Pai-tsu Tzu-chih-chou *see* Ta-li Pai Autonomous District
22 C3 Ta-li-su-lin *Dalisulin* Heilung.
14 C4 Ta-li-t'u *Dalitu* Kirin
23 E6 Ta-li-t'u *Dalitu* Kirin
Talitze *see* Ta-li-tzu
15 G6 Ta-li-tzu *Dalizi* Kirin
119 B4 Ta-liu *Daliu* Taiwan
103 D2 T'a-liu-ch'ang *Taliuchang* Sink.
55 F4 Ta-liu-chuang *Daliuzhuang* Honan
62 F1 Ta-liu-t'a *Daliuta* Shensi
55 E4 Ta-liu-tien *Daliudian* Honan
19 F2 Ta-liu-t'un *Daliutun* Liao.
46 D3 Ta-li-yüan *Daliyuan* Anhwei
94 C5 Ta-lo *Daluo* Yun.
11 D4 Ta-lo-chen *Daluozhen* Heilung.
103 D2 Ta-lo-li-k'o *Daluolike* Sink.
11 E5 Ta-lo-mi *Daluomi* Heilung.
79 C2 Ta-lo Shan *Daluo Shan* (mt) Kwangt.
91 E2 Ta-lou Shan *Dalou Shan* (mts) Kwei.
99 G3 Ta-lu *Dalu* Kansu
14 F6 Ta-lu *Dalu* Kirin
82 E3 Ta-lü *Dalü* Kwangsi
35 F2 Ta-lü-chia *Dalüjia* Shant.
27 E4 Ta-lu-hao *Daluhao* In. Mong.
70 A4 Ta-lu-li *Daluli* Kiangsi
71 B5 Ta-lung *Dalong* Kiangsi
111 D3 Ta-lung *Dalong* Tibet
30 C4 Ta-lung-hua *Dalonghua* Hopeh
79 D1 Ta-lung-t'ien *Dalongtian* Kwangt.
111 D3 Ta-lun Ts'o *Dalun Cuo* (lake) Tibet
19 G5 Ta-lu Tao *Dalu Dao* (island) Liao.
47 E4 Ta-ma-ch'ang *Damachang* Anhwei
30 C2 Ta-ma-chün Shan *Damajun Shan* (mts) Hopeh
39 C4 Ta-mai-chiao *Damaijiao* Shansi
119 B4 T'a-ma-li *Tamali* Taiwan
70 E3 Ta-mao Shan *Damao Shan* (mt) Kiangsi
106 D2 Ta-mei-kou *Dameigou* Tsing.
11 E3 Ta-mei-lin *Dameilin* Heilung.
38 D3 Ta-meng *Dameng* Shansi
46 C3 Ta-meng-lung *Damenglong* Yun.
94 B4 Ta-meng-o *Damenge* Yun.
51 E5 Ta-men Tao *Damen Dao* (island) Chek.
30 E2 Ta-miao *Damiao* Hopeh
26 B5 Ta-miao *Damiao* In. Mong.
26 D4 Ta-miao *Damiao* In. Mong.
70 B3 Ta-miao *Damiao* Kiangsi
42 B1 Ta-miao *Damiao* Kiangsu
18 B2 Ta-miao *Damiao* Liao.
87 G2 Ta-miao *Damiao* Szech.
75 D5 Ta-miao-k'ou *Damiaokou* Hunan
Ta-miao-shan *see* Jung-shui
67 A5 Ta-ming *Daming* Fukien
31 C7 Ta-ming *Daming* Hopeh
19 G2 Ta-ming-p'ei *Damingbei* Liao.
83 E4 Ta-ming Shan *Daming Shan* (mt) Kwangsi
19 F3 Ta-min-t'un *Damintun* Liao.
58 C2 Ta-mu-ch'ang *Damuchang* Hupeh
67 D4 Ta-mu-chih Shan *Damuzhi Shan* (mt) Fukien
114 B1 T'a-mu-su-pu-lu-ko *Tamusubuluge* Ningsia
70 F3 Ta-nan *Danan* Kiangsi
119 C4 Ta-nan *Danan* Taiwan
103 F2 Ta-nan-hu *Dananhu* Sink.
14 F4 Ta-nan-t'un *Danantun* Kirin
38 C2 Tan-chai *Danzhai* Shansi
91 E4 Tan-chai Hsien *Danzhai Xian* Kwei.
102 H2 T'an-ch'ang *Tanchang* Sink.
51 E3 Tan-ch'eng *Dancheng* Chek.
55 G4 Tan-ch'eng *Dancheng* Honan
34 D5 T'an-ch'eng *Tancheng* Shant.
42 B1 Tan-chi *Danji* Kiangsu
74 B3 T'an-ch'i *Tanqi* Hunan
70 C3 T'an-ch'i *Tanqi* Kiangsi
91 F2 T'an-chia-ch'ang *Tanjiachang* Kwei.
47 E6 T'an-chia-ch'iao *Tanjiaqiao* Anhwei
99 F3 T'an-chia-ching *Tanjiajing* Kansu
34 D3 T'an-chia-fang *Tanjiafang* Shant.
75 D6 Tan-chiang *Danjiang* Hunan
58 D2 Tan-chia.ıg *Danjiang* Hupeh
63 F7 Tan Chiang *Dan Jiang* (river) Shensi
79 C2 T'an Chiang *Tan Jiang* (river) Kwangt.
59 E4 T'an-ch'iao *Tanqiao* Hupeh
74 C3 T'an-chia-wan *Tanjiawan* Hunan
70 C4 T'an-ch'iu *Tanqiu* Kiangsi
83 F2 Tan-chou *Danzhou* Kwangsi
83 G4 Tan-chu *Danzhu* Kiangsi
55 F4 T'an-chuang *Tanzhuang* Honan
119 B3 Ta-nei *Danei* Taiwan
70 D4 T'an-fang *Tanfang* Kiangsi
95 D3 Tan-feng *Danfeng* Yun.
63 F7 Tan-feng Hsien *Danfeng Xian* Shensi
Tangar *see* Huang-yüan
43 E3 T'ang-cha *Tangzha* Kiangsu
99 G5 Tang-ch'ang *Dangchang* Kansu
31 B5 T'ang-ch'eng *Dangcheng* Hopeh
39 D5 T'ang-ch'eng *Tangcheng* Shansi
98 B2 Tang-ch'eng-wan *Dangchengwan* Kansu
50 C3 T'ang-ch'i *Tangqi* Chek.
43 D2 T'ang-chi *Tangji* Kiangsu
34 B3 Tang-chia-chuang *Dangjiazhuang* Shant.
30 F4 T'ang-chia-chuang *Tangjiazhuang* Hopeh
47 D6 T'ang-chia-kou *Tangjiagou* Anhwei
47 E5 T'ang-chia-kou *Tangjiakou* Anhwei
110 C3 T'ang-chia La *Tangjia La* (pass) Tibet
106 D4 T'ang-chiang *Dangjiang* Tsing.
71 B6 T'ang-chiang *Tangjiang* Kiangsi
35 F2 T'ang-chia-p'o *Tangjiapo* Shant.
62 F4 Tang-chia-wan *Dangjiawan* Shensi
50 C2 T'ang-chia-wan *Tangjiawan* Chek.
79 C2 T'ang-chia-wan *Tangjiawan* Kwangt.
107 G4 T'ang-ch'ien-kou *Tangqiangou* Tsing.
11 B4 T'ang-ch'ih *Tangchi* Heilung.
23 E4 T'ang-ch'ih *Tangchi* Heilung.
111 D3 T'ang-ch'ing *Dangqing* Tibet
106 D1 Tang-chin Shan-k'ou *Dangjin Shankou* (pass) Tsing.
31 B6 T'ang-ch'iu *Tangqiu* Hopeh
106 C4 Tang Ch'ü *Dang Qu* (river) Tsing.
99 H4 Tang-ch'uan *Dangchuan* Kansu
67 C5 T'ang-ch'üan *Tangquan* Fukien
67 D4 T'ang-ch'uan *Tangchuan* Fukien
34 D5 T'ang-chuang *Tangzhuang* Shant.
31 D4 T'ang-erh-li *Tangerli* Hopeh
71 D5 T'ang-fang *Tangfang* Kiangsi
30 F4 T'ang-feng *Tangfeng* Hopeh
98 B2 Tang Ho *Dang He* (river) Kansu
54 D5 T'ang-ho *Tanghe* Honan
46 D3 T'ang Ho *Tang He* (river) Anhwei
31 C5 T'ang Ho *Tang He* (river) Hopeh
30 D3 T'ang-ho-k'ou *Tanghekou* Hopeh
Tang-ho Nan-shan *see* Wu-lan-ta-pan Shan
18 D3 T'ang-ho-tzu *Tanghezi* Liao.
51 D2 T'ang-hsi *Tangxi* Chek.
51 D5 T'ang-hsia *Tangxia* Chek.
75 F6 T'ang-hsia *Tangxia* Hunan
51 D3 T'ang-hsien *Tangxian* Chek.
31 B5 T'ang-hsien *Tangxian* Hopeh
59 F3 T'ang-hsien-chen *Tangxianzhen* Hupeh
111 D3 Tang-hsiung *Dangxiung* Tibet
111 D3 Tang-hsü *Dangxu* Tibet
71 B5 T'ang-hu *Tanghu* Kiangsi
83 E4 T'ang-hung *Tanghong* Kwangsi
34 A3 T'ang-i *Tangyi* Shant.
Tangin Pass *see* Tang-chin Shan-k'ou
19 F3 T'ang-kang-tzu *Tanggangzi* Liao.
Tangkiachwan *see* T'ang-chia-chuang
86 D1 T'ang-k'o *Tangke* Szech.
107 G2 T'ang-ko-mu *Tanggemu* Tsing.
47 E6 T'ang-k'ou *Tangkou* Anhwei
42 C2 T'ang-kou *Tanggou* Kiangsu
43 E4 T'ang-k'ou *Tangkou* Kiangsu
31 E4 T'ang-ku *Tanggu* Hopeh
31 D5 T'ang-kuan-t'un *Tangguantun* Hopeh
106 C4 T'ang-ku-la-chia-k'a *Tanggulajiaka* Tsing.
111 D2 T'ang-ku-la Shan-k'ou *Tanggula Shankou* (pass) Tibet
106 B4 T'ang-ku-la Shan-k'ou *Tanggula Shankou* Tsing.
111 D3 T'ang-ku-la Shan-mo *Tanggula Shanmo* (mts) Tibet
110 C3 T'ang-ku-la-yu-mu Ts'o *Tanggulayoumu Cuo* (lake) Tibet
111 E3 T'ang-kuo *Tangguo* Tibet
102 C3 T'ang-ku-tzu-pa-ssu-t'e *Tangguzibasite* Sink.
27 E4 Tang-lang-hu-t'ung *Danglanghutong* In. Mong.
Tanglha Range *see* T'ang-ku-la Shan-mo
42 A1 T'ang-lou *Tanglou* Kiangsu
107 F3 Tang-lu *Danglu* TS1Tsinghai
63 E6 Tang-mu *Dangmu* Shensi
105 G3 T'ang-nai-hai *Tangnaihai* Tsing.
46 D3 T'ang-nan-chi *Tangnanji* Anhwei
86 C3 T'ang-o *Tange* Szech.
30 F3 Tang-pa *Dangba* Hopeh
87 E2 T'ang-pa *Tangba* Szech.
78 B3 T'ang-p'eng *Tangpeng* Kwangt.
11 G5 T'ang-pi-chen *Dangbizhen* Heilung.
51 D3 T'ang-p'u *Tangpu* Chek.
70 B3 T'ang-p'u *Tangpu* Kiangsi
70 C3 T'ang-pu *Tangbu* Kiangsi
Tangra Tso *see* T'ang-k'u-la-yu-mu Ts'o
19 F4 T'ang-sha *Tangsha* Liao.
46 C2 Tang-shan *Dangshan* Anhwei
30 F4 T'ang-shan *Tangshan* Hopeh
43 D3 T'ang-shan *Tangshan* Kiangsu
19 H4 T'ang-shan-ch'eng *Tangshancheng* Liao.
19 H4 T'ang-sha-tzu *Tangshazi* Liao.
43 E4 T'ang-shih *Tangshi* Kiangsu
10 E3 Tang-shih-ho *Dangshihe* Heilung.
82 D2 T'ang-tan *Tangdan* Yun.
95 E2 T'ang-t'ang *Tangtang* Yun.
30 F3 T'ang-tao-ho *Tangdaohe* Hopeh
75 F5 T'ang-t'ien *Tangtian* Hunan
75 D5 T'ang-t'ien-shih *Tangtianshi* Hunan
91 F3 T'ang-t'ou *Tangtou* Kwei.
34 D4 T'ang-t'ou *Tangtou* Shant.
79 D2 T'ang-t'ou-hsia *Tangtouxia* Kwangt.
30 E2 T'ang-t'ou-kou *Tangtougou* Hopeh
50 B3 T'ang-ts'un *Tangcun* Chek.
50 C3 T'ang-ts'un *Tangcun* Chek.
34 C4 T'ang-ts'un *Tangcun* Shant.
75 E6 T'ang-ts'un-yü *Tangcunyu* Hunan
47 E5 Tang-t'u *Dangtu* Anhwei
75 D5 T'ang-tu-k'ou *Tangdukou* Hunan
30 E3 T'ang-tzu-chuang *Tangzizhuang* Hopeh
75 C4 T'ang-wan *Tangwan* Hunan
43 D3 T'ang-wan *Tangwan* Kiangsu
10 E3 T'ang-wang *Tangwang* Heilung.
11 E4 T'ang-wang Ho *Tangwang He* (river) Heilung.
35 D3 T'ang-wu *Tangwu* Shant.
51 C3 Tang-ya *Tangya* Chek.
58 D4 Tang-yang *Dangyang* Hupeh
43 E3 T'ang-yang *Tangyang* Kiangsu
55 F2 T'ang-yin *Tangyin* Honan
71 D4 T'ang-yin *Tangyin* Kiangsi
63 E7 T'ang-yü *Tangyu* Shensi
11 E4 T'ang-yüan *Tangyuan* Heilung.

T'ien-yen-cha-kan – Tung-ching Wan 23

23 F4 T'ien-yen-cha-kan *Tianyanzhagan* Heilung.
Ti-erh-sung-hua Chiang *see* Sung-hua Chiang
34 C4 Ti-fang *Difang* Shant.
95 E3 Ti-hsü *Dixu* Yun.
Ti-huo *see* Wu-lu-mu-ch'i
Tihwa *see* Wu-lu-mu-ch'i
102 I2 Ti-k'an-erh *Dikaner* Sink.
103 E2 Ti-k'an-erh *Dikaner* Sink.
47 E5 Ti-kang *Digang* Anhwei
Tikelik Tagh *see* T'ieh-k'o-li-k'o Shan
Tikenlik *see* T'ieh-kan-li-k'o
55 F3 Ti-ko *Dige* Honan
66 D4 Ti-k'ou *Dikou* Fukien
46 B4 Ti-li-ch'eng *Dilicheng* Anhwei
Timurlik *see* T'ieh-mu-li-k'o
82 B3 Ting-an *Dingan* Kwangsi
78 B4 Ting-an *Dingan* Kwangt.
58 B5 Ting-chai *Dingzhai* Hupeh
46 C4 Ting-chi *Dingji* Anhwei
55 F4 Ting-chi *Dingji* Honan
71 C4 Ting-chiang *Dingjiang* Kiangsi
67 B5 T'ing Chiang *Ting Jiang* (river) Fukien
43 E3 Ting-chia-so *Dingjiasuo* Kiangsu
110 D3 Ting-chieh *Dingjie* Tibet
110 C3 Ting-chieh Hsien *Dingjie Xian* Tibet
59 H4 T'ing-ch'ien *Tingqian* Hupeh
111 E3 Ting-ch'ing *Dingqing* Tibet
86 B3 Ting-ch'ü Ch'ü *Dingqu Qu* (river) Szech.
63 B7 Ting-chün Shan *Dingjun Shan* (mt) Shensi
Tingfan *see* Hui-shui
51 F2 Ting-hai *Dinghai* Chek.
54 C4 Ting-ho *Dinghe* Honan
99 G4 Ting-hsi *Dingxi* Kansu
51 E3 T'ing-hsia *Tingxia* Chek.
38 D3 Ting-hsiang *Dingxiang* Shansi
47 D6 Ting-hsiang-shu *Dingxiangshu* Anhwei
90 C5 Ting-hsiao *Dingxiao* Kwei.
31 B5 Ting-hsien *Dingxian* Hopeh
74 D2 T'ing-hsien-tu *Tingxiandu* Hunan
98 D1 Ting-hsin *Dingxin* Kansu
30 C4 Ting-hsing *Dingxing* Hopeh
79 C2 Ting-hu *Dinghu* Kwangt.
62 E3 Ting-hui Ch'ü *Dinghui Qu* (canal) Shensi
Ting-jih *see* Hsieh-ko-erh
110 C3 Ting-jih *Dingri* Tibet
110 C3 Ting-jih Hsien *Dingri Xian* Tibet
111 F2 Ting-k'o *Dingke* Tibet
Tingkou *see* Chiu-teng-k'ou
43 D3 Ting-kou *Dinggou* Kiangsu
63 C5 T'ing-k'ou-chen *Tingkouzhen* Shensi
82 D5 T'ing-liang *Tingliang* Kwangsi
43 F5 T'ing-lin *Tinglin* Kiangsu
30 F4 T'ing-liu-ho *Tingliuhe* Hopeh
55 F2 Ting-luan *Dingluan* Honan
71 C7 Ting-nan *Dingnan* Kiangsi
51 E3 T'ing-p'ang *Tingpang* Chek.
62 C3 Ting-pien *Dingbian* Shensi
75 C5 T'ing-p'ing *Tingping* Hunan
47 B5 Ting-pu-chieh *Dingbujie* Anhwei
Tingri *see* Ting-jih
103 D1 Ting-shan *Dingshan* Sink.
43 D4 Ting-shu-chen *Dingshuzhen* Kiangsu
59 G5 T'ing-ssu-ch'iao *Tingsiqiao* Hupeh
91 F5 Ting-tan *Dingdan* Kwei.
51 E3 Ting-t'ang *Dingtang* Chek.
82 D4 Ting-tang *Dingdang* Kwangsi
34 A4 Ting-t'ao *Dingtao* Shant.
110 A2 Ting-to *Dingduo* Tibet
51 D5 Ting-ts'ao Yü *Dingcao Yu* (island) Chek.
66 C3 Ting-ts'o *Dingcuo* Fukien
91 F5 T'ing-tung *Tingdong* Kwei.
82 E5 T'ing-tzu *Tingzi* Kwangsi
35 F3 Ting-tzu Kang *Dingzi Gang* (inlet) Shant.
106 C1 Ting-tzu-k'ou *Dingzikou* Tsing.
43 E3 Ting-yen *Dingyan* Kiangsu
55 E4 Ting-ying *Dingying* Honan
46 D4 Ting-yüan *Dingyuan* Anhwei
Ting-yüan-ying *see* Pa-yen-hao-t'e
Tinki *see* Ting-chieh
Tinkye Dzong *see* Ting-chieh
Tinpak *see* Tien-pai
Tinq-chieh *see* Chiang-ka
38 B3 Ti-pa-pao *Dibabao* Shansi
22 D3 Ti-san-chan *Disanzhan* Heilung.
38 D2 Ti-san-tso *Disanzuo* Shansi
102 I1 Ti-shui Ch'üan *Dishui Quan* (spring) Sink.
51 E2 Ti-t'ang *Ditang* Chek.
11 F5 Ti-tao *Didao* Heilung.
39 B6 Ti-tien *Didian* Shansi
43 E3 Ti-to *Diduo* Kiangsu
Titsing Tibetan Autonomous District *see* Ti-ch'ing Tibetan Autonomous District
15 K4 Ti-yin-kou *Diyingou* Kirin
115 C4 Tizard Bank China Sea
110 D3 To-cha-chung *Duozhazhong* Tibet
22 E2 T'o-cha-ming *Tuozhaming* Heilung.
10 B2 T'o-cha-min-nu-t'u-k'o *Tuozhaminnutuke* Heilung.
79 D1 T'o-ch'eng *Tuocheng* Kwangt.
75 D6 T'o-chiang *Tuojiang* Hunan
87 E2 T'o Chiang *Tuo Jiang* (river) Szech.
90 C4 To-chiao *Duojiao* Kwei.
35 F1 T'o-chi Tao *Tuoji Dao* (island) Shant.
79 D2 To-chu *Duozhu* Kwangt.
34 D4 To-chuang *Duozhuang* Shant.
70 C3 T'o-ch'uan-pu *Tuochuanbu* Kiangsi
107 G3 To-fu-tun *Duofudun* Tsing.
Tamiin Süme *see* T'u-ho-mu-miao
46 D3 T'o Ho *Tuo He* Anhwei
46 D3 T'o-ho-chi *Tuoheji* Anhwei
110 B2 T'o-ho-p'ing Ts'o *Tuoheping Cuo* (lake) Tibet
74 B3 To-hsi *Duoxi* Hunan
To Huping Lake *see* T'o-ho-p'ing Ts'o
Toishan *see* T'ai-shan
Tokak *see* To-k'a-k'o
106 C2 To-k'a-k'o *Duokake* Tsing.
106 C2 To-k'a-k'o Ho *Duokake He* (river) Tsing.
102 I2 T'o-k'o-hsün *Tuokexun* Sink.
103 E2 T'o-k'o-hsün *Tuokexun* Sink.
110 C2 T'o-k'o-ting-ling *Tuokedingling* Tibet
26 D4 T'o-k'o-t'o *Tuoketuo* In. Mong.
75 B4 To-k'ou *Duokou* Hunan
Toksun *see* T'o-k'o-hsün
Toktomal Ulan Muran *see* T'o-t'o Ho
106 D2 T'o-la *Tuola* Tsing.
106 C4 To-la-hsing-ko *Duolaxingge* Tsing.
T'o-lai-kung-chuang *see* T'o-le
T'o-lai-mu-ch'ang *see* T'o-le
107 F1 T'o-lai Nan-shan *Tuolai Nanshan* (mts) Tsing.
106 E4 To-la-ma-k'ang *Duolamakang* Tsing.
106 D2 T'o-la-t'o-la-lin *Tuolatuolalin* Tsing.
106 D2 T'o-le *Tuole* Tsing.
107 F1 T'o-le *Tuole* Tsing.
102 C1 T'o-li *Tuoli* Sink.
119 B4 To-liang *Duoliang* Taiwan
110 A3 T'o-lin *Tuolin* Tibet
Ting *see* T'o-lin
106 C2 T'o-lo-i *Tuoluoyi* Tsing.
82 D5 T'o-lu *Tuolu* Kwangsi
27 G3 To-lun *Duolun* In. Mong.
106 C4 T'o-lun-ch'ih-p'ing-erh *Tuolunchipinger* Tsing.
110 A2 T'o-ma-erh *Tuomaer* Tibet
Tomar *see* To-ma-erh
86 D4 T'o-mu-kou *Tuomugou* Szech.
110 B2 To-mu-la *Duomula* Tibet
11 B4 To-nai *Duonai* Heilung.
23 E4 To-nai *Duonai* Heilung.
Tonga *see* T'a-ku-k'o
Tongkow *see* Chiu-teng-k'ou
Tongkyuk *see* Tung-chiu
Tonguz Baste *see* T'ang-ku-tzu-pa-ssu-t'e
82 B3 T'o-niang Chiang *Tuoniang Jiang* (river) Kwangsi
Tonori Tso Nor *see* T'o-so Hu (sic)
107 G2 To-pa *Duoba* Tsing.
59 E4 To-pao-wan *Duobaowan* Hupeh
10 C2 To-pu-k'u-erh *Duobukuer* Heilung.
10 C2 To-pu-k'u-erh Ho *Duobukuer He* (river) Heilung.
22 F2 To-pu-k'u-erh Ho *Duobukuer He* (river) Heilung.
63 B6 T'o-shih *Tuoshi* Shensi
102 B2 T'o-shih-kan Ho *Tuoshigan He* (river) Sink.
107 F3 T'o-so Hu *Tuosuo Hu* (lake) Tsing.
Toson Nuur *see* T'o-su Hu (sic)
Tossun Nor *see* T'o-su Hu
107 E2 T'o-su Hu *Tuosu Hu* (lake) Tsing.
Totalyn Gol *see* T'a-t'a-leng Ho
58 E4 To-tao *Duodao* Hupeh
Totling *see* T'o-lin
102 C1 T'o-t'o *Tuotuo* Sink.
106 B3 T'o-t'o Ho *Tuotuo He* (river) Tsing.
106 C3 T'o-t'o-ho *Tuotuohe* Tsing.
107 E2 T'o-t'u *Tuotu* Tsing.
30 D4 Tou-chang-chuang *Douzhangzhuang* Hopeh
118 C2 T'ou-ch'eng *Toucheng* Taiwan
83 F2 Tou-chiang *Doujiang* Kwangsi
118 B2 T'ou-fen *Toufen* Taiwan
19 H2 Tou-hu-t'un *Douhutun* Liao.
34 A3 Tou-hu-t'un *Douhutun* Shant.
94 C4 Tou-ko *Douge* Yun.
55 F5 Tou-kou *Dougou* Honan
87 E1 Tou-k'ou *Doukou* Szech.
11 E6 Tou-kou-tzu *Dougouzi* Heilung.
55 F1 Tou-kung *Dougong* Honan
98 B1 T'ou-kung *Tougong* Kansu
102 I1 T'ou-kung *Tougong* Sink.
11 G4 T'ou-lin *Toulin* Heilung.
118 B3 Tou-liu *Douliu* Taiwan
38 D3 Tou-lo *Douluo* Shansi
55 F3 Tou-men *Doumen* Honan
79 C2 Tou-men *Doumen* Kwangt.
63 D6 Tou-men-chen *Doumenzhen* Shensi
79 C2 Tou-men Hsien *Doumen Xian* Kwangt.
74 D3 Tou-mu-hu *Doumuhu* Hunan
95 D4 Tou-mu-ko *Doumuge* Yun.
118 B3 Tou-nan *Dounan* Taiwan
83 G3 Tou-p'ai *Doupai* Kwangsi
30 B3 T'ou-pai-hu *Toubaihu* Hopeh
51 D2 T'ou-p'eng *Toupeng* Chek.
71 D5 T'ou-p'o *Toupo* Kiangsi
95 E1 Tou-sha-kuan *Doushaguan* Yun.
58 E4 Tou-shih *Doushi* Hupeh
71 B6 Tou-shui *Doushui* Kiangsi
11 C5 T'ou-t'ai *Toutai* Heilung.
102 H1 T'ou-t'ai *Toutai* Sink.
14 F6 T'ou-tao *Toudao* Kirin
15 H5 T'ou-tao Chiang *Toudao Jiang* (river) Kirin
26 B4 T'ou-tao-ch'iao *Toudaoqiao* In. Mong.
18 E3 T'ou-tao-ho *Toudaohe* Liao.
102 I2 T'ou-tao-ho *Toudaohe* Sink.
62 E2 T'ou-tao-ho-tzu *Toudaohezi* Shensi
114 C2 T'ou-tao-hu *Toudaohu* Ningsia
15 J5 T'ou-tao-kou *Toudaogou* Kirin
38 E3 Tou-ts'un *Doucun* Shansi
102 H2 T'ou-t'un Ho *Toutun He* (river) Sink.
102 H2 T'ou-t'un-ho *Toutunhe* Sink.
114 C3 T'ou-ying *Touying* Ningsia
31 B6 Tou-yü *Douyu* Hopeh
78 A4 To-wen *Duowen* Kwangt.
86 D3 T'o-wu *Tuowu* Szech.
110 B3 T'o-ya *Tuoya* Tibet
106 D2 To-ya-ho *Duoyahe* Tsing.
14 F5 T'o-yao-ling *Tuoyaoling* Kirin
11 F4 T'o-yao-tzu *Tuoyaozi* Heilung.
107 E3 To-yün Ho *Duoyun He* (river) Tsing.
Tradom *see* Cha-tung
115 C2 Tree Island China Sea
115 C4 Trident Shoal China Sea
115 B3 Triton Island China Sea
Tsa-ch'u Ho *see* Ya-lung Chiang
Tsagaan Tologoy Hudag *see* Ch'a-kan-t'ao-le-kai-hu-tu-ko
Tsagaan Us *see* Ch'ai-ta-mu Ho
67 B5 Ts'ai-ch'i *Caiqi* Fukien
75 D5 Ts'ai-chia *Caijia* Hunan
35 E3 Ts'ai-chia-chuang *Caijiazhuang* Shant.
59 H4 Ts'ai-chia-ho *Caijiahe* Hupeh
46 C4 Ts'ai-chia-lan *Caijialan* Anhwei
63 C6 Ts'ai-chia-p'o *Caijiapo* Shensi
30 C2 Ts'ai-chia-ying *Caijiaying* Hopeh
55 F3 Ts'ai-chuang *Caizhuang* Honan
30 F3 Ts'ai-chuang *Caizhuang* Hopeh
Tsaidam Basin *see* Ch'ai-ta-mu P'en-ti
39 B7 Ts'ai-hsia *Caixia* Shansi
58 C4 Ts'ai-hua *Caihua* Hupeh
107 F3 Ts'ai-jih-wa *Cairiwa* Tsing.
55 F4 Ts'ai-kou *Caigou* Honan
118 C2 Ts'ai-lien *Cailian* Taiwan
91 F4 Tsai-ma *Zaima* Kwei.
82 D5 Tsai-miao *Zaimiao* Kwangsi
91 F5 Tsai-pien *Zaibian* Kwei.
90 B3 Ts'ai-shen-t'ang *Caishentang* Kwei.
47 E5 Ts'ai-shih *Caishi* Anhwei
59 G4 Ts'ai-tien *Caidian* Hupeh
30 E4 Ts'ai-t'ing-ch'iao *Caitingqiao* Hopeh
47 E6 Ts'ai-ts'un-pa *Caicunba* Anhwei
47 D6 Ts'ai-tzu Hu *Caizi Hu* (lake) Anhwei
14 D3 Ts'ai-tzu-kung *Caizigong* Kirin
83 G2 Ts'ai-wan *Caiwan* Kwangsi
51 F2 Ts'ai-yüan-chen *Caiyuanzhen* Chek.
86 D2 Tsa-ku-nao *Zagunao* Szech.
Tsamkong *see* Chan-chiang
55 H4 Tsan-ch'eng *Zancheng* Honan
14 E4 Tsan-chia *Zanjia* Kirin
35 F2 Ts'an-chuang *Canzhuang* Shant.
87 E2 Ts'ang-ch'i *Cangqi* Szech.
55 E5 Tsang-chi *Zangji* Honan
31 D5 Tsang-chia-ch'iao *Zangjiaqiao* Hopeh
66 D4 Ts'ang-ch'ien *Cangqian* Fukien
31 D5 Ts'ang-chou *Cangzhou* Hopeh
Tsangchow *see* Ts'ang-chou
39 C4 Ts'ang-erh-hui *Cangerhui* Shansi
31 D5 Ts'ang Hsien *Cang Xian* Hopeh
74 D3 Ts'ang-kang *Canggang* Hunan
90 B6 Ts'ang-keng *Canggeng* Kwei.
35 F2 Ts'ang-ko-chuang *Canggezhuang* Shant.
35 F3 Ts'ang-k'ou *Cangkou* Shant.
102 B3 Tsang-kui *Zanggui* Sink.
Tsangpo *see* Brahmaputra
59 G4 Ts'ang-pu *Cangbu* Hupeh
10 B2 Ts'ang-shan *Cangshan* Heilung.
87 E2 Ts'ang-shan-chen *Cangshanzhen* Szech.
34 D5 Ts'ang-shan Hsien *Cangshan Xian* Shant.
19 H3 Ts'ang-shih *Cangshi* Liao.
74 E3 Ts'ang-shui-p'u *Cangshuipu* Hunan
110 C3 Tsang-to *Zangduo* Tibet
47 D5 Ts'ang-t'ou *Cangtou* Anhwei
38 D1 Ts'ang-t'ou Ho *Cangtou He* (river) Shansi
Ts'ang-wu *see* Lung-hsü
83 H4 Ts'ang-wu Hsien *Cangwu Xian* Kwangsi
94 B4 Ts'ang-yüan *Cangyuan* Yun.
94 B4 Ts'ang-yüan Wa Autonomous Hsien Yun.
Ts'ang-yüan Wa-tsu Tzu-chih-hsien *see* Ts'ang-yüan Wa Autonomous Hsien
31 B6 Tsan-huang *Zanhuang* Hopeh
Tsan-lan *see* Yin-ch'uan
31 D4 Tsan-lan *Zanlan* Hopeh
46 D4 Ts'ao-an *Caoan* Anhwei
70 E3 Ts'ao-ch'i *Caoqi* Kiangsi
50 C2 Tsao-ch'i *Zaoqi* Chek.
46 B4 Ts'ao-chia-chi *Caojiaji* Anhwei
39 C7 Ts'ao-chia-ch'uan *Caojiachuan* Shansi
59 H4 Ts'ao-chia-ho *Caojiahe* Hupeh
31 C6 Tsao-ch'iang *Zaoqiang* Hopeh
43 D4 Ts'ao-ch'iao *Caoqiao* Kiangsu
118 B2 Tsao-ch'iao *Zaoqiao* Taiwan
107 G2 Ts'ao-chia-pao *Caojiabao* Tsing.
63 E7 Ts'ao-chia-p'ing *Caojiaping* Shensi
63 B6 Ts'ao-chia-wan *Caojiawan* Shensi
94 B3 Ts'ao-chien *Caojian* Yun.
39 B5 Ts'ao-ching *Caojing* Shansi
Tsaochow *see* Ho-tse
34 D5 Ts'ao-chuang *Caozhuang* Shant.
34 C5 Tsao-chuang *Zaozhuang* Shant.
Tsaochwang *see* Tsao-chuang
90 B4 Ts'ao Hai *Caohai* (lake) Kwei.
31 C5 Ts'ao-ho *Caohe* Hopeh
19 H4 Ts'ao Ho *Cao He* (river) Liao.
42 C1 Tsao-ho *Zaohe* Kaingsu
19 H3 Ts'ao-ho-chang *Caohezhang* Liao.
19 H4 Ts'ao-ho-ch'eng *Caohecheng* Liao.
19 G4 Ts'ao-ho-k'ou *Caohekou* Liao.
71 B5 Tsao-ho-shih *Zaoheshi* Kiangsi
34 A5 Ts'ao-hsien *Caoxian* Shant.
102 D2 Ts'ao-hu *Caohu* Sink.
34 C2 Tsao-hu-li *Zaohuli* Shant.
106 D2 Tsao-huo Ho *Zaohuo He* (river) Tsing.
46 D3 Ts'ao-kou *Caogou* Anhwei
30 B4 Ts'ao-kou-pao *Caogoubao* Hopeh
46 D3 Ts'ao-lao-chi *Caolaoji* Anhwei
118 C1 Ts'ao-li *Caoli* Taiwan
71 B5 Tsao-lin *Zaolin* Kiangsi
38 E2 Tsao-lin *Zaolin* Shansi
62 F3 Tsao-lin-p'ing *Zaolinping* Shensi
34 B5 Ts'ao-ma-chi *Caomaji* Shant.
114 C3 Ts'ao-miao *Caomiao* Ningsia
Tsaongo River *see* Ts'ao-o Chiang
43 E3 Ts'ao-nien *Caonian* Kiangsu
51 D3 Ts'ao-o *Caoe* Chek.
51 D3 Ts'ao-o Chiang *Caoe Jiang* (river) Chek.
86 D3 Ts'ao-pa *Caoba* Szech.
95 D4 Ts'ao-pa *Caoba* Yun.
59 H4 Ts'ao-p'an-ti *Caopandi* Hupeh
63 C6 Ts'ao-pi-chen *Caobizhen* Shensi
43 E3 Ts'ao-p'ieh *Caopie* Kiangsu
75 F4 Tsao-p'o *Zaopo* Hunan
42 C1 Ts'ao-p'u *Caopu* Kiangsu
119 B4 Ts'ao-pu *Caobu* Taiwan
99 I4 Tsao-sheng *Zaosheng* Kansu
46 C3 Ts'ao-shih *Caoshi* Anhwei
75 F5 Ts'ao-shih *Caoshi* Hunan
19 I2 Ts'ao-shih *Caoshi* Liao.
74 D2 Tsao-shih *Zaoshi* Hunan
75 E5 Tsao-shih *Zaoshi* Hunan
59 F4 Tsao-shih *Zaoshi* Hupeh
51 D3 Ts'ao-t'a *Caota* Chek.
78 A3 Ts'ao-t'an *Caotan* Kwangt.
91 E3 Ts'ao-t'ang *Caotang* Kwei.
87 G2 Ts'ao-t'ang-pa *Caotangba* Szech.
58 D2 Ts'ao-tien *Caodian* Hupeh
43 D2 Ts'ao-tien *Caodian* Kiangsu
46 D2 Ts'ao-ts'un *Caocun* Anhwei
63 E5 Ts'ao-ts'un *Caocun* Shensi
91 E5 Ts'ao-tu Ho *Caodu He* (river) Kwei.
118 B3 Ts'ao-t'un *Caotun* Taiwan
30 G4 Ts'ao-tung-chuang *Caodongzhuang* Hopeh
74 E2 Ts'ao-wei *Caowei* Hunan
59 E2 Tsao-yang *Zaoyang* Hupeh
43 D2 Ts'ao-yen *Caoyan* Kiangsu
67 E5 Ts'ao Yü *Cao Yu* (islet) Fukien
102 H1 Ts'ao-yüan *Caoyuan* Sink.
31 C7 Tsao-yüan *Zaoyuan* Hopeh
34 C3 Tsao-yüan *Zaoyuan* Shant.
62 E4 Tsao-yüan *Zaoyuan* Shensi
Tsaring Nor *see* Cha-ling Hu
Tsa-to *see* Yü-yü-jih-pen
106 D4 Tsa-to Hsien *Zaduo Xian* Tsing.
Tsaydamiin Uula *see* Ch'ai-ta-mu Shan
39 C6 Tse-chang *Zezhang* Shansi
74 B3 Tse-chia-hu *Zejiahu* Hunan
Tsehchowfu *see* Chin-ch'eng
Ts'e-heng Pu-i-tsu Tzu-chih-hsien *see* Ts'e-heng Puyi Autonomous Hsien
90 C6 Ts'e-heng Puyi Autonomous Hsien Kwei.
Tsehleh *see* Ts'e-le
Tsehpu *see* Tse-p'u
98 E1 Ts'e-k'o *Ceke* Kansu
Tse-k'u *see* So-nai-hai
107 G3 Tse-k'u Hsien *Zeku Xian* Tsing.
51 E4 Tse-kuo *Zeguo* Chek.
111 E3 Tse-la *Zela* Tibet
100 C3 Ts'e-le *Cele* Sink.
82 D3 Tse-ling *Zeling* Kwangsi
107 E2 Tse-ling-kou *Zelinggou* Tsing.
83 H5 Ts'en-ch'i *Cenqi* Kwangsi
79 C2 Tseng-ch'eng *Zengcheng* Kwangt.
79 C2 Tseng Chiang *Zeng Jiang* (river) Kwangt.
15 I5 Tseng-feng Shan *Zengfeng Shan* (mt) Kirin
115 C5 Tseng-hai An-sha *Zenghai Ansha* China Sea
34 D5 Ts'eng-shan *Cengshan* Shant.
14 F3 Tseng-sheng *Zengsheng* Kirin
Tsengshing *see* Tseng-ch'eng
79 D1 Ts'eng-t'ien *Cengtian* Kwangt.
71 C4 Tseng-t'ien *Zengtian* Kiangsi
119 B3 Ts'eng-wen Ch'i *Cengwen* (river) Taiwan
59 E4 Ts'en-ho *Cenhe* Hupeh
91 F3 Ts'en-kung Hsien *Cengong Xian* Kwei.
102 B3 Tse-p'u *Zepu* Sink.
38 E4 Ts'e-shih *Ceshi* Shansi
111 D3 Tse-tang *Zedang* Tibet
102 D2 Ts'e-ta-ya *Cedaya* Sink.
Tsethang *see* Tse-tang
35 G2 Tse-t'ou-chi *Zetouji* Shant.
111 F3 Tse-wei *Zewei* Tibet
90 C6 Ts'e-yang *Ceyang* Kwei.
43 E4 Tse-yang-chen *Zeyangzhen* Kiangsu
31 B6 Ts'e-yü *Ceyu* Hopeh
Tsian *see* Chi-an
Tsiaotso *see* Chiao-tso
Tsientang River *see* Ch'ien-t'ang Chiang
Tsiho *see* Ch'i-ho
Tsimo *see* Chi-mo
Tsinan *see* Chi-nan
Tsinchow *see* Ch'in-hsien
Tsingan *see* Ching-an
Tsinghai Province *see* Pages 105-108
Tsingi *see* Ch'ing-i Chiang
Tsing-ki *see* Han-yüan
Tsingkiang *see* Ch'ing-chiang
Tsingpu *see* Ch'ing-p'u
Tsingshan *see* Ch'ing-shan
Tsingshih *see* Chin-shih
Tsingshui *see* Chang-chia-ch'uan
Tsingshui Ho *see* Ch'ing-shui Ho
Tsingsi *see* Ching-hsi
Tsingsing *see* Ching-hsing
Tsingtao *see* Ch'ing-tao
Tsingtien *see* Ch'ing-t'ien
Tsingtungsia *see* Ch'ing-t'ung-hsia
Tsing-yuen *see* Ching-yüan
Tsingyün *see* Ch'ing-yüan
Tsining *see* Chi-ning
Tsining *see* Chi-ning
Tsinkiang *see* Ch'üan-chou
Tsinkong *see* Ch'ien-chiang
Tsinling Mountains *see* Ch'in-ling Shan-mo
Tsinsien *see* Chin-hsien
Tsinyün *see* Chin-yün
Tsishih Shan *see* Chi-shih Shan
Tsitaokow *see* Ch'i-tao-kou
Tsitsihar *see* Ch'i-ch'i-ha-erh
Tsiyang *see* Chi-yang
71 B5 Tso-an *Zuoan* Kiangsi
47 D5 Ts'o-chen *Cuozhen* Anhwei
119 B3 Tso-chen *Zuozhen* Taiwan
55 F2 Tso-ch'eng *Zuocheng* Honan
14 G3 Tso-chia-chen *Zuojiazhen* Kirin
82 D5 Tso Chiang *Zuo Jiang* (river) Kwangsi
Ts'o-ch'in *see* Men-tung
110 C3 Ts'o-chin Hsien *Cuojin Xian* Tibet
82 D5 Tso-chou *Zuozhou* Kwangsi
39 E4 Tso-ch'üan *Zuoquan* Shansi
39 E5 Tso-hui *Zuohui* Shansi
22 C3 Ts'o-kang *Cuogang* Heilung.
110 B2 Ts'o-k'o-cha *Cuokezha* Tibet
Tso-kung *see* Ya-chung
111 F3 Tso-kung Hsien *Zuogong Xian* Tibet
63 D8 Tso-lung-kou *Zuolonggou* Shensi
Ts'o-mei *see* Tang-hsü
111 D3 Ts'o-mei Hsien *Cuomei Xian* Tibet
Ts'o-na *see* Hsüeh-hsia
111 D4 Ts'o-na Hsien *Cuona Xian* Tibet
Tsonji *see* Ch'üan-chi
111 F3 Tso-pa *Zuoba* Tibet
105 E3 Ts'o-pa-jih-ka-tse *Cuobarigaze* Tsing.
Tso-shui *see* Cha-shui
79 D2 Tso-t'an *Zuotan* Kwangt.
82 D4 Tso-teng *Zuodeng* Kwangsi
70 C2 Tsou-ch'iao *Zouqiao* Kiangsi
34 B4 Tsou-hsien *Zouxian* Shant.
107 F1 Tsou-lang Nan-shan *Zoulang Nanshan* (mts) Tsing.
83 G3 Tsou-ma *Zouma* Kwangsi
31 B4 Tsou-ma-i *Zoumayi* Hopeh
58 C5 Tsou-ma-p'ing *Zoumaping* Hupeh
34 C3 Tsou-p'ing *Zouping* Shant.
74 D2 Tsou-shih *Zoushi* Hunan
43 E3 Ts'ou-t'ung *Coutong* Kiangsu
34 C5 Tsou-wu *Zouwu* Shant.
30 B3 Tso-wei *Zuowei* Hopeh
38 D2 Tso-yün *Zuoyun* Shansi
63 D6 Tsu-an-chen *Zuanzhen* Shensi
119 B4 Tsu-chin *Zujin* Taiwan
110 B2 Tsu-hsia-kung-pu *Zuxiagongbu* Tibet
51 E3 Ts'ui-chia-ao *Cuijaao* Chek.
35 E3 Ts'ui-chia-chi *Cuijiaji* Shant.
55 F3 Ts'ui-ch'iao *Cuiqiao* Honan
58 B4 Ts'ui-chia-pa *Cuijiaba* Hupeh
34 D4 Ts'ui-chia-yü *Cuijiayu* Shant.
59 H5 Ts'ui-chou *Cuizhou* Hupeh
30 E4 Ts'ui-huang-k'ou *Cuihuangkou* Hopeh
10 C1 Ts'ui-kang *Cuigang* Heilung.
10 B2 Ts'ui-ling *Cuiling* Heilung.
11 E4 Ts'ui-luan *Cuiluan* Heilung.
Tsuimen *see* Hsü-wen
54 E3 Ts'ui-miao *Cuimiao* Honan
63 C6 Ts'ui-mu *Cuimu* Shensi
63 C6 Tsui-t'ou-chen *Zuitouzhen* Shensi
71 C5 Ts'ui-wei Feng *Cuiwei Feng* (mt) Kiangsi
82 C4 Tsu-jung *Zurong* Kwangsi
34 C3 Ts'u-lai Shan *Cilai Shan* (mt) Shant.
46 C2 Tsu-lou *Zulou* Anhwei
70 C3 Ts'un-ch'ien *Cunqian* Kiangsi
38 E3 Tsung-ai *Zongai* Shansi
98 D2 Tsung-chai *Zongzhai* Kansu
107 E2 Tsung-chia-fang-tzu *Zongjiafangzi* Tsing.
91 F5 Ts'ung-chiang Hsien *Congjiang Xian* Kwei.
83 F6 Tsung-chiang-k'ou *Zongjiangkou* Kwangsi
79 C2 Ts'ung-hua *Conghua* Kwangt.
110 C3 Tsung-ka *Zongga* Tibet
59 E4 Tsung-k'ou *Zongkou* Hupeh
38 B4 Ts'ung-lo-yü *Congluoyu* Shansi
46 D4 Tsung-p'u *Zongpu* Anhwei
Tsungteh *see* Ch'ung-te
39 D5 Ts'ung-tzu-yü *Congziyu* Shansi
107 E2 Tsung-wu-lung *Zongwulong* Tsing.
47 D6 Tsung-yang *Zongyang* Anhwei
30 E3 Tsun-hua *Zunhua* Hopeh
91 D3 Tsun-i *Zunyi* Kwei.
91 D3 Tsun-i Hsien *Zunyi Xian* Kwei.
Tsunyi *see* Tsun-i
35 E3 Tsuo-shan *Zuoshan* Shant.
119 B4 Tsu-shan *Zushan* Taiwan
31 C6 Tsu-yang-chuang *Zuyangzhuang* Hopeh
Tsuyung Yi Autonomous District *see* Ch'u-hsiung Yi Autonomous District
82 C4 Tu-an *Duan* Kwangsi
82 E4 Tu-an *Duan* Kwangsi
55 G6 Tuan-chi *Duanji* Honan
107 E1 T'uan-chieh Feng *Tuanjie Feng* (peak) Tsing.
39 C5 Tuan-ch'un *Duanchun* Shansi
59 G4 T'uan-feng *Tuanfeng* Hupeh
54 C5 Tuan Ho *Duan He* (river) Honan
91 E3 T'uan-hsi *Tuanxi* Kwei.
70 E2 Tuan-hsin *Duanxin* Kiangsi
50 C2 T'uan-k'ou *Tuankou* Chek.
58 E4 T'uan-lin *Tuanlin* Hupeh
14 G5 T'uan-lin *Tuanlin* Kirin
58 B4 T'uan-pao-ssu *Tuanbaosi* Hupeh
39 E4 T'uan-pi *Tuanbi* Shansi
59 H4 T'uan-p'o *Tuanpo* Hupeh
91 D5 Tuan-shan *Duanshan* Kwei.
59 E5 T'uan-shan-ssu *Tuanshansi* Hupeh
39 D6 Tuan-shih *Duanshi* Shansi
38 C4 T'uan-shui-t'ou *Tuanshuitou* Shansi
59 G4 Tuan-tien *Duandian* Hupeh
38 D4 Tuan-t'ing *Duanting* Shansi
39 D4 Tuan-ts'un *Duancun* Shansi
39 D5 Tuan-ts'un *Duancun* Shansi
35 F3 T'uan-wan *Tuanwan* Shant.
35 F3 T'uan-wang *Tuanwang* Shant.
83 G2 Tu-an Yao Autonomous Hsien Kwangsi
Tu-an Yao-tsu Tzu-chih-hsien *see* Tu-an Yao Autonomous Hsien
67 D6 T'u-chai *Tuzhai* Fukien
70 D2 Tu-ch'ang *Duchang* Kiangsi
118 C2 T'u-ch'ang *Tuchang* Taiwan
58 C3 T'u-ch'eng *Tucheng* Hupeh
91 C2 T'u-ch'eng *Tucheng* Kwei.
30 B2 T'u-ch'eng-tzu *Tuchengzi* Hopeh
30 D2 T'u-ch'eng-tzu *Tuchengzi* Hopeh
14 A5 T'u-ch'eng-tzu *Tuchengzi* Kirin
14 G3 T'u-ch'eng-tzu *Tuchengzi* Kirin
23 D6 T'u-ch'eng-tzu *Tuchengzi* Kirin
19 G4 T'u-ch'eng-tzu *Tuchengzi* Liao.
58 C4 Tu-chen-wan *Duzhenwan* Hupeh
55 G3 Tu-chi *Duji* Honan
34 B2 Tu-chi *Duji* Shant.
110 D3 Tu-chia-li *Dujiali* Tibet
91 F5 Tu-chiang *Dujiang* Kwei.
91 F5 Tu Chiang *Du Jiang* (river) Kwei.
75 C5 Tu-ch'iao *Duqiao* Hunan
47 D5 T'u-ch'iao *Tuqiao* Anhwei
43 D4 T'u-ch'iao *Tuqiao* Kiangsu
15 G3 T'u-ch'iao *Tuqiao* Kirin
34 B2 T'u-ch'iao *Tuqiao* Shant.
63 D5 T'u-ch'iao *Tuqiao* Shensi
63 D7 T'u-chia-p'ing *Tujiaping* Shensi
70 C2 T'u-chia-pu *Tujiabu* Kiangsi
59 F4 Tu-chia-t'ai *Dujiatai* Hupeh
82 D4 Tu-chieh *Dujie* Kwangsi
82 E3 Tu-chieh *Dujie* Kwangsi
90 B3 T'u-chieh-tzu *Tujiezi* Kwei.
50 B3 Tu-ching *Dujing* Chek.
31 D4 T'u-ch'ing-t'o *Tuqingtuo* Hopeh
14 B2 T'u-ch'üan *Tuquan* Kirin
23 D5 T'u-ch'üan *Tuquan* Kirin
38 E2 Tu-chuang *Duzhuang* Shansi
39 E4 Tu-chuang *Duzhuang* Shansi
78 A4 T'u-ch'ü Wan *Tuqu Wan* (bay) Kwangt.
Tu-erh-po-t'e *see* T'ai-k'ang
Tu-erh-po-t'e Meng-ku-tsu Tzu-chih-hsien *see* Durbet Mongol Autonomous Hsien
67 B5 T'u-fang *Tufang* Fukien
34 C2 T'u-hai Ho *Tuhai He* (river) Shant.
58 C2 Tu Ho *Du He* (river) Hupeh
26 D3 T'u-ho-mo-miao *Tuhemomiao* In. Mong.
91 E2 T'u-hsi *Tuxi* Kwei.
51 E4 Tu-hsia-ch'iao *Duxiaqiao* Chek.
87 G2 T'u-hsiang *Tuxiang* Szech.
102 C3 Tu-hsien-pai-pa-cha *Duxianbaibazha* Sink.
67 C7 Tu-hsün *Duxun* Fukien
79 C2 Tu-hu *Duhu* Kwangt.
115 C5 Tu-hu An-sha *Duhu Ansha* (shoal) China Sea
94 C2 T'u-huan-ts'un *Tuhuancun* Yun.
91 D5 Tu-i *Duyi* Kwei.
39 C4 Tui-chen *Duizhen* Shansi
71 B5 Tui-ch'ien *Duiqian* Kiangsi
11 D5 Tui-ch'ing-shan *Duiqingshan* Heilung.
26 D4 Tui-la-ma-miao *Duilamamiao* In. Mong.
Tui-lung-te-ch'ing *see* Lang-ka
111 D3 Tui-lung-te-ch'ing Hsien *Duilongdeqing Xian* Tibet
10 E4 Tui-mien Shan *Duimian Shan* (mt) Heilung.
15 H4 T'ui-po *Tuibo* Kirin
62 D3 Tui-tzu-liang *Duiziliang* Shensi
103 E1 Tu-je *Dure* Sink.
114 B2 Tu-jih-le-chi *Durileji* Ningsia
91 F2 Tu-ju *Duru* Kwei.
51 E4 Tu-kang *Dugang* Chek.
23 D5 T'u-ken-t'a-la-miao *Tugentalamiao* Liao.
31 B7 Tu-k'ou *Dukou* Hopeh
70 F3 Tu-k'ou *Dukou* Kiangsi
82 C2 Tu-k'ou *Dukou* Kwangsi
86 C4 Tu-k'ou *Dukou* Szech.
94 C2 Tu-k'ou *Dukou* Yun.
Tuktsitukar Tso *see* Ta-tse Ts'o
118 B3 T'u-k'u *Tuku* Taiwan
54 B3 Tu-kuan *Duguan* Honan
95 D3 T'u-kuan-chuang *Tuguanzhuang* Yun.
95 D3 T'u-kuan-ts'un *Tuguancun* Yun.
94 C4 Tu-kuei *Dugui* Yun.
26 C5 Tu-kuei-chia-han *Duguijiahan* In. Mong.
26 C4 Tu-kuei-t'e-la *Duguitela* In. Mong.
27 E4 T'u-kuei-wu-la *Tuguiwula* In. Mong.
114 C1 T'u-k'u-mu *Tukumu* Ningsia
103 D3 T'u-la *Tula* Sink.
Tu-lan *see* Ch'a-han-wu-su
119 C4 Tu-lan *Dulan* Taiwan
107 F2 Tu-lan Hsien *Dulan Xian* Tsing.
107 F2 Tu-lan-ssu *Dulansi* Tsing.
114 B2 T'u-lan-t'ai *Tulantai* Ningsia
91 D4 Tu-la-ying *Dulaying* Kwei.
102 C3 T'u-le-k'o-ch'i-k'u-le *Tulekeqikule* Sink.
14 A2 T'u-lieh-mao-tu *Tuliemaodu* Kirin
23 D5 T'u-lieh-mao-tu *Tuliemaodu* Kirin
22 D2 T'u-li-ho *Tulihe* Heilung.
30 D1 T'u-li-ken Ho *Tuligen He* (river) Hopeh
31 D5 Tu-lin *Dulin* Hopeh
54 C4 Tu-li-p'ing *Duliping* Honan
31 D4 Tu-liu *Duliu* Hopeh
46 C2 Tu-lou *Dulou* Anhwei
102 I2 T'u-lu-fan *Tulufan* Sink.
102 I2 T'u-lu-fan *Tulufan* Sink.
103 E2 T'u-lu-fan *Tulufan* Sink.
103 E2 T'u-lu-fan Chan *Tulufan Zhan* Sink.
11 F4 Tu-lu-ho *Duluhe* Heilung.
102 A2 T'u-lu-ka-erh-t'e Shan-k'ou *Tulugaerte Shankou* (pass) Sink.
95 E4 Tu-lung-hsin-chieh *Dulongxinjie* Yun.
103 E1 Tu-lung-ko-k'u-tu-k'o *Dulonggekuduke* Sink.
11 F4 T'u-lung-shan *Tulongshan* Heilung.
67 C6 Tu-mei *Dumei* Fukien
58 C1 T'u-men *Tumen* Hupeh
15 J5 T'u-men *Tumen* Kirin
63 F7 T'u-men *Tumen* Shensi
15 J5 T'u-men Chiang *Tumen Jiang* (river) Kirin
15 K5 T'u-men Chiang *Tumen Jiang* (river) Kirin
14 G3 T'u-men-ling *Tumenling* Kirin
30 G3 T'u-men-tzu *Tumenzi* Hopeh
99 F3 T'u-men-tzu *Tumenzi* Kansu
58 D4 T'u-men-ya *Tumenya* Hupeh
26 D4 Tumet East Banner In. Mong.
26 D4 Tumet West Banner In. Mong.
83 G3 Tu-mo *Dumo* Kwangsi
T'u-mo-t'e Tso-ch'i *see* Tumet East Banner
T'u-mo-t'e Yu-ch'i *see* Tumet West Banner
74 E4 Tu-mu-ch'iao *Dumuqiao* Hunan
27 E4 T'u-mu-erh-t'ai *Tumuertai* In. Mong.
11 G4 Tu-mu-ho *Dumuhe* Heilung.
102 B2 T'u-mu-hsiu-k'o *Tumuxiuke* Sink.
30 B2 T'u-mu-lu *Tumulu* Hopeh
78 B4 T'un-ch'ang *Tunchang* Kwangt.
47 E7 T'un-ch'i *Tunqi* Anhwei
90 C5 T'un-chiao *Tunjiao* Kwei.
83 F3 T'un-ch'iu *Tunqiu* Kwangsi
34 B3 Tung-a-chen *Dongazhen* Shant.
34 B3 Tung-a Hsien *Donga Xian* Shant.
47 E6 Tung-an *Dongan* Anhwei
11 H4 Tung-an *Dongan* Heilung.
67 D6 T'ung-an *Tongan* Fukien
70 B3 T'ung-an *Tongan* Kiangsi
83 G3 T'ung-an *Tongan* Kwangsi
86 D4 T'ung-an *Tongan* Szech.
43 F4 Tung-an-chen *Donganzhen* Kiangsu
75 D5 Tung-an Hsien *Dongan Xian* Hunan
75 D5 Tung-an Hsien *Dongan Xian* Hunan
99 G4 T'ung-an-i *Tonganyi* Kansu
118 C2 Tung-ao *Dongao* Taiwan
38 D3 Tung-chai *Dongzhai* Shansi
54 D5 T'ung-chai-p'u *Tongzhaipu* Honan
43 D3 Tung-ch'ang-chieh *Dongchangjie* Kiangsu
98 C1 T'ung-ch'ang-k'ou *Tongchangkou* Kansu
31 B5 Tung-ch'ang-shou *Dongchangshou* Hopeh
54 D3 Tung-chao-pao *Dongzhaobao* Honan
31 B6 Tung-chen *Dongzhen* Hopeh
99 F2 Tung-chen *Dongzhen* Kansu
43 E3 Tung-ch'en *Dongchen* Kiangsu
39 C6 Tung-chen *Dongzhen* Shansi
63 D7 Tung-chen-chieh *Dongzhenjie* Shensi
51 E4 Tung-cheng *Dongzheng* Chek.
30 B3 Tung-ch'eng *Dongcheng* Hopeh
102 I2 Tung-ch'eng *Dongcheng* Sink.
46 A3 T'ung-ch'eng *Tongcheng* Anhwei
46 E4 T'ung-ch'eng *Tongcheng* Anhwei
47 C5 T'ung-ch'eng *Tongcheng* Anhwei
59 F5 T'ung-ch'eng *Tongcheng* Hupeh
34 B3 T'ung-ch'eng *Tongcheng* Shant.
47 E5 T'ung-ch'eng-cha *Tongchengzha* Anhwei
58 D3 T'ung-ch'eng-ho *Tongchenghe* Hupeh
43 D1 Tung-chi *Dongji* Kiangsu
67 C7 Tung Ch'i *Dong Qi* (river) Fukien
67 D5 Tung Ch'i *Dong Qi* (river) Fukien
87 F3 Tung-ch'i *Dongqi* Szech.
70 C3 Tung-chia *Dongjia* Kiangsi
35 E3 Tung-chia *Dongjia* Shant.
70 E3 T'ung-chia *Tongjia* Kiangsi
30 C3 Tung-chia-fang *Dongjiafang* Hopeh
19 E5 Tung-chia-kou *Dongjiagou* Liao.
75 F6 Tung-chiang *Dongjiang* Hunan
82 E3 Tung-chiang *Dongjiang* Kwangsi
83 F2 Tung-chiang *Dongjiang* Kwangsi
79 D2 Tung Chiang *Dong Jiang* (river) Kwangt.
119 B4 Tung-chiang *Dongjiang* Taiwan
11 D4 T'ung-chiang *Tongjiang* Heilung.
11 G4 T'ung-chiang *Tongjiang* Heilung.
50 C3 T'ung-Chiang *Tong Jiang* (river) Chek.
87 F2 T'ung-chiang *Tongjiang* Szech.
63 D7 Tung-chiang-k'ou *Dongjiangkou* Shensi
19 G2 T'ung-chiang-k'ou *Tongjiangkou* Liao.
70 C2 T'ung-chiang-ling *Tongjiangling* Kiangsi
59 E3 Tung-ch'iao *Dongqiao* Hupeh
71 A4 Tung-ch'iao *Dongqiao* Kiangsi
43 D2 Tung-ch'iao *Dongqiao* Kiangsu
111 D3 Tung-ch'iao *Dongqiao* Tibet
14 D3 T'ung-chia-tien *Tongjiadian* Kirin
47 E6 Tung-chia-wan *Dongjiawan* Anhwei
87 F1 Tung-ch'i-chen *Dongqizhen* Szech.
54 D4 Tung-chieh *Dongjie* Honan
51 E3 Tung-ch'ien Hu *Dongqian Hu* (lake) Chek.
99 H4 Tung-chih *Dongzhi* Kansu
47 D6 Tung-chih Hsien *Dongzhi Xian* Anhwei
119 A3 Tung-chi Hsü *Dongji Xu* (island) Taiwan
38 E4 Tung-chih-t'ou *Dongzhitou* Shansi
11 D4 Tung-chin *Dongjin* Heilung.
83 F4 Tung-chin *Dongjin* Kwangsi
62 F2 T'ung-ch'in-chai *Tongqinzhai* Shensi
11 C4 Tung-ch'ing *Dongqing* Heilung.
119 C4 Tung-ch'ing *Dongqing* Taiwan
42 C4 T'ung-ching *Tongjing* Kiangsu
34 D4 T'ung-ching *Tongjing* Shant.
11 E5 Tung-ching-ch'eng *Dongjingcheng* Heilung.
30 B3 Tung-ching-chi *Dongjingji* Hopeh
114 B2 Tung-ch'ing-hu *Dongqinghu* Ningsia
19 G3 Tung-ching-ling *Dongjingling* Liao.
Tung-ching Wan *see* Gulf of Tongking

26
Yang-fang-lin – Yung-chia-wan

59 G5 Yang-fang-lin *Yangfanglin* Hupeh
42 C2 Yang-ho *Yanghe* Kiangsu
19 G4 Yang-ho *Yanghe* Liao.
114 C2 Yang-ho *Yanghe* Ningsia
30 C3 Yang Ho *Yang He* (river) Hopeh
58 D4 Yang-hsi *Yangxi* Hupeh
102 D2 Yang-hsia *Yangxia* Sink.
43 D4 Yang-hsiang *Yangxiang* Kiangsu
63 C7 Yang-hsien *Yangxian* Shensi
59 G5 Yang-hsin *Yangxin* Hupeh
59 H5 Yang-hsin *Yangxin* Hupeh
34 C2 Yang-hsin *Yangxin* Shant.
38 D3 Yang-hsing *Yangxing* Shansi
42 C2 Yang-hua *Yanghua* Kiangsu
90 B4 Yang-huai-shu *Yanghuaishu* Kwei.
46 C4 Yang-hu-chen *Yanghuzhen* Anhwei
31 A7 Yang-i *Yangyi* Hopeh
39 D4 Yang-i *Yangyi* Shansi
11 G5 Yang-kang *Yanggang* Heilung.
38 E1 Yang-kao *Yanggao* Shansi
Yangkiachangtze *see* Yang-chia-chang-tzu
Yangkiokow *see* Yang-chiao-kou
30 D3 Yang-ko-chuang *Yanggezhuang* Hopeh
66 C4 Yang-k'ou *Yangkou* Fukien
70 F3 Yang-k'ou *Yangkou* Kiangsi
50 B4 Yang-k'ou-shih *Yangkoushi* Chek.
55 F3 Yang-ku *Yanggu* Honan
34 A3 Yang-ku *Yanggu* Shant.
47 C5 Yang-kung-miao *Yanggongmiao* Anhwei
70 C3 Yang-kung-yü *Yanggongyu* Kiangsi
63 E6 Yang-kuo *Yangguo* Shensi
59 E5 Yang-lin *Yanglin* Hupeh
95 D3 Yang-lin *Yanglin* Yun.
74 E3 Yang-lin-chai *Yanglinzhai* Hunan
75 F4 Yang-lin-ch'iao *Yanglinqiao* Hunan
63 D6 Yang-ling *Yangling* Shensi
59 F4 Yang-lin-wei *Yanglinwei* Hupeh
91 E4 Yang-liu-chieh *Yangliujie* Kwei.
58 C4 Yang-liu-ch'ih *Yangliuchi* Hupeh
31 E4 Yang-liu-ch'ing *Yangliuqing* Hopeh
47 E6 Yang-liu-p'u *Yangliupu* Anhwei
34 B4 Yang-liu-tien *Yangliudian* Shant.
34 C3 Yang-liu-tien *Yangliudian* Shant.
59 G4 Yang-lo *Yangluo* Hupeh
46 C2 Yang-lou *Yanglou* Anhwei
34 B5 Yang-lou *Yanglou* Shant.
74 F2 Yang-lou-ssu *Yanglousi* Hunan
59 F5 Yang-lou-tung *Yangloudong* Hupeh
91 D3 Yang-lung-chan *Yanglongzhan* Kwei.
35 G2 Yang-ma Tao *Yangma Dao* (island) Shant.
83 G5 Yang-mei *Yangmei* Kwangsi
118 C2 Yang-mei *Yangmei* Taiwan
71 B6 Yang-mei-ssu *Yangmeisi* Kiangsi
55 F3 Yang-miao *Yangmiao* Honan
18 B3 Yang-mi Ho *Yangmi He* (river) Liao.
79 D1 Yang-ming *Yangming* Kwangt.
38 D2 Yang-ming-pao *Yangmingbao* Shansi
75 D5 Yang-ming Shan *Yangming Shan* (mt) Hunan
118 C1 Yang-ming-shan *Yangmingshan* Taiwan
11 G5 Yang-mu-kang *Yangmugang* Heilung.
14 F5 Yang-mu-lin *Yangmulin* Kirin
91 C6 Yang-pa *Yangba* Kwei.
111 D3 Yang-pa-ching *Yangbajing* Tibet
94 B3 Yang-pi *Yangbi* Yun.
54 B3 Yang-p'ing *Yangping* Honan
58 D3 Yang-p'ing *Yangping* Hupeh
91 F3 Yang-p'ing *Yangping* Kwei.
38 C3 Yang-p'ing *Yangping* Shansi
63 B8 Yang-p'ing-kuan *Yangpingguan* Shensi
38 D3 Yang-p'o *Yangpo* Shansi
51 C1 Yang-p'u *Yangpu* Chek.
55 F5 Yang-pu *Yangbu* Honan
78 A4 Yang-p'u Wan *Yangpu Wan* (bay) Kwangt.
67 D5 Yang-shan *Yangshan* Fukien
79 C1 Yang-shan *Yangshan* Kwangt.
18 D3 Yang-shan *Yangshan* Liao.
34 B4 Yang-shan *Yangshan* Shant.
26 D4 Yang-shan Shan-mo *Yangshan Shanmo* (mts) In. Mong.
54 C3 Yang-shao *Yangshao* (site) Honan
43 E4 Yang-she *Yangshe* Kiangsu
30 F2 Yang-shu-ling *Yangshuling* Hopeh
83 G3 Yang-shuo *Yangshuo* Kwangsi
Yangsin *see* Yang-hsin
Yangsiu *see* Yung-hsiu
14 E4 Yang-ta-ch'eng-tzu *Yangdachengzi* Kirin
23 F6 Yang-ta-ch'eng-tzu *Yangdachengzi* Kirin
102 C2 Yang-t'a-k'o-k'u-tu-k'o *Yangtakekuduke* Sink.
47 F6 Yang-t'an *Yangtan* Anhwei
39 C6 Yang-t'an *Yangtan* Shansi
59 E2 Yang-tang *Yangdang* Hupeh
27 F3 Yang-tao-su-mu *Yangdaosumu* In. Mong.
103 E3 Yang-ta-shih-k'o *Yangdashike* Sink.
91 D2 Yang-teng *Yangdeng* Kwei.
54 B3 Yang-tien *Yangdian* Honan
59 G3 Yang-tien *Yangdian* Hupeh
43 D4 Yang-tien *Yangdian* Kiangsu
30 F3 Yang-tien-tzu *Yangdianzi* Hopeh
46 D3 Yang-t'ing *Yangting* Anhwei
35 H2 Yang-t'ing *Yangting* Shant.
94 C3 Yang-t'ou-yen *Yangtouyan* Yun.
54 E5 Yang-ts'e *Yangce* Honan
110 B2 Yang Ts'o *Yangcuo* (lake) Tibet
30 E4 Yang-ts'un *Yangcun* Hopeh
31 C4 Yang-ts'un *Yangcun* Hopeh
70 E3 Yang-ts'un *Yangcun* Kiangsi
71 B7 Yang-ts'un *Yangcun* Kiangsi
79 D2 Yang-ts'un *Yangcun* Kwangt.
46 E4 Yang-ts'un-chen *Yangcunzhen* Anhwei
50 C3 Yang-ts'un-ch'iao *Yangcunqiao* Chek.
Yangtze *see* T'ung-t'ien Ho
Yangtze *see* Chin-sha Chiang
Yangtze *see* Ch'ang Chiang
Yangtze *see* Ch'ang Chiang
Yangtze *see* Ch'ang Chiang
Yangtze *see* Chin-sha Chiang
Yangtze *see* Ch'ang Chiang
Yangtze *see* Ch'ang Chiang
59 E3 Yang-tzu *Yangzi* Hupeh
70 D2 Yang-tzu-ch'iao *Yangziqiao* Kiangsi
14 D2 Yang-tzu-ching *Yangzijing* Kirin
14 G5 Yang-tzu-shao *Yangzishao* Kirin
58 C2 Yang-wei *Yangwei* Hupeh
95 D4 Yang-wu *Yangwu* Yun.
82 C4 Yang-yü *Yangyu* Kwangsi
82 E4 Yang-yü *Yangyu* Kwangsi
30 B3 Yang-yüan Hsien *Yangyuan Xian* Hopeh
30 B3 Yang-yüan Hsien *Yangyuan Xian* Hopeh
Yanping *see* En-p'ing
34 A3 Yan-tien *Yandian* Shant.
94 C3 Yao-an *Yaoan* Yun.
82 D3 Yao-chai *Yaozhai* Kwangsi
10 C2 Yao-chan *Yaozhan* Heilung.
62 F2 Yao-chen *Yaozhen* Shensi
31 B6 Yao-ch'eng *Yaocheng* Hopeh
59 G3 Yao-chia-chi *Yaojiaji* Hupeh
74 F4 Yao-chia-pa *Yaojiaba* Hunan
91 D4 Yao-chia-shao *Yaojiashao* Kwei.
34 D4 Yao-chia-tien-tzu *Yaojiadianzi* Shant.
99 F3 Yao-chieh *Yaojie* Kansu
14 D3 Yao-ching *Yaojing* Kirin
98 C2 Yao-ch'üan-tzu *Yaoquanzi* Kansu
47 C5 Yao-hsiao-chuang *Yaoxiaozhuang* Anhwei
10 D3 Yao-hsiao-ling *Yaoxiaoling* Heilung.
63 D6 Yao-hsien *Yaoxian* Shensi
75 F6 Yao-kang-hsien *Yaogangxian* Hunan
35 E3 Yao-ko-chuang *Yaogezhuang* Shant.
47 D5 Yao-kou *Yaogou* Anhwei
34 D3 Yao-kou *Yaogou* Shant.
46 C4 Yao-k'ou-chi *Yaokouji* Anhwei
79 C2 Yao-ku *Yaogu* Kwangt.
94 B3 Yao-kuan *Yaoguan* Yun.
31 D5 Yao-kuan-t'un *Yaoguantun* Hopeh
70 E2 Yao-li *Yaoli* Kiangsi
14 C3 Yao-li-mao-tu *Yaolimaodu* Kirin
23 E5 Yao-li-mao-tu *Yaolimaodu* Kirin
47 C5 Yao-li-miao *Yaolimiao* Anhwei
15 G6 Yao-lin *Yaolin* Kirin
79 C1 Yao-ling *Yaoling* Kwangt.
47 B5 Yao-ling-t'ou *Yaolingtou* Anhwei
47 C5 Yao-lo-p'ing *Yaoluoping* Anhwei
18 C4 Yao-lu-kou *Yaolugou* Liao.
23 E5 Yao-min-wang-t'un *Yaominwangtun* Kirin
114 C2 Yao-pa *Yaoba* Ningsia
19 F2 Yao-pao *Yaobao* Liao.
75 F5 Yao-p'o *Yaopo* Hunan
46 E4 Yao-p'u *Yaopu* Anhwei
43 E2 Yao Sha *Yao Sha* (shoal) Kiangsu
67 B5 Yao-shan *Yaoshan* Fukien
79 C1 Yao-Shan *Yaoshan* (mts) Kwangt.
114 C3 Yao-shan *Yaoshan* Ningsia
30 E3 Yao-shang *Yaoshang* Hopeh
75 B5 Yao-shang *Yaoshang* Hunan
75 F6 Yao-shang *Yaoshang* Hunan
74 B4 Yao-shih *Yaoshi* Hunan
99 H4 Yao-tien *Yaodian* Kansu
62 E4 Yao-tien-tzu *Yaodianzi* Shensi
102 I2 Yao-tien-tzu *Yaodianzi* Sink.
71 B5 Yao-t'ou *Yaotou* Kiangsi
38 C3 Yao-t'ou *Yaotou* Shansi
39 B5 Yao-t'ou *Yaotou* Shansi
47 F6 Yao-ts'un *Yaocun* Anhwei
55 E1 Yao-ts'un *Yaocun* Honan
31 C4 Yao-ts'un *Yaocun* Hopeh
34 B4 Yao-ts'un *Yaocun* Shant.
47 D6 Yao-tu *Yaodu* Anhwei
10 D3 Yao-t'un *Yaotun* Heilung.
62 D4 Yao-tzu-ch'uan *Yaozichuan* Shensi
38 D2 Yao-tzu-t'ou *Yaozitou* Shansi
26 C4 Yao-tzu-wan *Yaoziwan* In. Mong.
42 C1 Yao-wan *Yaowan* Kiangsu
14 C2 Yao-yen *Yaoyan* Kirin
23 E5 Yao-yen *Yaoyan* Kirin
70 C4 Yao-yü *Yaoyu* Kiangsi
99 F2 Ya-pu-lai *Yabulai* Kansu
99 F2 Ya-pu-lai Shan *Yabulai Shan* (mts) Kansu
99 F2 Ya-pu-lai-yen-ch'ih *Yabulaiyanchi* Kansu
11 E5 Ya-pu-li *Yabuli* Heilung.
Yarkand *see* So-ch'e
Yarkand Darya *see* Yeh-erh-ch'iang Ho
47 E6 Ya-shan *Yashan* Anhwei
106 D2 Ya-sha-t'u *Yashatu* Tsing.
Yashil Tso *see* Ya-hsieh Ts'o
47 C6 Ya-t'an *Yatan* Anhwei
35 H2 Ya-t'ou *Yatou* Shant.
10 B3 Ya-tung *Yadong* Heilung.
22 E3 Ya-tung *Yadong* Heilung.
110 D4 Ya-tung *Yadong* Tibet
102 C3 Ya-t'ung-ku-tzu-lan-kan *Yatongguzilangan* Sink.
75 B5 Ya-t'un-pao *Yatunbao* Hunan
35 G2 Ya-tzu *Yazi* Shant.
74 E3 Ya-tzu-kang *Yazigang* Hunan
86 B2 Ya-wa *Yawa* Szech.
34 C3 Ya-wang-k'ou *Yawangkou* Shant.
106 C4 Ya-yün Ch'ü *Yayun Qu* (river) Tsing.
102 B3 Yeh-ch'eng *Yecheng* Sink.
30 F4 Yeh-chi-t'o *Yejituo* Hopeh
102 B3 Yeh-erh-ch'iang Ho *Yeerqiang He* (river) Sink.
54 E4 Yeh-hsien *Yexian* Honan
35 E2 Yeh-hsien *Yexian* Shant.
102 C3 Yeh-i-k'o *Yeyike* Sink.
111 E3 Yeh-kung *Yegong* Tibet
111 E3 Yeh-kung Ch'ü *Yegongqu* (river) Tibet
14 A5 Yeh-la-ma-t'u *Yelamatu* Kirin
23 D6 Yeh-la-ma-t'u *Yelamatu* Kirin
99 F4 Yeh-li-kuan *Yeliguan* Kansu
118 C1 Yeh-liu Chia *Yeliu Jia* (point) Taiwan
106 C3 Yeh-lu-su Hu *Yelusu Hu* (lake) Tsing.
90 B3 Yeh-ma-ch'uan *Yemachuan* Kwei.
98 C2 Yeh-ma Ho *Yema He* (river) Kansu
98 B2 Yeh-ma Nan-shan *Yema Nanshan* (mts) Kansu
19 F2 Yeh-mao-t'ai *Yemaotai* Liao.
105 E3 Yeh-ma-t'an *Yematan* Tsing.
107 F2 Yeh-ma-t'an *Yematan* Tsing.
14 B2 Yeh-ma-t'u *Yematu* Kirin
23 D5 Yeh-ma-t'u *Yematu* Kirin
106 B2 Yeh-men-k'o *Yemenke* Tsing.
107 E3 Yeh-niu-kou *Yeniugou* Tsing.
107 F1 Yeh-niu-kou *Yeniugou* Tsing.
18 C3 Yeh-pai-shou *Yebaishou* Liao.
71 D6 Yeh-p'ing *Yeping* Kiangsi
Yehposhow *see* Yeh-pai-shou
58 C4 Yeh-san-kuan *Yesanguan* Hupeh
106 D4 Yeh-ta Ch'ü *Yeda Qu* (river) Tsing.
31 B6 Yeh-ts'ao-wan *Yecaowan* Hopeh
63 F7 Yeh-ts'un *Yecun* Shensi
119 C4 Yeh-yu *Yeyou* Taiwan
102 D2 Yeh-yün-kou *Yeyungou* Sink.
Yellow River *see* Huang Ho
Yellow River *see* Huang Ho
35 G4 Yellow Sea Shant.
62 E4 Yen-an *Yanan* Shensi
62 E4 Yen-an Hsien *Yanan Xian* Shensi
39 D5 Yen-chai *Yanzhai* Shansi
39 C6 Yen-chang *Yanzhang* Shansi
62 F4 Yen-ch'ang *Yanchang* Shensi
62 C3 Yen-ch'ang-pao *Yanchangbao* Shensi
31 B5 Yen-chao *Yanzhao* Hopeh
119 B4 Yen-ch'ao *Yanchao* Taiwan
55 E4 Yen-ch'eng *Yancheng* Honan
43 E2 Yen-ch'eng *Yancheng* Kiangsu
34 B3 Yen-ch'eng *Yancheng* Shant.
67 C6 Yen-ch'i *Yanqi* Fukien
30 C3 Yen-ch'i *Yanqi* Hopeh
74 C3 Yen-ch'i *Yanqi* Hunan
70 C4 Yen-ch'i *Yanqi* Kiangsi
42 C1 Yen-chi *Yanji* Kiangsu
15 J5 Yen-chi *Yanji* Kirin
103 D2 Yen-ch'i *Yanqi* Sink.
18 E3 Yen-chia *Yanjia* Liao.
11 F4 Yen-chia *Yenjia* Heilung.
55 F6 Yen-chia-ho *Yanjiahe* Honan
63 B6 Yen-chia-ho *Yanjiahe* Shensi
82 D4 Yen-chiang *Yanjiang* Kwangsi
74 B4 Yen-ch'iao *Yanqiao* Hunan
90 C4 Yen-chiao *Yanjiao* Kwei.
66 C4 Yen-ch'ien *Yanqian* Fukien
67 B6 Yen-ch'ien *Yenqian* Fukien
114 D3 Yen-ch'ih *Yanchi* Ningsia
103 F2 Yen-ch'ih *Yanchi* Sink.
98 E2 Yen-chih Shan *Yanzhi Shan* (mt) Kansu
15 J5 Yen-chi Hsien *Yanji Xian* Kirin
Yen-ch'i Hui-tsu Tzu-chih-hsien *see* Yen-ch'i Hui Autonomous Hsien
98 B2 Yen-ch'ih-wan *Yanchiwan* Kansu
27 H2 Yen-chi-ko-miao *Yanjigemiao* In. Mong.
55 F2 Yen-chin *Yanjin* Honan
95 E1 Yen-chin *Yanjin* Yun.
30 C3 Yen-ch'ing *Yanqing* Hopeh
39 B6 Yen-ching *Yanjing* Shansi
87 F3 Yen-ching *Yanjing* Szech.
111 F3 Yen-ching *Yanjing* Tibet
71 B5 Yen-ch'i-tu *Yanqidu* Kiangsi
54 D3 Yen-ch'iu *Yanqiu* Honan
55 F2 Yen-chou *Yanzhou* Honan
34 B4 Yen-chou *Yanzhou* Shant.
Yenchow *see* Chien-te
62 F4 Yen-ch'uan *Yanchuan* Shensi
38 D3 Yen-chuang *Yanzhuang* Shansi
34 C3 Yen-chuang *Yanzhuang* Shant.
Yenchwan *see* Yen-ch'uan
38 E2 Yen-erh-yai *Yanerya* Shansi
95 E3 Yen-fang *Yanfang* Yun.
94 C3 Yen-feng *Yanfeng* Yun.
59 H3 Yen-ho *Yanhe* Hupeh
91 F2 Yen-ho *Yanhe* Kwei.
43 D2 Yen Ho *Yan He* (river) Kiangsu
62 F4 Yen Ho *Yan He* (river) Shensi
30 C3 Yen-ho-ch'eng *Yanhecheng* Hopeh
62 E4 Yen-ho-wan *Yanhewan* Shensi
30 G3 Yen-ho-ying *Yanheying* Hopeh
10 F4 Yen-hsing *Yanxing* Heilung.
102 I2 Yen-hu *Yanhu* Sink.
103 E2 Yen-hu *Yanhu* Sink.
106 D2 Yen-hu *Yanhu* Tsing.
38 E4 Yen-hui *Yanhui* Shansi
Yenki *see* Yen-chi
30 F4 Yen-ko-chuang *Yangezhuang* Hopeh
46 C4 Yen-k'ou *Yankou* Anhwei
43 D4 Yen-k'ou *Yankou* Kiangsu
51 D2 Yen-kuan *Yanguan* Chek.
99 G4 Yen-kuan *Yanguan* Kansu
83 G2 Yen-kuan-hsiang *Yanguanxiang* Kwangsi
47 E6 Yen-kung-t'ang *Yangongtang* Anhwei
82 D4 Yen-li *Yanli* Kwangsi
39 D6 Yen-li *Yanli* Shansi
63 E6 Yen-liang *Yanliang* Shensi
55 F3 Yen-ling *Yanling* Honan
43 D4 Yen-ling *Yanling* Kiangsu
47 C4 Yen-liu-miao *Yenliumiao* Anhwei
30 B4 Yen-mei-tung *Yenmeidong* Hopeh
74 B4 Yen-men *Yanmen* Hunan
87 E1 Yen-men-pa *Yanmenba* Szech.
38 E2 Yen-pei *Yanbei* Shansi
38 E1 Yen-pei Ti-ch'ü *Yanbei Diqu* Shansi
86 C4 Yen-pien *Yanbian* Szech.
Yen-pien Ch'ao-hsien-tsu Tzu-chih-chou *see* Yen-pien Korean Autonomous District
15 J4 Yen-pien Korean Autonomous District Kirin
119 C4 Yen-p'ing *Yanping* Taiwan
75 E4 Yen-p'o-ch'iao *Yanpoqiao* Hunan
74 C2 Yen-p'o-tu *Yanpodu* Hunan
119 B4 Yen-pu *Yanbu* Taiwan
59 H5 Yen-pu-t'ou *Yanbutou* Hupeh
59 G5 Yen-sha *Yansha* Hupeh
66 C3 Yen-shan *Yanshan* Fukien
22 D3 Yen-shan *Yanshan* Heilung.
31 E5 Yen-shan *Yanshan* Hopeh
83 G2 Yen-shan *Yanshan* Kwangsi
91 E4 Yen-shan *Yanshan* Kwei.
95 E4 Yen-shan *Yanshan* Yun.
54 D3 Yen-shih *Yanshi* Honan
106 C4 Yen-shih-p'ing *Yanshiping* Tsing.
11 E5 Yen-shou *Yanshou* Heilung.
75 F6 Yen-shou *Yanshou* Hunan
119 B3 Yen-shui *Yanshui* Taiwan
39 B5 Yen-shui-kuan *Yanshuiguan* Shansi
62 F4 Yen-shui-kuan *Yanshuiguan* Shensi
47 E7 Yen-ssu *Yensi* Anhwei
35 G2 Yen-t'ai* *Yantai* Shant.
51 D4 Yen-t'an *Yantan* Chek.
74 D4 Yen-t'ang *Yantang* Hunan
75 F5 Yen-t'ang *Yantang* Hunan
51 D4 Yen-tang Shan *Yandang Shan* (mts) Chek.
14 C3 Yen-teng-t'u *Yandengtu* Kirin
23 E5 Yen-teng-t'u *Yandengtu* Kirin
66 E4 Yen-t'ien *Yantian* Fukien
26 D5 Yen-tien *Yandian* In. Mong.
71 B4 Yen-t'ien *Yantian* Kiangsi
87 E2 Yen-t'ing *Yanting* Szech.
111 F3 Yen-to *Yanduo* Tibet
51 D4 Yen-t'ou *Yantou* Chek.
38 E2 Yen-t'ou *Yantou* Shansi
58 C3 Yen-tu-ho *Yenduhe* Hupeh
11 C4 Yen-t'un *Yantun* Heilung.
78 B4 Yen-tun *Yandun* Kwangt.
103 F2 Yen-tun *Yandun* Sink.
59 E4 Yen-tun-chi *Yandunji* Hupeh
82 C4 Yen-t'ung *Yantong* Kwangsi
82 D3 Yen-tung *Yandong* Kwangsi
14 G4 Yen-t'ung-shan *Yantongshan* Kirin
30 C3 Yen-t'ung Shan *Yantong Shan* (mts) Hopeh
11 C4 Yen-t'ung-t'un *Yantongtun* Heilung.
47 E6 Yen-tun-p'u *Yandunpu* Anhwei
42 C3 Yen-tzu-fan *Yanzifan* Kiangsu
90 C3 Yen-tzu-k'ou *Yanzikou* Kwei.
63 B8 Yen-tzu-pien *Yanzibian* Shensi
59 G4 Yen-tzu-wo *Yanziwo* Hupeh
94 B2 Yen-wa *Yanwa* Yun.
43 D1 Yen-wei-kang *Yanweigang* Kiangsu
39 C4 Yen-wu *Yanwu* Shansi
91 G3 Yen-wu-p'ing *Yanwuping* Kwei.
62 D5 Yen-yao-pien *Yanyaobian* Shensi
86 C4 Yen-yüan *Yanyuan* Szech.
Yen-yüan I-tsu Tzu-chih-hsien *see* Yen-yüan Yi Autonomous Hsien
86 C4 Yen-yüan Yi Autonomous Hsien *Yanyuan Yi* Szech.
Yeungchun *see* Yang-ch'un
Yeungkong *see* Yang-chiang
Yigrong Chu *see* Yek-kung Ch'ü
22 E2 Yin-a *Yina* Heilung.
82 D4 Yin-ch'a *Yincha* Kwangsi
79 C2 Yin-chan-yao *Yinzhanyao* Kwangt.
39 E6 Yin-ch'eng *Yincheng* Shansi
46 D3 Yin-chi *Yinji* Anhwei
34 B3 Yin-chi *Yinji* Shant.
47 D6 Yin-chia-hui *Yinjiahui* Anhwei
91 F2 Yin-chiang *Yinjiang* Kwei.
67 E5 Yin-ch'ien *Yinqian* Fukien
114 C2 Yin-ch'uan *Yinchuan* Ningsia
Yin-ch'uan - city plan *see* Page 136
Yinchwan *see* Yin-ch'uan
10 C3 Ying-ch'en *Yingchen* Heilung.
59 F4 Ying-ch'eng *Yingcheng* Hupeh
14 F3 Ying-ch'eng *Yingcheng* Kirin
14 F4 Ying-ch'eng-tzu *Yingchengzi* Kirin
18 E6 Ying-ch'eng-tzu *Yingchengzi* Liao.
19 H2 Ying-ch'eng-tzu *Yingchengzi* Liao.
83 H3 Ying-chia *Yingjia* Kwangsi
70 F3 Ying-chia-k'ou *Yingjiakou* Kiangsi
94 A3 Ying-chiang *Yingjiang* Yun.
55 E4 Ying-ch'iao *Yingqiao* Honan
71 B6 Ying-ch'ien *Yingqian* Kiangsi
86 D3 Ying-ching *Yingjing* Szech.
18 C2 Ying-chin Ho *Yingjin He* (river) Liao.
102 B3 Ying-chi-sha *Yingjisha* Sink.
Yingchow *see* Fu-yang
55 F2 Ying-chü *Yingju* Honan
50 C5 Ying-ch'uan *Yingchuan* Chek.
11 G4 Ying-ch'un *Yingchun* Heilung.
35 F3 Ying-fang *Yingfang* Shant.
74 E3 Ying-feng-ch'iao *Yingfengqiao* Hunan
54 C3 Ying-hao *Yinghao* Honan
46 C4 Ying-ho *Yinghe* Anhwei
46 B3 Ying Ho *Ying He* (river) Anhwei
38 E2 Ying-hsien *Yingxian* Shansi
14 D2 Ying-hua *Yinghua* Kirin
Yingkisha *see* Ying-chi-sha
118 C2 Ying-ko *Yingge* Taiwan
19 F4 Ying-k'ou *Yingkou* Liao.
19 F4 Ying-k'ou Hsien *Yingkou Xian* Liao.
Yingkow *see* Ying-k'ou
31 A5 Ying-li *Yingli* Hopeh
19 G5 Ying-na Ho *Yingna He* (river) Liao.
19 I2 Ying-o-men *Yingemen* Liao.
14 F6 Ying-o-pu *Yingebu* Kirin
83 F6 Ying-p'an *Yingpan* Kwangsi
19 H3 Ying-p'an *Yingpan* Liao.
94 B3 Ying-p'an *Yingpan* Yun.
63 E7 Ying-p'an-chieh *Yingpanjie* Shensi
94 B3 Ying-p'an-chieh *Yingpanjie* Yun.
114 B3 Ying-p'an-shui *Yingpanshui* Ningsia
59 F3 Ying-shan *Yingshan* Hupeh
59 H4 Ying-shan *Yingshan* Hupeh
87 F2 Ying-shan *Yingshan* Szech.
46 C4 Ying-shang *Yingshang* Anhwei
66 B4 Ying-shang *Yingshang* Fukien
35 F3 Ying-shang *Yingshang* Shant.
67 C5 Ying-shih *Yingshi* Fukien
67 C5 Ying-shih Ch'i *Yingshi Qi* (river) Fukien
30 E3 Ying-shou-ying-tzu *Yingshouyingzi* Hopeh
103 D2 Ying-su *Yingsu* Sink.
70 E3 Ying-t'an *Yingtan* Kiangsi
55 G2 Ying-t'ao-yüan *Yingtaoyuan* Honan
79 C1 Ying-te *Yingde* Kwangt.
74 E3 Ying-t'ien *Yingtian* Hunan
102 D2 Ying-t'ou-lai *Yingtoulai* Sink.
67 D6 Ying-tu *Yingdu* Fukien
62 E4 Ying-wang *Yingwang* Shensi
91 F2 Ying-wu-hsi *Yingwuxi* Kwei.
54 D3 Ying-yang *Yingyang* Honan
83 H3 Ying-yang Kuan *Yingyang Guan* (pass) Kwangsi
26 D4 Yin-hao *Yinhao* In. Mong.
10 B3 Yin Ho *Yin He* (river) Heilung.
63 E6 Yin-ho-hui *Yinhehui* Shensi
34 C2 Yin-hsiang *Yinxiang* Shant.
Yin-hsien *see* Ning-po
51 E3 Yin Hsien *Yin Xian* Chek.
46 C4 Yin-hsien-chi *Yinxianji* Anhwei
55 F1 Yin-hsü *Yinxu* (site) Honan
114 B1 Yin-ken *Yingen* Ningsia
71 C5 Yin-k'eng *Yinkeng* Kiangsi
34 A4 Yin-ma *Yinma* Shant.
98 C1 Yin-ma-ch'ang *Yinmachang* Kansu
14 F4 Yin-ma Ho *Yinma He* (river) Kirin
95 D2 Yin-min *Yinmin* Yun.
83 H4 Yin-nan *Yinnan* Kwangsi
42 C1 Yin-p'ing *Yinping* Kiangsu
87 E3 Yin-shan-chen *Yinshanzhen* Szech.
11 B4 Yin-te-erh *Yindeer* Heilung.
23 E4 Yin-te-erh *Yindeer* Heilung.
90 C3 Yin-ti *Yindi* Kwei.
75 E5 Yin-t'ien *Yintian* Hunan
59 F2 Yin-tien *Yindian* Hupeh
74 E4 Yin-t'ien-ssu *Yintiansi* Hunan
102 B4 Yin-ti-la-k'o-li Shan-k'ou *Yindilakeli Shankou* Sink.
59 G5 Yin-tsu *Yinzu* Hupeh
31 B6 Yin-ts'un *Yincun* Hopeh
35 H2 Yin-tzu-k'uang *Yinzikuang* Shant.
43 F4 Yin-yang *Yinyang* Kiangsu
38 E4 Yin-ying *Yinying* Shansi
Yisa *see* Hung-ho
Yitang *see* I-t'ang
Yitu *see* I-tu
Yiyang *see* I-yang
Yotsing *see* Lo-ch'ing
Yoyang *see* Yüeh-yang
58 D3 Yüan-an *Yuanan* Hupeh
118 B3 Yüan-ch'ang *Yuanchang* Taiwan
63 D7 Yüan-chia-chuang *Yuanjiazhuang* Shensi
46 B3 Yüan-ch'iang *Yuanqiang* Anhwei
74 E3 Yüan-chiang *Yuanjiang* Hunan
74 C3 Yüan Chiang *Yuan Jiang* (river) Hunan
94 D4 Yüan Chiang *Yuan Jiang* (river) Yun.
94 C4 Yüan-chiang *Yuanjiang* Yun.
51 E4 Yüan-ch'iao *Yuanqiao* Chek.
38 C3 Yüan-chia-ts'un *Yuanjiacun* Shansi
70 B3 Yüan-ch'ien *Yuanqian* Kiangsi
34 D3 Yüan-ch'üan *Yuanquan* Shant.
39 C6 Yüan-ch'ü Hsien *Yuanqu Xian* Shansi
55 F3 Yüan-fang *Yuanfang* Honan
91 C2 Yüan-hou *Yuanhou* Kwei.
55 G3 Yüan-hsiang *Yuanxiang* Honan
38 D4 Yüan-hsiang *Yuanxiang* Shansi
59 I5 Yüan Hu *Yuan Hu* (lake) Hupeh
87 F2 Yüan-i *Yuanyi* Szech.
66 C4 Yüan-k'eng *Yuankeng* Fukien
35 G2 Yüan-ko-chuang *Yuangezhuang* Shant.
91 G4 Yüan-k'ou *Yuankou* Kwei.
63 D8 Yüan-k'ou *Yuankou* Shensi
118 B2 Yüan-li *Yuanli* Taiwan
19 F3 Yüan-liang-tien *Yuanliangdian* Liao.
22 D3 Yüan-lin *Yuanlin* Heilung.
118 B3 Yüan-lin *Yuanlin* Taiwan
74 C3 Yüan-ling *Yuanling* Hunan
94 C3 Yüan-mou *Yuanmou* Yun.
63 B8 Yüan-pa *Yuanba* Shensi
11 E5 Yüan-pao *Yuanbao* Heilung.
18 C2 Yüan-pao-shan *Yuanbaoshan* Liao.
83 F2 Yüan-pao Shan *Yuanbao Shan* (mt) Kwangsi
26 C4 Yüan-pao-wan *Yuanbaowan* In. Mong.
38 D3 Yüan-p'ing *Yuanping* Shansi
87 E2 Yüan-shan *Yuanshan* Szech.
118 C2 Yüan-shan *Yuanshan* Taiwan
98 D2 Yüan-shan-tzu *Yuanshanzi* Kansu
31 B6 Yüan-shih *Yuanshi* Hopeh
70 B4 Yüan Shui *Yuan Shui* (river) Kiangsi
47 C6 Yüan-t'an *Yuantan* Anhwei
54 D5 Yüan-t'an *Yuantan* Honan
74 F2 Yüan-t'an *Yuantan* Hunan
79 C2 Yüan-t'an *Yuantan* Kwangt.
91 D2 Yüan-t'ien *Yuantian* Kwei.
31 B6 Yüan-t'ou *Yuantou* Hopeh
83 G3 Yüan-tou *Yuandou* Kwangsi
55 G1 Yüan-ts'un *Yuancun* Honan
99 F3 Yüan-tun *Yuandun* Kansu
38 D2 Yüan-tzu Ho *Yuanzi He* (river) Shansi
55 E2 Yüan-wu *Yuanwu* Honan
54 D3 Yüan-ya *Yuanya* Honan
55 E2 Yüan-yang *Yuanyang* Honan
95 D4 Yüan-yang *Yuanyang* Yun.
99 G4 Yüan-yang-chen *Yuanyangzhen* Kansu
94 C3 Yüan-yung-ching *Yuanyongjing* Yun.
Yüanyungtsing *see* Yüan-yung-ching
50 C5 Yü-chang *Yuzhang* Chek.
90 C5 Yü-chang *Yuzhang* Kwei.
55 F3 Yü-chen *Yuzhen* Honan
70 D2 Yu-ch'eng *Youcheng* Kiangsi
43 D1 Yü-ch'eng *Yucheng* Kiangsu
34 B3 Yü-ch'eng *Yucheng* Shant.
34 B5 Yü-ch'eng *Yucheng* Shant.
55 G3 Yü-ch'eng Hsien *Yucheng Xian* Honan
46 D3 Yu-chi *Youji* Anhwei
51 E4 Yu-ch'i *Youqi* Chek.
67 D4 Yu-ch'i *Youqi* Fukien
74 D4 Yu-ch'i *Youqi* Hunan
67 D4 Yu Ch'i *You Qi* (river) Fukien
87 F3 Yu-ch'i *Youqi* Szech.
67 E5 Yü-ch'i *Yuqi* Fukien
31 D6 Yü-chi *Yuji* Hopeh
58 D4 Yü-ch'i *Yuqi* Hupeh
43 E4 Yü-ch'i *Yuqi* Kiangsu
91 E2 Yü-ch'i *Yuqi* Kwei.
34 B3 Yü-chi *Yuji* Shant.
95 D3 Yü-ch'i *Yuqi* Yun.
70 D4 Yu-chia *Youjia* Kiangsi
70 D3 Yü-chia *Yujia* Kiangsi
74 C2 Yü-chia-ch'i *Yujiaqi* Hunan
47 C6 Yü-chia-ching *Yujiajing* Anhwei
70 D2 Yü-chia-i *Yujiayi* Kiangsi
82 D4 Yu Chiang *You Jiang* (river) Kwangsi
83 F5 Yü Chiang *Yu Jiang* (river) Kwangsi
70 D3 Yü-chiang Hsien *Yujiang Xian* Kiangsi
70 D4 Yu-chia-pien *Youjiabian* Kiangsi
59 E4 Yü-chia-pu *Yujiabu* Hupeh
15 G3 Yu-chia-t'un *Youjiatun* Kirin
74 D4 Yu-chia-wan *Youjiawan* Hunan
87 F2 Yu-ch'i-chen *Youqizhen* Szech.
118 B3 Yü-ch'ih *Yuchi* Taiwan
66 D4 Yu-ch'i-k'ou *Youqikou* Fukien
47 E5 Yü-ch'i-k'ou *Yuqikou* Anhwei
63 E6 Yü-chin-chen *Yujinzhen* Shensi
38 D2 Yü-ching *Yujing* Shansi
119 B3 Yü-ching *Yujing* Taiwan
91 E3 Yü-ch'ing Hsien *Yuqing Xian* Kwei.
70 B3 Yu-chü *Youju* Kiangsi
11 D5 Yü-ch'üan *Yuquan* Heilung.
38 D3 Yü-chuang *Yuzhuang* Shansi
91 E3 Yu-ch'üan-pa *Youquanba* Kwei.
58 D4 Yü-ch'üan-ssu *Yuquansi* Hupeh
106 B1 Yu-ch'üan-tzu *Youquanzi* Tsing.
99 G4 Yü-chung *Yuzhong* Kansu
86 C2 Yüeh-cha *Yuezha* Szech.
46 C4 Yüeh-chang-chi *Yuezhangji* Anhwei
55 F5 Yüeh-ch'eng *Yuecheng* Honan
31 B7 Yüeh-ch'eng *Yuecheng* Hopeh
79 C2 Yüeh-ch'eng *Yuecheng* Kwangt.
83 G1 Yüeh-ch'eng Ling *Yuecheng Ling* (mts) Kwangsi
30 F4 Yüeh-chih *Yuezhi* Hopeh
87 F2 Yüeh-ch'ih *Yuechi* Szech.
102 H1 Yüeh-chih-hsin-ts'un *Yuezhixincun* Sink.
102 H1 Yueh-chin Shui-k'u *Yuejin Shuiku* (res.) Sink.
Yüeh-chi-t'ai Ts'o *see* I-chi-t'ai Ts'o
110 D3 Yüeh-chu *Yuezhu* Tibet
34 D3 Yüeh-chuang *Yuezhuang* Shant.
103 F2 Yüeh-fei-ch'üan *Yuefeiquan* Sink.
55 E5 Yüeh-ho-tien *Yuehedian* Honan
86 D3 Yüeh-hsi *Yuexi* Szech.
47 C6 Yüeh-hsi Hsien *Yuexi Xian* Anhwei
Yüeh Kiang *see* Chu Chiang
59 F4 Yüeh-k'ou *Yuekou* Hupeh
70 D4 Yüeh-k'ou *Yuekou* Kiangsi
11 F4 Yüeh-lai *Yuelai* Heilung.
87 G2 Yüeh-lai *Yuelai* Szech.
87 F3 Yüeh-lai-ch'ang *Yuelaichang* Szech.
99 H3 Yüeh-le *Yuehle* Kansu
82 D2 Yüeh-li *Yueli* Kwangsi
14 D2 Yüeh-liang P'ao *Yueliangpao* (lake) Kirin
23 E5 Yüeh-liang P'ao *Yueliang Pao* (lake) Kirin
74 F3 Yüeh-lung-shih *Yuelongshi* Hunan
74 E3 Yüeh-lu Shan *Yuelu Shan* (mt) Hunan
106 B2 Yüeh-po-k'a-li-k'o *Yuebokalike* Tsing.
102 B3 Yüeh-p'u-hu *Yuepuhu* Sink.
47 C6 Yüeh-shan *Yueshan* Anhwei
74 E4 Yüeh-shan *Yueshan* Hunan
74 F2 Yüeh-t'ien *Yuetian* Hunan
71 C7 Yüeh-tzu *Yuezi* Kiangsi
114 C2 Yüeh-ya-hu *Yueyahu* Ningsia
74 F2 Yüeh-yang *Yueyang* Hunan
39 C5 Yüeh-yang *Yueyang* Shansi
Yüen King *see* Red River
30 F3 Yü-erh-yai *Yueryai* Hopeh
30 D4 Yü-fa *Yufa* Hopeh
31 C6 Yu-fang *Youfang* Hopeh
43 D3 Yu-fang *Youfang* Kiangsu
38 D2 Yu-fang *Youfang* Shansi
63 B6 Yu-fang-kou *Youfanggou* Shensi
63 E5 Yu-fang-t'ai *Youfangtai* Shensi
66 C4 Yü-fang-wei *Yufangwei* Fukien
82 D4 Yü-feng *Yufeng* Kwangsi
118 C2 Yü-feng *Yufeng* Taiwan
51 D2 Yü-hang Hsien *Yuhang Xian* Chek.
10 E4 Yu-hao *Youhao* Heilung.
87 F2 Yu-ho *Youhe* Szech.
55 E2 Yü-ho *Yuhe* Honan
38 E1 Yü Ho *Yu He* (river) Shansi
62 E3 Yü-ho-pao *Yuehebao* Shensi
Yü-hsi *see* Yü-ch'i
43 F3 Yü-hsi *Yuxi* Kiangsu
63 D6 Yü-hsia *Yuxia* Shensi
95 E3 Yü-hsia *Yuxia* Yun.
58 C4 Yü-hsia-k'ou *Yuxiakou* Hupeh
39 B7 Yü-hsiang *Yuxiang* Shansi
34 C2 Yü-hsiang *Yuxiang* Shant.
75 F4 Yu-hsien *Youxian* Hunan
54 E3 Yü-hsien *Yuxian* Honan
30 B4 Yü-hsien *Yuxian* Hopeh
38 E3 Yü-hsien *Yuxian* Shansi
59 F4 Yü-hsin *Yuxin* Hupeh
51 D5 Yü-hu *Yuhu* Chek.
43 E2 Yü-hua *Yuhua* Kiangsu
51 E4 Yü-huan Hsien *Yuhuan Xian* Chek.
51 E4 Yü-huan Tao *Yuhuan Dao* (island) Chek.
11 F4 Yu-i *Youyi* Heilung.
70 D3 Yü-i *Yuyi* Kiangsi
82 C6 Yu-i-kuan *Youyiguan* Kwangsi
106 D1 Yü-k'a *Yuka* Tsing.
106 D1 Yü-k'a Ho *Yuka He* (river) Tsing.
70 D3 Yü-kan *Yugan* Kiangsi
14 D2 Yu-kan-nao *Yougannao* Kirin
107 G3 Yu-kan-t'an *Yongantan* Tsing.
79 D1 Yü-k'eng *Yukeng* Kwangt.
Yüki *see* Yü-ch'i
Yü Kiang *see* Yü Chiang
Yükikow *see* Yü-ch'i-k'ou
31 C6 Yü-k'o *Yuke* Hopeh
86 C2 Yü-k'o *Yuke* Szech.
46 D3 Yü-kou *Yugou* Anhwei
30 E3 Yü-k'ou *Yukou* Hopeh
42 C2 Yü-kou *Yugou* Kiangsu
38 C4 Yü-k'ou *Yukou* Shansi
30 G4 Yü-kuan *Yuguan* Hopeh
11 F4 Yü-kung *Yugong* Heilung.
19 G3 Yü-kuo *Yuguo* Liao.
70 D3 Yu-lan *Youlan* Kiangsi
83 F3 Yu-lan *Youlan* Kwangsi
110 C2 Yu-lang-lo-p'u-chiang-ssu *Youlangluopujiangsi* Tibet
78 B2 Yü-lao *Yulao* Kwangt.
35 G2 Yü-li *Yuli* Shant.
103 D2 Yü-li *Yuli* Sink.
119 C3 Yü-li *Yuli* Taiwan
14 B4 Yü-liang-pao *Yuliangbao* Kirin
23 D6 Yü-liang-pao *Yuliangbao* Kirin
23 D6 Yü-liang-p'u *Yuliangpu* Kirin
35 D2 Yu-lin *Youlin* Shant.
22 D3 Yü-lin *Yulin* Heilung.
83 G5 Yü-lin *Yulin* Kwangsi
78 A4 Yü-lin *Yulin* Kwangt.
62 E2 Yü-lin *Yulin* Shensi
11 D4 Yü-lin-chen *Yulinzhen* Heilung.
62 E2 Yü-lin Ho *Yulin He* (river) Shensi
30 B3 Yü-lin-pao *Yulinbao* Hopeh
119 C3 Yü-li Shan *Yuli Shan* (mt) Taiwan
Yülung *see* Ya-lung Chiang
86 B2 Yü-lung *Yulong* Szech.
87 E2 Yü-lung *Yulong* Szech.
102 B3 Yü-lung-k'a-shih Ho *Yulongkashi He* (river) Sink.
94 C2 Yü-lung Shan *Yulong Shan* (mt) Yun.
83 G4 Yu-ma *Youma* Kwangsi
83 G3 Yu-ma-k'ou *Youmakou* Kwangsi
98 C2 Yü-men *Yumen* Kansu
98 C1 Yü-men-chen *Yumenzhen* Kansu
39 B6 Yü-men-k'ou *Yumenkou* Shansi
98 A1 Yü-men-kuan *Yumenguan* Kansu
98 C2 Yü-men Tung-chan *Yumen Dongzhan* Kansu
Yü-min *see* Ha-la-pu-la
102 C1 Yü-min Hsien *Yumin Xian* Sink.
Yumrang Lopchang *see* Yu-lang-lo-p'u-ch'iang-ssu
15 G4 Yü-mu-ch'iao-tzu *Yumuqiaozi* Kirin
78 B2 Yü-nan *Yunan* Kwangt.
87 G2 Yün-an-chen *Yunanzhen* Szech.
31 B5 Yün-ch'eng *Yuncheng* Hopeh
39 B6 Yün-ch'eng *Yuncheng* Shansi
34 A4 Yün-ch'eng *Yuncheng* Shant.
74 F2 Yün-ch'i *Yunqi* Hunan
83 F3 Yün-chiang *Yunjiang* Kwangsi
94 C5 Yün-ching-hung *Yunjinghong* Yun.
30 C2 Yün-chou *Yunzhou* Hopeh
39 D4 Yün-chou-hsi-ts'un *Yunzhouxicun* Shansi
38 D3 Yün-chung Shan *Yunzhong Shan* (mt) Shansi
38 D3 Yün-chung Shan *Yunzhong Shan* (mts) Shansi
Yün-fou *see* Yün-fu
79 C2 Yün-fu *Yunfu* Kwangt.
46 D3 Yung-an *Yongan* Anhwei
67 C5 Yung-an *Yongan* Fukien
11 D4 Yung-an *Yongan* Heilung.
11 F5 Yung-an *Yongan* Heilung.
75 E6 Yung-an *Yongan* Hunan
82 E2 Yung-an *Yongan* Kwangsi
91 E2 Yung-an *Yongan* Kwei.
34 D2 Yung-an *Yongan* Shant.
119 B4 Yung-an *Yongan* Taiwan
51 D4 Yung-an Ch'i *Yongan Qi* (river) Chek.
75 D6 Yung-an Kuan *Yongan Guan* (pass) Hunan
83 H2 Yung-an Kuan *Yongan Guan* (pass) Kwangsi
74 F3 Yung-an-shih *Yonganshi* Hunan
50 C3 Yung-ch'ang *Yongchang* Chek.
71 B5 Yung-ch'ang *Yongchang* Kiangsi
55 H4 Yung-ch'eng *Yongcheng* Honan
39 B7 Yung-chi *Yongji* Shansi
Yung-chia *see* Wen-chou
51 D4 Yung-chia *Yongjia* Chek.
51 E2 Yung Chiang *Yong Jiang* Chek.
38 F1 Yung-chia-pao *Yongjiabao* Shansi
74 F2 Yung-chia-wan *Yongjiawan* Hunan

Sources

Historical maps: In the absence of any adequate modern historical atlas of China, extensive use has been made in the compilation of the historical maps of *An Historical Atlas of China* by Albert Herrmann, Edinburgh University Press, Edinburgh, 1966; and *Ajia rekishi chizu* edited by Matsuda and Mori, Heibonsha, Tokyo, 1966.

Province maps and city plans: The base for all province maps and most of the town plans in this atlas is *Chung-kuo Ti-t'u-ts'e* (Collection of Maps of China), Peking, 1966. The following later sources: *Chung-hua Jen-min Kung-ho-kuo Ti-t'u-chi* (Atlas of the People's Republic of China), Peking, 1972, and *Chung-hua Jen-min Kung-ho-kuo Ti-t'u* (Map of the People's Republic of China), Peking, (a) 1:4,000,000, Dec. 1971 (b) 1:6,000,000, Jan. 1973, have been used extensively to update the province maps in respect of communications and administrative information, including internal boundary changes, and to provide a considerable number of new and additional names. The following sources for city plans have also been used: the *Hong Kong Official Guide Map* (2nd edition), 1:100,000, Crown Lands and Survey office, Hong Kong, 1973; and Portuguese Chart No. 520: *Provincia de Macau. Plano hidrográfico de Macau, Taipa e Coloane* (2a Edição), 1:20,000 Lisbon, 1972.

Ai-pi Hu
I-li Ho
K'ung-chi-ssu Ho
Wu-lu-mu-ch'i
140
Tarim
SINKIANG
102-103
Yarkand
Ho-t'ien Ho
K'ung-ch'iao Ho
Lop Nor
6-7
Aksai Chin
2-3
KANSU
98-99
NINGSIA
114-115
Yin-ch'uan
136
Koko Nor
(Ch'ing Hai)
Hsi-ning
140
TSINGHAI
106-107
Lan-chou
135
Huang Ho
Wei Ho
TIBET
110-111
Ch'i-lin Hu
Na-mu Hu
La-sa
140
Brahmaputra
Salween
(Nu Chiang)
Chin-sha Chiang
Min Chiang
Ya-lung Chiang
Chia-ling Chiang
Ch'eng-tu
139
SZECHWAN
86-87
Ch'ung-ch'ing
139
Mekong (Lan-ts'ang Chiang)
KWEICH
90-91
Kuei-yang
137
K'un-ming
139
YUNNAN
94-95

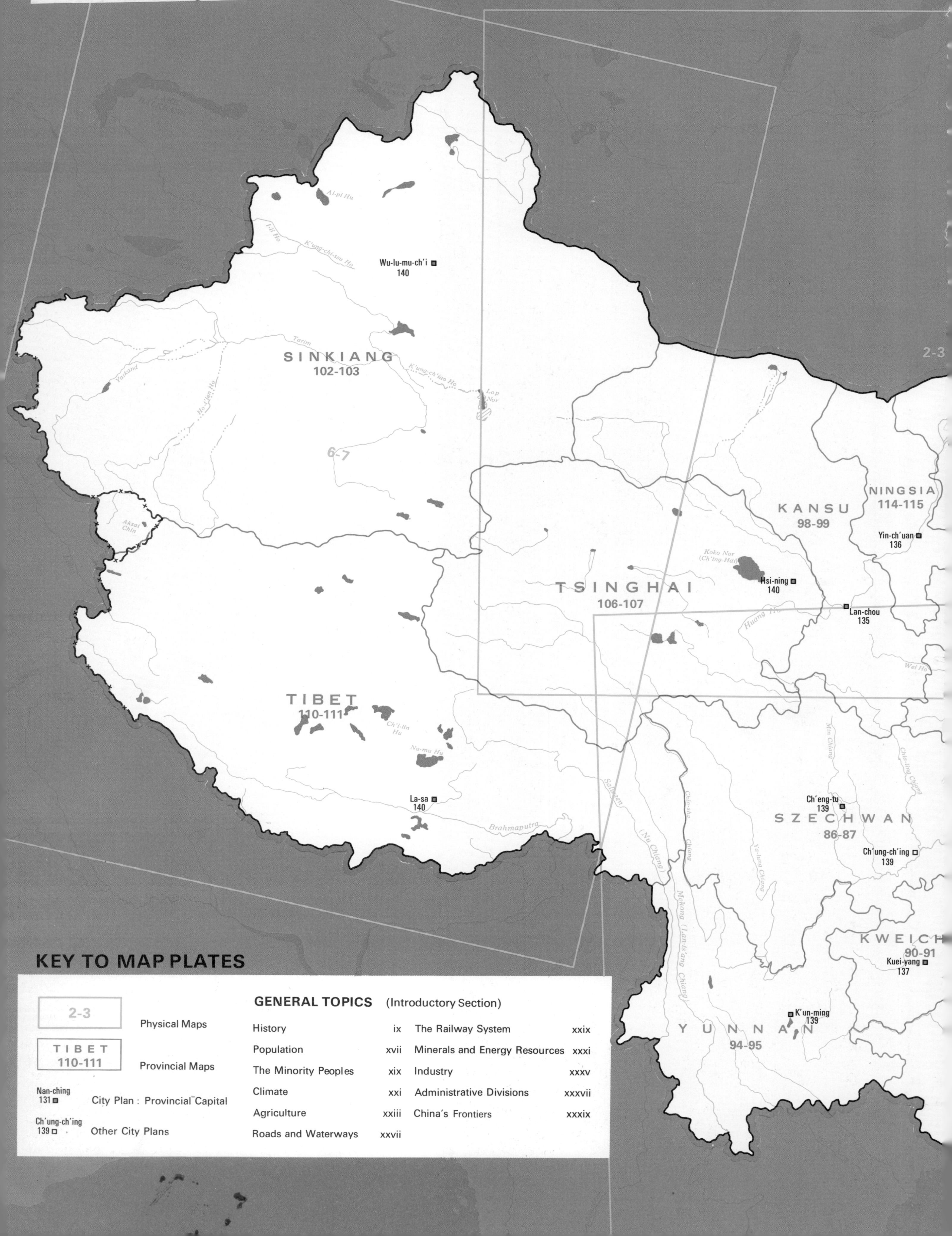

KEY TO MAP PLATES

2-3	Physical Maps
TIBET 110-111	Provincial Maps
Nan-ching 131 ■	City Plan : Provincial Capital
Ch'ung-ch'ing 139 □	Other City Plans

GENERAL TOPICS (Introductory Section)